T0139953

IFIP Advances in Information and Communication Technology

463

Editor-in-Chief

Kai Rannenberg, Goethe University Frankfurt, Germany

Editorial Board

IFIP – The International Federation for Information Processing

IFIP was founded in 1960 under the auspices of UNESCO, following the First World Computer Congress held in Paris the previous year. An umbrella organization for societies working in information processing, IFIP's aim is two-fold: to support information processing within its member countries and to encourage technology transfer to developing nations. As its mission statement clearly states,

> IFIP's mission is to be the leading, truly international, apolitical organization which encourages and assists in the development, exploitation and application of information technology for the benefit of all people.

IFIP is a non-profitmaking organization, run almost solely by 2500 volunteers. It operates through a number of technical committees, which organize events and publications. IFIP's events range from an international congress to local seminars, but the most important are:

- The IFIP World Computer Congress, held every second year;
- Open conferences;
- Working conferences.

The flagship event is the IFIP World Computer Congress, at which both invited and contributed papers are presented. Contributed papers are rigorously refereed and the rejection rate is high.

As with the Congress, participation in the open conferences is open to all and papers may be invited or submitted. Again, submitted papers are stringently refereed.

The working conferences are structured differently. They are usually run by a working group and attendance is small and by invitation only. Their purpose is to create an atmosphere conducive to innovation and development. Refereeing is also rigorous and papers are subjected to extensive group discussion.

Publications arising from IFIP events vary. The papers presented at the IFIP World Computer Congress and at open conferences are published as conference proceedings, while the results of the working conferences are often published as collections of selected and edited papers.

Any national society whose primary activity is about information processing may apply to become a full member of IFIP, although full membership is restricted to one society per country. Full members are entitled to vote at the annual General Assembly, National societies preferring a less committed involvement may apply for associate or corresponding membership. Associate members enjoy the same benefits as full members, but without voting rights. Corresponding members are not represented in IFIP bodies. Affiliated membership is open to non-national societies, and individual and honorary membership schemes are also offered.

More information about this series at http://www.springer.com/series/6102

Luis M. Camarinha-Matos · Frédérick Bénaben
Willy Picard (Eds.)

Risks and Resilience of Collaborative Networks

16th IFIP WG 5.5 Working Conference
on Virtual Enterprises, PRO-VE 2015
Albi, France, October 5–7, 2015
Proceedings

 Springer

Editors
Luis M. Camarinha-Matos
Universidade Nova de Lisboa
Monte Caparica
Portugal

Willy Picard
Poznan University of Economics
Poznan
Poland

Frédérick Bénaben
Ecole des Mines Albi Carmaux
Albi
France

ISSN 1868-4238   ISSN 1868-422X   (electronic)
IFIP Advances in Information and Communication Technology
ISBN 978-3-319-79585-0   ISBN 978-3-319-24141-8   (eBook)
DOI 10.1007/978-3-319-24141-8

Springer Cham Heidelberg New York Dordrecht London

Printed on acid-free paper

Springer International Publishing AG Switzerland is part of Springer Science+Business Media
(www.springer.com)

Preface

Societies in general, and enterprises in particular, are increasingly challenged by unexpected disruptive events occurring at a continuously rising frequency and causing more and more damages. The acceleration of globalization, demographic shifts, regional economic crises, changes in regulations, and rapid technological evolution, are factors that have led to turbulences and instability. Additional factors contributing to these changes include global warming, terrorism, cyber-attacks, scarcity of resources, and a rise in nationalism, racism, and religious conflicts, among others. Consequently, nowadays, instability may be considered as the "norm" or the default status, which naturally raises the question of how organizations and enterprises, as driving societal forces, can strive to gain in such disruptive environments. Collaborative Networks (CNs) provide tools to help organizations cope with unexpected changes and disruptions, particularly when exploring rapid consortia formation and dynamic structural re-organization. CNs also support addressing new business opportunities in these highly dynamic scenarios.

Although a vast amount of literature highlights the potential benefits of collaboration in general, only a few works have addressed the risks faced by organizations involved in collaborative networks, such as material flow related risks, financial risks, information misappropriation, insufficient performance of a partner, relational behavior related risks, or technological dependency, to name a few. The fear of such risks is often an obstacle to an effective involvement in collaborative processes. Furthermore, risks are not static, and as collaborative networks evolve, so do the risks. This is particularly true for long-duration networks, such as service provision networks for products that need to remain operational for many years. In these cases, the issue of sustainability of the collaboration becomes highly relevant.

It is therefore timely to progress in understanding risks and resilience of networks, to develop new assessment metrics and tools, and to devise proper governance methods towards a new generation of collaborative environments. Such developments require contributions from multiple and diverse knowledge areas (social sciences, organization science, technologies, etc.), which is well in line with the interdisciplinary spirit of the PRO-VE working conferences. This series of annual events provide an important opportunity for the collaborative networks community to share experiences, discuss research approaches, and identify future R&D directions. The selected theme for PRO-VE 2015, focusing on risks and resilience, stimulated this community to address the following challenging questions:

- In which ways can CNs support agility and resilience?
- How can CNs mitigate risks of collaboration in turbulent disruptive environments?

- What are significant examples of application cases and advanced ICT support systems supporting agile and resilient CNs?

PRO-VE 2015 held in Albi, France, was the 16th event in a series of successful conferences, including PRO-VE 1999 (Porto, Portugal), PRO-VE 2000 (Florianopolis, Brazil), PRO-VE 2002 (Sesimbra, Portugal), PRO-VE 2003 (Lugano, Switzerland), PRO-VE 2004 (Toulouse, France), PRO-VE 2005 (Valencia, Spain), PRO-VE 2006 (Helsinki, Finland), PRO-VE 2007 (Guimarães, Portugal), PRO-VE 2008 (Poznań, Poland), PRO-VE 2009 (Thessaloniki, Greece), PRO-VE 2010 (St. Étienne, France), PRO-VE 2011 (São Paulo, Brazil), PRO-VE 2012 (Bournemouth, UK), PRO-VE 2013 (Dresden, Germany), and PRO-VE 2014 (Amsterdam, The Netherlands).

This book includes selected papers from the PRO-VE 2015 conference, providing a comprehensive overview of major challenges and recent advances in various CN-related domains and their applications, with a strong focus on the following areas related to the selected main theme:

- risks in CNs,
- agility and resilience,
- collaboration frameworks,
- logistics and transportation,
- innovation networks,
- governance in CNs,
- collaborative communities,
- information and assets sharing,
- business processes,
- performance and optimization in networks, and
- network formation.

Finally, we would like to thank all the authors, both from academia/research as well as industry, for their contributions. We hope this collection of papers represents a valuable tool for everybody interested in research advances, emerging applications, and future challenges for R&D in collaborative networks. We also appreciate the dedication of the members of the PRO-VE International Program Committee who supported the selection of articles and provided valuable and constructive comments to help authors improve the quality of their papers.

July 2015   Luis M. Camarinha-Matos
                                                 Frédérick Bénaben
                                                 Willy Picard

Organization

PRO-VE 2015 – 16th IFIP Working Conference on
VIRTUAL ENTERPRISES
Albi, France, 5–7 Oct 2015

Conference Chair

Frédérick Bénaben, France

Program Committee Chair

Luis M. Camarinha-Matos, Portugal

Program Committee Co-chair

Willy Picard, Poland

Program Committee

Antonio Abreu, Portugal
Hamideh Afsarmanesh, Netherlands
Cesar Analide, Portugal
Samuil Angelov, Netherlands
Dario Antonelli, Italy
Bernard Archimede, France
Américo Azevedo, Portugal
Youakim Badr, France
Panagiotis Bamidis, Greece
José Barata, Portugal
Frédérick Bénaben, France
Peter Bertok, Australia
Xavier Boucher, France
Jean Pierre Bourey, France
Jeremy Bryans, UK
Luis M. Camarinha-Matos, Portugal
Tiago Cardoso, Portugal

Wojciech Cellary, Poland
Vincent Chapurlat, France
Naoufel Cheikhrouhou, Switzerland
Alok Choudhary, UK
Nicolas Daclin, France
Andrea Delgado, Uruguay
Yves Ducq, France
Schahram Dustdar, Netherlands
Jens Eschenbaecher, Germany
Elsa Estevez, Argentina
John Fitzgerald, UK
Franck Fontanili, France
Rosanna Fornasiero, Italy
Cesar Garita, Costa Rica
Ted Goranson, USA
Paul Grefen, Netherlands
Jorge E. Hernandez, UK

Technical Sponsors

IFIP WG 5.5 COVE
Co-Operation infrastructure for Virtual Enterprises and
electronic business

 **Society of Collaborative Networks**

Organizational Co-sponsors

Nova University of Lisbon

Contents

Collaboration Frameworks

Logistics and Transportation

Innovation Networks

Governance in Collaborative Networks

Collaborative Communities

Information and Assets Sharing

Business Processes

Performance and Optimization

Network Formation

Risks in Collaborative Networks

Towards an Integrated Model of Supply Chain Risks: An Alignment Between Supply Chain Characteristics and Risk Dimensions

Arij Lahmar[1,2(✉)], François Galasso[2], Habib Chabchoub[1], and Jacques Lamothe[2]

[1] Unit of Logistic, Industrial and Quality Management (LOGIQ),
Faculty of Economics Sciences and Management,
University of Sfax, Sfax, Tunisia
Arij.lahmar@hotmail.fr

[2] Industrial Engineering Center (CGI), University of Toulouse, Mines Albi,
Campus Jarlard, 81013 Albi, France
{francois.galasso,jacques.lamothe}@mines-albi.fr

Abstract. Within any Supply Chain Risk Management (SCRM) approach, the concept "Risk" occupies a central interest. Numerous frameworks which differ by the provided definitions and relationships between supply chain risk dimensions and metrics are available. This article provides an outline of the most common SCRM methodologies, in order to suggest an "integrated conceptual model". The objective of such an integrated model is not to describe yet another conceptual model of Risk, but rather to offer a concrete structure incorporating the characteristics of the supply chain in the risk management process. The proposed alignment allows a better understanding of the dynamic of risk management strategies. Firstly, the model was analyzed through its positioning and its contributions compared to existing tools and models in the literature. This comparison highlights the critical points overlooked in the past. Secondly, the model was applied on case studies of major supply chain crisis.

Keywords: Supply chain risk management · Supply chain risk dimensions · Risk management methodologies · SCRIM model

1 Introduction

As risks at different levels of the supply chain, crises and organizational weaknesses and the complexity of interactions are increasing [1]. Risk Management has become, in recent years, a fundamental and a better control factor of the supply chain as well as a necessity to ensure the sustainability and the survival of organizations and businesses [1–4]. This term *"Supply Chain Risk"* is used in a variety of contexts and domains. References to notions like "risk identification", "risk evaluation", "risk treatment", "risk management", "risk discovery" and so forth have been found. Extensive research over the past 30 years by academics, practitioners and others, has greatly attempted to improve the understanding of Supply Chain Risk (SCR) profiles and Supply Chain Risk Management (SCRM) approaches and actions.

© IFIP International Federation for Information Processing 2015
L.M. Camarinha-Matos et al. (Eds.): PRO-VE 2015, IFIP AICT 463, pp. 3–16, 2015.
DOI: 10.1007/978-3-319-24141-8_1

Numerous conceptual and analytical frameworks and mitigation techniques, tools and standards are now available to help managers and supply chain organizations to manage risk and to assure robustness and resilience of their networks. [5] state that managers seek to create an effective and efficient supply chain to ensure a competitive advantage. For this reason, they need to find a balance between costs, efficiency, effectiveness, resource use and therefore, risk management has become a reality for businesses to succeed. Thus, the SCRM is a support to the SCM in order to maintain the creation of value through the supply chain [6, 7]. This highlighted the link between risk management and supply chains in order to ensure the sustainability and survival of organizations and businesses, in a dynamic and unstable environment.

Therefore, more proactive and predictive risk management approach and strategy are needed [8]. This explains why supply chain risk management and resilience – robustness approaches have become such an attractive and powerful scientific and empirical discipline [9].

There is a common consensus amongst researchers in this field about the needs to develop a better understanding of risk and how it affects supply chain continuity. Every type of risk introduces different mechanisms of disruption, exposure level, impacts severity and poses different challenges for supply chain adaptability and recovery [10]. This creates the need for broader studies on supply chain risk decomposition and conceptualization within the context of dynamic supply chain networks [11].

Informed by the above critical aspects of the field and stressing the need for a better understanding of the concept of SCR, this article proposes a conceptual integrated model (SCRIM model) that helps in understanding, evaluating, measuring and managing these disruptions. In order to achieve this objective, the organization of the paper is as follows. After the introduction, Sect. 2 presents an overview of the most common conceptualization and decomposition of SCR and identifies SCRM implied methodologies. Then, an integrated conceptual model "SCRIM model" associated with SCRM domain and enriched with appropriate supply chain metrics is suggested in Sect. 3. The SCRIM model does not attempt to describe yet another model of Supply Chain Risk, but rather to offer a concrete structure incorporating the characteristics of the supply chain in the risk management process. In Sect. 4 experiments and results of model application are reviewed. Finally, Sect. 5 details the conclusions, limitations, and future directions regarding our conceptual model.

2 Supply Chain Risk Methodologies

SCRM has received during the last decade a considerable interest from researchers, practitioners and organizations. This led to the development of a plethora of different models and methods under the label of supply chain risk management and mitigation.

Drawing from the literature review, this section presents an analysis of the most common SCRM frameworks. Only methodologies and tools that define decompose and conceptualize risks or their constructs are selected. These latter has been investigated from a variety of aspects, summarized in the Table 1.

Several common themes emerge from reviewing these methodologies. First, different kinds of methods, processes, models and approaches are identified in order,

Table 1. SCRM Methodologies.

SCRM Methodologies	Generic models	The supply chain is analyzed from two possible states: normal or disturbed functioning of the chain They are based on the estimates of risk targets and decisions to make The objective of these models is the optimization of the supply chain and is not the risk management Limitations: the logistics processes can have the same probability of risk, but with different risk situations
	Risk analysis and assessment models	The aims are: Evaluation of risks and disturbances and their effects Evaluation of some configurations (locations, capacities, etc.) and strategies for supply chain networks, integrating one (or more) risk. Comparison between different logistics strategies or risk management, enabling the reduction of the level of risk

either to avoid future risks, or to mitigate the impact of identified risks. The extent to which the various approaches differ or complement each other is often unclear. The problem partly relies in the absence of common conceptual framework of supply chain risks. Many researchers viewed risk as a product of the probability of occurrence and severity of impact [12, 13]. According to this point of view, they establish that risk could be measured through the following formula:

$$\text{Supply Chain Risk} = \text{Probability} * \text{Impact.} \tag{1}$$

This method of risk measurement has a well-established place in the supply chain risk management domain. 67 % scientific articles follow this formula [9, 14]. However, Williams [15] and Levi [7] demonstrated that "calculating risk as a probability-impact matrix to quantify and prioritize risks is misleading" [15]. Reference [16] affirm that risk analysis need not to use probabilities because these latter may be irrelevant. Dani et al. [8] have suggested that this simple calculation of supply chain risk need to be re-considered. Furthermore, they suggested also that companies need to use more appropriate measures for supply chain risks and to develop programs to manage the critical risks [5].

A second commonality among these methodologies is that they propose a guide for managing supply chain risks, including the following procedures: identifying sources of risk, evaluating and estimating the severity of consequences and damages, and providing the approaches to mitigating and managing these risks.

However, few methodologies or studies explore the key elements, dimensions or constructs for managing supply chain risks.

The ability to identify which dimension of a Supply Chain Disruption often significantly impacts the supply chain is a critical factor in managing this disruption [19–21] highlights the lack of a common tool to identify SCR and their interrelations within supply chain networks. They affirm that understanding dynamic development of risks and their causal factors are essentials for effective SCRM strategies, helping managers making the right decisions. According to their work, each SCR is not an isolated event. Moreover, these prior frameworks focus on formalized and sophisticated tools for SCRM [1]. Such frameworks are difficult to implement without mathematical expertise or specialized tools, focus on quantifying networks vulnerabilities, provide little insight into underlying risk mechanisms and do not facilitate including supply chain factors in risk ratings. [22] stated: "*supply chain risk has been explored from one perspective, neglecting the sequences of various dimensions and constructs. Even methods that have taken into account the source-event relationship have failed to reflect the possible interactions among separated risk scenarios. Authors discussed the importance of studying the combination of diverse risks in the form of possible cause effects scenarios and made encouraging efforts*". Reference [23] highlighted the importance of a framework developed in the field of vulnerability studies and risk modeling. But he stressed the need for a common research structure that combines these two themes. According to [24], there are two main shortcomings related to the SCRM research, which are the missing of an integrated model that address the interactions between SCR factors and how this model can be integrated in the process of SCRM. Authors such as [21, 25–27] highlight the importance for gaining a more complete picture of SCR [17, 18] drawing the key variables, relationships, interactions and dynamic development of the SCR [28], down to revealing its impacts on the structure of the supply chain [19, 25, 29].

The study of these different methodologies highlights the need for specific model to address the main shortcomings identified, such as:

1. The need to capture the causal factors and the dynamic development of the Supply Chain Risk.
2. The impacts of mentioned risks on SC networks.
3. The need for a holistic and generic methodology for managing risks in the supply chain.

In order to address the issues identified, the SCRIM model is developed in Sect. 3.

3   Supply Chain Risk Integrated Model

The analysis of different methodologies is helpful in presenting several research explorations and orientations that have been used to provide a basis for our SCRIM model and depicted in Fig. 1. This model is mainly focused on the relationship between SC characteristics [30, 33] and risk dimensions and constructs [31, 32, 34]. In this section, the approach followed (see Fig. 1) in order to develop the SCRIM model is described. This approach improves the classical process of SCR model, with the appropriate SC metrics and Risks dimensions. Firstly, we started by investigating how risk is described, analyzed and modeled in the previous frameworks, in order to identify the main causal factors and to shed light over the development path of SCR. This analysis is incomplete without highlighting the SC networks vulnerability [21, 25]. So, a step is added regarding the modeling of the vulnerability factors. This step considered as a preparedness step that supply chain managers can apply in order to accelerate the risk analysis phase. These two previous steps "vulnerability and risk analysis" are combined and integrated into an alignment phase. The objective here is to present or measure the "Key Risk Indicators" (KRI).

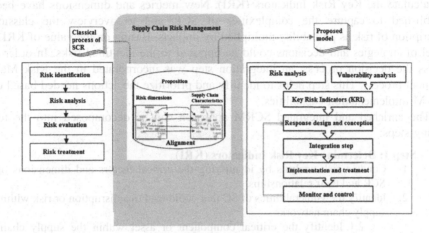

Fig. 1. Approach for SCRIM model

Another salient feature is the incorporation of "Integration step" into the traditional process of SCRM. During this phase, the characteristics of supply chain are integrated into the results of the previous step (response design and conception) and a suitable strategy is selected. As mentioned earlier, a variety of tools, approaches and strategies exist to mitigate or to prevent SCR [19, 35]. The choice inside this amount of frameworks is not easy and could present an important issue for managers [21].

In some cases, a wrong decision can aggravate the level of risk instead of mitigate it. References [34, 41, 42] highlight through their framework the impacts of SC design characteristics on the severity of SCR. However not only the structural characteristics of SC networks could affect risk management approach and strategy selection. References [38–40], have proved through their studies, that relationship dimensions between SC actors could influence the decision process and even the risk level and SCRM efficiency [45]. According to [5], the success of any SCRM strategy relies on the "SCRM culture" shared between SC entities. This could be achieved only through sharing knowledge and information about SCR. These two sharing mechanisms are concerned with three main SCM principles, which are collaboration [44, 45], trust [46, 47] and visibility [43, 48] within SC networks [49, 50].

As a result, when selecting one or more methods or actions for a given set of risks, one should also take into the account the capabilities. Any choice of SCRM method should not be made before verifying if the SC structure is compatible with the implementation requirements of the selected tool.

The SCRIM model is proposed as an enriched and integrated SCRM approach. Risk identification is the first and the crucial step in the risk management process. However, the nature and the complexity of the SC network make risk identification becoming a challenging task. Therefore, there is a need for a tool to assist organizations in identifying risk in their SC network. Given that, we suggest an interface for additional analysis of the SCR based on the alignment of two known steps: risk and vulnerability analysis. The interaction between these two phases allows to estimate and to calculate the Key Risk Indicators (KRI). New metrics and dimensions have been established to capture the complexities of SCR and to overview the classical description of risk as probability multiplied by impacts. Basing on the value of KRI, a panel of strategies and decisions could be opposed to the identified risks. In order to assess the decision process, an integration step was incorporated in the Risk Management process. This step helps to identify and prioritize the actions needed based on SCRM implementation capabilities.

The enriched and integrated SCRM approach can be decomposed into the following steps:

Step 1: Determine Key Risk Indicators (KRI)
1. Conduct risk analysis by identifying the critical factors and dimensions of SCR and their relationships.
2. Identify the vulnerabilities of SC that could lead to a disruption or risk within supply chain networks
   2.1. Identify the critical component or asset within the supply chain networks
   2.2. Identify the possible weakness causes for selected assets or components
3. Developing risk measurement criteria and define KRI

Step 2: Develop response design and conception:
1. Develop risk management strategies and actions to mitigate identified risks basing on the KRI measured in previous step

Step 3: Integration step
1. Identify the SCRM capabilities to applied the chosen strategies

      If

          SCRM capabilities < capabilities needed for RM strategy, then return in
step 2

      Else

          Move to step 3.2
2. Selection and prioritization of mitigation strategies and actions.

Step 4: Implementation and treatment

Step 5: Review and control
Control the KRI after implementing the actions and monitor:
4.1. **If** Risk is reduced,   **Then**   continue the treatment process until risk disappears.
4.2. **If** Risk is eliminated, **Then**   go back to step 2
4.3. **If** New risk appears,   **Then**   repeat the process

All these steps are supported by a class model detailing the parameters identified through the literature and depicted in Fig. 2.

The concepts presented, in the SCRIM class model, are considered as the most common key factors reoccurring amongst different SCRM frameworks and could be classified into three main subcategories:

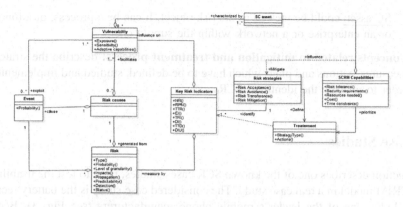

Fig. 2. SCRIM class model

i. **Concepts related to SCR:** include the dimensions, metrics and the main attributes that are relevant to SCR analysis and could be used when defining and assessing risks:

> Event: is defined as a negative change or outcome that causes deviation or disruption and triggers risks. It is characterized by the probability of occurrence.
>
> Risk cause: is a description of how risk can be generated and propagated. It could be viewed as an associative entity between risk event and vulnerability.
>
> Risk: is defined as one or more unforeseen events, with a probability of occurrence varies between o and 1, that have a financial, human, legal, managerial consequences (positive or negative), on logistics networks, ranging from, a probability of gain, to a failure of logistics organizations.
>
> Key Risk Indicators (RKI): is a set of measures or indicators (NR: Negative Result, RPN: Risk Priority Number, TTR: Time To Recovery, EI: Exposure Index, TRI: Total Risk Impact, TTD: Time To Detection, DIU: Losses Impacts, DI: Detection Impacts) that could be used to evaluate the SCR and thus to define the appropriate risk mitigation strategies.

ii. **Concepts related to Supply Chain:** It can be characterized by two elements: Elements used or exploited, leading to one or more risks, and elements which enable or contribute to risk treatment:

> The vulnerability: is a characteristic of an entity or a system within the supply chain, which measure the sensitivity level to external or internal disruptive events. It can be assessed in terms of three attributes: Exposure (the extent to which an asset is exposed to risk), Sensitivity (degree to which the asset is affected) and adaptive capabilities (The ability of an asset to react or to adapt to unexpected event).
>
> SCRM Capabilities: to manage risks in terms of objectives, requirements and constraints.

SC asset: could be viewed as the risk object. It can be a process, or a function, or an enterprise or a network within the supply chain.

iii. **Concepts related to mitigation and treatment process:** describe the strategies, measures, actions and plans which have to be defined, studied and implemented in order to manage the identified SCRs.

4 Case Studies

This section describes one of the known SCR cases studies, used to test the usability of the SCRIM model in a real case study. The considered case study is the battery recall of Nokia India, one of the leader's mobile phone manufacturers (see Fig. 3). Because overheating problems affecting battery during charging, Nokia announced the recall of batteries for its handsets from India markets. A total of 46 million batteries were recalled [36, 37].

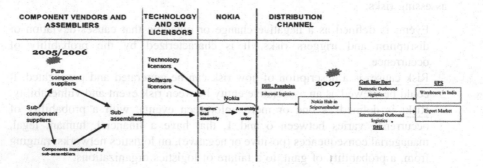

Fig. 3. Nokia supply chain

We followed the process described in Fig. 3 in order to identify the severity of situation that Nokia had to deal with it. From the first investigation, Nokia have detected the risk after two years of the first occurrence sign. Unfortunately, no prevention measures were applied. As result, Nokia has recalled 46 million handsets [37]. The first estimation of possible impacts was around 180 million dollars. Measuring the severity of this incident on the company's performance, the classical formula (probability multiplied by impacts) was applied. But, the given results do not represent the critical situation that Nokia managers have to face. With the low value of the involved risk, the severity was high. So, another calculation logic was needed to: firstly represent the real severity of risk and secondly, to help managers to make the mitigation decisions. As result, we adopt the logic of "Key Risk Indicators" to overcome this shortcoming. Basing on the value of Key Risk Indicators, managers ought to mitigate the supply risk for two main reasons: risk is critical, and the affected asset is crucial for Nokia supply chain (following vulnerability analysis). But, what Nokia managers haven't taken into account when they did apply their mitigation strategy is their implementation capabilities. This has led to decelerate the response time, from 15 days to 4 months [37]. Moreover in this case, Nokia was finally constrained to recall 46 million batteries leading to in depth modifications of schedules.

Based on the collected data from this case study and application of SCRIM model, the summary of the key results can be found in Table 2.

Table 2 illustrates the application results of SCRIM methodology to the Nokia's case. With limited data, the analysis is reduced to few risk dimensions and supply chain metrics. The result was supported by a class diagram, with the objective of giving a simple, complete and holistic picture of supply risk within the Nokia supply chain. The class diagram representation is depicted in Fig. 4.

Table 2. Summary of the key results presented in Nokia case study.

			Case: Nokia India: Recall battery (2007)
Description			Nokia issued a 'product advisory' for these BL-5C batteries for getting overheated and bursting during charging. 46 million batteries were recalled to prevent any damage to customer's life and to protect the Nokia reputation. This problem was caused by a defective battery produced by the main Nokia's supplier
The application of SCRIM model	**Risk analysis**	Event	Quality default in supplier's product
		Risk	Supply risk (low probability, high impact, unpredictable, cause transportation problem, low, at operational level)
	Vulnerability analysis	Sensitivity factors	Critical component Sourcing strategy
		Protection system	Quality standard protocol
		Exposure	Low
	Key Risk Indicators	EI : exposure index	EI = NR * TTR = 3 * 20.8 = 62.4 million USD
		DI : detection impact	DI = DIU * TTD = 3.5 * 20.2 = 70.7 million USD
		TRI: total risk impact	TRI = EI + DI = 62.4 + 70.7 = 133.1 million USD
		RPN: risk priority number	1
	Possible strategies		Mitigation strategy Avoidance strategy
	SCRM Capabilities		Customer protection
	Selected strategy		Mitigation strategy
	Actions		Recall of 46 million batteries
	Results		800 million USD loses

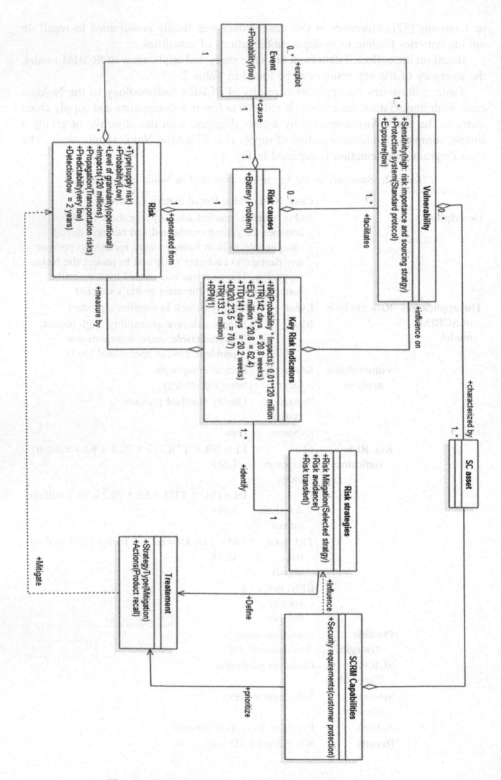

Fig. 4. Class diagram of supply risk within Nokia network

5 Conclusion

SCRM is a critical process for the business continuity within supply chain. Nevertheless, most of the existing frameworks deal with this research as a two separated area. Another concern is the classical view of supply chain risk. There is a shortage of calculation and interpretation of risk. Most of the developed frameworks were typically structured around the probability of risk and the possible impacts of its occurrence. However, no indication for using this formula in order to assess SCR is given. To overcome these gaps, we have proposed the SCRIM model as an enriched and integrated risk management approach within supply chain networks. In order to achieve our objective, several steps, each associated with an intermediate objective, were adopted. This model is used in order to align supply chain risk dimension with supply chain characteristics required for a better understanding and managing of SCR.

Considering the risk dimensions, a set of measures or indicators (NR: Negative Result, RPN: Risk Priority Number, TTR: Time To Recovery, EI: Exposure Index, TRI: Total Risk Impact, TTD: Time To Detection, DIU: Losses Impacts, DI: Detection Impacts) is built and create a Key Risk Indicators (KRI) which encompass the usual measure: Probability * Impact. The SC side is fully part of the SCRIM as each asset has an impact on the Risk Profile. Particularly, the supply chain characteristics have a strong influence on the selection process for the mitigation strategies. Such a choice relies on the intrinsic risk management capabilities of the SC as a whole. Thus, the level of collaboration, information sharing and trust within such a supply chain has been pointed out as an improvement issue for the SCRM capabilities.

The usability of the SCRIM model is investigated referring to Nokia [36] as an application case study. The application of the proposed model on the Nokia case showed that the model could be used in order to identify and to evaluate the supply chain risks and for giving an overall picture of the risk exposure situation. In this case, the supplier risk was underestimated by Nokia and led to the use of a mitigation strategy and a reactive strategy of avoidance instead of a proactive one. An improvement of the SCRM capabilities may have reduced the final impact. In that sense, a better sharing of information and knowledge about the SC could have led to a new evaluation of the vulnerability in which the exposure was graded as low.

Unfortunately, this study is still very limited. First of all, it is only focused on the few factors of both risk and supply chain on purpose of simplicity. Other metrics may contribute to further development of the SCRIM model. Secondly, the main difficulty encountered in this study was the limited amount of data available in the literature regarding the case Nokia. This statement could be identified as a common point between other case studies we identified in the literature.

Thus, future studies and more empirical investigations may allow the SCRIM model to be deeply improved.

References

1. Zsidisin, G.A.: A grounded definition of supply risk. J. Purchasing Supply Manage. 9, 217–224 (2003)

2. Kouvelis, P., Milner, J.M.: Supply chain capacity and outsourcing decisions: the dynamic interplay of demand and supply uncertainty. IIE Trans. **34**, 717–728 (2002)
3. Singhal, P., Agarwal, G., LalMittal, M.: Supply chain risk management: review, classification and future research directions. Int. J. Bus. Sci. Appl. Manage. **6**, 15–42 (2011)
4. Boote, D., Bailey, P.: Scholars before researchers on the centrality of the literature review in research preparation. Edu. Res. **34**, 3–15 (2005)
5. Christopher, M., Peck, H.: Building the resilient supply chain. Int. J. Logist. Manage. **15**(2), 1–14 (2004)
6. Marques, G., Gourc, D., Lamothe, J., Thierry, C.: Collaboration and risk management support in uncertain supply chain context. In: International Conference on Information Systems, Logistics and Supply Chain (ILS 2010). Facultés Universitaires Catholiques de Mons, Casablanca, 13 April 2010–16 April 2010
7. Simchi-Levi, D., Schmidt, W., Wei, Y.: From super storms to factory fires. Harvard Bus. Rev. **92**, 96–101 (2014)
8. Dani, S., Ghadge, A., Kalawsky, R.: Supply chain risk management: present and future scope. Int. J. Logist. Manage. **23**(3), 313–339 (2012)
9. Yang, Z., Aydin, G., Babich, V., Beil, D.R.: Supply disruptions, asymmetric information, and a backup production option. Manage. Sci. **55**(2), 192–209 (2009)
10. Zegordi, S.H., Davarzani, H.: Developing a supply chain disruption analysis model: application of colored petri-nets. Expert Syst. Appl. **39**(2), 2102–2111 (2012)
11. Gaonkar, R., Nukala, V.: A conceptual and analytical framework for the management of risk in supply chains. In: 2004 IEEE International Conference on Robotics and Automation Proceedings ICRA 2004, vol. 3 (2004)
12. Klibi, W., Martel, A., Guitouni, A.: The design of robust value-creating supply chain networks: a critical review. Eur. J. Oper. Res. **203**, 283–293 (2010)
13. Wu, T., Jennifer, B., Vellayappan, C.: A model for inbound supply risk analysis. Comput. Ind. **57**(4), 350–365 (2006)
14. Heckmann, I., Comes, T., Nickel, S.: A critical review on supply chain risk–definition, measure and modeling. Omega **52**, 119–132 (2015)
15. Williams, Z., Lueg, J.E., Lemay, S.A.: Supply chain security: an overview and research agenda. Int. J. Logist. Manage. **19**(2), 254–281 (2008)
16. Chapman, C.B., Cooper, D.F.: Risk engineering: basic controlled interval and memory models. J. Oper. Res. Soc. **34**, 51–60 (1983)
17. Paulsson, U., Nilsson, C.H., Wandel, S.: Estimation of disruption risk exposure in supply chains. Int. J. Bus. Continuity Risk Manage. **2**(1), 1–19 (2011)
18. Li, Z.P., Yee, Q.M.G., Tan, P.S., Lee, S.G.: An extended risk matrix approach for supply chain risk assessment. In: 2013 IEEE International Conference on Industrial Engineering and Engineering Management (IEEM), pp. 1699–1704, December 2013
19. Ouabouch, L., Gilles, P.: Risk management in the supply chain: characterization and empirical analysis. J. Appl. Bus. Res. (JABR) **30**(2), 329–340 (2014)
20. Parker, D.B., Zsidisin, A.G., Gary, L.R.: Timing and extent of supplier integration in new product development: a contingency approach. J. Supply Chain Manage. **44**(1), 71–83 (2008)
21. Karningsih, P.D., Berman, K., Sami, K.: Development of SCRIS: a knowledge based system tool for assisting organizations in managing supply chain risks. In: 2010 IEEE 24th International Conference on Advanced Information Networking and Applications Workshops (WAINA). IEEE (2010)
22. Fidan, G., Dikmen, I., Tanyer, A.M., Birgonul, M.T.: Ontology for relating risk and vulnerability to cost overrun in international projects. J. Comput. Civ. Eng. **25**(4), 302–315 (2011)

23. Fidan, G.: A risk and vulnerability ontology for construction projects. Ph.D. dissertation, Middle East Technical University (2008)
24. Oehmen, J., Ziegenbein, A., Alard, R., Schönsleben, P.: System-oriented supply chain risk management. Prod. Plan. Control **20**(4), 343–361 (2009)
25. Datta, P.P.: A complex system, agent based model for studying and improving the resilience of production and distribution networks. Ph.D. thesis, Cranfield University (2007)
26. Hallikas, J., Karvonen, I., Pulkkinen, U., Virolainen, V.M., Tuominen, M.: Risk management processes in supplier networks. Int. J. Prod. Econ. **90**(1), 47–58 (2004)
27. Sodhi, M.S., Son, B.G., Tang, C.S.: Researchers' perspectives on supply chain risk management. Prod. Oper. Manage. **21**(1), 1–13 (2012)
28. Chopra, S., Sodhi, M.S.: Managing risk to avoid supply-chain breakdown. MIT Sloan Manage. Rev. **46**, 53–61 (2004)
29. Faisal, M.N., Banwet, D.K., Shankar, R.: Supply chain risk management in SMEs: analysing the barriers. Int. J. Manage. Enterp. Dev. **4**(5), 588–607 (2007)
30. Ritchie, B., Brindley, C.: Supply chain risk management and performance: a guiding framework for future development. Int. J. Oper. Prod. Manage. **27**(3), 303–322 (2007)
31. Ellis, S.C., Henry, R.M., Shockley, J.: Buyer perceptions of supply disruption risk: a behavioral view and empirical assessment. J. Oper. Manage. **28**(1), 34–46 (2010)
32. Wagner, S.M., Bode, C.: An empirical investigation into supply chain vulnerability. J. Purchasing Supply Manage. **12**(6), 301–312 (2006)
33. Blackhurst, J., Craighead, C.W., Elkins, D., Handfield, R.B.: An empirically derived agenda of critical research issues for managing supply-chain disruptions. Int. J. Prod. Res. **43**(19), 4067–4081 (2005)
34. Craighead, C.W., Blackhurst, J., Rungtusanatham, M.J., Handfield, R.B.: The severity of supply chain disruptions: design characteristics and mitigation capabilities. Decis. Sci. **38**(1), 131–156 (2007)
35. Tang, C.S.: Perspectives in supply chain risk management. Int. J. Prod. Econ. **103**(2), 451–488 (2006)
36. Desai, P., Patel, D.N.: Identifying backfire of communication on perceived hazard level during product recall. Int. J. Retail. Rural Bus. Perspect. **3**(2), 969–977 (2014)
37. Charles, D., Narendar, S., Johnson, P.F., Monali, M.: Nokia India: Battery Recall Logistics, pp. 1–13. Ivey Publishing (2011)
38. Badea, A., Prostean, G., Goncalves, G., Allaoui, H.: Assessing risk factors in collaborative supply chain with the analytic hierarchy process (AHP). Procedia Soc. Behav. Sci. **124**, 114–123 (2014)
39. Chen, J., Sohal, A.S., Prajogo, D.I.: Supply chain operational risk mitigation: a collaborative approach. Int. J. Prod. Res. **51**(7), 2186–2199 (2013)
40. Li, G., Fan, H., Lee, P.K., Cheng, T.C.E.: Joint supply chain risk management: an agency and collaboration perspective. Int. J. Prod. Econ. **164**, 83–94 (2015)
41. Song, J., Bai, L., Yang, C.: Risk control research framework of supply chain of embeddedness structure based on perspective of risk conduction. In: 2012 Fifth International Joint Conference on Computational Sciences and Optimization (CSO), pp. 751–754. IEEE (2012)
42. Vermeulen, E.M., Spronk, J., van der Wijst, N.: Analyzing risk and performance using the multi-factor concept. Eur. J. Oper. Res. **93**(1), 173–184 (1996)
43. Goh, R.S.M., Wang, Z., Yin, X., Fu, X., Ponnambalam, L., Lu, S., Li, X.: RiskVis: supply chain visualization with risk management and real-time monitoring. In: IEEE International Conference on Automation Science and Engineering (CASE), pp. 207–212 (2013)

44. Grudinschi, D., Sintonen, S., Hallikas, J.: Relationship risk perception and determinants of the collaboration fluency of buyer–supplier relationships in public service procurement. J. Purchasing Supply Manage. **20**(2), 82–91 (2014)

45. Lavastre, O., Gunasekaran, A., Spalanzani, A.: Effect of firm characteristics, supplier relationships and techniques used on supply chain risk management (SCRM): an empirical investigation on French industrial firms. Int. J. Prod. Res. **52**(11), 3381–3403 (2014)

46. Hou, Y., Xiong, Y., Liang, X.: The effects of a trust mechanism on a dynamic supply chain network. Expert Syst. Appl. **41**(6), 3060–3068 (2014)

47. Wang, Q., Craighead, C.W., Li, J.J.: Justice served: Mitigating damaged trust stemming from supply chain disruptions. J. Oper. Manage. **32**(6), 374–386 (2014)

48. Yu, M.C., Goh, M.: A multi-objective approach to supply chain visibility and risk. Eur. J. Oper. Res. **233**(1), 125–130 (2014)

49. Scholten, K., Schilder, S.: The role of collaboration in supply chain resilience. Supply Chain Manage. Int. J. **20**(4), 471–484 (2015)

50. Fayezi, S., Zutshi, A., O'Loughlin, A.: Collaboration and risk mitigation capability in supply chains: a conceptual framework. In: 24th Annual Australian and New Zealand Academy of Management (ANZAM) (2010)

Risk Management in Hierarchical Production Planning Using Inter-enterprise Architecture

Alix Vargas[1(✉)], Andres Boza[1], Shushma Patel[2], Dilip Patel[2],
Llanos Cuenca[1], and Angel Ortiz[1]

[1] Centro de Investigación en Gestión e Ingeniería de Producción (CIGIP),
Universitat Politècnica de València, Camino de Vera s/n Ed 8G -1° y 4° planta
Acc D (Ciudad Politécnica de la Innovación), Valencia, Spain
alvarlo@posgrado.upv.es,
{aboza,llcuenca,aortiz}@cigip.upv.es
[2] School of Engineering, London South Bank University,
103 Borough Road, London SE1 0AA, UK
{shushma,dilip}@lsbu.ac.uk

Abstract. Unexpected events in hierarchical production planning, such as rush orders, labor problems, lack of availability of materials and faulty machines have to be managed efficiently because they represent a risk for business continuity, based on their impact and duration. The use of inter-enterprise architecture offers multiple benefits for collaborative networks, including: business strategy and information technology alignment, joint process integration and synchronization, supply chain cost reduction, risk and redundancy minimization and customer services improvement. Therefore, the use of inter-enterprise architecture to address the problem of unexpected events in hierarchical production planning supporting operational risk management is proposed. This paper presents a model for inter-enterprise architecture that addresses the problem of handling unexpected events in hierarchical production planning and how the inter-enterprise framework is embedded into the model.

Keywords: Inter-enterprise architecture · Hierarchical production planning · Collaborative networks · Unexpected events · Risk management

1 Introduction

The current dynamic environment forces enterprises to create collaborative networks (CN) in order to survive and maintain a competitive advantage. Collaborative networks are manifested in a variety of forms [1]: virtual enterprises, virtual organizations, extended enterprises, virtual communities and virtual teams. Inter-enterprise architecture allows CNs to: integrate business processes, align business with information systems and technology, increase responsiveness, reduce risks, inventory and redundancies, create synergies to achieve common goals, minimize cost of the supply chain, among other benefits [2].

Inter-enterprise architecture can be used to approach different issues that CNs have to address on a daily basis, such as: procurement planning, production planning,

© IFIP International Federation for Information Processing 2015
L.M. Camarinha-Matos et al. (Eds.): PRO-VE 2015, IFIP AICT 463, pp. 17–26, 2015.
DOI: 10.1007/978-3-319-24141-8_2

inventory planning, scheduling and controlling, and logistics and delivery planning. In this paper, our focus is production planning and specifically hierarchical production planning that facilitates decision-making in CNs by decomposing the decision problem into sub-problems. The sub-problems are related to the organizational structure at the highest levels of the hierarchy imposing restrictions at the lower levels [3].

In hierarchical production planning, the use of decision support systems (DSS) has increased considerably as these systems provide decision makers with better and more accurate real time information using mathematical and optimization models [4]. However, these systems are not designed to handle unexpected events that threaten business continuity. Thus, decision makers are forced to take decisions based on their knowledge and expertise, and the original plans have to change resulting in inefficiencies, increased inventory levels and costs, reducing customer service satisfaction and even risking business continuity.

Taking into account a holistic view of hierarchical production planning and decision support needs for unexpected events handling, poses the research question: Can the use of inter-enterprise architecture solve the problem of the arrival of unexpected events in hierarchical production planning supporting operational risk management? This paper proposes a model of inter-enterprise architecture to address the problem of handling unexpected events in hierarchical production planning enabling operational risk management in CNs and the validation of how the inter-enterprise framework is mapped into this model.

The paper is structured as follows: Sect. 2 describes the related work in the fields of: hierarchical production planning and operational risk, decision support systems and inter-enterprise architecture, with the latter describing the main findings of the research to date. Section 3 presents the proposed model that describes the problem of handling unexpected events in hierarchical production planning to support risk management. Section 4 maps the framework proposed in our ongoing research with the risk management model. Finally Sect. 5 presents the main conclusions and future work.

2   Related Work

2.1   Hierarchical Production Planning and Operational Risk

Collaborative and productive activities, especially planning and control, should follow a hierarchical approach that allows coordination between the objectives, plans and activities of the strategic, tactical and operational levels, in order to reduce the complexity of the system [5]. This means that each level will pursue their own goals, but take into account the higher level, on which it depends, and the lower level, which is restricted [4]. In hierarchical production planning (HPP) systems, the problems are split into sub-problems. Each sub-problem is related to a decision-making level in the organizational structure and a mathematical model is constructed for solving each sub-problem, which has different planning horizons, with aggregated and disaggregated information across hierarchical levels [3].

Operational risk is associated with the execution of companies' business functions. Risk management is the process devoted to protecting the organizations and augmenting its capability to achieve its stated strategic objectives [6]. In the context of production planning, the risk is associated with the arrival of unexpected events that affect the normal performance planning. Effectively preparing for unexpected events, such as the lack of available materials, rush orders, faulty machines, etc., is vital to guaranteeing business continuity. Therefore, the ability to cope with these changes and helping decision makers react in the best way, are important issues that must be taken into account in the systems and planning processes. Some studies have proposed that manufacturing systems should be sufficiently flexible and robust in order to efficiently handle unexpected events [7, 8] and new proposals arise for a better information management in production, such as Internet of Things [9]. However, most of the work in these areas only considers certain types of unexpected events, or provides limited assistance to manage how people react to them. There is limited research that takes into account the management of different types of unexpected events in an integrated way.

Darmoul et al. [7], define a typology of the different kinds of unexpected events that can occur in a manufacturing system and therefore affect production planning. This typology states that unexpected events could originate from the following entities: suppliers, resources, production and customers. The specific events reported for each kind of origin are:

- In suppliers: delays, difference in quantity ordered and quality problems
- In resources: machine breakdowns, tools breakage, workers sickness, workers under performance, workers high performance and strike
- In production: low raw material utilization, high raw material utilization, quality problems, low performance in production, high performance in production, returns for low quality, returns for delay in delivery and refunds for early delivery
- In customers: rush orders, order modification and order cancelation

In order to manage each and every specific unexpected event in an integrated way, it is necessary to consider different factors for its management, such as, duration of the disturbance (estimation of how long an unexpected event can last) and the criticality of the resources involved (which relates to substitution of resources), as well as the impact (high: related to strategic decisions, or low: related to operational or tactical decisions).

2.2 Decision Support Systems and Hierarchical Production Planning

Information systems, which provide necessary information for managers to make decisions, have become key elements in the decision-making process. Therefore, decision support systems are indispensable tools not only to obtain an optimal solution, but also to obtain a broader and deeper understanding of the problem.

A hierarchical production planning system should be able to detect abnormal behaviour, determine the type of disruption and continually propose alternatives depending on the type of event. Determining the type of unexpected event is important because the process will be affected differently and will require different decisions to be made. In this context, the way the decision maker understands the information can accelerate his/her perception, provide better insight and control, and harness the large volume of valuable data to gain a competitive advantage by making improved decisions [10].

Hierarchical production planning systems need to be sufficiently flexible in order to adapt to dynamic environments. The area of flexibility within the context of hierarchical production planning systems has been studied and different solutions proposed [11, 12], which demonstrate how the data model can be integrated with the hierarchical planning system. In addition, Boza et al. [4] state the logical building blocks that play an interactive role in the information system and decision technologies for hierarchical production planning, which are: Data Modelling (DaM), which represents the internal structure and the external presentation of the data; Decision Modelling (DeM) defines the models that represent the problem to be addressed. These models are used to evaluate possible decisions in a problem domain; and Model Analysis and Research (MAR), which is the instantiation of the decision model with data, model evaluation and results.

To date, there is little evidence of research using decision support systems for hierarchical production planning that includes handling unexpected events allowing for business continuity. Therefore, the ongoing research of inter-enterprise architecture aims to address this gap.

2.3   Inter-enterprise Architecture

In our ongoing research, the concept of inter-enterprise architecture (IEA) has been proposed by investigating the application of enterprise architecture in CNs [13]. The main elements of inter-enterprise architecture are: framework, methodology, and modelling language [2]. The framework represents a simple, graphical structure of the elements that make up the enterprise [14] and shows how the elements are integrated and related. The modelling language allows for modelling, organizing and understanding the relationships between elements of the enterprise, using building blocks to describe them [15]. The methodology facilitates the implementation of the framework, step-by-step, through the use of the building blocks defined by the modelling language [16].

Vargas et al. [17] proposed a framework for IEA comprising of four life cycle phases (identification, conceptualization, definition and action plan) and seven modelling views (business, organization, resources, process, decision, data and IS/IT). The framework is also represented by its eighteen building blocks, which constitute the modelling language proposed. The extended and revised framework and its building blocks are illustrated in Table 1.

In proposing a useful framework for modelling an inter-enterprise architecture, to facilitate unexpected events management on hierarchical production planning, IE-GIP (the Spanish acronym that translates to 'Enterprise Integration - Business Processes and Integrated Management') [18] is the foundation of the general framework used to propose a partial framework to solve this problem. The proposed partial framework maintains the life cycle phases of IE-GIP adapted to the specific context and the modelling views have been merged, added or evolved as it is explained in [17].

Through this framework, we believe it is possible to use inter-enterprise architecture for modelling the problem of handling unexpected events in hierarchical production planning. In order to validate this assertion, the next section describes the risk

Table 1. Definition framework of IEA and building blocks

Modelling views / Life cycle phases	Business	Organization	Resources	Process	Decision	Data	IS/IT
Identification	Domain Stakeholder	Cell Unit	Worker				
Conceptualization	Business strategy Stakeholder	Cell Unit	Worker				IS/IT strategy
Definition	Objetive Performance assessment Stakeholder	Cell Unit	Resource Worker	AS-IS processes CN processes Unexpected events	Decision model	Data model	Portfolio app AS-IS Portfolio app CN Analysis model
Action plan	Performance assessment Stakeholder	Cell Unit	Resource Worker	CN processes Unexpected events	Decision model	Data model	Portfolio app CN Analysis model

management model for hierarchical production planning and Sect. 4 illustrates how the framework is mapped to the risk management model.

3 Proposed Risk Management Model for HPP

Collaborative networks have to handle different kinds of unexpected events in hierarchical production planning, which can originate from: suppliers, customers, resources or production. In this section, the risk management model for HPP is presented taking into account a collaborative network made up of 2 companies, having two levels of decisions: Planning (strategic and tactical) and operational. The planning level is supported by the planning DSS (PDSS) that provides companies with information on quantities to produce per period, quantities to buy, stock levels, etc. Unexpected events occur at the operational level and the decision maker needs to analyse the information and propose solutions to solve the problems that arise. The decision maker needs to use his/her own expertise and knowledge to solve the specific situation causing inefficiencies, bottlenecks and chaos. In order to provide support to the decision maker, the ideal operational DSS (ODSS) would provide alternative solutions depending on the event and its duration and impact. Figure 1 shows the proposed model, which represents our vision of how events should be handled, supported by ODSS that allows enterprises to have contingency plans showing the decision maker ways to manage specific events through rules or models that check the events' impact and analyse historical data stored in the data warehouse. The numbers in the model below represent the order in which processes occur and are described below:

(1) The upper level is the planning level that sends to the operational level production plans.
(2) The risk for the arrival of unexpected events occurs at the operational level.
(3) The event causes a distortion in operational plans that the decision makers have to report to an ODSS (These specifics events have been predefined according to the literature review of Sect. 3)

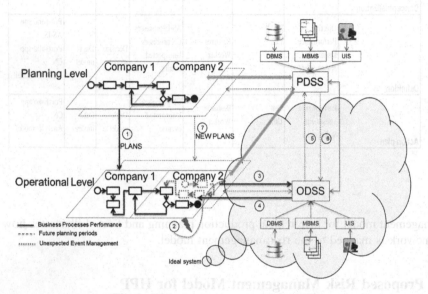

Fig. 1. Risk management model for HPP

(4) The ODSS system must provide an alternative solution based on specific rules, past experiences or models. The ODSS has to be flexible and provide fast and feasible solutions at the operational level.
(5) At the same time, the solution must be relayed to the upper level, because the solution has changed the inputs to decisions made at the planning level.
(6) The PDSS modifies the decision model in order to handle the specific event in the future in long term basis; this modification is reported to the ODSS that storage the solution information into the application. In this way, any decision makers belonging to the collaborative network, can access through the ODSS to this information in real time, allowing them sharing vital information to help them to take better decisions when an event occurs.
(7) PDSS will run again with this feedback and propose new plans for subsequent periods. The new plans are sent to the operational level that has already taken into account the impact of the event.

This model represents widely, how is our vision to handle different kind of unexpected events through the support of an ODSS that allows decision makers to access in real time to solution alternatives that occurred in the past as a mean to provide with accurate, validated and measurable information for a specific event, helping to decision makers gather, filter and analysing information that enable making better decisions when a new unexpected event occurs. This information can be accessed by any of the decisions makers belonging to the collaborative network, allowing transfer and generation of knowledge.

One of the limitations is the kind of unexpected events analysed. The unexpected events that have been analysed (Sect. 2.1) do not relate soft and catastrophic issues. Soft issues associated to availability of personnel and their level of competence. Catastrophic issues associated to earthquakes, adverse weather conditions, terrorist attacks and political conflicts.

4 Mapping the IEA Framework to the Risk Management Model in HPP

The framework described in Sect. 2.3 is made up of 18 building blocks. These building blocks are represented in the model proposed in Sect. 3. Figure 2 shows how the 18 building blocks of the proposed IEA framework represents the problem of handling unexpected events in HPP and how they are described in each of the elements of the model. This shows how the IEA framework embeds the elements needed to describe the problem of unexpected events in HPP.

Each building block is represented in a rectangle with borders depending on which modelling view it is associated with. Thus:

- Domain represents the boundaries of the CN in the collaborative context of hierarchical production planning to solve the problem of unexpected events handling.
- Stakeholders represent the number or nodes in the CN that participate in the collaborative domain.
- Organizational cell represents the teams of the CN.
- Organizational unit represents the workstation of the CN and its roles. Each unit must belong to at least one cell and each team must have at least one member.
- Resources represent all those physical resources necessary to carry out the operation of the CN.
- Worker represents a member from each stakeholder that participates in the collaborative process. The difference between worker and organizational unit is that the latest is related to the CN and worker is related to each stakeholder.
- Business strategy represents the mission, vision, values, goals, strategy, plans, critical success factors, policies and parameters of the CN that are agreed at a business level and have to be aligned with the IS/IT strategy.
- IS/IT strategy represents policies and parameters of the CN that are agreed at the technological level and have to be aligned with the business strategy.
- Objectives represent the goals of the CN for modelling the domain.
- Performance assessment helps to measure the performance of the CN through Key Performance Indicators (KPIs) that are assigned to measure each of the objectives of the CN.

Domain of hierarchical production planning and unexpected events management

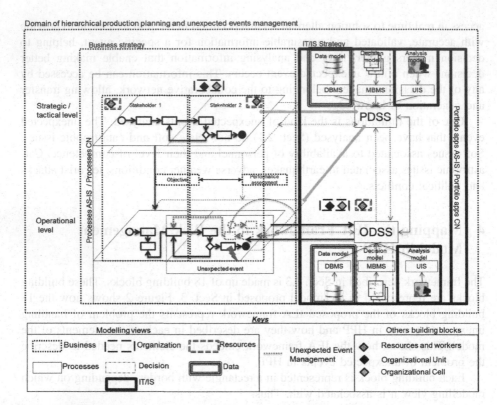

Fig. 2. Mapping IEA framework validation to risk management model in HPP

- AS-IS process defines at a macro-level the processes that are currently being developed in the domain of the CN at a local level.
- CN process defines the processes TO-BE of the CN in the global domain.
- Unexpected events allow establishing the management to support the decision process when unexpected events occur that affect production planning; there are four different origins of an event: customer, supplier, production and resource.
- Decision modelling, through this building block the decision models of the CN are defined, taking into account the organizational hierarchy of the CN.
- Data modelling defines the data structure related to the decision modelling and its relationship with the analysis model.
- Analysis model defines the operation and interaction of decision modelling and data modelling.
- AS-IS Application Portfolio helps to identify the information associated with each current local application, and its importance to support the global operations of the CN.
- CN Application Portfolio represents the list of applications or services with which the CN supports joint business processes in a TO-BE state.

5 Conclusions

This paper proposes a risk management model for hierarchical production planning for a collaborative network for handling unexpected events. The paper also maps the IEA framework with the risk management model.

The key contribution is that it enables collaborative networks to address the problem of handling unexpected events in hierarchical production planning, thus ensuring management of risks at the operational level. The impact of this work is to support decision makers to respond effectively and efficiently to risk events using the operational decision support system that provides alternative solutions and contingency plans to ensure business continuity, taking into account a wide range of risk based events, their impact and duration. As the model is currently being evaluated in a collaborative network in the Spanish ceramic tile sector, the collected results will provide the necessary information for hypothesis validation and research question satisfaction. There are some limitations relating to the kind of unexpected events analyzed that must be taken into account for future research including, but not limited to: the soft and catastrophic events. The initial findings suggest that the proposed model is a good representation of hierarchical production planning and unexpected events handling for risk management, at the conceptual level.

Acknowledgments. This paper has been developed as a result of a mobility stay funded by the Erasmus + Mundus in framework of Traineeship Program. This research has been carried out in the framework of the project ADENPRO-PJP (Ref. PAID-06-21) funded by the Universitat Politècnica de València.

References

1. Camarinha-Matos, L., Afsarmanesh, H., Ollus, M.: ECOLEAD and CNO base concepts. In: Camarinha-Matos, L.M., Afsarmanesh, H., Ollus, M. (eds.) Methods and Tools for Collaborative Networked Organizations. Springer, New York (2008)
2. Vargas, A., Boza, A., Cuenca, L., Ortiz, A.: Towards a framework for inter-enterprise architecture to boost collaborative networks. In: Demey, Y.T., Panetto, H. (eds.) OTM 2013 Workshops 2013. LNCS, vol. 8186, pp. 179–188. Springer, Heidelberg (2013)
3. Vicens, E., Alemany, M., Andrés, C., Guarch, J.: A design and application methodology for hierarchical production planning decision support systems in an enterprise integration context. Int. J. Prod. Econ. **74**(1), 5–20 (2001)
4. Boza, A., Ortiz, A., Vicens, E., Poler, R.: A framework for a decision support system in a hierarchical extended enterprise decision context. In: Poler, R., van Sinderen, M., Sanchis, R. (eds.) IWEI 2009. LNBIP, vol. 38, pp. 113–124. Springer, Heidelberg (2009)
5. Jüngen, F., Kowalczyk, W.: An intelligent interactive project management support system. Eur. J. Oper. Res. **84**(1), 60–81 (1995)
6. Borghesi, A., Gaudenzi, B.: Operational risk and supply chain risk management. In: Risk Management, pp. 117–137. Springer, Milan (2013)
7. Darmoul, S., Pierreval, H., Hajri-Gabouj, S.: Handling disruptions in manufacturing systems: an immune perspective. Eng. Appli. Artif. Intell. **26**, 110–121 (2013)

8. Bearzotti, L., Salomone, E., Chiotti, O.: An autonomous multi-agent approach to supply chain event management. Int. J. Prod. Econ. **135**(1), 468–478 (2012)

9. Boza, A., Cortes, B., Cuenca, L., Alarcón, F.: Internet of things applications in production systems. In: 17th International Conference on Enterprise Information Systems (ICEIS), Barcelona (2015)

10. Al-Kassab, J., Ouertani, Z., Schiuma, G., Neely, A.: Information visualization to support management decisions. Int. J. Inf. Technol. Decis. Mak. **13**(2), 407–428 (2014)

11. Weinstein, L., Chung, C.: Integrating maintenance and production decision in a hierarchical production planning environment. Comput. Oper. Res. **26**(10), 1059–1074 (1999)

12. Hurtubise, S., Olivier, C., Gharbi, A.: Planning tools for managing the supply chain. Comput. Ind. Eng. **46**(4), 763–779 (2004)

13. Vargas, A., Boza, A., Cuenca, L., Sacala, I.: Inter-enterprise architecture and internet of the future. In: Camarinha-Matos, L.M., Tomic, S., Graça, P. (eds.) DoCEIS 2013. IFIP AICT, vol. 394, pp. 25–32. Springer, Heidelberg (2013)

14. Cuenca, L., Boza, A., Ortiz, A.: An enterprise engineering approach for the alignment of business and information technology strategy. Int. J. Comput. Integr. Manufact. **24**(11), 974–992 (2011)

15. Vargas, A., Boza, A., Cuenca, L.: Towards interoperability through inter-enterprise collaboration architectures. In: Meersman, R., Dillon, T., Herrero, P. (eds.) OTM-WS 2011. LNCS, vol. 7046, pp. 102–111. Springer, Heidelberg (2011)

16. Bernard, S.: An Introduction to Enterprise Architecture. AuthorHouse, Bloomington (2012)

17. Vargas, A., Boza, A., Cuenca, L., Ortiz, A.: Using inter enterprise architecture as an instrument for decision-making under the arrival of unexpected events in hierarchical production planning. Int. J. Eng. Manage. Econ. **5**(1/2), 73–88 (2015)

18. Ortiz, A., Lario, F., Ros, L.: Enterprise integration—business processes integrated management: a proposal for a methodology to develop enterprise integration programs. Comput. Ind. **40**, 155–171 (1999)

Risk Assessment in Open Innovation Networks

João Rosas[1,2(✉)], Patrícia Macedo[2,3], Alexandra Tenera[1,4],
António Abreu[2,5], and Paula Urze[1,6]

[1] FCT/UNL, Faculdade de Ciências e Tecnologia da Universidade Nova de
Lisboa, Caparica, Portugal
jrosas@uninova.pt, {abt,pcu}@fct.unl.pt
[2] Uninova Institute, Centre of Technology and Systems, Caparica, Portugal
patricia.macedo@estsetubal.ips.pt,
ajfa@dem.isel.ipl.pt
[3] School of Technology of Setubal, Polytechnic Institute of Setubal, Setúbal,
Portugal
[4] Mechanical and Industrial Engineering Department,
UNIDEMI/FCT/UNL, Caparica, Portugal
[5] ISEL/IPL – Instituto Superior de Engenharia de Lisboa do Instituto Politécnico
de Lisboa, Lisbon, Portugal
[6] CIUHCT – Centro Interuniversitário de História das Ciências e da Tecnologia,
Caparica, Portugal

Abstract. Innovation is considered crucial for enterprises survival and current economic environment demands the best ways of achieving it. However, the development of complex products and services require the utilization of diverse know-how and technology, which enterprises may not hold. An effective strategy for achieving them is to rely in open innovation. Still, open innovation projects may fail for many causes, e.g. due to the dynamics of collaboration between partners. To effectively benefit from open innovation, it is recommended the utilization of adequate risk models. For achieving such models, a preliminary conceptualization of open innovation and risk is necessary, which includes modeling experiments with existing risk models, such as the FMEA.

Keywords: Open innovation · Risk assessment · Collaborative networks · FMEA

1 Introduction

Nowadays, Innovation is crucial for the enterprises survival and current economic environment demands the best ways of achieving it. Open innovation is a useful strategy enterprises adopt to seek knowledge and value from outside of their boundaries. In such way, enterprises share technology and knowledge with their suppliers and customers to develop innovative and improved products, and leveraging value creation. Assuming this strategy, enterprises may even disclose secrete technology or free intellectual property, for the sake of obtaining such benefits. But this is not done without risks, as open innovation projects might fail for diverse reasons. For instance, the appropriation of others' know-how or trying to take unmerited benefits from a technology are considered disruptive behaviors in open innovation projects.

© IFIP International Federation for Information Processing 2015
L.M. Camarinha-Matos et al. (Eds.): PRO-VE 2015, IFIP AICT 463, pp. 27–38, 2015.
DOI: 10.1007/978-3-319-24141-8_3

To effectively benefit from open innovation, it is recommended the utilization of adequate risk models. Open innovation is essentially a collaborative strategy. There is a significant number of risk-like assessment approaches for collaborative networks already, but few specifically addressing risk in open innovation.

Our aim is to develop research work towards developing a risk assessment approach for open innovation. As explained in Sect. 3, this problem has had little attention by the research community. Given this scarcity, we considered a research question, which can be stated as: *How to model open innovation risk assessment?* Our effort is, therefore, devoted to contribute to provide an answer to this question.

Our research method starts by problem formulation. It is followed by the conceptualization of open innovation and risk and by the related research analysis. The next phase is devoted to work on risk modeling in open innovation. In this regard, our risk assessment approach is based on a widely used risk model, namely, FMEA. The obtained approach is illustrated through an application example, followed by result analysis.

In the next section, we provide the relevant concepts regarding open innovation and risk. We briefly describe a few existing risk assessment models. A research on the state of the art related to risk in open innovation is presented in Sect. 3, aiming at identify and characterize risk assessment models in open innovation. In Sect. 4, we illustrate how we could model risk assessment using the FMEA model. We also provide an illustrative application example. We finish the results analysis, conclusions and future work.

2 Base Concepts

2.1 Open Innovation

The concept of open innovation, coined by Chesbrough in 2003 [1], has become relevant in practice and in academia. Open innovation is now a mainstream research focus in innovation literature [2]. One of the reasons for the advance of the open innovation paradigm is based on the principle that today´s problems are often complex and require a wide range of expertise. To create and implement solutions it is required that collaboration occurs among different areas and people with a variety of experience and knowledge. It is very difficult for organizations to build solutions and create knowledge by themselves. The basic assumption of open innovation is opening up the innovation process. This means to treat research and development as an open system. Open innovation is usually put in contrast to closed innovation, supposedly its precursor, where companies generate their own innovation ideas, and then develop, build, market, distribute, service, finance, and support them on their own [1].

Open innovation suggests that valuable ideas can come from inside or outside the company as well. The mobility of competencies, the increasing presence of venture-capital, the emergence start-ups and the role of university research and its linkages give rise to a more open approach towards innovation. Collaboration is argued to facilitate the production of new knowledge more than just transferring it. Chesbrough [3] has referred to open innovation not only as being a business model, but also as a way of promoting and sharing knowledge. This means that open innovation can go beyond the idea of knowledge transaction and of in/outsourcing ideas, but promote the creation of new knowledge.

Companies can develop and bring ideas to the market using channels outside of their current businesses, in order to generate value for the organization. A path for accomplishing this can involve new businesses and licensing agreements. These might be financed and staffed with the existing company's personnel. In addition, ideas can also be originated outside the company and be brought inside it, for commercialization [4]. In other words, the connection between a company and its environment is more permeable, enabling innovative ideas to transfer easily where boundaries once existed.

As argued by Felin and Zenger [5], the mechanisms for accessing external knowledge and promoting open innovation encompass a range of alternatives including alliances and joint ventures, corporate venture capital, licensing, open source platforms, and participation in various development communities. Each of the modalities brings distinct benefits, implies distinct levels of openness, and various risks. For instance, they vary in terms of intellectual property ownership, from Joint-ventures, created by formal-agreements, and "open-source models", in which IP is given away to a (large and open) software development community.

An open innovation strategy can generate a positive result, but, it also involves some risks. Therefore, companies should have a policy to secure open innovation within their organization, to create interfaces and make achievements measureable. The way employees manage their external partners is also very important and plays a central role.

2.2 Risk Models in Engineering

Proceeding as specified in our research method, we now address the concept of risk in an engineering context. To overcome global competition and rapid technological advances, in order to predict and positively respond to changes, the development of organizational capability to innovate has become one of the prime strategy in SMEs. This has been done despite the lack on practical models, metrics and tools to assist their risk management efforts [6].

For many years, organizations risk has been seen mainly as a combination of the probability of occurrence of harms and the severity of these harms. Nowadays, such in project management, risk is viewed as related to uncertain events or conditions that, when they occur, pose positive or negative effects on projects objectives. Similarly, as the uncertainty associated with innovative processes is bonded not only to inherent risk of failure, but also to inherent chance of success, these subsequently bring on the necessity of adequate risk management in innovative processes [7]. Thereby, and since the purpose of an integrated risk management is to facilitate innovation rather than stifle it, innovating firms require a strategy not of risk avoidance, but of early risk diagnosis and management [8, 9], which should be spread through organizations and collaborative networks.

Based on general project management practices, several frequently used risk assessment models can be identified, such as the Balanced Scorecard (BSC), Failure Mode Effects Analysis (FMEA), Fault Tree Analysis (FTA), Analytic Hierarchy Process (AHP) and Risk Diagnosing Methodology (RDM).

The BSC model is typically used to facilitate the monitoring of the firm's success factors, which can be viewed as opportunities as well as risks, meaning that the BSC is by nature an instrument close to the risk's grounds function [10].

Another commonly used risk assessment approach is the Failure Mode Effects Analysis (FMEA), which is a systemic approach suited to help identify and reduce critical aspects in early stages of products and processes conception. Due to its role in the context of our research work, this risk assessment technic is explained in more depth in the next section.

The Fault Tree Analysis (FTA) can be both used as a risk identification method or as a risk analysis instrument. In this approach, the probability of negative events can be estimated and their causes deducted from a named Fault Tree, in which the probabilities of alternative situations are assessed. These situations are organized using Boolean logic, in which lower-level events are fed into upper-level ones [10].

Another used risk assessment approach is the Analytic Hierarchy Process (AHP). AHP is considered a multivariate analysis technique that aims to decrease the randomness of subjective assessments, by having in consideration different objectives grounded on distinct criteria [11]. It is predominantly used in scenario selection and evaluation [12].

Another risk assessment approach is Risk Diagnosing Methodology (RDM) which main purpose is to help provide strategies that will support and improve the chance of projects success, by identifying and managing their potential risks [8, 13]. It is used to support the systematic diagnosis of companies, considering issues such as consumer and trade acceptance, commercial viability, competitive responses, external influential responses, product technology and manufacturing technology [8], in which the assessment of project risk is determined not only by risk likelihood and its effects, but also by the companies' ability to influence the course of the risk actions.

2.3 The FMEA Risk Assessment

FMEA is widely used risk assessment approach. It was original developed inside Aeronautic Industry in the 50's to guide the design process. But it has been widely used in a broader sense, not only to assess physical systems but also organizational ones, such as those in the areas of Knowledge Management [14] and supply-chain management [15]. The FMEA can be used as a design tool to systematically analyze postulated component failures and identify the resultant effects on system operations. A failure at a lower level may very well cause a larger failure on the higher level. Therefore, it is essential to find them as fast as possible [16].

With FMEA, we can quantify the risk level of each identified failure, whether known or potential. Then, an estimate of its likelihood of occurrence, severity, and detectability is made for each one. At this point, an evaluation of the necessary actions is performed, namely, they can be taken, planned or ignored. The emphasis is to minimize the probability of failures or to minimize their effects. The main constituents of the FMEA model are described as:

Failure - Event/process in which any part of the organizational system does not perform according to the prescribed behavior. Example: absence of knowledge sharing when it was expected.

Failure mode - The specific manner by which a failure occurs in terms of the failure of some part of the organization. It shall at least clearly describe the end state of the item under consideration. It is the result of the failure mechanism (see next). Example: An enterprise owing key knowledge left the project.

Failure cause and/or mechanism - Defects/problems detected in the elements of the organizational system which are the underlying cause or sequence of causes that initiate behaviors leading to a failure mode over a certain time. A failure mode may have several causes. Example: Inadequate organizational rules adoption may cause network weaknesses.

Failure effect - Immediate consequence of a failure. Example: Lack of knowledge sharing decreases the quality of a project and increases its duration.

Likelihood of occurrence (L) - The Likelihood of occurrence is the probability that a specific failure mode, which is the result of a specific cause under current open-innovation network, will happen. Failure Likelihood is a relative ranking within the scope of an individual FMEA. A suggested likelihood scale is given in Table 1.

Table 1. Risk guidelines rank.

Rank	Failure likelihood	Severity of effects	Detection processes
5	Frequent	Maximum severity - failure leads to the end of the open-innovation process	Extremely unlikely - management processes will almost certainly not detect the potential failure before it occurs.
4	Reasonably probable	Very High Severity – open innovation network performance severely affected. Members very dissatisfied. Network members will be able to correct the failure/situation with some constraints	Remote likelihood – management process more likely will not detect the existence of a potential failure before it occurs
3	Occasional	Moderate - reduced performance with gradual performance degradation. Network members dissatisfied. Network members will be able to correct the failure/situation	Moderate – management process may detect the potential failure before it occurs
2	Remote	Minor – network members will probably notice the effect, it is considered negligible	High: management processes have a good chance of detecting the potential failure before it occurs
1	Extremely unlikely	Very slight – insignificant/negligible effect	Very high: management processes almost certainly will detect the potential failure before it occurs

Severity (S) - Severity is an assessment of the most serious effect for a given failure mode. Example: The severity of problematic partners can be reduced through their exchange. If such an exchange is attainable, the failure can be minimized eliminated. Severity is also a relative ranking within the scope of an individual FMEA.

Detectability (D) - Detectability is an assessment of the ability to identify any potential failure modes, case they occur. Detectability is a relative ranking within the scope of an individual FMEA.

The suggested risk guidelines for severity, occurrence and detection are given in Table 1.

Risk Priority Number (RPN) - The Risk Priority Number defines the priority of each failure. RPNs have no value or meaning by themselves. They are used only to rank (define) the potential open- innovation network deficiencies. The RPN is calculated by multiplying these three ratings:

$$RPN = \text{Failure Likelihood} \times \text{Severity} \times \text{Detectability}. \tag{1}$$

In this equation, failure Likelihood, Severity and detectability must have a value greater than zero. A suggested RPN ranking is provided in Table 2.

Recommended Action - The recommended action may be specific action(s) or it may correspond to major changes in the operating process of an open innovation project or network. The idea of the recommended actions in FMEA is to reduce the severity, occurrence, detection or them all.

Table 2. Risk category guidelines.

Heading level	Risk category
90–125	Extreme
60–89	Significant
40–59	Major
18–39	Moderate
1–17	Low

3   Depicting Existing Approaches of Risk Assessment in Open Innovation

During our research work, it was relatively difficult to find related research concerning risk assessment in open innovation. This difficulty led us to formulate the hypothesis that such models might be currently scarce. But this is an assumption that is difficult to demonstrate. Frequently in science, we can more easily prove that something exists than proving that it does not [17, 18].

In order to overcome this difficulty, we devised an approach to estimate the amount of research work concerning risk in open innovation. For such, a small content analysis based on the utilization of "Publish or Perish" search engine was performed.

"Publish or Perish" allows flexible searches of published research works. In our approach, we looked for papers with certain words in their titles. For instance, when a research intends to publish a paper related to risk modeling or assessment, the word "risk" or "uncertainty" is likely to appear in its title. Similarly, this is also true for researchers aiming to write papers on innovation. In this case, the word "innovation" or its synonymous would appear in the title.

The search was restricted to publications written since 2004, as the term "open innovation" was coined in 2003. After initial trials, we perceived that many results were unrelated to open innovation, so we tuned the search engine to filter out papers containing the words: "financial", "bank", "credit", "price", "climate" and "drug". We performed similar searches for words in areas that are considered consolidated, to serve as a comparison basis. The obtained results are summarized in Table 3.

Table 3. Publications regarding risk in open innovation, with comparison examples.

Keywords	Papers found	Number of citations
Risk innovation	901	2446
Risk innovation model	48	74
Risk innovation modeling	5	12
Risk innovation assessment	44	93
Risk innovation management	182	461
Open innovation Risk	7	4
Open innovation Risk model	1	0
Open innovation risk management	0	0
Open innovation FMEA	0	0
Virtual organizations risk	6	12
Collaborative networks risk	6	22
Collaborative FMEA	2	0
Collaboration FMEA	2	0
Business risk model	146	361
Risk portfolio selection	280	1672
Failure mode effects analysis	406	2829
FMEA	above 1000	6602 (of these 1000)
Risk management	above 1000	71809 (of these 1000)
Organizational behavior	above 1000	44648 (of these 1000)

The mentioned table is split in three groups of results. The first group indicates there is a significant number of papers addressing risk in either closed and open innovation, and that some of them (could be up to 48) are more specific to risk models. The second group indicates there are few papers which consider risk in open innovation, about 7, and that only one has got the word "model" in title. Concerning risk, such areas of collaborative networks also present similar numbers. The last group of results serves as comparison basis, as it provides figures for areas that are more stabilized. The approach can be repeated and extended with more words. For instance, the number of papers with "uncertainty" and "innovation" in their titles was 308. But if we include the word "open", we only obtain 6 publications. A reader is right stating that the approach may not provide very rigorous figures. But the divergence of values between open innovation and other consolidated areas provides support to our claim, that such models for risk in open innovation might be scarce.

As to establish a theoretical bases for our research in open innovation risk assessment models, we performed an analysis of the more promising publications among the few ones which were obtained during our context analysis:

Research works addressing risks, whiteout risk assessment models: In [19], a risk-based technology management approach was proposed. In this approach, risk is considered as an inherent aspect of the product development. It simultaneously considers both quantitative innovation objectives and quantitative product delivery objectives, such as cost, schedule and performance, enabling to establish formal quantitative technology innovation objectives and to track and monitoring them during a product development cycle. In [20], the external technology dependence, complex process management, difficulty in intellectual property protection, market information leakage, and mismatched resources capacity are identified as situations that pose risks in open innovation projects. In [21], several factors related to intellectual property competition in open innovation are highlighted. The study reveals the likelihood that open and proprietary competitors will clash, according to the industry type, e.g. radio and television, Medical, Electric motors, food and beverages, etc.

Identified risk models in open innovation: The research work in [22] is focused on the risk evaluation of customer integration in new product development. A number of risk factors of customer integration in new product development were identified, namely, organization risk, capacity risk, knowledge risk, and market risk. Their goal was to develop a risk evaluation method. The approach is based on rough set theory to handle vagueness. In [23], a research was conducted towards developing methodologies for managing risks of open-source software adoption in a context of an ecosystem of developers. The approach combined risk monitoring methods in order to provide early warnings of risks and their mitigation. The developed tools also included Bayesian networks and social network analysis. In [24], a risk management approach for crowdsourcing innovation is proposed. It provided overall guidelines to managing risks associated with crowdsourcing strategy, and a risk model suited for small and medium enterprises.

4 Application of FMEA to Open Innovation

4.1 Factors of Risk in Open Innovation

As mentioned in previous section, there are many definitions of risk according to the respective contexts in consideration. For all that matters in this research work, we can assume one of these general descriptions, in which risk can be seen as a probability or threat of damage, injury, liability, loss, or any other negative occurrence that is caused by external or internal vulnerabilities, and that may be avoided through preemptive action [25].

There are several innovation modalities, which as described before, are characterized by several aspects, like degree of openness to external partners. Each of these modalities pose distinct risk types. Envisaging a risk assessment instrument requires the identification of these risk types. Table 4 presents an initial characterization of these risks, which affect enterprises participating in open innovation.

Table 4. Situations posing risks in innovation, based on [20].

Situations	Description
External technology dependence	When enterprises rely excessively on their partners for technology and knowledge, they might get in weaker situation if cooperation with these partners fail
Complex process management	The absence of organizational boundaries and the interaction with autonomous partners increases the difficulty of process control and management. Conflicts and uncooperative behavior might manifest
Intellectual property protection	When a partner gives away its knowledge to its peers, core knowledge is difficult to protect. Enterprises risk lose control of knowledge ownership, and may not collect the desired benefits
Market information leakage	When participating in open innovation, enterprises may need to disclosure knowledge and business secrets to peers. They risk product and user information being stolen by its peers
Resources capacity mismatch	When resources and capacity of several partner are mismatched, it creates obstacles for innovation activity

For each risk of a failure, we can identify its causes, its effects and corresponding degree of impact, and the likelihood of its occurrence, as illustrated in Table 5.

Table 5. Characterization of open innovation risks

Failure	Failure mode	Effect	Failure mechanisms
Partner needs competency not available within the network	A partner left the project	Loss of core competencies vital for the project	Excessive reliance on external partners; Low technological/competence independence
Cooperation issues	Uncooperative behavior	Project disruption	Conflicting goals and expectations; values misalignment
Intellectual property protection (IP)	Abuse of IP by peers	Loss of trust among network partners; loss of competiveness	Inadequate IP laws and regulations
Market information sharing	Insecure disclosure of core market knowledge	Theft of product and customers information	Information leakage occurs during customers and suppliers participation in the innovation process
Resource allocation	Mismatched resource capacity	Costs increment; project delay	Wrong perception of resources capacity and complementarity

4.2 Assessing Risk Example

The information regarding the risk factors described in previous section can be used to illustrate how we could assess risks in open innovation using.

Let us suppose the existence of an open innovation project aiming at developing an Internet of Things application for health care. In an initial stage of the project, the set of potential failures where identified and analyzed. The corresponding values for the likelihood of occurrences, severity and detectability of each failure were estimated. The obtained risk assessment results are presented in Table 6. The values in the table were merely chosen for illustrative purposes.

Table 6. Open innovation risk assessment illustration with FMEA method

Failure Mode	Likelihood of occurrence (L)	Severity of consequence (S)	Detectability of the failure (D)	RPN (L × S × D)
Partner with key technology left the project	5	3	4	60 (significant)
Uncooperative behavior	2	2	3	12 (low)
Abuse of IP by peers	4	5	5	100 (Extreme)
Insecure disclosure of core knowledge	4	4	2	32 (moderate)
Mismatched resource capacity	2	3	3	18 (moderate)

The obtained risk priority numbers provide indication of which failures must receive more attention. For instance, the RPN for "uncooperative behavior" is low, while the risk of abuse of IP by peers is extreme (see Table 2). Based on this assessment, a project manager can take preventive actions in order to minimize the likelihood of these failures and minimize the effects of their eventual occurrence. For instance, reducing the risk that some peers may abuse of intellectual property during the project implies establishing agreements with effective rules to protect IP, as well as the monitoring processes to ensure the compliance with these rules.

5   Conclusions

We described an approach for risk assessment towards providing an answer to the formulated research question, which is concerned on how to access risk in open innovation. Although existing research works address risk in open Innovation, specific works considering risk assessment models seem scarce.

After an initial conceptualization and related research analysis, we identified illustrative examples of failures in open innovation projects from literature. As a way to illustrate how to assess open innovation risks, we characterized these failures according to one widely used risk model, namely the FMEA. To our knowledge, the FMEA model had never been used in the concrete "open innovation" realm. An application example of FMEA illustrated the approach.

The study and development of our approach led us to conclude that it is necessary further research for an adequate open innovation risk assessment, including a more comprehensive characterization of open innovation risks. In this regards, we should assume a more holistic perspective. Furthermore, open innovation is inherently collaborative. Therefore, one line of research for future work may include the adaptation of existing collaborative risk models, so they could suit in open innovation. In the area of collaborative networks, there is a variety of collaboration-related key performance indicators already, as well as assessment models of more soft nature, such as value systems, benefits sharing methods, and collaboration preparedness. Encompassing these elements into a tailored and holistic approach to risk assessment in open innovation is planned for the next phase of this research work.

Acknowledgments. This work was funded in part by the Center of Technology and Systems and FCT-PEST program UID/EEA/00066/2013 (Impactor project), by DEMI/FCT/UNL and by CIUHCT: Interuniversity Center for the History of Science and Technology.

References

1. Chesbrough, Henry: Open Innovation: The New Imperative for Creating and Profiting from Technology. Harvard Business School Press, Boston (2003)
2. Elmquist, M., Fredberg, T., Ollila, S.: Exploring the field of open innovation. Eur. J. Innov. Manage. **12**(3), 326–345 (2009)
3. Chesbrough, H.: Open Services Innovation: Rethinking Your Business to Grow and Compete in a New Era. Jossey-Bass, San Francisco (2010)
4. Chesbrough, H., Vanhaverbeke, W., West, J. (eds.): Open Innovation: Researching a New Paradigm. Oxford University Press, Oxford (2006)
5. Felin, T., Zenger, T.R.: Open or closed innovation? Prob. Solving Gov. Choice Res. Policy **43**(5), 914–925 (2014)
6. Aleixo, G., Tenera, A.: New product development process on high-tech innovation life cycle. World Acad. Sci. Eng. Technol. **58**, 794–800 (2009)
7. Vargas-hernández, J.G., García-santillán, A.: Management in the innovation project. J. Knowl. Manage. Econ. Inf. Technol. **1**(7), 1–24 (2011)
8. Keizer, J., Halman, J., Song, M.: From experience: applying the risk diagnosing methodology. J. Prod. Innov. Manage. **19**(3), 213–232 (2002)
9. Pereira, L., Tenera, A., Wemans, J.: Insights on individual's risk perception for risk assessment in web-based risk management tools. Procedia Technol. **9**, 886–892 (2013)
10. Henschel, T.: Risk Management Practices of SMEs: Evaluating and Implementing Effective Risk Management Systems. ESV- Erich Schmidt Verlag, Berlin (2008). Edwards and Bowen, 2005

11. Goodwin, P., Wright, G.: Decision Analysis for Management Judgment, 3rd edn. Wiley, New York (2004)
12. Hülle, J., Kaspar, R., Möller, K.: Analytic network process - an overview of applications in research and practice. Int. J. Oper. Res. (IJOR) **16**(2), 172–213 (2013)
13. Pereira, L., Tenera, A., Bispo, J., Wemans, J.: A risk diagnosing methodology web-based platform for micro, small and medium businesses: remarks and enhancements. In: Fred, A., Dietz, J.L.G., Liu, K., Filipe, J. (eds.) IC3 K 2013. CCIS, vol. 454, pp. 340–356. Springer, Heidelberg (2015)
14. Trafialek, J., Kolanowski, W.: Application of failure mode and effect analysis (FMEA) for audit of HACCP system. Food Control **44**, 35–44 (2014)
15. Gary Teng, S., Michael Ho, S., Shumar, Debra, Liu, Paul C.: Implementing FMEA in a collaborative supply chain environment. Int. J. Qual. Reliab. Manage. **23**(2), 179–196 (2006)
16. IEC 60812 Technical Committee: IEC 60812, analysis techniques for system reliability - procedure for failure mode and effects analysis (FMEA). IEC (2006)
17. Alderson, P.: Absence of evidence is not evidence of absence: we need to report uncertain results and do it clearly. BMJ Br. Med. J. **328**(7438), 476 (2004)
18. Walton, D.: Nonfallacious arguments from ignorance. Am. Philos. Q. **29**(4), 381–387 (1992)
19. Sleefe, G.E.: Quantification of technology innovation using a risk-based framework. Proc. World Acad. Sci. Eng. Technol. **66**, 589–593 (2010)
20. Xiaoren, Z., Ling, D., Xiangdong, C.: Interaction of open innovation and business ecosystem. Int. J. u- e-Serv. Sci. Technol. **7**(1), 51–64 (2014)
21. Alexy, O., Reitzig, M.: Managing the business risks of open innovation. McKinsey Q. **1**, 17–21 (2012)
22. Song, W., Ming, X., Xu, Z.: Risk evaluation of customer integration in new product development under uncertainty. Comput. Ind. Eng. **65**(3), 402–412 (2013)
23. Rossi, B., Russo, B., Succi, G.: Adoption of free/libre open source software in public organizations: factors of impact. Inf. Technol. People **25**(2), 156–187 (2012)
24. Souza, L., Ramos, I., Esteves, J.: Crowdsourcing innovation: a risk management approach. In: MCIS, p. 67 (2009)
25. Business dictionary. http://www.businessdictionary.com/definition/risk.html. Accessed 15 April 2015

Bayesian Network-Based Risk Prediction in Virtual Organizations

Hamideh Afsarmanesh[✉] and Mahdieh Shadi

Federated Collaborative Networks Group, Informatics Institute,
Computer Science Department, University of Amsterdam,
Amsterdam, The Netherlands
{h.afsarmanesh,m.shadi}@uva.nl

Abstract. To support and increase the success rate of collaboration in Virtual Organizations (VOs), usually formed within Virtual organizations Breeding Environments (VBEs), their operation stage and performance of their tasks must be continuously monitored and supervised. A task in the VO is either planned to be performed by an individual partner or jointly by a group of partners, and typically consists of several sub-tasks defining the day-to-day activities of its involved partners. However, VOs are dynamic and therefore detailed activities related to sub-tasks are defined gradually during their operation phase. In this paper, as the base for discovery of potential task failures, past performance and record of previous sub-tasks' fulfillment of each partner (so-called agent) is considered for appraisal of its trustworthiness. Furthermore, the communication characteristic of the agent and its current workload in all its involved VOs within the VBE are also considered as input for measuring its potential probability of failure on currently assigned sub-tasks. For tasks that involve several partners, a Bayesian network is created during the VO's operation phase, and used for measuring their failure probabilities. These two potential risk measurements in VOs enable their coordinators to appropriately identify the weak points in their planning of upcoming VO activities, as well as assisting them with advice on how to intervene and change the situation.

Keywords: Virtual Organizations · VO supervision/coordination · Failure risk prediction · Task performance promises · Trustworthiness · Responsibility template

1 Introduction

To respond to the emerging opportunities in the market, some autonomous and heterogeneous agents registered in a Virtual organization Breeding Environment join forces and form a VO. Research on the success rate of Virtual Enterprises in business show that at least 30 % of the established VOs end up either in failure or operate under the pressure of high risks for failure [1]. Primarily, three categories of risks for organizations involved in a virtual organization are highlighted in the literature [2], including: internal, external, and network-related, in relation to the success rate of virtual organizations.

© IFIP International Federation for Information Processing 2015
L.M. Camarinha-Matos et al. (Eds.): PRO-VE 2015, IFIP AICT 463, pp. 39–52, 2015.
DOI: 10.1007/978-3-319-24141-8_4

Network-related risks are those addressing collaborative relationships among organizations, and are typically caused by lack of trust, insufficient information sharing, clash of cultures, etc. To support the success of collaboration among the involved organizations in the VOs, it is necessary to define a framework and provide support functionality through which the risks can be mitigated.

VO is a goal-oriented network, which means during its formation/creation stage, a set of targets are gradually defined, and the main sub-goals and their tasks to be performed for achieving those targets are pre-planned. However, during the operation/ evolution stage of the VO's life-cycle, these high level sub-goals and their tasks need to be detailed out into a set of specific sub-tasks, to be each performed either by a specific partner, or jointly by a group of partners. In our research, we focus on risks that mostly rise during the operation phase of the VOs, when large number of tasks and sub-tasks are planned and scheduled (or are being gradually planned), each to be performed either individually by one partner, or jointly by a group of partners. To support the success of collaboration in VOs, it is necessary that its planned activities are monitored, supervised, and coordinated, in order to discover and/or predict potential risks of failure in their fulfillment. Our novel approach to forecasting and managing potential risks of failure in VOs is founded on analyzing partners' past and present behavior in performing the tasks to which they have committed. Our approach contributes to developing novel methods and mechanisms for monitoring both individual behavior and collective behavior of partners in VOs [3]. The factors that are considered for potential risk in VOs in our research are focused on three specific risks, including: low trustworthiness, insufficient communication, and heavy workload. These three factors play a major role as causes for risk during the operation phase of the VO's life cycle. Therefore, our approach concentrates on measuring the trust level, communication level, and workload level of each VO partner, acting as an agent, within a VBE [4]. These are used as the criteria for discovering potential probability of activity failures in currently assigned sub-tasks to agents.

Trust is commonly considered as a main countering factor to the risks that may rise in networks, due to agents' opportunistic behavior, creating uncertainty and ambiguity, and thus an agent's low trustworthiness influences its risk of failure in fulfilling its responsibilities, while agent's high trust level positively influences its successful completion of assigned sub-tasks and being cooperative in the VO. In our approach [5], a set of trust-related norms are already defined that can be monitored for VO partners, depending on the importance and timeliness of responsibilities assigned to them. There is also a direct relationship between trust and communication in VOs. More trust is established in the network when there is effective communication, and insufficient or failing communication among partners in a VO, is typically followed by its failure. A third risk factor considered in our approach is the current workload on the staff and resources that are owned by the VO partners, and this considers the workload of each agent within the entire VBE and in relation to all its commitments. For instance, if a VO partner is simultaneously involved in several VOs, its workload may become too heavy and its resources and staff overloaded, which must be considered when measuring its potential risk to fail the already committed responsibilities or when volunteering to undertake new responsibilities.

It should be noted that the main goals and sub-goals of the VOs are usually reflected through high level tasks to be undertaken by its partners. These are typically included in the VO contracts, which are agreed and signed during the VO's creation phase among its partners. Nevertheless, considering that VOs are dynamic organizations, typically the sub-tasks related to daily activities to be performed by the partners are gradually defined during the VO's operation phase [5]. Furthermore, some sub-tasks need to be executed sequentially, while some others concurrently, which implies the existence of certain causal relationships among different tasks and sub-tasks. The responsibilities accepted by different VO partners in performing each sub-task constitute promises from partners to perform those sub-tasks. A responsibility template can represent task/sub-tasks, with the related promises/commitments from VO partners to perform them, as well as inter-relationships among the sub-tasks. Promises made to perform sub-tasks, are formulized as the norms for the promising partner. These causal inter-relationships can be modeled through a Bayesian network. When and if a VO partner violates one of its related norms, the risk prediction process discovers if there are other sub-tasks assigned to that partner, which will now become risky. For calculating the failure probability of every individual sub-task, the above mentioned factors are considered. For joint tasks and sub-tasks, promised by a group of partners, the Bayesian network provides their failure probabilities at any point in time, which in turn enables the VO coordinator to identify their associated potential risks, and possibly to decide reassigning the risky tasks and sub-tasks, for which our approach also facilitates finding the best-fit candidates for the reassignment.

The remaining structure of this paper is as follows: Sect. 2 provides the related works. Section 3 addresses risk factors considered in this. How to find the weakest/most risky planned task/sub-task in the VO is investigated in Sect. 4. Finally, Sect. 5 provides the conclusion of this research.

2 Related Works

Coordinating a Virtual Organizations (VO), with the awareness about any potential risk of failure in fulfilling some of its tasks, clearly increases the chance of its success, and thus the effective achieving of its goals and sub-goals. Literature review illustrates different definitions for risks in various environments. Risk in an organization is defined in [6] as the probability of an event that can influence the organizations' objectives, either negatively or positively.

In our research, we seek to identify risks in the VOs, due to the VO partners who may violate some of their norms (promises they have made to fulfill some sub-tasks), and consequently threatening the success of the VO.

Factors Related to Risk. Three risk factors related to the supply chains, including the internal, external and network-related risks are identified in [2]. Changes in industry market, political situation, social atmosphere, etc. are categorized as the sources for external risks threatening the involved organizations, while events such as strikes, machine failure, etc. are placed in the internal risks categories. All other risks raised from the collaborative relationships among organizations in a VO, are clustered under the network-related risk category. Being two forms of collaborative networks, there is a large similarity on internal and external risk factors between the supply chains and virtual organizations. However, the factors related to their network-related risks are different between the virtual organizations and supply chains. In supply chains, every organization is one member in the chain, thus knowing about and dependent on two other organizations, which appear before and after it in the chain. Also, every organization is contracted to perform its own sub-task within the chain, so the success/failure of each organization depends primarily on receiving the needed output from its predecessor organization in the chain as well as performing its own contracted tasks well. The case of VOs however is very different. All its partners are jointly responsible for achieving the goals and sub-goals of the VO, and therefore, the success or failure of every one of its involved organizations is directly dependent on the success or failure of the VO as a whole. This joint responsibility is the main reason why even when one partner cannot perform its sub-task in the VO, other partners volunteer to perform it instead, so that the VO as a whole can succeed. The joint responsibility notion in turn creates complex inter-relationships among the involved partners. Modeling the individual and collective cooperative behavior of organizations that are involved in VOs is challenging. Once an organization's behavior is monitored and modeled within a VBE, and through its involvement in a number of VOs, its patterns can be established, and used for reasoning about predication of its behavior in its forthcoming sub-tasks.

In [2] a list of important sources/causes for network-related risks in VOs is provided, which includes: lack of trust, lack of clarity in the agreements/commitments, partners heterogeneity, loss of communication, lack of information sharing, heavy workload, ontology differences, heterogeneity in structure and design, cultural differences, and geographic distance, etc. In other words, any of these sources represents the existence of a risk in the VO, and depending on its severity can contribute to its failure. From this list of risk sources, trust, commitment, and information sharing are investigated further in [7], specifically focused on the creation phase of the VOs, and finding the potential risk of collaboration for the industrial partners and logistics operators that wish to get involved in the formation of a new VO.

In our research, we focus on three factors of trust, communication, and workload of the organizations (considered as agents), in order to predict the probability of failure for each of these agents in fulfilling their individual assigned sub-tasks during the VO operation phase. As such, violation of a trust-related norm by an agent triggers the risk prediction process to consider further involvement of that agent in the responsibility template of the VO. Our algorithm focuses on dynamic measurement of agent's trustworthiness and potential risks associated with it during the operation phase of the VOs, and therefore very different from approaches applied during the VO creation phase [7, 8].

Risk Prediction Approaches. A number of approaches, some of which parameterized, are employed for modeling and prediction of risks, such as the FTA (Fault Tree Analysis), the ETA (Event Tree Analysis) and the ANP (Analytic Network Process). FTA uses the combination of AND and OR gates to build the failure model [9]. It calculates the probability of failing for the top level event(s), based on the data extracted from their lower level events. This method is however limited to a binary prediction, and it only treats instantaneous failures, i.e. it does not include and/or consider any delays in time. Furthermore, a main drawback of FTA is related to building the accurate tree which requires a great effort.

In [7], estimation of the failure risk for individual partners is routed in ETA. ETA addresses all potential consequences resulted by an initiating event, to which the probability for their occurring can be assigned. In addition to individual risk, collective risk is also addressed in [7] which is evaluated through fault tree analysis. The limitation of the ETA approach is however related to the number of event trees that it generates, since one event tree is needed for assessment of risks for each partner, therefore the time complexity of the approach and its algorithm is high.

ANP is a multi-criteria decision making method that produces a structured influence network of clusters containing nodes. The network contains source node, intermediate nodes and sink nodes indicating different criteria. The origin of the influence path is shown by a source node, while the destination of influence path is illustrated by a sink node. In [10], the authors compare ANP with other multi-criteria decision making methods. However, the ANP model has also the limitation to require filling up many questionnaires as input.

In our approach, a Bayesian Network (BN) is developed, which consists of a set of nodes representing its variables and a set of directed arcs representing relationships between those variables. If variable A causes B then there is a directed arc from A to B and A is the parent of B. To each node, a conditional probability is assigned which indicates the probability of the variable associated to the node, given the probability of the variables associated to its parents. In our research, nodes represent the failure in fulfilling the sub-tasks, tasks, or goals. The probability of occurring failure in fulfilling of the individual sub-tasks is measured based on the trustworthiness, communication level and workload of the responsible agents. Then, the probability of failure occurring in joint-tasks is calculated according to the Bayesian network rules.

The benefits of BN to assess risks in natural hazards are illustrated in [11]. Roed et al. in [12] propose a framework considering human and organizational factors in hybrid causal logic (HCL) to perform a risk analysis. This framework is developed based on traditional risk analysis tools (FTA and ETA) accompanied by the Bayesian Network. In our approach, we use BN to recognize risky tasks to support the success of collaboration in VOs. The BN is built during VO operation phase, and if task planning is changed then the graph representing BN is easily updated, which is not easy in other mentioned approaches that need more effort to stay up-to-date with changes in task planning.

3   Risk Factors

The ability to predict the reasons of particular events is crucial in risk management. Based on the state-of-the-art in the area, different risk sources can be identified, among which three specific ones are considered in our research, including: lack of trust, lack of communication, and heavy workload. These three play a vital role as causes for risk during the operation phases of the VO's life cycle, and are addressed in more details in the following paragraphs.

3.1 Trust Level

Trust plays an important role in virtual organizations and in relation to identification of risk factors. Establishing trust is primarily rooted in the behavior of involved partners. Therefore, monitoring the behavior of organizations involved in the VO and how they are performing their commitments can provide good indications for predicting some of the weak points in the near future plan of activities, which can cause risks in the VOs. Subsequently, notifying the VO coordinator about such weaknesses and the risks that are associated with them assists the coordinator with taking timely and appropriate strategic actions. For this objective, we have developed a framework, addressed in [3], which enables formalizing responsibilities and commitments of agents to perform their sub-tasks in the VOs. It further supports the VO coordinator with monitoring partners' behavior through identification of any potential violation in the set of defined norms for the VO.

In support of the VO coordinator with monitoring partners' behavior, we have earlier defined in [5] three kinds of behavioral norms, including the socio-legal norms, the functional norms, and the activity-related norms, which in one way or another constrain the partners' behavior in the VO. The socio-legal norms are related to aspects such as leadership rights that are agreed and signed by all partners usually through a so called consortium agreement.

During the VO formation/creation stage, partners commit themselves to collectively fulfill the objectives of the VO. Then through negotiating contracts, the general terms of each partner's main responsibilities in the VO are indicated as its coarse-grained tasks. The assignment of coarse-grained tasks to partners (frequently assigned as joint tasks for a number of partners to perform together) corresponds to the functional norms in the VO. However, and mostly due to the dynamic nature of VOs, these contracts cannot and do not determine the details of partners' day-to-day sub-task assignments and activities that they perform. Therefore, a template is only extracted in this phase which is called in our research Goals-Tasks-Interdependency-Template (GTIT) which is instantiated during the VO operation phase.

At different times during the VO operation phase, definition and assignment of day-to-day sub-tasks to each partner are achieved, complying with its general responsibilities, as specified in its VO contract. To assign the day-to-day sub-tasks, agreements are made within the VO between each partner who commits to perform the sub-task and its task leader. Every such agreement to commit to a sub-task, generates a promise in the VO. Fulfillment of these promises in the VO corresponds to the activity-related norms. Clearly, the activity-related norms are in conformance with the functional norms in the VO. We have implemented the behavior monitoring functionality of our approach in a tool called VOSAT (Virtual Organization Supervisory Assistant Tool) [5], within which the focus of behavior monitoring is on the activity-related norms. VOSAT is applied to assist the VO coordinator by giving useful information about the VO partners' behavior as monitored during the operation phase of the VO.

To enable monitoring and reasoning about the activity-related norms, promises must be concisely defined and formalized. In our proposed framework, a set of rules are defined according to which the state of each promise is changed, and adding new facts to the knowledge base. Every promise goes through different states during its life cycle [3], some of which are briefly described below. The state of a promise which requires a priori fulfillment of some conditions is called conditional. This means, only when any/ all required conditions are fulfilled (before their deadlines), that the state of a promise is/becomes unconditional. Otherwise, if the a priori conditions for a promise are not fulfilled on time, then the state of the promise is/becomes dissolved. If a sub-task for which a promise is made is fulfilled before/on its deadline, then the state of the promise is/become kept and if the deadline is passed and the sub-task is not fulfilled, then the state of the promise is/become not kept. If the reason for the failure in fulfilling a sub-task is beyond its promiser's control, then the state of the promise is/become invalidated, and finally a promise is/becomes released when the promisee cancels it, which requires pre-agreement with the task leader.

To evaluate the overall trust value of each agent, the VOSAT framework applies a comprehensive fuzzy evaluation method. This method is a multi-criteria decision making approach that evaluates the influences of various factors on a certain element, applying fuzzy mathematical methods [13]. For example, construction project management can be evaluated using fuzzy comprehensive evaluation in which three evaluation factors are the degree of controlling project objectives, the need of supporting of the owners and support ability of the owners and contractors. In our approach, we apply two specific fuzzy factors, namely the personal norm abidance, and collective norm abidance. To evaluate the personal norm abidance for an agent A, the past interaction/ collaboration experiences of agent A with all other agents in the VBE are considered, e.g. the number of all kept promises made by A to other agents, and the number of all violated promises. To evaluate the collective norm abidance for an agent A, all ranking suggestions received for an agent A from other agents are aggregated. Through applying this method, it is possible to measure the violation of trust-related norm for each agent, which is then used to predict the potential risk of failure for this agent.

3.2 Communication Level

The second important risk factor in virtual organizations after trust is related to failing needed communication with other partners, which is typically followed by failure in virtual organizations [14]. In other words, agents' timely and periodic reporting on the status of progress in activities under their responsibilities, e.g. by email in relation to performing a sub-task to both the task-leader and other involved partners in joint tasks, by email in relation to a Work Package to the VO coordinator, etc. is vital to the success of the VO.

Communication processes in VOs complements the VO's structures. In other words, goals of the VO as well as the partners responsibilities are reflected and clarified through their effective communication. There is in fact a direct relationship between trust and communication, meaning that more trust can be established in a collaborative networks, as a consequence of better communication.

Nevertheless, sometimes communications among agents fail. The Ratio of Failure for an agent in its required communication, is calculated through the following equation:

$$RFC\left(A_1\right) = \frac{n_f}{N}$$

A_1 shows the agent for whom we calculate the potential Risk of Failure in Communication (RFC), related to fulfilling the sub-tasks under its responsibility in the VO. The n_f shows the number of his failed communications in this VO, and the N shows the total number of required communications by this agent in the VO.

In our approach we consider that a threshold percentage for tolerating failures in communications can be defined in each VO, by its coordinator. This threshold is then compared against the RFC of an agent. If the RCF is larger than the pre-defined threshold, then their difference indicates the percentage of not-tolerated lack of communication by the agent in that VO. This difference represents the probability of Lack of Communication (LC) for the agent A_1.

3.3 Heavy Work Load

When a partner is involved in two or more VOs simultaneously, there is a risk of resources and/or staff insufficiency to undertake all its responsibilities. There is not much related work referring to this aspect, however in [8] an agent's bidding for tasks in several VOs is considered as a source of risk. In our approach, we define a Ratio of Over-workload Commitment for each agent $ROC(A_1)$, as a risk factor. If positive, this shows the percentage of over commitment of an agent A_1, when considering all its commitments to different VOs in the VBE, in comparison to the real person-months in a year that the agent has planned to invest in this VBE. Equation below:

$$ROC(A_1) = \frac{\sum_{i=1}^{n} \frac{PM_i}{y_i} - N}{N}$$

Where PM_i shows the Person-Month that organization A_1 commits in VO_i, y_i is the duration of VO_i in years, n shows the number of VOs in which A_1 is involved, and N is the maximum person-month that A_1 has planned for being involved in the VBE, as specified in its profile/competency information at the VBE. In our approach we consider that a threshold percentage for tolerating over-commitment can be defined in each VO. If the $ROC(A_1)$ is larger than this pre-defined threshold for an agent, then their difference indicates the probability of Heavy Workload (HW).

3.4 Relative Weights Comparing Risk Factors

To determine the three criteria weights used to calculate the probability of the risk, related to individual sub-tasks, an Analytic Hierarchy Process (AHP) [15] is adopted. The approach ponders a set of evaluation criteria, and a set of alternative options through which the best decision is to be made. The AHP produces a weight for each evaluation criterion according to the decision maker's criteria paired comparisons. The higher the weight, the more important is the related criterion. In order to compute the weights of the different criteria, the approach initiates the creation of a paired comparison matrix A.

The matrix A is an $m \times m$ matrix, where m is the count of evaluation criteria considered to be compared. Let us assume that each a_{jk} indicates the relative importance of the jth factor to k^{th} factor, so there are three possibilities:

$a_{jk} > 1$, if the jth factor is more important than the kth factor

$a_{jk} < 1$, if the jth factor is less important than the kth factor

$a_{jk} = 1$, if the two criteria have the same importance

There are two constraints: $a_{jk} \times a_{kj} = 1$ and $a_{jj} = 1$ for all j.

Table 1 indicates suggestive numerical scales for relative importance between any two factors [15].

Table 1. Relative importance where comparing every two factors [15]

Status	Value
Equally important	1
Slightly more important	3
More important	5
Greatly more important	7
Fully more important	9
For comparison between margins mentioned above	2, 4, 6, 8

After building the matrix A, it is possible to derive from this matrix a normalized paired comparison matrix, by making the sum of the entries on each column equal to 1. Therefore, each entry in column i is divided by the sum of the entries of that column. Ultimately, the criteria weight vector w (that is an m-dimensional column vector) is constructed by averaging the entries on each row of the normalized matrix. Of course, the consistency among assigned weights should be checked as explained in [15].

Generally, the AHP computations are directed by the decision maker's experience, hence AHP can be considered as a means to translate the decision maker's evaluations into a multi criteria ranking. Figure 1(a) shows an example of VO coordinator's opinion about comparing the influences of Lack of Trust (LT), Lack of Communication (LC), and Heavy Workload (HW) on the failure probability of individual tasks. Weights in Fig. 1(a) are selected by the area experts, based on the weights they suggested in Table 1, e.g. in this example the VO coordinator has decided that the weight of lack of trust is 7 times more important than the lack of communication (which also indicates the former is greatly more important than the latter), consequently the weight for the lack of communication in contrast to the lack of trust is 1/7 which equals to 0.14.

Considering the weight matrix shown in Fig. 1(a), the sum of entries in columns from left to right are respectively 8.33, 1.25, and 13. Then in order to normalize these values, each entry in column i is divided by the sum of the entries of that column. Consequently, the matrix is changed as shown in Fig. 1(b).

	LC	LT	HW
LC	1	.14	3
LT	7	1	9
HW	.33	.11	1

(a)

	LC	LT	HW
LC	1/8.33=0.12	.14/1.25=0.112	3/13=.23
LT	7/8.33=0.84	1/1.25=0.8	9/13=.69
HW	.33/8.33=.039	.11/1.25=0.088	1/13=.076

(b)

Fig. 1. (a) An example of weights suggested for comparing the LT, LC, and HW based on the values defined in Table 1. (b) The normalized version of the matrix in (a)

The resulted weight vector is then {(.12 + .112 + .23)/3 = 0.15, (.84 + .8 + .69)/3 = 0.78, (.039 + .088 + .076)/3 = 0.07}. This in turn means that for example, the probability of failure in fulfillment of an individual task, given the violation of trust-worthiness of the responsible agent, and when there is no lack of communication and heavy workload, is 78 %. These weights are then used in the Conditional Probability Tables (CPT), explained in the next section.

4   Proposed Approach for Risk Prediction

In the VO contracts, some general tasks are defined for the partners, in order to fulfill the VO goals and sub-goals. As illustrated in Fig. 2, we define one template called the Goals-Tasks-Interdependency-Template (GTIT) for a VO during its creation phase. The GTIT reflects the pre-defined goals and main tasks hierarchy and their inter-relationships to the VO partners, as they are typically specified in the VO contract. During the VO operation stage however, each of the main task is divided into several sub-tasks, and the sub-tasks are committed by specific partners, thus representing their different day-to-day activities. Therefore, the GTIT of a VO will dynamically get instantiated and expanded with more details during the operation phase of the VO, generating the Partner-Responsibility-Interdependency-Tree (PRIT) that represent current activities of the VO. At any time, there is only one current PRIT at the VO, which can be dynamically updated to either reflect new assignment of subtasks to partners, reassignment of main VO tasks or sub-tasks from one partner to another, or even due to higher level changes in the VO's goals and sub-goals.

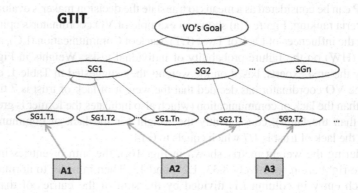

Fig. 2. The Goals-Tasks-Interdependency-Template, created during the VO creation phase. **T** is for a task, **SG** is for a Sub-Goal, and **A** is for an agent who is responsible for a particular sub-task.

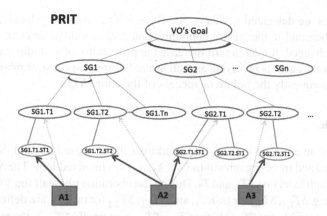

Fig. 3. An example of current Partner-Responsibility-Interdependency-Tree, created during the VO operation phase

A simple case of the extended GTIT template, called Partner-Responsibility-Interdependency-Tree (PRIT) is illustrated in Fig. 3.

In our research, the causal inter-relationships among sub-tasks, tasks, and goals are modeled through a Bayesian network. As mentioned before, three main sources of risks regarding VOs are taken into account, focused on: *trust*, *communication*, and *work-load*, and then the Bayesian network is applied to find the failure probabilities of joint-tasks or joint-sub tasks at each point in time, and subsequently the VO coordinator can properly recognize and reassign risky tasks.

Clearly, the risk analysis can be addressed during all phases of the VO life cycle, i.e. creation, operation, evolution, and dissolution. However, the focus of our work is on the operation and evolution phases.

4.1 Bayesian Network

Bayesian networks are frequently used for modeling of complex systems. A Bayesian network is a DAG (Directed Acyclic Graph). This graph consists of some nodes that representing variables and some edges representing relationships between the variables. A directed edge from variable A to variable B is considered if A is the parent of B meaning A causes B. To each node, a conditional probability is assigned which indicates the probability of the variable associated to node given the probability of the variables associated to its parents.

In this research, each node in Bayesian network represents the failure in fulfillment of a task/sub-task. The conditional probability table related to each node shows a basis for identifying how much responsibility an involved agent or group of agents have committed toward a task fulfillment.

During the VO operation phase, when the sub-tasks are defined in details or dynamically changed, the Bayesian network is established and changed accordingly. For instance, when the PRIT for the VO is changed to represent that a new partner has entered to the VO with certain new responsibilities, or when a partner leaves the VO while its responsibilities are delegated to others, the Bayesian network is updated accordingly. Moreover, when and if the trust, communication and workload level of an agent is dramatically changed, it may in turn increase the probability of its failure or success in tasks in which the agent is involved, as well as the failure or success of other dependent tasks, and consequently the failure or success of the entire VO.

4.2 Example

In this section, an example is presented to address the proposed method. Suppose that a VO is created and three organizations (A_1, A_2, A_3) are involved in it. The VO's goal is to fulfill two high level tasks T_1, and T_2. During the operation phase of the VO, a number of sub-tasks, e.g. $ST_{1,1}, ST_{1,2}$ for task T_1, and $ST_{2,1}, ST_{2,2}$ for task T_2, are defined. Furthermore, A_1 is responsible for $ST_{1,1}$, A_2 for $ST_{1,2}, ST_{2,1}$, and finally $ST_{2,2}$ is the responsibility of A_3. The purpose here is to find out if there are any tasks at risk caused for instance by any decrease in the level of trust or communication, or any increase in the workload of related agents. The Bayesian network representing this example is shown in Fig. 4(a), which represents these three performance criteria concentrated only on agent A_1. Here, $F_{ST_{1,1}}$ for Agent A_1, refers to the potential failure of sub-task $ST_{1,1}$, where LT_{A1}, LC_{A1}, and HW_{A1} respectively represent the lack of trust, lack of communication, and heavy workload, related to this agent, and calculated based on the approaches respectively explained in Sects. 3.1–3.3.

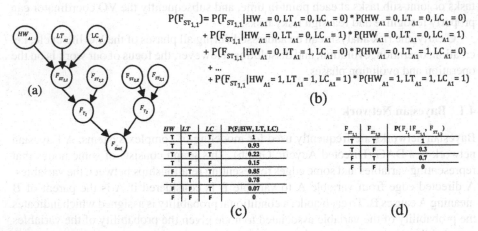

(a)

(b)

(c)

(d)

Fig. 4. (a) Bayesian network for finding the failure risk of the VO's goal, represented by F_{Goal}. (b) An example of BN rules to find the probability of $F_{ST_{1,1}}$. (c) The Conditional Probability Table (CPT) for nodes showing failure in individual sub-tasks shown by F_i. (d) The CPT for node F_{T_i}.

The CPT related to the conditional probabilities of failure in individual tasks is then calculated based on the weights explained in Sect. 3.4 as shown in Fig. 4(c). Therefore, for example, if the ratio of agent's failed communication is more than the tolerated threshold, the percentage of its committed person-month in a year is more than pre-defined threshold, and also the agent violates its trust-related norm then the conditional probability of failure in its individual task is 100 % (15 % + 78 % + 7 %). This situation is shown in the first row of the CPT shown in Fig. 4(c).

Assume that the responsibility of A_1, and A_2 in fulfillment of task T_1 are 30 %, and 70 % respectively, while the responsibility of A_2 and A_3 in fulfillment of task T_2 might be 80 % and 20 % respectively. Now we can establish the CPTs for F_{T_1}, and F_{T_2} based on how much responsibility each involved agent or group of agents have in their fulfillment. For example, the CPT for F_{T_1} based on this assumption is shown in Fig. 4(d).

An example of the communication, trust, and workload values for A_1, A_2, and A_3 both at time t_0 and time t_1 are shown in Table 2. The failure probabilities of tasks T_1 and T_2 are then calculated based on the Bayesian network rules as shown in Fig. 4(b). Furthermore, a threshold for risky tasks is considered, to identify which VO task is risky. For example, if this threshold is 0.7 then at time t_0 none of the tasks are at risk, but at time t_1 both tasks T_1 and T_2 are considered risky. However, task T_1 is more risky than T_2 because both of its involved agents, i.e. A_1 and A_2, have high level of trust violation at this time, while the values of these three criteria for A_3 that is involved in T_2 are improved in contrast to the other two, to time t_0.

Table 2. Task probabilities for the Bayesian network of Fig. 4(a).

Time step	Agent	$P(C), P(T), P(W)$	$P(F_{ST_{1,1}})$ [A_1]	$P(F_{ST_{1,2}})$ [A_2]	$P(F_{ST_{2,1}})$ [A_2]	$P(F_{ST_{2,2}})$ [A_3]	$P(F_{T_1})$ [A_1,A_2]	$P(F_{T_2})$ [A_2,A_3]
t_0	A_1	0.5, 0.7, 0.5						
	A_2	0.5, 0.6, 0.5	0.657	0.5785	0.5785	0.5	0.602	0.5628
	A_3	0.5, 0.5, 0.5						
t_1	A_1	0.5, 0.7, 0.5						
	A_2	0.5, 0.9, 0.5	0.657	0.814	0.814	0.3636	**0.7669**	0.7239
	A_3	0.2, 0.4, 0.3						

5 Conclusions

This paper addresses an extension to our earlier work on the VOSAT framework, emphasizing and supporting prediction of risk in VOs related to joint-tasks. Considering the VO's goals, identifying sources of risk in relation to the performance of planned daily activities of VO partners is critical in the risk analysis process for the success of the VO. The VOSAT framework provides mechanisms to reason about partner's trust-related norms, and their influence on VO risk analysis. Besides the trustworthiness, two other factors, the communication level and the workload level of each agent are also considered for calculating the failure probability of individual sub-tasks and in turn as potential sources for risks in VOs. Our proposed model for measuring the risk of failure related to joint-tasks, not only presents the inter-relationship among the main relevant factors, but also captures the causality among them. Therefore, based on the Partner-Responsibility-Interdependency-Tree (PRIT) which is developed during the VO's operation phase, a Bayesian network is created and kept up to date, in order to assist and enable the VO coordinator with identifying the weakest points and the high risk tasks in the VO's plan of activities.

References

1. Gao, W.: Study on the Construction and Benefits and Risks of Virtual Enterprise. Harbin Institute of Technology, Harbin (2004)
2. Alawamleh, M., Popplewell, K.: Risk sources identification in virtual organisation. In: Popplewell, K., Harding, J., Poler, R., Chalmeta, R. (eds.) Enterprise Interoperability IV, pp. 265–277. Springer, London (2010)
3. Shadi, M., Afsarmanesh, H., Dastani, M.: Agent behaviour monitoring in virtual organizations. In: Enabling Technologies: Infrastructure for Collaborative Enterprises (WETICE). IEEE (2013)
4. Afsarmanesh, H., Camarinha-Matos, L.M., Msanjila, S.S.: On management of 2nd generation virtual organizations breeding environments. J. Ann. Rev. Control **33**(2), 209–219 (2009). Elsevier
5. Shadi, M., Afsarmanesh, H.: Behavioral norms in virtual organizations. In: Camarinha-Matos, L.M., Afsarmanesh, H. (eds.) Collaborative Systems for Smart Networked Environments. IFIP AICT, vol. 434, pp. 48–59. Springer, Heidelberg (2014)
6. Vose, D.: Risk Analysis: a Quantitative Guide. Wiley, Hoboken (2008)
7. Vieira, R.G., Alves-Junior, O.C., Rabelo, R.J., Fiorese, A.: A risk analysis method to support virtual organization partners' selection. In: Camarinha-Matos, L.M., Afsarmanesh, H. (eds.) Collaborative Systems for Smart Networked Environments. IFIP AICT, vol. 434, pp. 597–609. Springer, Heidelberg (2014)
8. Alawamleh, M., Popplewell, K.: Analysing virtual organisation risk sources: an analytical network process approach. Int. J. Networking Virtual Organ. **10**(1), 18–39 (2012)
9. Xing, L., Amari, S.V.: Fault tree analysis. In: Misra, K.B. (ed.) Handbook of Performability Engineering, pp. 595–620. Springer, London (2008)
10. Saaty, T.L.: Fundamentals of the analytic network process - dependence and feedback in decision-making with a single network. J. Syst. Sci. Syst. Eng. **13**(2), 129–157 (2004)
11. Straub, D.: Natural hazards risk assessment using Bayesian networks. In: 9th International Conference on Structural Safety and Reliability (ICOSSAR 2005), Rome, Italy (2005)
12. Røed, W., Mosleh, A., Vinnem, J.E., Aven, T.: On the use of hybrid causal logic method in offshore risk analysis. Reliab. Eng. Syst. Saf. **94**(2), 445–455 (2008)
13. Li, L.J., Shen, L.T.: An improved multilevel fuzzy comprehensive evaluation algorithm for security performance. J. China Univ. Posts Telecommun. **13**(4), 48–53 (2006)
14. Westphal, I., Thoben, K.-D., Seifert, M.: Measuring collaboration performance in virtual organizations. In: Camarinha-Matos, L.M., Afsarmanesh, H., Novais, P., Analide, C. (eds.) Establishing the Foundation of Collaborative Networks, pp. 33–42. Springer, Boston (2007)
15. Saaty, T.L.: Decision making with the analytic hierarchy process. Int. J. Serv. Sci. **1**(1), 83–98 (2008)

A New Decision Support Tool for Dynamic Risks Analysis in Collaborative Networks

Afshin Jamshidi[1(✉)], Samira Abbasgholizadeh Rahimi[1],
Daoud Ait-kadi[1], and Angel Ruiz[2]

[1] Department of Mechanical Engineering, Université Laval, Quebec, Canada
Afshin.jamshidi.1@ulaval.ca
[2] Department of Operations and Decision Systems, Quebec, Canada

Abstract. Collaborative networks are complex systems and consist of many factors with dependencies among them. Although the number of collaborative networks such as advanced supply chains or virtual organizations/laboratories/ e-science is growing and their significance is increasing in the world, many of them are unsuccessful. In addition, very little attention has been paid to the risk analysis of collaborative networks by considering the dependencies among risk factors. So, the precise risks analysis associated with collaborative networks projects is crucial to attain a satisfactory performance. To address this, we are proposing an advanced decision support tool called "Fuzzy Cognitive Maps" (FCM) which can deal with risks of such complicated systems by considering the interrelationships between factors. FCM states the behaviour of complex systems accurately and illustrate any complex environment based on the experts' perceptions and by graphical representations. It is able to consider uncertainties, imprecise information, the interactions between risk factors, Information scarcity, and several decision maker's opinions. FCM is not only able to evaluate risks more precisely in collaborative networks, but also it could be applied in different decision makings problems related to collaborative networks such as partner selection and forecasting behaviors, policy analysis, modeling collaboration preparedness assessment, etc. Hence, the proposed tool would help practitioners to manage collaborative network risks and decision making problems effectively and proactively.

Keywords: Risks analysis · Collaborative networks · Fuzzy cognitive maps · Virtual enterprises · Expert knowledge

1 Introduction

Collaborative networks (CNs) such as virtual organizations, dynamic supply chains, professional virtual communities, collaborative virtual laboratories, etc. are complex systems associated with uncertainties in dynamic business environments. This uncertainty and complexity could lead to critical risks which could influence on the enterprises' performance [28–30]. According to Munyon and Perryman [1], failure rate of alliances are estimated between 60 % and 70 %. Risk evaluation of CNs is a complex and critical task since several tangible and intangible risk factors should be considered in this process. In addition, there are always some dependencies among risks that can

© IFIP International Federation for Information Processing 2015
L.M. Camarinha-Matos et al. (Eds.): PRO-VE 2015, IFIP AICT 463, pp. 53–62, 2015.
DOI: 10.1007/978-3-319-24141-8_5

influence each other mutually and these dependencies make the evaluation process more complex and challenging. Therefore, an effective method for evaluating the risks is fundamental and essential. In recent decade, many problems related to CNs such as partner selection [2–4], modeling collaboration preparedness assessment [5], etc. have been investigated. However, very little attention has been paid to the risk analysis of collaborative networks by considering the dependencies among risk factors [6, 7].

Li and Liao [6] identified all possible risks which could influence on the operation of alliance and measured their priority numbers using three criteria; probability of risk, severity of risk and risk detection number. Das and Teng [8] developed a risk perception model. The model consists of the following components: the antecedents of risk perception, relational risk and performance risk, risk perception and structural preference, and the resolution of preferences. Ip et al. [9] described and modeled a risk-based partner selection method by taking into account risk of failure, due date and the precedence of sub-project. In addition, a rule-based genetic algorithm with embedded project scheduling was proposed to solve the problem. Huang et al. [10] developed a risk management model for virtual enterprises (VE) and presented a tabu search algorithm by considering uncertainties in experts' opinions. Huang et al. [11] proposed a two level Distributed Decision Making (DDM) model for the risk management of dynamic alliance. A Particle Swarm Optimization (PSO) algorithm is used to solve the resulting optimization problem. Their proposed model improves the description of the relationship between the owner and the partners.

However, research about the risk assessment of CNs by considering the interrelationships among risks factors and forecasting the impact of each risk on the other risks don't exist in the literature of CNs and further research in this field is required. Considering the interdependencies among risks could lead to more accurate risk assessment to enterprises. In addition, during the risk assessment process, there are lots of uncertainties and imprecise information associated with experts opinions that should be taken into account [28–30]. Recently, Zhou and Lu [7] presented a methodology for choosing a coalition partner using Fuzzy Analytic Network Process (FANP) and by considering the interaction and feedback relationships between risk factors. Although ANP is able to consider interdependencies among factors, it has some disadvantages. Sometimes it is not easy even for experts to compare the importance of a factor to another [12]. In addition, different structures could lead to the different rankings and it is usually difficult for experts to provide the true relationship structure by taking into account several factors. Moreover, ANP is time-consuming due to the large number of pair-wise comparisons needed for comparing the risk factors.

Therefore, this paper deals with risk assessment of CNs as the most important phase of risk management, and proposes an advanced decision support tool called "FCM" to overcome the shortcomings of current risk evaluation tools applied in CNs. FCM is a useful tool that states and evaluate the dynamic behaviour of complex systems by considering the interrelationships among factors [13]. It considers the uncertainties and imprecise information by using linguistic variables. Hence, expert perception is considered in the model more precisely. Moreover, FCM can even be used when the information is scarce. This tool recently has been applied successfully in evaluating risks in complex and critical environments such as Enterprise Resource Planning (ERP) maintenance [14, 15] and IT projects [16], and therefore we think it has a good

potential to be applied in complex CNs for evaluating risks and forecasting the impact
of each risk.

The reminder of this paper is organized as follows. Section 2 introduces the FCM
fundamentals. Section 3 explains the proposed tool with an example related to risk
evolution in dynamic alliance and conclusions are drawn in Sect. 4.

2 FCM Fundamentals

Fuzzy Cognitive Map (FCM) was originally introduced by Kosko in 1986 [17] as a tool
for modeling complex systems, able to consider dependencies among different criteria
and based on experience and knowledge of experts. In the last decade, FCM has been
widely employed in the variety of applications such as, decision analysis, engineering
science, political decision making, failure detection, process control, and medical
diagnosis [18]. More information about the different applications of FCM are available
in [19, 20] books.

FCMs are a combination of fuzzy logic and neural networks and are able to represent both quantitative and qualitative data. An FCM consists of some nodes/concepts
which indicate the main features of the system and some edges/arcs between nodes
showing the relationships between them [18]. Figure 1 shows a simple FCM diagram
with five nodes and nine weighted edges, where each node C_i takes values in the range
$A_i \in [0, 1]$, and each edge between two nodes, C_i and C_j, has a weight, W_{ij} in the
interval $[-1, 1]$ which denotes the influence of each node on the others.

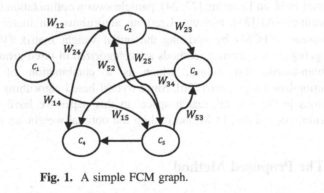

Fig. 1. A simple FCM graph.

The sign of arcs' weights $(+W_{ij}/ - W_{ij})$ states the increase/decrease between
concepts in the same or opposite directions. In the other words, if an increase in
concept C_i results in an increase in concept C_j (same directions), the sign of W_{ij} will be
positive, and vice versa. The types of concepts and dependencies among them,
directions of dependencies, and initial weights of concepts and arcs are significantly
based on the experience and knowledge of experts [21].

After assigning initial values to the concepts and weights, the FCM converges to a
steady state through the interaction of Eq. (1). At each step, the value A_i of the concept
C_i is influenced by the values of concepts connected to it and it is updated [22].

$$A_i^{k+1} = f(A_i^{(k)} + \sum_{\substack{j=1 \\ j \neq i}}^{n} W_{ij} A_j^{(k)}), \qquad (1)$$

where,

- W_{ij} is the initial weight of the arc between concepts C_i and C_j;
- A_i^{k+1} is the value of concept C_i at step $k+1$;
- k stands for the iteration counter;
- f is a threshold or barrier function, which is used to restrict the concept value into [0,1] range. Different types of threshold function f could be applied in Eq. 1 depending on the concepts interval. The most common types are; tangent hyperbolic ($f(x) = tanh(x)$), bivalent function (f(x) = 0 or 1), sigmoid function ($f(x) = 1/(1 + e^{-\lambda x})$), and trivalent function (f(x) = -1, 0 or 1).

At each iteration, Eq. 1 produces a new value for the concepts and when FCM arrives at one of the following three states, the iterations end and it results in a steady state [20];

(1) The value of concepts have stabilized at a fixed value (fixed equilibrium point),
(2) A limited state cycle is reached,
(3) Chaotic behavior has appeared.

As mentioned by Papageorgiou et al. [21], one of main drawbacks of FCMs is the potential convergence to undesired steady states. In the recent decade, several authors have tried to resolve this drawback by developing learning algorithms such as Differential Hebbian Learning [23, 24], particle swarm optimization (PSO) [21], Simulated Annealing (SA) [25], and etc. Learning algorithms can increase the efficiency and robustness of FCMs by updating the initial weight matrix ($W^{Initial}$). According to Papageorgiou, the training methods are categorized in three groups; population-based, Hebbian-based, and hybrid, which is a combination of Hebbian-based and evolution-based algorithms [26]. Since hybrid based algorithms ensure near-optimum solutions in the weights search space, in this paper we have applied hybrid based algorithm for training FCM and finding the optimal weight set of the FCM.

3 The Proposed Method

In order to illustrate the proposed tool, we adopted the risks identified in Li and Liau [6] study regarding dynamic alliance. Dynamic alliance or VE is a temporary network of specialised individuals and independent institutes who work together and share skills and costs in order to better respond to fast changing market opportunities [6]. The identified risks are shown in Table 1 and the related FCM graph is depicted in Fig. 2. The definitions of these risks are available in study [6].

The FCM graph is depicted based on experts' opinions in order to show the dependencies and feedbacks among factors. To make the initial weight matrix (W_{ij}), each expert individually determines the dependencies between concepts, using fuzzy linguistic terms such as Very High (VH), Low (L), etc. Then, the linguistic variables

Table 1. Risk factors in dynamic alliance [6].

Risk	Sub-risks	Index
Market risk	Demand fluctuation risk	C1
	Competition risk	C2
	Spillover effect risk	C3
Financial risk	Interest rate risk	C4
	Exchange rate risk	C5
Natural risk	Natural risk	C6
Relational risk	Trust risk	C7
	Moral risk	C8
	Motivation risk	C9
	Communication risk	C10
	Organization risk	C11
Operational risk	Information sharing risk	C12
	Information integration risk	C13
	Information conveyance risk	C14
Political risk	Social risk	C15
	Policy risk	C16
Competency risk	Quality risk	C17
	Cost risk	C18
	Time risk	C19
	Technologic risk	C20
Investment risk	Investment recovery risk	C21
	Investment implementation risk	C22

are aggregated and defuzzified to numerical values [21]. The initial weight matrix, is shown in Table 2.

In order to deffuzify a triangular fuzzy number (l, m, u) the following Equation is usually applied:

$$t = \frac{l + m + m + u}{4} \tag{2}$$

4 FCM Building Process

Two types of FCM model could be developed for evaluating risks. The first type is scenario-based which is used in this paper and the second type is based on initial concept values obtained from multi criteria decision making tools such as AHP/ANP or eigenvalue approach. Scenario-based FCM is a new method recently presented by different authors and it is becoming popular in complex and fast-changing domains such as business environment, therefore it is critical to predict the impact of potential risks that could be happened in the future. In order to evaluate the impact of risks in a

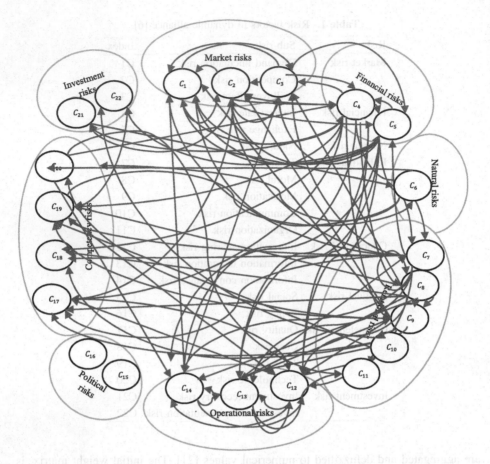

Fig. 2. FCM for risk analysis on dynamic alliance.

scenario-based FCM model, several what-if analysis scenarios should be developed using different initial concept values (c). In each scenario, a risk or a set of risks are activated and using Eq. 1 and using learning algorithms the initial vector (c) is updated in order to show the impact of activated risks on the other risks. Note that when a risk is activated, its value in the initial vector (c) is considered 1. This number is 0 for the rest of the risk factors which are not activated.

In second type of FCM modeling, the initial concept values (c) is updated by using initial weight matrix (W_{ij}) and Eq. 1 until it converges to the steady state condition. The updated concept values C^* shows the importance of each risk. Since this type of FCM is unable to assess the impact of each risk on the other risks, we propose to apply the first type in evaluating the risk of CNs. To illustrate the risk evaluation process, in this paper we only assess the impact of "Market risks" on other risks.

In this scenario, at the initial time only risks related to market risks including "Demand fluctuation risk (C1)", "Competition risk (C2)", and "Spillover effect risk (C3)" are activated.

Table 2. Initial weight matrix.

W^{Aug}	C1	C2	C3	C4	C5	..	C18	C19	C20	C21	C22
C1	0	0.2	0.5	0	1	..	0	0	1	0	0.3
C2	0.2	0	0.6	0.5	0	..	0.26	0	0	0.1	0.3
C3	1	0	0	0	0	..	0	0	0.8	0	0.3
C4	0.8	0.9	0	0	0.2	..	0.12	0	0	0.1	0
C5	0.7	0	0.8	0.4	0	..	0	0	0.4	0	0
C6	0.8	1	0	0	0.2	..	0	0.1	0	0	0
C7	0.8	0	0	0.6	0.6	..	0.78	0	0	1	0.38
C8	0	0.2	0	0.5	0	..	0	0	0.5	0.1	0.1
C9	0.7	0.3	0.8	0.8	0.5	..	0	0.78	0	0.99	0
C10	0.1	0.35	0.2	0.1	0.9	..	0	0	0	0	0
C11	0.4	0	0.2	0	0	..	0	0	0.1	0.1	0
C12	0	1	0.1	0	0	..	0.5	0.3	0	0	0.9
C13	0	0.3	1	0.2	0	..	0	0	0.2	0.1	-1
C14	0	0	0.5	0.5	0	..	0	0.6	0	0	0.8
C15	0.7	0.3	0.3	0	0.9	..	0	0	0	0.6	0.9
C16	0.2	0	0.1	0	0	..	1	0.67	0	0	0
C17	0.65	0.3	0	0.8	0.5	..	0	0	0.3	0.1	0
C18	0.7	0	0	0	0.1	..	0	0.6	0	0.5	0
C19	0.2	0.5	0	0.8	0	..	0.3	0	0	0.1	0
C20	0.6	0	0.3	0	0	..	0.9	0.7	0	0.1	0.56
C21	0	0.6	0.7	0	0	..	0.3	0.2	0.1	0	0.8
C22	0	0	1	0.5	0	..	0	0.7	0.1	0.5	0

$$c = [1, 1, 1, 0, 0, 0, 0, 0, 0, 0, 0, 0, 0, 0, 0, 0, 0, 0, 0, 0, 0, 0];$$

Using W_{ij} matrix, Initial concept vector c, Eq. (1) and learning algorithm, the training process starts. In this paper we applied NHL-DE algorithm for training FCM which is a combination of nonlinear Hebbian learning (NHL) and differential evolution (DE) algorithms. According to Papageorgiou [27], the hybrid training approaches such as NHL-DE emerge less limitations as they combine two training algorithms and inherit the benefits and shortcomings of both of them. The training process in NHL-DE has two steps. The first step starts with NHL algorithm and in the second step, the result of first step is used to seed the DE algorithm. We imported the data into Matlab code and we used MATLAB version R2012a software to obtain the updated concept matrix (C^*). In this paper, the values of learning rate parameter (η), mutation constant (μ), crossover constant (CR), and weight decay learning parameter (γ) have been selected 0.04, 0.5, 0.5, 0.98 respectively. The population size is considered 50. It should be noted we performed 1000 iterations for the algorithm per experiment and 100 independent experiments were performed.

$$C^* = [0.7, 0.47, 0.85, 0.7, \mathbf{0.98}, 0.4, 0, \mathbf{0.94}, 0, \mathbf{0.97}, 0.2, 0.49, 0.78, 0.21, \mathbf{0.93}, 0.7,$$
$$\mathbf{0.91}, 0.1, 0.78, \mathbf{0.99}, 0, 0.37];$$

The steady state vector C^* shows that activating C1, C2, and C3 risks have a strong influence over the remainder risks in particular risks C5, C8, C10, C15, C17, and C20. The same procedure should be done for all other risks by activating their sub-risks each time. The results reveals that which risks are critical. In addition, the proposed tool is able to predict the impact of each risk on the other risks more accurately because it take into account the multiple connections between risks. Therefore, decision makers will be able to manage the risks of CNs properly and accurately. It should be noted that the process for developing a FCM is strongly dependent on the experts' opinions. Then, special attention should be paid to matters such as the selection of experts' team and the feedback with them.

5 Conclusion

This paper proposes an advanced decision support tool called "Fuzzy Cognitive Maps" (FCM) which can deal with risks of collaborative networks by taking into account the interrelationships among factors. This tool can be adapted to a wide range of multi criteria decision making problems such as predicting behaviors in CNs, partner selection, policy analysis, modeling collaboration preparedness assessment, etc.

The main features of FCM in contrast with those of other existing methods are; (1) the relationships among variety of factors and also importance of factors could be considered, (2) uncertainties and imprecise information are taken into account on the decision-making process, (3) several experts can state their opinions, (4) it has capabilities to handle both qualitative and quantitative factors, (5) several alternatives can be considered in decision making about best partner and (6) by using the casual graphs in FCM, it is easier for decision makers and experts to understand the factors and their dependencies. Moreover, by relying on FCM models, the decision makers have a strong support, and therefore are able to decide more precisely and accurately when evaluating risks or choosing the partner. As a future research topic, application of other hybrid algorithms for training FCM could be considered. Currently, we are working on developing a comprehensive framework for partner selection problem in dynamic alliance by using an integrated FCM-based method.

Acknowledgements. This research was partially financed by grants [OPG 0293307 and OPG 0118062] from the Canadian Natural Sciences and Engineering Research Council (NSERC). This support is gratefully acknowledged.

References

1. Munyon, T.P., Perryman, A.A.: The dynamics of effective organization alliances. Org. Dyn. **40**, 96–103 (2011)

2. Hexin, H., Jim, C.: A partner selection method based on risk evaluation in virtual enterprises. In: Proceedings of ICSSSM (International Conference on Services Systems and Services Management) (2005)
3. Shah, R.H., Nathan, A.: Factors influencing partner selection in strategic alliances: the moderating role of alliance context. Strateg. Manag. J. **29**, 471–494 (2008)
4. Jarimo, T., Salo, A.: Optimal partner selection in virtual organisations with capacity risk and network interdependencies. IEEE J. Syst. Man Cybern. (2007). http://sal.aalto.fi/publications/pdf-files/mjar07.pdf. Accessed 12 April 2015
5. Rosas, J., Camarinha-Matos, L.M.: Modeling collaboration preparedness assessment. In: Camarinha-Matos, L.M., Afsarmanesh, H. (eds.) Collaborative Networks: Reference Modeling, pp. 227–252. Springer, Lisbon (2008)
6. Li, Y., Liao, X.: Decision support for risk analysis on dynamic alliance. Decis. Support Syst. **42**, 2043–2059 (2007)
7. Zhou, X., Lu, M.: Risk evaluation of dynamic alliance based on fuzzy analytic network process and fuzzy TOPSIS. J. Serv. Sci. Manage. **5**, 230–240 (2012)
8. Das, T.K., Teng, B.S.: A risk perception model of alliance structuring. J. Int. Manage. **7**(1), 1–29 (2001)
9. Ip, W.H., Huang, M., Yung, K.L., Wang, D.W.: Genetic algorithm solution for a risk-based partner selection problem in a virtual enterprise. Comput. Oper. Res. **30**(2), 213–231 (2003)
10. Huang, M., Ip, W.H., Yang, H.M., Wang, X.W., Lau, H.C.W.: A fuzzy synthetic evaluation embedded tabu search for risk programming of virtual enterprises. Int. J. Prod. Econ. **116**(1), 104–114 (2008)
11. Huang, M., Lu, F.Q., Ching, W.K., Siu, T.K.: A distributed decision making model for risk management of virtual enterprise. Expert Syst. Appl. **38**(10), 13208–13215 (2011)
12. Yu, G.T.R.: A soft computing method for multi-criteria decision making with dependence and feedback. Appl. Math. Comput. **180**, 63–75 (2006)
13. Kosko, B.: Fuzzy cognitive maps. Int. J. Man-Mach. Stud. **24**, 65–75 (1986)
14. Lopez, C., Salmeron, J.L.: Dynamic risks modelling in ERP maintenance projects with FCM. Inf. Sci. **256**, 25–45 (2014)
15. Ahmad, K., Kumar, A.: Forecasting risk and risk consequences on ERP maintenance. Int. J. Soft Comput. Eng. **2**(5), 13–18 (2012)
16. Salmeron, J.L.: Fuzzy cognitive maps-based IT projects risks scenarios. Stud. Fuzziness Soft Comput. **247**, 201–215 (2010)
17. Kosko, B.: Fuzzy cognitive maps. Int. J. Man Mach. Stud. **24**, 65–75 (1986)
18. Xiao, Z., Chen, W., Li, L.: An integrated FCM and fuzzy soft set for supplier selection problem based on risk evaluation. Appl. Math. Model. **36**, 1444–1454 (2012)
19. Glykas, M.: Fuzzy Cognitive Maps, Advances in Theory, Methodologies, Tools and Applications. Springer, Greece (2010)
20. Papageorgiou, E.I.: Fuzzy Cognitive Maps for Applied Sciences and Engineering (From Fundamentals to Extensions and Learning Algorithms). Springer, Berlin (2014)
21. Papageorgiou, E.I., Parsopoulos, K.E., Stylios, C.S., Groumpos, P.P., Vrahatis, M.N.: Fuzzy cognitive maps learning using particle swarm optimization. Intell. Inf. Syst. **25**(1), 95–121 (2005)
22. Kosko, B.: Fuzzy Engineering. Prentice Hall, NewYork (1997)
23. Papageorgiou, C.S.P.G.E.I.: Active Hebbian learning algorithm to train fuzzy cognitive maps. Int. J. Approximate Reasoning **37**, 219–249 (2004)
24. Papakostas, G.A., Polydoros, A.S., Koulouriotis, D.E., Tourassis, V.D.: Training fuzzy cognitive maps by using hebbian learning algorithms: a comparative study. In: IEEE International Conference on Fuzzy Systems, Taipei, Taiwan (2011)

25. Alizadeh, S., Ghazanfari, M.: Learning FCM by chaotic simulated annealing. Chaos, Solitons and Fractals **41**, 1182–1190 (2009)
26. Papageorgiou, E.: Learning algorithms for fuzzy cognitive maps: a review study. IEEE Trans. **42**(2), 150–163 (2012)
27. Papageorgiou, E.I.: Fuzzy Cognitive Maps for Applied Sciences and Engineering. Springer, Greece (2014)
28. Jamshidi, A., Rahimi, S.A., Ait-Kadi, D., Ruiz, A.: A comprehensive fuzzy risk-based maintenance framework for prioritization of medical devices. Appl. Soft Comput. **32**, 322–334 (2015)
29. Jamshidi, A., Rahimi, S.A., Ait-Kadi, D., Ruiz, A.: Using fuzzy cost-based FMEA, GRA and profitability theory for minimizing failures at a healthcare diagnosis service. Qual. Reliab. Eng. **31**(4), 601–615 (2013)
30. Jamshidi, A., Rahimi, S.A., Bartolome, A.R., Ait-kadi, D.: A new framework for risk assessment in ERP maintenance. In: Reliability and Maintainability Symposium (RAMS), Annual, Colorado Springs (2014)

Interaction Protocols for Human-Driven Crisis Resolution Processes

Eric Andonoff, Chihab Hanachi[✉], Nguyen Le Tuan Thanh,
and Christophe Sibertin-Blanc

University of Toulouse 1 Capitole, IRIT laboratory 2 rue du Doyen Gabriel Marty,
31042 Toulouse Cedex, France
{Eric.Andonoff,Chihab.Hanachi,Nguyen.Le,
Christophe.Sibertin-Blanc}@irit.fr

Abstract. This work aims at providing a crisis cell with process-oriented tools to manage crisis resolutions. Indeed, the crisis cell members have to define the crisis resolution process, adapt it to face crisis evolutions, and guide its execution. Crisis resolution processes are interaction-intensive processes: they not only coordinate the performance of tasks to be undertaken on the impacted world, but they also support regulatory interactions between possibly geographically distributed crisis cell members. In order to deal with such an interweaving, this paper proposes to use Interaction Protocols to both model formal interactions and ease a cooperative adaptation and guidance of crisis resolution processes. After highlighting the benefits of Interaction Protocols to support this human and collective dimension, the paper presents a protocol meta-model for their specification. It then shows how to suitably integrate specified protocols into crisis resolution processes and how to implement this conceptual framework into a service oriented architecture.

Keywords: Crisis resolution process · Interaction protocols · Process flexibility

1 Introduction

In crisis situations (natural or industrial disasters, explosions of violence ...), the various actors driving the crisis resolution have to act immediately and simultaneously in order to reduce its impacts on the real world. To achieve this common goal as quickly and efficiently as possible, these actors (police, military forces, medical organizations ...) have to collaborate and act in a coordinated way [1]. The coordination of a crisis resolution process is difficult since it needs to adhere to the evolving requirements of the crisis.

In the framework of the Génépi project[1], we adopt a computer-based approach to support the coordination of actors; it is based on the following requirements:

- A Mediator Information System (MIS, [1]) should be set up within the crisis cell to support the crisis resolution;

---

[1] Project funded by the French Research National Agency (ANR).

© IFIP International Federation for Information Processing 2015
L.M. Camarinha-Matos et al. (Eds.): PRO-VE 2015, IFIP AICT 463, pp. 63–76, 2015.
DOI: 10.1007/978-3-319-24141-8_6

- The partners' Information Systems have to be connected to the MIS in order to declare by means of services, the concrete actions they are able to perform;
- A Crisis Resolution Process (CRP) is to be defined and monitored for orchestrating partners' actions;
- The MIS runs in a Service Oriented Architecture (SOA), which is known for easily dealing with distribution and inter-operability issues;
- Given the dynamic, uncertain and unpredictable actual environment of the crisis, the MIS should also ease the flexibility of the CRP.

In France, a MIS is under the responsibility of a Command and Control Center, called a *crisis cell*, headed either by the local "Préfet" or the Interior Minister, depending on the regional or national scope of the crisis. This crisis cell is composed of representatives of the different public organizations involved in the crisis resolution. The cell, which may be geographically distributed, is in charge of adapting and applying a resolution plan framed by the law and implemented into the Crisis Resolution Process.

According to the Génépi project requirements, the main issue for a crisis cell is to define, maintain and adapt a CRP in a collective way. More precisely, crisis cell actors have to interact with each other (vote, negotiate, delegate, sub-contract ...) to guide the CRP execution and adaptation, removing its indeterminism and deciding between the available options. Interactions between the crisis cell members and the actors in the field should also be formalized to guarantee both a good understanding of the orders and a correct interpretation of the feedback information and also to ascribe responsibilities. Consequently, CRPs are interaction-intensive processes. The information, knowledge and decisions shared between the actors are heavily reliant on the interactions between them and they must be logged in order to keep trace of the responsibility of each actor in the crisis management. Interactions in the course of a CRP are almost as important as the coordination of activities. Given all these considerations, the problem addressed in this paper is *how to build and monitor flexible crisis resolution processes, i.e. easily adaptable and integrating a human and collective dimension through interaction support between the actors?*

Flexibility of processes is not a new issue [2, 3]. It is defined in [2] as the "ability to deal with both foreseen and unforeseen changes in the environment in which processes operate". Reference [2] also proposes a taxonomy defining several types of process flexibility along with techniques to support them – flexibility by design, flexibility by deviation, flexibility by under-specification and flexibility by change – techniques which are obviously useful to face the dynamic and unstable context of crises.

However, all the crisis cell members share a CRP and this brings a new requirement. The CRP mode of execution, along with the different alternatives it considers, should be subject to consultation and collective decisions at run-time, since they engage the responsibility of cell members. Hence, in this context, flexibility must also take into account this *human* and *institutional* dimension and integrate interaction places to ease decision-making within the crisis cell.

To address this problem, we propose to coherently combine conventional flexibility techniques with interaction mechanisms into CRPs. These interaction mechanisms are described by means of an Interaction Protocol (IP) [3], defined as a set of structured communication acts, following a recurrent schema, and aiming at coordinating interventions of involved actors to reach specific objectives. In our context, an IP may correspond to the selection of actors who will execute specific tasks according to their roles, the vote of an important decision between actors, or the negotiation of the service quality of tasks. Consequently, IPs can guide the execution of CRPs and facilitates their adaptation.

Following the typology provided by [11], business process systems can be divided into two classes: Person-to-Person (P2P) process-based systems corresponding to groupware and Person-to-Computer (P2C) process-based systems corresponding to workflow. Our proposition merges these two classes in combing suitably the P2P approach with the P2C one. To this end, the contribution of the paper is threefold: (1) a meta-model for the declarative specification of IPs along with means to integrate these protocols into CRPs; (2) requirements and new functionalities for a workflow-process engine in charge of executing CRPs; (3) a Service Oriented Architecture implementation of our propositions.

The paper is organized as follows. Section 2 discusses CRP flexibility and highlights the benefits of IPs for introducing a human and collective dimension in crisis processes. Section 3 presents a meta-model of protocols and also explains protocol integration into CRPs using conventional flexible techniques. Section 4 defines the requirements that a process/workflow engine has to meet to execute such CRPs. Section 5 presents an implementation of our solution in PEtALs, a specific service-oriented architecture. Finally, Sect. 6 discusses our propositions and concludes the paper.

2 Flexibility of the Crisis Resolution Process

A Crisis Resolution Process describes the coordination of actions performed by actors involved in crisis resolution. A CRP is executed by the Mediator Information System [1] whose aim is to drive the CRP lifecycle: define, adapt, orchestrate and supervise its execution according to the crisis model, which is an accurate representation of the crisis and its evolution. CRP flexibility is supported at two abstraction levels. At the MIS level, CRP flexibility is supported by the dynamicity of its life cycle, while, at the CRP level, it is supported by flexibility techniques both used to adapt the CRP and support formal interactions between the possibly geographically distributed crisis cell members.

2.1 Life Cycle for the Dynamic Management of a Crisis Resolution Process

The process driving the execution of the CRP, called Driving Process (DP), includes a *perception-decision-action* loop. Indeed, it provides means to capture information about the impacted world, to support the definition and the adaptation of the CRP managing the crisis reduction, and to coordinate and assign to each participant the actions to be undertaken. These actions modify the real world and lead to a new iteration, where these tasks are performed again, taking into account the new crisis context. Figure 1 illustrates, through a BPMN diagram, the dynamics of the DP.

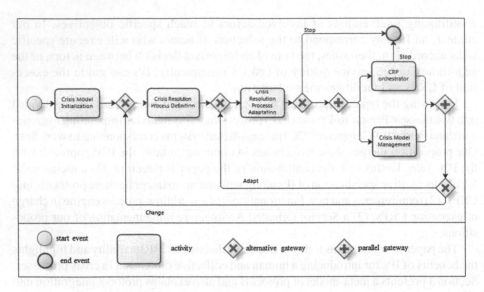

Fig. 1. PMN diagram of the driving process.

The DP structure should be read as follows. Once a crisis cell, responsible for the crisis management, is set up, the Crisis Model Initialization task records into the crisis model the observations of the impacted real world. This crisis model is compliant with a crisis meta-model such as defined in [4].

Using this crisis model, the *Crisis Resolution Process Definition* activity defines the initial CRP. Then, this initial CRP may be adapted in order to introduce human controls into the loop (through interaction protocols) or to take into account specific organizational requirements expressed by actors involved in crisis resolution. More precisely, this adaptation may consist in removing, adding or reordering actions or interaction protocols, or in selecting, among several alternatives, the most relevant one to guide the CRP execution. Then, either the DP stops or continues. In the first case, this means that the crisis is reduced or considered as being solved. In the second case, two activities are concurrently performed: the first one executes of the CRP, while the second updates the crisis model representative of the real world situation. The orchestration of the CRP may be suspended to be either adapted or changed according to the evolution of the crisis model. The *Adapt* case corresponds to a simple update of the CRP and then a new <Orchestration // Crisis Model Management> step is started. The *Change* case corresponds to an evolution of the crisis and a deep modification of the CRP. Consequently, the *Crisis Resolution Process Definition* activity is again performed in order to define a new CRP in line with the new crisis model. Section 4.1 will explain how the *Crisis Model Management* activity impacts CRP *Orchestration*.

The DP structure requires to control the functioning of the orchestrator responsible for the execution of the CRP. This orchestrator must be able to suspend its execution and restart it. Section 4 presents the solutions we provide for that.

2.2   Flexibility Techniques for Adapting the Crisis Resolution Process

Flexibility of a Crisis Resolution Process corresponds to its ability to face changes, i.e. to be adapted in the course of its life cycle. Some of these changes are foreseen and consequently are taken into account when designing the CRP, while others are not and are consequently performed at run-time. We present below appropriate techniques for CRPs flexibility. We distinguish those proposed by the Business Process Community in the context of activity-oriented processes (e.g. [5, 6]), from the one we propose in the paper: interaction mechanisms, involving human groups having to collectively guide the execution of the CRP, remove its indeterminism, discuss its execution options or decide actions to undertake.

Conventional Techniques for CRP Flexibility. Four types of flexibility are identified in [2] and are convenient for CRP. The types of flexibility are: flexibility by *design*, flexibility by *deviation*, flexibility by *under-specification* and flexibility by *change*. Flexibility by design corresponds to foreseen changes in processes that can be modelled when designing them. This type of flexibility depends on the modelling power of the language used for process description. Flexibility by derivation handles, at run-time and at the instance level, unforeseen changes and where the differences with the initial process are minimal. Flexibility by under-specification deals with foreseen changes that cannot be defined at design-time but rather at run-time. This type of flexibility corresponds to the notions of late binding and late modelling [2]. Regarding late binding, a process designer specifies several ways to implement a process or an activity of the process, and postpones the choice of one of these ways until its execution. Late modelling is different from late binding since the designer postpones the way to model the process to its execution. Consequently, the user who will execute the process will have to define it before its execution. Finally, flexibility by change corresponds to unforeseen changes at run-time, which require occasional or permanent modification of process schema. In the context of CRPs adaptation, and as illustrated later, we propose to use flexibility by change and flexibility by under-specification (and more precisely late binding) techniques [5, 6].

Flexibility by Integration of Interaction Protocols. As defended in the introduction, the previous techniques must be supplemented with collaborative facilities in order to integrate interaction places to support crisis cell members' decision-making. Consequently, we propose to use Interaction Protocols [17] to integrate such a dimension into CRPs. In the crisis context, IPs are for instance used to select actors who will execute specific actions (e.g. which hospitals are available for receiving injured people), to organize votes about important decisions between possibly geographically distributed crisis cell members, or to negotiate criteria to perform specific actions. Consequently, IPs within a CRP influences its execution and thus participates to its dynamic guidance and adaptation.

3 Integration of Interaction Protocols into Crisis Resolution Processes

This section first introduces a meta-model of protocols devoted to declarative specification of Interaction Protocols. It then explains protocol integration into CRPs using conventional flexible techniques.

3.1 Declarative Specification of Interaction Protocols

An Interaction Protocol (IP) is defined as a service through its profile and its behaviour. The profile provides all the necessary information for an IP to be found and possibly selected, while the behaviour of an IP defines the operations it performs. As this paper mainly focuses on IP behaviour specification and integration into CRPs, Fig. 2 only introduces concepts for behaviour description, i.e. the concepts of roles, messages exchanged between roles, actions performed within roles, and the way these actions and messages are connected together.

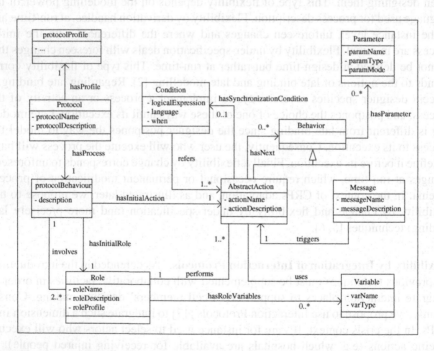

Fig. 2. Protocol meta-model as a UML class diagram.

More precisely, a *protocolBehaviour* has a *description* and involves several roles; it is initiated by one of these roles (*hasInitialRole* association), and it starts triggering an initial action (*hasInitialAction* association). Each *Role* has a name (*roleName* attribute), a description (*roleDescription* attribute), a profile (*hasProfile* attribute), performs actions (*performs* association), and uses some local variables (*hasRoleVariables* association). We distinguish two kinds of actions for IPs: *AbstractActions*, which correspond to internal actions of roles, and *Messages*, which correspond to messages exchanged between roles. Regarding messages, we specify their name (*messageName* attribute), their description (*messageDescription* attribute) along with the abstract actions (of a role) they trigger (*triggers* association), the local variables they use (*uses* association), and the parameters sent to these abstract actions (*hasParameter* association). Regarding abstract actions, we specify their name (*actionName* attribute), their description (*actionDescription* attribute), and the parameters they receive or send. The code of an action, i.e. the code that will be executed when the action will be performed, will be defined later, at the implementation level (see Sect. 5). We also indicate how actions and messages are connected together (*hasNext* association), along with the synchronization condition when an action follows several previous ones (in order to be able to model join and fork patterns for parallelized actions, if pattern for alternative actions …).

3.2 Flexibility Techniques for Interaction Protocol Integration

Two flexibility techniques among the ones proposed by the Business Process Management community can be used for IP integration. The first technique, flexibility by change, enables the integration of a concrete IP whose profile and behaviour are known at design time. This technique consists in adding an activity into the CRP whose role is to call the IP to be integrated. As illustrated in Fig. 3, we have added the Protocol activity between two conventional activities (Activity-1 and Activity-2) of a CRP.

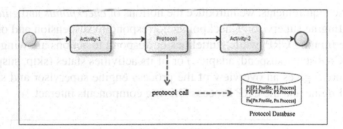

Fig. 3. Flexibility by adding concrete interaction protocols.

As illustrated in Fig. 4, the second technique, combining both flexibility by change and under-specification (late binding) approaches, differs from the previous one since it enables the integration of abstract IPs, for which only the profile is known at design-time. The idea is to postpone the choice of an IP behaviour at run-time. Thus, this technique consists in adding the Protocol Selection activity into the CRP whose role is to select a convenient protocol among the IPs recorded in the Protocol database. When executing this activity, the most convenient protocol, in terms of IP' profile and behaviour is chosen and then executed.

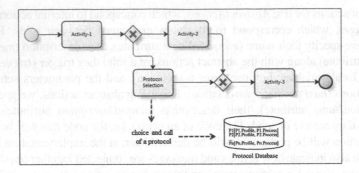

Fig. 4. Flexibility by adding abstract interaction protocols.

4 Crisis Resolution Process Engine Requirements

The two previous techniques may be used both at design-time and run-time. Adding IPs at run time requires that the Process Engine executing the CRP is able to suspend and restart its execution. This section states requirements the Process Engine should meet for this integration.

4.1 Overview of the Process Engine Supervisor

To meet these requirements, we introduce the notions of *checkpoints* and *guidelines* for the Process Engine supervisor. Checkpoints correspond to suspension and observation points of the running CRP, while guidelines correspond to actions allowing modifications of the CRP state (suspend, adapt…) or of its activities states (skip, suspend, allocate…). Figure 5 gives an overview of the process engine supervisor and shows how the Process Engine and the CRP Process Driving components interact.

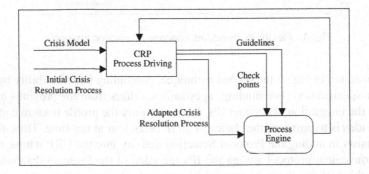

Fig. 5. Process engine supervisor

Let us recall that the Mediator Information System activity consists mainly in CRP definition, adaptation and supervision. The Process Engine performs CRP execution while supervision is left to the CRP Process Driving component. This component inputs are the initial CRP and the Crisis model (cf. Sect. 2) and its outputs are an eventually adapted CRP (integrating new activities or protocols for instance), execution checkpoints and guidelines for the Process Engine.

4.2 Checkpoints and Guidelines

These two notions support Process Engine supervision. However, we first have to define the states of a CRP and its activities.

States of a CRP and its Activities. Figure 6 presents the different states of a CRP and indicates which transitions are available between them. These states are *defined* (the CRP is defined), *executed* (the CRP is running), *suspended* (the execution of the RCP is suspended in order to adapt or redefine it), *adapted* (the CRP is changed in order to face crisis evolution), or *finished* (the CRP execution is terminated and the crisis is reduced). This state is the final one.

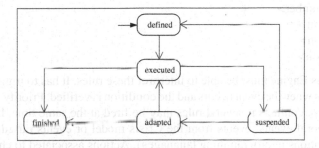

Fig. 6. The CRP states

In the same way, we define the states of CRP activities which have to be performed by actors to reduce the crisis. The different possible states of an activity are: *defined* to indicate that the activity is defined in the CRP, *sensible* to indicate that it will possibly be executed, *allocated* to indicate that it will be executed soon, *executed* for a running activity, *suspended* when its execution is suspended, *finished* to indicate that its execution is terminated, *failed* to indicate that its execution failed, *skipped* to indicate that it will not be executed, and *aborted* to indicate that its execution has been aborted. The possible final states are skipped, finished, failed and aborted. Figure 7 presents the transitions between states.

Checkpoints and Guidelines. Now, we indicate how to supervise the execution of a CRP through the use of checkpoints and guidelines. Guidelines correspond to orders given to the Process Engine to modify the state of the CRP or the state of a CRP activity. Checkpoints correspond to breaks introduced in the CRP. These breaks are associated with activities included in the CRP. When the Process Engine meets a checkpoint, it suspends the execution of the CRP, and the crisis cell may adapt or redefine it by introducing new activities or interaction protocols. Guidelines and checkpoints are expressed as active rules [7] defined as follows:

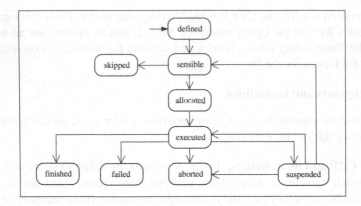

Fig. 7. The states of a CRP activity

Rule   <RuleName>
Priority <Number>
When   <Event>
If   <Condition>
Then   <Action>

The Process Engine must be able to interpret these rules. It has to trigger the action part of the rules when the event occurs and the condition is verified. Priority is introduced in order to solve conflicts if several rules may be fired at the same time. Events correspond to temporal events, events from the Crisis model or events raised by the CRP itself (as exceptions in programming languages). Actions associated to checkpoints or guidelines differ. Regarding checkpoints, the triggered action suspends the execution of the CRP; then the crisis cell may analyze the CRP state, redefine it or adapt it by adding new activities or integrating interaction protocols as indicated in Sect. 3.2. Regarding guidelines, the triggered action may modify an activity state or may correspond to notifications sent to the crisis cell.

We can note that this idea of integrating events into processes to make them more flexible is also used in [8] for cross-organizational business processes.

5   A Service Oriented Architecture Implementation

We have implemented our propositions in PEtALs, an open source Service Oriented Architecture on top of an Enterprise Service Bus technology based on JBI (Java Business Integration), JMS (Java Message Service), XSLT (eXtensible Stylesheet Language Transformation) and web services standards (SOAP, WSDL, BPEL).

PEtALs supports mediation and interoperability between software components using adaptors, and provides an engine, called Maestro, for orchestrating BPEL services. In the context of Génépi, PEtALs connects information systems of partners (actors) involved in crisis resolution and orchestrates the CRP. More precisely, partners publish the actions they are able to perform on the impacted world (e.g. stop a fire) as web services through their information systems. After real world situation analysis, the crisis cell defines a first CRP, which connects the different web services published by partners. This CRP is specified in BPMN and automatically derived in a BPEL process using UML as a pivot model and ATL (Atlas transformation Language) for the derivation [9]. Then, these elements (i.e. the BPEL process and the Maestro engine) are deployed on PEtALs. When running, the CRP triggers services corresponding to either external services such as web services published by partners, web services implementing inter-action protocols as BPEL processes, web services supporting the update of the crisis model after collecting information from actors on the field, or internal services such as the Service Retriever component used for finding services. Figure 8 illustrates the connexion between internal and external services within PEtALs.

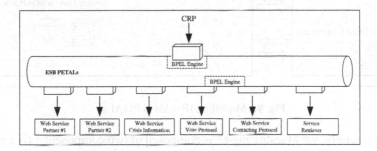

Fig. 8. Conceptual architecture of PEtALs

More precisely, internal and external services are deployed in PEtALs as service units. Each service unit has an endpoint along with its corresponding WSDL (web Service Description Language) specification. An external service is deployed by two service units: the first one for the service itself and the second one for its access through the web (using a SOAP binding component). As indicated above, interaction protocols are mapped onto BPEL processes and encapsulated into web services. Moreover, these BPEL processes are completed with a set of packaged operations that includes the (Java) code concretizing the different abstract actions of protocol roles. Consequently, an IP is deployed in PEtALs by three service units for each of its role: one for the BPEL process corresponding to the considered role, a second one for the operations (Java code) concretizing the different abstract operations of the role, and a third one for accessing the role through the web. Figure 9 illustrates this idea considering a *Contracting Protocol* involving two roles: manager and contractor. Several instances of the *Contractor* role are visualised in this figure.

Regarding the integration of IPs as BEPL process, static integration of IPs (i.e. when defining the CRP) raises no difficulty. On the other hand, dynamic integration of IPs is more difficult and requires being able to suspend the execution of the CP, and then eventually take it up again. The PEtALs Maestro engine supports this functionality. Indeed, this engine uses the results of the work carried out in the context of the Fractal open source project (http://fractal.objectweb.org/), and as any component architecture based on Fractal, Maestro has capacities for introspection.

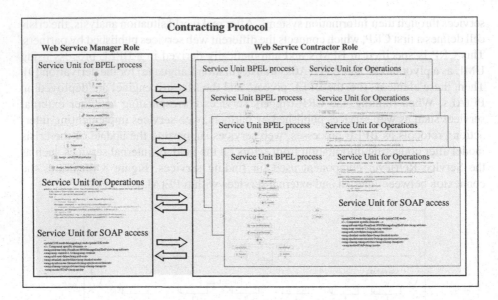

Fig. 9. Modelling IP roles in PEtALs

More precisely, the Maestro engine is composed of two components: (i) a wrapper that translates a BPEL process into a Java class, and (ii) a Process Virtual Machine (PVM) that is responsible for this Java class execution. The process activities included in the Java class are packed as Fractal components. So, thanks to the capability of Maestro to account for the Fractal facilities of the components, users can supervise processes execution, and through predefined or specific controllers, they can drive the CRP using checkpoints and guidelines.

Moreover, Maestro collaborates with a rule engine in order to take into account checkpoints and guidelines. These checkpoints and guidelines are defined as XML rules recorded in a configuration file (rules.xml) and are loaded by the BPEL file of the CRP.

6   Discussion and Conclusion

To deal with the need of a human and collaborative dimension in CRPs, the paper has shown how to integrate interaction places that ease coordination within the crisis cell, the guidance of process execution and collaborative decision-making.

For that purpose, we have defined a Protocol meta-model for the declarative specification of Interaction Protocols (IPs) and have shown how to implement them by means of conventional flexibility techniques (flexibility by change and under-specification [2, 5, 6]). Moreover, the paper proposes new functionalities that a Process Engine should offer to orchestrate flexible CRPs. Finally, to complete this conceptual and platform independent framework, we provide an implementation on a Service Oriented Architecture environment, namely PEtALs. This implementation has required the development of the specific Process Engine Maestro.

The outcomes of IP interaction places that are integrated into a CRP impact and guide the course of the CRP itself. This provides a level of human and collaborative flexibility, which has never been proposed in previous works, while the flexibility of processes is an important issue for the effectiveness of information systems processes [10].

Regarding the state of the art in the Crisis Information System domain, even though a lot of information systems have been developed to support crisis management, most of them are specific to a type of crisis [12], focus on the influence of innovative tools [13], or are limited to simulation or geographic information management and visualization [14]. Collaborative tools (such as CSCW) have also been developed in the Crisis Management domain [15]. Most often they are used just to support interactions among partners and document sharing because such tools do not offer a process management perspective. In this regard, the closest work to ours is [16], developed in the context of the WORKPAD project (http://www.workpad-project.eu). In this work, a P2P architecture is designed from users requirements, and it includes data storage and communication, middleware and user layers. This architecture also manages processes and allows workflow patterns mining. Unlike the architecture proposed in [16], a CRP is a first class citizen component for the supervision, guidance and mastering of a crisis. Finally, our approach remains conceptual and does not impose any technological choice (P2P, Web Services, Grid…), even if this paper reports a SOA-based implementation.

So far, several protocols – a vote protocol, a Matchmaker protocol and an iterative Contract-net protocol – have been implemented. We plan to integrate them and to make them work into the flood of the Loire (longest river in France) CRP, in the context of a simulation exercise involving real crisis cell and actors (firemen, police, medical organizations).

Acknowledgements. Authors thank Nicolas Salatgé, Cecile Faure and Tom Jorquera for their help in the implementation phase of this work. The study was made possible thanks to the financial support of the ANR (French Research National Agency).

References

1. Truptil, S., Bénaben, F., Salatge, N., Hanachi, C., Chapurlat, V., Pignon, J.P., Pingaud, H.: Mediation information system engineering for interoperability support in crisis management. In: I-ESA, pp. 187–197 (2010)
2. Schoneneberg, H., Mans, R., Russell, N., Mulyar, N., van der Aalst, W.: Process flexibility: a survey of contemporary approaches. In: International Workshop on CIAO/EOMAS, at International Conference on Advanced Information Systems, pp. 16–30, Montpellier, France (2008)
3. Rantrua, A., Gleizes, M.P., Hanachi, C.: Flexible and emergent workflows using adaptive agents. In: Proceedings of the 5th International Conference on Computational Collective Intelligence, Technologies and Application, pp. 185–194, Craiova, Romania (2013)
4. Benaben, F., Hanachi, C., Lauras, M., Couget, P., Chapurlat, V.: A Metamodel and its ontology to guide crisis charaterization and its collaborative management. In: International Conference on Information systems for Crisis response and Management, pp. 189–196, Washington, USA (2008)

5. Reichert, M., Dadam, P.: ADEPTflex: supporting dynamic changes of workflow without losing control. Int. J. Intell. Inf. Syst. **10**(2), 93–129 (1998)
6. Adams, M., ter Hofstede, A., Edmond, D., van der Aalst, W.: Worklets: a service-oriented implementation of dynamic flexibility in workflows. In: International Conference on Cooperative Information Systems, pp. 291–306, Montpellier, France (2006)
7. Widom, J., Ceri, S.: Active Database Systems: Triggers and Rules for Advanced Database Processing. Morgan Kaufmann publishers, Burlington (1996)
8. Chakravarty, P., Singh, M.: Incorporating events into cross-organizational business processes. IEEE Int. J. Internet Comput. **12**(2), 46–53 (2008)
9. Trupil, S., Benaben, F., Pingaud, H.: Collaborative process design for mediation information system engineering. In: International Conference on Information System for Crisis Response and Management, Gothenburg, Sweden (2009)
10. Reijers, H.: Workflow flexibility: the forlorn promise. In: International Workshop on Enabling Technologies: Infrastructure for Collaborative Enterprises, pp. 271–272, Manchester, United Kingdom (2006)
11. Ellis, C., Barthelmess, P., Chen, J., Wainer, J.: Person-to-person processes: computer-supported collaborative work. In: Dumas, M., van der Aalst, W., Ter Hofstede, A. (eds.) Process-Aware Information Systems: Bridging People and Software through Process Technology, pp. 37–60. Wiley, Hoboken (2005)
12. de Addams-Moring, R.: Tsunami self-evacuation of a group of western travelers and resulting requirements for multi-hazard early warning. In: International Conference on Information System for Crisis Response and Management, Delft, The Netherlands (2007)
13. Avery-Gomez, E., Turoff, M.: Interoperable communication: an analysis of SMS text-message exchange. In: International Conference on Information System for Crisis Response and Management, Delft, The Netherlands (2007)
14. Dilekli, N., Rashed, T.: Towards a GIS data model for improving the emergency response in the least developing countries: challenges and opportunities. In: International Conference on Information System for Crisis Response and Management, Delft, The Netherlands (2007)
15. Cai, G.: Extending distributed GIS to support geo-collaborative crisis management. Geogr. Inf. Sci. **11**(1), 4–14 (2005)
16. Catarci, T., de Leoni, M., Marrella, A., Mecella, M., Russo, A., Steinmann, R., Bortenschlager, M.: Workpad: process management and geo-collaboration help disaster response. Int. J. Inf. Syst. Crisis Response Manage. (IJISCRAM) **3**(1), 32–49 (2011)
17. Hanachi, C., Sibertin-Blanc, C.: Protocol moderators as active middle-agents in multi-agent systems. Int. J. Auton. Agents Multi-Agent Syst. **8**(3), 131–164 (2004)

Agility and Resilience in Collaborative Networks

Resilient and Robust Human-Agent Collectives: A Network Perspective

Willy Picard[✉]

Department of Information Technology, Poznań University of Economics
and Business, al. Niepodległości 10, 61-875 Poznań, Poland
picard@kti.ue.poznan.pl

Abstract. Human and software agents are more and more often interacting in groups in which directives are originated as well as addressed by humans or software agents. Among challenges raised by the rise of such heterogeneous groups, referred to as Human-Agent Collectives (HACs), resilience and robustness remain an open question. In this paper, the factors that influence the resilience and robustness of HACs are identified based on former research concerning interdependent and complex networks. The two main factors identified in the paper are (1) interactions between HACs with their open-networked environment, (2) the structure of the interactions among members of the HACs.

Keywords: Human-Agent collectives · HAC · Resilience, robustness, interdependent networks, small-world networks

1 Introduction

With the rise of the internet of think and the ubiquity of ICT, humans are interacting more and more with various electronic devices and information systems. These devices and systems provide not only means to sense and act on the surrounding world, they also allow for distant, often complex, interactions between humans. As such, humans and devices often collaborate within limited temporal frames to achieve a common goal. An example of such interactions is the process of online booking at airport during which many actions are performed by humans with the help of various systems, depending if the booking process is taken from the perspective of the traveler, of the airline company officer that checks the travelers, or the immigration officer.

The collaboration with devices and information systems may take different forms: in some cases, the human being is controlling the device, by asking the device to perform in a given manner. However, in more and more frequent cases, the device is asking the human to behave in a given manner: in the case of online booking at the airport, the information system instructs the traveler about the information to be provided to the system. Another example of a system that instruct human being are most hotlines, especially in the e-banking sector: the system directly asks the customer to press some keys to perform certain tasks.

Therefore collaboration may take place within groups whose members can be humans or agents. In the remaining of this paper, the word "agents" refers to electronic devices and information systems. Importantly, the social relations between humans and

© IFIP International Federation for Information Processing 2015
L.M. Camarinha-Matos et al. (Eds.): PRO-VE 2015, IFIP AICT 463, pp. 79–87, 2015.
DOI: 10.1007/978-3-319-24141-8_7

agents are not based on a fixed hierarchy: humans may instruct other humans or agents as well as agents may instruct other humans or agents.

Human-Agent Collectives (HACs) have been proposed by Jennings et al. [1] as a new concept to capture these type of collaborative systems. Jennings et al. define HAC as "a new class of socio-technical systems in which humans and smart software (agents) engage in flexible relationships in order to achieve both their individual and collective goals. Sometimes the humans take the lead, sometimes the computer does and this relationship can vary dynamically" [1]. Among key research challenges related to HACs, they have identified, among others, "achieving flexible autonomy between humans and the software, and constructing agile teams that conform and coordinate their activities".

Underpinning the question of flexible autonomy, the question of resilience and robustness for HACs is not mentioned in [1] although it has to be addressed, especially in the concept of open environments. There is a need to identify factors that influence the resilience and robustness of human-agent collectives. Although other aspects of HACs, such as flexibility, agility, efficiency, effectiveness, responsiveness, and stability, still need to be addressed, we choose to focus in this paper on the aspects of resilience and robustness.

In this paper, we will present an analysis of the problem of resilience and robustness of HACs from the perspective of networks and based on the results of former works on complex and interdependent networks. The basic concepts underlying this paper are presented in Sect. 2, starting from robustness and resilience, followed by human-agent collectives. In Sect. 3, the interactions between HACs with their open-networked environment are presented as an important factor influencing the resilience and robustness of HACs. In Sect. 4, the structure of the interactions among members of the HACs, especially when structured as small-world networks, are discussed as a second important factor influencing the resilience and robustness of HACs. Finally, Sect. 5 concludes this paper.

2   Basic Concepts

2.1   Robustness and Resilience

The concepts of robustness and resilience have been studied in various scientific fields such as ecology [2], transportation [3], digital forensics [4], or supply chains [5]. Currently, there is no consensus on a broadly accepted definition of these concepts.

Although these concepts are related, they are different and refer to two distinct characteristics of systems that should not be considered as synonyms. The concept of robustness refers to "the ability to withstand or survive external shocks" [6]. As an illustration, most nuclear plants are robust, as they may continue to operate even in the case of external shocks.

In this paper, we adopt the definition of resilience given by Haimes as "the ability of the system to withstand a major disruption within acceptable degradation parameters and to recover within an acceptable time and composite costs and risks" [7]. The concept of resilience is related with the idea that a resilient system may absorb shocks and adapt to the damages caused by these shocks. While a robust system withstands shocks *by construction*, thanks to its internal constitution, a resilient system withstands shocks *by behavior*, thanks to its adaptation capabilities. As an example, urban road transportation systems are resilient as, although some traffic jam may congest a large part of a city, the traffic will be redirected to other streets and arterial roads to keep the transportation system working.

2.2   Human-Agent Collectives

The concept of Human-Agent Collectives (HACs) has been forged by Jennings et al. in [1]. The term HAC aims at reflecting "the close partnership and the flexible social interactions between the humans and the computers. As well as exhibiting increased autonomy, such systems are inherently open and social. This openness means participants need to continually and flexibly establish and manage a range of social relationships".

One may recognize in HACs characteristics of Collaborative Networks defined as "a network consisting of a variety of entities—organizations and individuals—that are largely autonomous, geographically distributed, and heterogeneous in terms of their operating environment, culture, social capital and goals, which collaborate to better achieve common or compatible goals, and whose interactions are supported by computer networks" [8]. Therefore HACs are CNs in which entities may be either humans or agents and the interactions are not only supported by computer networks, but they can also be initiated by entities existing only on computer networks (i.e., agents). In HACs, the control usually shifts between humans and agents in a flexible manner.

HACs exhibit the following characteristics as collaborative networks:

- *Socially Heterogeneous* – humans and agents are related by very different social bounds. Power is exerted in a different manner between humans, between humans and agents, and between agents;
- *Embedded in an Open Environment* – when both humans and agents are always connected to the Internet, HACs have to face the possibility of a broad variety of competitive entities (humans or agents) that may potentially perform the tasks of some entities of the HAC in a competitive manner;
- *Adaptive* – Not only humans have to react to changes in the HAC and its environment, but agents should also be able to adapt to highly adaptive human decision making processes. As a consequence, the whole HAC itself often has to adapt by changing its structure, shifting control from members to members.

These characteristics of HACs lead to a set of major research challenges, among which Jennings et al. pointed out:

1. *Flexible Autonomy* – "flexible autonomy [...] allows agents to sometimes take actions in a completely autonomous way without reference to humans, while at other times being guided by much closer human involvement".

2. *Agile Teaming* – agile teams should be able to "come together on an ad hoc basis to achieve joint goals and then disband once the cooperative action has been successful".
3. *Incentive Engineering* – as a result of incentive engineering, "the actors' rewards are designed so the actions the participants are encouraged to take generate socially desirable outcomes"
4. *Accountable Information Infrastructure* – an "accountable information infrastructure [...] allows the veracity and accuracy of seamlessly blended human and agent decisions, sensor data, and crowd-generated content to be confirmed and audited".

One may notice that the second and third points are objects of research for the community focusing on CNs, and that HACs could probably benefit from the results concerning CNs in these areas.

3 Robustness of HACs in Interdependent Networked Environments

3.1 Interdependent Networks

HACs operate in open, networked environments. In these networks, it is frequent to observe various networks, interacting one with another. A well-known example of this fact is the structure of IT networks according to the Open Systems Interconnection model, known as the OSI model [9]. In this model, 7 layers, corresponding to various networks, are defined and their potential interactions are defined. In HACs, agents are usually related to various networks, such as telecommunication networks, application networks, social networks, corporate networks....

Interdependent networks are defined as a set of networks whose nodes and links are connected by *epilinks*. We define an epilink as a link connecting two nodes, or two links, or a link and a node from two networks. The concept of an interdependent network captures the idea that various networks may influence each other. For, example, in metropolises, the exchange of ideas and information via social media relies on infrastructural networks, such as the wired and wireless Internet or cable television. Similarly, attendance of a child at a given school is often related with the existence of appropriate transportation means, which illustrates the interdependence between social networks and infrastructure networks. Interdependence between networks is usually reciprocal, i.e., if a network A influences a network B, then the network B often influences the network A as well. As an example, not only is the school attendance of children correlated with available transportation means, but also transportation means, especially the capacity and timetable of public transportation, are usually evolving to appropriately support the population of children attending schools.

3.2 Failure Propagation in HACs and Surrounding Interdependent Networks

Buldyrev et al. [10] have shown that the dynamics of interdependent networks is a novel surprising field of study. They have studied the robustness of a set of interdependent networks, i.e., the vulnerability of interdependent networks to the removal of nodes and links. The results of this study are that interdependent networks are less robust than each network is isolation due to cascades of failure from one network to another. And "surprisingly, analysing complex systems as a set of interdependent networks may destabilize the most basic assumptions that network theory has relied on for single networks" [10].

An exhaustive list of studies of interdependent networks is provided in [11, 12].

As HACs are embedded in interdependent open networks, they are also exposed to the weaknesses pointed out by Buldyrev et al.: as an HAC is connected to an interdependent network, the robustness of the HAC may be deeply affected by potential *cascades* and *propagations* in the surrounding interdependent network. The case studied by Buldyrev et al. was related with a failure in the Italian electric grid, which has propagated to the Italian Internet (Internet routers needed energy to work), which has propagated back to the electric grid (as power stations are controlled remotely via the Web). Other examples of cascades and propagations in interdependent networks may be found in the area of infrastructure networks, transportation networks, and the financial sector and its recent crisis.

In the scenario of a failure in the HAC, a similar scenario may happen: not only the other members of the HAC may be directly affected by the failure, but they may also be affected in an indirect manner: the member that fails may by connected by one network to the surrounding interdependent open environment. In the surrounding environment, the failure may propagate to another network via epilinks, which may further affect another member of the HAC. Figure 1 illustrates this scenario.

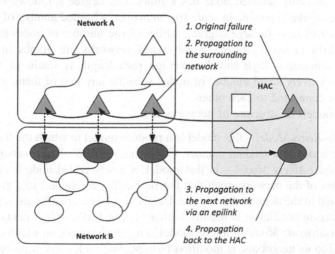

Fig. 1. Failure propagation in HACs and surrounding interdependent open networks

The risk that the surrounding open interdependent environment introduces for HACs may be mitigated:

(1) by reducing the number of interactions with the environment, which reduces the probability of a failure directly cause by the surrounding network. An entity may play the role of a façade to the HAC with regards to the surrounding environment, hiding the remaining member of the HAC from the environment, and therefore protecting them;

(2) by limiting the number of networks to which the various members of the HACs are connected to in the surrounding environment. As a result, failures propagated via epilinks will less probably cause failures to HAC members connected to the surrounding interdependent network.

4 Internal Structure of HACs as a Key Factor of Resilience

While the interdependent structure of the surrounding environment has an influence on the robustness of HACs, the key factor of resilience for HACs is related to their internal structure, which is defined, to a large extent, by its network structure.

4.1 Popular Network Structures

Networks have been the object of intense research works since the late 1990's. Among key characteristics of networks, the clustering coefficient, the scale-free and the small-world properties of some networks have been intensively scrutinized. The *clustering coefficient* is a measure of the tendency of nodes to connect to other nodes within groups of nodes. The highest the clustering coefficient, the highest the number of connected triplets of nodes. *Scale-free networks* are networks in which the probability that a randomly selected node has k links, i.e., degree k follows $P(k) \sim k^{-\gamma}$, where γ is the degree exponent. In *scale-free networks*, a limited number of nodes have a large number of links (a large degree), while a large number of nodes have a small number of links (a small degree). Small-world networks are graphs in which the clustering coefficient is high and the average path length is small. In small-world networks, a relatively small number of nodes separate any two of them, even if most nodes are not connected to each other.

Popular models of structure of networks are:

- *The Erdős–Rényi Model* – this model is a random model in which the links between nodes are added in a random manner. Clustering of Erdős–Rényi networks is low;
- *The Barabàsi-Albert Model* – in this model, a newly added node is connected to other nodes of the network, such that the probability to connect to a given node is proportional to the degree of this node. Barabàsi-Albert networks are scale-free and their clustering coefficient is usually higher than in Erdős–Rényi networks;
- *The Watts-Strogatz Model*: – in this model, a regular network, in which each node is connected to its neighbors, is modified by replacing with a given probability β the end destination node of each link by a randomly chosen different node. The

Watts-Strogatz model may generate random networks, similar to Erdős–Rényi networks, as well as regular networks, depending on the value of β. Even small values of β lead the generation of small-world networks, although not scale-free ones;

- *The Hierarchical Model*– in this model, a network pattern is iteratively replicated, leading to a hierarchical organization. Hierarchical networks may be both small-world networks and have a high clustering coefficient.

4.2 Resilience of Networks

The resilience of networks has been largely studied in the literature, mostly from a topological perspective. It has been shown that the resilience of a networks depends not only of its structure but also depends on the type of attack. Albert et al. [13] have demonstrated that scale-free networks are highly resistant to attacks focused on random nodes, but they are very vulnerable to attacks targeting the hubs, i.e., highly inter-connected nodes.

In [14], Watts provides an analysis of the 1997 Toyota-Aisin crisis with regards to resilience and network topology. On February 1, 1997, a fire started in the Toyota Aisin factory. This factory was producing almost all p-valves, a valve used to control the fluid pressure in brakes. Without almost any stock, the destruction of the Aisin factory may cause the interruption of the whole Toyota production. However, within 4 days, Toyota was producing its first p-valves with the help of its other factories and business partners [16].

According to Watts, the resilience of Toyota in the Aisin incident was due to the structure of the social and organizational network. On the one hand, the Japanese culture has imposed a strongly hierarchical organization within Toyota. On the second hand, due to internal policies providing strong incentives for employee mobility, many horizontal relations between various factories have been created by employees visiting other factories for a few months.

This particular network structure, consisting of a highly regular structure and many shortcuts, allows to control the exchange of information (on the regular structure) but

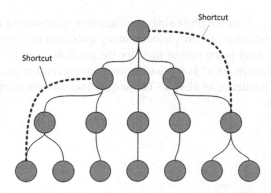

Fig. 2. A resilient network with a regular hierarchical network and shortcuts.

also to speed up and to *recover* from failure (with shortcuts) if the regular structure is partially destroyed. One may notice that the idea of a regular structure rewired with shortcuts is at the heart of small-world networks [15]. Figure 2 illustrates this type of network structure.

Following the Aisin-Toyota case, HACs could rely on their internal structure, especially shortcuts between their members to increase resilience. In case of a failure of an HAC member, shortcuts can be used to recover efficiently by increasing the speed of information exchange among HAC members.

5   Conclusions

HACs are a novel type of collaborative networks in which both humans and agents can ask their counterparts to take some actions. HACs requires additional works in many areas, including technical and business ones.

As far as resilience and robustness are concerned, HACs are facing various important challenges. For the robustness of HACs, the open interdependent networked environment in which they exist is an important challenge as the interdependency of the networks in the surrounding environment is potentially strongly degrading the robustness of HACs.

From a broader perspective, although interdependent networks have been studied in various contexts, e.g., critical infrastructure or population mobility, there is still a need for a unifying theory of interdependent networks that would encompass and largely extend former studies in a structured and organized manner.

For the resilience of HACs, their internal structure plays an important role: an appropriate structure, with shortcuts, may allow an HAC to rapidly recover from a failure by rapidly exchanging information among the remaining HAC members, which speed up the decision making process related with recovery.

The case of Toyota is a very interesting example of resilience within networks of networks. Or to be precise, Toyota may be considered as an organization consisting of various organizational entities. These organizational entities are collaborating in a similar way to collaborative networks. The case of the fire in the break factory of Toyota illustrates the idea that collaborative networks, if appropriately structured can be resilient.

Finally, this paper is in not proposing an exhaustive treatment of the hard question of robustness and resilience of HAC, leaving many questions not only unanswered but even unformulated: what is the role of trust for the resilience and robustness of HACs and how to measure/improve it? Is it possible to adopt preventive measures to improve the robustness and resilience of HACs? These questions remain open and are waiting for further attention.

References

1. Jennings, N.R., Moreau, L., Nicholson, D., Ramchurn, S., Roberts, S., Rodden, T., Rogers, A.: Human-agent collectives. Commun. ACM **57–12**, 80–88 (2014). doi:10.1145/2629559
2. Meerow, S., Newell, J.P.: Resilience and complexity: a bibliometric review and prospects for industrial ecology. J. Ind. Ecol. Spec. Issue Adv. Complex Adapt. Syst. Ind. Ecol. **19**(2), 236–251 (2015). doi:10.1111/jiec.12252
3. Gluchshenko, O.: Definitions of disturbance, resilience and robustness in ATM context. DLR report IB 112-2012/28, release 0.07 (2012). http://elib.dlr.de/79571/1/IB-112-2012-28_web_Gluchshenko_0.07.pdf
4. Kim, Y., Chen, Y.-S., Linderman, K.: Supply network disruption and resilience: a network structural perspective. J. Oper. Manage. **33–34**, 43–59 (2015). doi:10.1016/j.jom.2014.10.006
5. Amann, P., James, J.I.: Designing robustness and resilience in digital investigation laboratories. Digit. Invest. **12**(1), S111–S120 (2015) ISSN 1742-2876. doi:10.1016/j.diin.2015.01.015
6. Bankes, S.: Robustness, adaptivity, and resiliency analysis. In AAAI fall symposium: complex adaptive systems (2010). https://www.aaai.org/ocs/index.php/FSS/FSS10/paper/viewFile/2242/2643
7. Haimes, Y.Y.: On the definition of resilience in systems. Risk Anal. **29**(4), 49–501 (2009). doi:10.1111/j.1539-6924.2009.01216.x
8. Camarinha-Matos, L.M., Afsarmanesh, H., Ollus, M.: Ecolead and CNO base concepts. In: Methods and Tools for Collaborative Networked Organizations, pp. 3–32. Springer, New York (2008)
9. Zimmermann, H.: OSI reference model — the ISO model of architecture for open systems interconnection. IEEE Trans. Commun. **28**(4), 425–432 (1980). doi:10.1109/TCOM.1980.1094702
10. Buldyrev, S.V., Parshani, R., Paul, G., Stanley, H.E., Havlin, S.: Catastrophic cascade of failures in interdependent networks. Nature **464**(7291), 1025–1028 (2010). doi:10.1038/nature08932
11. Zio, E., Sansavini, G.: Modeling interdependent network systems for identifying cascade-safe operating margins. IEEE Trans. Reliab. **60**(1), 94–101 (2011). doi:10.1109/TR.2010.2104211
12. Gao, J., Buldyrev, S.V., Stanley, H.E., Havlin, S.: Networks formed from interdependent networks. Nat. Phys. **8**, 40–48 (2012). doi:10.1038/nphys2180
13. Albert, R., Jeong, H., Barabási, A.L.: Error and attack tolerance of complex networks. Nature **406**, 378–382 (2000)
14. Watts, D.J.: Six Degrees: The Science of a Connected Age. W.W. Norton & Company, New York (2004)
15. Watts, D.J., Strogatz, S.H.: Collective dynamics of 'small-world' networks. Nature **393**, 440–442 (1998). doi:10.1038/30918
16. Kakihara, M., Sørensen, C.: Exploring knowledge emergence: from chaos to organizational knowledge. J. Glob. Inf. Technol. Manage. **5**(3), 48–66 (2002). http://www.kakihara.org/papers/Kakihara&Sorensen_JGITM.pdf

Collaborative Strategies Alignment to Enhance the Collaborative Network Agility and Resilience

Beatriz Andres^(⊠), Raul Poler, and Raquel Sanchis

Research Centre on Production Management and Engineering (CIGIP),
Escuela Politécnica Superior de Alcoy, Centre d'Innovació i Investigació,
Universitat Politècnica de València (UPV), Calle Alarcón, 03801 Alcoy, Spain
{bandres, rpoler, rsanchis}@cigip.upv.es

Abstract. Current supply networks are embedded in dynamic and turbulent environments, and must face the appearance of some disruptive events throughout their life cycle. Disruptions are almost always accompanied by negative effects, resulting on performance loss for both, the enterprises and the network. The activation of proactive strategies will allow enterprises to reduce this loss when a disruption appears. Enterprises must be aware of that the activated strategies must be aligned, so that they positively influence the objectives and the performance indicators defined by all the network partners. This paper proposes a simulation model to support enterprises in the decision-making on which proactive strategies activate in order to be aligned, from a collaborative perspective. The main aim is to limit the adverse effects produced by the disruptions. Such aligned strategies allow collaborative enterprises to move in the same direction when a disruption appears. In addition the strategies enhance the resilience and agility of both the enterprises and the network as well as positively influence the objectives and the performance indicators defined by all the network partners

Keywords: Strategies Alignment · Disruptions · Collaborative Processes · Process Disruptions · System Dynamics · Proactive Actions · Resilience

1 Introduction

The current global business environment, characterised by being unpredictable and competitive, makes enterprises to be more exposed to disruptive events. This encourages enterprises to change the way they work and to be more flexible in the process of recovering themselves from disruptions. Thus, a new tendency is emerging through the enterprises participation in Collaborative Networks (CN) [1]. Such participation requires to restructure their internal operations, make information systems interoperable, coordinate their production processes, align their strategies, share goals, achieve suitable levels of trust, reach agreements in practices, and align values [2–4]. The benefits specifically associated with the strategies alignment have a great influence on the CN success, since they are becoming a relevant issue for achieving competitive advantages [4]. The participation in CNs allows enterprises to be more agile and

© IFIP International Federation for Information Processing 2015
L.M. Camarinha-Matos et al. (Eds.): PRO-VE 2015, IFIP AICT 463, pp. 88–99, 2015.
DOI: 10.1007/978-3-319-24141-8_8

resilient, and to increase the effectiveness in response to the effects of potential disruptive events [5]. Focusing on the strategies alignment process, carried out from a collaborative perspective, Andres and Poler [6] consider in their approach the strategies alignment to facilitate some of the conventional disruptions [7], such as the variability of networks, global competition, complexity in supply chain and greater variety in production.

When a disruption takes place, various independent enterprises are affected and each one defines a set of strategies to deal with the negative repercussions that impact its performance. These strategies can be proactively or reactively deployed [8]. Mitroff and Alpasan [9] stated that resilient organizations are proactive and they recover sooner and better from the disruptions. The decision of which proactive strategies to activate, in order to deal with the disruptions, can be made from a collaborative or non-collaborative perspective. This paper focuses on the proposal of a collaborative and proactive solution through the *Strategies Alignment Simulation Model* (SASM). SASM models the influences expected among the collaborative enterprises taking into account the objectives defined and the proactive strategies formulated by all the networked enterprises, modelling the influences exerted among them. The model is based on the System Dynamics (SD) method and promotes the activation of those proactive strategies that, being aligned, positively influence all objectives defined by all the network partners; enabling them to reduce the loss of business performance, after a disruptive event occurs.

In the light of this, the next research question appears:

What would be an adequate model to support enterprises in the decision making process of selecting proactive strategies to be aligned, in order to efficiently deal with the unexpected disruptive events, from a collaborative perspective?

The paper is organised as follows: Sect. 2 introduces the concept of disruption in supply networks as define in the literature. In Sect. 3, the *Strategies Alignment Simulation Model* (SASM) is presented. A numerical example is described in Sect. 4, applying the model to deal with a supply disruption. Finally in Sect. 5, conclusions and future research lines are considered.

2 Supply Networks Disruptions

The term disruption, outlined by Barroso et al. [10], is defined as a predictable, or in most cases unpredictable event that directly affects the common activity and stability of an enterprise, thereby its performance. Sheffi and Rice [7] model the loss of business performance, defining 8 phases that enterprises experience when a disruption occurs (see Fig. 1): (i) preparation: companies anticipation and proactive attitude, (ii) disruptive event: any situation that threatens the daily operation of a company, (iii) first response: decision after reaction, (iv) initial impact: immediately disruption repercussion, (v) total impact: medium or long term effects (once the disruption occurs, the performance decreases significantly), (vi) preparation for recovery: starts in parallel with the first response, (vii) recovery: the stage in which the company returns to the state before the disruption and (viii) long-term impact: the time companies need, after a disruptive event, to recover (depending on the severity of the consequences).

Work that can be highlighted in the scope of supply network disruptions are: Wu et al. [11] Disruption Analysis Network (DA_NET), determines how disruptions propagate and affect supply networks, through the methodology. Sheffi and Rice [7] focus their work on the disruptions classification so that can be easily identified and overcame. Ivanov et al. [12] focus on the potential disruptions identification using the Supply Chain Events Management (SCEM) or Sanchis and Poler [13] propose a categorization framework of disruptions as a starting point to evaluate the resilience capacity of enterprises.

3 Strategies Alignment to Deal with Supply Disruptions

In order to reduce the performance loss and be more resilient against any disruption, enterprises are encouraged to collaborate, and more concretely, to collaboratively align their strategies [6, 14]. Therefore, a simulation model to collaboratively carry out the strategies alignment process is developed. The strategies alignment model is designed based on the assumption that the networked partners individually formulate a set of proactive strategies to manage the appearance of potential disruptions. Thus, it is crucial to collaboratively work to select those proactive strategies that are aligned, allowing the network members to reduce the negative influences reflected in the Business Performance (Key Performance Indicators, KPIs), when a disruptive event occurs (Fig. 1, orange line). The SASM supports enterprises in the collaborative decision making process of which strategies to activate in order to align their own strategies with the strategies formulated by all the partners of the network.

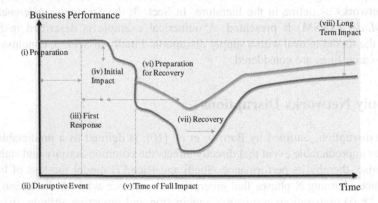

Fig. 1. Disruptions phases (adapted from Sheffi and Rice [7])

3.1 Strategies Alignment Concept

In order to give the reader a better understanding of how the strategies alignment process is treated in this paper, a definition of the concept *strategies alignment* is hereafter presented.

It is widely known that the strategies are the set of actions raised to achieve the defined objectives, i.e. minimise the performance loss derived from a disruption by reducing the recovery time or cost, etc. Considering the work developed in [15], it is assumed that the strategies alignment concept is defined as, the set of strategies, formulated by all the network enterprises, whose activation positively influence the achievement of all the objectives defined by all the partners, increasing their KPI levels. The activation of the aligned strategies will promote the maximization of the positive influences and the minimization of the negative influences, respectively at the network level. Note: the concept of alignment is not the same as compatibility. Strategies are compatible when they can be activated at the same time but do not have positive influences on each other. The total benefit corresponds to the sum of the benefit obtained by the activation of each strategy individually. Lets consider two enterprises e_i and e_j, each one defines one objective o_i and o_j and formulates one strategy, S_i and S_j. S_i and S_j are considered to be aligned when the activation of S_i has a positive influence on both objectives o_i and o_j and the same occurs with S_j. The strategies are aligned when the total benefit obtained is higher than the sum of the benefits obtained by the activation of each strategy individually. The strategies alignment concept is mathematically described in [4].

3.2 Strategies Alignment Simulation Model (SASM)

Despite the importance of aligning strategies in a CN, in terms of avoiding partnership conflicts and moving in the same direction when dealing with disruptive events, a gap has been found in the literature with respect to the contributions of a holistic approach. An approach that considers all the strategies formulated by all the partners, when deciding which aligned strategies to activate in order deal with a disruption. To fill this gap, this research aims to support the decision making process of identifying which of the proactive strategies have to be activated, by a simulation model. The holistic perspective, will allow modelling the strategies alignment process regardless the strategies' nature and the type of disruption facing, considering the CN context. The proposed SASM allows the modelling the CN considering the elements that define the strategies alignment process. These elements and the relations established among them are represented through a causal and flow chart according to the SD Method [16]. For the model formulation, the following considerations have been taken into account:

- Each networked enterprise defines a set of objectives, which will be measured before and after a disruption occurs. The extent into which the objectives are achieved is measured through KPIs. The enterprises' aim is to achieve the maximum level of each KPI (what means to minimise the performance reduction), and to obtain, as fast and at lowest costly possible, the maximum levels of network performance in the recovery phase and in the long term, once a potential disruptive event occurs.
- A set of proactive strategies is formulated by each network enterprise, with the main objective of dealing with future potential disruptions and minimise the performance loss of the defined objectives (KPIs). The strategies are devoted to improve the

performance level of each KPI, and consequently to improve the network performance.

- The use of KPIs allows computing the increase/decrease of the network and enterprises performance when a specific set of strategies is activated.
- Not all the proactive strategies formulated will be activated; the enterprises will only carry out those that are aligned.

The SASM will allow analysing, describing, explaining, simulating, assessing, monitoring and predicting misalignments among the strategies specifically those formulated to deal with disruptions. Moreover, the simulation model is proposed as a supporting tool for the enterprise decision makers, to identify which proactive strategies to activate in order to obtain higher levels of alignment, and consequently of performance, not only at the intra-enterprise level but also with the rest of enterprises of the network, that is the inter-enterprise level. In the light of this, recovery time and cost will be reduced, increasing the levels of resilience of both the enterprises and the network.

System Dynamics Method (SD). Solving the strategies alignment model through analytical methods implies to face tedious procedures involving large number of iterations. For that reason the use of the SD method is considered. SD method, outlined by Forrester [16], allows to analyse the characteristics of the feedbacks of the represented system (CN), allowing to understand how the elements, belonging to the system, interact with each other, influencing in its performance. Generally, SD allows to understand the causal relationships of systems' behaviour by bringing together sets of elements that are interrelated in such a way that a change in one element affects a whole series of elements [17]. In the context of strategies alignment, SD allows representing the influences that the activated strategies have on the KPIs level. The relations of influences are represented in the SASM. Depending on the strategies activated, the KPIs level will be positively or negatively influenced. In the particular scenario considered in this paper, the SD method allows to simulate all the elements of the system (proactive strategies formulated, objectives defined and their relations) by simultaneously changing the *decision variables*, which are defined by (i) the *units of strategies to activate* (u_Sis) and (ii) the *time when to activate them* (ti_Sis). This will enable the SASM to identify the proactive strategies appropriate to be activated, so that positive influences are obtained in all the KPIs defined by all the networked enterprises

The causal loop diagram allows representing the elements and relationships of the modelled system, based on an influence on effects (+ and − loops) [17]. The flow diagram translates the information depicted in the causal loop diagram into a terminology that helps writing equations in the computer. The representation of the flow diagram involves classifying the parameters and variables defined in the model into stock variables (which are a mental photograph of the system), flow variables (elements determining the variation of levels), parameters and auxiliary variables (Table 1 and Fig. 2). The equations used to model the SASM are formulated in Table 2 from the SD method perspective, a general notation has been considered.

Thus, the strategies alignment process is modelled using the SD method. The simulation software used to represent the SASM in the SD simulation approach is

Table 1. Stock, flow, parameter and auxiliary variables in the SASM

	Elements	Definition
Parameter	u_Sis	Units of strategy [u.s] *Sis* to be activated
	ti_Sis	Initial time of activation of *Sis*
	c_Sis	Cost of the strategy
	KPIixk_min	Minimum increase that the enterprise estimates for the *KPI_{ixk}*
	Threshold_KPIixk	Value from which the associated *KPI_{ixk}* is affected by the activation of a strategy *Sis*
	val_Sis_KPIixk	Value that registers the increase or decrease of the *KPI_{ixk}* when one unit of *Sis* is activated (*u_Sis*)
	Wikx	Relevance that the *KPI_{ixk}* has for enterprise *i*
	d1_Sis	Delay time of activation of the strategy *s* in enterprise *i Sis*
	d2_Sis	Time between the *Sis* starts to influence the *KPI_{ixk}* until the maximum level of influence in is achieved
	d4_Sis	Total duration of *Sis*
Auxiliary Variable	d3_Sis	Time period in which *Sis* is exerting the highest influence (**val_Sis_KPIixk**) on the *KPI_{ixk}*
	Sis_mu	Monetary units invested in the activation of *Sis*
	tf_Sis	Time unit when *Sis* is finished [t.u.]
	slope_Sis_KPIikx	Slope of the ramp in represented in **curve_KPIixk**
	fulfill_KPIixk_min	Minimum increase that the enterprise estimates for the *KPI_{ixk}*,
	KPI_i	Increase experienced by the KPI defined at enterprise level
	KPI_GLOBAL	Increase experienced KPI defined at network level
Stock	KPIixk	Increase observed in the *KPI_{ixk}* when the *Sis* is activated: *Sis* activated in the same enterprise (intra-enterprise) and *Sjs* activated by other enterprises (inter-enterprise)
	KPIixk_T	Increase experienced by the *KPI_{ixk}* once the *Threshold_kpi_{ixk}* is computed
	bi	Budget owned by the enterprise *i* to invest in the activation of the strategies *Sis*
Flow	curve_KPIixk	Function that models the increase of *KPI_{ixk}* considering all the activated strategies
	curve_KPIixk_T	Function that models the increase of *KPI_{ixk}* when *Threshold_kpi_{ixk}* value is computed
	Inf_Sis_KPIixk	Function that models the behaviour of the *KPI_{ixk}* when *Sis* is activated

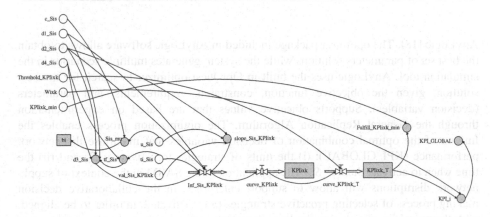

Fig. 2. SASM: flow diagram

Table 2. Equations for the SASM in SD

Dimensions
`dimension_KPIixk`, representing the indexes of the KPIs defined in the model `index_KPIixk`
`dimension_Sis`, representing the indexes of the strategies defined in the model `index_Sis`
Budget
`bi - ΣSis_mu`
Monetary units invested in the activation of str_{is}
`Sis_mu = u_Sis · c_Sis.get(index_Sis)`
Unit of time when str_{is} is finished
`tf_Sis = ti_Sis + d4_Sis.get(index_Sis)`
Time period in which str_{is} is exerting the highest influence ($inf\_str_{is\_}kpi_{ixk}$) on the kpi_{ixk}
`d3_Sis = d4_Sis.get(index_Sis) - d1_Sis.get(index_Sis) -` `(2·d2_Sis.get(index_Sis))`
Slope of the ramp in represented in $f\_inf\_str_{is\_}kpi_{ixk}(t)$
`slope_Sis_KPIixk = (u_Sis · val_Sis_KPIixk [dimension_KPIixk])/` `d2_Sis.get(index_Sis)`
Function that models the behaviour of the kpi_{ixk} when str_{is} is activated[1]
`Inf_Sis_KPIixk = delay (ramp (slope_Sis_KPIixk[dimension_KPIixk], ti_Sis,` `ti_Sis + d2_Sis.get(index_Sis)) - ramp (slope_Sis_KPIixk[dimension_KPIixk],` `ti_Sis + d2_Sis.get(index_Sis) + d3_Sis, ti_Sis + 2 · d2_Sis.get(index_Sis)` `+ d3_Sis) , d1_Sis.get(index_Sis))`
Function that models the overall behaviour of the kpi_{ixk} considering all the activated strategies
`curve_KPIixk = ΣInf_S11_KPIixk[dimension_KPIixk]`
Increase observed in the kpi_{ixk}
`KPIixk = ∫ curve_KPIixk[dimension_KPIixk]`
Function that models the curve of the behaviour of the kpi_{ixk} when the $Threshold\_kpi_{ixk}$ value is rested
`Curve_KPIixk_T = IF ((curve_KPIixk[dimension_KPIixk] >=` `Threshold_KPIixk[dimension_KPIixk]) THEN (curve_KPIixk[dimension_KPIixk] -` `Threshold_KPIixk[dimension_KPIixk]) ELSE (IF` `(curve_KPIixk[dimension_KPIixk]<0) THEN curve_KPIixk[dimension_KPIixk] ELSE` `0))`
Increase experienced by the kpi_{ixk} once the $Threshold\_kpi_{ixk}$ is computed
`KPIixk_T = ∫ curve_KPIixk_T[ dimension_KPIixk ]`
Acomplishment of the minimum increase that the enterprise determines for the kpi_{ixk}, once the $Threshold\_kpi_{ixk}$ is computed
`fulfill_KPIixk_min = IF ((KPIixk_T[ dimension_KPIixk ] >= KPIixk_min[` `dimension_KPIixk ]) THEN 1 ELSE 0)`
Increase experienced by the KPI defined at enterprise i level
`KPI_i = Σ KPIixk_T.get(index_KPixk) · Wixk[dimension_KPIixk]`
Increase experienced KPI defined at network net level
`KPI_GLOBAL = Σ KPI_i / n`

AnyLogic [18]. The optimiser package included in AnyLogic software allows to obtain the best set of parameters solutions while the system generates multiple scenarios in the simulation tool. AnyLogic uses the built-in OptQuest optimizer to search for the best solution, given the objective function, constraints, requirements, and parameters (decision variables). Supports objective values that are based on experimentation through the General Replication Algorithm. The optimization process enables the finding of the optimal combination of decision variables that maximise the network performance (KPI_GLOBAL): (i) the units of strategies to activate u_S_{is} and (ii) the time when to activate them ti_S_{is}. The application of the SASM in the context of supply network disruptions will allow to support enterprises in the collaborative decision making process of selecting proactive strategies to be activated, in order to be aligned, with the main aim of reducing the loss of performance as well as the time and cost of recovery when a disruption occurs.

4 Illustrative Example

In this section, an illustrative example is presented in order to demonstrate the application of the SASM to deal with disruptive events and enhance resilience and agility in the CN and its enterprises. In this example, two enterprises are considered acquiring the roles of supplier (enterprise 1) and manufacturer (enterprise 2). Each enterprise defines two proactive strategies in order to deal with a production process disruption due to the interruption of material supply caused by a machine breakdown in the supplier plant (the supplier cannot provide the required products with the requirements specified by the focal company) [13].

Supplier

- Strategy 1($S11$): Increase the level of Safety Stock
- Strategy 2($S12$): Total Productive Maintenance

Manufacturer

- Strategy 1($S21$): Increase Suppliers Base
- Strategy 2($S22$): Increase the level of Safety Stock

Moreover, each enterprise defines two KPIs to measure the influence that the strategies have on the recovery phase. These indicators are related to the cost and the time of recovery for each of the enterprises participating in the CN. Accordingly KPI_{111} (of the supplier) and KPI_{211} (of the manufacturer) refer to the reduction of recovery cost ($KPI_{i11} = \frac{recoveryCost_{t-1} - recoveryCost_t}{recoveryCost_{t-1}}$) and KPI_{121} (of the supplier) and KPI_{221} (of the manufacturer) refer to the reduction of recovery time ($KPI_{i21} = \frac{recoveryTime_{t-1} - recoveryTime_t}{recoveryTime_{t-1}}$). Table 3 shows all the data required by SASM. First, the budget that each enterprise owns to activate the proactive strategies is defined. Regarding the strategies characterisation, the activation cost of the strategies and the duration parameters are estimated by the enterprises. With respect to the performance

Table 3. Illustrative example: data

Supplier (e_1) $b_1 = 3$													kpi$_{111}$		kpi$_{121}$	
													w_{111}	0,5	w_{121}	0,5
													Threshold_kpi$_{111}$	0,2	Threshold_kpi$_{121}$	0,1
S_{11}	u_S_{11}	?	tl_S_{11}	?	c_S_{11}	1	$d_1\_S_{11}$	0,05	$d_2\_S_{11}$	0,01	$d_4\_S_{21}$	0,3	$val\_S_{11}\_kpi_{111}$	0,9	$val\_S_{11}\_kpi_{121}$	-0,02
S_{12}	u_S_{12}	?	tl_S_{12}	?	c_S_{12}	2	$d_1\_S_{12}$	0,2	$d_2\_S_{12}$	0,03	$d_4\_S_{21}$	0,6	$val\_S_{12}\_kpi_{111}$	0,5	$val\_S_{12}\_kpi_{121}$	0,4
													$val\_S_{21}\_kpi_{111}$	-0,8	$val\_S_{21}\_kpi_{121}$	-0,4
													$val\_S_{22}\_kpi_{111}$	0,8	$val\_S_{22}\_kpi_{121}$	0,8

Manufacturer (e_2) $b_2 = 6$													kpi$_{211}$		kpi$_{221}$	
													w_{211}	0,5	w_{221}	0,5
													Threshold_kpi$_{211}$	0,3	Threshold_kpi$_{221}$	0,15
S_{21}	u_S_{21}	?	tl_S_{21}	?	c_S_{21}	5	$d_1\_S_{11}$	0,05	$d_2\_S_{21}$	0,02	$d_4\_S_{21}$	0,75	$val\_S_{21}\_kpi_{211}$	1	$val\_S_{21}\_kpi_{221}$	0
S_{22}	u_S_{22}	?	tl_S_{22}	?	c_S_{22}	6	$d_1\_S_{21}$	0,1	$d_2\_S_{21}$	0,01	$d_4\_S_{21}$	0,5	$val\_S_{22}\_kpi_{211}$	0,8	$val\_S_{22}\_kpi_{221}$	0,8
													$val\_S_{11}\_kpi_{211}$	-0,7	$val\_S_{11}\_kpi_{221}$	-0,2
													$val\_S_{12}\_kpi_{211}$	0,8	$val\_S_{12}\_kpi_{221}$	0,8

indicators, the weight and the threshold values are given. Finally, the values of influence are estimated by each enterprise (*val_Sis_KPIixk*).

In this case, the collaborative scenario modelled takes into account all the values of influence. Considering the data provided and introducing this data in the SASM simulation software (AnyLogic) in which the SASM is modelled, the optimisation experiment is done to obtain the decision variables that maximise the network performance level (KPI_GLOBAL). The results of the decision variables concerning (i) the units of strategies to activate u_S_{is} and (ii) the time when to activate them ti_S_{is} are shown in Fig. 3. The result of the collaborative scenario shows that, in order to have an efficient recovery and increase the levels of resilience and agility of the network, the supplier must activate the two defined strategies. The activation time of the supplier's strategies will be ti_S11 = 0.162 and ti_S12 = 0.063, considering that the unit refers to one year, strategy S11 will be initialised at the day 59 (0.162 · 365days) and strategy S12 will be initialised at the day 23, from the beginning of the year. Whilst, the manufacturer must only activate the strategy S22 at the day 59'5.

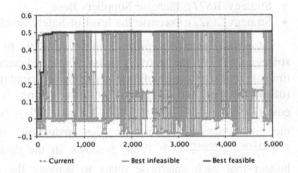

Fig. 3. SASM: flow diagram

Table 4 presents a comparison of the results obtained in the collaborative scenario with those obtained in the non-collaborative scenario, in both cases using the SASM. In the non-collaborative scenario the supplier only considers his own estimated values of influence, without considering how the strategies formulated by the manufacturer influence the performance level of his own indicators (shaded with grey in Table 3); the same happens to the manufacturer. In this regard, the non-collaborative scenario only considers intra-enterprise influences. The collaborative scenario is a more realistic one considering both intra and inter-enterprise influences, in which the supplier not only considers his own estimated values of influence, but also considers how the strategies formulated by the manufacturer influence the performance level of his own indicators, the same happens to the manufacturer.

From Table 4, it can be concluded that in the proposed illustrative example, the optimised solution of the collaborative scenario generates a level of network performance significantly higher than the performance resulting from the solution obtained in the non-collaborative scenario. Moreover, the solution obtained in the non-collaborative scenario breach the restriction of non-negativity values of KPI111

Table 4. SASM comparison of the results: non-collaborative vs. collaborative scenario

	Non-collaborative Scenario	Collaborative Scenario
u_S11	1	1
ti_S11	0,169	0,162
u_S12	1	1
ti_S12	0	0,063
u_S21	1	0
ti_S21	0,239	0,199
u_S22	0	1
ti_S22	0	0,163
KPI111_T	-0,195	0,663
Fulfill_KPI111_min	0	1
KPI121_T	-0,139	0,45
Fulfill_KPI121_min	0	1
KPI211_T	0,587	0,357
Fulfill_KPI211_min	1	1
KPI221_T	0,189	0,533
Fulfill_KPI221_min	1	1
KPI_1(distributor)	-0,167	0,557
KPI_2 (manufacturer)	0,388	0,445
KPI_GLOBAL	**0,1105**	**0,501**

and KPI121. Whereas that the solution of the collaborative scenario complies with the non-negativity restriction so that all the performance indicators are larger than 0. Making collaboratively decisions of which strategies to activate in order to deal with a certain disruption, using the SASM provides better solutions than if this decision is performed individually.

The SASM serves as a supporting tool, for enterprises participating in CN, to deal with disruptive events, so that the activation of aligned proactive strategies involves an improvement in time and cost of recovery. Consequently, the application of SASM is an effective tool to increase the resilience and agility of CN in terms of identifying the aligned strategies that will allow dealing with potential disruptions.

5   Conclusions

This paper proposes the Strategies Alignment Simulation Model (SASM) for aligning the proactive strategies formulated in order to reduce the recovery time and cost in the case of a process disruption, in the CN context. It has been proved, in the illustrative example, that deciding about the activation of aligned strategies from a collaborative perspective provides better results in terms of disruption recovery time and cost. Ultimately, the results obtained using the SASM allow increasing the resilience and agility of the CN. The main drawback considered is the data collection, especially with respect to the values of influence (val_Sis_KPIixk), which the enterprises have to estimate. As the enterprise may face up to a disruption that has never occurred, this estimation could become very difficult. In the light of the results obtained, future research lines lead to propose guidelines to support enterprises on the data gathering and sharing along the strategies alignment process. In the collaborative scenario, the exchange of information is considered a key factor; therefore, future work will be also devoted to enhance the information sharing process. Finally, the SASM will be applied in a real case study in order to obtain the proper feedback from the enterprises and improve the simulation model.

Acknowledgments. This work was funded in part by the European Community's 7FP programme (FP7/2007-2013) under the grant agreement n° NMP2-SL-2009- 229333 and the *Programa Val i + d para investigadores en formación* (ACIF)

References

1. Camarinha-Matos, L.M., Afsarmanesh, H.: Collaborative networks: a new scientific discipline. J. Intell. Manuf. **16**(4–5), 439–452 (2005)
2. Bititci, U., Turnera, T., Mackaya, D., Kearneyc, D., Parunga, J., Waltersb, D.: Managing synergy in collaborative enterprises. Prod. Plan. Control Manage. Oper. **18**(6), 454–465 (2007)
3. Macedo, P., Abreu, A., Camarinha-Matos, L.M.: A method to analyse the alignment of core values in collaborative networked organisations. Prod. Plan. Control **21**(2), 145–159 (2010)
4. Andres, B., Poler, R.: Computing the strategies alignment in collaborative networks. In: Mertins, K., Bénaben, F., Poler, R., Bourrières, J.-P. (eds.) Enterprise Interoperability VI, pp. 29–40. Springer, Cham (2014)
5. Shamsuzzoha, A.H.M., Kankaanpaa, T., Helo, P., Carneiro, L.M., Almeida, R., Fornasiero, R.: Non-hierarchical collaboration in dynamic business communities. In: Camarinha-Matos, L.M., Boucher, X., Afsarmanesh, H. (eds.) PRO-VE 2010. IFIP AICT, vol. 336, pp. 609–618. Springer, Heidelberg (2010)
6. Andres, B., Poler, R.: Enhancing enterprise resilience through enterprise collaboration. In: IFAC Proceedings, vol. 7, no. 1, pp. 688–693 (2013)
7. Sheffi, Y., Rice, J.B.: A supply chain view of the resilient enterprise. A supply chain view of the resilient enterprise. MIT Sloan Manage. Rev. **47**(1), 41–48 (2005)
8. Chorn, N.H.: The alignment theory: creating strategic fit. Manage. Decis. **29**(1), 20–24 (1991)
9. Mitroff, I., Alpasan, M.: Preparing for the evil. Harvard Bus. Rev. **81**(4), 109–115 (2003)
10. Barroso, A.P., Machado, V.H., Cruz-Machado, V.: Supply chain resilience using the mapping approach. In: Pengzhong, L. (ed.) Supply Chain Management, pp. 161–184. InTech, Rijeka (2011)
11. Wu, T., Blackhurst, J., O'grady, P.: Methodology for supply chain disruption analysis. Int. J. Prod. Res. **45**(7), 1665–1682 (2007)
12. Ivanov, D., Sokolov, B. Dolgui, A., Solovyeva, I.: Application of control theoretic tools to supply chain disruptions management. In: Proceedings of the IFAC Conference on Manufacturing Modelling, Management and Control, pp. 1926–1931 (2013)
13. Sanchis, R., Poler, R.: Enterprise resilience assessment: a categorisation framework of disruptions. Dirección y Organización **54**, 45–53 (2014)
14. Sanchis, R., Poler, R.: Definition of a framework to support strategic decisions to improve enterprise resilience. In: IFAC Proceedings, vol. 7, no. 1, pp. 700–705 (2013)

15. Andres, B., Poler, R.: Dealing with the alignment of strategies within the collaborative networked partners. In: Camarinha-Matos, L.M., Baldissera, T.A., Di Orio, G., Marques, F. (eds.) DoCEIS 2015. IFIP AICT, vol. 450, pp. 13–21. Springer, Heidelberg (2015)
16. Forrester, J.W.: Industrial Dynamics. MIT press, Cambridge (1961)
17. Campuzano, F., Mula, J.: Supply Chain Simulation. A System Dynamics Approach for Improving Performance, p. 106. Springer, London (2011)
18. AnyLogic: AnyLogic ® (2015). http://www.anylogic.com/

Creating Agility in Traffic Management by Collaborative Service-Dominant Business Engineering

Paul Grefen[1], Oktay Turetken[1(✉)], Kostas Traganos[1],
Aafke den Hollander[2], and Rik Eshuis[1]

[1] School of Industrial Engineering, Eindhoven University of Technology,
5600 MB Eindhoven, The Netherlands
{p.w.p.j.grefen,o.turetken,k.traganos,
h.eshuis}@tue.nl
[2] Ingenieursbureau Amsterdam, Amsterdam, The Netherlands
A.den.Hollander@amsterdam.nl

Abstract. Traffic management is a business domain characterized by an infrastructure-dominant approach to new developments: the focus is typically on innovating assets such as traffic detection systems, road signage and traffic information systems. This domain also has a large number of involved stakeholders, such as road authorities, municipalities, technology providers and road users of various kinds. Faster changing traffic management requirements and increasing complexity of the collaborative networks required to meet these requirements render traditional approaches to business design in traffic management too rigid. We have applied collaborative, service-dominant business engineering to prototype a basis for new levels of business agility in multi-stakeholder traffic management. Collaborative workshops have shown to be a useful means to quickly arrive at agile, customer-centric business models that allow decoupling from long-term infrastructure considerations. This paper demonstrates that service-dominant business engineering can be effective in an asset-dominant domain to increase business resilience in complex environments.

Keywords: Service-dominant business · Collaborative business network · Business model · Traffic management

1 Introduction

Like most large cities, Amsterdam is characterized by extensive road traffic problems. These traffic problems are bad during daily rush hours, but reach their worst peaks when large events are held that attract large volumes of traffic in a small window of time in a specific area of the city. Examples of these events are major soccer matches and large rock concerts – or even the combination of both. The southeast section of Amsterdam is a location where a number of large event locations is clustered and that consequently meets these traffic problems at a regular pace. To try and counter these problems collaboratively, the main involved stakeholders have joined in the PPA/ZO project: the practice trial for traffic management in the southeast of Amsterdam. A large

© IFIP International Federation for Information Processing 2015
L.M. Camarinha-Matos et al. (Eds.): PRO-VE 2015, IFIP AICT 463, pp. 100–109, 2015.
DOI: 10.1007/978-3-319-24141-8_9

variety of stakeholders is involved, both of the public, the private and the individual kind. The public kind includes the city of Amsterdam, the province of North-Holland and the Dutch road authority. The private kind includes several event locations in the city section, organizers of events at these locations, local retailers, parking providers and transport providers. The individual kind is formed by individual road users, both car drivers and other users influenced by car traffic.

Traffic management is a business domain that is traditionally characterized by an infrastructure-dominant approach to new developments. The focus in innovation is typically on developing and realizing new assets such as roads, traffic detection systems, road signage, and traffic management information systems. This asset-dominant orientation has two main drawbacks. Firstly, the assets are typically very costly to develop and deploy, which means that they must be designed for strategic, long-term use. This long-term approach is, however, hard to combine with much faster changing user requirements, which are strongly related to emerging transport patterns. Organizations developing or deploying the assets observe the situation from their own, isolated perspective. Secondly, the end users of traffic management solutions are not interested in the characteristics of the individual assets, but in the added value that the use of combinations of assets brings them. As an example, car drivers are not so much interested in algorithms that determine traffic information on roadside signage, but in travel time reduction that they may realize by any means of traffic management. The fact that there are multiple groups of end users (private drivers, professional drivers, institutions that need to remain accessible, the city that wants to uphold a good image) further complicates the situation. Consequently, there is a problem in the design of multi-stakeholder, collaborative business models in this traffic management context.

To try and counter this problem, we have introduced service-dominant business engineering as a new approach to collaborative business model design in the traffic management arena. To do so, we have applied part of the BASE/X approach that has been developed for service engineering in other business domains than traffic management [1]. Following the service-dominant line of thinking [2], BASE/X puts the added value for a specific group of service-based solutions at the center-point, called *value-in-use*. From this value-in-use, a collaborative network of organizations is designed that can realize this value-in-use and that has a realistic combination of costs and benefits for the involved organizations. The contributions of organizations to the value-in-use are mapped to their capabilities, which in turn are based on existing or future assets (infrastructures). Multiple combination of value-in-use and customer groups can co-exist, forming multiple collaborative business models that can be executed by *instant virtual enterprises* [3]. These business models use the same assets 'under the hood', thereby enabling an explicit decoupling of the strategic approach to asset management and the tactic approach to business model design.

This paper describes the application of BASE/X business model design in the PPA/ZO project. It demonstrates that a collaborative approach to business design can be efficient in a complex, multi-stakeholder context. On a higher level, it shows that a service-dominant approach to business engineering can be effective in asset-dominant domains, such as traffic management, to increase business resilience.

The remainder of the paper is structured as follows. In Sect. 2, we lay the basis for the paper by introducing service-dominant business engineering and the BASE/X approach. In Sect. 3, we explain the collaborative approach to apply BASE/X in the practical context for the design of prototype business models. In Sect. 4, we discuss the execution of the approach and the realized results. We end the paper with conclusions in Sect. 5.

2   Service-Dominant Business Engineering and BASE/X

Business in many domains has transitioned towards a service-dominant setting where the provisioning of solution-oriented services to the customers is the focal point [4]. This can be compared to the traditional setting where the emphasis is on the delivery of products (assets) [5]. The services may require the deployment of products, but these products become part of the delivery channel of services, not the central point. This transition has shifted the emphasis from the value of the product to the value of the use of the product in an integrated context – the so-called *value-in-use* [6].

In a highly dynamic business environment, the customer expectations from solution-oriented services evolve faster than the capabilities of the underlying products. Customers expect coherent solutions (as opposed to stand-alone solution fragments), which require the integration of the capabilities of multiple service providers. This introduces the necessity of explicitly managed business networks [7].

For a solution-oriented service provider, however, it is not only about what services to offer, but also about how to get them delivered. Managing service complexity and business agility requires a tight integration between the business strategy and models on the one hand and the structure of business operation and information management on the other hand. Truly agile service provisioning business is not achievable if these elements are treated in isolation.

BASE/X is a business engineering framework that puts the service management at the forefront [1]. It adapts a holistic view and covers the entire spectrum from high-level business strategy definition to business information system architecture design, including elements, such as business strategy definition, business model conception, business service specification and business process modeling. It distinguishes between (i) business goals (the 'what' of business) and business operations (the 'how' of business), and (ii) the stable essence of an organization (i.e. business strategy and business services) and its agile market offerings (i.e. business models and service compositions). This leads to a model with four layers as shown in Fig. 1.

The top half of the pyramid covers business goal engineering, which contains two layers: the service-dominant business strategy and business models. The strategy describes the identity of an organization in a service-dominant market [8, 9]. The identity is relatively stable over time: the strategy evolves. A service-dominant business model describes a market offering in the form of an integrated, solution-oriented complex service: they describe a concrete value-in-use. Business models follow fluid market dynamics and are agile: they revolve – they are conceived, modified, and discarded as required. Business models are specialized from the strategy as they implement part of the strategy in a more specific way. They are operationalizations of the strategy as they are more concrete.

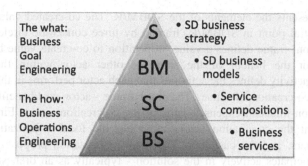

Fig. 1. BASE/X business pyramid

The bottom half of the pyramid covers business operations engineering, which contains business services and service composition. Each business service encloses a core service capability of the organization. As these capabilities are related to the resources (covering both personnel and large-scale technical infrastructures), they are relatively stable over time: they evolve. In the service compositions layer, business services are composed to realize the service functionality required by a business model: they implement a concrete value-in-use. The composition includes business services from the organization's own set, but also business services of partner organizations in a business network. As service combinations follow business models, they are agile: they revolve with their associated business models [1].

2.1   Service-Dominant Business Models

A business model describes the way in which an organization along with its providers and partners creates value for all its stakeholders [10]. Well-designed business models that ensure harmonization among business strategy, business processes, and information system are crucial for any business organization to survive and to succeed [11].

Business models can be designed using methods, such as the Business Model Canvas (BMC) [12], E3-value [13] or Service-Dominant Business Model Radar (SDBM/R) of BASE/X [1]. BMC is a visual chart with elements describing a company's or product's value proposition, customers, infrastructure -including its partnerships, and financial aspects. Although, it considers cross-organizational relations and the importance of partnerships, BMC is an organization-centric model that reasons mainly from the perspective of a *single* company. Unlike the BMC, the SDBM/R has a *network-centric* design at its core, allowing the composition of service design in multi-party business networks. It defines how the actors in the business ecosystem participate in value co-creation and what the cost–benefits distribution is.

Another network-centric approach to business model design is the E3-value e-business model, which describes the value exchanges among actors of a business network [13]. It focuses on the interactions between the actors of the network in terms of the value exchanges. However, contrasting the SDBM/R, E3-value does not consider the alignment between the business strategy, model, process and the information systems/technology as a harmonized package [10].

Figure 2 presents the elements of the SDBM/R. The co-created value-in-use constitutes the central point in SDBM/R, framed by three concentric circles. The 'actor value proposition' frame defines a value proposition to co-create value by an actor to the solution for the benefit of the same or other actor within the ecosystem. Co-production activity defines the activities that each actor performs in the business for achieving the co-creation of value. The third frame –actor cost/benefits defines the financial and non-financial expenses/gains of the co-creation actors. Finally, the 'pie slices' represent the co-creation actors including the focal organization, core and enriching partners, and the customer. The focal organization proposes the business model and participates actively in the solution - typically as an orchestrator. A core partner contributes actively to the essentials of the solution, while an enriching partner enhances solution's added value-in-use. SDBM/R accommodates an arbitrary number of actors, suiting the network-centric character of service-dominant business.

Each business model is operationalized by a service composition in the third level; i.e., it is implemented by composing a number of services from the business services layer of the BASE/X pyramid (refer to Fig. 1). The activities that take place in a service composition originate from or are tightly coupled with the 'actor coproduction activities' layer of the business model radar.

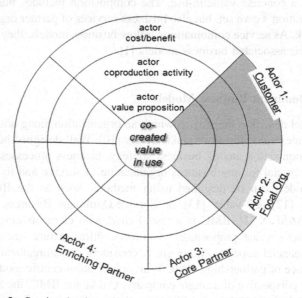

Fig. 2. Service dominant business model radar (SDBM/R) template.

3   Collaborative Approach to Agile Business Model Design

The infrastructure- and technology-dominant view and the diversity of stakeholders in traffic management pose challenges in designing multi-stakeholder, collaborative business models. Following an approach with a service-dominant line of thinking becomes essential for such initiatives. Therefore, we employ the SDBM/R in designing agile business models.

The BASE/X approach and its tools have been applied in diverse business domains (e.g. [1, 14]). However, effective application of tools in specific domains, such as traffic management, requires explicit guidelines to operationalize the concepts in practical business settings. We introduce the following steps in using SDBM/R for a collaborative design of business models:

i. *Stakeholder Field Analysis:* Business domains in contemporary markets, like traffic management, are characterized by a large number of stakeholders. Structuring the domain in terms of stakeholders through a field analysis helps significantly in understanding the dynamics and relationships in a particular business domain. It gives insight into the possible roles and their capabilities in potential business models in collaborative business networks.

ii. *Awareness Creation and Knowledge Transfer to Stakeholders:* Traditional asset-oriented mindset is still prevalent in many business domains. Creating awareness over the involved stakeholders on the service-dominant thinking, and on concepts such as value in-use, as well as on the use of relevant techniques and tools is essential before any attempt for a collaborative design of business models.

iii. *Workshops with Stakeholders for Collaborative Business Model Design:* The first two steps provide hints for business models and potential collaborators. The next step is to bring together selected stakeholders (typically 6 to 8 experts) to conduct workshops for interactive and collaborative business model design. The objective is to select a prospective business scenario, and design blueprint business models using the SDBM/R as a guiding template. The effectiveness of these workshop sessions depends heavily on the ability of the *moderator* in engaging the stakeholders in active communication and collaboration for innovative ideas.

The initial step in using the SDBM/R is to define and agree on the co-created 'value-in-use'. This goes in line with identifying the customer of the service and the focal organization that orchestrates its provisioning. Next, core and enriching partners that contribute to the proposed value-in-use are discussed and identified. These parties offer their 'actor value propositions' and 'co-production activities' to achieve the co-creation of value. As a final step, parties identify the costs and benefits (monetary or non-monetary) involved in the creation of value-in-use.

iv. *Business Model Refinement and Validation:* Workshop sessions typically result 'draft' business models on which the parties agree on the essential components. These models go through a round of refinements through offline/online discussions with involved parties. The finalized business models, which are represented using the SDBM/R, are validated by all stakeholders and act as a critical component of the agreement between the relevant parties.

4 Executing the Approach

The extensive number of prototypical technologies/services to be developed and tested, and the diversity of the stakeholders involved in their provisioning makes the PPA/ZO project a suitable context for applying the approach we introduced for collaborative design of business models.

As the first step, we performed a stakeholder analysis with domain experts in the field. We used two dimensions in classifying the parties: 'public vs. private' and 'service providers vs. consumers'. While the first dimension is mutually exclusive, the second category involves parties that play a dual role depending on a specific business model. Following this line, we defined main categories of stakeholders (such as governmental bodies, traffic service providers, technology suppliers, event organizers, etc.) and identified concrete parties under each category, which led to a set of over 30 parties. This analysis has not only brought a structure and a high level understanding of the market but also helped focal parties in identifying opportunities for collaboration with various parties in diverse business scenarios.

Based on the potential scenarios, a set of experts representing selected stakeholders were invited for a 2-h workshop organized in the Municipality of Amsterdam. We conducted 3 workshops for the design of 3 draft SDBM/R blueprints and were able to bring together around 20 stakeholders operating in this domain. Workshops constituted two phases. The first phase involved a tutorial on the concept of service-dominant business, BASE/X framework, and on the use of SDBM/R. The second phase comprised the core of the interactive design of a particular business model using the SDBM/R. Following a practical approach, large posters and 'post-its' were used to represent the SDBM/R blueprints and its specific elements (see Fig. 3).

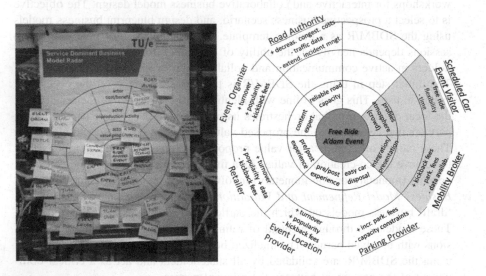

Fig. 3. The picture on the left shows the use of the SDBM/R poster and 'post-it's during the workshops. The figure on the right shows the first digital version of the *draft* business model.

The draft blueprints that were interactively designed in the workshops were later refined and communicated with involved parties for validation. Figure 4 presents an example of a completed SDBM/R blueprint for a business model. The *Free Ride Amsterdam Event* value-in-use contributes to the positive experience of event visitors who plan their arrival by car. The idea behind the model is to attract visitors at a much

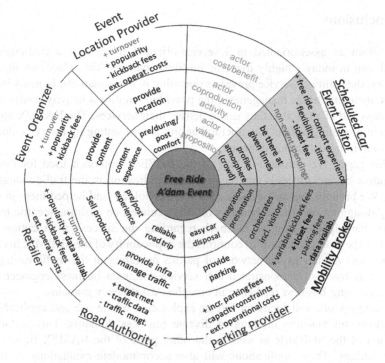

Fig. 4. A business model in SDBM/R: free ride Amsterdam event

earlier time than the beginning of the event, which helps reduce the traffic just before the event. This is facilitated by offering free parking, funded by parties benefiting from the early presence of the visitors (such as retailers). A number of stakeholders in the network contributes to this service. The Mobility Broker acts as the focal organization orchestrating the traffic-related parties. The Parking Provider provides parking services for an easy car disposal, while the Road Authority provides the road infrastructure and traffic management before and after the event for a reliable and safe trip. Retailers are also involved by contributing to customer's experience with pre- and post-event convenience (shopping, eating, etc.).

After each workshop session, we gathered feedback from the participants regarding the use of the approach and its effectiveness. All participants agreed that following an explicit approach that structures the interactive design of business models fostered the creation of innovative ideas. Participants indicated SDBM/R as an effective means for that purpose. They further agreed that it created awareness on the value of agile, service-dominant business thinking and provided inspiration for collaboration with different stakeholders. Feedback also included improvement suggestions regarding –for instance, the representation of cost-benefit flow between parties in the SDBM/R, which was incorporated in the new edition of the radar. Further details regarding the setup of the workshops, participants, and all three blueprints are available in [15].

5 Conclusions

Moving from an asset-oriented to a service-oriented mindset is a challenging yet essential step in today's highly dynamic business markets. This places an increasing demand on the agility of service providers operating in these markets. In many business domains, including traffic management, the providers' agility is heavily constrained by the business and IT platforms they use to deliver their services. The BASE/X approach can help in providing a basis for structural agility and in setting up a service-dominant business environment in this domain.

In this paper, we introduce a *part* of the BASE/X approach used for designing collaborative business models and report on its application in the traffic management domain. We brought together a diverse set of stakeholders and helped them in collaboratively designing innovative business models centered on customer-centric business solutions. Participants' positive feedback regarding the successful execution of the approach in the workshop sessions confirms the applicability of the SDBM/R in creating novel business models in the network of parties operating in the traffic management domain. This has also demonstrated that service-dominant business engineering can help in increasing business resilience in complex, asset-heavy domains.

Our future work will focus on further exploration of the use and applicability of service-dominant business thinking in diverse business domains. This includes the application of the SDBM/R as well as the other parts of the BASE/X framework in real-life settings. These applications will also accommodate evaluations on the perceived usability and ease of use of the method (through employing the techniques in the research field of technology acceptance [16]), and the benefits in terms of the degree in which the method fosters developing innovative and effective business models. Research and development on the tools and the guidelines to support the entire spectrum of the BASE/X pyramid is another key research direction.

References

1. Grefen, P., Luftenegger, E., Linden, E. v.d., Weisleder, C.: Business agility through cross-organizational service engineering - the business and service design approach developed in the CoProFind project. Beta working papers, vol. 414. Eindhoven University of Technology (2013)
2. Vargo, S.L., Lusch, R.F.: Service-dominant logic: continuing the evolution. J. Acad. Mark. Sci. **36**, 1–10 (2007)
3. Mehandjiev, N., Grefen, P.: Dynamic Business Process Formation for Instant Virtual Enterprises. Springer, London (2010)
4. Ostrom, A.L., Bitner, M.J., Brown, S.W., Burkhard, K.A., Goul, M., Smith-Daniels, V., Demirkan, H., Rabinovich, E.: Moving forward and making a difference: research priorities for the science of service. J. Serv. Res. **13**, 4–36 (2010)
5. Lusch, R.F., Vargo, S.L.: The service-dominant mindset. In: Hefley, B., Murphy, W. (eds.) Service Science, Management and Engineering Education for the 21st Century, pp. 89–96. Springer, Boston (2008)
6. Lusch, R.F.: Service-dominant logic: reactions, reflections and refinements. Mark. Theor. **6**, 281–288 (2006)

7. Camarinha-Matos, L.M., Afsarmanesh, H.: Collaborative networks: a new scientific discipline. J. Intell. Manuf. **16**, 439–452 (2005)
8. Lüftenegger, E., Grefen, P., Weisleder, C.: The service dominant strategy canvas: towards networked business models. In: Camarinha-Matos, L.M., Xu, L., Afsarmanesh, H. (eds.) Collaborative Networks in the Internet of Services. IFIP AICT, vol. 380, pp. 207–215. Springer, Heidelberg (2012)
9. Lüftenegger, E., Comuzzi, M., Grefen, P.: The service-dominant ecosystem: mapping a service dominant strategy to a product-service ecosystem. In: Camarinha-Matos, L.M., Scherer, R.J. (eds.) PRO-VE 2013. IFIP AICT, vol. 408, pp. 22–30. Springer, Heidelberg (2013)
10. Al-Debei, M.M., Avison, D.: Developing a unified framework of the business model concept. Eur. J. Inf. Syst. **19**, 359–376 (2010)
11. Magretta, J.: Why business models matter. Harvard Bus. Rev. **80**, 86–92 (2002)
12. Osterwalder, A., Pigneur, I.: Business Model Generation: A handbook for Visionaries, Game Changers and Challengers. Willey, New Jersey (2010)
13. Gordijn, J., Akkermans, H.: Designing and evaluating e-business models. IEEE Intell. Syst. **16**, 11–17 (2001)
14. Luftenegger, E.: Service-dominant business design. Ph.D. thesis (2014)
15. Traganos, K., Grefen, P., den Hollander, A., Turetken, O., Eshuis, R.: Business model prototyping for intelligent transport systems: a service-dominant approach. Beta working papers, Eindhoven University of Technology (2015)
16. Davis, F.D.: Perceived usefulness, perceived ease of use, and user acceptance of information technology. MIS Q. **13**, 319 (1989)

An Analysis of Resilience of a Cloud Based Incident Notification Process

Paul de Vrieze[✉] and Lai Xu

Faculty of Science and Technology,
Bournemouth University, Poole House, Talbot Campus, Fern Barrow,
Poole, BH12 5BB, UK
{pdvrieze,lxu}@bournemouth.ac.uk

Abstract. Cloud based Business Process Management (BPM) systems have provided SMEs with BPM in a pay-per-use manner. Previous work has focused on looking at cloud based BPM from the perspectives of distribution of data, activity or/and process engine and related issues, such as scalability of system, security of data, distribution of data and activities. To achieve business agility, business process collaboration needs to seamlessly connect local BPM systems and cloud based BPM systems. In this paper we look at BPM in the cloud from a user perspective: how can they support the fast pace of change of business collaborations and how to determine a resilience of a cloud based BPM solution. The paper proposes a distribution solution in which the shared process model can be discovered at the design time from a process repository, and adapted to local needs. At run-time the selected collaborative process model provides a global view, but is executed by multiple mashup engines of the participating parties. A real world case is used to explain our design. Collaborative processes for incident notifications are built to work across different organizations. Resilience of the solution are analysed accordingly.

Keywords: Business process as a service · Incident management · Business process mashup · Resilience of cloud based processes

1 Introduction

Cloud based Business Process Management (BPM) provides the distributed infrastructure as well as computing power to connect different partners towards a common goal. Cloud based BPM is therefore an ideal solution for collaborative BPM. In this paper, we look at the resilience of cloud based business process incident notification processes.

The Internet is a conduit for information exchange. In this role it has fundamentally changed how business is conducted. Cloud computing has enabled users to use computing resources in a pay-per-use manner and to treat these resources as unlimited [1]. In the cloud computing age, business process management systems have also adapted themselves to cloud environments. Business Processes as a Service (BPaaS) as a relative new concept can be any type of business process that is delivered based on a cloud provisioning model. BPaaS can be seen as a new trend for Business Process Management [2, 3].

© IFIP International Federation for Information Processing 2015
L.M. Camarinha-Matos et al. (Eds.): PRO-VE 2015, IFIP AICT 463, pp. 110–121, 2015.
DOI: 10.1007/978-3-319-24141-8_10

Incident notification processes normally are collaborative processes because industrial incident management most of time involves multiple parties. This kind of ad-hoc notification process is not supported by traditional BPM systems.

Looking at the incident notification process exposes the limitations of existing cloud-based business process service patterns. Executable business process models represent how the common business goals are achieved in a computer understandable way. Business process models thus are important assets for many organisations [4, 5]. Business processes encapsulate business drivers and policies. Therefore, business process models should be seen as an important component BPaaS. Traditionally, process models are created and deployed on a process engine by IT specialists. Today organisations face fast changes of their business environment. They need to be able to rapidly react to the changes. As such it is often desirable for Non-IT people to be able to select and modify process models to adapt to business needs.

In materials science, resilience represents the ability of a material to recover its original shape following a deformation [6]. In the corporate world, resilience refers to the ability of a company to bounce back from, or even resist, a large disruption – this includes, for instance the speed with which it returns to normal performance level (production, services, fill rate, etc.) [7]. Within cloud computing, the characteristic of resiliency can refer to redundant IT resources within the same cloud (but in different physical locations) or across multiple clouds [8]. In this paper, we analyse the resilience of a cloud based BPM solution for incident notification.

This paper is organized as follows: Sect. 2 presents related work; Sect. 3 briefly introduces our motivating case; Sect. 4 presents overview of analysis of resilience of the proposed solution; Sect. 5, data dependence of the case is presented; Sect. 6 address the proposed architecture; Sect. 7 presents an analysis of the resilience of our incident notification solution. Finally, the paper reviews related works and concludes with a future research direction.

2 Related Work

In recent years a good amount of work on providing BPM capabilities in the cloud has appeared. It specially attracts SME's (Small and Medium Enterprise), as they now can use scalable BPM services in a pay-per-use manner without incurring large maintenance costs [9]. Major IT vendors have begun to provide cloud based BPM services, such as Salesforce's Sales cloud, Market cloud [10], IBM's Blue Works [11], Vitria's M3O [12], and a solution based upon Amazon EC2 cloud [13]. These services are at different cloud levels.

Helo et al. [14] have proposal and implement a prototype, NetMES system for distributed manufacturing. The cloud-based solution runs on a PaaS layer in the cloud architecture. NetMES builds a manufacturing execution system on Web services and provides a standard for information sharing/transferring environment. Cloud technology is adopted in order to support monitoring, information exchange and also other real-time interactions. Our proposed BPaaS solution goes further, which does not only treat the cloud as a platform, but also allows a collaborative business process model shared, data, and activities running among participating parties in cloud environment.

Duipmans et al. [15, 16] present a cloud-based solution for a television broadcast organization. The organization allows users to submit their program ideas, which include users' personal information as well as text description and a short video of their ideas. The activities of the video conversion and analysis are computation-intensive activities which are assigned to the cloud. As well as video storages are allocated to the cloud. The original business processes within the organization have thus transformed into collaborating business processes. The main benefit of stockholders in choosing a cloud-based solution is that organization can utilise the flexibility of cloud resources dynamically to meet peak demand without investing in in-house resources. Their solution includes only distributed activities and related data of a process involved in a single organization. The significant difference from their work, our solution is supporting multi-partners involved collaborative business processes in cloud. Therefore, not only certainly activities and related data within an organization are running in cloud, but also each individual organisation is running a shared process collaboratively in cloud.

Chen and Hsu [17] implemented a decentralized collaborative process management system. Although collaborative process execution is based on business process model which is same as our solution, the design of an inter-enterprise collaborative business process management integrates E-Carry with E-Speak, which leads to lake of supporting of handling ad-hoc collaborative business processes in cloud. Our solution supports to support distributed collaborative processes in a flexible way, i.e. it means that the collaboration among partners are not hard code in a framework, but potential collaboration can be formed using service-oriented principles.

Our research includes the design and implementation of a business process mashup engine [18] and lightweight business process modelling language [19, 20]. Special attention is paid to the end-user aspect which is orthogonal to extending our designs for cloud based BPM. In [21] we look at data as a service in a cloud environment. The paper includes a data central solution for the same case. In our previous research, we have designed and implemented business process mashup for incident notification in a cloud environment. Further work in [22] presents a BPaaS solution for the same case. In this research, we extend a BPaaS pattern for collaborative business processes; provide more analysis of our solution; and a detailed performance evaluation.

3 Motivating Case

The Spanish electricity system is generally formed of a high-voltage electric power transmission network and grid connecting power stations and substations to transport electricity from where it is generated to where it is needed.

There are a number of stakeholders in the Spanish electricity system, each fulfilling various roles in the overall process of electricity generation and delivery. Many of the well-established, former government, parties play many of the roles in the system. The unavoidably monopolistic and critical roles of market operator (OMEL) and system operator (REE) remain in government hands. There are three main energy producers, one market operator, three main distributors, eighteen substations, and 32 marketers [23].

The process of delivering electricity to a single customer involves the entire chain of roles (and therefore actors). The delivery of electricity to a single geographic group (for example, a street) of customers likely involves many more marketers. Given that most distributors are also active as marketers on a national level these distributors generally act both as each other's collaborators/customers and competitors.

Incidents in the electricity system can occur anywhere and anytime. These incidents, ranging from signal errors, cabling problems to serious substation overloads, will affect energy supply, lead to power cuts or even generate a further huge impact to the community and economy.

Large industrial customers directly connected to the 132 kV network are generally on interruptible contracts. As their electricity demands can have significant impact on the network there is frequent and well-established contact with these customers that could be used for incident notification. Domestic customers and smaller business users however are often only known by name to marketers. The distributors and market operator generally only have knowledge of the address. As a result, domestic and small business users are currently not notified of incidents directly (for larger disruptions they may be informed indirectly through the local press).

To improve customer satisfaction, it becomes clear that effective incident management includes effective and timely informing of customers without relying on suddenly overloaded call-centers. The information provided should not only acknowledge the existence of an issue but also provide information on progress and estimated resolution timelines. When appropriate, follow-up notifications should be sent to all or interested customers.

4   Resilience

The resilience of the incident notification case is a multi-faceted problem. Resilience is required to handle normal problems, as well as abnormal problems. Normal problems are when the systems themselves continue to function properly (but need to handle external incidents and may be stretched beyond their ability to handle). Abnormal problems are when the systems to handle incidents themselves are compromised.

While the next sections focus on resilience in normal cases, this section will briefly discuss the resilience in abnormal cases. In discussing the resilience an important consideration is the degradation behaviour of the solution. Catastrophic failure as such can be defined as a failure that completely prevents the system from notifying customers. Partial degradation is when either a subset of customers cannot be notified, the notifications cannot be as detailed as required, or when a superset of affected customers is notified even if they are not affected. The incident notification systems are passive, as such worse-than-catastrophic failure with the systems actively countermanding out of bounds notification does not need to be considered.

Considering catastrophic failure, a significant driver of this would be single points of failure. Primary candidates would be either OMEL or the incident sources (such as substations). In case of substation failure, this would be rapidly noticed, not the least due to customers contacting their suppliers, but also through a sudden reduced energy usage within the network. OMEL has a unique responsibility however, and could potentially fail. Within its marketer role OMEL however already has a high-resilience infrastructure for the management of the power supply. The incident notification processes could be linked to this infrastructure. In addition, as notification by OMEL is not directly to end-users notification could be performed through human intervention by directly contacting the relevant parties (such as the distributors) based upon pre-prepared contact protocols (e.g. a phone-list printed out for these cases).

For the other parties involved complete failure is less significant, with the largest impact on critical failure of marketer systems. Whereas substation information is available in multiple parts of the system (and not commercially sensitive), customer information could be only available at the marketers. The customer systems can however be split into two parts, where one part is the raw contact information (address, contact details) and the other is the marketers related systems. Given the raw contact information an alternative, cloud based, notification system can easily be used as fallback with reduced functionality (for example not taking customer contact preferences into account). As the customer details are of significant commercial value to the marketers it should be expected that regular provision of this data in escrow is feasible, if not directly in the interest of the marketers.

As to the cloud systems it is clear that these are resilient to localised failures. Unfortunately, systematic failure (e.g. software errors that affect all instances) can not be excluded. The loosely coupled nature of the architecture does however mitigate this to the extent that many cases can be treated as failure of a single node in the system.

Missing parties can in general be handled through bypassing the affected parties. This does degrade the experience of incident notification but not catastrophically so. The head of the chain (OMEL) and tail (the marketers) can be handled through an existing high-resilience system (and manual intervention) in the case of OMEL and escrow of customer details in the case of the marketers. With these measures, which need to be taken into account in the detailed design and implementation of the system, the notification system can be resilient against abnormal failure.

5 Data Dependence

In terms of normal failure, it is necessary that the systems can meet their requirements even in case of an abnormally large amount of failures. A possible disruption of the energy supply, that could be caused by varying circumstances, creates the need to inform to the customers affected. According to Gas Natural Fenosa, the information sent to customers affected is not immediate. The energy-distribution area has two distinct data bases named SGC and BDI. The SGC is an operational system and contains a list of Transformers Centers (CT in Spanish) and the customers are associated with one CT. This database also contains the name of the marketer that provides the billing service to the consumer. Therefore, a CT has several consumers and a consumer is charged by one marketer. This information allows Gas Natural Fenosa (Distributor) to charge the marketer directly for the energy consumption of this consumer. Consequently, the marketer will charge its customers using this information.

The other information system, named BDI, has information about distribution substations and contains the list of positions inside the substation. For each position, it has a CT list. Therefore, a distribution substation has several positions or lines, and each line/position has several CTs. By aggregating this information from those two sources and the list of substations affected, a list of affected customers and streets can be created. Figure 1 shows the data dependencies involved.

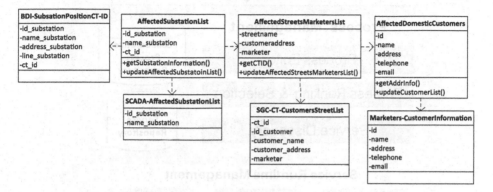

Fig. 1. Data dependence between distributors

The CRM stores all the information considered important in relation to the customers, offers, marketing campaigns, etc. However, the information that is needed for customer notification is just basic information about the customer such as, address, name, telephone number, etc. The list of affected customers and streets can then be combined with customer data from the CRM and used for notification.

6   Architecture of the Case

The incident notification process used as our case is based upon the use of business process oriented mashup engines. These business process oriented mashup engines are deployed for all distributors and marketers. This insures that all involved stakeholders can flexibly deal with appeared incidents (the engines can also be used for other situational applications).

Figure 2 shows the architecture of the Cloud-based Incident Notification Process Solution (CINPS). Within the CINPS, user management provides access control for all stakeholders. The process management subsystem handles process uploading, process editing, process ranking and selection, as well as service discovery. The service runtime management subsystems handle monitoring, reporting and service invocation at the runtime. Furthermore the CINPS also has two repositories which enumerate collaborative processes and services related to incident notification.

Business process oriented mashup engines are deployed for all stakeholders. The business process model repository contains collaborative business process models. This repository is managed by the overall system owner OMEL and enables sharing and reusing of existing collaborative process models. The business process editor allows modifying, verifying, and ranking process models. Each stakeholder has access to the process editor and is able to make changes to its processes as long as that does not

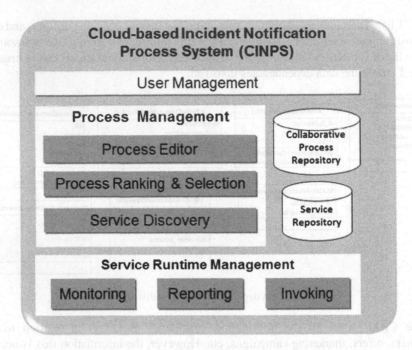

Fig. 2. Architecture of cloud-based incident notification processes

compromise the integrity of the overall system. The collaborative process models can be downloaded or uploaded to the business process model repository as desired. Process models are instantiated into process instances after all data sources and invoked services are (semi-) automatically identified.

The decentralised execution of process instances is a core aspect of the incident notification system in the Spanish electricity system case. While the information needed from both distributors and marketers is not large in terms of data size (so transfer would not be a technical challenge), there are data sensitivity issues. While the information from the distributors is not commercially sensitive, the data from the marketers is. For the purpose of incident notification, marketers could download a common process model from the process model repository on the cloud. Starting with the downloaded process model, the marketers can make modifications; for example to adopt different notification channels, such as sending Facebook messages as well as SMS messages. The marketers can use a local process editor to allocate the data (affected customers' mobile phone number, Facebook ID, or Twitter ID) and run the business process on a private process-oriented mashup engine. For the distributors, incidents or interruptions can be caused or observed in different parts of the organization. Therefore a sample process model can be modified according to the situation. The process can keep monitoring the process of the repair and ensure information is consistently published on the Web using the private process engine. Figure 3 presents such a process model.

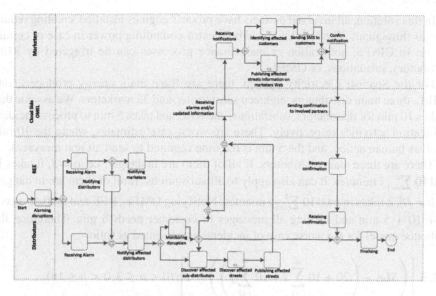

Fig. 3. Cloud-based incident notification process model for SES

The solution owner (in this case OMEL) mainly concentrates on maintaining the process model repository and on providing some common Web services. OMEL also provides a process editor and a process engine for users testing the process model. The other users are certainly able to upload their data for running their processes in case the private process engine is out of order. A collaborative process which runs in the cloud can be supported for special cases, e.g. monitoring the collaborative process.

7   Resilience of Incident Notification Solution

Marcon et al. [8] deal with an on-going authorization model UCN_{ABC}, which provides resilience to the re-evaluation of usage policies of individual users. The meaning of resilience is providing the model with the ability to deal with some individual user authorization attributes exceeding, while the SLA for the respective consumption service is under the contracted amount. Our proposed resilience model is adapted from that paper.

Let R be the resilience of the solution. *SLA* is a service level agreement of the maximum time to notify domestic customers. $T(i)$ represents the process notification time of each partner. The resilience of the incident notification solution is defined only if *SLA* minus the sum of time cost of each partner for processing the incident is greater than t. The constant is a spare quota freely defined by the consumer for the notification services.

$$R:\exists \left[\left(SLA - \left(\sum_{i=1}^{n} T(i)\right)\right) > t\right]$$

In this solution, all involved partners have process engines installed, creating redundancies throughout. The solution could hold extra computing power in case of certain failure. In CINPS, notification or maintenance processes can be triggered by REE, distributors, substations, or OMEL.

For the Spanish Electricity System, there are three main energy producers, one OMEL, three main distributors, eighteen substations, and 32 marketers. We assume that it takes 10 min for distributors, substations, and REE and takes 5 min to process incident notification activities respectively. These are worst-case estimates, where the 10 min involves human action, and the 5 min is the time required to send all text messages.

There are three main distributors. If all of them are in danger, i.e. $a = 3$, it takes in total $10 \sum_{i=1}^{a} i$ minutes. It can also apply to all substations. If all of them are in danger, i.e. $b = 18$, it takes in total $10 \sum_{i=1}^{b} j$ minutes. Notifying OMEL, REE and markets needs $10 + 10 + 5$ min and sending all messages to customer needs 5 min. Therefore, the resilience model for the worse case of incidents is presented as follow,

$$R{:}\exists \left[\left(SLA - \left(20 + 10 \sum_{i=1}^{a} i + 10 \sum_{j=1}^{b} j \right) \right) > t \right], (0 < a \le 3, 0 < b \le 18)$$

Table 1 shows total time of processing incident notification, i.e. $20 + 10 \sum_{i=1}^{a} i + 10 \sum_{j=1}^{b} j$. The row represents how many substations have trouble. The column indicates how many main distributors are in trouble. This table can be used to determine SLA.

Table 1. Total time cost of different incident sizes

(b, a)	0	1	2	3	4	5	6	7	8	9
0	0	10	30	60	100	150	210	280	360	450
1	10	20	40	70	110	160	220	290	370	460
2	30	40	60	90	130	180	240	310	390	480
3	60	70	90	120	160	210	270	340	420	510
(b, a)	**10**	**11**	**12**	**13**	**14**	**15**	**16**	**17**	**18**	
0	550	660	780	910	1050	1200	1360	1530	1710	
1	560	670	790	920	1060	1210	1370	1540	1720	
2	580	690	810	940	1080	1230	1390	1560	1740	
3	610	720	840	970	1110	1260	1420	1590	1770	

The x-axis of Fig. 4 presents the numbers of substations in danger; y-axis of Fig. 4 notes the number of main distributors in dangers; and z-axis of Fig. 4 presents total time of processing incident notification in minutes.

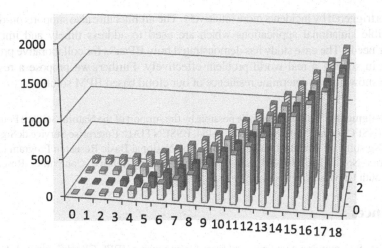

Fig. 4. Total time cost of different incident effect

8 Conclusion

Cloud-based BPM systems bring many benefits to business users. They provide a good opportunity for organizations which seek scalable and flexible solutions. Cloud-based BPM systems are not likely to replace all local BPM systems. To achieve business agility business process collaboration needs to seamlessly connect local BPM systems and cloud-based BPM systems. Business process models as assets for many organizations are important to supporting business agility. The lightweight business process modeling technologies, lightweight business process mashup engines, and large collections of process models are providing possible solutions for end-user oriented BPM and BPaaS.

In this paper, we have provided an analysis of the resilience of a BPaaS solution to incident notification in the electricity supply market. Careful design with manual over-rides allows for graceful degradation (in some cases only resulting in - short - additional delays due to manual processes). We have addressed both abnormal failures, where the system itself is compromised, as normal failures where the electricity supply is compromised, but not the notification system. It is clear that the system can be designed to be highly resilient, only to fail in extreme circumstances. These circumstances however are likely to be such extreme that traditional broadcast solutions (radio cars, door-to-door leaflets) are acceptable.

The use of loosely coupled cloud solutions provides for resilience and fallback, effective cooperation while not limiting competition, innovation and variety in the usage by the parties involved.

Effective incident management can be considered as a more cost-effective solution to reduce the negative impact on the community and economy after an industrial incident occurs. From the end-user perspective, this relies on instant situation awareness and response. The core concept of the architecture is that it uses verified incident notification process models and a business mashup engine to help organizations respond to emerging situations triggered by incidents more intuitively. The architecture also supports on-demand and flexible situational applications which are used to address timely and immediate customer needs. The case study has demonstrated how BPaaSs for collaborative processes facilitate in solving a real world problem effectively. Further, we propose a resilience model to show how to determine resilience of our cloud based BPM solution.

Acknowledgments. This work is made possible by the support of the Natural Science Foundation of China (NSFC) under Grant No. 61150110484, ESSENTIAL: Enterprise Service deSign based on ExistiNg software Architectural knowLedge, the National Basic Research Program of China under Gran No. 2014CB340404, and FIF Strengthening Service Computing Research in Bournemouth University, UK.

References

1. Bouvry, P.: Emerging paradigms and areas for expansion. IEEE Cloud Comput. **1**(1), 58–61 (2014)
2. Sun, Y., Su, J., Yang, J.: Separating execution and data management: a key to business-process-as-a-service (BPaaS). In: Sadiq, S., Soffer, P., Völzer, H. (eds.) BPM 2014. LNCS, vol. 8659, pp. 374–382. Springer, Heidelberg (2014)
3. Zhang, L.-J., Qun, Z.: CCOA: Cloud computing open architecture. In: IEEE International Conference on Web Services, ICWS 2009, pp. 607–616. IEEE (2009)
4. Raduescu, C., Tan, H.M., Jayaganesh, M., Bandara, W., zur Muehlen, M., Lippe, S.: A framework of issues in large process modeling projects. In: ECIS, pp. 1594–1605 (2006)
5. Dijkman, R.M., La Rosa, M., Reijers, H.A.: Managing large collections of business process models-current techniques and challenges. Comput. Ind. **63**(2), 91–97 (2012)
6. Campbell, F.C. (ed.): Elements of Metallurgy and Engineering Alloys. ASM International, Russell (2008)
7. Sheffi, Y.: Building a resilient supply chain. Harvard Bus. Rev. **1**, 1–4 (2005)
8. Marcon, A.L., Olivo Santin, A., Stihler, M., Bachtold, J.: A UCON$_{ABC}$ resilient authorization evaluation for cloud computing. IEEE Trans. Parallel Distrib. Syst. **25**(2), 457–467 (2014)
9. Buyya, R., Yeo, C.S., Venugopal, S.: Market-oriented cloud computing: vision, hype, and reality for delivering it services as computing utilities. In: 10th IEEE International Conference on High Performance Computing and Communications, HPCC 2008, pp. 5–13. IEEE (2008)
10. Salesforce: Salesforce: sales cloud, marketing cloud (2012)
11. IBM: Blueworkslive (2013)
12. VitriaCloud: Vitriacloud m3o in the cloud (2013)
13. Amazon: Amazon elastic compute cloud (amazon ec2) (2013)
14. Helo, P., Suorsa, M., Hao, Y., Anussornnitisarn, P.: Toward a cloud-based manufacturing execution system for distributed manufacturing. Comput. Ind. **65**(4), 646–656 (2014)
15. Duipmans, E.F., Pires, L.F., da Silva Santos, L.O.B.: Towards a BPM cloud architecture with data and activity distribution. In: 2012 IEEE 16th International Enterprise Distributed Object Computing Conference Workshops (EDOCW), pp. 165–171. IEEE (2012)
16. Duipmans, E.F., Pires, L.F., da Silva Santos, L.O.B.: A transformation-based approach to business process management in the cloud. J. Grid Comput. **12**(2), 191–219 (2014)
17. Chen, Q., Hsu, M.: Inter-enterprise collaborative business process management. In: Proceedings of 17th International Conference on Data Engineering, pp. 253–260. IEEE (2001)

18. de Vrieze, P., Xu, L., Bouguettaya, A., Yang, J., Chen, J.: Building enterprise mashups. Future Gener. Comput. Syst. **27**(5), 637–642 (2011)
19. Xie, L., Xu, L., de Vrieze, P.: Lightweight business process modelling. In: 2010 International Conference on E-Business and E-Government (ICEE), pp. 183–186. IEEE (2010)
20. Xu, L., de Vrieze, P., Phalp, K., Jeary, S., Liang, P.: Lightweight process modeling for virtual enterprise process collaboration. In: Camarinha-Matos, L.M., Boucher, X., Afsarmanesh, H. (eds.) PRO-VE 2010. IFIP AICT, vol. 336, pp. 501–508. Springer, Heidelberg (2010)
21. Jiang, N., Xu, L., de Vrieze, P., Lim, M.-G., Jarabo, O.: A cloud based data integration framework. In: Camarinha-Matos, L.M., Xu, L., Afsarmanesh, H. (eds.) Collaborative Networks in the Internet of Services. IFIP AICT, vol. 380, pp. 177–185. Springer, Heidelberg (2012)
22. Xu, L., de Vrieze, P., Jiang, N.: Incident notification process as a service for electricity supply systems. In: 2013 IEEE 6th International Conference on Cloud Computing (CLOUD), pp. 926–933. IEEE (2013)
23. Bilbao, J., Bravo, E., Garcia, O., Varela, C., Rodriguez, M., Gonzalez, P.: Electric system in Spain: generation capacity, electricity production and market shares. Int. J. Tech. Phys. Probl. Eng. **9**(3), 91–96 (2011)

Cloud Service Brokerage: Strengthening Service Resilience in Cloud-Based Virtual Enterprises

Simeon Veloudis[✉], Iraklis Paraskakis, and Christos Petsos

South East European Research Centre (SEERC), CITY College International
Faculty of the University of Sheffield, 24 Proxenou Koromila St,
54622 Thessaloniki, Greece
{sveloudis,iparaskakis,chrpetsos}@seerc.org

Abstract. We argue that the incorporation of cloud service brokerage (CSB) mechanisms will strengthen the resilience of services in cloud-based VEs. In this respect, we present the Service Completeness-Compliance Checker (SC^3), a mechanism which offers capabilities with respect to the Quality Assurance dimension of CSB. More specifically, SC^3 strengthens the resilience of cloud services by evaluating their compliance with pre-specified policies concerning the business aspects of their delivery. By relying on an ontology-based representation of policies and services, SC^3 achieves a proper separation of concerns between policy definition and policy enforcement. This effectively enables SC^3 to perform policy evaluation in a manner generic and agnostic to the underlying cloud delivery platform utilised by a cloud-based VE.

Keywords: Virtual enterprises · Cloud computing · Cloud service brokerage · Governance · Quality control · Ontologies · Linked USDL

1 Introduction

Cloud computing has evolved out of Grid computing [1, 2] as a result of a shift in focus from an infrastructure aiming to deliver mainly storage and compute resources, to an economy-based computing paradigm aiming to deliver a wide range of resources abstracted as services [2]. Such a shift is anticipated to impact the manner in which businesses and organisations share skills and core competencies within a distributed collaborative network [3]. More specifically, activities performed by a dynamic multi-institutional virtual enterprise (VE) may involve the use of heterogeneous, externally-sourced cloud services which span different clouds and capability levels (IaaS, PaaS, and SaaS) [4], and which are entrusted by their users with data, software, and computation; we shall term such a VE a *cloud-based* one.

As an example, consider the following scenario. An industrial consortium is formed to collaboratively process the data produced as part of a seismic survey. Such processing integrates software components, offered as a service, by different consortium participants (SaaS offerings). Each component may be operating on a participant's proprietary infrastructure or, alternatively, on infrastructure provisioned as a cloud

© IFIP International Federation for Information Processing 2015
L.M. Camarinha-Matos et al. (Eds.): PRO-VE 2015, IFIP AICT 463, pp. 122–135, 2015.
DOI: 10.1007/978-3-319-24141-8_11

service (IaaS offering). At the same time, the simulation requires the development of new specialised software components. To this end, the consortium is provisioned the necessary software platform for developing these applications as a service (PaaS offering).

Evidently, the IT environment of a cloud-based VE is transformed into a complex ecosystem of intertwined infrastructure, platform, and application services delivered remotely, over the Internet, by diverse service providers. As the number of services proliferates, it becomes increasingly difficult to keep track of when and how they evolve over time, either through intentional changes, initiated by their providers, or through unintentional changes, such as variations in their performance and availability. Moreover, it becomes increasingly difficult to accurately predict the potential reper-cussions that such an evolution has with respect to a service's compliance to policies and regulations, and its conformance to service level agreements (SLAs).

In order to strengthen the resilience of the services in such an ecosystem, cloud-based VEs are anticipated to increasingly rely on *cloud service brokerage* (CSB) [5]. In this respect, the work in [3] proposed a conceptual architecture of a framework which offers capabilities with respect to two dimensions of CSB, namely *Quality Assurance Service Brokerage*, and *Service Customisation Brokerage*. These capabilities revolve around the following themes: (i) *governance and quality control*; (ii) *failure prevention and recovery*, and (iii) *optimisation*. The 1st theme is concerned with checking the compliance of services with a set of policies and regulations; it is also concerned with testing services for conformance with their expected behaviour. The 2nd theme is concerned with the reactive and proactive detection of service fail-ures, and the selection of suitable strategies to prevent, or recover from, such failures. The 3rd theme is concerned with continuously identifying opportunities to optimise service consumption.

Continuing the work in [3], this paper reports on the implementation of a particular mechanism of the aforementioned framework, namely the Service Completeness-Compliance Checker (SC^3), which offers capabilities with respect to the *governance and quality control* theme. More specifically, SC^3 strengthens the resilience of cloud services by continuously evaluating their compliance with pre-specified policies con-cerning their business aspects of delivery. By relying on a *declarative* representation of policies and services, one which is based on an RDF(S) ontology, SC^3 achieves a clear separation of concerns: policies are represented independently of the code that SC^3 employs for enforcing them. SC^3 is thereby kept generic and orthogonal to any underlying cloud delivery platform employed by a cloud-based VE. Such a separation of concerns is generally absent in contemporary governance mechanisms [6], with negative repercussions on their portability, as well as on their ability to represent and reason about, policy interrelations.

The rest of this paper is structured as follows. Section 2 presents a motivating scenario. Section 3 outlines our declarative approach to policy representation and explains how SC^3 extracts from this representation the necessary information for the subsequent policy enforcement process. Section 4 describes this process, and Sect. 5 outlines related work. Finally, Sect. 6 presents conclusions and future work.

2 Motivating Scenario

The work in [3] proposed a conceptual architecture of a CSB framework offering capabilities spanning the main phases of a service's lifecycle, namely Service On-boarding, Service Operation, and Service Evolution. SC^3 offers capabilities with respect to the *Service On-boarding* phase[1]. Below we identify these capabilities through the prism of the example of Sect. 1.

Let CPx (stands for Cloud Platform x) be a cloud delivery platform that hosts various services that are potentially used by the industrial consortium. The platform houses a variety of apps developed by CPx's network of ecosystem partners. CPx also allows advanced users to develop and deploy custom applications on the platform, and to create rich compositions of applications (mash-ups) offered by third-party service providers.

Table 1. Entry-level criteria

Service-level Attribute	Acceptable Values	SLO	Comments
storage	[100,1000)	Gold storage	
	[10,100)	Silver storage	Size in TB
	[0,10)	Bronze storage	
availabil-ity	[0.99999,1)	Gold availability	
	[0.9999,1)	Silver availability	Total uptime ratio
	[0.999,1)	Bronze availability	
encryption	256	Gold encryption	
	192	Silver encryption	Key-length in bits
	128	Bronze encryption	

Suppose that an ecosystem partner offers a new service on CPx, call it StoreCloud, which provides an encrypted and versioned persistence layer for storing the results during the various phases of the seismic survey. In order for the new service to be on-boarded on CPx, a number of entry-level criteria must be satisfied. These crucially capture a set of *service-level objectives* (SLOs) expressed in terms of restrictions on relevant *service-level attributes* (see Table 1). These SLOs essentially form CPx's *business* (or *broker*[2]) *policy* (BP) with respect to on-boarding StoreCloud.

We assume that the ecosystem partner who offers StoreCloud, hereafter referred to as the *service provider* (SP), submits a service description (SD) which details the manner in which StoreCloud is to be deployed on CPx. The SC^3 mechanism offers a

---

[1] SC^3 also offers capabilities with respect to the Service Operation phase and, in particular, with respect to continuously monitoring the behaviour of a service. These capabilities shall not, however, concern us in this paper.

[2] We use the term "*broker*" to emphasise that, in our work, such a business policy is formulated according to the declarative approach of our *brokerage* framework (see Sect. 3.3).

policy evaluation capability which essentially allows the cloud-based VE to determine whether this SD is compliant with CPx's BP. Such a capability entails two kinds of evaluation: SD *completeness* evaluation and SD *compliance* evaluation. The former kind of evaluation aims at determining whether the SD specifies values for *all* required service-level attributes. For example, an SD which does not specify a value for the `encryption` attribute cannot be considered complete. The latter kind of evaluation aims at determining whether the specified attribute values fall within the corresponding ranges prescribed in the BP. For example, an SD which specifies a 64-bit value for the `encryption` attribute cannot be considered compliant. Clearly, the aforementioned evaluations seek to determine whether StoreCloud attains the SLOs specified in CPx's BP. In this respect, they strengthen the service's resilience.

3   Parsing BPs: The SC³ Approach

This section describes how the SC³ mechanism parses a BP in order to extract the necessary information for evaluating the completeness and compliance of SDs. A brief description of a conceptual architecture for SC³ is, however, first in order.

3.1   Conceptual Architecture

As depicted in Fig. 1, the SP submits StoreCloud's SD through the SP-facing component – an interface which exposes an editor for facilitating the construction of the SD. The SD is then transported to the SC³ mechanism, and also stored in the Governance Registry (GReg) depicted in Fig. 1; the transportation takes place through a Publish/subscribe (Pub/sub) system. An explanation of the reasons for opting for the open-source WSO₂ Carbon platform [7] (see Fig. 1), as well as for advocating a Pub/sub system for transporting SDs, is omitted here due to space limitations; a relevant discussion can be found in [8, 9].

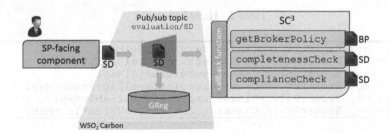

Fig. 1. SC3 conceptual architecture

The SC³ exposes a callback function for subscribing to the appropriate topic of the Pub/sub system and (asynchronously) receiving the SD. More specifically, this callback function exposes the `EvaluationComponentSDSubscriber` class which is responsible for orchestrating all the actions required for creating connections to the Pub/sub system and subscribing to its topics. This class triggers the SC³ mechanism when a fresh SD arrives. In particular, it invokes an object of the class `Policy-CompletenessCompliance`, one which is parameterised with the appropriate BP against which the evaluation will take place. The `PolicyCompletenessCompliance` class is one of the core classes of the SC^3 mechanism. It offers three main methods: `getBrokerPolicy`, `completenessCheck`, and `compliance-Check`. The first method extracts all the required information from the BP for the subsequent SD completeness and compliance evaluations to take place (see Sect. 3.2), whilst the last two implement these evaluations (see Sect. 4). All three methods are implemented in Java using the Apache Jena (Core and ARQ) APIs [10].

3.2   The `getBrokerPolicy` Process

The `getBrokerPolicy` process parses the BP and places the information that it extracts in the bp object of the class `BrokerPolicy`. This class encompasses a number of Java HashMap objects as attributes; Table 2 depicts these attributes for the scenario of Sect. 2. The HashMap objects reflect our *declarative framework* for representing the SLOs incorporated in the BP and, effectively, the BP itself. As already mentioned, through the incorporation of this framework, SC^3 achieves a clear separation of concerns between policy representation and policy enforcement: BPs are represented independently of the code that SC^3 employs for enforcing them. SC^3 is thus kept generic and orthogonal to the underlying cloud delivery platform.

The declarative framework is based upon Linked USDL [11] and, in particular, upon Linked USDL's SLA schema. Linked USDL is a lightweight ontology which provides an RDF vocabulary for the description of the business aspects of policies and services; it draws upon a number of widely-adopted vocabularies such as GoodRelations, SKOS, and FOAF. The reasons for opting for Linked USDL are outlined in Sect. 5.1; a more complete discussion can be found in [12]. A brief account of our framework is in order; such an account is necessary here for understanding the implementation of `getBrokerPolicy`. The account is based on the scenario of Sect. 2.

Table 2. HashMap objects

```
Map<String, BrokerPolicyClass> serviceModelMap;
Map<String, BrokerPolicyClass> serviceLevelProfileMap;
Map<String, BrokerPolicyClass> serviceLevelMap;
Map<String, BrokerPolicyClass> serviceLevelExpressionMap;
Map<String, BrokerPolicyClass> expressionVariableMap;
Map<String, BrokerPolicyClass> quantitativeValueFloatMap;
```

3.3   Declarative Representation of BPs and SLOs

We model the SLOs of a BP, hence the BP itself, through a *specialisation process* which constructs a framework of suitable subclasses and sub-properties of the Linked USDL SLA classes and properties depicted in Fig. 2. These subclasses are then populated by instances specified in StoreCloud's SD. Below we outline this process for the 'gold' SLO of StoreCloud's `availability` attribute[3] (see Sect. 2); a more complete account of this process can be found in [9, 12].

SLO Representation. For each service-level attribute, the BP offers a subclass of the class `ServiceLevel` for accommodating the attribute's SLOs. For example, for accommodating the SLOs of the `availability` attribute (i.e. the 'gold', 'silver', and 'bronze' SLOs of Table 1), it offers the class `SL-Availability` (see Fig. 2). SLOs appear as instances of this class – e.g., the `SL-GoldAvailability` instance specified in StoreCloud's SD (see Fig. 2).

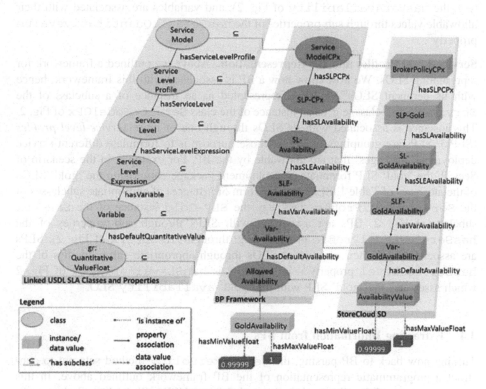

Fig. 2. Linked USDL SLA for the gold availability SLO

Each SLO is defined in terms of a *service-level expression* (SLE) which specifies the conditions that must be satisfied in order for the SLO to be met. SLEs are modelled as instances of suitable subclasses of the `ServiceLevelExpression` class (see Fig. 2). For example, the SLEs that correspond to the availability-related SLOs are modelled as instances of the class `SLE-Availability`. SLOs are associated with their corresponding SLEs through appropriate sub-properties of the `hasService-LevelExpression` property. In particular, the availability-related SLOs are associated with their SLEs through the `hasSLEAvailability` property (see Fig. 2).

---

[3] Of course, an analogous account applies to the rest of the attributes and SLOs of Table 1.

Each SLE binds a *variable* that corresponds to a particular attribute, one which is associated with an allowable range of values. Following an approach entirely symmetrical to the one outlined above for SLOs and SLEs, variables are modelled as instances of appropriate subclacess of the class `Variable`, whilst value ranges are modelled as instances of appropriate subclasses of the GoodRelations class `QuantitativeValueFloat`[4]. Figure 2 depicts these subclasses (`Var-Availability`, `AllowedAvailability`), and instances (`Var-GoldAvailability`, `AvailabilityValue`), for the 'gold' `availability` attribute. SLEs are associated with their corresponding variables through sub-properties of the `hasVariable` property (e.g. the `hasVarAvailability` of Fig. 2), and variables are associated with their allowable values through sub-properties of the `hasDefaultQuantitativeValue` property[5].

Service-Level Profiles and BP Representation. Above we outlined a framework for representing SLOs. We now show how a BP is associated with this framework, hence with its pertinent SLOs[6]. A BP is represented as an instance of a subclass of the `ServiceModel` class, e.g. as an instance of the class `ServiceModelCPx` of Fig. 2. This instance is associated with its SLOs through one or more *service-level profiles* (SLPs). SLPs are groupings of SLOs whose purpose is to formulate different service deployment 'packages' that are allowable by the BP. For example, in the scenario of Sect. 2, the 'gold' SLP formulates a deployment package comprising the 'gold' SLOs of the attributes of Table 1. SLPs take the form of instances of appropriate subclasses of the `ServiceLevelProfile` class, e.g. the `SLP-Gold` instance of the `SLP-CPx` subclass of Fig. 2. BPs are associated with SLPs through sub-properties of the `hasServiceLevelProfile` property (e.g. through `hasSLPCPx` of Fig. 2). SLPs are associated with their constituent SLOs through appropriate sub-properties of the `hasServiceLevel` property – an example is `hasSLAvailability` of Fig. 2 which associates the 'gold' SLP with the 'gold' `availability` SLO.

3.4   Extracting Information from BPs

Turning now back to BP parsing, the `getBrokerPolicy` method sets out to construct a programmatic representation of the BP framework outlined above. In this respect, it starts off by discovering, for each Linked USDL SLA class *C*, those subclasses *S* of *C* that appear in the BP. It then instantiates the HashMap attributes of the bp object (see Table 2) with the corresponding subclasses. This instantiation takes place through the method `getBrokerPolicyClassMap` as indicated in the 1st row of Table 3 for the `ServiceLevel` class (the rest of the instantiations are entirely analogous and thus omitted). The `getBrokerPolicy` method then proceeds to

---

[4] Or of the class `QualitativeValue`, in case of qualitative variables.

[5] Or through sub-properties of the `hasDefaultQualitativeValue`, in case of qualitative values.

[6] Recall from Sect. 2 that a BP is essentially a set of SLOs.

construct a list of string objects holding the URIs of all QuantitativeValue-Float instances found in the BP (e.g. the GoldAvailability instance depicted in Fig. 2); an excerpt of the code that populates this list is shown in the 2nd row of Table 3.

Table 3. Storing BP subclasses and QuantitativeValueFloat instances

```
bp.setServiceLevelMap(getBrokerPolicyClassMap(USDL_SLA,
                                    "ServiceLevel"));
```

```
1. List<String> qvSubclassList = new ArrayList<String>();
2. Iterator<BrokerPolicyClass> iterFl =
   bp.getQuantitativeValueFloatMap().values().iterator();
3. while (iterFl.hasNext()) {
4.    qvSubclassList.add((iterFl.next()).getUri());}
```

Subsequently, the getBrokerPolicy method discovers all properties in the BP, along with their corresponding ranges, which have as a domain one of the subclasses *S*; these are effectively all the *sub-properties* that appear in the BP. For each sub-property, an object of the class Subproperty is constructed (see Table 4 for an excerpt of the relevant code).

Table 4. Discovering ranges of sub-properties

```
1. while (riIn.hasNext()) {
2.    Resource subclassPropertyResource = riIn.next();
3.    Subproperty prop =
      new Subpropety(subclassPropertyResource.toString());
4.    prop.setDomainUri(subclassResource.toString());
5.    Property rangeProperty =
      ResourceFactory.createProperty(RDFS + "range");
6.    NodeIterator riIn2 =
      modelMem.listObjectsOfProperty(subclassPropertyResour
         ce,rangeProperty);
7.    prop.setRangeUri(riIn2.next().toString());}
```

4 SD Completeness and Compliance Checking

An SD is effectively a framework of instances that populate the subclasses of the BP framework (see Fig. 2). Below we outline the processes that determine whether an SD is *complete* and *compliant* with respect to the BP.

4.1   The `completenessCheck` Method

The `completenessCheck` algorithm starts off by determining whether there is a corresponding instance I_S for each class S discovered by the `getBrokerPolicy` method (see Sect. 4.2). Then, for each object property P_o discovered by `getBrokerPolicy` such that $\text{dom}(P_o) = S$, it determines if I_S is associated (via P_o) with exactly one instance $I_{S'}$ of the class $S' = \text{ran}(P_o)$. Similarly, for each data property P_d, such that $\text{dom}(P_d) = S$, it determines whether I_S is associated via P_d with a data value from $\text{ran}(P_d)$. An excerpt of the code that checks these associations is shown in Table 5. For example, let S = SL-Availability (see Fig. 2). The algorithm initially checks if the SD contains an instance of S (in this case SL-GoldAvailability). Let now P_o = hasSLEAvailability. The algorithm checks if SL-GoldAvailability is associated, via P_o, with an instance of SLE-Availability (an association which exists with SLE-GoldAvailability). Analogous checks are performed for the rest of the instances in the SD framework.

Table 5. Sample code for checking instance associations

```
1.    Subproperty prop = null;
2.    while (propertyIter.hasNext()) {
3.       prop = propertyIter.next();
4.       int countNli = countQuery("{ <"+instance_uri+">
         <"+prop.getUri()+"> ?var}");
5.       String nli_uri = null;
6.       if (countNli == 0) {
7.          System.err.println("Error no connections");
8.          throw new CompletenessException();}
9.       if (countNli > 1) {
10.         System.err.println("Error > 1 connections");
11.         throw new CompletenessException();}
12.      else if (countNli == 1) {
13.         System.out.println("OK Instance");}
14.      RDFNode node = oneVarOneSolutionQuery("
         {<"+instance_uri+"> <"+prop.getUri()+"> ?var}");
15.      nli_uri = node.toString();}
```

4.2   The `complianceCheck` Method

The compliance checking algorithm proceeds by determining whether the values, or value ranges, specified in the SD are in accordance with the allowable values, or value ranges, specified in the BP. More specifically, the algorithm starts off by determining the number of values that are associated with a QuantitativeValueFloat instance (e.g. the instance Var-GoldAvailability of Fig. 2) via each of the properties `hasMinValueFloat` and `hasMaxValueFloat`. If this number is not equal to 1, an exception is raised (see lines 1–3 in the 1st row of Table 6). Otherwise, the algorithm proceeds to check that the range associated with the `Quantita-tiveValueFloat` instance is indeed subsumed by the corresponding range declared in the BP (see 2nd row of Table 6). For example, the algorithm checks whether the range $[0.99999, 1)$ associated with `Var-GoldAvailability`, is subsumed by the range $[0.9999, 1)$ associated with the corresponding `AvailabilityValue` instance in the BP (see Fig. 2).

Table 6. Sample code for compliance checking

```
1.  int minMaxFloatValueCount =
    countQuery("{<"+instance_uri + ">
                   gr:hasMinValueFloat ?someMinValue; " +
             "gr:hasMaxValueFloat ?someMaxValue}");
2.  if (minMaxFloatValueCount != 1) {
3.      System.err.println("Erroneous range associa-
        tion");}
```

```
1.  QuantitativeValueInstance bpQvInstance = null;
2.  while (bpInstancesIter.hasNext()) {
3.      bpQvInstance = bpInstancesIter.next();
4.      if (((Float) vObj.getMaxValue() <
            (Float) bpQvInstance.getMaxValue()) &&
           ((Float) vObj.getMinValue() >=
            (Float) bpQvInstance.getMinValue())) {
5.          System.out.println("OK - Instance ");
6.          break;}}
```

5 Related Work

To the best of our knowledge, no works other than [4] address the quality assurance dimension of CSB in the context of VEs. [4] recognises the need for frameworks that guide the creation, execution, and management of services in cloud-based VEs; it does not, however, address the quality assurance aspect of such frameworks. The rest of this section outlines work related to service description languages and to ontology-driven policy-based cloud service governance and quality control.

5.1 Service Description Languages

We provide an overview of different strands of service description formalisms. More specifically we outline approaches that: focus on syntactic service descriptions; consider the underlying semantics of web services; capture business aspects of services.

Syntactic service descriptions aim, primarily, at facilitating the interoperable data exchange between service registries (notably UDDI), service providers, and service consumers. The most prominent example is, perhaps, WSDL [13]. Nevertheless, syntactic service descriptions can only aid manual discovery, selection, and composition of services. In an attempt to automate these processes, a new breed of service description languages was introduced that enable Semantic Web Services [14]. These use ontologies in order to capture the functionality of web services in terms of an underlying, domain-specific, vocabulary. The rationale is that since both service descriptions and consumer demands rely on a common semantics, automatic service discovery and composition is, in principle, feasible. Prominent examples of standardisation efforts in this area include WSMO [15], OWL-S [16], SAWSDL [17], and SA-REST [18].

Whilst focusing on aspects which are important for the automatic composition and invocation of web services, the aforementioned approaches neglect any pertinent business details or, at best, address them as non-functional properties. This renders service descriptions cumbersome for service consumers and third-party intermediaries who are often interested in both business details and technical specifications in order to create added value by deploying, aggregating, customising, and integrating services. A third strand of description languages has therefore emerged, one which focuses on the business aspect of services. A prominent example is the Unified Service Description Language (USDL) [19]. USDL aims at unifying the business, operational, and technical aspects of a service in one coherent description. Although it provides a comprehensive framework, USDL has received limited adoption due mainly to its complexity and limited support for extensibility.

To overcome these limitations, Linked USDL [11] has been proposed. Linked USDL is a remodelled version of USDL which offers the following advantages [20, 21]. Firstly, it uses a light-weight RDF(S) vocabulary which provides a framework of concepts and properties for modelling, comparing, and trading services and service bundles, as well as for specifying, tracking, and reasoning about the involvement of entities in service delivery chains. This framework can be easily extended through linking to other RDF(S) ontologies. Secondly, it supports large-scale, efficient, multi-party interactions by: (i) capitalising on widely-adopted, general-purpose vocabularies such as Dublin Core, GoodRelations, SKOS, and FOAF; (ii) embracing Linked Data as the core means for capturing facts about people, organisations, resources, and services. It is to be noted here that these advantages facilitate the evaluation of the compliance of cloud services with pre-specified policies concerning the business aspects of service delivery and deployment. They are thus particularly significant from the standpoint of strengthening the *resilience* of cloud services.

5.2   Ontology-Driven Policy-Based Cloud Service Governance and Quality Control

Cloud service governance refers to policy-based management of cloud services with emphasis on quality assurance [22]. Current practice [23, 24] focuses on the use of registry and repository systems combined with purpose-built software to check the conformance of services with relevant policies [25]. A major weakness in these systems is failure to achieve a separation of concerns between defining policies and evaluating data against these policies [22, 25]. This has a number of negative repercussions such as lack of portability and lack of explicit representation of policy interrelations. Several works have attempted to address these shortcomings [26–29]. These generally employ bespoke languages, and ontologies, for capturing policies; the policies are then enforced at run-time typically through the use of a reference monitor. Closer to our approach are the works in [27–29] which embrace Semantic Web representations for capturing the knowledge encoded in policies.

In [27], the authors present KAoS – a general-purpose policy management framework which exhibits a three-layered architecture comprising: (i) a *human interface layer*, which provides a graphical interface for policy specification; (ii) a *policy management layer*, which uses OWL to encode and manage policy-related knowledge; (iii) a *policy monitoring and enforcement layer*, which automatically grounds OWL policies to a programmatic format suitable for policy-based monitoring and policy enforcement. In [28] the authors propose Rei – a policy specification language expressed in OWL-Lite. It allows the declarative representation of a wide range of policies which are purportedly understandable – hence enforceable – by a wide range of autonomous entities in open, dynamic environments. In [29], POLICYTAB is proposed for supporting trust negotiation in Semantic Web environments. POLICY-TAB advocates an ontology-based approach for describing policies that drive a trust negotiation process aiming at providing controlled access to Web resources.

Whilst achieving a proper separation of concerns between policy specification and policy enforcement, the aforementioned semantically-enhanced approaches rely on bespoke, non-standards-based, ontologies for the representation of policies. Such ontologies generally lack the expressivity for addressing the business details that characterise web and cloud services. They are therefore inadequate, as they stand, for capturing the business policies on which this work reports. In this respect, in our work, we have opted for Linked USDL: a language which readily provides the necessary constructs for capturing the required business policies.

6 Conclusions and Future Work

We have presented SC^3, a mechanism which offers capabilities with respect to the *Quality Assurance* dimension of CSB. SC^3 strengthens the resilience of services in cloud-based VEs by evaluating their compliance with pre-specified policies concerning the business aspects of their delivery. By representing policies declaratively, in terms of an ontology, and not as part of the code of SC^3, a separation of concerns between policy definition and policy enforcement is achieved. This effectively enables SC^3 to operate in a manner generic and agnostic to the underlying cloud delivery platform.

This paper has focused on the policy evaluation capabilities of SC^3 during the On-boarding phase of a service's lifecycle (see Sect. 2). Nevertheless, SC^3 offers a number of additional relevant capabilities which have been omitted here for reasons of space. These are: (i) an SLA monitoring capability which enables SC^3 to *continuously* check whether a service complies with the BP during the service Operation phase (i.e. during its consumption); (ii) a *standalone policy evaluation* capability, which assesses the correctness of a BP. In addition, SC^3 can be used for strengthening the resilience not only of application services (as demonstrated in this paper), but also of infrastructure and platform services.

SC^3 has been successfully used, in the frame of EU's Broker@Cloud project [30], for evaluating the quality of CRM services that are on-boarded on an existing commercial cloud application platform – namely the CAS Open [31] platform. In the future we intend to further assess the effectiveness of SC^3 by incorporating it in a number of additional cloud platforms, in particular platforms that provide infrastructure and platform services.

Acknowledgements. This research is funded by the EU 7th Framework Programme under the Broker@Cloud project (www.broker-cloud.eu), grant agreement n°328392.

References

1. Vaquero, L.M., Rodero-Merino, L., Caceres, J., Lindner, M.: A break in the clouds: towards a cloud definition. SIGCOMM Comput. Commun. Rev. **39**(1), 50–55 (2008)
2. Foster, I., Zhao, Y., Raicu, I. Lu, S.: Cloud computing and grid computing 360-degree compared. In: IEEE Grid Computing Workshop 2008, pp. 1–10. IEEE (2008)
3. Veloudis, S., Paraskakis, I., Friesen, A., Verginadis, Y., Patiniotakis, I., Rossini, A.: Continuous quality assurance and optimisation in cloud-based virtual enterprises. In: Camarinha-Matos, L.M., Afsarmanesh, H. (eds.) Collaborative Systems for Smart Networked Environments. IFIP AICT, vol. 434, pp. 621–632. Springer, Heidelberg (2014)
4. Cretu, L.G.: Cloud-based virtual organization engineering. Informatica Economică **16**(1), 98–109 (2012)
5. Cloud computing reference architecture. Technical report, NIST (2011)
6. Veloudis, S., Friesen, A., Paraskakis, I., Verginadis, Y., Patiniotakis, I.: Underpinning a cloud brokerage service framework for quality assurance and optimization. In: 6th IEEE International Conference on Cloud Computing Technology and Science, pp. 660–663. IEEE Press, New York (2014)
7. WSO_2 Carbon – 100% Open source middleware platform. http://wso2.com/products/carbon/
8. Broker@Cloud project deliverable 30.3. http://www.broker-cloud.eu/documents
9. Broker@Cloud project deliverable 40.1. http://www.broker-cloud.eu/documents
10. Apache Jena. https://jena.apache.org/
11. Linked USDL. http://www.linked-usdl.org/
12. Broker@Cloud project deliverable 30.2. http://www.broker-cloud.eu/documents
13. W3C recommendation: web services description language (WSDL) 1.1 (2001). http://www. w3.org/TR/wsdl
14. McIlraith, S.A., Son, T.C., Zeng, H.: Semantic web services. IEEE Intel. Syst. **16**(2), 46–53 (2001). doi:10.1109/5254.920599
15. W3C Member Submission.: Web Service Modelling Ontology (WSMO) (2005). http://www.w3.org/Submission/WSMO
16. W3C Member Submission: OWL-S: semantic markup for web languages (2004). http://www.w3.org/Submission/OWL-S
17. W3C Recommendation: Semantic annotations for WSDL and XML schema (2007). http://www.w3.org/TR/sawsdl

18. W3C Member Submission: SA-REST: semantic annotations for web resources (2010). http://www.w3.org/Submission/SA-REST
19. Oberle, D., Barros, A., Kylau, U., Heinzl, S.: A unified description language for human to automated services. Inf. Syst. **38**(1), 155–181 (2013). doi:10.1016/j.is.2012.06.004
20. Pedrinaci, C., Cardoso, J., Leidig, T.: Linked USDL: a vocabulary for web-scale service trading. In: Presutti, V., d'Amato, C., Gandon, F., d'Aquin, M., Staab, S., Tordai, A. (eds.) ESWC 2014. LNCS, vol. 8465, pp. 68–82. Springer, Heidelberg (2014)
21. Cardoso, J., Pedrinaci, C., Leidig, T., Rupino, P., De Leenheer, P.: Foundations of open semantic service networks. Int. J. Serv. Sci. Manag. Eng. Technol. **4**(2), 1–16 (2013). doi:10. 4018/jssmet.2013040101
22. Kourtesis, D., Parakakis, I., Simons, A.J.H.: Policy-driven governance in cloud application platforms: an ontology-based approach. In: 4th International Workshop on Ontology-Driven Information Systems Engineering (2012)
23. Marks, E.A.: Service-Oriented Architecture Governance for the Services Driven Enterprise. Wiley, New York (2008)
24. Zhang, L.J., Zhou, Q.: CCOA: cloud computing open architecture. In: IEEE International Conference on Web Services, pp. 607–616. IEEE Press, New York (2009)
25. Kourtesis, D., Paraskakis, I.: A registry and repository system supporting cloud application platform governance. In: Pallis, G., Jmaiel, M., Charfi, A., Graupner, S., Karabulut, Y., Guinea, S., Rosenberg, F., Sheng, Q.Z., Pautasso, C., Ben Mokhtar, S. (eds.) ICSOC 2011 Workshops. LNCS, vol. 7221, pp. 255–256. Springer, Heidelberg (2012)
26. Damianou, N., Dulay, N., Lupu, E.C., Sloman, M.: The ponder policy specification language. In: Sloman, M., Lobo, J., Lupu, E.C. (eds.) POLICY 2001. LNCS, vol. 1995, pp. 18–38. Springer, Heidelberg (2001)
27. Uszok, A., Bradshaw, J., Jeffers, R., Johnson, M., Tate, A., Dalton, J., Aitken, S.: KAoS policy management for semantic web services. IEEE Intell. Sys. **19**(4), 32–41 (2004)
28. Kagal, L., Finin, T., Joshi, A.: A policy language for a pervasive computing environment. In: 4th IEEE International Workshop on Policies for Distributed Systems and Networks (POLICY 2003), pp. 63–74. IEEE Computer Society, Washington DC (2003)
29. Nejdl, W., Olmedilla, D., Winslett, M., Zhang, C.C.: Ontology-based policy specification and management. In: Gómez-Pérez, A., Euzenat, J. (eds.) ESWC 2005. LNCS, vol. 3532, pp. 290–302. Springer, Heidelberg (2005)
30. Broker@Cloud project. http://www.broker-cloud.eu/
31. CAS CRM. http://www.cas-crm.com/

How to Maintain the Network Resilience and Effectiveness in Case of Resources Reduction? A Covering Set Location Approach

Lionel Dupont[1(✉)], Matthieu Lauras[1], and Claude Yugma[2]

[1] Mines Albi – University of Toulouse,
Campus Jarlard, Route de Teillet, 81000 Albi, France
{lionel.dupont,matthieu.lauras}@mines-albi.fr
[2] Ecole des Mines de Saint-Etienne,
880 Route de Mimet, 13451 Gardanne, France
yugma@emse.fr

Abstract. The objective of covering set location models consists in designing or modifying a network (commercial shops, antennas, drugstores, etc.) in order to cover totally or partially the demand related to a given area. When an area is covered by several activities (multi coverage), this can improve the responsiveness of the network (in case of congestion traffic for example) but this can also have negative effects such as customers' cannibalization. In this paper, we propose an innovative covering set location model able to support decision makers to design networks that have a high resiliency level (i.e. ability to maintain service level despite hazards or failures) in a context of resources reduction (i.e. closing-down of network installations). Basically, the proposal allows studying the benefits and limits of multi coverage on each part of the network. Heuristic and exact methods are suggested to solve this problem.

Keywords: Location model · Resiliency · Effectiveness · Network · Resources reduction · Covering location model

1 Introduction and Research Statement

Many investment projects can be supported through facility location models. The general principle of these models consists in supplying customer demands (goods or services) from one or more facilities spatially distributed on a given area. A facility is defined as a large variety of entities.

Many practical problems can be formulated as covering problems. Here is a non-exhaustive list of real-life problems: police stations, hospitals, radar installations, shop centers, location of retail facilities, etc. For recent surveys on this topic, see Berman et al. (2010) and Farahani et al. (2012). Opening or using a facility is cost expensive (regarding investment and/or use). That is why most of the companies must optimize their networks in order to be competitive. The localization decisions are critical due to the time and expenses that any further change would induce. One particular issue of modern networks consists in avoiding network overcosts by limiting the number of facilities that are necessary to work. Another particular issue is the fact

© IFIP International Federation for Information Processing 2015
L.M. Camarinha-Matos et al. (Eds.): PRO-VE 2015, IFIP AICT 463, pp. 136–145, 2015.
DOI: 10.1007/978-3-319-24141-8_12

that networks are more and more subjected to hazards. Thus, in a general context of means' reduction, networks should maintain a capability regarding uncertainties. In other words, the challenge is to maximize the efficiency of a network while maintaining the resiliency of this network.

One particular illustration of this problem statement is the rationalization of a banking network on a given territory. Actually, bank companies are currently trying to limit the number of their agencies in order to reduce their costs. But at a same time, they want to propose a high service level to high-potential customers and to improve their resiliency in particular zones that are considered strategic or sensitive (for instance a business district or a shopping area). To do that, the decision-makers have to design a network that is characterized by (i) a limited number of facilities, (ii) a minimum service-level in nominal situation in the whole concerned territory and (iii) a redundancy capability in high-potential areas in order to manage uncertainties. This is the purpose of the current research work.

Classically, the paper is split up into 4 sections. The first one proposes a brief background on the multi-covering facility location problem. The second one formulates the studied problem. The third section develops the proposed model and gives some information regarding the solving step. Finally, the fourth section discusses the results obtained on a numerical application.

2 Background

One of the most popular models in the research area of facility location is the covering problem. In this problem, the customer can receive service from each facility, of which the distance to the customer is equal or less than a predefined number. This predefined distance is called service distance, coverage distance, or coverage radius R – Fallah et al. (2009). The customer demand is then defined as a discrete set of demand nodes. Demands at a node i are "covered" by a candidate facility site j if the distance between i and j is less than R. On one hand, the Location Set Covering Problem (LSCP) minimizes the number of facilities that are required to cover, at least once, each node. On the other hand, considering a fixed number of facilities available, the Maximal Covering Location Problems (MCLP) maximizes the number of customers reached. Since seventies, many authors have discussed these covering problems such as Toregas et al. (1971), Berlin and Liebman (1974), Church and ReVelle (1974), Church and Roberts (1983) or ReVelle et al. (2008).

The problem that we studied in this paper is related to multiple-coverage problems. By multiple-coverage is meant the presence of more than one facility within the coverage distance. Hogan and ReVelle (1986) introduced the multiple-coverage concept. Kolen and Tamir (1990) worked on multiple coverage problems. In this paper, the author considers that each existing demand node has to be delivered by a set of new facilities and this set depends on the type of new facilities. He introduces also an upper bound for the number of facilities that have to be located at a given place. From his side, Kim and Murray (2008) considered a problem in which the number of facilities on a continuous space is predetermined. He proposed a model, based on two objective functions, able to maximize primary and secondary coverage in such a context. Erdemir et al. (2010) developed a set-covering problem through a MCLP in order to optimize aero medical and ground ambulance services. The originality of this approach is the fact that the allocated budget is not sufficient to satisfy all the demand with the good level of service. To solve this issue, the author proposed to maximize the amount of demand covered within the acceptable service distance by locating a given fixed number of new facilities. Erdemir et al. (2010) developed a covering model that is a combination of response and total service times. Three complementary service coverage have been considered: (i) the field emergency medical one, (ii) the air emergency medical one and (iii) the joint coverage ground air emergency medical thorough transfer point one. Based on those, the model assesses if a node can be fulfilled by an emergency medical service in the frame of the response and service time limits. Then, the proposed model covers both crash nodes and paths (i.e. nodes and links of network).

Multiple-coverage can be suitable or prejudicial. When an area is covered by several activities (multi coverage), this improves the responsiveness and resilience of the system (in case of congestion traffic for example) but some also have negative effects (cannibalization customer for example). In the case of service or emergency facility, multi-coverage is suitable: with high levels of multiple coverage a congested system may more often be able to respond to demand even if the most desirable facility is busy. In the case of antenna placement, on the contrary, it is prejudicial: it creates electromagnetic interference due to multiple uses of frequencies at the node.

3 Problem Formulation

In this research work, a new extension of the multi-covering facility location problem is proposed. Here, the decision-maker wants to develop a multi-covering solution in particular areas and to avoid it in other ones. Let's consider the following example to underline the interests of such an objective. A company has opened during the years 50 stores in a urban area. Considering the population and competitors' evolutions, the network is not adapted anymore. The company wants to keep only 20 of its 50 shops. The urban area has been split up into a 20 × 20 square. We make the assumption that a shop covers a square of 5 × 5 (25 spots). The Fig. 1 hereafter gives the forecasted turnover for each spot and the position of the 50 current shops.

Following a study, the urban area has been shared into three zones:

1. A zone characterized by a strong demand (in red). This is the most profitable one, where the competition is very intense. The objective is to have an important presence in any circumstance. The decision-maker wants to favor multi-covering solution able to offer a high-service level even when a hazard occurs.
2. A zone characterized by a medium demand (in orange). In this zone, there are few competitors and the decision-maker wants to be present.
3. A zone characterized by a low demand (in white). The decision-maker wants to keep a minimal presence on this area.

Each shop has a rental cost which varies depending on the location. In this example, we have considered proportional costs to turnovers (resp 4, 9, 14). Considering this

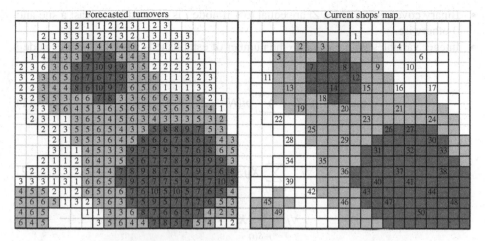

Fig. 1. Forecasted turnovers and the current shops' map

network, the problem will consist in reducing the number of facilities from 50 to 20 while maintaining a high level of resiliency (evaluated through a multi-covering rate) and a high level of service (evaluated through a unsatisfied demand rate).

4 Scientific Proposition

If a demand node i is not covered by any facility, there is a gain of g_i. Conversely, if a demand node i is covered by q facilities, it is an additional (or redundancy) value that is proportional to the number of extra facilities. This value is equal to $(q-1).p_i$ where p_i is the unit additional value. This value will be positive value (a gain) if multiple-coverage is suitable. Otherwise, it is a negative value (cost).

The capacity of a facility is assumed to be unlimited. Establishing a facility on a site j has a fixed cost f_j.

The problem can be formulated through a Mixed Integer Linear Programming (MILP) with binaries variables and the mathematical integer programming written as follows.

Let:

    i: index of demand nodes
    j: index of potential sites
    $S(i)$: set of sites that can cover the demand at node i
    $N(j)$: set of nodes that can be covered by site j

Let us now define the set of decision variables:

- Binary allocation variables X_{ij} are equal to 1 if node i is covered by site j and 0 otherwise.
- Binary location variables Y_j are equal to 1 if a facility is located at site j and 0 otherwise.

- Binary coverage variables Zi are equal to 1 if node i is covered by at least a site and 0 otherwise.
- Integer variables Wi are equal to the number of established sites which cover node i

$$\max \sum_i gi.Zi + \sum_i pi(Ni - Zi) - \sum_j fj.Yj \tag{1}$$

subject to:

$$\forall j \quad \sum_{i \in N(j)} Xij \leq |N(j).Yj| \tag{2}$$

$$\forall j \quad \sum_{j \in S(i)} Xij = Wi \tag{3}$$

$$\forall i, \quad Zi \leq Wi \tag{4}$$

$$\forall i, \quad Wi \leq |S(i)|.Zi \tag{5}$$

$$\sum_j Yj \leq PMax \tag{6}$$

Constraint (2) expresses the location and allocation variables and indicates that site j is established if it covers at least one node of $N(j)$. Constraints (3) determine the number of sites that cover node i. Constraints (4) and (5) state that Zi is equal to 0 if Wi is equal to 0, and Zi is equal to 1 if Wi is greater than or equal to 1. Constraint (6) limits the number of located facilities at $PMax$.

This formulation uses 4 kinds of integer and binary variables. This formulation does not allow building a concise enumeration tree useable by a branch and bound technique. The integer variables Wi can easily be replaced by their expression (see Eq. 3). To limit the number of binary variables, we start by re-formulating this problem. Then, we call "main" facility of node i one and only one of the facility covering i. The other facilities covering i are "extra" facilities. They induce the multiple-coverage cost. The issue is then to select the main facilities. Let us introduce the binary allocation variables $XMij$. $XMij$ are equal to 1 if site j is established ($Yj = 1$) and site j is the main facility for node i, and 0 otherwise (site j is established and is extra facility of i or site j is not establish).

Within these variables $XMij$, the objective function can be written as following:

$$\sum_j \sum_{S(j)} gi.XMij + \sum_j \sum_{S(j)} pi.(Yj - XMij) - \sum_j fj.Yj$$
$$= \sum_i \sum_j (gi. - pi).XMij - \sum_j Yj.\left(fj - \sum_{S(j)} pi\right)$$

Let:

$$ai = gi. - pi.$$

$$bj = fj - \sum_{S(j)} pi$$

The problem can be formulated:

$$\max \sum_i \sum_j ai.XMij - \sum_j bj.Yj. \tag{7}$$

The constraints become:

$$\forall j \quad \sum_{i \in N(j)} XMij \leq |N(j).Yj| \tag{8}$$

$$\forall i \quad \sum_{j \in S(i)} Xij \leq 1 \tag{9}$$

$$\sum_j Yj \leq PMax \tag{10}$$

The objective function (7) maximizes the gain. Constraints (8) assure that $Yj = 1$ if and only if a demand node has j as a main facility. Equation (9) ensures that at most one facility is the main facility of node i. Constraint (10) limits the number of located facilities.

5 Solving Issue

This kind of MILP problem can be solved by current software only if the problem has a limited size. That's why we propose to use here a branch and bound method:

Usually, the branch and bound algorithm performance is based on:

1. The search tree enumeration,
2. The lower bound determination,
3. A heuristic or polynomial method that makes it possible to construct a good feasible solution.

5.1 Search Tree Enumeration

The enumeration tree is constructed by adding a new facility j at each step k. This facility becomes the main facility of the nodes $M(j,k)$ of $N(j)$ not yet covered and a extra facility for the others. Let's consider now the objective function. On one hand, we pay bj to position j. On the other hand, we gain $vjk = \sum_{M(j,k)} ai.$

The profit is so $pjk = bj - vjk$. If $pjk < 0$, site j can be rejected from the solution. The ratio $rjk = bj/ajk$ measures the profitability of the facility selection j in step k. The sites' selection is based on a prioritization list. This list can be static (when it is once and for all fixed at the beginning of the enumeration) or dynamic (when it is reconstructed each time a decision is taken). Here the enumeration tree is built dynamically by considering the facilities with a decreasing profitability rjk.

5.2   Heuristics

Two greedy heuristics have been retained here.

The first one consists in choosing in every step the site j given that the maximum profitability rjk and in taking it as the main facility of all nodes that are not yet covered.

The second heuristic is built on the same principle by retaining the site j with the maximum profit pjk.

5.3   Upper Bound

Here again we have retained two greedy heuristics:

- The first is based on the demand nodes,
- The second is based on the facilities.

To obtain the first upper bound, we retain as main facility of any node i not covered the site j not selected of maximum profitability

To obtain the second upper bound, we retain at step k, the $PMax-k$ facilities not selected with maximum gain.

We do not detail here the branch and bound and its performances. Nevertheless, up to 60 facilities, the optimal solutions have been obtained in less than 15 min (fixed time deadline).

6   Numerical Application and Discussion

Let's consider the problem described in Sect. 3 and the model proposed to solve it. If we are looking to maximize the profit (turnover minus rental costs), then we obtain the following solution (Fig. 2). The left side of the figure indicates the opened facilities while the right side gives the number of facilities that cover a spot.

Within this solution, 18 demands on 1544 are not satisfied (1.17 %) and the multi-coverage is more or less similar in the 3 zones. This result is presented in Table 1.

The Fig. 3 proposes an alternative solution, also for 20 facilities (black spots). Regarding this second solution, a light increase of the unsatisfied demand appears (21 instead of 18, or 1.36 %). The zone 3 is now favored comparing to zone 1 (see Table 1). Moreover, if we consider the uncertainty that exists on the demand associated to each part of the network, the decision-maker should retain this second solution. Our

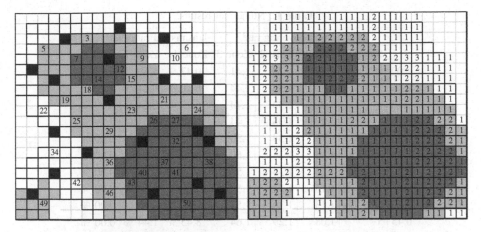

Fig. 2. First solution for 20 facilities: solution 1 in Table 1.

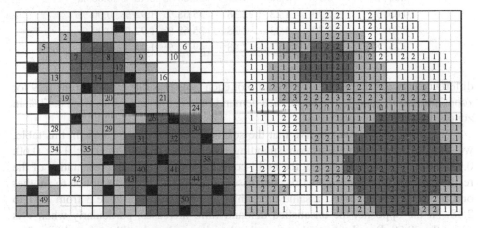

Fig. 3. Second solution for 20 facilities: solution 3 on Table 1.

objective consists in supporting decision by proposing to the decision-maker several alternatives and their associated impacts in terms of effectiveness and resiliency.

The Table 1 shows an experiment plan on which we have applied a value $p1 = -v$ to zone 1, $p2 = 0$ to zone 2 and $p3 = +v$ to zone 3. The objective is to find a solution that allows maximizing the resiliency (multi-covering) of the strategic zone (zone 3 in this case) and limiting the unsatisfied demand of low-potential zone (zone 1 in this case), despite of resources reduction (from 50 to 20 facilities).

The first part of the Table 1 (multi-covering ratio) gives the average number of facilities that cover a slot of each zone 1, 2 or 3. The second part (unsatisfied demand ratio) indicates the percentage of turnover that has been lost in each zone.

If $v = 0$, then we are just looking for to maximize the profit (turnover minus rental costs of the shops). Without favoring a zone regarding another one, there is very few

Table 1. Numerical results.

v	Solution	Multi-covering rate			Unsatisfied rate (%)		
		Zone 1	Zone 2	Zone 3	Zone 1	Zone 2	Zone 3
0.00	1	1.34	1.29	1.41	0.47 %	1.60 %	0.99 %
0.05	2	1.20	1.33	1.44	6.10 %	0.64 %	0.99 %
0.10		1.20	1.33	1.44	6.10 %	0.64 %	0.99 %
0.15		1.20	1.33	1.44	6.10 %	0.64 %	0.99 %
0.20	3	1.15	1.34	1.50	4.69 %	1.76 %	0.00 %
0.25		1.15	1.34	1.50	4.69 %	1.76 %	0.00 %
0.30		1.15	1.34	1.50	4.69 %	1.76 %	0.00 %
0.35		1.15	1.34	1.50	4.69 %	1.76 %	0.00 %
0.40	4	1.13	1.36	1.54	6.10 %	0.80 %	0.00 %
0.45	5	1.08	1.29	1.64	8.45 %	1.44 %	0.00 %
0.50		1.08	1.29	1.64	8.45 %	1.44 %	0.00 %
0.55		1.08	1.29	1.64	8.45 %	1.44 %	0.00 %
0.60	6	0.90	1.30	1.99	20.66 %	0.48 %	0.00 %
0.65	7	0.70	1.23	2.38	35.68 %	1.92 %	0.00 %
0.70		0.70	1.23	2.38	35.68 %	1.92 %	0.00 %
0.75	8	0.52	1.27	2.48	49.77 %	1.44 %	0.00 %

difference between the multi-covering ratio of each slot. This rate evolves from 1.29 for zone 2 to 1.41 to zone 3. The unsatisfied demand ratio is low and varies from 0.47 % in zone 1 to 1.60 % in zone 2.

When v increases, we observe that the solutions evolve step by step. In this table, we show 8 different solutions corresponding to $v = \{0; 0.05; 0.20; 0.40; 0.45; 0.60; 0.65; 0.75\}$. We can remark that the multi-covering ratio – that is representative of the resiliency capability of the network - decreases continuously from a solution to another one (from 1.34 to 0.52). At a same time, this ratio increases for zone 3 from 1.41 to 2.48. At the opposite, the unsatisfied demand ratio increases, particularly when v is upper than 0.60. Based on our objective, the decision-maker should retain solution 3 or 4.

This paper presents a simplified case, treating each facility equally in terms of operating costs, benefits and homogeneous coverage. In further works, we will propose a new model able to avoid this limitation and to get closer to reality. Another perspective consists in considering randomly distributed demand points.

References

Berlin, G.M., Liebman, J.C.: Mathematical analysis of emergency ambulance location. Socio-Econ. Plan. Sci. **8**, 323–328 (1974)

Berman, O., Drezner, Z., Krass, D.: Generalized coverage: new developments in covering location models. Comput. Oper. Res. **37**(10), 1675–1687 (2010)

Church, R.L., ReVelle, C.S.: The maximal covering location problem. Pap. Reg. Sci. Assoc. **32**, 101–118 (1974)

Church, R., Roberts, K.: Generalized coverage models and public facility location. Pap. Reg. Sci. Assoc. **53**, 117–135 (1983)

Erdemir, E.T., Batta, R., Spielman, S., Rogerson, P.A., Blatt, A., Flanigan, M.: Joint ground and air emergency medical services coverage models: a greedy heuristic solution approach. Eur. J. Oper. Res. **207**(4), 736–749 (2010)

Fallah, H., NaimiSadigh, A., Aslanzadeh, M.: Covering problem. Facility Location: Concepts, Models, Algorithms and Case Studies. Physica Verlag, Heidelberg (2009)

Farahani, R., Asgari, N., Heidari, N.: Covering problems in facility location: a review -. Comput. Ind. Eng. **62**(1), 368–407 (2012)

Hogan, K., ReVelle, C.: Concepts and applications of backup coverage. Manag. Sci. **32**, 1434–1444 (1986)

Kim, K., Murray, A.T.: Enhancing spatial representation in primary and secondary coverage location modeling. J. Reg. Sci. **48**(4), 745–768 (2008)

Kolen, A., Tamir, A.: Covering problems. In: Mirchandani, P.B., Francis, R.L. (eds.) Discrete Location Theory, pp. 263–304. Wiley-Inderscience, New York (1990)

Toregas, C., Swain, R., ReVelle, C.S., Bergman, L.: The location of emergency service facilities. Oper. Res. **19**, 1363–1373 (1971)

ReVelle, C.S., Eiselt, H.A., Daskin, M.S.: A bibliography for some fundamental problem categories in discrete location science. Eur. J. Oper. Res. **184**, 817–848 (2008)

A Framework for Evaluation of Resilience of Disaster Rescue Networks

Javad Jassbi[1,2(✉)], Luis M. Camarinha-Matos[1], and Jose Barata[1]

[1] Faculty of Sciences and Technology, Uninova - CTS and Nova University
of Lisbon, 2829 - 516 Caparica, Portugal
{j.jassbi, cam, jab}@uninova.pt
[2] Azad University, Science and Research Branch, Tehran, Iran

Abstract. Disasters by their very nature are unpredictable so being prepared to react in short time and with high efficiency is vital. The adoption of the collaborative networks paradigm in disaster management can lead to a new generation of rescue teams so called Disaster Rescue Network (DRN). During the first hours after a disaster, and before external help can arrive, it is the DRN implanted in the incident area that can perform the first rescue tasks. But the DRN is itself affected by the disaster and often gets its operational level drastically reduced. The main objective of this work is to propose an evaluation model, through employing experts' knowledge, for measuring a resilience index in DRNs. In this paper, a Fuzzy Inference System is used to achieve the mentioned objective. This will help in evaluating the resilience of DRNs and provide the opportunity to simulate policies to improve that resilience.

Keywords: Resilience · Fuzzy inference system · Disaster rescue network

1 Introduction

In the first hours after a large scale disaster and before a disaster rescue team is operational, social networks play crucial roles [1]. This means that professional rescue teams implanted in the incident area are not resilient enough to recover and accomplish their mission. Recently this problem has attracted the attention of researchers as on one hand professionals are empowered to deal with crisis situations and on the other hand response time is crucial. Having an effective recovering process after being impacted could make huge difference.

Rescue networks due to their functionality and mission have to face challenges which are not predictable. In case of disasters not only we face complex and dynamic phenomena but also the multiplicity and multifunction of actors, whether individuals or organizations, needed to deal with the situation [2]. Traditional leadership structures cannot be of much help in crisis, while a resilient response needs to be institutionalized in Disaster Rescue Networks (DRN) [3]. Resilience is an important decisive factor in terms of survivability of the system in unpredictable situations. It is sourced in basic systems theory concepts such as equilibrium, adoptability and stability [4]. Both individual and collective responses to unexpected and radical changes are interesting for researchers in the area of resilience [5].

© IFIP International Federation for Information Processing 2015
L.M. Camarinha-Matos et al. (Eds.): PRO-VE 2015, IFIP AICT 463, pp. 146–158, 2015.
DOI: 10.1007/978-3-319-24141-8_13

Resilience in hazard management systems has attracted the researchers' attention and many works confirm the importance of the subject when the focus is on developing strategies for building resilient societies. Macro Level is the dominant perspective in this area and achieving a resilient society the focal point. Something which is less considered is that DRNs are also affected by disasters while we are expecting them to react quickly to recover and help the victims. In all natural or human provoked disasters, the first hours are crucial and life of people depends on how the rescue networks react when the network and its members are also suffering, both as a team and as individuals, from the same disaster. Imagine there is earthquake in a big city. Most of the infrastructures could be damaged and at the same time the hierarchy and authority structure of different organizations, responsible to help in these cases, could be hardly attacked or unable to work properly due to many reasons. What is important here is the way the DRNs could recover and start to operate efficiently.

One relevant research challenge in resilient DRNs is the development of a **framework for resilience assessment**. It is clear that rescue networks have to be restructured to work as collaborative networks to increase the resilience of the system [6]. The aim is to achieve a model of resilience that keeps a record of rescue networks and how they are achieving adequate levels of resilience. Having a conceptual model with the characterization of all relevant factors is a necessary but not sufficient step. To fulfill the mission, a quantitative model is also needed. A conceptual model could provide a big picture of what is essential and the strategy to be adopted. However, with no measuring system it is not possible to understand the weaknesses and strengths as the basis for improvement. The main concern of this paper is thus the measurability of DRNs' resilience in case of natural or human provoked disasters.

The paper is organized as follows: in next section the related literature is reviewed; section three deals with a conceptual model and in section four the process of developing hybrid intelligent system for evaluating resilience of DRNs is introduced. In section five the applicability of the model is presented by an illustrative example and implementing the proposed model into a real case study. Section six presents the discussion and future direction of the work.

2 Literature Review

It is claimed that Collaborative Networks could help achieving better operation against threats and risks and bringing a new approach to adapt to crisis situations [2]. Typically emergency management networks have multiplex relationships, follow flat decision-making process, and involve both formal and informal groups with a combination of vertical and horizontal relations [7]. Rescue teams, seen as a form of collaborative network, need a strategic and operational plan to enhance the capacity of the system to deal with critical situations. Traditional risk-based approach is insufficient and resilience analysis should be part of all catastrophe management plans [8]. The main difference between these two approaches is the way they look into future. In risk-based approaches the centre of attention is risk factor identification and mitigation, while in the resilience-based approach the assumption is that hazards are indefinable and internal preparedness and readiness for unexpected situations are necessary.

Adaptability is one of the most important capabilities which would guarantee the survival of a system while agility and resilience are the representatives of this capability of the system [9]. Resilience, as an emerging research field, is being analyzed from different perspectives and as a result there are different meanings and perceptions which sometimes are contested or contrasted [10, 11]. Resilience is used in different contexts, including ecology management, psychology, supply chain management, safety engineering, crisis management, and collaborative networks [5, 12]. Nevertheless it is important to avoid common pitfalls of synonyms and distinguish between resilience and other characteristics of the system such as flexibility, agility, and robustness [13]. In this work, a definition from [14] is taken as more appropriate to present the concept of resilience for Disaster Rescue Networks:

"Resilience can be understood as the ability of the system to reduce the chances of a shock, to absorb a shock if it occurs (abrupt reduction of performance) and to recover quickly after a shock (re-establish normal performance)" [14].

The benefit of a holistic perspective is the relation-hood view, so needless to say that the collective capability of a system is not just the additive composition of individuals, but more related to interactions and interrelations between individuals. To take advantage of the synergies in DRNs as collaborative networks, we are aiming resilience at both individual and collective levels [15]. This brings complexity and dynamism to the resilience evaluation model. Resilience is more than just capacity to provide sufficient response to uncertainty, which is the minimum expectation. It is a process of learning from doing and building a knowledge repository from tough experiences [16]. The nature of all systems is imperfect and, as such, resilient networks need to adopt a process of improvement through learning from events [17]. Furthermore, and unlike traditional views, resilience is not any more limited to the concept of distinctive and discontinuous events but it is recognized as a capability or capacity of organizations related to ordinary adoptive practices that lead the system to higher levels of efficiency [18]. Resilience in disaster management could be discussed at different levels, while most research works are focused on the resilience of the society or citizens especially in the first hours and days after large scale disasters [3].

Measurement systems associated to resilience indicators could be classified in two categories, pre-event or post-event models [4]. Pre-event models endeavor to use indicators to present the estimated level of resilience and post-event models show the actual level of resilience after analyzing the reaction of the system to real cases when a catastrophe actually happens [19]. Developing a model for pre-event estimation is a hard task that includes designing process, measurement of specific factors, and an aggregation model.

Planning, benchmarking, or a strategic move to enhance the resilience of any type of organization need an assessment model, including clear indicators. The aimed model should present the resilience of the system in a way to enable decision makers to have a clear picture of what the current situation is and the gap to meet desired state. It is difficult to develop a general mathematical model due to the variety of classes of affecting variables, while dealing with imprecise data is also indispensable [20].

The number of proposed models in the literature is still limited when most of the works concentrate on meaning, and on the conceptual part of the resilience model. There are also some attempts to use fuzzy logic, or statistical methods by employing questionnaires [4, 20–23]. The scope of our work, different from previous approaches, can be summarized as follows: First, it considers the concept of resilience at micro-level (comparing with society level), targeting Disaster Rescue Networks in case of large scale catastrophes and second, developing an intelligent decision-support system to measure the level of resilience in DRNs.

3 Conceptual Model for Resilience Evaluation

There are several evaluation frameworks offering different methodologies for resilience evaluation in an organization or network [14, 15]. Some of them are more focused on organizations, while some others try to propose a wider perspective to make it appropriate to cover from individuals to collective systems, such as teams, organizations, or societies. The main challenge in the proposed models is the **measurability** of the adopted criteria. This requires a trade-off analysis, as on one hand we need a comprehensive model with enough criteria covering all aspects and domains, while on the other hand non-measurable criteria are tricky. If we cannot measure it, it could not help us in reality to evaluate the level of resilience and thus it is useless for strategy selection.

In this paper, the conceptual model introduced in [24] is adopted and used as a basis to develop a quantitative model. The mentioned model is well accepted by experts in the area and provides a comprehensive framework for understanding resilience. In fact, in several other research works, the same model was employed on different occasions. As a result, there is an adequate number of empirical studies and satisfactory guidelines for measurability of the used criteria, which is very important for quantitative models [4, 15, 16, 18, 24]. Figure 1 presents the mentioned model.

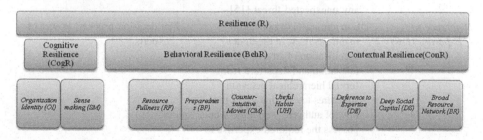

Fig. 1. Resilience Evaluation Model (adapted from [24])

The value of each main criterion is a result of aggregation of sub-criteria values which could make the process of measurement applicable. Table 1 presents all criteria in the model and their description.

Table 1. Explanation of Resilience Evaluation Model

Criteria	Definition	
Organization Identity (OI)	OI encompasses the core values and beliefs of an organization that its members deem to be the most central, distinctive, and symbolic, through which an organization reveals its identity to stakeholders [25]	Mission, core values, Common vocabulary, Group commitment
Sense making (SM)	The process through which individuals work to understand novel, unexpected, or confusing events [26]	Balance of confidence and scepticism, Positive perception, Experience interpretation
Resource Fullness (RF)	The ability to identify problems, establish priorities, and mobilize resources when disaster occurs; resourcefulness can be further regarded as flexible plans, strategies and procedures to apply or coordinate resources [27]	Creativity, Balance of originality and initiative
Preparedness (BP)	BP is taking actions and making investments before they are needed to ensure that an organization is able to benefit from situations that emerge [24]	Prepared infrastructure, Cooperation in noncritical situations, Training
Counter-intuitive Moves (CM)	The ability to follow a dramatically different course of action from the one which is the norm [15]	Variety of strategies, Scenario planning, Non-aligned activities, Learning from events
Useful Habits (UH)	Useful, practical habits, especially repetitive, over-learned routines that provide the first response to any unexpected threat [15]	Flat decision process, Power of experts
Deference to Expertise (DE)	DE in a mindful organization manifests itself in the under specification of structures, relaxation and departure from formal hierarchical decision structures to one that gives the flow of authority to people who possess the required expertise to deal with the problem at hand [28]	Flat decision process, Power of experts
Deep Social Capital (DS)	DS is attained through well-maintained interpersonal relationships within an organizational community. It focuses on long term partnership	Member communication and cooperation, Resource sharing

(Continued)

Table 1. (*Continued*)

Criteria	Definition	
	that benefits parties beyond immediate transaction interests [29]	
Broad Resource Network (BR)	Resilient firms are able to utilize relationships with supplier contacts, loyal customers, and strategic alliance partners to secure needed resources to support adaptive initiatives [24]	Resource network, Meta organizational resources

4 Developing a Hybrid Intelligent System for Evaluation

One of the main problems in social or human based systems is the lack of tools to map from an input space to an output space. This is due to the complexity of the system and shortage of knowledge about its components and their relations. It is a challenging mission when there is neither sufficient historical data nor knowledge about the structure of the system. To tackle these types of problems, the knowledge of experts could be the only source of information.

Fuzzy Inference System (FIS) is a powerful tool to deal with expert's knowledge and for approximate reasoning [30]. To develop a FIS, knowledge is extracted and represented in a set of rules that express the relations between components of the system. For the case of resilience measurement, due to the lack of information and unclear equation between the criteria, FIS seems to be more effective comparing with other possible methods. Most of the other methods need historical behavior (information) or clear relation for aggregating. In this work, FIS is employed to develop an evaluation model for DRNs' resilience. As it can been inferred from Fig. 1, we need to have a hybrid system including four FISs to aggregate the criteria in two steps. In the first step, three FISs are built to aggregate the sub-criteria to determine the three main criteria, Cognitive Resilience, Behavioral Resilience, and Contextual Resilience. In a second step, the result will be the output of criteria fusion from first step. To do that, and for each FIS, we follow the procedure presented in Fig. 2.

The first step is to determine input and output, for which two important decisions should be taken: the number of fuzzy sets and the membership function. In this work we selected five fuzzy sets and a Gaussian membership function. This membership function is more complex in comparison with a triangle-shaped function, but with better results in most cases [31]. Afterwards, the experts' knowledge, in a form of a set of rules, is extracted. This is based on the experts' experience, using questionnaires/interviews. The final rule set can be refined using an experts' panel. Below some sample rules for Cognitive Resilience FIS are presented:

(a) If "*Organization Identity*" is very high and "*Sense making*" is very high then the "*Cognitive Resilience*" is very high.

Fig. 2. The process of developing FIS for evaluation of resilience in DRN

(b) If *"Organization high"* is high and *"Sense making"* is medium then the *"Cognitive Resilience"* is Medium.
(c) If *"Organization Identity"* is very how and *"Sense making"* is very low then the *"Cognitive Resilience"* is Medium.
(d) If *"Organization Identity"* is high and *"Sense making"* is Low then the *"Cognitive Resilience"* is Medium.
(e) If *"Organization Identity"* is very Low and *"Sense making"* is very Low then the *"Cognitive Resilience"* is very Low.

The last three steps comprise an iterative process to make sure that the model will work properly.

In order to confirm the validity of the model, a typical three-step process was used which includes face validity, extreme conditions test, and behavior analysis. In "face validity" the rules are rechecked to make sure they are acceptable and satisfy the logic of relationships between the variables. Extreme conditions test is used to make sure that the model could respond properly to critical situations which are usually on the border, such as extreme conditions of variables. Finally, behavioral analysis is a way to analyze the behavior of the system when values of input variables are increasing, at a constant rate, from their minimum to their maximum (or from max to min) one by one while the others remain constant. This can provide detailed information about the system and its performance so any deviation from expected situation or illogical behavior should be analyzed and by imposing new rules the model could be corrected to be acceptable. Figure 3 shows the high-level view of the model.

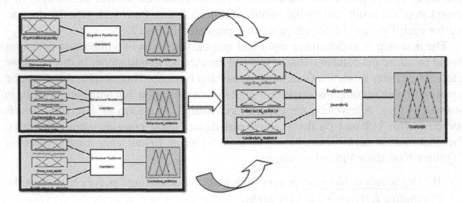

Fig. 3. Architecture of Resilience Evaluation model (Hybrid Intelligent system)

As mentioned above, four FISs are developed and all should be analyzed one by one, while the hybrid system also needs to be verified as it could be an erroneous infusion model. Figure 4 depicts the rules and output surface for "Behavioral Resilience", presenting the relation between "Preparedness" and "Resourcefulness". This is an example and by analyzing each relation unacceptable conditions/rules could be recognized.

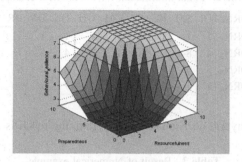

Fig. 4. Graphical representation of the rules for behavioral resilience

Figure 5 shows the example of behavioral analysis which is used in this work. As it can be seen, the behavior of the system when one of the indicators (preparedness) is increasing from minimum to maximum value (0 to 10) and the others are fixed (5) is presented. Similarly, different combinations should be analyzed to verify the model.

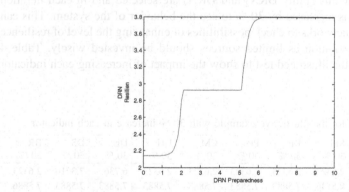

Fig. 5. The behavior of the system in case of change in preparedness while all other indicators remain constant

The key benefits of the introduced model, more than measuring the level of resilience, is the ability to simulate different scenarios to recognize which indicator could affect more the resilience of the network in each condition to be investigated. This can help managers to select appropriate combinations of solutions to enhance the resilience of the network in an efficient way.

5 Case Study

In this section, the applicability of the proposed model is demonstrated by using an illustrative example and real case study. For numerical example four types of DRNs with the following information are considered (Table 2).

Table 2. Initial information for a numerical example

DRN$_i$	OI	SM	RF	PP	CM	UH	DE	DS	BR
DRN$_1$	1	1	1	1	1	1	1	1	1
DRN$_2$	4	8	8	4	4	3	4	6	7
DRN$_3$	3	5	6	5	6	6	6	4	5
DRN$_4$	7	7	7	7	7	7	7	7	7

By employing a hybrid decision-support system, the result is as below (Table 3).

Table 3. Result of Numerical example

DRN$_1$ Resilience	DRN$_2$ Resilience	DRN$_3$ Resilience	DRN$_4$ Resilience
0.9084	2.6323	3.7788	7.5883

As discussed in previous section, the advantage of the proposed model is the ability to simulate different scenarios to investigate which indicator affects more the resilience in each case and should be in priority of investment to increase the level of resilience of the network. To show this ability DRN$_2$ and DRN$_4$ are selected and in each iteration one of the indicators is increased by 30 % to see the behavior of the system. This can help managers of the networks to check possibilities of enhancing the level of resilience and find an optimal solution as limited sources should be invested wisely. Table 4 presents the result of the illustrated test to show the impact of increasing each indicator (one by one).

Table 4. Result for the illustrative example with 30 % increase in each indicator

	OI 30 %	SM 30 %	RF 30 %	PP 30 %	CM 30 %	UH 30 %	DE 30 %	DS 30 %	BR 30 %
DRN$_2$	2.6324	2.6323	2.6323	2.6323	2.6323	2.6323	6.736	7.3716	2.6323
DRN$_4$ Resilience	7.5883	8.5746	7.5883	7.5883	7.5883	7.5883	7.5883	7.5883	7.5886

As it can be seen, for DRN$_2$, the best strategies are investment on Deference to Expertise (DE) and Deep Social Capital (DS), while for DRN$_4$ Sense Making (SM) is the best investment target.

After demonstrating the capability of the introduced model by an illustrative example, a real case study was implemented. Red Crescent/Red Cross organizations due to their nature have to be prepared for prompt action to disasters. They are usually the first formal group to respond in natural disasters and increasing the level of resilience is part of their strategic plan. They include a combination of professionals and volunteers while, at the same time, they have several organizations to support their activities. For the case study, a Red Crescent organization from a Middle Eastern country was selected. The selected country has a long history in natural disasters such as earth quakes and floods. In several cases the rescue network was affected while as a rescue team they had to keep operation going on. The first step was to measure the level of criteria and process them to feed the model. Each criterion from Fig. 1 (details in Table 1) was "measured" by questions which were representing the sub-criteria. Seven selected managers who are experts in the organization answered questionnaires. The final scores to be used by model resulted from the aggregation of information in the questionnaires using the average of sub-criteria (which were expressed in the form of questions).

For instance, Organizational Identity (OI) had five sub-criteria which were turned into questions. Each person had to answer all questions and give a number between 0 and 100 (percentage). Below you can find an example of question.

"How strong is the sense of visions, goals and values in the organization?"

Then the average of all five criteria/answers is calculated.

OI_{Qi} = Average(C_j) wheere C_j is representing the jth criterion, j = [1:5] and i = [1:7].

In the last step information from all questionnaires should be aggregated and here average of the values were used. Final value, OI_{total} is the average of OI_{Qi} where max " i" is the number of filled-in questionnaires.

OI_{total} = Average (OI_{Qi}), where i = [1:7].

Table 5 presents the result of this measurement process.

Table 5. Information for the case study in percentage

DRN	OI	SM	RF	PP	CM	UH	DE	DS	BR
DRN$_{Red\ Crescent}$	62 %	60 %	63 %	50 %	56 %	53 %	58 %	55 %	59 %

Table 6 presents the level of resilience using introduced model:

Table 6. Level of Resilience in the Case Study (from 0 to 10)

Resilience	Contextual Resilience	Behavioral Resilience	Cognitive Resilience
3.7920	3.2353	7.4051	5.0017

Finally, for scenario planning, the value of each criterion is increased 30 % and the impact on total resilience is calculated. Table 7 shows the result and, as it can be seen, "Broad Resource Network" is the most relevant criteria for investment in this case.

Table 7. Red Crescent Resilience in case of 30 % increase in each indicator (From 0 to 10)

30 % increase in main criteria	OI	SM	RF	PP	CM	UH	DE	DS	BR
DRN$_{Red\ Crescent}$	3.7920	3.7920	3.7924	3.6640	3.7942	3.7942	3.7920	3.7920	7.2976

6 Discussion and Future Work

Collaborative Networks, as an emerging discipline, open a new window to enhance our capability to confront complex problems. One of the most difficult cases is to work under stressful conditions of post hazards situation. Rescue Networks have to work in critical situations while, as a member of society, they are also under the influence of the event. Disasters are unpredictable and it is crucial to make sure DRNs work as resilient structures able to recover immediately from any crisis and to start their mission with minimum delay. In this paper a conceptual model based on contextual, behavioral, and cognitive resilience was employed to develop an intelligent hybrid decision system for assessing the level of resilience of DRNs. Face validity of the rules, extreme condition test, and behavioral analysis of the system were used to verify the model. At the end, the applicability of the model was illustrated by using a case study. The model not only helps to quantify the concept of resilience for DRNs but it also gives us a tool for scenario planning/testing in a virtual environment. The most important reason to select the "Fuzzy Inference System" was its ability to deal with imprecise data and the capability to make a bridge between knowledge of experts (as the only available source of data in this case) and decision support system. Other alternatives such as MCDM or statistical methods have their own strengths and weaknesses for information fusion but are not suitable for this type of problem which has characteristics such as unclear relation between variables, no knowledge about synergies or redundancies between them and lack of historical data to recognize the pattern.

As future work, the plan is to implement the introduced model in more real cases to improve the system. Further we are planning to improve the capability of the model by considering the role of time and interrelation between resilience indicators.

Acknowledgements. This work was partially funded by the Center of Technology and Systems and FCT- PEST program UID/EEA/00066/2013 (Impactor project).

References

1. Yondong, Z.: Social networks and reduction of risk in disasters: an example of Wenchuan earthquake. In: Yeung, W.J.J., Yap, M.T. (eds.) Economic Stress, Human Capital, and Families in Asia, vol. 4, pp. 171–182. Springer, Berlin (2013)
2. Camarinha-Matos, L.M., Afsarmanesh, H., Boucher, X.: The role of collaborative networks in sustainability. In: Camarinha-Matos, L.M., Boucher, X., Afsarmanesh, H. (eds.) PRO-VE 2010. IFIP AICT, vol. 336, pp. 1–16. Springer, Heidelberg (2010)
3. Boin, A., McConnell, A.: Preparing for Critical infrastructure breakdowns: the limits of crisis management and the need for resilience. J. Contingencies Crisis Manag. **15**, 50–59 (2007)
4. Arsovski, S.; Andre, P.; Đordevic, M.; Aleksic, A.: Resilience of automotive sector: a case study. In: Proceedings of 4th International Quality Conference, Kragujevac, Serbia (May 2010), pp. 89–104. http://www.cqm.rs/2010/3.html
5. Bhamra, R., Dani, S., Burnard, K.: Resilience: the concept, a literature review and future directions. Int. J. Prod. Res. **49**(18), 5375–5393 (2011)

6. Camarinha-Matos, L.M.: Collaborative networks in industry and the role of PRO-VE. Int. J. Prod. Manag. Eng. **2**(2), 53–56 (2014)
7. Kapucu, N., Hu, Q.: Understanding multiplexity of collaborative emergency management networks. Am. Rev. Public Adm. [Internet], 23 Oct 2014. http://arp.sagepub.com/content/early/2014/10/23/0275074014555645
8. Park, J., Seager, T.P., Rao, P.S., Convertino, M., Linkov, I.: Integrating risk and resilience approaches to catastrophe management in engineering systems. Risk Anal. **33**(3), 356–376 (2013)
9. Noran, O.: Collaborative disaster management: an interdisciplinary approach. J. Comput. Ind. **65**(6), 1032–1040 (2014)
10. Brown, K.: Global environmental change I: a social turn for resilience? Prog. Hum. Geogr. **38**, 107–117 (2014)
11. Folke, C., Hahn, T., Olsson, P., Norberg, J.: Adaptive governance of social-ecological systems. Ann. Rev. Environ. Resour. **30**, 441–473 (2005)
12. Ponis, S., Koronis, E.: Supply chain resilience: definition of concept and its formative elements. J. Appl. Bus. Res. **28**(5), 921–930 (2012)
13. Christopher, M., Peck, H.: Building the resilient supply chain. Int. J. Logist. Manag. **15**(2), 1–13 (2004)
14. Francis, R., Bekera, B.: A metric and frameworks for resilience analysis of engineered and infrastructure systems. Reliab. Eng. Syst. Safety **121**, 90–103 (2014)
15. Lengnick-Hall, C.A., Beck, T.E., Lengnick-Hall, M.L.: Developing a capacity for organizational resilience through strategic human resource management. Hum. Resour. Manag. Rev. **21**, 243–255 (2011)
16. Lengnick-Hall, C.A., Beck, T.E.: Adaptive fit versus robust transformation: how organizations respond to environmental change. J. Manag. **31**(5), 538–575 (2005)
17. Vogus, T.J.; Sutcliffe, K.M.: Organizational resilience: towards a theory and research agenda. In: IEEE International Conference on Systems, Man and Cybernetics, pp 3418–3422, Montreal, Canada (2–7 October 2007)
18. Akgün, A.E., Keskin, H.: Organisational resilience capacity and firm product innovativeness and performance. Int. J. Prod. Res. **52**(23), 6918–6937 (2014)
19. Rose, A.: Economic resilience to natural and man-made disasters: multidisciplinary origins and contextual dimensions. Environ. Hazards **7**(4), 383–398 (2007)
20. Aleksić, A., Stefanović, M., Arsovski, S., Tadić, D.: An assessment of organizational resilience potential in SMEs of the process industry, a fuzzy approach. J. Loss Prev. Process Ind. **26**(6), 1238–1245 (2013)
21. Azusa, K., Hiroyuki, Y.: Organizational resilience: an investigation of key factors that promote the rapid recovery of organizations. Acad. J. Interdiscip. Stud. **2**(9), 188–194 (2013)
22. Huber, G.J., Gomes, J.O., de Carvalho, P.V.: A program to support the construction and evaluation of resilience indicators. Work **41**, 2810–2816 (2012)
23. Azadeh, A., Salehi, V., Arvan, M., Dolatkhah, M.: Assessment of resilience engineering factors in high-risk environments by fuzzy cognitive maps: a petrochemical plant. Saf. Sci. **68**, 99–107 (2014)
24. Lengnick-Hall, C.A., Beck, T.E.: Resilience capacity and strategic agility: prerequisites for thriving in a dynamic environment (2009). http://business.utsa.edu/wps/mgt/0059MGT-199-2009.pdf
25. Zellweger, T.M., Nason, R.S., Nordqvist, M., Brush, C.G.: Why do family firms strive for nonfinancial goals? An organizational identity perspective. Entrepreneurship Theor. Pract. **37**(2), 229–248 (2013)

26. Maitlis, S., Christianson, M.: Sensemaking in organizations: taking stock and moving forward. Acad. Manag. Ann. **8**(1), 57–125 (2014)
27. Zhong, S.: Developing an evaluation framework for hospital disaster resilience: tertiary hospitals of Shandong province, China. PhD thesis (2014). http://eprints.qut.edu.au/76090/
28. Khan, S.A., Lederer, A.L., Mirchandani, D.A.: Top management support, collective mindfulness, and information systems performance. J. Int. Technol. Inf. Manag. **22**, 94–122 (2013)
29. DuBrin, A.J.: Handbook of Research on Crisis leadership in Organizations. Edward Elgar Pub, Cheltenham (2013)
30. Jassbi, J., Alavi, S.H., Serra, P.J.A., Ribeiro R.A.: Transformation of a Mamdani FIS to first order Sugeno FIS. In: Fuzzy Systems Conference (FUZZ-IEEE 2007). IEEE (2007)
31. Markowski, A.S., Mannan, M.: S: Fuzzy risk matrix. J. Hazard. Mater. **159**(1), 152–157 (2008)

Building Resilient SCs: Mapping and Measuring Key Value Drivers Through a Multi-perspective and Multi-stakeholder Value Creation Framework Based on Intangible Assets

Stephane Pagano[✉] and Gilles Neubert

EMLYON Business School,
UMR5600, 23, Avenue G. de Collongue, 69134 Ecully, France
{Pagano,GNeubert}@EM-Lyon.com

Abstract. Until recently, the evolution of strategy and of business models mainly focused on shareholder Value Creation with global offshoring and outsourcing. The competitive cost models of globalized flows, translated in worldwide Supply Chains, with intensive energy consumption of fossil fuels and optimized processes with outsourcing to specialized agents, highly dependent on globalized infrastructures resources and markets. Our approach is that to build resilient companies and networks, all the stakeholders of the Supply Chain must be able to shift and align their perspectives, understand, map, value and document the key drivers that constitute the core competences needed, the appropriate intangible assets. Our proposition is a methodology to analyze, map and measure the key drivers of Value Creation through of multi-perspective and multi-stakeholder framework, based on intangible assets.

Keywords: Value creation · Collaborative ecosystems · Resilient SC · Intangible assets · Stakeholders

1 Introduction

In a rapidly changing environment, companies have to face many challenges while the competitive and technological environment keeps evolving at a fast pace: Globalization of markets through trade agreements and communication technologies, consumers' maturity and power of influence, strong trend towards a service-focused and dematerialized economy. Beyond a direct confrontation on their markets, with a particular focus on costs, firms have seen their competitiveness being challenged over new dimensions [1]. Consumers and non-profit organizations' pressure, legislation from states trying to limit externalities and reduce climate change impacts, real time information technologies being exploited by versatile consumers and investors. In a time where cost based competition remains harder and harder to maintain, the integration of stakes such as those addressed by Corporate Social Responsibility sets new standards for innovating strategies and competitiveness [2]. These concepts acknowledge that failing to do so inevitably leads to higher pressure from stakeholders, rising costs of environmental issues, and development of legal

© IFIP International Federation for Information Processing 2015
L.M. Camarinha-Matos et al. (Eds.): PRO-VE 2015, IFIP AICT 463, pp. 159–169, 2015.
DOI: 10.1007/978-3-319-24141-8_14

measures from states enforcing companies to share more of the value they create. All of these rising global risks on value creation, if not destroying value by rising sources of pressure on competitiveness.

The paper is organized as follow: after the introduction, the second part reviews essential concepts underlying our approach, the third part presents our framework and gives some details on our research and propositions. The fourth part presents some findings, while the conclusion draws expected contributions and future operational outputs.

2   Context

Today's value chains consist of globally spread stakeholders, globally spread production processes, global distribution and retail channels to reach clients. It is very fragile in essence, either because of geopolitical bottlenecks, environmental and social issues or because of natural disasters [3]. As part of the procurement process, the purchasing function is a fundamental hub for the firms, upstream of the Supply Chain, orchestrating and managing fundamental inputs in term of value creation, adapting to business models evolutions by configuring the SC to create and capture value.

2.1   Value and Value Creation

Value is a multi-perspective concept that extends beyond the limits of the firm. Globalization and technological innovation have reorganized the way value is created and delivered through dynamic networks or chains of interconnected firms or supply chain. This raises the question on how a particular relationship helps a firm creating value in terms of offerings, and what factor(s) are essential to successfully establish a particular relationship [4]. In a globalized Supply Chain, the strategic models of Value Creation based on arms-length confrontation with suppliers has led many companies on a short term value creation path, which meant value destruction for many suppliers and their economic ecosystem, impacting their entire value chain and their stakeholders. The value proposition is a strategic concept that allows firms to better analyze and describe their competencies and capacities, on the strategic as well as on the operational levels [5]. The deployment of the concept of Value Proposition had a significant impact on operational models of firms [6, 7].

To take into consideration these impacts, we position the Supply Management and the Supply Chain at the heart of the strategic models of firms.

2.2   Corporate Social Responsibility

There's an increasing pressure to consider the environmental and social aspects in purchasing policies: expectations are rising from stakeholders such as customers, the general public, NGOs, and governments who now hold companies responsible, not only for their own actions, but also all the partners within the supply chain [8–11].

Corporate Social Responsibility is a concept that is becoming mainstream because it raises the question of establishing sound and balanced relationships between companies, a wider type of stakeholders, and their environment, at all different levels: global, regional and local, but also strategic, tactical and operational. CSR approach advocates the idea that companies need to change their business models and value propositions, actually integrating the idea of creating value not only for themselves, but also for a larger number of stakeholders. The Strategic Intention of the firm can practically be translated into strategic, tactical and operational actions.

The translation of this focus in the Supply Chain and the purchasing process reflects in a growing number of international recommendations and is now common in academics [12]. The focus on sustainability reporting initiatives and on CSR shows the necessity for companies to adopt a multi-perspective approach on the supplier selection and management: purchasing process and supply chain play a strategic role, which must go beyond optimization of processes, and take into account the temporal dimensions of the ROI (short, mid and long term) and the management of intangibles.

2.3 Relationships and Risks Mitigation

Usual competitive strategies based on competitive advantage, such as Porter's models [13] or Resource Based View [14], can't last. To address this issue, firms have investigated other domains: process optimization to save resources, flexibility, changes in relationship with other partners to secure exclusive access to suppliers because upsurge in globalized externalization and sourcing of trade, and the use of the Internet, has enlarged purchasers' accesses. Changes in organizational forms involve more decision-makers. These developments impact the complexity and importance of purchasing decisions [15–17]. Supplier management is a key issue in supply chain performances and this reflects in a continuing growth of publications [18–21]. Since suppliers can represent up to 90 % of firms turnover in industrial companies, the potential impact of inappropriate portfolio of suppliers can seriously impact the value of a company. The question of risks, systemic and global, predictable or not, strategic or external must be part of the strategy of firms [22].

At first, firms developed collaborative strategies, internal then between business units and departments, based on information sharing, and co-development of products and services. Instead of becoming experts, firms managed to collaborate with partners that could provide a competitive advantage [23]. Collaboration became a model for buyer-supplier relationship. Still, this remained in a narrow scope, without considering other stakeholders and that it's at a strategic level that is designed the Value Proposition for which the tactical and operational actions are translated. Firms are interconnected with their societal, natural and economic environment [24] thus depending on these in term of competitiveness: trained employees, infrastructures, communications, political stability. The state of the environment impacts the firms activity, the operational costs, the availability of the resources, and the value of the firms viewed by the stakeholders. Global environment is not just about financial crises and competitions: human operations and natural catastrophes can generate "future simultaneous shocks to systems (that) could trigger the 'perfect global storm', with potentially insurmountable consequences" [25]. These risks are putting a high pressure on companies that need to adapt rapidly to innovative or disruptive situations.

Companies, their suppliers and networks of partners need to be aligned to fulfill the strategy to deliver the value and adapt rapidly whatever challenge arises, and in this situation, a power relation may turn irrelevant if not destructive. To be resilient, companies and their networks have to build business ecosystems in a systemic thinking with relationships that are beyond transactional, with constant feedback, collaborative models, creating and extracting value in cascade and in interaction.

3   Research Framework and Method

The purchasing function is the architect of the globally spread value chain: many functions are now outsourced. In this regard, the value of the firm largely depends on the value purchased from the suppliers and appropriately delivered to internal customers, hence giving purchasing departments a fundamental role to build collaborative, cooperative and successful relationships both internally and externally.

3.1   Focusing on Intangibles

As we see it, creating value extends beyond the limits of the firm and must question the different dimensions and boundaries of the firm, their strategies and business models, what value they place at the heart of their value proposition and how they intend to create, capture and share value (Fig. 1). This requires considering internal organization of the firm, its networks of connections and partners, strategic models, its tangible and intangible assets and the notions of capital and investment. It is possible to comprise in the same model different values such as economic, financial, marketing but also intangible assets such as, management, services, strategic position or technical performance [26].

Though there is an abundant literature in economy and management on intangibles assets [27], we think that there is still a great work to do to operationalize intangible assets management with value creation for firms, according to a multi-perspective view, namely time frames, and according to a multi-stakeholder view, that is, in term of value created or destroyed by the firm for the different stakeholders in the firm's ecosystem. Our objective is to identify the value drivers in the organizational processes, going beyond the drivers already mastered by the buyers and more broadly the supply-chain: cost, quality, lead-time, financial performances and risk mitigation. The stake here is to demonstrate the contribution of intangible assets in the processes, seen here as drivers of successful relationships, by identifying their strategic importance in the interactions taking place in the processes. Finally, our applied research proposition is to build tools for the management of value creation in the buying and supply-chain processes that integrate these new perspectives.

Measure, management and value creation in the firm are spread over time and must take into account the stakeholders. To ensure the longevity of the firm, the following dimensions and perspective must be included in the processes:

– The time horizon of the firms' strategies;
– Value creation/destruction for the firm and its ecosystem;
– Actual place of intangible assets as drivers of competitiveness and value creation.

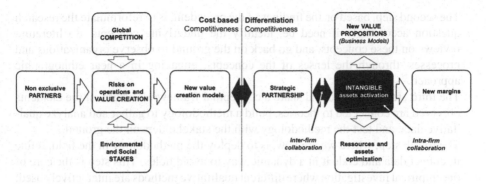

Fig. 1. Placing intangible assets at the heart of renewed value propositions.

To achieve this, we are constructing on an approach by value "enablers" or "drivers" for future value creation [28], mapping intangible assets, processes and stakeholders through events that will eventually generate economic value and performance for the firm.

3.2 Ground for the Research

The global research ground for our projects is based on several companies operating in different industries. For this specific project, three companies offered the ground for initial explorations. Later on, among the three initial, two offered a long-standing partic- ipation for the conduct of the full research project for a period of two years.

- The first company, company A, is a food-products corporation operating on the global markets of waters, specialized nutrition and dairy products.
- The second company, company B, is an affiliate of the first, operating in France, specialized in dairy food and infant nutrition.
- The third company, company C, is an international family-owned group, operating in 13 countries, specialized in aerolic and thermal systems for the building industry.

3.3 Empirical Method

Our position is that "the organizational world is socially constructed" and that "the people constructing their organizational realities are *knowledgeable agents* (…) and can explain their thoughts, intentions, and actions" [29]. We build an iterative process where in each step, fieldwork confronts hypothesis and theory constructs elaborated on the previous ground observation. It borrows empirical investigation methodologies found in cases study methods specifically qualitative, in an interactive way so that the compo- nents of the research, i.e. purpose, context, questions, methods and validity of the research are always considered simultaneously at each step.

- The first step of the research is an exploration where we confront our initial question, "value creation and collaborative relationships" to the stakeholders of the research ground. We state a hypothesis and test it.

- The second step, based on the findings of the precedent, is to reformulate the research question accordingly if need be, identify the underlying concepts, do literature reviews on these concepts, and go back on the ground to observe organizations and processes, through the lenses of the concepts, engaging in a near ethnographic approach.
- The third step is to build and share a conceptual framework where all the elements observed are connected to theories, build a methodology to gather and analyze qualitative data, and test the methodology with the stakeholders on the ground.
- The fourth step, where we are now, is to deploy the methodology in the field, refine it, collect data and code it in a dynamic way to avoid holes. This step is the core of the empirical investigation where different qualitative methods are interactively used: observation, interviews, questionnaires and documents analysis.
- The fifth and last step is two-fold: in terms of scientific research, we will have to decide which form will take the conclusion. In terms of applied research, we will negotiate on outputs that help companies that provided the ground to operationalize the scientific work.

4   Main Outcomes

As this research project is still ongoing, we only present partial findings from selected phases tested in the field. This communication wishes to present the research method, the principles of the practical output, and main outcomes of the empirical work.

4.1   Initial Outcomes

To initiate the research, we extended on a previous literature review on collaboration [26] and completed it with a literature review on value and on value creation. Then, we elaborated documents and presentations to share with the participating companies. Afterwards, we organized informal meetings with two groups of buyers from the three companies to share these views and gather some qualitative data regarding the proposed definitions and approaches.

The groups consisted in thirteen buyers from the company C, and two head of purchasing departments from companies A and B. These two meetings were conducted by asking open-ended questions to the audience and animating the discussions to gain insights. The initial open-ended questions were about the criteria used by the buyers and their managers to evaluate the success or the failure of a relationship with their suppliers.

While we were trying to find a pattern linking levels of collaboration and levels of (perceived) success, buyers seized the opportunity to focus on the fact that the "life" of the buyer-supplier relationship is as complex as any human based interaction between organizations and services, because, according to the buyers, it greatly relies on the "qualities" of the organization, carried and developed by persons of both sides of the relation (buyers, vendors, and other stakeholders involved).

We gathered structured data to complete the fuzzy findings of the meetings, by distributing formal surveys of the same questions, based on a pre-existing model [26] but providing this time precise criteria associated to likert-like scales. Buyers were asked to evaluate collaborative relationships criteria, for a relationship they estimated as successful, and for a relationship they estimated as failing. The results of criteria evaluation showed that certain collaboration criteria are consistently highly rated with a relationship considered as successful. On the opposite side, few criteria are consistently rated when it comes to failed relationships so buyers tend to have a more fuzzy perception, as far as criteria are concerned, of what characterizes a failed relationship.

The comments in the surveys were very consistent with the feedback from the meetings. In the cases of successful relationships, some buyers insisted in their comments on the facts that the personal behavior and skills of their corresponding contacts were the main reasons why they were satisfied with the relationship. In the cases of relationships considered as failing, it's the quality of the interpersonal relationships and organizational issues that were described.

Though in the same organization, each individual deals with a series of expectations and means to achieve them, according to different perception, interpretation and perspective. Participants proposed discussions based on their experience while we were biased trying to use a pre-conceived model: our assumptions assumed collaborative relationships *meant* successful relationships, which *meant* value creation.

4.2   Empirical Outcomes on the Tools Constructs

To help companies in creating value through a multi-perspective and multi-stakeholder model, we are building a practical methodology to analyze and manage value creation in the processes, to objectively link the activation of intangible assets to value creation and achieve performance. At the heart of the methodology, we want to analyze the drivers represented by intangible assets (human capital, relational capital, structural capital) to connect them with the value proposition made to the clients.

To do so, we need to clarify what happens in what we call a fuzzy box (Fig. 2) where players activate processes and stakeholders to achieve objectives and create value. Key steps here are to identify *helping* events occurring during the life of the project to evaluate the role and contribution of intangibles assets, and *breaking* events to capitalize on experience and construct feedback.

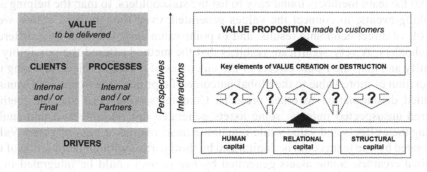

Fig. 2. The fuzzy box.

We have elaborated an interactive tool that allows the mapping, contextualization and linking of the stakeholders, their interactions and the value created or destroyed for each one of them (Fig. 3).

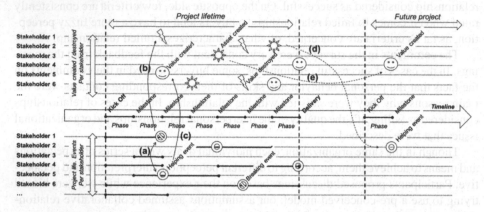

Fig. 3. Visual canvas, mapping events, value and stakeholders' interactions.

Helping and breaking points of a given projects' life are positioned on time-lines. Events' interactions (a) are visually mapped. It is possible to map the value destruction caused by breaking events (b) and value created by helping events (c). Assets created during one project can be identified as a significant source of a helping event in a future project (d), or directly create value (e). A concept that is at the core of our research work is that assets mobilized in one project are probably the result of a previous investment, just like assets generated in the current project can be drivers of future value.

To validate the method and the tools with the participating companies to the research project, we have organized a workshop with a team from each of the firms. The three teams add-up to a total of seven participants with varying profiles. To reinforce triangulation of this experience, we have asked the participating teams to bring to the workshop the story of a past project, that ended successfully or that failed.

All the team members found easy to list the stakeholders, to map the helping and breaking events, to connect the values generated, even though these values were outside of direct economic results, and to point value destructions for the different stakeholders. A very significant result is that the method offered the possibility to identify and map the ripple effects of the outcomes of a given project, allowing the affectation of more value to the global outcome of a project due to previously unaccounted dissemination to other projects. Comments were here that the method offered unsuspected outputs: some assets generated are reusable and thus multiplying their effects and value while remaining unaccounted or miss-affected. Value generated by one team could be capitalized by third parties without recognition of the original creators. Some assets generated by one project could be integrated in an innovative Business Models not foreseen before.

5 Conclusion

Two participating companies offered to follow one project each, during the full length of the projects. These two projects found their origin in the apparition of an important threat to their operations that needed urgent responses involving many internal and external stakeholders of their value and supply chain. When the incident or the pressure arises, the organizations temporarily reacts to respond to the issues in a resilient fashion: they appoint a project manager with appropriate credentials to mobilize all the departments of the company in a transversal team and mobilize the web of their partners, supply chain and value chain, to initiate multi-level tactical actions.

Their resiliency relies on an adaptive line:

1. Companies follow their normal operations;
2. They get hit by a stressful event that impacts their operations and puts them at risk in term of viability;
3. They create a temporary structure, mobilizing the full web of internal and external stakeholders;
4. They elaborate a multi tactical strategy to have appropriate responses, deploy them to adapt or rebuild the necessary flows;
5. Once the response has been delivered and the crisis resolved, the temporary project structure is dissolved;
6. They return to their "normal" operations.

This ability for firms to adapt, reconfigure and respond, greatly relies on the capacity of the different stakeholders involved to collaborate and mutually adjust to each-others, diffuse information and realign. All this relies almost exclusively on the very own capacities of the actors involved (human, relational and structural capital), thus illustrating the central importance of intangible assets.

Very formalized processes can alter the adaptive capacities of companies and networks, building the case for a transversal, project based organization of processes and a qualitative approach of relationships and information sharing, all these heavily relying on the intangible assets of companies. Our objective is to identify the value drivers in the organizational processes, going beyond the drivers already mastered by the buyers and more broadly the supply-chain: cost, quality, lead-time, financial performances and risk mitigation.

While purchasing managers often apply methods focused on savings, a focus that limits their scope of action, participants to our research acknowledged positively our approach and identified intangible assets that could be drivers of the overall "value" created, because "any factor that enhances operational performance" and allows strategic alignment of the actors potentially generates "value". This is consistent with the literature review [26].

This research builds meaningful and applied methods to track, document and manage intangibles assets in response to internal or external pressure on value creation. It provides tangible and practical ways to objectivate very qualitative concepts all actors recon as essential to maintain and develop successful operations but have very few if no tools to leverage on in an environment governed by quantitative methods.

Expected outputs are: a tool to analyze the strategy of the firm and how it is translated along the supply chain, an analysis grid to identify and take into account all the stakeholders, a tool for mapping, contextualizing and linking the stakeholders, their interactions and the value created or destroyed for each one of them. These deliverables are being developed and refined through fieldwork.

Among scientific contributions, we expect this research will contribute to Resource-Based View theory, to Knowledge Management, to Sustainable Supply Chain and to Supply Chain performance.

Acknowledgements. This project is part of the PEAK (Purchasing European Alliance for Knowledge). The authors would like to thank THESAME, the companies that co-finance this research project, and more generally the financial supporters of the PEAK program: member companies of the program, the F2I (Fund for Innovation and Industry) funding structure of the UIMM (Union of Metal Industries and Crafting), the UDIMERA (Rhône-Alpes' Union Of Metallurgical and Electrical Industries), the Research Division of the Regional Council of Rhône-Alpes, and the General Council of Haute-Savoie which provides support to the Arve Industries competitiveness cluster.

References

1. Kim, W., Mauborgne, R.: Value innovation. Harvard Bus. Rev. **82**(7/8), 172–180 (1997)
2. Lash, J., Wellington, F.: Competitive advantage on a warming planet. Harvard Bus. Rev. **85**, 94–102 (2007)
3. Ambulkar, S., Blackhurst, J., Grawe, S.: Firm's resilience to supply chain disruptions: scale development and empirical examination. J. Oper. Manage. **33–34**, 111122 (2015)
4. Srivastava, V., Singh, T.: Value creation through relationship closeness. J. Strateg. Mark. **18**, 3–17 (2010)
5. Martinez, V., Bititci, U.S.: Aligning value propositions in supply chains. Int. J. Value Chain Manage. **1**, 6–18 (2006)
6. O'Dell, C., Grayson Jr., C.J.: Knowledge transfer: discover your value proposition. Strat. Leadersh. **27**, 10 (1999)
7. Bititci, U.S., Martinez, V., Albores, P., Parung, J.: Creating and managing value in collaborative networks. Int. J. Phys. Distrib. Logistics Manage. **34**, 251–268 (2004)
8. Jiang, B.: The effects of interorganizational governance on supplier's compliance with SCC: an empirical examination of compliant and non-compliant suppliers. J. Oper. Manage. **27**, 267–280 (2009)
9. Kovács, G.: Corporate environmental responsibility in the supply chain. J. Cleaner Prod. **16**, 1571–1578 (2008)
10. Goebel, P., Reuter, C., Pibernik, R., Sichtmann, C.: The influence of ethical culture on su plier selection in the context of sustainable sourcing. Int. J. Prod. Econ. Sustain. Dev. Manuf. Serv. **140**, 7–17 (2012)
11. Igarashi, M., de Boer, L., Fet, A.M.: What is required for greener supplier selection? A literature review and conceptual model development. J. Purchasing Supply Manage. **19**, 247–263 (2013)
12. Linton, J., Klassen, R., Jayaraman, V.: Sustainable supply chains: an introduction. J. Oper. Manage. **25**(6), 10751082 (2007)

13. Porter, M.E.: Competitive Advantage: Creating and Sustaining Superior Performance with a New Introduction, 1st edn. Free Press, New York (1998)
14. Barney, J.: Firm resources and sustained competitive advantage. J. Manage. **17**, 99 (1991)
15. De Boer, L., Labro, E., Morlacchi, P.: A review of methods supporting supplier selection. Eur. J. Purchasing Supply Manage. **7**, 75–89 (2001)
16. van Weele, A.J.: Purchasing and Supply Chain Management: Analysis, Strategy, Planning and Practice. Cengage Learning, Andover (2010)
17. Oshri, I., Kotlarsky, J., Willcocks, P.L.P.: The Handbook of Global Outsourcing and Offshoring. Palgrave Macmillan, London (2011)
18. Ho, W., Xu, X., Dey, P.K.: Multi-criteria decision making approaches for supplier evaluation and selection: a literature review. Eur. J. Oper. Res. **202**, 16–24 (2010)
19. Cao, M., Zhang, Q.: Supply chain collaboration: impact on collaborative advantage and firm performance. J. Oper. Manage. **29**, 163–180 (2011)
20. Wu, C., Barnes, D.: A literature review of decision-making models and approaches for partner selection in agile supply chains. J. Purchasing Supply Manage. **17**, 256–274 (2011)
21. Chai, J., Liu, J.N.K., Ngai, E.W.T.: Application of decision-making techniques in supplier selection: a systematic review of literature. Expert Syst. Appl. **40**, 3872–3885 (2013)
22. Kaplan, R.S., Mikes, A.: Managing risks: a new framework. Harvard Bus. Rev. **90**, 48–60 (2012)
23. MacCormack, A., Forbath, T.: Learning the fine art of global collaboration. Harvard Bus. Rev. **86**, 24–26 (2008)
24. Porter, M.E., Kramer, M.R.: The competitive advantage of corporate philanthropy. Harvard Bus. Rev. **80**, 56–69 (2002)
25. Howell, W.L.: World economic forum. In: Risk Response Network, Global risks 2013, World Economic Forum, Cologny, Geneva, Switzerland (2013)
26. Parung, J., Bititci, U.S.: A metric for collaborative networks. Bus. Process Manage. J. **14**, 654–674 (2008)
27. Sveiby, K.-E.: Methods for measuring intangible assets. http://www.sveiby.com/articles/IntangibleMethods.htm. Accessed 16 May 14
28. Marr, B., Schiuma, G., Neely, A.: Intellectual capital - defining key performance indicators for organizational knowledge assets. Bus. Process Manage. J. **10**, 551–569 (2004)
29. Gioia, D., Corley, K., Hamilton, A.: Seeking qualitative rigor in inductive research: notes on the Gioia methodology. Organ. Res. Methods **16**(1), 1531 (2012)

Building Business Resilience with Social Media in B2B Environments: The Emergence of Responsive Customer Relationship Management Processes on Twitter

Jyotirmoyee Bhattacharjya[(⊠)] and Adrian B. Ellison

Institute of Transport and Logistics Studies,
The University of Sydney, Sydney, NSW 2006, Australia
{jyotirmoyee.bhattacharjya,
adrian.ellison}@sydney.edu.au

Abstract. Companies operating in the business-to-consumer (B2C) space have been increasingly using the social media platform, Twitter, to conduct customer relationship management activities. Similar practices are also gradually emerging in business-to-business (B2B) environments. However, B2B service providers are yet to incorporate social media into their overall business strategy to the extent that this has become common practice amongst B2C companies. Engaging with customers over social media poses both risks and opportunities for companies. This paper examines the customer relationship management activities of a B2B service provider, Shopify, to identify opportunities for improving brand perception and business resilience.

Keywords: Business-to-business services · Social media · Twitter · Customer relationship management · Brand resilience · Shopify

1 Introduction

In recent years, there has been a rapid growth in the adoption of social media platforms for conducting B2C interactions. This is largely because companies around the world have recognized the need to build and protect their brands in the virtual environments in which consumers express their opinions and engage with their peer groups. The microblogging site, Twitter, has become the social media platform most widely adopted by Fortune 500 companies [2]. Previous research undertaken by the authors [1] has demonstrated that these companies are not only using Twitter for promotional purposes but for the provision of customer service as well. However, companies operating in the B2B space have not as yet adopted social media as extensively as their B2C counterparts and there is a lack of understanding amongst these firms regarding how social media could help the resilience of their brands [3, 4].

Nevertheless, some B2B service providers are beginning to take a strategic approach to their social media. This paper presents findings in relation to the customer relationship management (CRM) activities of a B2B company. The data presented here is part of a larger ongoing project initiated in December 2014 which has now collected

© IFIP International Federation for Information Processing 2015
L.M. Camarinha-Matos et al. (Eds.): PRO-VE 2015, IFIP AICT 463, pp. 170–177, 2015.
DOI: 10.1007/978-3-319-24141-8_15

over 5 million tweets (microblogs) from B2B and B2C companies. The uniqueness of the project lies in the fact that, unlike previous studies, it is designed to extract entire conversations rather than just tweets on a large scale.

2 Background and Literature Review

Social CRM or CRM 2.0, is a term coined by president of The 56 Group and leading CRM thinker, Paul Greenberg describes "a philosophy and a business strategy, supported by a technology platform, business rules, workflow, processes and social characteristics, designed to engage the customer in a collaborative conversation in order to provide mutually beneficial value in a trusted and transparent business environment. It's the company's response to the customer's ownership of the conversation" ([5, 6]). This definition highlights the need for a shift in focus from customer management to customer engagement in an era where the customer is in increasing control of the narrative due to the proliferation of social media platforms.

The combination of rapid technological changes and regulatory and geopolitical upheavals over the past decade have led companies to recognize the need for resilient strategies that allow them to adapt their business models as well as their marketing approaches as their local or global contexts evolve ([17, 18]). As an increasing number consumers around the world build their presence on social media platforms, companies have recognized that news travels fast through social networking sites and complacency is not an option in ensuring the resilience of their brands [7]. Dell, for instance, has a Social Media Listening Command Center to monitor customer conversations about its brand on social media platforms [8]. Online retailer Amazon has also been at the forefront of customer engagement via social media and attempts to address customer complaints through its Twitter based channel as quickly as possible [1]. PepsiCo and Gap are also amongst other big brand owners and retailers engaging customers in conversations about their products in order to keep abreast of brand perceptions and ensure brand resilience ([9, 10]).

However, as previously stated, while B2C companies have begun using social media sites to their advantage, B2B companies have been slow on the uptake ([3, 4]). The business software industry is the leading B2B sector in terms of social media activity, with Intel, Oracle and IBM being key players in the sector. The medical and pharmaceutical sector, with leaders such as Pfizer, Merck and GlaxoSmithKlein is the second most active sector. Other sectors, such as the B2B logistics sector are much less active on social media with only a few companies in each sector making a noticeable effort. For instance, the container shipping company, Maersk, is one of the few companies in the B2B logistics space that has been recognized for building its presence across social media channels [11]. It has over 34,000 followers on Twitter and over 2.2 million likes on Facebook. However, while B2B companies are beginning to building their presence on social media, few are using these platforms to provide customer service and build closer ties with customers. This is in significant contrast to the growing number of B2C companies who have dedicated customer service accounts on Twitter and are taking a proactive approach to engaging in conversations with customers to manage satisfaction and brand perception.

3 Research Method

Twitter allows users to post microblogs or tweets which are limited to 140 characters in length. A user's timeline consists of tweets from accounts the user has chosen to follow on Twitter. These tweets can be accompanied by links, photos and videos and may be retweeted or replied to by the user. Tweets, retweets and responses are generally visible to the general public unless a direct message (DM) is sent by one user to another. The public nature of most of these interactions has led a diverse range of companies to monitor discussions about themselves and reach out to customers using this platform. The limitations posed by the Twitter application programming interface (API) on the extraction of tweets along a user's timeline along with a lack of tweet extraction tools with appropriate capabilities has led to most research till date being focused on the sentiment analysis of individual tweets ([12, 13]) rather than the conversations between interacting parties on this platform. For this research, a custom application package was developed to extract tweets from the timelines of companies of interest along with the conversations associated with these tweets. Each tweet on Twitter is allocated a unique identification number. The package developed for this research allows the tweets to be written to a MySQL database allocates identification numbers for the conversations thus allowing the subsequent analysis of not just tweets but conversations as well. Since December 2014, the package has been used to collect over 5 million tweets from companies and their customers. The data collection methodology is discussed in more detail by the authors in another paper [16]. The conversations are subsequently extracted from Twitter and uploaded to the text mining tool for coding and analysis.

4 Findings

One company that has both undergone business model transformation and adapted its marketing strategies to the proliferation of social media is the billion dollar Canadian ecommerce solution provider Shopify. The company started out as an online store for selling snowboards. It later developed its own e-commerce solution and developed into an e-commerce platform because of interest from other online retailers. As an e-commerce company, it allows businesses to set up online stores organize products, accept payments, and track orders. Its ecosystem comprises of small businesses, developers and end consumers. Although, its accounts on Twitter are oriented towards business customers, the platform allows it to get exposure to end consumers as well, thus giving it wider brand recognition. Its site received about 15-20 million visits per month in the last six months [15]. Around 10.5 % of the visits in the last three months have been from Twitter. It not only encourages customers to use the power of social media to create greater awareness of their offerings but has also been making a concerted effort to build its own presence on social media. As outlined in Table 1, it maintains a number of accounts on Twitter.

By way of comparison, Amazon, which has been on Twitter since February 2009, has over 13,400 tweets on its main account and over 1.84 million followers. Its customer service account, operational since October 2009, has over 242,000 tweets and 24,000 followers. The differences in the numbers are indicators of the different levels of

Table 1. Shopify's accounts on Twitter.

Account	Purpose	Tweets	Followers
@Shopify	Main account which also addresses customer service queries	16,900	157,000
@ShopifySupport	Dedicated customer service account	2,051	3,276
@ShopifyPicks	Product stream curated from over 160,000 Shopify powered stores around the world	4,542	28,100
@ShopifyDevs	News for developers about the Shopify API	687	3897
@ShopifyMasters	Advice on growing store traffic and sales based on success stories of Shopify customers	3552	5697
@ShopifyPartners	Account for the Shopify Partners Program	4602	7165

activity on Twitter in B2C and B2B contexts but both companies appear to take their presence on Twitter seriously as suggested by their verified accounts on Twitter. A Twitter verified account has a blue verified badge associated with the account [14]. Twitter does not accept verification requests but prioritizes highly sought users as part of their ongoing verification process.

4.1 Customer Service Interactions

As shown in Table 2, customers generally post tweets to make Shopify aware of problems with their system that are interrupting or slowing down business processes. Such tweets may also be accompanied by photos that communicate the problem. Monitoring the Twitter accounts allows Shopify to respond quickly on a public platform, thus allowing it to demonstrate its responsiveness to a wider customer base. The company also uses its Twitter accounts to provide information or direct customers to websites where the information may be available.

Table 2. A conversation with a customer following a system problem.

User	Tweet	UTC Date, Time
@notrab	Just spent 30 min editing a file with @Shopify templates and then it errors on save. Doh	5:22 am, Feb 20, 2015
@Shopify	@notrab Oh no! So sorry about that Jamie. We are working on getting everything back up as soon as possible!	5:35 am, Feb 20, 2015
@notrab	@Shopify That's ok! :)	5:35 am, Feb 20, 2015

In the previous example Shopify was able to inform the customer that it was working on the problem. In other instances the platform allows the company to build goodwill by providing information that resolves a perceived problem (Table 3).

Like companies in the B2C space [1], Shopify uses Twitter in conjunction with other traditional channels for providing customer service such as email and phone.

Table 3. A conversation with a customer following a system problem.

User	Tweet	UTC Date, Time
@Misc_Goods_Co	@Shopify y?! [Image of popup error message]	7:27 am, Dec 19, 2014
@Misc_Goods_Co	@Shopify @ShopifySupport I'm very frustrated about this new POS fee. I only need to use POS a few times a year.	8:43 am, Dec 19, 2014
@Misc_Goods_Co	@Shopify @ShopifySupport I've been sitting here at my last minute pop up like a bozo trying to figure out why it's not working.	8:44 am, Dec 19, 2014
@Misc_Goods_Co	@Shopify @Shopifysupport very bad taste in my mouth right now	8:45 am, Dec 19, 2014
@Shopify	@Misc_Goods_Co Thank you for the feedback and very sorry for any frustration. It is free to process on Shopify Mobile.	8:51 am, Dec 19, 2014
@Misc_Goods_Co	@Shopify well that's cool. went from frustrated to pretty chill. wasn't aware of that change	9:00 am, Dec 19, 2014
@Shopify	@Misc_Goods_Co Thanks for letting us know. We are happy to help with other questions.	9:49 am, Dec 19, 2014

However, there are some risks associated with a social media presence. Customers may contact the company via Twitter if satisfactory customer service is not received promptly via other less public media but it may not be possible for the company to provide a resolution via the platform (e.g., Table 4). Thus while the conversation may suggest that the company hasn't been able to resolve problems promptly, someone (e.g., a potential customer) visiting its Twitter account may be left wondering whether the query was resolved to the customer's satisfaction. As with B2C companies, customers are found to rarely return to thank a company via the Twitter platform if the query is resolved via a more private channel.

Table 4. A conversation with a customer following a system problem that was originally communicated through a traditional channel.

User	Tweet	UTC Date, Time
@gooderdle	@ShopifySupport – as an early supporter of Shopify, we'd like to upgrade but keep our grandfathered "No transaction fee"… cc @Shopify	8:15 am, Jan 16, 2015
@Shopify	@gooderdle We'd be happy to look into that. Can you please contact our billing team – billing[at]shopify[dot]com..	8:52 am, Jan 16, 2015
@Shopify	What is your open ticket number?	8:54 am, Jan 16, 2015
@gooderdle	No open ticket number – been going back and forth over email and phone for a week with a "Sales Lead"	8:58 am, Jan 16, 2015

Even if a conversation starts on Twitter, Shopify may still divert the query to email (Table 5). Unlike B2C companies, Shopify makes very limited use of Twitter's direct messaging (DM) service to address problems that cannot be resolved in public.

Table 5. A conversation that starts on Twitter but has to be diverted to a different channel.

User	Tweet	UTC Date, Time
@Schappi	@Shopify heads up that I'm getting multiple reports of shipping methods not loading at checkout	8:40 pm, Dec 10, 2014
@Shopify	@Schappi Apologies for the delay. Are you still experiencing issues?	6:56 am, Dec 11, 2014
@Schappi	@Shopify yup we are still experiencing issues... 3 people today complained. Just migrated all stores to responsive to see if that fixes it.	8:04 pm, Dec 11, 2014
@Shopify	@Schappi Thanks for getting back to us. Please email support[at]shopify[dot]com with more info and respond with the ticket number.	8:34 am, Dec 12, 2014

4.2 Collaborative Approach to Marketing

The company appears to recognize the fact that the resilience of its ecosystem which comprises of a large number of small businesses is essential for its own resilience. It takes a collaborative approach to its marketing activities and uses its @ShopifyPicks account on Twitter to highlight products sold by companies that use Shopify as their ecommerce solution (Table 1). This allows small companies with modest resources, such as Stitch and Locke, to focus on their core businesses and provide customers with links to Shopify's main Twitter account instead of maintaining their own. There is both a downside and an upside to this approach. End consumers may approach Shopify directly with queries regarding products and services provided by Shopify's customers. The upside is that if it is handled well, this may create a positive impression of its brand beyond the B2B environment in which it operates (Table 6). In the conversation below, the customer adds a hashtag #brandPlus to show his appreciation for the prompt response. Hashtags are searchable on Twitter and allow users to easily find comments on particular topics.

The company also engages with developers via Twitter in two ways. On the one hand it keeps developers informed about changes to its API using the @ShopifyDevs and @ShopifyPartners accounts so they can continue to support and build solutions for their customers. On the other hand it encourages them to earn money by developing apps, designing themes or referring clients to the Shopify platform. The @Shopify-Partners account helps to highlight successful activities of partners and create a community atmosphere.

Table 6. Shopify's exposure to the B2C interface via Twitter.

User	Tweet	UTC Date, Time
@Marcus Kouric	@Shopify Hi there. I bought from stich and locke. My delivery address needs to be changed though, how do I go about this?	9:13 am, Dec 11, 2014
@Shopify	@MarcusKourie Please try contacting the store through their about us page or the original order notification.	9:24 am, Dec 11, 2014
@Marcus Kourie	@Shopify Thank you! Appreciate you prompt response. #brandPlus	3:19 am, Dec 12, 2014

5 Discussions

In the B2B environment there continues to be lower uptake of social media platforms for customer service and promotional activities that might help these companies build wider brand recognition and resilience. Those B2B companies who are present on social media are largely engaged in a one-way communication where the provision of news and updates seems to be the only purpose for maintaining the Twitter accounts. However, even though their levels of activity may be noticeably lower than those of the more active B2C companies on Twitter (e.g. Amazon), a small number of B2B companies such as Shopify are beginning to take a more strategic approach to this platform. In Shopify's case, this involves structuring its engagement with the members of its ecosystem using a number of dedicated accounts for specific purposes. Adequate resourcing of a social media strategy is essential for its success. For instance, Shopify was generally found to respond to customer and developer queries within the hour. The company's two-way engagement with small business customers, developers and consumers and its attempts to approach benefits to its ecosystem holistically through its accounts on Twitter makes it an exemplar amongst B2B companies. The ongoing longitudinal data collection project will examine the emerging trends in the practices of B2B companies around the world and provide further insights into how these practices can help to nurture resilient business ecosystems.

References

1. Bhattacharjya, J., Tripathi, S., Ellison A.B., Kitratporn, N.: Creation using social media in a virtual business model: how Amazon approaches customer service on Twitter. In: 24th International Business Information Management Association Conference on Crafting Global Competitive Economies: 2020 Vision Strategic Planning and Smart Implementation, pp. 2208–2215. Milan, Italy (2014)
2. Culnan, M., McHugh, P.J., Zubillaga, J.I.: How large U.S. companies can use Twitter and other social to gain business value. MIS Q. Executive **9**, 243–259 (2010)

3. Michaelidou, N., Siamagka, N.T., Christodoulides, G.: Usage, barriers and measurement of social media marketing: an exploratory investigation of small and medium brands. Ind. Mark. Manag. **40**, 1153–1159 (2011)
4. Swani, K., Brown, B.P., Milne, G.R.: Should tweets differ for B2B and B2C? An analysis of Fortune 500 companies' Twitter communications. Ind. Mark. Manag. **9**, 243–259 (2014)
5. Greenberg, P.: CRM at the Speed of Light: Social CRM Strategies, Tools, and Techniques for Engaging Your Customers. McGraw-Hill, New York (2009)
6. PGreenblog (2009). http://the56group.typepad.com/pgreenblog/2009/07/time-to-put-a-stake-in-the-ground-on-social-crm.html
7. Copulsky, J., Fritz, A., White, M.: Protecting your brand from saboteurs in a high-speed world. Deloitte Rev. **9**, 88–101 (2011)
8. Menchacha, L.: Dell's next step: The social media command center (2010). http://en.community.dell.com/dell-blogs/Direct2Dell/b/direct2dell/archive/2010/12/08/dell-s-next-step-the-social-media-listening-command-center
9. Bauerlein, V.: Gatorade's mission: sell more drinks. Wall Street J. (2010). http://www.wsj.com/articles/SB10001424052748703466704575489673244784924
10. Morales, G., Nemer, N., Bhattacharjya, J.: The impact of Twitter on customer relationship management within Mexican value chains. In: 1st International Conference on Value Chain Management - Modelling Value, Pre-Proceedings, vol. 2, pp. 219–239. Shaker Verlag, Aachen, Germany (2011)
11. Maersk Social. http://www.maersk.com/en/social
12. Jansen, B.J., Zhang, M., Sobel, K., Chowdhury, A.: Twitter power: Tweets as electronic word of mouth. J. Am. Soc. Inf. Sci. Technol. **60**, 2169–2188 (2009)
13. Liau, B.Y., Tan, P.P.: Gaining customer knowledge in low cost airlines through text mining. Ind. Manag. Data Syst. **114**, 1344–1359 (2014)
14. Twitter. https://support.twitter.com/articles/119135-faqs-about-verified-accounts#
15. Similarweb. http://www.similarweb.com/website/shopify.com?utm_source=checkpagerank.net&utm_medium=SourcesWidget&utm_campaign=mb_SourcesWidget_checkpagerank.net
16. Bhattacharjya, J., Ellison, A.B., Tripathi, S.: An exploration of logistics related customer service provision on Twitter: the case of e-tailers. Int. J. Phys. Distrib. Logist. Manag. (2015, accepted)
17. Hamel, G., Välikangas, L.: The quest for resilience. Harvard Bus. Rev. **81**, 52–63 (2003)
18. Day, G.S.: Closing the marketing capabilities gap. J. Mark. **75**, 183–195 (2011)

Collaboration Frameworks

Supporting Collaborative Networks
for Complex Service-Enhanced Products

Luis M. Camarinha-Matos[✉], Ana Inês Oliveira, and Filipa Ferrada

Faculty of Sciences and Technology and Uninova – CTS,
Nova University of Lisbon, 2829-516 Monte Caparica, Portugal
cam@uninova.pt

Abstract. Several collaborative networks need to be involved in supporting the life cycle of complex service-enhanced products. When addressing highly customized products, these networks need to consider the involvement of the customer and local stakeholders close to the customer. In this context, a set of integrated subsystems supporting both long-term strategic networks and goal-oriented virtual organizations is proposed. Experimental results are presented in the context of service-enhanced products in the solar energy sector.

Keywords: Collaborative networks · Service-enhanced product · Consortia formation · Collective emotions

1 Introduction

The development of complex and highly customized products such as a solar power plant, an intelligent building, or a special purpose complex machine, typically require contributions from several stakeholders from diverse knowledge sectors. Greater levels of efficiency could be achieved when these contributors are organized under the form of a collaborative network in order to better integrate their parts. In fact, most companies in these sectors are small and medium enterprises (SMEs), which can only cope with the complexity of the projects and reach markets in different geographical regions if collaborating with others.

Seeking business opportunities in different geographical regions in these domains often requires the involvement of the customer (co-creation) and collaboration with local suppliers in those target markets [1, 2]. This need motivated the emergence of the term *glocal enterprise*, to reflect the idea of thinking and acting globally, while being aware and responding adequately to the local preferences and constraints.

Furthermore, a growing number of business services are needed in association with the various phases of the product life-cycle, which led to the notion of service-enhanced product. For instance, in the case of solar energy, such business services can include: services for operation monitoring (energy monitoring, monitoring reports, system performance testing, site security, data analytics), preventive maintenance (panel cleaning, vegetation management, wildlife prevention, water drainage, retro-commissioning, upkeep of systems), corrective/reactive maintenance (on-site monitoring/mitigation, critical reactive repair, warranty enforcement), condition-based monitoring, other support (training, audit), etc. [3, 4]. These services add value to the

© IFIP International Federation for Information Processing 2015
L.M. Camarinha-Matos et al. (Eds.): PRO-VE 2015, IFIP AICT 463, pp. 181–192, 2015.
DOI: 10.1007/978-3-319-24141-8_16

physical product, representing a great differentiation factor and creating space for new business opportunities.

With the exception of a few large companies, the market offer is rather fragmented while, from the customer side, there is a clear demand for the provision of integrated services (Fig. 1). The provision of integrated services also calls for collaboration among multiple stakeholders.

Fig. 1. The need for integrated business services

In this context, there is a need to deal with different collaborative networks, operating at different stages of the life-cycle of the product and associated business services, which motivates the following research question:

What is a suitable platform and associated tools to support collaborative enterprise networks involved in the life-cycle of complex service-enhanced products?

This work was performed in the framework of the European research project GloNet which addressed the development of an agile virtual enterprise environment for networks of SMEs involved in highly customized and service-enhanced products [5].

The project developed a cloud-based system, which comprises a cloud-based platform offering multiple collaboration spaces [6], and a collaborative networking framework including functionalities for specification of products and business services, and management of collaborative networks (Fig. 2). This paper is mainly focused on the implemented subsystems for management of the various networks.

2   Collaborative Networks Management

A number of sub-systems are provided in GloNet to support both long-term strategic networks and goal-oriented networks.

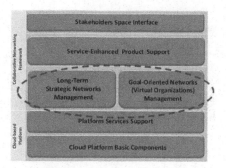

Fig. 2. GloNet system architecture

Long-Term Strategic Networks Management. The main purpose of this sub-system is to promote preparedness of its members for collaboration [7]. In the context of this network a growing number of service-enhanced products are created, leading to a product portfolio of the network.

Although this network is a typical virtual organizations breeding environment (VBE), the aim of supporting the *glocal* enterprise concept led to the involvement of the customer and other local stakeholders in the target market. In other words, for each target market the core VBE is extended with the inclusion of local members. In fact, the selection of partners for each goal-oriented virtual organization (VO) considers the extended recruitment space, as illustrated in Fig. 3.

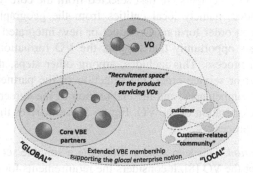

Fig. 3. Extended VBE

The functionalities developed for this component support the main steps illustrated in Fig. 4:

- *members' recruitment*, including basic management services of admission and withdrawal of members;
- *members' profiling*, with members and network profile and competencies definition, network performance management, among other functionalities; and

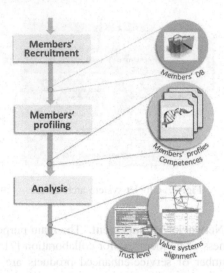

Fig. 4. Business ecosystem management

- *VBE analysis*, through services that enhance the VBE life-cycle, including functionalities for trust management among VBE members and assessment of the
  alignment of their value systems. Additional analysis tools could be plugged here
  through a web services interface.

Virtual Organizations Creation and Negotiation Subsystem. As mentioned above,
for the creation of VOs, members are first selected from the core VBE, but additional
members can be added, namely local entities from the geographical region of the
customer [8]. When an order for a new product or new integrated business service is
received (the business opportunity that triggers the VO formation), the VO Planner
initiates the creation process. This includes, among other steps, the detailed specification of the product or service order, the selection of the partners according to the
necessary skills and competences, and the elaboration of the agreements and contracts
that will regulate the operation of the VO. Figure 5 summarizes the main steps of the
consortium creation process:

- *Consortia generation.* This step aims at choosing a suitable set of partners to form
  the consortium for the VO [8]. It considers the requirements for the new VO, which
  depend on the specification of the new product or service, namely the necessary
  competences the potential VO Partners need to have. This is done performing a
  match with the existing competences in the VBE to identify the members that are
  suitable candidates to be part of the VO [7]. Then, a list of all possible VO combinations is generated automatically out of the members that can satisfy each goal.
  Furthermore, there is the possibility to manually impose "mandatory" or "preferred"
  partners in all possible consortia.
- *Filtering and selection.* In order to select the most appropriate consortium out of the
  list of previously generated consortia, the VO Planner can identify and assess, to
  certain extent, the risk level of each potential consortium [9]. In the current

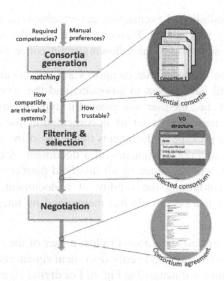

Fig. 5. Partners' selection and negotiation

implementation, the system can infer the alignment level of the value systems of potential partners, as well as their level of trustworthiness [10]. Depending on the application domain, additional criteria could be added here. For instance, in the case of logistics-related goals, it could make sense to consider the geographical location of the potential partner. Nevertheless, the system provides a ranking of the potential consortia according to the selected criteria, being the final selection done by the human planner.

- *Negotiation*. After having selected suitable partners to form the consortium, it is also important to have a negotiation mechanism that supports the process of achieving agreements among them during the VO formation. These agreements will then be the basis for the governance principles of the VO during its operation phase. The implemented negotiation support functionalities facilitate the participation of multiple stakeholders in the negotiation of different subjects via a set of mechanisms that ensure the privacy and confidentiality ("virtual negotiation spaces (VNSs)") [8]. For each topic/clause that needs to be negotiated, the VO Planner can invite a subset of (potential) partners into a specific VNS. The agreement can be built following either a default or customized template. Templates contain general information agreed by all involved partners, but also specific clauses agreed by a set of partners. The agreement is represented in the form of a readable document.

After the VO agreement is reached, the VO Planner can create a dossier comprising all relevant documentation related to the specific consortium agreement. This package of documents is stored in an electronic notary system to which all VO partners need to access in order to digitally sign the agreement. The existence of an e-notary system at the level of a VBE is particularly relevant in a *glocal* (multi-cultural) context in order to avoid future misunderstandings during the operation of the VO. The developed Electronic Notary and Conservatory Sub-system provides mechanisms for signing documents and the possibility of exchanging agreements-related documentation with warranty of authenticity and validity. Furthermore, it provides a safe archive for such documentation. In this sub-system, the following main concepts are used:

- Dossier: a collection or folder that comprises several documents. Only a limited number of users will have access to a dossier, and the access is managed by the owner of the dossier, i.e., the user who created it (typically a VO Planner). In other words, the dossier represents a set of documentation for a specific consortium agreement, that is, a package of documents that support the consortium agreement;
- Signature: referring to a digital signature of a document. A consortium agreement, in order to be valid, will be signed by all involved partners; and
- File Certification: confirming the validity of a document. An authorized VBE Member may verify if a certain file has maintained its integrity or if it has been deceived.

Depending on the corresponding access rights, a user of the e-notary system is able to properly manage dossiers, sign and verify document signatures, etc. The sequence of use of these functionalities is illustrated in Fig. 6. For digital signatures and certification an asymmetric keys mechanism is used.

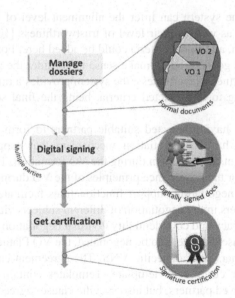

Fig. 6. e-Notary services

Supporting Co-creation Networks. In order to facilitate co-creation/co-design processes, a collaborative environment for multi-stakeholder based design of new business services, the Services Co-Design Negotiation (CoDeN) sub-system, was developed [11]. The involved participants (including the customer) in this process are initially selected by the initiator of the co-creation process. Similar to the Negotiation support sub-system for VO creation (mentioned above), this sub-system is also intended to generate an agreement that represents all consensus reached on the characteristics of a new business service. However, in this case, the process of reaching consensus is based on the *service design methodology* [12] that serves as a guide for the negotiation.

As illustrated in Fig. 7, a number of templates are used: *stakeholders mapping*, to identify the relevant stakeholders that have to be considered for direct and indirect contact with the new business service; *service blueprint diagrams*, considering: *User*, highlighting what the customer of the new business service does; *Touchpoints*, to identify the moments and places when the customer gets into direct contact with the new business service; *Service direct contact* and *Service back office*, to detect what should be the behaviour of the new business service staff; and *Means and processes*, to identify what else can be involved with the new business service.

The co-design involves thus a specialized iterative negotiation process, guided by the mentioned templates.

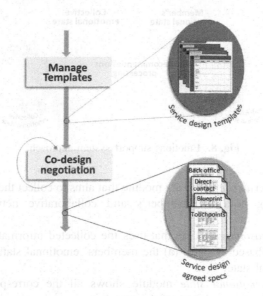

Fig. 7. Service co-design support

Supporting the Emotional Equilibrium of the Network. The emotional equilibrium of a network contributes to supporting a healthy and sustainable collaboration among all the involved parties and in this way leverage the success rate of the collaborative network. Emotions play an important role in promoting the effective management of communications and interactions among participants, namely in what concerns dealing with *soft* issues such as inter- and inter-organizational abilities, problems in keeping team cohesion, leadership, decision-making, involvement of customers, potential conflicts resolution, etc. [13, 14]. Furthermore, it is assumed that emotions also contribute to the sustainability of the network, so the more positive the emotion is, the healthier the collaboration becomes and on the other hand, negative emotions constitute a risk factor [15].

In this context, an emotions-based supervision sub-system was also developed. This sub-system uses a collection of non-intrusive mechanisms to estimate the level of emotion of each member individually and of the collaborative network as a whole (collective emotion). Figure 8 illustrates the adopted approach which comprises:

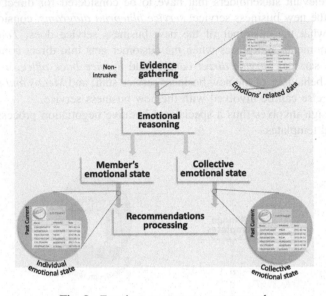

Fig. 8. Emotions support system approach

- a non-intrusive *evidence gathering* module that aims to collect the emotions' related data comprising both the member's and collaborative network's emotional information;
- an *emotional reasoning* module that uses the collected information and estimates (through a rule-based system): (a) the members' emotional state, and (b) the collective emotional state;
- the *members' emotional state* module shows all the corresponding evidences information and emotional state of the member;
- the *collective emotional state* module on its turn presents the evidences regarding the network as a whole and the collective emotional state;
- a *recommendations' processing* module that aims to give support to the network administrator by suggesting a plan of actions to enhance the collective emotional state of the network. These actions are merely suggestions and it is up to the administrator to put them in practice.

All these sub-systems are part of the GloNet system [16], which provides a cloud-based collaborative environment and includes other functionalities developed by the other partners of the GloNet consortium, such as a product specification subsystem, a business services specification sub-system, sub-product/service recommendation sub-system, complex product portfolio repository, collaboration spaces, and workflow subsystem.

3 Validation

The developed functionalities and methodological guidelines were evaluated through the implementation of a realistic demonstrator in the solar energy sector. For this purpose, GloNet selected as case study the Charanka solar park in Gujarat, India, a contemporary project in which the iPLON partner participated in the Operations and Maintenance system. The Charanka project started during the early phases of GloNet, when relevant research results were not available yet, and thus it was mostly implemented through traditional methods in this sector. At that stage, only a small influence of GloNet could be noticed in terms of the use of the CNs concepts to help iPLON structure the various partnerships under the notions of VBE and VO. But the involved processes were essentially manual at that stage.

Nevertheless, the available data, acquired experience, and lessons learned, that are recent and thus easily recalled, constituted an important basis to help assessing the potential impacts of adopting GloNet results in similar future projects. As such, the strategy was to use Charanka solar park as a reference case and to replicate, through the use of GloNet results, some relevant business scenarios selected from this case and to compare them with the traditional approaches (Fig. 9).

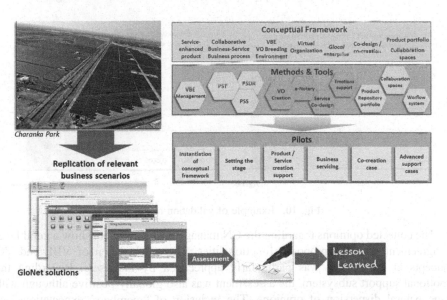

Fig. 9. Demonstration and validation pilot

This case, where a European SME expanded its business to another continent in collaboration with local stakeholders, also provided insights on the implementation of the *glocal* enterprise concept.

According to the assessment made by the end-users, the platform and collaboration support tools fit well the needs of the use case, although some improvements in the user interface style could be considered when evolving to a commercial product. Although the needed organizational changes are significant, the expected potential benefits are also very high, at least as it can be estimated at this stage. Furthermore, the conceptual framework for collaborative networks and service-enhanced products proposed by GloNet:

- Offers SMEs the opportunity to implement new business models based on collaboration;
- Certainly requires a change in the mind-set of companies operating in the solar energy and intelligent buildings sectors, which are more used to sub-contracting relationships; this also requires an extensive training plan;
- Offers SMEs the possibility of jointly having a more agile response in dynamic market contexts; and
- Provides an effective way of implementing the *glocal* enterprise concept, allowing SMEs to expand into new markets in other regions.

As part of the validation process, a group of external enterprises, i.e. members of the solar energy VBE (including about 40 enterprises), were invited to get a closer understanding of GloNet vision and solutions. This process involved a couple of training actions and an extensive workshop with demonstration of the implemented system. These external users were then invited to assess the various functionalities of the GloNet system. A partial example of their assessment is shown in Fig. 10.

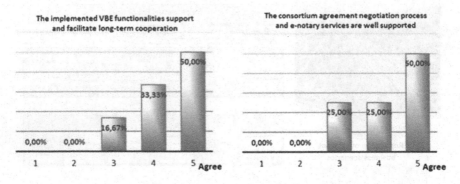

Fig. 10. Example of validation results

The collected opinions regarding the CN management subsystem show a good level of agreement with the proposed functionalities. The combination of VBE and VO concepts in the system was particularly appreciated by the users. Regarding the emotional support subsystem, the assessment was also globally positive although with some natural dispersion of opinions. The inclusion of "members' expectations" as inputs for the tool was particularly appreciated by participants.

4 Conclusions and Further Work

GloNet developed an integrated environment to support complex and highly customized products. Particularly in the case of solar power plants, the collaborative enterprises networking, the notion of *glocal* enterprise, and the focus on supporting multi-stakeholder integrated business services, appear as very promising for future developments in this sector. The solutions developed in GloNet and demonstrated in the implemented pilot confirmed this expectation, and proved a very good fit with the identified needs. Furthermore, the developed functionalities contributed to point out new directions for achieving higher levels of effectiveness in the core business processes. Of particular relevance to the end-users is the set of mechanisms, environment, and tools to support multi-stakeholder co-creation/co-innovation in collaboration with the customer and local entities close to the customer.

As future work, this use case also showed the need to further address the needs of multi-cultural business ecosystems involving members from different geographical regions.

Acknowledgments. This work was funded in part by the European Commission through the GloNet project (FP7 programme), and in part by the Center of Technology and Systems and FCT- PEST program UID/EEA/00066/2013 (Impactor project). The authors also thank the contributions from their partners in the GloNet project.

References

1. Romero, D., Molina, A.: Collaborative networked organisations and customer communities: value co-creation and co-innovation in the networking era. Prod. Plann. Control **22**(5 6), 447–472 (2011)
2. Afsarmanesh, H., Thamburaj, V.: ICT requirements analysis for enterprise networks supporting solar power plants. In: Camarinha-Matos, L.M., Xu, L., Afsarmanesh, H. (eds.) Collaborative Networks in the Internet of Services. IFIP AICT, vol. 380, pp. 149–157. Springer, Heidelberg (2012)
3. EPRI. Addressing Solar Photovoltaic Operations and Maintenance Challenges - A Survey of Current Knowledge and Practices. Electric Power Research Institute white paper. www.smartgridnews.com/artman/uploads/1/1021496AddressingPVOaMChallenges7-2010_1_.pdf, July 2010
4. Camarinha-Matos, L.M., Afsarmanesh, H., Oliveira, A.I., Ferrada, F.: Cloud-based collaborative business services provision. In: Hammoudi, S., Cordeiro, J., Maciaszek, L.A., Filipe, J. (eds.) ICEIS 2013. LNBIP, vol. 190, pp. 366–384. Springer, Heidelberg (2014)
5. Camarinha-Matos, L.M., Afsarmanesh, H., Koelmel, B.: Collaborative networks in support of service-enhanced products. In: Camarinha-Matos, L.M., Pereira-Klen, A., Afsarmanesh, H. (eds.) PRO-VE 2011. IFIP AICT, vol. 362, pp. 95–104. Springer, Heidelberg (2011)
6. Surajbali, B., Bauer, M., Bär, H., Alexakis, S.: A cloud–based approach for collaborative networks supporting serviced-enhanced products. In: Camarinha-Matos, L.M., Scherer, R.J. (eds.) PRO-VE 2013. IFIP AICT, vol. 408, pp. 61–70. Springer, Heidelberg (2013)
7. Camarinha-Matos, L.M., Ferrada, F., Oliveira, A.I.: Interplay of collaborative networks in product servicing. In: Camarinha-Matos, L.M., Scherer, R.J. (eds.) PRO-VE 2013. IFIP AICT, vol. 408, pp. 51–60. Springer, Heidelberg (2013)
8. Oliveira, A.I., Camarinha-Matos, L.M.: Electronic negotiation support environment in collaborative networks. In: Camarinha-Matos, L.M., Shahamatnia, Ehsan, Nunes, Gonçalo (eds.) DoCEIS 2012. IFIP AICT, vol. 372, pp. 21–32. Springer, Heidelberg (2012)

9. Harland, C., Brenchley, R., Walker, H.: Risk in supply networks. J. Purchasing Supply Manage. **9**(2), 51–62 (2003)
10. Camarinha-Matos, L.M., Oliveira, A.I, Ferrada, F., Sobotka, P., Vataščinová, A., Thamburaj, V.: Collaborative enterprise networks for solar energy. In: ICCCT 2015 - IEEE International Conference on Computing and Communications Technologies, Chennai, India, 26–27 Feb 2015
11. Oliveira, A.I., Camarinha-Matos, L.M.: Negotiation support for co-design of business services. In: Camarinha-Matos, L.M., Afsarmanesh, H. (eds.) Collaborative Systems for Smart Networked Environments. IFIP AICT, vol. 434, pp. 98–106. Springer, Heidelberg (2014)
12. Mager, B., Sung, T.: Special issue editorial: designing for services. Int. J. Des. **5**(2), 1–3 (2011)
13. Bar-Tal, D., Halperin, E., de Rivera, J.: Collective emotions in conflict situations: societal implications. J. Soc. Issues **63**(2), 441–460 (2007)
14. Mackie, D.M., Devos, T., Smith, E.: Intergroup emotions: explaining offensive actions in an intergroup context. J. Pers. Soc. Psychol. **79**, 602–616 (2000)
15. Ferrada, F., Camarinha-Matos, L.: An emotional support system for collaborative networks. In: Technological Innovation for Cloud-based Engineering Systems, pp. 42–53. IFIP AICT Series 450/2015. Springer, Berlin
16. Camarinha-Matos, L.M., Macedo, P., Ferrada, F., Oliveira, A.I.: Collaborative business scenarios in a service-enhanced products ecosystem. In: Camarinha-Matos, L.M., Xu, L., Afsarmanesh, H. (eds.) Collaborative Networks in the Internet of Services. IFIP AICT, vol. 380, pp. 13–25. Springer, Heidelberg (2012)

Framework Conditions for Forming Collaborative Networks on Smart Service Platforms

Volker Stich, Michael Kurz, and Felix Optehostert[✉]

Institute for Industrial Management, RWTH Aachen University, Campus-Boulevard 55,
52074 Aachen, Germany
{Volker.Stich,Michael.Kurz,Felix.Optehostert}@fir.rwth-aachen.de

Abstract. Smart Products are ubiquitous in enterprise's businesses. They communicate over cross-company networks and generate a large quantity of data. By analyzing and filtering these data, enterprises are enabled to create innovative business models. These service innovations are offered to companies on service platforms. Furthermore, these platforms can be integrated in the innovation process. Users are enabled to voice their needs with respect to a particular service on this platform. A group of service enterprises address these demands by using the platform as a collaborative network and form a short-term virtual enterprise. They jointly develop a customer-specific service. There are some obstacles that need to be overcome in order to operate such platforms and form collaborative networks on them. This paper identifies and analyses the platform's framework conditions which are required to address this issue and allow the enterprises to form a short-term virtual enterprise. Based on this work, the concept of such a platform can be defined in a next step.

Keywords: Service innovation · Collaborative network · Service platform · Smart service

1 Introduction

The use of information- and communication technologies in business and society are nowadays taken for granted [1]. Especially concerning the consumer service industry, the disruptive force of digitalization has changed business fundamentally. New digital platforms have changed the business structure for example in the music industry as well as the cinema and television industry. Old value added structures have been abolished and replaced by new innovative business models. Dominant players, ruling the market in this field by establishing platforms are e.g. Apple (iTunes), amazon and Netflix [2, 3]. In comparison to consumer services, industrial services are executed in a business to business relationship. They are characterized by a high connection to the industrial good [3, 4]. However, the obstacles for the digitalization of the business models of indusial services are much higher than in the consumer services. Three reasons for this can be identified. On the one hand the complexity of products and services is much higher in the business to business relationship. Industrial services have much higher requirements with regards to the qualifications of a service provider. Furthermore the

© IFIP International Federation for Information Processing 2015
L.M. Camarinha-Matos et al. (Eds.): PRO-VE 2015, IFIP AICT 463, pp. 193–200, 2015.
DOI: 10.1007/978-3-319-24141-8_17

markets for industrial services are much smaller and regional focused. Developing costs and market-introduction costs for new digital solutions do not seem to amortize. Finally entering the industrial service market is often very difficult. Consumer services can be offered and executed via internet whereas the connection of small and regionally focused service providers is more difficult.

However, these obstacles should not be seen as a general hindrance for the digitalization of the industrial service industry. These obstacles rather explain why the digitalization is growing fast in some markets whereas other markets are still lagging behind. However, in the industrial sector fundamentally changing forces already appear [5, 6]. Established value creating chains will be changed fundamentally or will completely vanish. They will be substituted by value creating networks and virtual enterprises formed on platforms [7]. These value creating networks will not only change the process of executing services, but also the organizational structures and most importantly the way services are being engineered. The division of labor between producer, supplier and service provider as well as their business models will be changed by digitalization [6, 7].

The place where producer, industrial service provider and software companies cooperate and form networks are upcoming digital ecosystems. Every company changing their way of thinking on value creation and using these ecosystems for their business models will have a competitive advantage [7]. Therefore the ongoing transformation of business models by digitalization will not only be a challenge but simultaneously a chance for small to medium sized businesses [7].

Now small to medium sized businesses have the chance to participate in building value creating networks. This can be achieved for e.g. by establishing new digital standards and enabling the access to data and information. One of the new digital standards can be platforms on which innovative services are engineered by a network of companies forming a short-term virtual enterprise. This platform can either be operated by one company or otherwise by a consortium of firms, in order to avoid a dominant party. These kinds of platforms can be an important part of the new digital value creating in networks. In the following paper the framework requirements for such a platform will be discussed and illustrated by a use case.

2 Background

Platforms are building the new digital infrastructure of our economy by offering new types of collaboration within value creating networks. It means that platforms map business systems in which actors and their products as well as processes become independent from the used hardware. Regarding product-service-systems platforms provide the specific cooperation between product manufacturer and service providers. Services platforms are a perfect opportunity to combine physical and digital services as a so called smart service. Meanwhile platforms define standards, tools, processes and interfaces. Therewith they characterize the game rules of interaction between the actors and objects [6, 7]. To get to the bottom of platforms hereinafter the basics of service engineering, service networks and virtual enterprises. Service Engineering deals with the question of how to develop new services including product-service-systems.

Service Engineering describes the target orientated planning and design of services [8, 9]. According to intelligences from product and software development the core element of service engineering is the process design of services [10]. Therefore service engineering follows an iterative approach, utilizes methods and tools to measure efficiency as well as effectiveness of services. The target is to provide high quality services [11, 12]. Based on the work of JASCHINSKI [13] a DIN-standard (DIN is the German Institute for Standardization) had been developed in the form of a reference process. Due to the fact that services are more and more provided within a service networks [14] the question of cooperation and collaboration becomes a key challenge. Though the reference process by DIN enables service development for networks the research landscape on cooperation and networks cannot be seen as homogeneous in general. There are rather various theories which in each case are based on insights from different business sectors [15, 16]. Nevertheless the research field of networks can be divided by three main characteristics. The relation between network partners can be seen as the main characteristic. Further the examined phase within the evolution process of a network helps to structure research on networks. As the third characteristic the perspective on the network is quoted [10].

A closer look should be taken into virtual enterprise structures because these are also aiming at collaboration between different organizations. Matos lines out that those virtual enterprises are information centered and its concepts had been developed to maximize reactivity between the actors. For instance in engineering this goes hand in hand with concurrent and co-engineering. Virtual enterprises request a management system to organize its activities and procedures. On the working level technical constraints like interoperability can be seen quite often but in general there is a strong need to define interfaces on all levels [17]. To prevent a large, complex and uncontrollable system MATOS proposes need-oriented acting. Therefor he divides virtual enterprises structures into three different classes by its complexity and lifetime. The first type of structures is based on a single market opportunity with a short term perspective. These need only a few co-working activities and work mostly in asynchronous collaborative phases. The system controls on a high level while sub-activities have to be managed by the internal departments. Each sub-activity than has to be assigned to a specific virtual enterprise member who confirms on in- and output. The states of synchronization, resources and the actors themselves have to be determined by the global control system. In the result the system has to provide information by an Inter-Organizational Information System (IOIS) and a partner management system. The second type of virtual enterprises is characterized by more complex collaborations crossing company boundaries meaning collaborations between companies, its partners, customers, suppliers and whole markets [17]. This implies a possible global exchange, partnership or even subcontracting. In the resulting increase of coordination expenditure these types of extended enterprises have to connect external supply chains and information systems with internal systems. In addition the requirement of a high flexibility comes up. For partnerships where robustness and reactivity are the main focus, virtual enterprise structures as a consortium are recommended. Here internal competition could lead to more efficient resource consumption but results simultaneously to less flexibility.

Platforms are tackling a hand full of challenges within service design, value-adding networks and especially in digitalized virtual enterprises. They allow new business models and extend value streams. It is foreseen that platforms become dominant in value-adding networks by defining standards of collaboration. Existing manufacturer and service providers have to be aware of the upcoming risk of their replaceability in value streams or networks. Especially small and medium enterprises should use the opportunity to use open platform structures. These also prevent monopoly-like structures with in a single digital market. Summarizing platforms save employment and make growth potential accessible by providing optimal and modular types of collaboration.

3   Framework Conditions Forming Collaborative Networks on Smart Service Platforms

Innovative service-engineering provided by two or more companies forming collaborative networks on service platforms is hindered by some challenges. These challenges can be addressed and overcome by framework conditions which the platform must meet. In this chapter these framework conditions will be introduced and explained. In the following chapter these frameworks are illustrated by a use-case, covering the service engineering of maintenance services.

As stated above, some approaches (BAUER and SCHOBERT as well as ZAHN and STANIK [18, 19]) described service engineering in collaborative networks. However, the smart service platforms face other challenges and therefore need other framework conditions.

Service engineering by collaborative networks on service platforms unleashes its potential by integrating cyber physical systems. Therefore each company connects its cyber physical system with the platform. By doing so these cyber physical systems are enabled to autonomously provide data on the platform, for the use of service engineering processes and simultaneously ask for service solutions on the platform. Therefore the platform has to provide different interfaces in order to enable every company to connect their cyber physical system to the platform. As these sensitive connections and data are exposed to the platform, a data security concept has to be developed in order to protect companies' data and IT-systems. This can be achieved by software programming, independent servers and server location as well as specific entry requirements for the platform which have to be passed by every participant. Additionally the availability of data has to be guaranteed. The engineering process on the platform can only be executed if the needed data is provided by the companies and their cyber physical systems [7].

Usually the data generated by cyber physical systems is unstructured information [7]. As the service engineering process on the platform can only handle structured and refined data.

Another framework condition is the critical mass of platform participants. A critical mass is achieved when the platform participants provide all the competencies, which allow them to form a collaborative network on the platform and engineer an innovative service for the demand of the costumer. This critical mass allows the access to all relevant data for the service engineering process.

Another framework condition is the operation of the platform itself. The platform can be operated by a third impendent party, by some participates of the platform or by all participants of the platform. However, a neutral operator establishes an atmosphere of trust for the participants of the platform [7].

Another framework condition are the entry requirements. Data security is a very important issue for smart service platforms, as they are connected to the cyber physical systems and infrastructure of each participant. The definition of entry requirements, which every participant has to pass, allows the operator to control the platform and help the participants to gain trust in to the platform.

The platform has also to provide framework conditions on the process level. First the platform needs a standardized process for enquiring demands of services. Basic characteristics need to be defined, which help the platform-management-system to match the service provider's competencies profile with the enquiry. Furthermore the platform has to provide framework conditions on how the collaborative network is formed on the platform. It has to define whether a party is included or excluded. Furthermore, framework conditions with regards to the service engineering process itself need to be defined. Requirements, competencies and restrictions need to be cleared by the platform in order to transfer relevant subtasks to the appropriate service provider.

An overview of the mentioned framework conditions is pictured in Fig. 1. They are arranged under three generic terms which are data, participants and process. In the following chapter a use case is presented focusing on a complex maintenance task. The use case demonstrates the framework conditions in the course of an example.

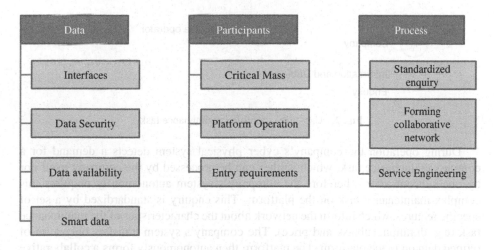

Fig. 1. Framework conditions

4   Use Case – Complex Maintenance Task

In the previous chapter, the framework conditions which provide the platforms required to facilitate a smart service engineering process were described and explained. This chapter exemplary demonstrates these framework conditions on the basis of a use case, focusing on a company, which has machines and software forming a cyber physical system. The company wants to be a participant of a smart service engineering platform, which has a critical mass of participants and an independent platform operator. Here the participants can form collaborative networks in order to engineer innovative services.

At first the company has to pass the entry requirements for the platform. This allows the platform operator to guarantee the data security and data availability of the platform. In the next step, a connection between the company's cyber physical system and the platform has to be established (Fig. 2).

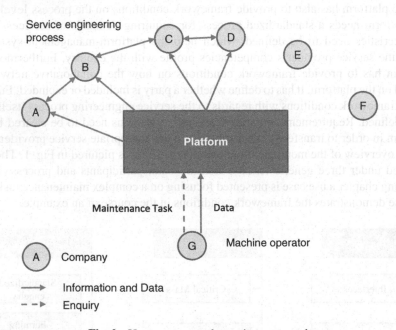

Fig. 2. Use-case – complex maintenance task

During operation the company's cyber physical system detects a demand for a complex maintenance task, which neither can be processed by the company itself nor by one subcontractor. Therefore the company's system autonomously enquires this complex maintenance task on the platform. This enquiry is standardized by a set of specific features, which inform the network about the characteristics of the maintenance task (e.g. duration, subtask and price). The company's system transfers only a set of refined data on to the platform. The platform then autonomously forms a collaborative network of specific service providers (participants of the platform) whose competencies match the characteristics of the maintenance task. They share the provided data on the platform in order to engineer the service for the costumer.

5   Conclusion

Digitalization is changing the value adding structure in various industries. (cf. iTunes, amazon and Uber) However, some obstacles for digitalization can be identified, which define the pace of the digitalization especially in the industrial service sector. Value adding networks form digital ecosystems where producer, industrial service provider and software companies collaborate and engineer innovative services. The data need for the service engineering process is generated by the cyber physical systems of each company participating with the platform.

The paper introduced ten framework conditions. They arranged under three generic terms named data, participants and process. The framework conditions interfaces, data security, data availability and smart data are sorted under the term "data". The term "participants" include critical mass, platform operation and entry requirements. The last term is "process". This term aggregates standardized enquiry, process of forming collaborative network and service engineering process. Platforms meeting these conditions, allow a collaborative service engineering process with data generated form cyber physical systems. In chapter four these framework conditions are illustrated by a use case.

In a next step the framework conditions can be used in order to design and program a platform for collaborative service engineering processes.

References

1. Institut für Demoskopie Allensbach (Ed.): Die Zukunft der digitalen Gesellschaft. Ergebnisse einer repräsentativen Befragung (2014)
2. Kreutzer, R.T., Land, K.-H.: Digitaler Darwinismus. Der stille Angriff auf Ihr Geschäftsmodell und Ihre Marke. Das Think!Book. In: Digitaler Darwinismus (2013)
3. Redlich, T., Wulfsberg, J.P.: Wertschöpfung in der Bottom-up-Ökonomie. Springer-Verlag (VDI-Buch), Heidelberg, New York (2011)
4. Meier, H.: Integrierte Industrielle Sach- und Dienstleistungen. Vermarktung, Entwicklung und Erbringung hybrider Leistungsbündel. Springer, Berlin, Heidelberg (2012)
5. Brynjolfsson, E., McAfee, A.: The Second Machine Age. Work, Progress and Prosperity in a Time of Brilliant Technologies, 1st edn. Norton, New York (2014)
6. Westkämper, E.: Digitale Produktion. Springer Vieweg, Berlin (2013)
7. Kagermann, H., Riemensperger, F.: Smart Service Welt. Umsetzungsempfehlungen für das Zukunftsprojekt Internetbasierte Dienste für die Wirtschaft. acatech - Deutsche Akademie der Technikwissenschaften - Arbeitskreis Smart Service Welt, Berlin (2014)
8. Liestmann, V.: Dienstleistungsentwicklung durch Service Engineering. Von der Idee zum Produkt. Aachen, p. 23 (2001)
9. Bullinger, H., Scheer, A.: Service Engineering - Entwicklung und Gestaltung innovativer Dienstleistungen. In: Bullinger, H., Scheer, A. (eds.) Service Engineering: Entwicklung und Gestaltung innovativer Dienstleistungen, 2nd edn, pp. 3–17. Springer, Berlin (2006)
10. Thomassen, P.: Kooperationskonzepte für Servicenetzwerke am Beispiel der erneuerbaren Energien. Apprimus Verlag, Aachen (2013)
11. Gudergan, G.: Service engineering: multiperspective and Interdisciplinary framework for new solution design. In: Maglio, P.P., Kieliszewski, C.A., Spohrer, J.C. (eds.) Handbook of Service Science, pp. 387–418. Springer Science + Business Media, LLC, Boston (2010)
12. Schuh, G., Friedli, T., Gebauer, H.: Fit for Service: Industrie als Dienstleister. Hanser, München (2004)
13. Jaschinski, C.: Qualitätsorientiertes Redesign von Dienstleistungen. Shaker, Aachen (1998)
14. DIN - Deutsches Institut für Normung e.V.: Standardisierter Prozess zur Entwicklung industrieller Dienstleistungen in Netzwerken. DIN PAS 1082. Beuth, Berlin (2008)

15. Nawatzki, J.: Integriertes Informationsmanagement. Die Koordination von Informations verarbeitung, Organisation und Personalwirtschaft bei der Planung, Durchführung, Kontrolle und Steuerung des Einsatzes neuer Informationstechnologie in der Unternehmung. Eul, Bergisch Gladbach (1994)
16. Cooper, R.G., Edgeti, S.J.: Product Development for the Service Sector. Lessons from Market Leaders. Perseus, Cambridge (1999)
17. Camarinha-Matos, L.M., Afsarmanesh, H.: Matos collaborative networks: a new scientific discipline. J. Intell. Manuf. **16**, 439–452 (2005)
18. Bauer, C., Schobert, A.: Auftragsinduzierte Konfiguration von Produktionsnetzwerken in der Dienstleistungswirtschaft. Arbeitsbericht Wirtschaftsinformatik II Nr. 01/2002, Universität Nürnberg, Nürnberg (2002)
19. Zahn, E., Stanik, M.: Integrierte Entwicklung von Dienstleistungen und Netzwerken-Dienstleistungskooperationen als strategischer Erfolgsfaktor. In: Bullinger, H., Scheer, A. (eds.) Service Engineering. Entwicklung und Gestaltung innovativer Dienstleistungen, pp. 309–328. Springer, Berlin (2006)

Improving Collaboration Between Large and Small Enterprises Using Networked Services

Wolfgang Gräther[1(✉)], Isabel Matranga[2], Vincenzo Savarino[2], Karol Furdik[3],
and Martin Tomášek[3]

[1] Fraunhofer FIT, St. Augustin, Germany
wolfgang.graether@fit.fraunhofer.de
[2] Ingegneria Informatica, Palermo, Italy
{isabel.matranga,vincenzo.savarino}@eng.it
[3] Intersoft, a.s., Kosice, Slovakia
{karol.furdik,martin.tomasek}@intersoft.sk

Abstract. Collaboration between large and small & medium-sized enterprises is still not adequately supported by current groupware solutions. In this paper, we present a novel approach that addresses the challenges of inter-enterprise collaboration. Key elements of our approach are: interoperability to legacy applications to retain current working styles, basic services for sharing and management of shared collaboration spaces, use of email for collaboration especially on the SME's side, information extraction to enable semantic search in inter-enterprise collaborations and automatic tagging of documents, and integration of business process models. We evaluated the approach on three application cases in the workplace: new product development, software development supply chain, and supply chain collaboration between SMEs and LEs. Our results suggest that the implemented services are beneficial in typical cooperation situations between enterprises.

Keywords: Groupware · Interoperability · Lightweight semantics · Virtual enterprise

1 Introduction

Collaboration between large enterprises (LE) and small and medium-sized enterprises (SME) is often solely based on exchanging documents via email. The advantage of email usage is the interoperability of email clients, which means that it is straight forward and easy to distribute documents and other information to co-workers even if they are using different email clients. There are drawbacks with email usage: for example, email usage could lead to divergent document versions, does not provide awareness about activities of co-workers, and could overwhelm users with messages.

However, even if some of the cooperating enterprises are using collaboration suites (groupware), there exist several reasons to collaborate via email:

- the cooperating enterprises are using different collaboration systems that are not interoperable,

© IFIP International Federation for Information Processing 2015
L.M. Camarinha-Matos et al. (Eds.): PRO-VE 2015, IFIP AICT 463, pp. 201–208, 2015.
DOI: 10.1007/978-3-319-24141-8_18

- even if the cooperating partners agree on a common collaboration system, then especially SMEs often do not have the resources to buy, install and use all the different collaboration suites of their LE partners,
- if one partner is already using a collaboration system, then often external partners are not allowed to register with the partner's collaboration suite,
- the compliance rules of the cooperating enterprises do not allow to use services in the cloud, such as Doodle for scheduling or Dropbox for sharing.

In this paper, we present a novel solution to this interoperability problem. After a section with related work, we will report the details of our approach. The description of the VENIS application cases, the method and settings for the evaluation as well as the presentation of the evaluation results follow. Finally, we present a conclusion and future work.

2 Related Work

Interoperability of collaborative working environments (CWE) has been previously studied and prototypically tested in several research projects. A Reference architecture for interoperable CWE systems as well as concrete implementations can be found in [1] and [2]. This generic architecture is still inspiring; however, our approach focuses on integration of modularized services and connects to enterprise repositories and legacy systems.

Email is still widely used today even if there are problems and implications of message-based patterns for organizing collaboration [3, 4]. For example, exchange of documents as email attachments cause extra coordination work for the co-workers and multiple copies of the documents are stored in the users' email inboxes. In addition, information overload could be a problem especially when distribution lists are used. This research supports our decision to integrate email in inter-enterprise collaborations.

In [5] a model for automatic suggestion of shared spaces when a user composes an email is presented, i.e. email is posted to relevant shared spaces such as wikis, for example. This approach preserves email usage as our approach does, but we go further and integrate attachment stripping and named entity recognition to support semantic search. Our work on email analysis, information extraction, enterprise search, and lightweight semantics has been reported earlier [6–9].

3 The VENIS Approach

The requirements for the VENIS approach were elicited from an analysis of LE-SME collaboration settings and the three application cases. These requirements informed our design that was mainly driven by the desire to combine the ad hoc features of email, lightweight semantic technologies, and business process support into distributed services to enabling interoperability and collaboration between enterprises.

The VENIS services for interoperability (VSI) are included in so-called VSI nodes, which are connected in a network, see Fig. 1. Usually each collaborating enterprise hosts its own VSI node, but, for example, very small SMEs could be invited to connect to a VSI node of an enterprise they are collaborating with. At the network level, the VENIS network administrator manages the Yellow Pages Server and keeps the network configuration up to date.

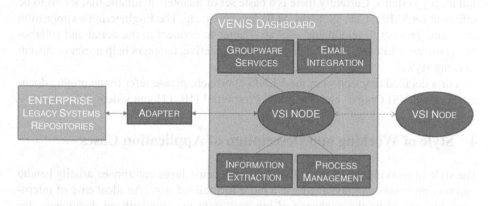

Fig. 1. Conceptual model and components of VENIS.

The VENIS services for interoperability comprise basic groupware services: sharing of artifacts, management of shared collaboration spaces, membership management, and means to notify members about ongoing activities of co-workers. The traditional login-password access mechanism is replaced by tokens, which enable collaboration members to access and to revise shared artifacts as well as to upload new artifacts.

The VENIS approach integrates email into collaborative processes. For example, tokens to access artifacts are sent via email. In addition, attached documents are automatically stripped of and become thus part of the addressed collaboration space. Furthermore, email conversations are input for indexing and information extraction.

The means for searching are based on indexing and information extraction services from emails and human-readable documents in collaborative processes. The extracted semantic information is stored in a semantic network as a free collection of types. In earlier research work [9] default annotation types for business documents have been identified: organization, person, address, product, document, inventory, etc. The type organization, for example, is sub-structured into attributes such as name, organization identifier and tax registration number. The type of a document could be invoice, order, contract, or change request. The extracted semantic information enables rich semantic search over emails and collaboration artifacts.

The VENIS approach facilitates usage of business process models in collaborative processes, i.e. management and control of the collaboration flow is supported by notifications and task lists. Assume, for example, that a LE-SME business process model has been created, then the execution triggers an event and an email will be sent to the SME employee containing the token for a particular document. The SME will receive the token and will get access to the business document to work on it. After finishing the work and uploading the updated document, other co-workers are informed and the business process continues with the next steps.

There is, of course, a graphical user interface – the VENIS dashboard – available that offers all basic groupware functions, search functions as well as functions for task management to co-workers and it displays an activity stream.

The concept of adapters is used to connect VENIS services to enterprise repositories and legacy systems. Currently there is a basic set of adapters available that seems to be sufficient for SMEs: FTP, WebDav, SQL data bases, etc. The Engineering's application case 'new product development' uses an adapter to connect to the portal and collaboration software Liferay. From an end-user's perspective, adapters help preserve current working styles.

For a detailed description of the VENIS approach, please refer to the project documents 'D5.3 VSI Online' and 'D6.2 VSI Prototype' [10, 11] and videos [11].

4   Style of Working and Description of Application Cases

The style of working for LEs and SMEs differ because large enterprises usually handle business processes and documents in a more formalized way. An ideal case of interoperability would be the exchange of business data via standardized documents, for example, using CoreComponents, EDI or ebXML. However, SMEs often handle business documents in human-readable format such as doc, pdf or html and the fixed working procedures driven by legacy applications are missed. These procedures are replaced by the SME employee's decisions and actions taken according to the usual unwritten way of working [6].

The three application cases reflect these different working practices. For example, the application case depicted in Fig. 2 focuses on the exchange of resources between SMEs and LE and the interaction of distributed working groups within a business process. Collaboration steps between a prime contractor, a partner company and a supplier are shown.

The application case 'software development supply chain' illustrates the situation that a provider, requiring an implementation of a complex software project, needs additional resources from suppliers. In this application case the VENIS support focuses on the quick identification of suppliers by their skills and on easy management of technical and contractual aspects between provider and supplier.

The application case 'supply chain collaboration between SMEs and LE' stands for typical inter-enterprise collaboration. The SME supplies IT and Telematics software and hardware to the large enterprise as well as staff when required so as to fulfill the needs of their control room staffing requirements. The collaboration includes procedures of getting quotes and orders from the LE to the SME, while the SME provides either quotes or fulfills the orders that have been sent.

Altogether, the three application cases are typical for current LE and SME collaboration and require almost all features that are available in the VENIS services for enterprise interoperability: adapters to connect to legacy systems and enterprise repositories, basic groupware services, email for messaging and token-based access to shared documents, functions for searching and business process support.

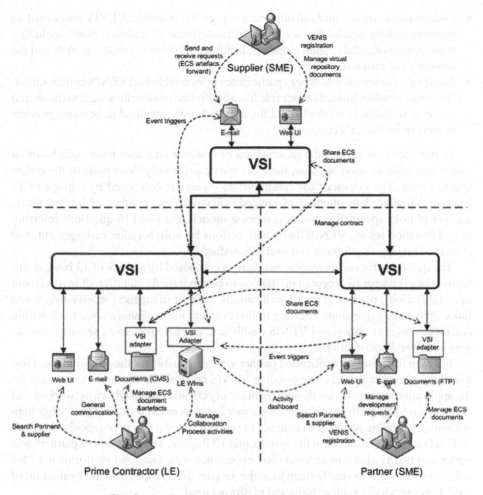

Fig. 2. Application case 'New product development'.

5   Evaluation Method and Settings for Application Cases

The VENIS approach was evaluated for all three application cases. The goal was to get findings about usability, user friendliness, benefits, and finally an overall business applicability of the VENIS approach as a whole. To evaluate these aspects, an on-line questionnaire was used. The questionnaire was designed with the aim to cover all phases of the software installation, configuration, deployment, and daily operation from various user perspectives. To evaluate the usability in all the identified phases, three user roles and their responsibilities were distinguished as follows:

- *Technical system administrator* - is responsible for the overall installation, configuration, and deployment of the VENIS network, as well as for the operational technical maintenance.

- *Collaboration owner and administrator* - uses the installed VENIS dashboard to perform actions needed for set up and maintenance of collaborations, including management of collaboration members, handling of business process models and the repository of artifacts.
- *Involved collaboration member* - participates in an established VENIS collaboration. By means of token links, this user role has a controlled read/write access to the shared space of artifacts, is notified about the required tasks specified in business process models or by owner's commands.

In this paper we restrict the presentation of results to the user roles *collaboration owner* and *collaboration member*, therefore we describe only these parts of the online questionnaire. The questions for *collaboration owners* is composed by a block of 13 basic quantitative data (number of created collaborations, number of invited users, number of tasks specified in business process models, etc.) and 16 questions referring to collaboration set up, VENIS dashboard, actions for collaboration management, and perceived security, usefulness and overall satisfaction.

The questions for *collaboration members* is composed by a block of 13 basic quantitative data (number of accepted invitations to collaborations, duration of involvement in collaborations, number of email notifications, number of artifacts received via token links, etc.) and 23 questions referring to involvement into collaborations, work within collaborations, navigation and VENIS dashboard, and also perceived security, usefulness and overall satisfaction.

For each use case one application partner was responsible for the evaluation and had to set up and customize the corresponding VENIS network. For example, the setting for the application case 'software development supply chain' comprised two networked VSI nodes. Two SME partners and one LE partner have accessed a shared space of collaborations, employing adapters to connect to respective local resource repositories such as TestTrack application, local file system, and FTP space. The selection of partners was performed taking also into account their experience with tools and platforms used for collaboration, so as to enable them to make an effective comparison and evaluation of the VENIS services vs. other tools and platforms used.

6   Results from Evaluation

During winter 2015 the three VENIS networks were used by 24 people; one application case involved 12 people, the other two involved 6 users each. 14 shared spaces for collaborations were created and 120 artifacts were stored. Two application cases used the support for business process models with 4 tasks on average.

The evaluation confirmed that the VENIS services could be successfully used for all the three application cases and that usage of the VSI network has been beneficial (overall effective and useful) to the different collaborative business processes. However, the ratings from involved small and medium-sized enterprises were better than that from the large enterprise, which is only little better than *neither agree nor disagree*. Moreover, the evaluation results indicate that the VENIS services are generally applicable to a large amount of typical collaboration situations involving large and small and medium-sized enterprises through its adaptability, integration of email and business process models. For example, results from application case 'supply chain collaboration between SMEs and LE' indicate that request for purchasing processes seem to be adequately supported by automating manual tasks.

The deep integration of email into collaborative processes is beneficial for all enterprises. Sharing of artefacts by sending them as attachments was mentioned by the large enterprise as most frequently used method, the SMEs rely on token-based upload of documents.

Tokens are used to access or upload documents, with the advantage that no login is needed. The tokens are sent via email that implies a certain security risk. Despite this situation our evaluation shows a rather positive rating and also confirms the usefulness of the tokens for uploading documents.

The means for searching are based on indexing and information extraction services and are automatically performed on email and other human-readable documents that are shared in collaborative processes. Those services support annotation of documents and enable full text as well as semantic search. The evaluation shows for *collaboration owners* as well as for *collaboration members* a slight superiority of full text search over the innovative semantic search.

The evaluation of the means for business process modeling and management of the collaboration flow shows that the users see the potential of the business process support. The robustness and easy to use aspect of the business process support is slightly positive. For the participating SMEs the evaluation indicates that the VENIS services are able to manage contractual aspects, support purchasing processes and make interaction with suppliers easy than what it is in the usual way of working. For the participating large enterprise the results for those questions are neither positive nor negative.

7 Conclusion and Future Work

Conducting the evaluation with three application cases provided valuable insights from our users and suggestions how to further improve the VENIS services for interoperability. For example, the overall evaluation of the VENIS dashboard was positive but additional functions such as move, copy, or mark as read for artifacts were requested. The integrated support of business process models was appreciated, but the results suggest simplifying the creation of the process models. The semantic search seems to be too complex for *collaboration members* and an improved user interaction is requested.

Currently the project team is working on improving the VENIS services. We believe that the VENIS approach combining email, lightweight semantics and business process support in a unified manner has sufficient potential to improve current styles of working between large and small and medium-sized enterprises.

Acknowledgement. Our thanks are due to all partners of the VENIS (Virtual Enterprises by Networked Interoperability Services) project that is partially funded by the EU under grant number 284984. Special thanks go to Marco Alessi, Bruno Casali, Štefan Dlugolinský, Martin Šeleng, Harry Trigazis, and Gicomo Vecere as well as to all test persons for their contribution to this work.

References

1. Peristeras, V., Fradinho, M., Lee, D., Prinz, W., Ruland, R., Iqbal, K., Decker, S.: CERA: a collaborative environment reference architecture for interoperable CWE systems. SOCA **3**(1), 3–23 (2009)
2. Prinz, W., Löh, H., Pallot, M., Schaffers, H., Skarmeta, A., Decker, S.: ECOSPACE - towards an integrated collaboration space for eProfessionals. In: 2006 International Conference on Collaborative Computing: Networking, Applications and Worksharing. IEEE Press (2006)
3. Prinz, W., Jeners, N., Ruland, R., Villa, M.: Supporting the change of cooperation patterns by integrated collaboration tools. In: Camarinha-Matos, L.M., Paraskakis, I., Afsarmanesh, H. (eds.) PRO-VE 2009. IFIP AICT, vol. 307, pp. 651–658. Springer, Heidelberg (2009)
4. Zhang, A.X., Ackerman, M.S., Karger, D.R.: Mailing lists: why are they still here, what's wrong with them, and how can we fix them? In: 33rd Annual ACM Conference on Human Factors in Computing Systems, pp. 4009–4018. ACM (2015)
5. Mahmud, L., Matthews, T., Whittaker, S., Moran, T.P., Lau, T.: Topika: integrating collaborative sharing with email. In: SIGCHI Conference on Human Factors in Computing Systems, pp. 3161–3164. ACM (2011)
6. Seleng, M., Laclavik, M., Dlugolinsky, S., Ciglan, M., Tomasek, M., Hluchy, L.: Approach for enterprise search and interoperability using lightweight semantic. In: 2014 18th International Conference on Intelligent Engineering Systems (INES), pp. 73–78. IEEE (2014)
7. Dlugolinsky, S., Krammer, P., Ciglan, M., Laclavik, M.: MSM2013 IE Challenge: Annotowatch. Making Sense of Microposts (# MSM2013) (2013)
8. Laclavik, M., Ciglan, M., Dlugolinsky, S., Seleng, Hluchy, L.: Emails as graph: relation discovery in email archive. In: 21st International Conference Companion on World Wide Web, pp. 841–846. ACM (2012)
9. Laclavik, M., Dlugolinsky, S., Seleng, M., Kvassay, M., Gatial, E., Balogh, Z., Hluchy, L.: Email analysis and information extraction for enterprise benefit. Comput. Inform. **30**(1), 57–87 (2012)
10. VENIS Deliverables. http://www.venis-project.eu/deliverables
11. VENIS Video. http://www.venis-project.eu/video

Towards a Customer-Driven Value Chain Framework – A Set-Based Oriented Approach

João Bastos[1,2(✉)], Américo Azevedo[1], and Paulo Ávila[2]

[1] INESC TEC – INESC Technology and Science and FEUP -
Faculty of Engineering, University of Porto,
Campus da FEUP, Rua Dr Roberto Frias, 4200-465 Porto, Portugal
{jsbastos,ala}@fe.up.pt
[2] ISEP/IPP - School of Engineering, Polytechnic Institute of Porto,
Rua Dr. António Bernardino de Almeida, 431, 4249-015 Porto, Portugal
psa@isep.ipp.pt

Abstract. In today's business, consumers are challenging manufacturers by increasingly demanding low volumes of innovative, fashionable and inexpensive products; adopting high quality standards; responding in smaller intervals of time, and with high configurability and parameterization. This omnipresent scenario poses challenging opportunities for collaborative networked organizations. The present paper addresses the main collaborative business processes tailored for responsiveness and efficient use of knowledge on customized manufacturing environments through a lean-based framework proposal for collaborative networks inspired in the Set-Based Concurrent Engineering (SBCE) methodology. In particular this work describes the ongoing implementation of the proposed concepts through a web-based collaborative portal.

Keywords: Collaborative networks · Customer-driven · Framework · Set-based design

1 Introduction

The recent decades have shown at manufacturing level an expansion of collaborative strategies addressing the small batches to lot one production of highly-customized complex products. This is especially critical for innovative and/or fashionable products with short to micro life-cycles. In fact, consumer needs and expectations are arising as challenging opportunities for worldwide manufacturing companies which are required to put more emphasis on the service levels they provide, by reducing response times and by tackling customers' specific demand needs of small series of innovative/ fashionable inexpensive high quality products, in shorter periods of time.

Facing a competitive market, companies' managers are constantly challenged to reduce the lead time between technical or market opportunity arising and satisfying the customer need with full-rate production of a quality product. The time to market on the case of innovative and fashionable goods is a critical factor, since all competitors get access to new technical ideas and new market information at about the same time.

© IFIP International Federation for Information Processing 2015
L.M. Camarinha-Matos et al. (Eds.): PRO-VE 2015, IFIP AICT 463, pp. 209–222, 2015.
DOI: 10.1007/978-3-319-24141-8_19

On the other hand, with the increasing empowerment of the user/customer role, the design focus has been shifting from a designer-centered approach to a co-designing attitude in which the roles of the designer, the researcher and the 'customer' have been moving increasingly closer. The implications of this shift for traditional manufacturing networks are enormous. The current evolution in the design approach has a significant impact in the product configurations, product volumes and response time, changing the landscape of collaborative networking.

In order to conceive, design, develop, manufacture and supply such products, new approaches and underneath supporting services for collaborative networking are increasingly mandatory in order to companies succeed in addressing the market demand through customer-driven value chains.

This paper addresses the multidisciplinary complexity of customer-driven value chains creation for innovative/fashionable products, in particular, by tackling the main collaborative business processes tailored for responsiveness and efficient use of knowledge on customized manufacturing environments through a lean-based framework proposal.

The proposed framework extends the lean product development principles followed by the Toyota Motor Corporation and presented by D. Sobek as Set-Based Concurrent Engineering (SBCE) [1] to the presently growing and increasingly significant environment of Collaborative Networks (CNs).

This innovative *lean*-based framework is intended to cope with the challenges posed by the omnipresent consumers demand of products with manufacturing of low volume, high variability and increasingly reduced time-to-market expectations.

The remaining sections of this paper are organized as follows: primarily the existing related literature and research questions are presented as background and research topics, followed by the presentation of the set-based principles in collaborative networks. Afterwards, the customer-driven value chain framework is portrayed. Finally, conclusions and future developments are presented regarding the framework instantiation and further improvement.

2 Background and Research Topics

The acceleration of globalization and rapid technological evolution are leading to an increased unpredictability and instability. The emergence of global and competitive markets are forcing the companies, especially in the case of SMEs, to adjust to this new aggressive environment in order to proactively respond to challenging market requirements with increased responsiveness and flexibility [2].

This competitive reality is intensified by the fact that the demand of consumer goods, especially innovative and fashion products, have in the recent past forcing manufacturers into delivering an increased number of product variants with a dramatic reduction of products life-cycle. Furthermore, paradigms such as mass customization and personalization are forcing companies to increased flexibility in order to produce small batches, till one-of-a-kind product, to satisfy customer demand.

In many industries, an ever growing number of new products (often only incremented modified) are introduced within increasingly shorter time intervals. In many cases, product life-cycles have been cut to one third or even one fourth over the past decades [3]. Briefly, the modern business landscape is characterized by small batches, short to micro product life-cycles, fast-passed new product releases designed to attend increasingly knowledgeable, well informed, and demanding customers.

All these issues create a challenge for companies' managers: how to address this present-day consumers' demand for personalized value-added products, but also cope with it in terms of high quality levels, innovative functionalities and responsiveness?

Certainly, aligned with the objective to address this new customer demand challenges, there is a pressing need of new methods and tools for manufacturing value chains supported in the collaborative network organizational paradigm [4]. This new forms of networked organizations present a promising approach to deal with the need to customer driven focus, reduced time to market of new products and cost effective manufacturing in a cooperative and collaborative environment.

2.1 Customer-Driven Value Chains

Nowadays competition within the innovative and fashionable goods sectors is between global networks and one of the critical matters are on how to put and execute innovative managerial models and methods to provide and sustain collaborative practices, especially among SMEs, which represents the majority of companies in Europe [5, 6].

The most recent research in the topic of supply networks addressed distinct forms of business organizations that participate in value creation. They are distinguished for example, by the degree of virtualization or hierarchical structure (hierarchical vs. non-hierarchical networks), the value chain orientation (horizontal, vertical, lateral) and life span (long-term vs. short-term) [7].

Research in collaborative networks of innovative and fashionable products have identified six key phases in order to organizations address a specific market need till final dispatch to the customer (see Fig. 1). It also have shown that each one of these phases present relevant challenges regarding their complexity, time constraints and resources consumption [8].

Fig. 1. Market oriented manufacturing network phases

In face of these critical impact phases, the prevailing market environment asks for flexible and reactive organizational structures which rapidly adjust to new manufacturing challenges and revise the business requirements accordingly. These new market characteristics are compelling manufacturing networks to embody shorter life-time existences and take advantage of new infrastructure technologies to support distributed decision making, information sharing and knowledge management [2].

In order to answer to the consumer's pressing needs and expectations, the paradigm of customer-driven value chains is emerging in literature as a collaborative approach [9–11]. Based on this new paradigm, new approaches to address and engage market demand are envisioned. These approaches are based not only on traditional sales distribution channels (as stores or sellers) but increasingly on an Internet mediated interaction with consumers covering aspects such as product co-design, product customization till final sale.

Exploratory work provided evidence to researchers that responsiveness is intrinsically related to competiveness. Namely, organizations can increase their ability to compete based on product innovation, low time to market, low price and high delivery dependability by increasing the firms' responsiveness [12].

A direct outcome of firms and by extension collaborative networks responsiveness is the reduction of the time to market. The time to market is the lead time between a technical or market opportunity arising and satisfying the customer need with full-rate production of quality products. The time to market lead time is critical since all competitors eventually get access to new technical ideas and new market information at about same time. The winner is the one which is consistently faster than competition. As Li et al. states: "time to market is the ability of an organization to introduce new products faster than major competitors" [13]. In reality there is a extensive acknowledgment that time to market is a fundamental determinant for competitive advantage [14].

According to Ward [15] the time to market can be decomposed into the sum of four periods: **reaction time** (period between the opportunity appearing and company decision to invest); **exploration time** (period which the development team explores alternative implementations); **lock-in time** (during which a final solution is detailed); and fix-up time (during which the company tries to deal with the problems aroused during the implementation of the solution) (see Fig. 2).

Fig. 2. Time to market periods (based in [15]).

Inversely to the concept of 'time to market' there is the concept of 'market miss'. In reality, markets are missed because the development team fails to understand the customer, or because it is not innovative enough and therefore missing the customer needs on time or generating cost and quality problems [15].

Customarily, the development of a value stream inside companies or inside collaborative networks, produces operational value streams. Operational value streams run from suppliers to manufacturers, into product characteristics, and finally out to customers. Manufacturing units are the primary customers of the development value streams. Actuality, the development process only has value if it enables manufacturing operations to deliver better products to the final customer.

In conventional development processes the approach followed is the "waterfall" or "V" methodology. In this approach, starting from the concept specification, first it is designed the system, freezing the interfaces between the subsystems, then designed the subsystems, following a top down method.

A similar "waterfall" approach is followed in the development process of collaborative networks. The initial definition of the business opportunity leads to the collaborative design of the product and subsequently to the process planning and the network configuration definition. The Fig. 3 presents the similarities between the product design process and the collaborative network formation process using the conventional "waterfall" approach.

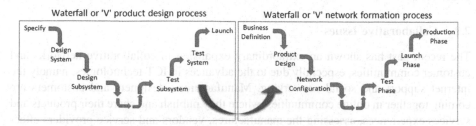

Fig. 3. Waterfall or traditional approach

Although abundantly used this "waterfall" approach, it presents for several researchers significant drawbacks. The followed top down approach means that critical systems decisions about module or subsystems interfaces are made on the basis of early insufficient data about what is possible. The resulting designs on products, processes or network configurations are usually distorted and inconsistent, leading to usually low levels of reutilization of parts, manufacturing systems or reconfiguration of networks [16–18].

In reality, is common for companies select suppliers through a bid process usually based on cost. This approach requires the release of product specifications or drawings. In many cases, this practice blocks the opportunity to identify what suppliers and partners can actually do, and therefore which system design, module specification or network configuration actually makes sense. Also, since the selection of network members is based in many cases on the basis of quotation, which is in many cases, is more a "promise" than a commitment.

A major consequence of the typical product development cycle based on the "waterfall" approach in supply networks is the occurrence of problems that are discovered late or in advanced phases of the design process. These problems force design loopbacks and network reconfiguration (see Fig. 4) which often consumes 50–75 % of engineering resources [19].

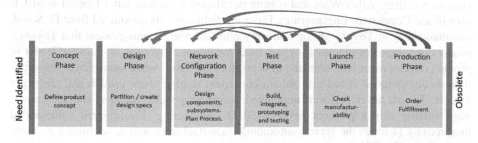

Fig. 4. Loopbacks in "waterfall" collaborative networks formation

In summary, the traditional "waterfall" approach presents several drawbacks which include: **inefficient use of resources** due to the late problems discovery and the necessary loopbacks; the **discard of knowledge** due to the early product concept definition and design specifications which limits the network partners involvement and knowledge generation; and finally generates **poor and unreliable solutions** in terms of products and network configurations since it is based before the customer interests are understood.

2.2   Collaborative Issues

The recent past has shown an extraordinary expansion in collaborative networks and customer communities, especially due to the advances in ICT technologies, namely the internet support and social networking. Manufacturers, designers and customers are coming together in online communities, where they publish and share their products and services experiences, assessing the manufactures, vendors and service providers effectiveness [20]. Increasingly, consumers are participating both in the front-end period with contributions to the idea generation and conceptualization, and the back-end period with involvement in the sketch, design and testing phases of new product development by enhancing the innovation process and thus co-creating value [21].

Simultaneously, due to the business increasing emphasis on technological innovation and the improvements in ICT technologies, a growing number of designers and network stakeholders use knowledge management tools and integrated systems to support innovation in collaborative design [22].

The recent research shows that collaborative design is a knowledge-based path, requiring not only experts with knowledge and experience on different multidisciplinary areas, but also requiring the integration and coordination of the design and development phases of different actors. The challenge of providing reliable and fully operational collaborative design and knowledge management systems increasingly relies in integrated platforms but also practices and methods that promote and sustain the development coordinately [23].

3   Set-Based Approach in Collaborative Networks

The concept of set based thinking was initially conceived by researchers from MIT and University of Michigan in the late 90's. Starting from Toyota's product development success practices, Allen Ward and is team developed what they latter labeled as SBCE (Set-Based Concurrent Engineering). From the field analysis conducted from D. Sobek simultaneously at Toyota Motor Company and Chrysler, it was evident that Toyota's product development practices surpass its competitors. Toyota is an industry leader in product development lead time and new product launches, while using fewer resources than its competitors. It has also shown consistent market share growth and profit per vehicle. Toyota never performs unplanned design loopbacks; had a systematic knowledge sharing across projects; achieve 80 % engineering development value-added productivity (4 times the typical automobile manufacturer); and never misses its milestones dates [24, 25].

Sobek summarized the definition of SBCE as engineers and product designers "reasoning, developing, and communicating about sets of solutions in parallel and relatively independent" [1]. In fact, according to the lean approach from Toyota, the most important input to production is knowledge. Starting from this paradigm, Toyota doesn't understood product development as a series of steps that result in a final product, but rather as an inclusive environment that yield a stream of products.

In order to acquire this 'knowledge breeding environment', the set-based approach followed by Toyota seeks continuously to obtain usable knowledge from the following sources:

- Integration knowledge - includes learning about customers, suppliers, partners, designers, the manufacturing network, the market;
- Innovation knowledge - the conception of new ideas and solutions;
- Feasibility knowledge - allows comprehension of the manufacturing constraints and capabilities enabling better decisions among the possible solutions.

The effort to collect this knowledge starts immediately at the customer requirements early definition. Traditionally, using the "waterfall" approach, the customer requirements are frozen early, followed by a more detailed design and interface specification of the process. In contrast, in the set-based approach, Toyota builds a set of possibilities to satisfy their customer needs, and through a series of experimentation, combination and knowledge acquisition, they narrow the possibilities until arriving at final solution (see Fig. 5).

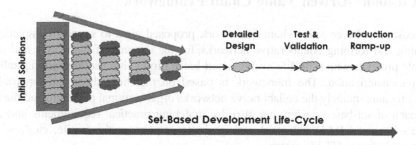

Fig. 5. Set-based development life-cycle

In order to the set-based development approach be successful, it relies on basic tools. As is usual in the lean philosophy, the tools should be simple and as possible rely on visual sense. Understanding and documenting technical knowledge in the case of the set-based approach is achieved in the forms of trade-off curves, checklists and limit curves. This form of representation naturally transfers tacit to explicit knowledge. Afterwards the approach integrates the knowledge through causal mapping for problem solving as depicted in Fig. 6.

In summary, a set-based development approach enhances early and efficient learning so that enough information is attained before decision making. It requires collaborative learning and the involvement of many areas of expertise, but also the relevant stakeholders' commitment. In addition, by allowing delayed decision-making,

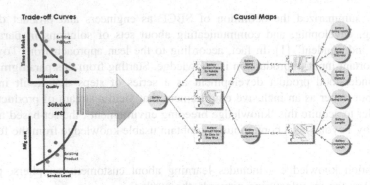

Fig. 6. Set-based development supporting tools

until enough knowledge is acquired, enables wise decisions and not guessing. It also supports collaborative, converging decision-making by assuring that decisions in one area will not impact decisions on others areas.

Collaborative networks due to their intrinsic characteristics have immensely to benefit from this comprehensive approach proposed by the set-based development theory. The following chapter details how it is possible to apply set-based theory and methods in the collaborative networks environment through a customer-driven value chain framework.

4 Customer-Driven Value Chain Framework

The customer-driven value chain framework proposed aims to support companies in defining and forming collaborative networks for the demand of innovative and fashionable products with short life-cycles, small batch production and high configurability and parameterization. The framework is based on matching theoretical approaches from literature, namely the collaborative networks organizational paradigm and the lean approach of set-based design, but also, by matching practical requirements and constraints observed R&D industrial case projects namely on the textile, clothing and footwear industry (TCFI) sector.

The emerged needs from the analyzed business cases consider three different decision levels: strategic, tactical and operative. Figure 7 presents the overall conceptual view of this proposed framework mapping its decisional levels with the three framework structural dimensions considered, namely concepts, methods and tools. All these levels are instantiated along the dimensions and are embedded with the contributions from the collaborative networks paradigm and the lean set-based development system approach.

The customer-driven value chain framework proposal relies on two basic elements: methods and tools. The **methods** define guidelines which are instantiated though the definition of the business processes mainly through BPMN notation. On the other hand, in order to support the realization of the designed methods, specific ICT tools based mainly in web-technology are required and have been under design and implementation.

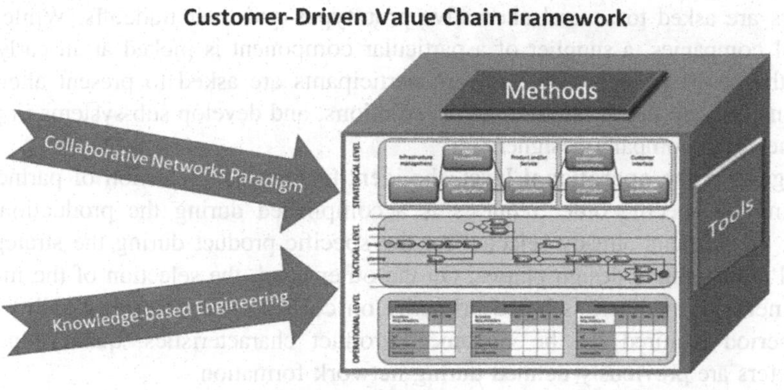

Customer-Driven Value Chain Framework

Fig. 7. Customer-driven value chain framework conceptual view

A critical element of the framework is related with the functional view of the value chain formation. Namely the partner search can occur in different phases of the network business scenarios namely at:

- **Strategic level:** during definition of the product portfolio when the manufacturer needs to select strategic partners which will support both the conception/design and the manufacturing of the products.
- **Tactical level:** collaboratively participating in the detailed product design and the matching production process design.
- **Operational level:** since a customer order is collected, it is necessary to select amongst the partners those who will be set off for that specific order.

For all of these three levels of collaborative work, different criteria and partner search capabilities shall be used, in order to ensure a comprehensive knowledge-based networked development engineering process.

In the case of the **strategic level**, the partner search is based on criteria for the identification and selection of partners based on a partner profile which summarizes the historical performance of the partner. The partner search at this early stage is useful in the definition of formal framework agreements. Namely, this formal agreements, bind partners in the commitment to reserve an amount of their production capacity for the production of a certain product along the production period and also participate in the early modular definition of products and respective interfaces. The selection of partners is based not only on the product characteristics but also on the historical performance of the partner in terms of quality, expertise, responsiveness and price. In this context, complementary indicators are flexibility and adaptability to requests from the focal company, which in summary is the ability to quickly reconfigure or set-up processes, to support new products variants or to vary quantities.

Concerning the **tactical level**, the collaboration is tighten and comprehensive. Each partner make drafts, simulate and conduct tests of solutions. The proponent of business opportunity expects that the network partners explore the trade-offs among different product requirements, support decisions with test data and validate designs by delivering fully functional prototypes as early as possible in the process. In some cases,

partners are asked to several alternative prototypes and their tradeoffs. While in traditional companies, a supplier of a particular component is picked at an early stage,
using the set-based approach, network participants are asked to present alternatives
solutions, present the feasibilities of the solutions, and develop sub-systems in parallel
with the focus company designers.

Regarding the **operational level**, the identification and selection of partners participating on specific order requests is accomplished during the production phase
among the partners already selected for the specific product during the strategic and
tactical collaborative design phases. On the other hand, the selection of the manufacturing network members is based primarily on costs and capacity availability for the
time period required by the customer. Product characteristics, quality and other
parameters are previously defined during network formation.

In order to test and validate the concepts presented in this new holistic framework, a
specific set of methods, tools and technologies were defined with the purpose to
support the formation and the operation of collaborative networks. This framework
supports the production of innovative and fashionable products by enabling collaborative product design, distributed manufacture and delivery of functional products
aligned with the consumer needs. A crucial element devised to set up these services for
the supply networks stakeholders is the Collaborative Portal (see Fig. 8).

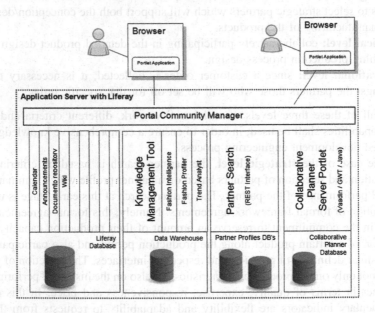

Fig. 8. Collaborative portal schema

The Collaborative Portal is a web-based front-end accessible through an Internet
browser application. Using the Liferay web content management framework, the collaborative portal application server supports legacy integration and messaging with
companies external applications such as MES and ERP's. Namely the collaborative

portal supports the partner search functionalities for collaborative networks formation based on the following technological components and data:

- An ontology for the description of KPI concepts and relations;
- A repository of skills and performance data;
- An collaborative algorithm to perform search and matching for network formation;
- Integration of set-based knowledge approach through the support of trade-off curves and causal maps definition;
- Integration with the ERP databases for collection and synchronization of relevant data;
- A tool for collaborative production of customer orders.

In order to support the operation formation of the collaborative network, the collaborative algorithm used to search and matching for network formation abides to the following steps:

- A potential customer present a business opportunity to the company front-office (focal company that identifies the business opportunity and hosts the interaction with the customer);
- Following the definition of the key requirements on the required custom made product, the front-office starts an elicitation process for the selection of the core-partners that will participate in the conception and design activities and are committed in responding to the overall business opportunity. This selection is based on their identifiable competencies, historical performance and availability through a knowledge based engineering approach;
- After the new product design activities, the required list of operations in the manufacturing network are instantiated by the focal company and core partners, added with a preliminary sequence plan with time restrictions (start and finish dates), which take into account the due date specified by the customer and aggregated capacities defined on each partner's profile (again using a knowledge based engineering approach);
- At the beginning of the planning phase, the criteria for partner selection is defined and agreed by the core partners and subsequently will be used to assess the final solution. The criteria take into account historical performance, time period availability and partner expertise and knowledge. Through a knowledge based engineering approach the defined criteria is imported to the partner search module;
- Several partners are asked to bid for several operations. The selection of the partners for the network configuration is accomplished through a multi-criteria process according to the guidelines of the set-based approach. This leads to a "rough" manufacturing plan that the focal company proposes to all the partners of the newly formed collaborative manufacturing network.
- Afterwards the initially "rough" plan is decomposed in a set of partial requests for quotation on each operation for each partner. Subsequently the partner performs a local time-framed analysis of their local capacity and availability in order to assess if it is possible to respond to the proposed dates and lead time. Later a response quotation is created stating if the proposed plan is accepted with the cost of it, or replying with alternative solutions for the request both in terms of quantities or time

constraints. Each response generates a possible plan that is assessed through a multi-criteria plan evaluation;

- The negotiation process continues until a satisfactory solution is achieved and a final manufacturing plan is accepted and implemented.

With this approach, it is addressed the role of the network ownership in an "elegant way". Even though, the proposed approach relies on a centralized infrastructure when considering the information and communication technology elements, in reality, it promotes a decentralized approach on the formation and operation of the manufacturing network. This decentralized approach seeks to embody the concept of collaborative networks in which each partner is capable of proposing and participating actively on the characterization of each required product and/or operation, by working together with high degrees of integration and with matching goals.

In conclusion, through the development of the Collaborative Portal, the proposed framework offers a set of methods based on a web-based toolset designed to assist network managers and stakeholders in face of business opportunities to: create, update and reuse knowledge in development of new products using the set-based approach; to assist the configuration and the formation of collaborative networks by supporting the manufacturers in the identification and selection of the network partners; by supporting the operation of the network and the construction of manufacturing plans; and by assessing past and present network members performance through the computation of key performance indicators.

5 Conclusions and Future Developments

This work proposes a customer-driven value chain framework in order to create innovative collaborative environments which enable manufacturing companies to produce and supply small series of specialized and customized high value added products. The empirical origin of the framework empowers it to address the time to market issue for innovative and fashionable goods as a critical factor and guarantees full applicability of its guiding principles through the use of a lean inspired knowledge-based engineering approach.

In particular, the framework represents the translation of a methodology that can be instantiated to companies with the support of methods and tools for product co-design, collaborative process planning, networked manufacturing planning activities and assessment of partners' collaborative performance. The framework aspires to assist collaborative networks in understanding consumer needs, engage consumers in product co-design activities, assist in the creation and reuse of knowledge in the formation of the networks, encourage joint collaboration with network partners, and support innovative knowledge-based engineering design of new products through a lean inspired set-based approach.

The conceptual model of the framework, developed from previous and ongoing R&D projects with industrial partners has been applied to the real cases of TCFI industry. The instantiations made according to the three levels of the framework covered the definition of new business models and the description of the most relevant dimensions involved in its application concerning the strategy definition, the collaborative network formation, the product and process design process and the knowledge gathering.

Through the development of the collaborative portal, specifically a web-based toolset, it was possible to instantiate the framework concepts in a practical tool which supported the necessary mechanisms for network formation, the co-design approach, the knowledge gathering and reutilization, and the proficiency in designing and manufacturing of small lots of products. The fundamental objective of this collaborative portal was to offer an integrated set of collaborative services that support the network managers and stakeholders of innovative and/or fashionable product manufacturers with the necessary guidance and assistance to address the multitude of processes, activities, functions, decisions, relationships and interactions alongside with the products, services and information flows.

The proposed customer-driven value chain framework for small series production represents a contribution towards the definition of adequate business models addressing responsiveness and efficient use of knowledge on customized manufacturing and collaborative environments.

As future developments, it is intended for the research team to pursue the refinement of the proposed framework based on the contributions of the industrial users and the ongoing development of more efficient and reliable knowledge-based tools embed on the lean approach of set-based design in collaborative environments.

Acknowledgments. This work was financed by the Project "NORTE-07-0124-FEDER-000057", financed by the North Portugal Regional Operational Programme (ON.2 - O Novo Norte), under the NSRF, through the European Regional Development Fund, and by national funds, through the Portuguese funding agency, FCT - Fundação para a Ciência e a Tecnologia.

References

1. Sobek, D.K., Ward, A.C., Liker, J.K.: Toyota's principles of set-based concurrent engineering. Sloan Manage. Rev. **40**(2), 67–84 (1999)
2. Zangiacomi, A., et al.: Reference model framework for production of small series of innovative and fashionable goods in manufacturing networks. In: Azevedo, A. (ed.) Advances in Sustainable and Competitive Manufacturing Systems, pp. 1291–1303. Springer, Switzerland (2013)
3. Trinkfass, G.: The Innovation Spiral: Launching New Products in Shorter Time Intervals. Springer-Verlag, Wiesbaden (2013)
4. Camarinha-Matos, L.M., Afsarmanesh, H.: Collaborative networks: value creation in a knowledge society. In: PROLAMAT 2006, IFIP International Conference on Knowledge Enterprise - New Challenges. Springer, Shanghai, China (2006)
5. Camarinha-Matos, L.M., Afsarmanesh, H., Boucher, X.: The role of collaborative networks in sustainability. In: Camarinha-Matos, L.M., Boucher, X., Afsarmanesh, H. (eds.) PRO-VE 2010. IFIP AICT, vol. 336, pp. 1–16. Springer, Heidelberg (2010)
6. Dyer, J.H., Singh, H.: The relational view: cooperative strategy and sources of interorganizational competitive advantage. Acad. Manage. Rev. **23**(4), 660–679 (1998)

7. Grefen, P., et al.: Dynamic business network process management in instant virtual enterprises. Comput. Ind. **60**(2), 86–103 (2009)
8. Fornasiero, R., Bastos, J., Franchini, V., Azevedo, A.: Collaborative networks model for clothing and footwear business sector. In: Camarinha-Matos, L.M., Xu, L., Afsarmanesh, H. (eds.) Collaborative Networks in the Internet of Services. IFIP AICT, vol. 380, pp. 349–359. Springer, Heidelberg (2012)
9. Childerhouse, P., Aitken, J., Towill, D.R.: Analysis and design of focused demand chains. J. Oper. Manage. **20**(6), 675–689 (2002)
10. de Treville, S., Shapiro, R.D., Hameri, A.-P.: From supply chain to demand chain: the role of lead time reduction in improving demand chain performance. J. Oper. Manage. **21**(6), 613–627 (2004)
11. Piller, F.T., Tseng, M.M.: New directions for mass customization. In: Tseng, M.M., Piller, F.T. (eds.) The Customer Centric Enterprise, pp. 519–535. Springer, Heidelberg (2003)
12. Thatte, A.A.: Competitive Advantage of a Firm Through Supply Chain Responsiveness and SCM Practices. University of Toledo, Ohio (2007)
13. Li, S., et al.: The impact of supply chain management practices on competitive advantage and organizational performance. Omega **34**(2), 107–124 (2006)
14. Holweg, M.: An investigation into supplier responsiveness: empirical evidence from the automotive industry. Int. J. Logistics Manage. **16**(1), 96–119 (2005)
15. Ward, A.C., Sobek II, D.K.: Lean Product and Process Development. Lean Enterprise Institute, Cambridge (2014)
16. Ward, A., et al.: Toyota, concurrent engineering, and set-based design. Ch **8**, 192–216 (1995)
17. Liker, J.K., et al.: Involving suppliers in product development in the United States and Japan: evidence for set-based concurrent engineering. IEEE Trans. Eng. Manage. **43**(2), 165–178 (1996)
18. Inoue, M., et al.: Collaborative engineering among designers with different preferences: Application of the preference set–based design to the design problem of an automotive front-side frame. Concurrent Engineering (2013). doi:10.1177/1063293X13493447
19. Kennedy, M.N., Harmon, K.: Ready, Set, Dominate: Implement Toyota's Set-based Learning For Developing Products And Nobody Can Catch You Author: Mich (2008)
20. Romero, D., Molina, A.: Collaborative networked organisations and customer communities: value co-creation and co-innovation in the networking era. Prod. Plann. Control **22**(5–6), 447–472 (2011)
21. Nambisan, S.: Designing virtual customer environments for new product development: toward a theory. Acad. Manage. Rev. **27**(3), 392–413 (2002)
22. Reimer, U., Margelisch, A., Staudt, M.: Eule: a knowledge-based system to support business processes. Knowl.-Based Syst. **13**(5), 261–269 (2000)
23. Chu, M., Tian, S.: Research on Knowledge Management of Collaborative Design. In: 2010 International Conference on E-Business and E-Government (ICEE), pp. 1890–1893 (2010)
24. Sobek, D.K.: Principles that shape product development systems: a Toyota-Chrysler comparison. Dissertation on Industrial and Operations Engineering in the University of Michigan (1997)
25. Kennedy, M.N., Ward, A.: Product Development for the Lean Enterprise: Why Toyota's System is Four Times More Productive and How You Can Implement It. Oaklea Press Richmond, VA (2003)

Conceptual Framework for Agent-Based Modeling of Customer-Oriented Supply Networks

Clara Mabel Solano-Vanegas[1], Angela Carrillo-Ramos[2],
and Jairo R. Montoya-Torres[3(✉)]

[1] Industrial Engineering Department, Pontificia Universidad Javeriana,
Bogotá, D.C., Colombia
solano.c@javeriana.edu.co

[2] Systems Engineering Department, Pontificia Universidad Javeriana,
Bogotá, D.C., Colombia
angela.carrillo@javeriana.edu.co

[3] School of Economics and Management Sciences, Universidad de La Sabana,
Chía (Cundinamarca), Colombia
jairo.montoya@unisabana.edu.co

Abstract. Supply Networks (SN) are complex systems involving the interaction of different actors, very often, with different objectives and goals. Among the different existing modeling approaches, agent-based systems can properly represent the autonomous behavior of SN links and, simultaneously, observe the general response of the system as a result of individual actions. Most of research using agent-based modeling in SN focuses on production issues. To the best of our knowledge, other relevant issues affecting SN competitiveness have not been fully studied such as the impact of customer's individual behavior or SN adaptability to changes in customer choices due to his/her decision-making context. In such a context, simulating SN oriented to the customer with context adaptability skills will allow researchers and practitioners to better look at ways to improve the relations between the SN and its customers, as well as to enhance SN's competitiveness. This paper presents our work in process about the design of an agent-based model of customer-oriented supply networks. Our focus is on the inclusion of the customer's purchase decision-making process and the SN adaptability. A preliminary model is developed based on a real-life case study from the floriculture sector in Colombia.

Keywords: Supply network · Multi-agent · Modeling · Simulation · Customer-oriented · Framework

1 Introduction

According to current definitions in the literature, a supply network "consists on all stages involved, directly or indirectly, in fulfilling a customer request. The SN not only includes manufacturers and suppliers, but also transporters, warehouses, retailers, and customers themselves" [1, p. 19]. The management of supply networks can be defined as all things required to influence the behavior of the SN and get the expected results [2].

© IFIP International Federation for Information Processing 2015
L.M. Camarinha-Matos et al. (Eds.): PRO-VE 2015, IFIP AICT 463, pp. 223–234, 2015.
DOI: 10.1007/978-3-319-24141-8_20

Effective management of these structures requires simultaneous improvement in both level of service to customers and efficiencies in internal operations of the organizations within the SN. Each supply network has its own unique set of market demands and operational challenges; each actor (company) of the SN must make decisions individually and collectively regarding production, inventory, facility location, transportation, and even information management [2]. The complexity of these decisions has increased in today's globalized markets; supply networks compete in multiple aggressive and changing environments. Continuous adaptation of their operating principles to search, face and act are paramount in response to new business challenges and opportunities in order to survive and remain competitive in the global market [3]. As a consequence, traditional SN's have evolved to become virtual, collaborative, complex and adaptive systems [4–6].

The academic literature has witnessed the proposition of multiple approaches for operational, tactical and strategic analyses of SN, including optimization (mathematical and/or heuristic), system dynamics, simulation and multi-agent modeling (e.g., [7–10]). Among those different modeling approaches, the multi-agent paradigm serves to model actors (agents) in the supply network as independent entities with a defined perception of their local environments, as well as to handle the impact of interconnectivity at a global level [3]. In other words, multi-agent systems (MAS) allow representing the system's behavior as result of the interactions between its members and the environment. The scientific literature has for a long time centered the study of SN structures on production, in which agents interact in response to messages sent and received in order to fulfill a demand requirement. However, this focus must be widened in order to actually respond to current needs and requirements of customers. It is hence necessary to analyze SN as costumer-oriented systems by taking into account the customers' decisional processes and their context. All this is done in order to improve the level of customers' satisfaction.

This paper aims at integrating the customers and their decisional processes into the analysis of SN. The goal is to exploit the benefits of multi-agent systems (MAS) as a tool of context-awareness analysis of supply networks in order to improve the SN competitiveness. At this point, the current paper presents our work in process on the design of an agent-based model of a customer-oriented SN. To illustrate the framework, a preliminary model is developed based on a real-life case study from the floriculture sector in Colombia.

This paper is organized as follows. Section 2 presents an overview of relevant related research. Section 3 describes the main features of a customer-oriented supply network. Section 4 is devoted to the description of the proposed multi-agent modeling framework in which the real-life case study is taken as an example of its implementation. The paper ends in Sect. 5 by presenting some concluding remarks and drawing directions for further research.

2   Overview of Related Literature

This section is devoted to present an overview of related academic works about modeling and simulation of supply networks using Multi-Agent Systems (MAS). For the purpose of this paper, we followed the principles of systematic literature review (SLR), in contrast to narrative reviews, by being more explicit in the selection of the studies and employing rigorous and reproducible evaluation methods [11, 12]. Indeed, from a methodological point of view, a literature review is a systematic, explicit, and reproducible approach for identifying, evaluating, and interpreting the existing body of documents [13, 14]. To this end, we defined relevant keywords ("Supply Networks" and "Multi-agents") and searched in academic databases (Proquest, Scopus, ISI Web of Knowledge/Science, IEEE) for research papers published in English since 2003. A total of 53 academic papers are finally shortlisted and analyzed (see [15]). A summary of findings of this review is presented next. Interested reader in the complete classification of reviewed papers is invited to check the internal project report at http://ashiy.javeriana.edu.co/~agora/.

The first important output from this review is that supply networks have mainly been product-oriented and process-oriented, mostly representing make-to-order configurations, while only one paper focusing on make-to-stock and another on built-to-stock. Focus of reviewed works has usually been on production planning and control. In addition, these topics have been modeled with a biased attention into software development and information technology implementation. As a consequence, evidence from the review shows that collaborative issues have been settled from a software-system development perspective.

Another interesting outcome from our literature review is that, although the MAS paradigm has been employed to model SN as complex systems, few real life applications have been employed to validate the approaches in industrial settings. Hence, there is still a gap between academic models and real-life environments.

Due to the continuous increase of global competitors, traditional product-centered and process-centered orientations of SN have not been successful. Hence, it is necessary to focus on customers considering the demand side of the SN [16]. As a matter of fact, only costumer-centered SN's will be successful thanks to the coordination between products, services, and plans all together oriented to the fulfillment of costumers' satisfaction [17]. At this point, it is important to note that existing agent-based SN models do not explicitly include the customer or his/her decision-making process; the MAS modeling paradigm has only been used for isolated simulations of customer's decision processes (e.g., [18–20]).

In addition, as stated in the literature [17, 21], it is of great importance to study the organizational adaptation to costumer changes due to cultural, social, individual and psychological factors that affect costumer's purchase behavior, as well as product utilization and disposition behaviors. Therefore, the SN scope must expand and focus primarily on the customers who finally determine the systems survival. This requires looking forward for the integration of costumers into the SN [21]. The current paper aims at fulfilling this gap in the academic literature. A case study from the Colombian floricultural sector is analyzed, but the modeling framework intends to be as general as possible to be applied to other industrial sectors.

3   The Customer-Oriented Supply Network

Before presenting the proposed conceptual MAS framework for customer-oriented SN, it is first required to identify the different processes within the supply network required to fulfill customer demands. To this end, the Supply Chain Operations Reference model

(SCOR®) will be employed [22]. In the SCOR® model, each company of the SN may perform five macro processes: Plan, Source, Make, Deliver and Return. Through the detailed performance of the activities within these processes, all companies interact through the SN, developing business relationships that finally accomplish both individual enterprise objectives and, most important, global profit. This is done by means of collaboration as a way to align individual companies towards this general objective. The processes supporting the scope of our model are presented in Table 1. In addition, the right side of Fig. 1 describes the relations and the processes occurring at each link between SN actors. Within the loop, arrows are centered in each SN company (some processes occur inside). However, these relations do not currently regard the customer; the customer appears as a passive SN actor. This behavior is far distant from real life. Customer's nature is active, and purchase decisions give sense and guarantee SN survival.

Table 1. Make-to-order processes codification according to SCOR® reference model [27].

Process-level 1	Process-level 2	
Plan	sP1. Plan supply chain	sP3. Plan make
	sP2. Plan source	sP4. Plan deliver
Source	sS2.1. Schedule product deliveries	sS2.4. Transfer product
	sS2.2. Receive product	sS2.5. Authorize supplier payment
	sS2.3. Verify product	
Distribution	sD2.1. Process inquiry and quote	sD2.8. Pick product
	sD2.2. Receive, configures, enter and validate order	sD2.9. Pack product
	sD2.3. Reserve inventory and determine delivery date	sD2.10. Load product and generate shipping documents
	sD2.4. Consolidate order	sD2.11. Ship product
	sD2.5. Build loads	sD2.12. Receive and verify product by customer
	sD2.6. Route shipments	sD2.13. Install product
	sD2.7. Receive product from source or make	sD2.14. Invoice
Make	sM2.1. Schedule production activities	sM2.4. Package
	sM2.2. Issue sourced/in-process product	sM2.5. Store finished product
	sM2.3. Produce and test	sM2.6. Release finished product for delivery

The proposed model of the SN including the customer can be seen in the right side of Fig. 1, in which the enhancing processes are highlighted with bolded lines. The processes included are the ones referred to the purchase decisions made by the customer (PDM) and the marketing processes: Consumer Analysis, Product Design, Distribution Channel Relations and Communication with the customer [19]. These are defined in the figure as MK 1, 2, 3, 4. When simulating these SN relations among multiple actors, and the impact of context-awareness on the processes, customer-facing metrics proposed by SCOR® reference model [22], such as Perfect Order fulfillment, order fulfillment cycle time, upside SN flexibility and adaptability (towards suppliers), Downside SN adaptability (towards de final consumer) will reflect its improvement, and measure reliability, responsiveness and agility of the SN under different scenarios.

4 Framework Based on Agents for Customer-Oriented SN

Multi-agent modeling is a tool that allows the simultaneous representation of multiple actors and their relationship. In the proposed model, further simulation will allow the customer decision-making agent to decide and generate a purchase order based on the context adapted information the SN offered initially. This section describes in detail the proposed agent-based system for customer oriented supply networks. As a matter of illustration, several parts of the framework will refer to a case study from the flori-cultural sector in Colombia.

4.1 Context-Aware Customer-Oriented Supply Networks: Considering Both Customer and Context Profiles

MAS modeling allows the creation of an agent able to perceive the customer's context and to change related SN processes in regard to the input received. In order to model this context-awareness functionality, following the ideas highlighted in [23], the context must be determined. In general terms, it can be defined by the customer's profile and the context profile. The former is the characterization of preferences, tastes, habits, interests, restrictions and benefits of the customer, while the later is characterized by several variables including spatial-temporal variables, infrastructure, as well as social technology, normative and environmental variables. All these describe the context in which the customer is immersed. These context characteristics are refined regarding each scenario. Some authors (e.g., [24]) have considered the context to be defined by the information registered in purchase orders, reception goods notes and shipment notes, but not the customer's environment itself. It is thus necessary to "capture" the customer's mental model of context [25].

In order to illustrate the inclusion of customer and context profiles within the proposed MAS model, the case personalized flower bouquet is considered. Figure 2 shows these two example profiles.

On the first hand (left side of Figure), the customer profile is explained. Tastes are customer's characteristics regarding the product due to past purchase and usage experiences. These include bouquet types, flowers, colors and varieties bought and the moments in which they were enjoyed. Preferences are customer choices from a list, for example ornaments to include in the bouquets, delivery options and costs (or prices). Interests are costumers' current trends (e.g., purchase motivation). Habits can be seen as customers' behavior regarding purchase frequency. Basic information as location and purchase type, recipients and restrictions variables determines the customer's specific profile. On the other hand (right side of Figure), the context profile is formed by the variables that characterize the processes context in which customers interact with

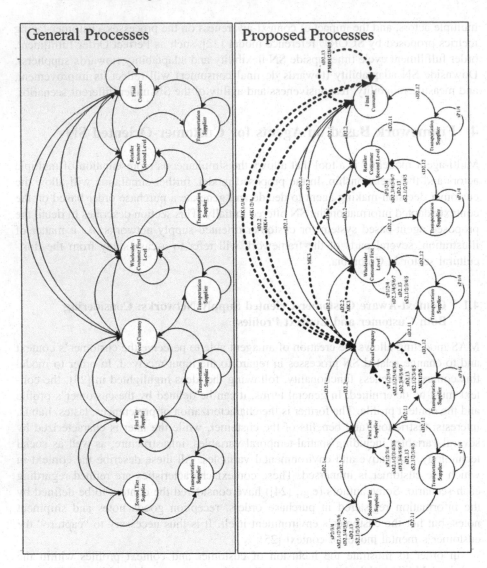

Fig. 1. General (left) and proposed (right) processes and relations diagrams.

the SN. The spatial and temporal characteristics regarding purchase occasions due to cultural situations, and the different taxes and customs regulations affect each customer. Also purchase channels, environmental issues (e.g., weather and humidity levels) affect the customers' possibilities towards his/her access to specific products.

The multi-agent model represents a set of customers defined by their individual profiles and contexts. Regarding this characterization, he/she will make a purchase decision. At the same time, the SN establishes a relation with the customer updating both profiles and context information in order to personalize the offers. In response, the system will adapt processes related to bouquet design and channel options impacting

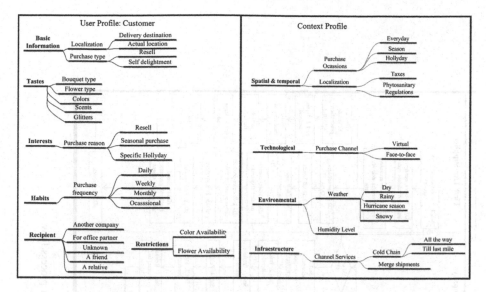

Fig. 2. User profile and context profiles applied to Flower Company Case.

upstream processes. As stated in [26], it is necessary to consider external conditions when simulating SN; they are the origin of complexities of these systems.

4.2   Multi-agent System: Illustrating the Order Fulfillment Process

In order to effectively model customer-oriented supply networks, a multi-agent modeling methodology has to be employed. In our case, we have chosen the so-called Organizational Approach for Agent Oriented Programming (AOPOA) methodology [27] in order to analyze, design and implement the model. Understanding the problem domain can be achieved by stating the process activity flow in which SCOR processes are defined (Fig. 3). Due to the page limitation of the current paper, the remainder of this subsection illustrates the AOPOA modeling methodology for the Order Fulfillment process. The agent definition is the result of the description of user case diagrams, functional and non-functional requirements, activities, objectives, abilities, resources, relations and roles tables. Finally, Fig. 4 shows how, for each SN actor in the MAS model, agents with different capabilities can assume different functions, regarding their role. For example, the focal company can be represented in the MAS model by either agent Plan (FC-P), charged of rules and strategies between actors, or agent Make (FC-M), responsible of assembly processes, or agent Source (FC-S) responsible of sourcing, or agent Distribution (FC-D) managing of delivery processes, or agent Adaptation (FC-Ad) responsible of the customers' feedback and communications between actors upstream the SN.

Supplier collaboration in order fulfillment processes is critical for the SN survival; hence, agility can be achieved as well as enhanced competitiveness. Suppliers' and focal company response to requirements from customers are modeled by considering their context. For instance, the Order Fulfillment Process is improved with initial communications from the focal company to the customer, taking into account his/her

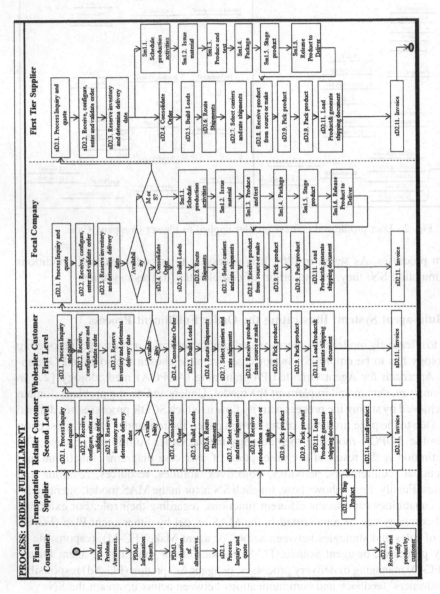

Fig. 3. Activities diagram of order fulfillment process flow.

context and the supplier's context. In our case, the agent adaptation sends, one or two days ahead to the historical request date, a personalized offer to the customer. This offer may respond to the environmental context profile in which the customer asks for flowers. The offering message considers customer's taste (e.g., bouquet and flower types, colors, and other preferences about ornaments).

Personalized offers will attend to production and sourcing availabilities and product design preferences. Furthermore, regarding the context information, future orders can be initiated directly from the customer. This information is used by the Production Agent in order to modify the product (for the case under study, future bouquets) by changing the percentages of colors, for example. Figure 5 presents an example of SN simulated performance of the whole supply network based on context-awareness.

Processes such as product design (in the illustrative case, bouquet and packing, channel options and prices) will be adapted regarding the costumers' decisions. As result of context awareness, personalized product offers, based on product availabilities considering customers preferences, habits, interests and additional variables from his/her context that affect the product design and packing, are presented to the

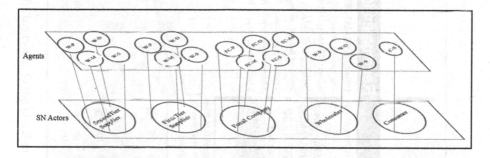

Fig. 4. Agent definition diagram.

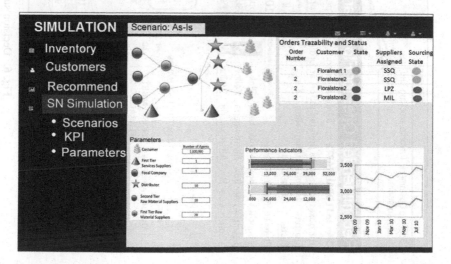

Fig. 5. Decision support tool: example of simulated key performance indicators.

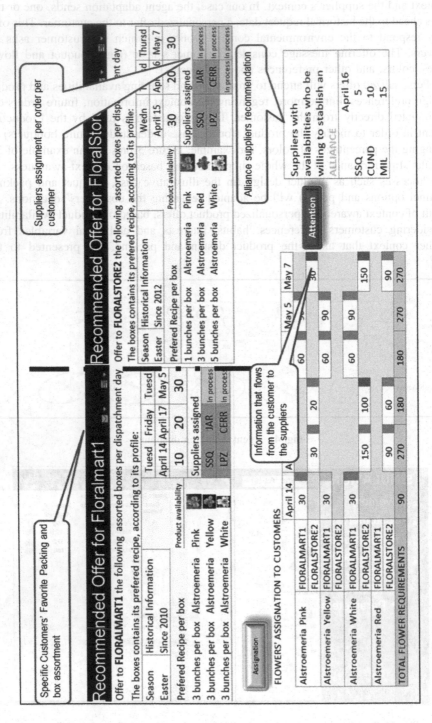

Fig. 6. Decision support tool: example of customized offering.

customers considering the incoming product, the requests already assigned to customer with assorted availabilities. Additionally, external conditions can be considered to adjust incoming product forecasting for example, weather conditions under different periods (daily, weekly, monthly, year). Figure 6 illustrates how personalized offers to customers can be taken into account by our decision support tool, considering suggested suppliers to be recommended as allied SN actors.

5   Conclusions and Further Research

In order to respond to current market conditions in which the customer's decision-making process does impact the performance of supply networks, this paper proposed a conceptual modeling of SN based on the multi-agent paradigm. The goal was to have more insights about the explicit consideration of the customer decision-making process and context in the modeling framework, in order to gain competitiveness. A computational decision support tool is under development allowing the test of different scenarios and the evaluation of SN key performance indicators. The aim is to have this tool able to consider customer decisional process and hence provide information to SN managers for adapting processes in response to customers' context.

As this is a first step in the modeling and simulation of a customer-oriented supply network under context awareness, further research is still needed. In particular, we are still on the data collection stage of the research and hence more numerical validation of the multi-agent system and the simulation tool are to be done. Additionally, our future research will also focus on the application of collaborative relations among different actors of the supply network and include the adaptive processes so as to evaluate the impact on key performance indicators. Finally, current insights for the design of the decision support tool are based from a particular case study from the floricultural industry in Colombia. More tests and feedback is needed in order to have a generic multi-agent model and computation tool, exploitable in different industrial settings.

Acknowledgments. We specially thank Ing. Luis Fernando Morales for assisting us with the Agora Project web page and system screenshots design.

References

1. Chopra, S., Meindl, P.: Supply Chain Management. Prentice Hall Inc, Upper Saddle River (2007)
2. Hugos, M.: Essentials of Supply Chain Management. Wiley, Hoboken (2011)
3. Medini, K., Rabénasolo, B.: Analysis of the performance of supply chains configurations using multi-agent systems. Int. J. Logistics Res. Appl. **17**, 441–458 (2014)
4. Camarinha-Matos, L., Afsarmanesh, H.: Collaborative Networked Organizations: a Research Agenda for Emerging Business Models. Springer, Berlin (2004)
5. Surana, A., Kumara, S., Greaves, M., Raghavan, U.N.: Supply-chain networks: a complex adaptive systems perspective. Int. J. Prod. Res. **43**(20), 4235–4265 (2005)
6. Pathak, S.D., Day, J.M., Nair, A., Sawaya, W.J., Kristal, M.M.: Complexity and adaptivity in supply networks: building supply network theory using a complex adaptive systems perspective. Decis. Sci. **38**(4), 547–580 (2007)

7. Labarthe, O., Espinasse, B., Ferrarini, A., Montreuil, B.: Towards a methodological framework for agent-based modeling and simulation of supply chains in a mass customization context. Simul. Model. Pract. Theor. **15**(2), 113–136 (2007)
8. Özbayrak, M., Papadopoulou, T.C., Akgun, M.: Systems dynamics modelling of a manufacturing supply chain system. Simul. Model. Pract. Theor. **15**(10), 1338–1355 (2007)
9. Melo, M.T., Nickel, S., Saldanha-da-Gama, F.: Facility location and supply chain management- a review. Europ. J. Oper. Res. **196**(2), 401–412 (2009)
10. Brandenburg, M., Govindan, K., Sarkis, J., Seuring, S.: Quantitative models for sustainable supply chain management: developments and directions. Euro. J. Oper. Res. **233**(2), 299–312 (2014)
11. Denyer, D., Tranfield, D.: Producing a systematic review. In: Buchanan, D.A., Bryman, A. (eds.) The Sage Handbook of Organizational Research Methods, pp. 671–689. Sage Publications, London (2009)
12. Delbufalo, E.: Outcomes of inter-organizational trust in supply chain relationships: a systematic literature review and a meta-analysis of the empirical evidence. Supply Chain Manag. Int. J. **17**(4), 377–402 (2012)
13. Fink, A.: Conducting Research Literature Reviews: From Paper to the Internet. Sage, Thousand Oaks (1998)
14. Badger, D., Nursten, J., Williams, P., Woodward, M.: Should all literature reviews be systematic? Eval. Res. Educ. **14**(3–4), 220–230 (2000)
15. Solano-Vanegas, C.M., Carrillo-Ramos, A., Montoya-Torres, J.R.: Agent-based supply network simulation: a literature review. Internal report, Pontificia Universidad Javeriana, Bogotá, Colombia (March 2015). http://ashiy.javeriana.edu.co/~agora/
16. Priem, R.L.: A consumer perspective on value creation. Acad. Manag. Rev. **32**(1), 219–235 (2007)
17. Fischer, L., Espejo, J.: Mercadotecnia, Cuarta edn. Mc Graw Hill, Mexico (2011)
18. Vag, A.: Simulating changing consumer preferences: a dynamic conjoint model. J. Bus. Res. **60**(8), 904–911 (2007)
19. Zhang, T., Zhang, D.: Agent-based simulation of consumer purchase decision-making and the decoy effect. J. Bus. Res. **60**, 912–922 (2007)
20. Roozmand, O., Ghasem-Aghaee, N., Hofstede, G.J., Nematbakhsh, M.A., Baraani, A., Verwaart, T.: Agent-based modeling of consumer decision making process based on power distance and personality. Knowl. Based Syst. **24**(7), 1075–1095 (2011)
21. Lamb, C., Hair, J.: Marketing. South-Western College/West, USA (2010)
22. APICS Supply Chain Council. The Supply Chain Operations Reference model (SCOR®). http://www.apics.org/sites/apics-supply-chain-council/frameworks/scor. Accessed April 2015
23. Wong, T.N., Fang, F.: A multi-agent protocol for multilateral negotiations in supply chain management. Int. J. Prod. Res. **48**(1), 271–299 (2010)
24. Hu, Y., Houde, J., Duong, T.-K.: A multi-agent model of cooperative and competitive strategies in supply chain. In: Proceedings of the IEEE International Conference on Automation and Logistics, pp. 2908–2913 (2008)
25. Zhang, X., Lesser, V., Wagner, T.: Integrative negotiation in complex organizational agent systems. In: Proceedings of the IEEE/WIC International Conference on Intelligent Agent Technology (IAT 2003), pp. 140–146 (2003)
26. Luck, M., McBurney, P., Preist, C.: A manifesto for agent technology: towards next generation computing. Auton. Agent. Multi-Agent Syst. **9**(3), 203–252 (2004)
27. Gonzalez, E., Bustacara, C.: AOPOA organizational approach for agent oriented programming. In: Proceedings of the 8th International Conference on Enterprise Information Systems (ICEIS 2006), Paphos-Cyprus (2006)

Towards a Workflow-Driven Multi-model BIM Collaboration Platform

Mario Gürtler[✉], Ken Baumgärtel, and Raimar J. Scherer

Institute of Construction Informatics, TU Dresden, 01062 Dresden, Germany
{mario.guertler,ken.baumgaertel,raimar.scherer}@tu-dresden.de

Abstract. Building Information Modelling (BIM) based way of work leads to increased data complexity in early phases of construction project and to higher effort in managing collaboration. In this context, techniques and methodologies have to be developed to support the participants in collaboration process. One technique is the integration of a workflow management system in a collaboration platform handling the data in an automatic way. This can be done if two approaches, the data exchange of an Industrial Foundation Classes (IFC) data model and a multi-model containing several data models also addressing non-IFC information, for collaboration in building industry are combined to form a multi-model BIM collaboration platform. The collaboration platform can be used to integrate and check relevant data models, which will be utilized by a workflow engine in a second step. This allows a very flexible and partly automated data and work management and facilitates the work of participants.

Keywords: BIM · IFC · IDM/MVD · BCF · Multi model · Workflow management

1   Introduction

The BIM based way of work wants to achieve a shift of effort from documentation and construction phase to concept and design phase. This has the advantage that in the construction phase can more effectively be responded on problems, which often happens due to the uniqueness of the production place of a building. This is described in [1, 2] and expressed as MacLeamy-curve [3]. Because of the digital way of work and the associated new possibilities to support design decisions and planning decisions by simulation and calculation, the effort increases in sense of data management as well as the management of participants and their software tools in collaboration process. When working with BIM the actors in a collaboration process are already confronted in the early phase with raising complexity of data. Furthermore, quality requirements concerning the work results have to be fulfilled so that the next collaborator is able to work with it. The data can be managed in a local or distributed folder structure as handled in many companies or they can be stored on a file server or model server. Each participant uses several software tools that can differ from other participant's tools. With regard to a computer aided way of work in a collaborative process, the respective software solutions should not be restricted but should support the way of work of the collaborators.

© IFIP International Federation for Information Processing 2015
L.M. Camarinha-Matos et al. (Eds.): PRO-VE 2015, IFIP AICT 463, pp. 235–242, 2015.
DOI: 10.1007/978-3-319-24141-8_21

In this context, the BIM-Manager is a new role within construction industry [4]. The upcoming of this new role confirms the raised effort regarding data management and associated problems during BIM based way of work. It is essential to develop techniques and software for automated data handling so that the new role will be supported in an efficient way.

Considering the changed way of work in concept and design phase, we look on already existing collaboration approaches to support the work of a BIM manager by proposing a more automatic way of interaction and data validation. The IFC based collaboration is based on following concepts: IFC, Information Delivery Manual (IDM), Exchange Requirement (ER), Model View Definition (MVD) and Open BIM Collaboration Format (BCF). IFC is an open data standard defined by buildingSMART and registered as ISO 16739 [5]. It represents the geometry of a building and its elements which compose it, a logical building structure and properties as well as quantities of building elements. It serves the exchange of digital building models and is widely used in open BIM environment to support high degree of interoperability. The Information Delivery Manuals is a standardized methodology to identify and to specify information flow during lifecycle of a facility. It has been developed by buildingSMART and is registered as ISO 29481-1:2010 and ISO 29481-2:2010. The methodology is used to describe information that has to be exchanged between parties working along a collaborative process [6]. Basis of the IDM methodology is a Process Map [7]. A Process Map documents the flow of activities of particular business use case and their required, consumed and produced information as well the actors involved [6]. The Process Map acts as fundament to identify each data exchange of a common information model between activities. They are documented as Exchange Requirements specifying a set of information. An ER describes the information in non-technical terms [6] normally in tabular or spread sheet applications [7]. The elaborated ERs are handed over to software implementation group specifying out of ERs a more technical, model/data-specific description of exchanged information documented as Model View Definition (MVD) [8]. A MVD defines a subset of the IFC schema that is needed to satisfy one or many ERs and is published by the software tool ifcDoc that was developed by BuildingSMART [5]. The Open BIM Collaboration Format enables a model-based communication between different users based on the standardized data model IFC. It has been adopted by BuildingSMART as standard. BCF can be used to exchange information between different software products [5]. While IDM describes and specifies the data flow within a collaboration process, BCF provides a technical solution for communication of the actors within collaboration process. BCF provides the opportunity to exchange issues, proposals or change requests on a particular topic. With BCF it is possible not only to address a specific IFC data model, but also to specify the location of the topic in form of snapshots or camera perspectives. It is possible to set up an own BCF server based on a RESTful API developed by the Institute of Applied Building Informatics (IABI) [9].

In contrast to described data-centric and very monolithic way of work, where collaborators work together on and exchange information about one single IFC data model, the multi-model approach assumes that one single data model (also called elementary model) is not sufficient during collaboration. The information space spreads over several data models during construction project, especially after design phase where other data models are added to the initially IFC data model like time models in the planning phase.

The individual elementary data models are composited to one multi-model (MM) and also exchanged in that way between collaborators. In addition, the multi-model approach pursues the idea to link the elements of the different data models to raise the information space of a multi-model [10]. The linkage of elements is described in a separate link model (LM). The common holistic approach in [11] can be used in all project phases, e.g. in the design phase for energy efficient simulations [12]. Regarding the technical implementation of multi-model approach and its use, the multi-model container (MMC) was developed to transfer multi-models between participants within a collaboration process [10]. On the other hand a higher semantic way of the multi-model approach based on ontologies is established. It does not mainly focus on the exchange of multi-models but it focuses on the centralized management of the distributed data models and the development of methods based the linkage of information. By means of ontology, rules can be defined for automatic validation of data quality [13] and automatic linkage of data models.

2 Multi-model BIM Collaboration Platform Based on IDM/MVD and BCF

Facing the changed way of work in concept and design phase of a construction project, there is a need to integrate the multi-model approach into conventional BIM collaboration platform based on the two standards, IDM/MVD and BCF. These established methodologies and techniques have to be advanced so they can also be used as basis of a distributed multi-model BIM collaboration platform. The potential of MVDs is not fully exploited in the validation and filtering of data in today's perspective. Today, mvdXML is mainly used for certification of software products primarily exporting IFC. A certification server is used to validate the exported data against mvdXML. The software tool ifcDoc has also a feature for data validation but there is no more implementation for data validation using mvdXML on the market. MVDs can also be used to filter IFC data [5] or to provide a partial model which can be an important feature in a collaboration platform regarding information security and data traffic. The word BimSnippet defined within BCF suggests that it should be also possible to address partial models. This snippet concept is supposed to prevent downloading and uploading of entire bulk of data model. Therefore, we see a potential to address predefined MVD integrated in the data management system.

The IDM methodology and the resulting ERs are independent from used data schemas because of their only documentary nature. BuildingSMART recommends using BPMN in an IDM specific way [5]. The Process Map is modeled as *Pool* including the actors as *Swim Lanes*. The Swim Lanes contain the activities assigned to the actors connected by the flow (see Fig. 1). The information model is also modeled as Swim Lane, the ER as document from or to the information model connected to the exchange point modeled as message event. This notation can be extended to cover the multi-model approach by splitting one common information model into elementary models and link models. An ER can be modeled by aggregating model-specific ER (see Fig. 1).

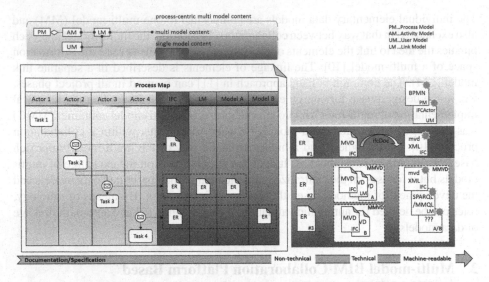

Fig. 1. Output of IDM/MVD based on Process Map (a) conventional single model (IFC) (b) multi-model approach (c) process-centric multi-model approach

Figure 1 shows that the IDM/MVD methodology produces a lot of documents that can be used as basis of a contractual collaboration but not as structured data for software interoperability. However focusing on technical interoperability, IDM/MVD only provides the computer-readable XML based format mvdXML that have to be laboriously created by entering the MVDs in ifcDoc tool and only works for IFC data schema. As far MVDs are used as document, there should be no problem to use this document structure to describe also the exchanged data of non-IFC data schemas. Regarding the technical utilization of MVD, like mvdXML for IFC data schema, we have to figure out what kind of other description languages of non-IFC data schemas exist and how they can be integrated. Furthermore, we have to elaborate methods how the model specific model views work together aggregating to one multi-model view definition (MMVD).

Regarding the usage of BCF in a multi-model based data management a BimSnippet addresses one specific data model mostly IFC. To use BCF for multi-models the fixed cardinality should be increased so that BCF itself can be used as container for all relevant models of multi-model. But this change can affect software products already using BCF. A MMC encapsulates the necessary data models and link models using XML based description and the concept to provide data models as raw format or to address data models via Uniform Resource Identifier (URI). Instead addressing all necessary data models of a multi-model, MMC makes it possible to use only one address. Hence, it fits perfectly to the BimSnippet of BCF and it would just impact the syntactical way and not the semantic way. Extending the standards BCF and IDM/MVD to support the multi-model approach as described in the sections before, a more dynamic architecture of a collaboration platform can be developed.

3   Workflow-Driven Multi-model BIM Collaboration Platform

The elaborated process of IDM/MVD methodology with its activities and their flows, even modeled in the standardized format BPMN, as well as the link information of an activity to its consumed and produced data and its assigned actor or executing service is only used as process documentation until now. This information is available and can be easily integrated in multi-model content management system by storing the process model and user model in a content management system using an ontology to link the activities to data models and actors (see Fig. 2). This process-centric data management can be used as basis of a process-driven collaboration platform by integrating a workflow management system (WMS) handling primarily the data flow. Considering the raising amount and complexity of data during early phases of a construction project, software solutions are needed to support the collaborators as well as the decision-maker and BIM manager in handling with data during collaboration process in the sense of an automatic data validation, data linkage, data filtering and data transfer/transport.

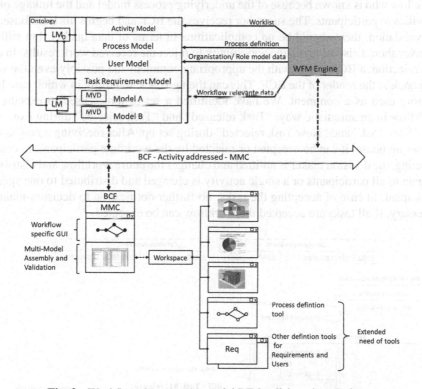

Fig. 2. Workflow-driven multi-model BIM collaboration platform

Thereby the requirement models introduced in [14] can have a major role. The requirement model specifies the requirements on a specific task e.g. the design of a building that an architect has to create or the resulting values of simulation that an engineer has to deliver and how they can be verified to guarantee data quality. These task requirements are also assigned to a task and could also be integrated in the ontology based content management and be linked with tasks (see Fig. 2).

The Workflow Management Coalition developed a Workflow Reference Model that describes the components and interfaces of a common WMS [15]. The core component is the workflow engine that provides the runtime environment for a workflow instance. During execution of a workflow instance the engine consumes and produces different data that is provided by the Workflow Enactment System. In Fig. 2 is illustrated that these data can be also provided by the described multi-model content. Figure 3 shows the UML sequence diagram of a common use case describing two interacting participants. The participants are using a collaboration client including the functionality of a multi-model client and a workflow engine. The workflow execution begins by editing the first or more than one task. After completing his task, the workflow participant releases his work results for the next participants in the workflow. A release leads to automatic validation of the results. When the validation fails the work results cannot be released. The work results are encapsulated and delivered to the next participants in the workflow who is known because of the underlying process model and the linkage of the activities to participants. The successor receives the BCF and begins his task. Based on the validation, there should be no complications in terms of data quality, but still the receiver should also be given the opportunity to reject the received work results. In case of a rejection, a BCF is sent with the appropriate comment and possibly even the same data back to the sender of the BCF. This can then go back and forth, in which case BCF is more used as a comment. We have identified a set of topics used to execute the workflow in an automatic way: "Task released" and "Task rejected" during execution and "New Task" and "New Task rejected" during set up. After receiving a new task in the set-up phase, it can be accepted or rejected by the workflow participant. In case of rejecting, the decision maker is notified and changes the entire workflow and distributes it again to all participants or a single activity is changed and distributed to one specific participant. In case of accepting the tasks, no further notification to decision-maker is necessary. If all tasks are accepted the workflow can be executed.

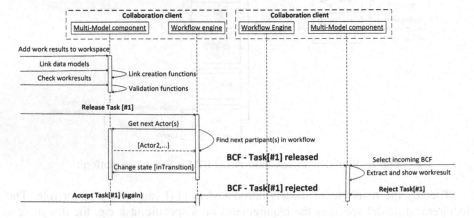

Fig. 3. Excerpt of UML sequence diagram of workflow execution

Based on the process, task and user information within the multi-model, the workflow engine takes over the function (1) to identify the next actor in the workflow, (2) to load the content of the activity based on previous finished tasks and (3) to identify all actors in a process they have to be informed during setting-up the workflow. In addition, the workflow engine is in charge (4) to manage the state of the activities and also the state of the process. The collaboration client has the functionality to fire the described BCF topics and to validate/check the quality of work results before they are released. Supporting the multi-model way of work, the collaboration client must be able to assemble multi-models by different elementary models and to link them. Especially the linkage of necessary information and tasks done by decision-maker is important.

4   Summary and Conclusion

This paper presented an approach for the integration of a workflow engine into a multi-model BIM collaboration platform. In a simple use case we showed how the workflow engine could be integrated to increase the degree of automation. In addition, the requirements on necessary software components were listed. It was also shown how a multi-model BIM collaboration platform based on ontologies and BCF can be formed, which made it possible to integrate workflow-specific data models. It was explained that MVDs are crucial factors in an automatic driven collaboration process. But their usage for validation and filtering of data is not fully evolved. It has been shown how the workflow specific data can be obtained from the multi-model IDM/MVD methodology, not only data relevant information but also process model and user model as well as their linkage information.

In next steps the sketched workflow-driven BIM collaboration platform will be implemented successively focusing on the workflow engine. First, a collaboration client will be developed including the functionalities of a workflow engine. Hence, the elaborated execution of a workflow can be proofed and be advanced. In a second step, the developed functionalities of a workflow engine are deployed as services in combination with BCF server.

Acknowledgments. We kindly acknowledge the support of the European Commission to the eeEmbedded project, Grant Agreement No. 609349, http://eeEmbedded.eu.

References

1. Fallon, K., Hagan, S.: Report on integrated practice - information for the facility life cycle. In: AIA National Convention, Los Angeles (2006)
2. Collaboration, integrated information and the project lifecycle in building design, construction and operation. In: Architectural/Engineering Productivity Committee of The Construction Users Roundtable (2004)
3. Zanchetta, C., Croatto, G., Paparella, R., Turrini, U.: Performance based building design to ensure building quality: from standardization to LEAN construction. TECHNE **8**, 62–69 (2014)

4. Barison, M.B., Santos, E.T.: An overview of BIM specialists, computing in civil and building engineering. In: Proceedings of the International Conference on Computing in Civil and Building Engineering. Nottingham University Press, UK (2010)
5. buildingSMART. http://www.buildingsmart.org
6. Wix, J., Karlshøj, J.: Information delivery manual - guide to components and development methods. buildingSMART International (2010)
7. See, R., Karlshoej, J., Davis, D.: An integrated process for delivering IFC based data exchange. buildingSMART International (2012)
8. Hietanen, J.: IFC model view definition format. International Alliance for Interoperability (2008)
9. BCF-API. https://github.com/BuildingSMART/BCF-API
10. Fuchs, S., Nityantoro, E.: BIM-management von multimodellen. In: Proceedings of 4. Fachkonferenz Bauinformatik - Baupraxis (2013)
11. Scherer, R.J., Schapke, S.-E.: A distributed multi-model-based management information system for simulation and decision making on construction projects. Adv. Eng. Inform. **25**, 582–599 (2011)
12. Baumgärtel, K., Kadolsky, M., Scherer, R.J.: An ontology framework for improving building energy performance by utilizing energy saving regulations. In: Proceedings of European Conference on Product and Process Modelling, pp. 519–526. CRC Press (2014)
13. Kadolsky, M.,Baumgärtel, K., Scherer, R.J.: An ontology framework for rule-based inspection of eeBIM-systems. In: Proceedings of Creative Construction Conference. Procedia Engineering, vol. 85, pp. 293–301 (2014)
14. Scherer, R.J., Guruz, R.: Towards a KPI-controlled holistic design method for eeBuildings. In: Proceedings of European Conference on Product and Process Modelling, pp 879–885. CRC Press (2014)
15. Hollingsworth, D.: The workflow reference model, workflow management coalition (1994)

Reference Model for Smart x Sensing Manufacturing Collaborative Networks - Formalization Using Unified Modeling Language

Dante Chavarría-Barrientos[✉], José Martín Molina Espinosa, Rafael Batres,
Miguel Ramírez-Cadena, and Arturo Molina

Tecnologico de Monterrey, Mexico City, Mexico
{dante.chavarria,jose.molina,rafael.batres,
miguel.ramirez,armolina}@itesm.mx

Abstract. This paper defines the Smart x Sensing reference model (S^2-RM) as a model that fulfills the requirements, characteristics and processes of a Manufacturing Collaborative Network to face the challenge of a digital economy. All the attributes have been formalized using Unified Modeling Language (UML). The S^2-RM allows a complete description using the five generic viewpoints stated in the Reference Model of Open Distributed Processing (RM-OPD): enterprise, information, computation, engineering and technology. A Collaborative Network Organization that produces micro-machines is used as pilot demonstration showing the specific purpose of each viewpoint and its relevance to achieve a smart and sensing environment.

Keywords: Collaborative networks · Smart organizations · Enterprise modelling · Sensing enterprise · Distributed systems · UML description · Manufacturing enterprise

1 Introduction

To compete in an ever-changing environment, enterprises face a number of challenges in the digital economy such as:

1. A connected economy and social networks as customers
2. Global clouds for share information services, data and applications
3. Worldwide real time design and on-site creation of product and services
4. International open innovation for new product and services
5. Universal global collaboration focuses on the right competencies
6. Collaborative networked organizations for manufacturing and services
7. Economical, ecological, and socially sustainable products and services

Collaborative systems play an important role in addressing these challenges. Smart environments require connecting all the smart and sensing objects of the physical and digital world [1]. There is a need for Enterprises or Collaborative Network Organizations to become aware of the global and physical context by means of sensing elements, which

© IFIP International Federation for Information Processing 2015
L.M. Camarinha-Matos et al. (Eds.): PRO-VE 2015, IFIP AICT 463, pp. 243–254, 2015.
DOI: 10.1007/978-3-319-24141-8_22

can be used to determine the actions needed to be agile and resilient. In PROVE 2014, we introduced the concept of the S^2-Enterprise (Smart x Sensing) reference model to address the above challenges [2]. According to Tolle et al. [3] a reference model is a model that captures characteristics and concepts common to several enterprises and organizations to capitalize on previous knowledge rather than developing the models from scratch. In brief, we designed a reference model using the RM-ODP as generic model to guide the design and development of Smart and Sensing Enterprises or Collaborative Networks Organizations in the manufacturing domain. An Enterprise in the context of this research is also a Collaborative Networked Organization (CNO) as described by [1]. Therefore the reference model could be used and applied in the creation of Smart and Sensing Collaborative Networked Organizations (Fig. 1). This paper develops further the reference model using UML as the formal language to model each of the five viewpoints of the RM-ODP standard: enterprise, information, computational, engineering and technology. Section 2 describes the general definitions of the S^2 Reference Model. Each of the viewpoints with their UML descriptions is presented in Sect. 3. A case study is presented in Sect. 4. Finally conclusions are drawn of the experiences of formalizing the reference model and experiences are shared on experiment with the pilot demonstration.

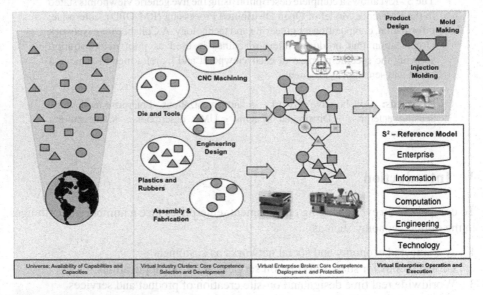

Fig. 1. The use of the S^2 Reference Model in the context of a Collaborative Networked Organization (Adapted from Molina et al. [13])

2   Smart x Sensing – Enterprise Reference Model (S^2-RM): Viewpoints Perspective

As stated by Putman [4], the use of 5 standard viewpoints proposed by the RM-OPD standard allows independence of business and architecture specification from technologies, therefore emerging technologies could be easily adopted by the enterprise without changing its elementary behaviour. The approach to the manufacturing system as an enterprise follows the description established by the RM-ODP standard; thus, the viewpoints inside the S²-RM are used as described below (See Fig. 2).

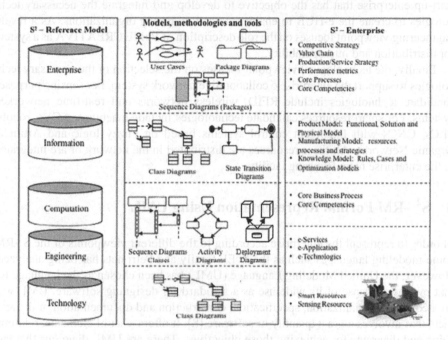

Fig. 2. The use of UML in the S² Reference Model and the definition of each viewpoint

The Enterprise viewpoint takes the perspective of a business model, so this viewpoint should be directly understandable to the stakeholders. As stated by Molina [2], this viewpoint represents the functionality that Smart and Sensing Enterprise is intended to achieve. Business concept creation, strategy formulation and action plan definition are the main issues identified for starting a description of the Enterprise, and thus, these components are proposed as the core of the enterprise viewpoint.

The information viewpoint focuses on describing the semantics of information and information processing functions in the system. Three information models are required in an enterprise to describe all data, information and knowledge required: Product, Manufacturing and Knowledge models [2].

The computational viewpoint represents a functional decomposition of the system; therefore this level represents the core business process and core competencies. Selecting the importance of business, customer and supplier related processes according to the Browne et al. [6] is important to know the level of detailed that must be represented. The internal processes of the business are: product development, obtaining customer commitment, order processing, and customer service. The interaction processes are co-engineering, co-design, and supplier and client relationships management.

The engineering viewpoint deals with the distributed nature of the system and the interoperability. This viewpoint offers the capability to support value added industrial networks or Collaborative Networked Organizations (CNOs). These networks rely on e-services in an open technological platform: e-HUB. PyME CREATIVA [7] is a project start-up enterprise that has the objective to develop and integrate the necessary technologies to create the e-HUB to enable interaction among organizations. As a result, engineering viewpoint focuses on the role description of PyME CREATIVA as a system for distribution and interoperability.

Finally, the technological viewpoint focuses on the selection of the necessary technologies to support the enterprise o collaborative network system. For sensing purposes candidate technologies include RFID, wireless networks and real-time networked systems. For smart resources candidate technologies include machines, AGVs, robots, PLCs, CNCs with Intelligent control systems based on Fuzzy logic and Artificial Organic Networks. All these resources are distributed in the network or are integrated in the enterprise manufacturing facility.

3 S^2 –RM Formal Representation Using UML

In order to represent the enterprise according to the different viewpoints of the S^2-RM some modeling languages such as the IDEF family and Petri nets has being analyzed. However, the Unified Modeling Language (UML) has been chosen as the language for that purpose because of its wide use as a standard for designing software. UML was created for the visualization, specification, construction and documentation of the artifacts that involves a great quantity of software [8]. It offers a set of elements, relationships and diagrams for achieving those objectives. There are UML diagrams that can describe the structural and behavioral perspectives of a system. UML has been efficiently used for software systems in banking, telecommunications, transport, commerce, medicine, space, etc. And because its flexibility, UML not only is useful for modeling software, but also for modeling juridical systems, security systems and hardware design [8]. And because UML has been used also in manufacturing systems [9], some diagrams will be proposed for the description of the S^2-RM.

For the representation enterprise viewpoint, Molina et al. [2] have proposed use-case diagrams and activity diagrams. In UML, use-case diagrams are used for representing actors and the actions they can accomplish. For the enterprise viewpoint case-diagrams specify actions such as defining and implementing the strategy (Fig. 3). Activity diagrams are used for the definition of the dynamics of a system. Then, it is used for the definition of the process suggested for defining the enterprise (Fig. 5).

The information viewpoint encompasses the product model, manufacturing model and knowledge model of the enterprise [10]. Because the object nature of the information in this viewpoint, UML class diagrams are convenient for modeling the information entities and their relationships.

In the computation viewpoint, key processes are nominated, so the business process strategy is defined. UML sequence diagrams and activity diagrams are used for this viewpoint (Fig. 2).

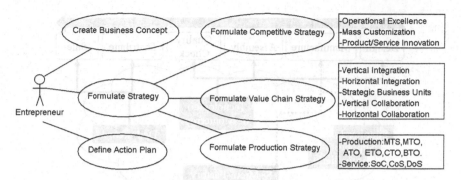

Fig. 3. Use case diagram for enterprise viewpoint activities

In the engineering viewpoint, information and communication technologies (ICTs) are seen as the key enabler for collaboration among SMEs, and consequently the creation of virtual enterprise [7]. PyME CREATIVA was born as an e-HUB to support e-part-nership, and e-commerce. The use of that platform is described with a deployment diagram because it shows the nodes that participate in the execution and the components inside.

The technology viewpoint defines choices of technologies, products, standards and tools. For example, PyME CREATIVA platform was chosen as the e-HUB but other platforms that offer e-services can be used. For the representation of this viewpoint class diagrams together with objects-diagram can be constructed.

4   Case Study

In order to evaluate the effectiveness of the S^2-RM model, we are studying its application to create a S^2-micro-factory that produces reconfigurable CNC-micro-machines [14] in collaboration with Tecnologico de Monterrey. The pilot has being selected due to its simplicity and completeness; it is a single product where the main concepts regarding CNs and manufacturing can be found. The product is designed according to the user needs. For example, if the user is a low-income college the micro-factory may be for academic only purposes. In this case study, the objective of the enterprise is to design a low cost micro-machine where the precision is not an issue. The micro-factory has the capability to produce small sized products (e.g. gears, screws, joints, etc.). In addition, collaboration is necessary in order to manage resources, (e.g. motors, computers, DAQs, structural profiles, etc.) in an effective way. Expert engineers and researchers from Tecnologico de Monterrey manage the product development process. And finally, De Lorenzo is in charge of the distribution and sales. The micro-factory, suppliers, Tecno-logico de Monterrey and De Lorenzo are the enterprises, which conform the temporary Virtual Enterprise (VE) for the creation of the micro-machine. The VE should accom-plish the competences of a smart organization: internetworked, virtual in concept, dynamically adaptive, knowledge driven and hierarchically flattened (Fig. 4).

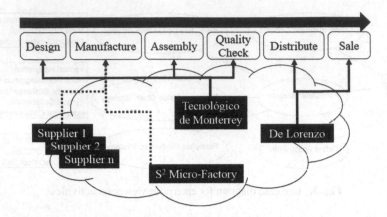

Fig. 4. Collaborative Networked Organization for the design, manufacture, assembly, distribution and sale of the reconfigurable CNC micro-machine.

4.1 Enterprise Viewpoint

For the definition of the enterprise a UML activity diagram is used (Fig. 5). It shows the steps to define the enterprise, the first one is the Business concept where the Canvas model, mission and vision, and values and policies are created. The second step is the strategy definition: competitive strategy, value chain strategy and product/service strategy. And finally the third step consist in the identification of core process and competences and the creation of the business plan.

Fig. 5. Activity diagram defining the enterprise.

Regarding the pilot case, the strategies are exemplified. A competitive strategy is defined depending on whether the goal is for Product Innovation, Operational Excellence or Mass Customization [5]. Product innovation and client customization were selected as the competitive strategy for the Manufacturing Collaborative Network. This decision was made based on the assumption that the enterprise has a strong R&D area. Therefore, the objective is to implement the best technology available according to the needs of a specific client. This requires a network of suppliers to manufacture the micro-machine components.

The value chain strategy allows the design and creation of Collaborative Networks Organization with all the SMEs required to support the design and fabrication of the

Micro-Machines. The Value Chain Strategy could define two collaborative approaches: Vertical and Horizontal. Vertical is used when the enterprise collaborate by aggregating its competencies to build components and parts of the Micro-Machine. Horizontal Collaboration is when the enterprises share their competence to design and build together a new component. In this particular scenario Vertical Collaboration has been defined, as the type of collaboration require for this particular CNO because there will be many suppliers for each part of the micro-machine. The Build to Order (BTO) was selected as production strategy because there is a design according to each client needs and specifications [5]. For evaluating the strategy, the global KPIs are: time to market, time for customization, delivery time, customer satisfaction, total costs and ROI per product.

4.2 Information Viewpoint

Figure 6 diagram shows an overview of the information viewpoint and its basic inter-actions and contents. Product Model, Manufacturing Model and Knowledge Model should be represented in this viewpoint.

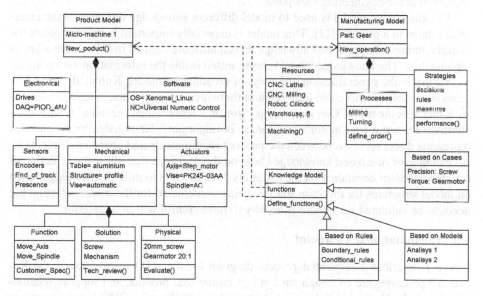

Fig. 6. Class diagram represents the information viewpoint of a micro-machine, manufacturing resources and knowledge to manufacture it.

The product model is divided into five different types of components due to the mechatronics nature of the reconfigurable micro-machine. Then within each type of component there are three different models. The functional model defines the set of functions the product has to accomplish. The solution model defines alternatives of solution to design the product. The physical model describes the final product with specific parts with restrictions and specifications. The technology used is a PLM system. Figure 6 illustrates how some functions for the mechanical components of the system are accomplished. A screw for a precision axis movement and a gear motor mechanism for high torque spindle movement. The specific design is stated in the physical model, where a 20 mm screw is selected for the Z axis for the specific micro-machine and a gear motor that increases the torque 20 times is selected.

The manufacturing model is presented as a class with three subclasses: manufacturing resources, manufacturing processes, and strategies of the company and operational rules. Figure 6 shows the case of a manufacturing model for the fabrication of a gear used for the gear motor. The resources listed are the components of the micro-factory, two reconfigurable CNC machines, a robotic arm, and a warehouse. Then the processes for the production of the machined product are stated: a milling and a turning operation for getting the gear. Finally the third part of the manufacturing model consist of a set of strategic decisions, operational rules, and performance measures on each of the levels i.e. factory, shop, cell, and station. This manufacturing model has being described within the capabilities of the micro-factory, nevertheless it offers resilience because the manufacturing model for collaborative networks has the ability to acquire manufacturing resources via e-services. The distribution nature of the collaborative networks that support this agile recovery in case of a failure of the micro-factory is explained in the engineering viewpoint.

The knowledge model is used to model different knowledge domains of the enterprise related to a product [11]. This model is especially important because it offers the manufacturing enterprise the knowledge driven attribute defined in [2] to have a Smart organization. The knowledge model is represented inside the information viewpoint by a class that is the generalization of 3 ways of creating the model. Knowledge based on cases is suitable for this case study because there are new micro-machines according to customer specifications. One example is "use of a screw when precision is important alternatively use a gear motor when torque is important." Knowledge based on rules represents direct relations between the product requirements and operation limits [12]. An example of rule based knowledge could be the decisions that allow the selection of the spindle motor depending on the materials the user want to mill. A knowledge based on model structures for this case study is being constructed for the motor selection but needs to be validated since there is no way to have control within its interior.

4.3 Computational Viewpoint

Figure 7 describes a sequential process diagram for the BTO micro-factory, the key external processes are co-design since it is a customized product, and supplier relationship due to the Vertical Collaboration strategy that will allow the CNO to have suppliers ready for operating the distributed manufacturing processes. The main internal process identified is customer satisfaction, related with the achievement of its loyalty defined as a KPI in the enterprise viewpoint. Once there is a selection of the process it is required to focus for designing the activity diagram. This diagram was selected because it captures de dynamic aspects of the system. It shows the flow control between activities. Figure 8 shows the creation of the micro-machine focusing on core processes.

The activity diagram describes the creation of the reconfigurable micro-machine tool for academic purposes and displays the importance of the core processes. As it can be seen co-design plays an important role, since there is a loop with the customer in the designing stage. This loop together with the *analyze clients* activity are sensing activities

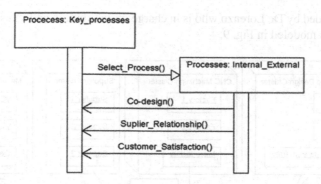

Fig. 7. Sequence process diagram showing the business process strategy selection for the S2-micro-factory that creates micro-machines.

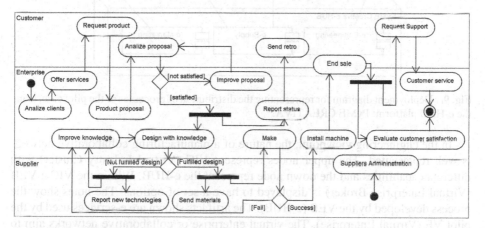

Fig. 8. Activity diagram specifies the enterprise activities according to business process strategy of the pilot demonstration.

since they makes the manufacturing collaborative network to be aware of its contexts in terms of client satisfaction and requirements. The supplier relationship is also important so there is an alternative start with no end that has supplier management activities. This activity is located between two swim lanes since it is an activity done by the Collaborative Network conformed by the enterprise and its suppliers. Finally, customer satisfaction stages have many related activities i.e. send retro, request support, customer service and evaluate customer satisfaction.

4.4 Engineering Viewpoint

The most important core processes are co-design, supplier – customer relationship management. The co-design process can be supported by expert engineers and researchers from Tecnologico de Monterrey. Then the supplier relationship will be supported by the e-Supply service provided by the e-HUB. Finally, e-Marketing services will be provided by De Lorenzo who is in charge of distribution and sales. This sharing of services is modeled in Fig. 9.

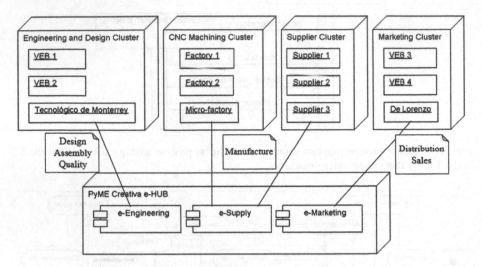

Fig. 9. Deployment diagram for representing the distribution of processes of the pilot case, using the e-HUB platform: PyME CREATIVA.

In the engineering viewpoint, the nature of a manufacturing collaborative network is well represented. The upper nodes represent VIC (Virtual Industry Cluster) with different capabilities and the down node represent the e-HUB. Within the VIC a VEB (Virtual Enterprise Broker) is displayed to have a set of options. The notes show the process developed by the VEB (e-HUB). The artifacts shown are e-services used by the pilot VE (Virtual Enterprise). The virtual enterprise or collaborative networks aim to capitalize individual capabilities by creating a temporary arrangement to share skills and core competences. And with platforms such as PyME CREATIVA the internetworking is easy to achieve, allowing the pilot enterprise to rapidly configure is competences to fulfill new customer requirements. Cooperation, ubiquity and ability to adapt are the main principles of this viewpoint that defines a smart organization.

4.5 Technology Viewpoint

A technology review is necessary before choosing any tool, since it guarantees smart and sensing capabilities of the organization. This paper presents the sensing and smart resources used by the collaborative network to produce the micro machine (Fig. 10). The sensing resources allows the acquiring of data and information. And the smart resources has to do with the efficient operation of the manufacturing. The independency of technology achieved with this viewpoint improves the resilience of an organization since a deficiency detected can be solved adopting new technology that deals with the shortage.

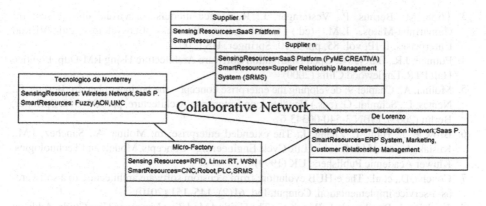

Fig. 10. Object diagram showing the actors with its smart and sensing resources for the fabrication of the micro-machine.

5   Conclusions

The S^2-RM defines a set of generic viewpoints to design and create Smart and Sensing Manufacturing Collaborative Networks using a structural approach by defining strategies, KPIs, core process and technologies. When applied to the pilot case it helps to have a better description of the system and hence identify the sources of advantage and key points for supporting collaborative networks. The functionality of each viewpoint can be formally represented using UML because its variety of diagrams. The enterprise and information viewpoints focus on the business perspective, strategies and core processes and core competencies. Therefore this viewpoint must define the smart and sensing concepts. The information computational and engineering defines the architecture of the system; especially the computational and engineering form a specific description of the core processes, and interactions inside the enterprise and the collaboration network. Here at these viewpoint the collaborative organization definition is established, and the advantages such as resilience and agility are identified. And finally, the technology viewpoint forms a constraint on the implementation of the system, but due to its independence it allows the integration of the latest technology to assure the best development of smart and sensing through all viewpoints.

References

1. Camarinha-Matos, L.M., Afsarmanesh, H.: Collaborative systems for smart environments: trends and challenges. In: Camarinha-Matos, L.M., Afsarmanesh, H. (eds.) Collaborative Systems for Smart Networked Environments. IFIP AICT, vol. 434, pp. 3–15. Springer, Heidelberg (2014)
2. Molina, A., Ponce, P., Ramirez, M., Sanchez-Ante, G.: Designing a S^2-enterprise (Smart x Sensing) reference model. In: Camarinha-Matos, L.M., Afsarmanesh, H. (eds.) Collaborative Systems for Smart Networked Environments. IFIP AICT, vol. 434, pp. 384–395. Springer, Heidelberg (2014)

3. Tolle, M., Bernus, P., Vesterager, J.: Reference models for virtual enterprises. In: Camarinha-Matos, L.M. (ed.) Collaborative Business Ecosystems and Virtual Enterprises. IFIP, vol. 85, pp. 3–10. Springer, US (2002)

4. Putman, J.R., Barry, W.: Open Distribution Software Architecture Using RM-Odp. Prentice Hall PTR, Englewood Cliffs (2000)

5. Molina, A.: Chapter 9: developing the enterprise concept – the business plan. In: Bernus, P., Nemes, L., Schmidt, G. (eds.) Handbook on Enterprise Architecture, pp. 333–369. Springer, Berlin (2003). ISBN 3-540-00343-6

6. Browne, J., Hunt, I., Zhang, J.: The extended enterprise. In: Molina, A., Sanchez, J.M., Kusiak, A. (eds.) Handbook of Life Cycle Engineering – Concepts, Models and Technologies. Kluwer Academic Publishers, UK (1999)

7. Concha, D., et al.: The e-HUB evolution: from a custom software architecture to a software-as-a-service implementation. Comput. Ind. **61**(2), 145–151 (2010)

8. Jacobson, I., Rumbaugh, J., Booch, G.: The Unified Modeling Language User Guide. Addison Wesley, Reading (1999)

9. Costa, C.A., Harding, J.A., Young, R.I.M.: The application of UML and an open distributed process framework to information system design. Comput. Ind. **46**, 33–48 (2001)

10. Molina, A., Velandia, M., Galeano, N.: Virtual enterprise brokerage: a structure driven strategy to achieve build to order supply chains. Int. J. Prod. Res. **45**(17), 3853–3880 (2007). doi:10.1080/00207540600818161. Taylor & Francis, London, ISSN: 0020-7543

11. Molina, A., Acosta, J., Romero, D.: A methodology for knowledge-based engineering systems implementations: two case studies. In: Horváth, I., Rusák, Z. (eds.) Proceedings of TMCE 2014, May 19–23, 2014, Budapest, Hungary, © Organizing Committee of TMCE 2014, ISBN 978-94-6186-177-1 (2014)

12. Waheed, A., Adeli, H.: Case-based reasoning in steel bridge engineering. Knowl. Based Syst. **18**(1), 37–46 (2005)

13. Molina, A., Mejía, R., Galeano, N., Najera, T., Velandia, M.: The HUB as an enabling IT strategy to achieve smart organizations. In: Mezgar, I. (ed.) Integration of ICT in Smart Organizations, pp. 64–95. Idea Group Publishing, USA (2006). ISBN 1-59140-390-1

14. Pérez, R., Molina, A., Ramírez-Cadena, M.: Development of an integrated approach to the design of reconfigurable micro/mesoscale CNC machine tools. J. Manufact. Sci. Eng. **136** (2014)

Supporting Knowledge-Centered Business Collaboration for Wind Power Plants

Christian Zinke[1(✉)], Johannes Schmidt[1,2], and Andreas Nareike[1]

[1] University of Leipzig, Augustsplatz 10, 04109 Leipzig, Germany
{zinke,jschmidt,nareike}@informatik.uni-leipzig.de
[2] Institute for Applied Informatics (InfAI) e.V., University of Leipzig,
Hainstraße 11, 04109 Leipzig, Germany

Abstract. In Germany, the importance of renewable energy resources increased significantly within the last years. In contrast to conventional power plants, there are highly interactive and complex value-added networks around such an energy resource. Today, the members of these networks mainly have to cope with information gaps or other issues regarding documentation quality. These challenges become critical in the context of knowledge intensive business-to-business processes. To encourage better business collaboration, a holistic knowledge-centered approach is needed. The digital Plant Lifecycle Record (PLR) addresses the given challenges in the context of wind turbines. Based on this approach, the members of the value-added networks cooperatively manage a plant-related knowledge base. By means of a use case, the general concepts of the Plant Lifecycle Record are introduced. Furthermore, empirically collected expectations of the most important stakeholders are discussed.

Keywords: Renewable energy · Business collaboration · Documentation · Knowledge management · Plant lifecycle record

1 Introduction

In Germany, the number of wind power plants (WPP) increased significantly within the last decade [1]. In contrast to conventional power plants, WPPs are widely distributed. Remote monitoring and remote services of WPPs enable an unattended operation. Thus, no permanent on-site staff is required. If needed, the plant owner can commission local service providers, which are often specialized on knowledge intensive business tasks. For example, maintenance services depend on up-to-date and complete information about the structure of the WPP and a complete maintenance history. Another example are surveyor services, which require a complete and comprehensive list of certificates and the latest technical documentation. All these service providers interact within a dynamic market whereas WPPs are incorporated in a highly flexible value-added network.

Today, most challenges in business collaboration and service commission result from missing information as well as from the lack of standardized business processes, services, and information technology. The digital Plant Lifecycle Record (PLR)

© IFIP International Federation for Information Processing 2015
L.M. Camarinha-Matos et al. (Eds.): PRO-VE 2015, IFIP AICT 463, pp. 255–262, 2015.
DOI: 10.1007/978-3-319-24141-8_23

addresses these challenges by providing a shared knowledge base that satisfies the specific information needs of every stakeholder. Based on this approach, the members of the valued-added network can cooperatively share and manage plant-related knowledge. This results in lower process costs and improved collaboration within the network.

This paper addresses the following research questions. (1) Which requirements, potentials, and stakeholder types are important for a knowledge-based approach in the wind energy domain? (2) What are the most relevant structural elements of the PLR? Therefore, this paper has the following structure. Firstly, the used methodology is introduced. Secondly, the theoretical framework of the Business Collaboration Pyramid by Ewig [2] is discussed, including a short discourse about the dependencies between organizational structure, knowledge and information technology. Thirdly, in Sect. 4, empirical based requirements and innovation potentials are presented and the overall structure of the digital PLR is introduced. Finally, a use case and an outlook on further research will be given.

2 Methods and Methodological Remarks

The methodology of this work is oriented towards the design science[1] with the aim "to create things that serve human purposes" [3]. The resulting artefacts need to be designed and evaluated [4]. Therefore, methods and knowledge of natural and social sciences are applied.

Following a middle-out strategy, the presented findings result from two sources. The first source is the relevant literature, which provides a theoretical description of the problem and the context (top-down). The second source is an explorative semi-structured expert survey (bottom-up) which aims to identify different stakeholder viewpoints (called ideal-types) and their particular requirements on the PLR. The extracted ideal-types help to understand the specific information needs of the stakeholders as well as the practical potential of the PLR approach.

3 Related Work

Collaboration in value-added networks is a young phenomenon with growing interest. Due to organizational specialization and outsourcing activities in the industry, collaboration issues emerged. This work mainly refers to the business collaboration framework developed by Ewig [2] that is introduced below. Additionally, other related works in the field of organizational theory and knowledge management are presented.

3.1 Business Collaboration Pyramid

Ewig [2] introduced a framework to describe the transformation process of business and value-chains towards business collaboration. The current state of this transformation can be described with the help of the Collaborative Business Pyramid. This pyramid consists of five dimensions (strategy, organizational operations, organizational structure, information

---

[1] In contrast to natural sciences and social sciences, which try to understand the reality.

structure, and information technology) with three maturity levels each. In this work, only three dimensions and their mutual relations are investigated (see Fig. 1).

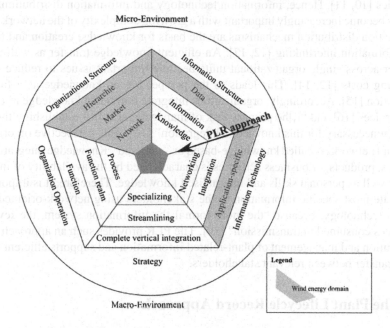

Fig. 1. Business transformation pyramid following Ewig [2]

Within the complete lifecycle of a WPP, numerous stakeholders cooperate, especially in the operation phase. Hence, the *organizational structure* can be classified as a network. Although, most of the business tasks and services are knowledge intensive, the quality of the available information is often insufficient and the data exchange is only semi structured. Thus, the type of *information structure* is on the level of data. One reason for this situation is the low maturity of *information technology*. Individual proprietary software products are prevalent, due to low company ages or sizes. No common information system integration approach is established.

To reach more efficient business collaboration in the wind energy domain, the maturity of the information structure and information technology should be increased. The PLR approach explicitly addresses these two dimensions.

For a better understanding of the connection between technology and knowledge, a short excurse to organizational theory is introduced below.

3.2 Network Organization, Knowledge and Technology[2]

Scott describes a direct dependence of technical and structural complexity: "The structural response to technical diversity is organizational differentiation." [9]. A high degree

---

[2] The presented theoretical background is very similar to virtual organization approaches (e.g. [5–8], which will not discussed here.

of organizational differentiation also means a high degree of network complexity, which results in a substantial amount of required information in specialized business network activities [10, 11]. Hence, information technology and information distribution mechanisms become increasingly important with a growing complexity of the network. These information distribution mechanisms are the basis for knowledge creation and transfer via information interlinking [12, 13]. An efficient knowledge transfer as well as skill transfer across single organizational units become important issues to reduce overall operating costs [12, 14]. This leads to the perspective on knowledge as a factor of production [15]. Accordingly, organizations integrate individual knowledge into goods and services [16] and "[t]he primary task of management is [to] establishing the coordination necessary for this knowledge integration" [16]. This perspective on organizations and networks is called knowledge-based or –centered[3]. Knowledge integration into services, products, or business activities is characterised by the availability of information as well as personal skills and internalised knowledge. Therefore, it is important to distribute most specific information to the stakeholders using network-oriented information technology, because "the more formal the information system, the fewer the resources consumed in transmission" [10]. The PLR provides such an approach for the distribution and management of plant-related information and supports efficient knowledge transfer between relevant stakeholders.

4   The Plant Lifecycle Record Approach

Stakeholders can have different objectives in a value-added network. As a result of a qualitative survey, four ideal-types can be distinguished which refer to their specific needs as well as their expectations on a knowledge-based approach. The structure of the PLR considers these expectations and is introduced shortly in the following. Finally, the application of the PLR is shown by a use case.

4.1   Stakeholder Expectations and Requirements

To explore requirements and potentials of a knowledge-centered approach in the wind energy domain, experts have been questioned with the help of an explorative semi-structured survey. The qualitative analysis (cross-case and case immanent analysis) of the interviews results in four preliminary types of stakeholder viewpoints (called ideal-types[4]):

1. Stakeholders with an *information-oriented* point of view are mainly interested in structural properties of information. Unification, completeness, comprehensibility and centralisation of information have been mentioned as most important functions

---

[3] This definition of knowledge-centered approaches is similar to [17] and other researcher in the domain of Knowledge Management, which define it "as any approach which can be applied in KM and facilitates the knowledge activities in KM" [17].

[4] An ideal-type is a stakeholder with empirically extracted and exaggerated properties. The ideal-types are disjoint in their interpretations.

for a knowledge-based approach. This leads in the innovation potentials of improved information flows and higher efficiency in general. It can be assumed, that this ideal-type only has insufficient access to required information and seeks for improvements in information organization. Maybe this is the reason why this ideal-type is –in context of a knowledge-centered approach– not interested in dimensions like legal evidence, processes, or business.

2. Stakeholders with a *documentation-oriented* point of view focus on documentations, particularly on information exchange, historisation, and completeness. A documented history enables transparency and leads to the identified innovation potentials of an improved information flow and higher traceability. The special importance of the documentations suggests that this ideal-type mainly works with (technical) documents and does not depend on specific contents that might not be available in general.

3. Stakeholders with a *process-oriented* point of view concentrate on business processes, activities, and activity data. They refer to information distribution and (legal) evidence instead of information exchange. Furthermore, these stakeholders are interested in activity-tracing. They act as a networking hub of process-based information. From their point of view, the innovation potentials of a knowledge-based approach are the better availability and reusability of process information as well as the improved (legal) safety.

4. Stakeholders with a *systemic* point of view follow a holistic and systematic understanding of business processes and their structure. Especially, the comparability and effectiveness of information logistics are important concepts for these stakeholders. Probably, they are not actively involved in business process operations, but rather perform managerial functions.

4.2 Concepts of the PLR

According to Ewig [2], common information concepts as well as better information system integration are needed to reach a high level of business collaboration maturity. The technical specification DIN SPEC 91303 [19] introduces a generic structure of a Plant Lifecycle Record for sustainable energy resources based on international technical standards. A PLR is defined as a collection of information sets, which consist of an amount of documents, data or both of them. These information sets refer to the following concepts: (1) the plant structure, (2) the product structure, (3) one or more views, (4) the lifecycle phase, and (5) the responsible stakeholders.

The most important concept of the PLR is the plant structure definition. All information must refer to that structure. In the wind energy domain, the so called Reference Designation System for Power Plants (RDS-PP®) is relevant [18]. It defines a standardized language to describe the e.g. functional components of the WPP system. Furthermore, it defines a syntax to designate relations between information and the plant structure. The actual product structure of the WPP is managed separately. This enables an overview of every installed product that realized a specific function for the complete lifecycle of the WPP.

A special characteristic of the PLR is the view concept. Based on a classification of the stakeholder information needs, five basic views have been defined. They refer to scopes of responsibilities like commercial, technical, or legal aspects. Every information can be annotated using a set of view meta-data. Accordingly, the stakeholders can access and filter the PLR based on their responsibility with respect to their activity based information needs.

The DIN SPEC 91303 only defines the top level concepts of the PLR. No detailed meta-data is defined. To qualify these concepts, existing and standardized meta-data definitions and information models are applied. This ensures a high degree of interoperability, comprehensibility, and acceptance. The designation and semantics of services for the operation of sustainable energy resources can be found in DIN SPEC 91310 [20]. For WPPs, the ZEUS approach by FGW renewable energies [21] defines the semantics of the plant state. Based on this classification, the actual health and possible resulting tasks can be described in a generally understandable notation. Furthermore, existing complex information models have been taken into account, like the Common Information Model by the IEC [22], or the ISO 15926 and IEC 61400-25 standards [23].

The *digital* PLR concretises and implements the given concepts of the DIN SPEC 91303. It provides a scalable and highly integrated knowledge base that can be accessed by every member of the value-added network. The digital PLR is an integrated information system that can be used by every stakeholder to manage plant-related information. A common information model ensures consistent data and information linking.

4.3 Use Case

The owner is responsible for the secure operation of a WPP. In the operation lifecycle phase, a so-called operator often undertakes the operation tasks in the name of the owner. In this case, the owner's point of view is systemic, whereas the operator is a process-oriented stakeholder. Based on the PLR, the owner can supervise the operator and compare the information of different WPPs. The operator can use the digital PLR to coordinate the information distribution as well as to analyse the quality and completeness of the available information.

In the context of maintenance and repair, the operator has to coordinate the pending processes of the service providers in charge. The PLR represents a common knowledge base for every partner involved. The service providers take an information-oriented perspective on the PLR. They can directly access the required information and file new documents. The information sets can be exchanged directly between the partners. No information conversion or restructuring is needed. The operator only has to check the quality of the new information and can add new links to other relevant information in the PLR. This shared management leads to better information quality, higher actuality of the information and reduced workloads for all involved stakeholders.

The digital PLR approach provides the basis for a structured information exchange between the stakeholders. The improved availability of information reduces the efforts for service preparation and completion. The digital PLR ensures an improved system integration and supports the automation of data exchanges. In total, the business collaboration is strengthen by an improved information technology support.

5   Conclusion

Value-added networks for WPPs are complex and highly dynamic. Today, business collaboration between the stakeholders is amendable because of inefficient or broken information flows, which are results of immature information technologies and an insufficient inter-company knowledge management. The digital Plant Lifecycle Record approach addresses these challenges by providing a shared knowledge base whose concepts are premised on international technical standards and information models.

To identify the main innovation potentials and the requirements of the PLR, experts have been questioned. The resulting four preliminary ideal-types are introduced. These types can help to create a theoretical framework to describe the stakeholder-network and interactions for WPPs and beyond. Furthermore, the main concepts of the PLR are derived from the requirements of the ideal-types.

A demonstration implementation of the digital PLR is under development and will be evaluated in different practical use cases. In contrast to DIN SPEC 91303, this prototype will consider requirements like security or system availability in more detail and will provide some decision support methodology.

Acknowledgments. This work is a result of the CVtec project, supported by the Federal Ministry of Education and Research (BMBF) as grant 01IS14016C.

References

1. Fraunhofer Institute for Wind Energy and Energy System Technology (IWES): Wind energy report Germany 2013, Kassel (2014). http://publica.fraunhofer.de/dokumente/N-287408.html
2. Ewig, M.: Der Transformationsprozess zum collaborative business. Eine strategische, organisatorische und informatorische Betrachtung. Schriften zur Wirtschaftsinformatik, Bd. 17. Lang, Frankfurt am Main, New York (2006) (German)
3. March, S.T., Smith, G.F.: Design and natural science research on information technology. Decis. Support Syst. **15**(4), 251–266 (1995). doi:10.1016/0167-9236(94)00041-2
4. Peffers, K., Tuunanen, T., Rothenberger, M.A., Chatterjee, S.: A design science research methodology for information systems research. J. Manage. Inf. Syst. **24**(3), 45–77 (2008)
5. Chai, H., Liu, L., Luo, S.: Knowledge transferring in virtual organization. In: 2011 2nd International Conference on Artificial Intelligence, Management Science and Electronic Commerce (AIMSEC), Dengfeng, China, pp. 3089–3092 (2011). doi:10.1109/AIMSEC.2011.6010369
6. Katzy, B.R.: Design and implementation of virtual organizations. In: Proceedings of the Thirty-First Annual Hawaii International Conference on System Sciences, HICSS 1998, Kohala Coast, Hawaii, USA, p. 142, 6–9 January 1998
7. Ahuja, M., Carley, K.M.: Network structure in virtual organizations. J. Comput. Mediated Commun. **3**(4), 0 (1998). doi:10.1111/j.1083-6101.1998.tb00079.x
8. DeSanctis, G., Monge, P.: Introduction to the special issue: communication processes for virtual organizations. Organ. Sci. **10**(6), 693–703 (1999). doi:10.1287/orsc.10.6.693
9. Scott, W.R., Davis, G.F.: Organizations and Organizing. Rational, Natural, and Open System Perspectives, 1st edn. Pearson Prentice Hall, Upper Saddle River (2007)

10. Galbraith, J.R.: Organization design: an information processing view. Organ. Effectiveness Cent. Sch. **21**, 21–26 (1977)
11. Gulløv, T.: Structural Limitations in organizational design. In: Burton, R., Håkonsson, D., Eriksen, B., Snow, C. (eds.) Organization Design. Information and Organization Design Series, vol. 6, pp. 67–83. Springer, New York (2006)
12. Tsai, W.: Knowledge transfer in intraorganizational networks: effects of network position and absorptive capacity on business unit innovation and performance. Acad. Manage. J. **44**(5), 996–1004 (2001). doi:10.2307/3069443
13. Walter, S.: Logistik in Dienstleistungsunternehmen. Deutscher Universitätsverlag, Wiesbaden (2003). (German)
14. Hill, C.W.L., Hitt, M.A., Hoskisson, R.E.: Cooperative versus competitive structures in related and unrelated diversified firms. Organ. Sci. **3**(4), 501–521 (1992). doi:10.1287/orsc. 3.4.501
15. Sydow, J., van Well, B.: Wissensintensiv durch Netzwerkorganisation — Strukturationstheoretische Analyse eines wissensintensiven Netzwerkes. In: Sydow, J. (ed.) Management von Netzwerkorganisationen, pp. 143–186. Gabler Verlag, Wiesbaden (2010) (German)
16. Grant, R.M.: Toward a knowledge-based theory of the firm. Strat. Manage. J. **17**(S2), 109–122 (1996). doi:10.1002/smj.4250171110
17. Ding, W., Liang, P., Tang, A., van Vliet, H.: Knowledge-based approaches in software documentation: a systematic literature review. Inf. Softw. Technol. **56**(6), 545–567 (2014). doi:10.1016/j.infsof.2014.01.008
18. VGB PowerTec: RDS-PP – Application Guideline; Part 32: Wind Power Plants (VGB-S-823-32-2014-03-EN-DE-0) (2014)
19. DIN: Components and structure of a plant documentation system for renewable energy plants, Berlin (DIN SPEC 91303) (2015) (German)
20. DIN: Classification of services for the technical management of renewable energy plants (DIN SPEC 91310) (2014) (German)
21. FGW: Betrieb und Instandhaltung von Kraftwerken für Erneuerbare Energien - Teil 7 Rubrik D2: Zustands-Ereignis-Ursachen-Schlüssel für Erzeugungseinheiten (ZEUS) (FGW TR 7 D2) (2013) (German)
22. Uslar, M., Specht, M., Rohjans, S., Trefke, J., Gonzalez, J.M.V.: Introduction. In: Uslar, M., Specht, M., Rohjans, S., Trefke, J., Vasquez Gonzalez, J.M. (eds.) The Common Information Model CIM. POWSYS, vol. 2, pp. 3–48. Springer, Heidelberg (2012)
23. IEC: Wind turbine generator systems - ALL PARTS (IEC 61400-SER ed1.0) (2011)

Logistics and Transportation

ECoNet Platform for Collaborative Logistics and Transport

Luis A. Osório[1(✉)], Luis M. Camarinha-Matos[2], and Hamideh Afsarmanesh[3]

[1] ISEL - Instituto Superior de Engenharia de Lisboa, Instituto Politécnico de Lisboa,
Lisbon, Portugal
lo@isel.ipl.pt

[2] Faculdade de Ciências e Tecnologia, Universidade Nova de Lisboa, Lisbon, Portugal
cam@uninova.pt

[3] University of Amsterdam (UvA), Amsterdam, The Netherlands
h.afsarmanesh@uva.nl

Abstract. The development of the Port Community System (PCS) concept, as a single access point to a port, offering integrated logistics and transport services, is a complex and challenging endeavour. Effective value creation in PCS requires the integration of stakeholder's internal processes with the collaborative activities/processes, under an open framework. The establishment of such community thus requires a well-founded collaborative framework to integrate and coordinate the diverse IT-systems of the participating stakeholders. These IT-systems, in most of the cases, were not designed and developed for a cooperation context, leading to a complex overpriced web of disconnected systems that are difficult to manage, maintain, and adapt to the fast evolution of technologies and collaboration models. In this context, an enhanced Enterprise Collaborative Network platform is presented and discussed as an approach to support PCS.

Keywords: Collaborative networks infrastructures · Business ecosystems · Service oriented computing · System of systems

1 Introduction

An increasing pressure for organizations to participate in collaborative business processes has created new research challenges on how to adapt the IT-systems to effectively cope with this fast emerging dynamics. This trend is observed in diverse domains, including manufacturing supply chains, services sector, and also logistics networks. For instance, a collaborative logistics framework for the integration and collaboration among stakeholders in logistics chains is proposed in [1]. A particularly relevant sector, due to its economic relevance, is the logistics ecosystems associated to ports. Stakeholders in this area are under the pressure to adopt electronic data exchange with peers, private or governmental, while at the same time their success depends on their strategies regarding business partnerships.

© IFIP International Federation for Information Processing 2015
L.M. Camarinha-Matos et al. (Eds.): PRO-VE 2015, IFIP AICT 463, pp. 265–276, 2015.
DOI: 10.1007/978-3-319-24141-8_24

The difficulties here are related to the large number of services each partners has to offer/participate in, associated to the adoption of a total electronic data management and exchange. The electronic data exchanges can take many forms in terms of protocols and technologies (e.g. HTTP, FTP, SOAP, RESTful, WCF/.NET, JEE, DNS), and data models structure and semantics (e.g. STEP, HL7, DATEX, SWIFT, IMO, GS1), to mention only a few. Furthermore, business requirements are commonly directly mapped to software development needs without strong enough component models. This is recurrently identified as a process to technology "gap", representing the lack of well-founded approaches to automatically manage all steps from the inception/design of new business services/processes to their execution, management and evolution.

This challenge requires multi-disciplinary contributions from processes/business to technology/engineering domains. Although modularity is recognized as of paramount importance to reduce lifecycle complexity, promote collaborative developments, and allow competitive complex IT-systems composed of components supplied by diverse software developers, typical software systems lack sufficient adaptability to the world diversity [2], i.e. generated solutions tend to be specific. As a result, making adaptations is a needed time consuming process, aggravated by the associated risks of potential errors that might be introduced through changes. The research community is for long tackling this problem from complementary approaches. One of those approaches is the component-based software engineering (CBSE) initiative [3], focused on efficiency issues like performance and reliability. The certification of components is argued as a valuable contributor to the increase of reusability, and model behaviour prediction. Another approach is related to a formal modelling, using domain analysis (FORMULA) [4, 5]. The establishment of model driven strategies to address formal structuration of the complex technology bindings were since long proposed by the Object Management Group (OMG). A concretization of the OMG's Model Architecture (MDA) vision, where platform independent models (PIM) are automatically mapped to platform specific models (PSM), is proposed and discussed in [5]. Nevertheless, given the underlying complexity, the proposed modelling approach and tools offer only partial specialized automation, lacking a whole and consistent integrated development workbench (e.g. popular frameworks/tools like OSGi, Maven, Eclipse and interdependent plug-ins, are not consistently integrated).

Considering this context, this paper presents and discusses the ECoNet platform [7], and its application to support a port community business case. Unlike an initial suite of concepts to model collaborations in the context of the Logistics Single Window (LSW), introduced and demonstrated in our previous research [7], in this paper we enhance the ECoNet platform with the concept of Virtual Collaboration Context (VCC). The experience with the development of a PCS demonstrator, involving the integration of a large amount of heterogeneous open source code, is discussed. It further argues for the need to move towards a total coordinated collaboration integration, and discusses the strengths, weaknesses and needed further research.

2   The Port Community System Business Case

The MIELE project has established the strategy to develop a Port Community System (PCS) as an enhanced version of the existing *port single window* (in Portuguese, *Janela Única Portuária* - JUP). The PCS, as defined by the EPCSA[1] association:

(i)   *"a neutral and open electronic platform, enabling intelligent and secure exchange of information between public and private stakeholders in order to improve the competitive position of the sea and air ports' communities"*, and

(ii) *"it optimises, manages and automates port and logistics efficient processes through a single submission of data and connecting transport and logistics chains"* [6].

The Portuguese port single window (PSW/JUP) system is developed based on the National Reference Model (NRM) [12], a set of business processes models associated to its offered services, and their supporting functionalities. The NRM processes, while following a model-driven approach, soon became outdated in relation to the operating PSW/JUP. This is a common problem as it is difficult to maintain the models updated along the lifecycle (inception, design, development, operations/maintenance, evolution) of complex IT-system. A suite of good practices regulating the changes required during the development and evolution, based on the operation experience and the identification of required changes, is necessary. The difficulties to maintain the consistency of the mapping between the platform independent model (PIM) and the platform specific model (PSM) are recognized and commonly associated to the weakness of the supporting tools. Existing development tools (e.g. Eclipse, Maven, plugins) are not complete enough to manage changes (refactoring at any level) and maintain the consistency of all supporting models (and meta-models).

This is a common situation considering that the implementations usually have to adopt specific approaches in order to answer requirements not identified during the design phase. Furthermore, the PSW/JUP system has different implementations for at least the Lisbon and Leixões ports. In fact one identified difference is the approach to manage the port gates. A port gate is a physical place where freight trucks or trains are registered and controlled. In Leixões there is an automated and reliable gate that registers all freight/transport flows using road transportation (trucks). On the other hand, in Lisbon the role of the gate is played by the IT-system of the port operator (concession managed under a pubic private partnership). This situation makes us to question the current PSW/JUP system and identify the need to rethink its architecture in order to promote similar computational responsibilities for all the ports.

3   ECoNet Platform Concepts, Services and Validation

The Enterprise Collaborative Network (ECoNet) platform supports preserving electronic relationships between an organization and its partners [7]. It follows an analogy with the classic correspondence management department, responsible to manage the inbound/outbond surface mail. The Enterprise Collaborative Manager (ECoM) IT-system is the

---

[1] European Port Community Systems Association.

component of the ECoNet platform responsible to manage the electronic exchanges. It can be seen as a formal abstraction for the current panoply of adapters necessary to support business message exchanges specific needs. For such abstraction, the ECoM implements a suite of Collaboration Contexts (CoC) specialized in managing the semantics of specific electronic message exchanges (EDIFACT, GS1, STEP, and HL7) developed to support distinct application domains. The ECoM component has therefore the following main computational responsibilities:

- Based on the Collaboration Context zero (CoC$_0$), a common secure and reliable communication infrastructure is made available to be shared by the other collaboration contexts;
- The other collaboration contexts {CoC$_1$, ..., CoC$_N$} are responsible to manage specific electronic data exchanges, share common services with the CoC$_0$ (also representing system collaboration context) and might establish secure direct communication links depending on specific communication requirements (e.g., fast FTPS large files exchange);
- The collaboration context might evolve to incorporate standard messaging (MOM[2]) with publish/subscribe capabilities, transactions management for atomic (reliable) coordination, and other specialized mechanisms depending on specific requirements of a particular message exchange.

By computational responsibility we define the abstraction that models a mapping between requirements and capabilities that are (completely) fulfilled by an IT-system (made of software or software and hardware, under a unique supplier responsibility).

In the ECoNet platform model, the ECoM component plays a core role as the unique IT-system of the organization responsible for the coordination of the electronic message exchanges. In fact, ECoM is the inbound/outbound endpoint of an ECoNet-enabled organization (or ECoNet node). The proposed approach adopts a unified coordination of message exchanges between an organization and its peer partners (other ECoNet members). This raises two complementary concerns: i) the establishment and lifecycle management of the ECoNet network, and ii) the relations to the IT-systems of an ECoNet member.

Current approaches in this sector are based on proprietary architectures, usually positioned as B2B integration platforms associated to specialized services to access existing repositories in a diversity of formats to make effective the exchange of business messages (e.g., GXS platform). Depending on the scale/complexity, large business companies commonly establish their own standards for business partners to access electronic exchanges (INTTRA, DHL). Also large logistics and transport companies usually hold expensive enterprise resource planning IT-systems already embedding the capabilities to manage business messages exchange in a diversity of formats. The (Enterprise Application) IT-system to IT-system data exchange faces three main concerns:

(i)   How can an IT-system data be retrieved/stored (outbound/inbound);
(ii)   What is the format of the exchanged data (payload) and;
(iii) What is the transport protocol, Fig. 1.

---

[2] Message Oriented Middleware.

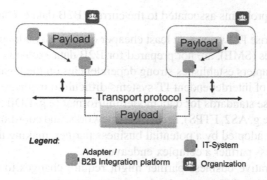

Fig. 1. Exchange of data between organizations

This scenario establishes a complex distributed system where a source IT-system needs to be accessed to generate the payload message. If the IT-system has B2B data exchange embedded capabilities, the adapter might not be necessary. Nevertheless the question is what should be the adopted format (e.g. EDIFACT/X.12, GS1) considering that the potential partners might have adopted different IT-systems and so different data formats.

The fast growing of business exchanges makes interoperability, maintenance, and adaptability to a new business partner, a difficult and error prone process, not only at setup time but along the overall life cycle. Furthermore, as legacy IT-systems are usually not prepared for cooperation, the integration of B2B adapters or platforms requires, in most of the cases, a tight integration process by accessing internal data models to retrieve/store data. This process contributes to potential problems (and additional costs) when integrated systems are updated or new versions are installed, [13]. The growing complexity associated to the number and diversity of specialized IT-systems (adapters, B2B platforms), contributes to increase costs and the operational risks. Figure 2 illustrates a group of organizations linked by such adapters or B2B integration platforms as a traditional approach to establish B2B relations among organizations.

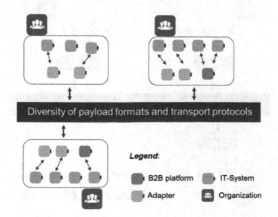

Fig. 2. Current B2B interoperability based on adapters

Some of the main problems associated to the current B2B data exchange are:

- Existing enterprise IT-systems, at least cheaper ones mostly adopted by medium and small enterprises (SME), are not prepared for B2B data exchange;
- Adoption of adapters establishes strong dependencies on the legated systems. They generate a web of interdependent IT-systems difficult to maintain and evolve;
- There are diverse standards for data modelling/format (e.g. EDIFACT, GS1), transport protocols (e.g. AS2, FTPS), security frameworks, and coordination frameworks, which might be adopted by a potential business partner, making the joining process of a new business partner a complex endeavour;
- A new collaborative business partner might require changes to the installed B2B adapters if adopting different payload or transport formats.

The ECoNet collaboration platform aims to answer to the formulated weaknesses of existing approaches. Instead of putting pressure on unification of existing standards or proprietary models and protocols, ECoNet assumes *diverse cultures* (processes or technology), establishing a unified adapters framework, the collaboration context (CoC). In fact a collaboration context provides a unified framework for the adapters/B2B platforms as shown in Fig. 3. Instead of specialized adapters, vendors are invited to adopt the open specification of the ECoNet collaboration context mechanism and publish the newly created CoC at the ECoNet root portal (providers of certified CoC as products). In this way, any organization that decides to initiate a business relationships with new business partners, if they are ECoNet-enabled (if they have a certified ECoM instance installed or accessible through a cloud provider) they only have to install an interoperable collaboration context. At a higher abstraction level, the ECoNet establishes a kind of unified B2B logical bus. As such, ECoNet contributes to the collaboration preparedness of the members of the business ecosystem [8].

Based on these principles, a prototype of a generic file/message exchange and a Port Community System IT-system were developed. The file/message exchange system was the first reference implementation of the ECoM subsystem. The collaboration context

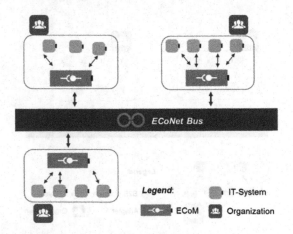

Fig. 3. The ECoNet collaboration platform as a unified B2B bus

zero is based on the CIPA reference implementation of the PEPPOL EU project as already discussed in [7].

Considering the complexity of the PEPPOL approach, a simpler generic secure and adaptive communication management is currently being evaluated. An alternative reference implementation was studied, OXALIS, promoted as an open source by Difi[3]. Nevertheless, there is a significant conceptual different between PEPPOL, OASIS/Business Document Exchange Architecture [9] and the ECoNet strategy. In PEPPOL, the access points need to expose compatible transport protocols (START, LIME, AS2) while for ECoNet nodes, the transport protocol is internal to ECoM. The transport protocol is transparent for the IT-systems and also for the collaboration contexts (CoC), considering it is abstracted by the collaborative context zero (CoC_0). The CoC_0 maintains the concept of access point (AP) as defined by OASIS/BusDox [14]. The plans are to (re)implement a simplified secure and reliable message exchange mechanism between ECoNet nodes eventually reusing some parts from the PEPPOL reference implementation but based exclusively on ECoNet requirements. There is a common idea about the simplicity to use nomadic commodities (smartphones or tablets) and the Web Services technology to support collaborations. In fact, those facilities offer services to the users of some organization of some service provider (e.g., Facebook). The ECoNet infrastructure addresses the business data exchange needs, but only those with origin in the IT-systems that automate the enterprise's business processes. Those IT-systems in fact are being enhanced with new communication channels beyond classic user interfaces (web based or not), to support nomadic and things (Internet of Things) interactions, e.g., a transponder (thing) in a container to support real-time tracking.

Introduction of the Virtual Collaboration Context (VCC) concept

A collaboration Context was defined in [7] as:

- Collaboration Context (CoC) – abstracts a specific collaboration and is made of one or more collaboration context services (CCS), where $CCS_A = \{CCS_0, CCS_1 \ldots CCS_k\}$, for $k > 0$, is the set of the CCS of the collaboration context CoC_A. The collaboration context service zero (CCS_0) is a mandatory (system) service and establishes the CoC entry point.

It establishes a bounded collaboration semantics as far as data formats and semantics of source and target IT-systems are concerned. As mentioned, it plays a similar role to a specialized adapter for the management of the exchanges of data between IT-systems in two organizations. Nevertheless, in the initial model, if an IT-system that accesses peer IT-systems through an interoperable CoC needs to establish multitenant spaces for groups of ECoNet nodes (partners), there was no mechanism available. To solve this weakness, the model was improved to support the concept of Virtual Collaboration Context (VCC). A VCC establishes one or more groups (multitenant spaces) from the ECoNet ecosystem members able to establish restricted view only accessible to nodes that joined the VCC. It is important to clarify here that a VCC is to be managed by IT-systems that access one or more CoC to exchange business date with a peer IT-system

---

[3] http://www.difi.no/; https://github.com/difi/oxalis.

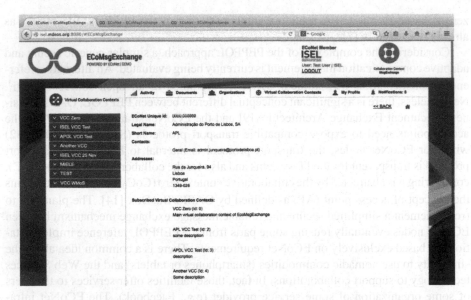

Fig. 4. A snapshot of the ECoMsgExchange ECoNet reference IT-system

(from a business partner). For an ECoNet node (from the initiative of an IT-system) to join a VCC it needs to be accepted by the VCC owner, i.e. the node that created it. Formally this new concept enhances the CoC with the newly created virtual collaboration context (VCC):

- Collaboration Context (CoC) – also abstracts one or more virtual collaboration context services (VCC), where $VCC_A = \{VCC_0, VCC_1... VCC_m\}$, for m > 0, is the set of the VCC of the collaboration context CoC_A
- A Collaboration Context (CoC) is therefore (e.g. for the collaboration context A):
  - $CoC_A = CCS_A \cup VCC_A$; i.e., the set of all the CCS and VCC of the collaboration context CoC_A;
- The Virtual Collaboration Context zero (VCC_0) exists by default and includes all the ECoNet nodes that have the respective collaboration context installed and belongs to the same business partnership.

The visibility of an ECoNet node is restricted to the peer ECoNet nodes that accepted to be business partners (same business partnership). This means that each ECoM instance maintains a list of the ECoNet nodes that were trusted to be considered as business partners. The ECoMsgExchange reference implementation already supports the virtual collaboration contexts making possible for ECoNet members to establish restricted file or message exchange share spaces, Fig. 4.

From the ECoMsgExchange web interface a user from the organization can create and invite ECoNet members to join a VCC. For a selected VCC, a user can share files or messages (currently limited to 10 Kb). For both the ECoMsgExchange and PCS IT-systems, presented in the next chapter, two distinct specialized CoC were developed: (i) the $CoC_{ECoMsgExchange}$, and (ii) the CoC_{PCS}.

4   The PCS Validation Business Cases

The Port Community System was developed as a complement to the current PSW/JUP system. The objective is to develop a wider port community of service providers with a single access point for both electronic exchanges and web access. A snapshot of a transportation container tracking inquire is shown in Fig. 5. The proposal of an extended approach to the management of formalities in a sea port, as worked in the MIELE project are related to the application of the Directive 2010/65/EU[4] and the need for an enhanced collaboration among EU ports promoting, in this way, single procedures for stakeholders and thus simplify processes while maintaining the required security. A first prototype implementing container tracking as an initial service for the new a PCS was developed, Fig. 5.

Fig. 5. A snapshot of the PCS ECoNet demonstrator IT-system

One of the main challenges in this domain is related to the need for a generalized cooperation among a panoply of IT-systems supporting transport and logistics processes from business stakeholders and interactions with customs and other authorities. By establishing a unified adaptive business collaborative framework, the ECoNet infrastructure is expected to make easier the adaptation of the participating IT-systems from a diversity of (with multiple cultures) stakeholders on answering the requirements established by Directive 65 for single authorization/control procedures inside Eurozone. The port community system is from inception integrated to ECoNet being this way interoperable with port administrations and other regulators IT-systems along the transport chain. Such common interoperable platform plays a key role for the agility of door-to-door integrated transport and logistics services offered by the concept of logistics single window (LSW) as discussed in [7].

---

[4] Directive 2010/65/EU of the European Parliament and Council of 20 October 2010 on reporting formalities for ships arriving in and/or departing from ports of the Member States.

The need for efficiency on the exchange of logistics information between information systems is discussed in [10] by proposing guidelines to promote collaboration processes among stakeholders of maritime transport and regulatory procedures for Single Window Systems. In fact, the ECoNet open specifications aim at contributing to establish a structured multi-supplier technology landscape able to reduce costs and risks associated to existing models to make effective electronic data exchanges.

The ECoNet proposal emphasises a separation between intra-organization and inter-organization issues. While focused on the inter-organization perspective by postulating a well-founded model (a common virtual breeding environment - VBE) to manage collaborative relations among groups of organization with different organizational, processes, and technology cultures, the intra-organization is also being considered. The difficulty to adapt complex legacy IT-systems to the newly proposed ECoNet services has motivated the (re)construction of PCS as a wrapper of JUP, Fig. 6. Nevertheless, further enhanced integrated models and validations are necessary, namely a high level modularity abstractions in line with the Cooperation Enabled System [11] as a strategy to contribute for a reduction of the growing technology dependencies (vendor lock-in situations).

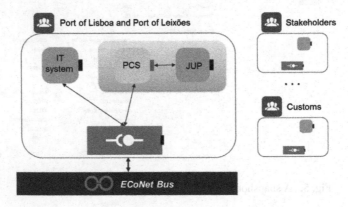

Fig. 6. The new PCS IT-system wraps the legated PSW/JUP

5   Conclusions and Further Research

The collaborative logistics and transport involves large-scale complex distributed systems that must be reliable, maintainable (panoply of technology suppliers), competitive, auditable, and secure. Additionally, it is necessary to get the confidence of all stakeholders for the management of their critical business processes. The ECoNet platform is developed in support of a holistic framework able to speed up the adoption of competitive business collaborative networks and at the same time it contributes to a new generation of dynamic and agile IT product and services. Unlike the first prototype of ECoNet focused on demonstrating the potential of a unified coordination of B2B exchanges, as discussed in our previous research [7], in this paper both an enhanced model of the ECoNet platform as well as a reference implementation for its PCS prototype were presented. Furthermore, the complexity of adopting the open source PEPPOL/CIPA reference implementation and the need for a simple approach to the communication layer was discussed.

The need for novel distributed systems technology able to cope with the growing complexity of collaborative logistics and transport was confirmed by a great level of adherence of stakeholders to the ECoNet proposition. Further validation of the implemented system regarding the exchange of traffic data involving DATEX2 format and payment security enforcement for a competing gas distribution networks (forecourts) is now under planning and development. Nevertheless, some weaknesses can be identified in the current implementation, namely:

- The proposed model is not yet validated for large data sets under diverse formats and semantics. Existing approaches while proprietary are quite complete and credible to manage complex exchanges;
- The ECoNet strategy might challenge the value of well-established business platforms (or products) considering that with the adoption of ECoNet by main stakeholders such unique solutions might have to move to the open ECoNet environment. Nevertheless this change needs to get the approval and confidence of stakeholders about its competitive advantage against current proprietary approaches (even if they adopt existing standards).

The EcoNet infrastructure is to underlie professional business to business data exchanges. While possible, it is not expected to be installed in a personal laptop or in a nomadic (smartphone or tablet) to support the establishment of personal or even business data exchanges. For those case other simple technology approaches are available (from single Web Service mechanism to platforms specialized for personal interactions support). Nevertheless, it is expected that through the new enhanced ECoNet enabled IT-systems (integrated to the ECoNet platform) a suite of new APP based services indirectly using the ECoNet infrastructure, might be available.

Acknowledgements. This work has been partially supported by Administration of the Port of Lisbon and the visionary support of Clara Xavier and Luis Marinho Dias in the MIELE project, Brisa Innovation and Technology, through a yearly research grant, Galpgest and BP through the Hórus project and ANSR (National Road Security Authority) through the SINCRO project. Reference implementation of ECoNet has been supported by Paula Graça, Ana Mourato and Tiago Dias. Partial support was also provided by the Center of Technology and Systems and FCT- PEST program. Concepts from the European project GloNet were also adopted.

References

1. Ascencio, L.M., González-Ramírez, R.G., Bearzotti, L.A., Smith, N.R., Camacho-Vallejo, J.F.: A collaborative supply chain management system for a maritime port logistics chain. J. Appl. Res. Technol. **12**(3), 444–458 (2014)
2. Halmans, G., Pohl, K.: Software product family variability: essential capabilities and realization aspects. In: Proceedings of the 3rd International Workshop on Software Product Lines: Economics, Architectures, and Implications, ICSE 2002, Orlando, USA, 21 May 2002

3. Becker, S., Koziolek, H., Reussner, R.H.: Model-based performance prediction with the palladio component model. In: WOSP 2007: Proceedings of the 6th International Workshop on Software and performance, pp. 54–65. ACM, New York, NY, USA, 5–8 February 2007
4. Jackson, E.K., Sztipanovits, J.: Towards a formal foundation for domain specific modeling languages. In: Proceedings of the 6th ACM and IEEE International Conference on Embedded Software, EMSOFT 2006, pp. 53–62. ACM, New York, NY, USA (2006)
5. Jackson, E.K., Kang, E., Dahlweid, M., Seifert, D., Santen, T.: Components, platforms and possibilities: towards generic automation for MDA. In: Proceedings of 10th ACM International Conference on Embedded Software, EMSOFT 2010, pp. 39–48. ACM, New York, USA (2010)
6. EPCSA: White paper - the role of port community systems in the development of single window. Technical report, European Port Community Systems Association EEIG (2011)
7. Osório, A.L., Camarinha-Matos, L.M., Afsarmanesh, H.: Enterprise collaboration network for transport and logistics services. In: Camarinha-Matos, L.M., Scherer, R.J. (eds.) PRO-VE 2013. IFIP AICT, vol. 408, pp. 267–278. Springer, Heidelberg (2013)
8. Afsarmanesh, H., Camarinha-Matos, L.M., Ermilova, E.: VBE reference framework. In: Camarinha-Matos, L.M., Afsarmanesh, H., Ollus, M. (eds.) Methods and Tools for Collaborative Networked Organizations, pp. 35–68. Springer, New York (2008). doi: 10.1007/978-0-387-79424-2_2
9. Oasis BEDA: Business document exchange architecture - BEDA, March 2011
10. Ahn, K.: The study of single window model for maritime logistics. In: 2010 6th International Conference on Advanced Information Management and Service (IMS), pp. 106–111 (2010)
11. Osório, A.L., Camarinha-Matos, L.M., Afsarmanesh, H.: Cooperation enabled systems for collaborative networks. In: Camarinha-Matos, L.M., Pereira-Klen, A., Afsarmanesh, H. (eds.) PRO-VE 2011. IFIP AICT, vol. 362, pp. 400–409. Springer, Heidelberg (2011)
12. APL and APDL National Reference Model, with port and customs operations processes - report and models – MRN V4.1, internal working documents (2008)
13. Habich, D, Lehner, W., Bohm, M., Bittner, J., Wloka, U.: Model-driven generation of dynamic adapters for integration platforms. In: Proceedings of the First International Workshop on Model Driven Interoperability for Sustainable Information Systems (MDISIS 2008), CEUR Workshop Proceedings, vol. 340, pp. 105–119, June 2008. http://CEUR-WS.org
14. OASIS-BusDox BEDA. Business document exchange architecture - BEDA, March 2011

A Software Architecture for Transportation Planning and Monitoring in a Collaborative Network

Anne Baumgraß[1], Remco Dijkman[2(✉)], Paul Grefen[2], Shaya Pourmirza[2],
Hagen Völzer[3], and Mathias Weske[1]

[1] Hasso Plattner Institut, University of Potsdam, Potsdam, Germany
{anne.baumgrass,mathias.weske}@hpi.de
[2] Eindhoven University of Technology, Eindhoven, The Netherlands
{r.m.dijkman,p.w.p.j.grefen,s.pourmirza}@tue.nl
[3] IBM Zurich Research Lab, Zurich, Switzerland
hvo@zurich.ibm.com

Abstract. Transportation planners require software support to easily monitor and dispatch transportation resources, especially when transportation is multi-modal and when resources from different companies in their network are being used. We call such an application a transportation control tower. This paper presents a software architecture for transportation control towers. It focuses in particular on the novel aspects of the software architecture. These are: the ability to easily configure the monitoring of resources and tasks; the ability to create the statements for monitoring resources and tasks based on the transportation plan; and the ability to dynamically adjust the monitoring statements. A prototype of the software architecture is implemented and evaluated on three usage scenarios.

Keywords: Collaborative networks · Transportation · Transportation management system · Control tower · Transportation planning

1 Introduction

On a daily basis, planners at transportation companies are working on the assignment of transportation resources to transportation orders. Each transportation order involves a large variety of activities and may involve many different parties. Of course, activities include the actual transportation of the goods, either by the company of the planner or by partner companies. However, they also include logistic activities around the transportation, such as collecting an empty container to transport the goods in, temporary storage of the goods in a partner of a warehouse, and transshipment by a terminal. They also include administrative tasks, such as reserving resources of transportation partners,

---

A working version of this paper is available as A. Baumgrass, R.M. Dijkman, P.W.P.J. Grefen, S. Pourmirza, H. Voelzer, M. Weske. A Software Architecture for a Transportation Control Tower. BETA Working Paper WP-461. Eindhoven University of Technology, Eindhoven, The Netherlands, 2014.

© IFIP International Federation for Information Processing 2015
L.M. Camarinha-Matos et al. (Eds.): PRO-VE 2015, IFIP AICT 463, pp. 277–284, 2015.
DOI: 10.1007/978-3-319-24141-8_25

filling out forms, inspection of the goods by customs, and billing. Transportation planners are responsible for planning and monitoring these activities. This task is made more complex by the fact that the transportation plan for a transportation order often changes, for example, due to changes in the availability or cost of transportation resources. This may have a rippling effect on other transportation orders as well.

To support these tasks, a transportation planner would benefit from software that helps him monitor the tasks that have been performed for the transportation order, the tasks that still have to be performed, and the transportation resources that are assigned to, or are available for, the transportation orders. We also call such software a 'transportation control tower' analogous to the control towers that monitor transportation resources in aviation.

There exist a large number of transportation management systems (TMS), which provide functionality for monitoring transportation resources. In previous work [4], we did a thorough analysis of a collection of 49 of these tools. The difference between such more traditional TMS and a control tower is that a control tower provides a more open ecosystem with advanced facilities for incorporating monitoring capabilities of partner resources and other data.

This paper presents an architecture for a transportation control tower. The architecture is based on an analysis of transportation scenarios from practice.

2   Usage Scenarios

This section presents three scenarios that were developed in collaboration with industry partners [9]. The scenarios represent situations that occur on a daily basis and that require advanced (control tower) functionality from transportation management systems to properly support transportation planners. The section ends with an overview of this functionality.

2.1   Multi-modal Planning

A transportation planner can plan a multi-modal route for a full container load. To do that effectively, the planner needs to have insight into real-time information about the transportation infrastructure, including both the current traffic conditions and transportation-related events, such as the waiting time at customs or the gate at the harbor.

Often, transportation companies make use of partners to do the transportation. To that end, the transportation planner needs insight into the availability of transportation partners. Using this information, the transportation planner can select the trucks that are closest to the pick-up location of the goods. These trucks can either be own assets or assets owned by transportation partners or single drivers.

After the transportation plan is created, the planner should be able to automatically distribute the transportation plan to the parties that are involved, including transportation partners. Subsequently, the execution of the transportation must be monitored, the geographical position of the resources involved must be tracked, as well as the status of the transportation steps that have been performed and the steps that still must be performed.

2.2 Freight Shift

It happens every day that transportation capacity or demand shifts from one location to another. For example, an airplane that carries 10 containers may have to land at a different airport unexpectedly due to weather conditions. As another example, an airplane may suddenly have more transportation capacity available, because of the cancellation of a transportation order.

Such freight-shifts should be detected as quickly as possible to properly act on them. Nowadays, transportation companies often hear about it at a late stage, for example, when the airplane has already landed at another airport.

Once the freight-shift has been detected, transportation planners must change the plans around the affected locations. This involves re-planning the resources that were originally planned to pick-up or drop-of the cargo, possibly even if they are already en-route. It also involves re-planning additional capacity to pick-up or drop-of the cargo at the new location.

2.3 Inland Waterways

The use of inland waterway transportation usually is associated with transportation cost advantages and positive environmental performance. However, its reliability is influenced by varying water levels which might lead to restrictions or complete close down of the waterway for days. Since such situations can, to an extent, be foreseen, the creation of robust offline plans, which consider the risk of low or high water levels, and careful monitoring and prediction of water levels, can mitigate the need for ad-hoc online re-planning.

Based on historical data and information about the current water levels and their development, situations in which the planned transportation by inland waterway might lead to problems due to insufficient water depth can be detected. Since this information can be transmitted to the planner in ample time before the start of the transportation, the planned route can still be changed using other transportation alternatives.

The choice of other transportation alternatives is facilitated by the consideration of existing alternatives based on schedules as well as on information about the available capacities and routes shared by transportation partners or by assigning free vehicles to new routes.

2.4 Required Functionality

The scenarios above, point to a number of requirements that transportation control tower software should support. A detailed analysis of requirements can be found in [9], but on a high level of abstraction, a transportation control tower should support:

- the provisioning of information on the availability of transportation resources, including own resources, and partner resources;
- the provisioning of information on infrastructure availability;
- automated detection and prediction of disruptions of transportation infrastructure and resources;

- offline planning (before the transportation is executed);
- online planning (while the transportation is executed and taking real-time information about resource availability and disruption into account);
- robust planning (taking into account likely changes to a transportation plan);
- multi-party tracking and tracing based on a transportation plan; and
- automated reconfiguration of the tracking and tracing facilities based on changes to a transportation plan.

3 Architecture Overview

Considering the requirements that are explained in the previous section, we developed a software architecture for a transportation control tower. Figure 1 shows the high level components that are provided by this architecture. The architecture is described in detail in [10].

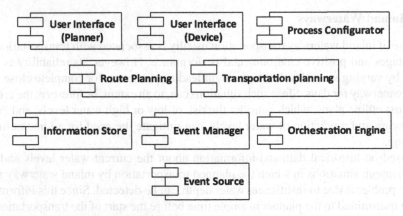

Fig. 1. Architecture for a transportation control tower.

The architecture is layered and shows the following components. There are user interfaces for both the planner and for devices that drivers of transportation resources use. In addition, there is a process configurator that can be used by a designer, to describe the activities that must be executed for various types and legs of transportation routes in terms of processes. Through the user interface, the planner has access to various types of planning algorithms.

Both the planning algorithms and the user interfaces make use of information that is either accessible from an (external) information store such as a database or via an event manager. The event manager is a publish-subscribe mechanism that can be used to monitor events that are published by event sources, such as board computers of trucks, road management systems, and AIS transponders of ships.

The tasks that must be executed and monitored during the execution of a transportation plan, are determined by composing them based on the transportation plan and the processes that are designed in the process configurator. These tasks are subsequently managed by the orchestration engine, which also takes care of subscribing (and unsubscribing) to events that are relevant in different stages of the transportation plan and must be shown on the various user interfaces.

4   Detailed Architecture Operations

In the usage scenarios, the architecture components work together as follows.

In order to plan the fulfilment of a transportation order, the *route planning* component is used to create a, possibly intermodal, routing for the transportation order or each consignment thereof. Such an intermodal routing is an alternating sequence of transportation legs and transshipments that connects the pick-up point with the delivery point of the consignment. Optionally, multiple transportation orders can be planned together, e.g. to benefit from optimal sharing of resources, by using the *transportation planning* component. The transportation plan must then be refined into a detailed actionable plan, which we also call a transportation process.

Figure 2 shows a section of a transportation process. This section corresponds to two legs: first an empty container is procured by a truck and then the truck picks up the goods and drives them to a train terminal for further shipment.

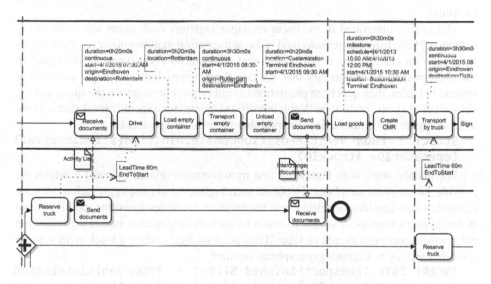

Fig. 2. Initial part of transportation process example.

To construct the transportation process from the transportation plan, we follow the idea that a process model is composed of process snippets, where we have essentially one snippet for each segment (i.e., leg or transshipment) of the transportation routing. For example, in Fig. 2, the vertical dashed red lines show the boundaries of the snippets. Functions to create models from snippets, i.e., creating a snippet from scratch, registering it to the repository using index attributes, searching for snippets with transportation routing segments and composing snippets together, are integrated into the *process configurator* component.

The *orchestration engine* provides a means to enact transportation processes. The orchestration engine has a task handler to monitor the state of transportation tasks that are derived from the transportation order and to enable different users, e.g. a planner, to perform the tasks that need to be done. To this end the orchestration engine also has access to the static *information store*. Optionally, it can activate external applications to perform certain tasks (not in the architecture).

The transportation resources that are being monitored may vary per process or per task. For example, during a truck leg, a truck is being monitored, while during a train leg, a train of a partner company is being monitored. In order to receive notifications from the *event monitoring* component about the status of the resources, the orchestration engine has to subscribe to predefined queries. The transportation process itself as well as all of its tasks can be annotated by these predefined queries as shown in Fig. 2. The orchestration then ensures that a subscription becomes active when the corresponding task or process becomes active.

To process the queries, we implemented an *event manager* responsible for collecting events from different sources and processing them. The event manager is based on 'complex event processing' [3, 6, 7] and builds on Esper [2, 5]. In this paper, we focus on the usage of event subscriptions during transportation execution and refer the interested reader for the technical details of the event manager to [1] and the corresponding tutorials[1].

The engine integrated in the event manager registers each event subscription via listeners. These listeners get informed if the subscription matches observed event types from relevant *event sources*. We assume that all required event types are registered in the event manager. The queries that activate the listeners look like SQL queries, but instead of tables, they query the pre-defined event types. For example, the query below, subscribes to events of the type 'VehiclePositionUpdate' for a specific truck that is given as a parameter and within a time interval that is given as a parameter.

```
SELECT * FROM VehiclePositionUpdate.win:time($timeInterval)
(operatorID= $truckID)
```

We mainly work with high-level and transportation-related events for which we provide subscription templates. To obtain such high-level events, aggregation rules are defined, which combine or select event information contained in events, possibly from different event sources. A simple example of such an aggregation rule is the following rule, which generates events of type 'TransportFinished', when a truck with a given identifier arrives at a certain geographical position.

```
INSERT INTO TransportFinished SELECT * FROM VehicleLocation
(operatorID=$truckID,latitude=$lat,longitude=$lon)
```

The planning algorithms are made accessible to the end-users via *user interfaces*. The user interfaces also show information on the status of transportation orders, the tasks that must be performed for these transportation orders, the status of resources that are needed for executing the transportation orders, and related information such as the weather conditions, traffic congestion or low water levels that might affect container transport on barges.

---

[1] http://bpt.hpi.uni-potsdam.de/Public/EPP.

5   Evaluation

We have done an initial evaluation of the architecture, using a questionnaire in which we asked practitioners about the use and usefulness of particular aspects of the transportation control tower. In particular we asked them to rank the importance of completeness, time-liness and accuracy of different types of information in their system on a five-point Likert scale. We also asked them whether their current systems provided the information in a complete, timely and accurate manner. The questionnaire was filled out by three practi-tioners from different logistics service providers during this initial evaluation. We are currently working to have it filled out by a much larger number of respondents. The prac-titioners ranked the importance of completeness, timeliness and accuracy of all types of information as high or very high. Interestingly, they also indicated that timeliness is a problem with many types of information. In a discussion with them, we found that this was because planners often need to resort to searching for information on, for example, delays of trains on a web-site and they need to ask for availability of partner vehicles by calling their partner organization. In a transportation control tower, that information is available in a more timely manner, because it is directly fed into the system through event aggregators. More detail on the setup of the evaluation, including the questionnaire can be found in [8].

6   Conclusion

This paper presented an architecture for software that transportation planners can use to manage and monitor their transportation orders. Using a publish-subscribe mechanism, information on transportation resources of the company itself, on the transportation resources of transportation partners, and on other transportation-related events can be made available in a flexible manner. Subscriptions are associated with tasks in the process model that is derived from the transportation planning. In that way, information subscriptions are highly configurable and will adapt to the context of the tasks that are being executed for the transportation order.

The architecture has been implemented in a prototype, of which a demo is available on-line[2].

This paper focuses on introducing the overall architecture of a transportation control tower and the information aggregation component of the architecture. We acknowledge that there are other aspects that are important to ensure the collaboration of partners in such a platform, including security and technical and conceptual data translation. These aspects have, to an extent, been addressed in the work described in [1, 9, 10] of which this paper is a summary.

Acknowledgement. The research leading to these results is part of the GET Service project (http://www.getservice-project.eu) and has received funding from the European Commission

---

[2] http://is.ieis.tue.nl/research/getservice/.

under the 7th Framework Programme (FP7) for Research and Technological Development under grant agreement no 2012-318275.

References

1. Baumgrass, A., et al.: Conceptual architecture specification of an information aggregation engine. Deliverable D6.2, GET Service, Service Platform for Green European Transportation (2014)
2. Bernhardt, T., Vasseur, A.: Esper: event stream processing and correlation (2007). http://www.onjava.com/lpt/a/6955. (Accessed on 25 August 2015)
3. Cabanillas, C., Baumgrass, A., Mendling, J., Rogetzer, P., Bellovoda, B.: Towards the enhancement of business process monitoring for complex logistics chains. In: Lohmann, N., Song, M., Wohed, P. (eds.) BPM 2013 Workshops. LNBIP, vol. 171, pp. 305–317. Springer, Heidelberg (2014)
4. Demir, E., et al.: A review of transportation planning tools. Deliverable D5.1, GET Service, Service Platform for Green European Transportation (2013)
5. EsperTech: Esper - complex event processing, July 2014
6. Herzberg, N., Meyer, A., Weske, M.: An event processing platform for business process management. In: Enterprise Distributed Object Computing Conference (EDOC), pp. 107–116. IEEE (2013)
7. Luckham, D.C.: Event Processing for Business: Organizing the Real-Time Enterprise. Wiley, Hoboken (2011)
8. Schmiele, J., et al.: Evaluation plan. Deliverable D1.4.1, GET Service, Service Platform for Green European Transportation (2014)
9. Treitl, S., et al.: Use cases, success criteria and usage scenarios. Deliverable D1.2, Get Service, Service Platform for Green European Transportation (2014)
10. van der Velde, M., Saraber, P., Grefen, P., Ernst, A.C.: Get architecture definition. Deliverable D2.2.1, Get Service, Service Platform for Green European Transportation (2014)

An Adaptive IoT Management Infrastructure for EcoTransport Networks

J.M.F. Calado[1,2(✉)], Luís A. Osório[1], and Ricardo Prata[3]

[1] IPL – Instituto Politécnico de Lisboa, ISEL – Instituto Superior de Engenharia de Lisboa, Rua Conselheiro Emídio Navarro, 1959-007 Lisbon, Portugal
jcalado@dem.isel.ipl.pt, lo@isel.ipl.pt
[2] IDMEC/LAETA - IST, Universidade de Lisboa, Avenida Rovisco Pais, 1049-001 Lisbon, Portugal
[3] DailyWork – Investigação e Desenvolvimento Lda, Zona Industrial, Rua da Bélgica, Lote 18, Edifício OPEN, 2430-028 Marinha Grande, Portugal
ricardo.prata@dailywork.pt

Abstract. The complexity associated with fast growing of B2B and the lack of a (complete) suite of open standards makes difficulty to maintain the underlying collaborative processes. Aligned to this challenge, this paper aims to be a contribution to an open architecture of logistics and transport processes management system. A model of an open integrated system is being defined as an open computational responsibility from the embedded systems (on-board) as well as a reference implementation (prototype) of a host system to validate the proposed open interfaces. Embedded subsystem can, natively, be prepared to cooperate with other on-board units and with IT-systems in an infrastructure commonly referred to as a center information system or back-office. In interaction with a central system the proposal is to adopt an open framework for cooperation where the embedded unit or the unit placed somewhere (land/sea) interacts in response to a set of implemented capabilities.

Keywords: Logistics · Transports · Service oriented computing · Internet of things · Location based services/devices

1 Introduction

The idea of open systems has been placed with increasing acuity wherein the need for new services and their supporting processes require overall integration of a disparity of systems. By open system within a framework of complex information systems (IT-Systems) is understood by a system (of systems) in which its subsystems implement a responsibility framework, or set of computational capabilities, where for each of those subsystems there are at least two implementations that compete in the market. In an architectural service oriented framework it could be considered that each subsystem implements a set of services whose interface corresponds to an open specification or even a norm when a specification is required by a formal standardization [12].

The generalization of sensors/actuators as intelligent systems with an increasing degree of autonomy, adaptability and may be permanently connected, has motivated a

© IFIP International Federation for Information Processing 2015
L.M. Camarinha-Matos et al. (Eds.): PRO-VE 2015, IFIP AICT 463, pp. 285–296, 2015.
DOI: 10.1007/978-3-319-24141-8_26

number of works in the area of Internet of Things (IoT), [1]. As defined in [1], "The Proliferation of These Devices in the Communicating-actuating Network Creates the Internet of Things (IoT),…", which means that the growing number of networked devices form the growing capacity and distributed intelligence in the perception of environment where devices are always connected to any decision system (IT-System).

Although expectations are high concerning the widespread potential adoption of a network of "things", the success depends on the establishment of a "business eco-systems" as a multiplier of devices installed settling the contribution to the development of Big-Data concepts in supporting business and decision processes. Although being a recent topic, the first use with the designation of network of things (IoT) dates back to 1999–2002 being referred in the Forbes Magazine as "We need an internet for things, a standardized way for computers to understand the real world" as an interaction strategy with the real world [2]. In the same paper is identified a set of capabilities that could help reduce the gap between the physical and virtual worlds:

- **Communication and cooperation** - either among different units in close spaces or in communication/cooperation with the infrastructure side systems in connection to central information systems (back-office). Recent developments in technologies such as GSM/UMTS/LTE, Wi-Fi, Bluetooth, ZigBee, DSRC-MDR (Dedicated short-range communication – Medium Data Rate), Sigfox, NFC (Near Field Communication), among others, has established facilitators (production capacity and costs) in the generalization of devices, with more potential to incorporate more functionalities;
- **Addressing capability (Addressability)** - the devices must be able to be addressed for what a reference must be located (sought) in any directory or by any search (discovery/lookup) process with or without the use of a centralized repository (peer-to-peer);
- **Identification** - looks for an agreement under a unique identification framework or through any qualification that allows the conflict resolution between identical addresses;
- **Sensing** - collection of information about the physical environment, its local store and forward for information systems when available a communication channel for this purpose (adaptive communication);
- **Actuation** - generation of actuation signals over physical systems, where such a responsibility could require a processes coordination with local autonomy (in a framework of Programmable Logical Controllers - PLC);
- **Embedded information processing** - the increasing ability of processors provided by Advanced RISC Machine (ARM) architectures, allow the incorporation of local intelligence;
- **Location** - the emergence of intelligent "things" with localization capabilities either by geo-positioning (GPS/EGNOS) or by identification from stations in the infrastructure, being the accuracy of the positioning dependent on the triangulation techniques used;

Thus, this paper aims to be a contribution to an open architecture of logistics and transport processes management system, as a model of an open integrated systems, being defined a computational responsibility associated with the embedded system (on-board) as well as a reference implementation (prototype) of a host system to validate the interface. The idea is that the embedded subsystem can, natively, be prepared to cooperate (cooperative systems [11]) with other on-board units and with systems in an infrastructure commonly referred to as a center information system or back-office. The interaction under a framework of cooperation between equals (peer-to-peer) can occur through a virtual connection point to point communication. In interaction with a central system the proposal is to adopt an open framework for cooperation where the embedded unit or the unit placed somewhere on land or sea environment, which has been called the Mobile Services Unit (MSU), interacts in response to a set of implemented capabilities in cooperation with a monitoring infrastructure ensuring its operability and response in case of failure (prognosis). This research presents the results from the SASPORT project, namely the nomadic unit (MSU) as an initial prototype.

The paper is organized as follows: Sect. 2 provides a discussion about open interfaces for communication; Sect. 3 describes the proposed approach architecture; Sect. 4 presents the concluding remarks and highlights few future lines of research.

2 Open Interfaces for Communication

This section is concerned with the establishment of a theoretical framework that underpins the architectural options, with special emphasis on scientific and technological work streamlined by the scientific community and industry, in promoting heavily based solutions in electronics, telecommunications and computer and information systems, in an open architectures framework for communication between devices and a host (the central of back-office system). In fact the trio, people, "things" and Internet can be connected via mediators' devices as shown in Fig. 1.

Although the devices tend to be simple and specialized, either in the number of sensors/actuators or in the computational and communication resources, the trend with the increasing competitiveness at the hardware level is to implement increasingly intelligent and autonomous units or "things" [3].

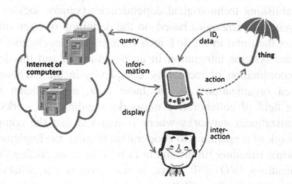

Fig. 1. The Smartphone as a mediator between people, "things" and Internet [2].

However, all this potential requires the definition of a set of open specifications and even the definition of new standards so that the devices within a framework of IoT can participate in transport processes, logistics, decision support approaches and others. As a strategy to respond to the increasing network complexity of smart devices [4] and [5] proposes a network management architecture of intelligent "things" through a multi-agents architecture. The architecture presented and discussed in [4] and [5] was framed in the project called Platform for Transport Management Systems (P4TMS) considering the transport of goods in an inter-modal way. The P4TMS aimed at the management of transport processes involving multiple modes (road and rail). The models of a transport process includes activities and their interdependencies. An activity involves one or more services under a pre-established contract celebrated by a service provider that implements an open interface. A service provider is referred to as its implementation and its operationalization through a computational agent (intelligent entity or not). Thus, in a services oriented architecture, all are services, being understood as computational entities with which other services can establish dependency relationships.

Although one of the platform's goals was an agile response (intelligent) to transport planning and associated logistics, the platform aspect most closely with this paper's topic refers to the network management methodology of devices that is intended to be adaptive and intelligent. Thus, we propose a component, as another IT-system with the management responsibility of a network of devices through the implementation of a component called intelligent Transport Unit (iTU) Technological Infrastructure Management Services (iTIMS) [4]. This component is in charge of the devices network management through the concept of "surrogate" as a mediator mechanism in managing unique identifiers applied to the data base management [6] and later in devices abstraction with limited resources that are unable to manage state information or advanced features [7].

In addition to devices network management strategies in maintaining updated global state information, a key aspect is the establishment of open interfaces to minimize the need for adapters. In the electronic information exchange between heterogeneous systems has been a common practice the integration based on adapters. However, the costs and risks associated with the development of integrated systems, in particular by establishing technological dependencies (vendor lock-in solutions) suggests the development of strategies based on the definition of open interfaces.

In recent years the trend in the IoT area includes the development of open architectures aiming the systems integration in an organization and the definition of new models for the coordination of increasing complexity in the exchange of electronic messages between organizations. In the latter case, a significant work has been developed in the field of collaborative networks standing out works leading to the structure of organizational networks where is required that the companies progress towards a framework of preparation to cooperation through the implementation of what is known as a Virtual Breeding Environment (VBE) [8] in supporting the establishment of virtual organizations (VO) [9]. Thus, it was proposed a collaborative platform ECoNet aiming to structure the collaboration between organizations in the transports and logistics domains where the members of this network can share and exchange information using a common middleware infrastructure [10].

3 Proposed Approach Architecture

The definition of a communication open interface between devices and the host of the approach proposed in this paper, it is an opportunity for the projection of some of the above listed concerns. Thus, for the open interface definition, the following guidelines are considered:

- Characterization of requirements and its generalization in an accountability framework formulation (capabilities) of a MSU unit:
  - Functional model: Data model; Exceptions; Tests/Compliance (conformance tests); Interface and semantics/coordination of access operations.
  - Monitoring model: Data model; Operational quality assessment rules.
- Decoupling strategy of MSU units through surrogate services (MSU-S) being the development management responsibility of each unit as follows:
  - Coordination server of a set of surrogates through a gateway server (MSU-G): Responsible by communications with the network of MSUs.
  - Implementation strategy of each MSU-S: Pairs lifecycle (MSU, MSU-S); Pair monitoring (MSU, MSU-S), where a MSU-S may or may not reflect a MSU (based upon availability and status update rate of the status of these two systems (tandem).
  - Set of interfaces to be made available as open specifications and may evolve in the context of standardization processes.

As a first approximation, it will be considered the overall architecture of the proposed approach into its main components, Fig. 2. It will be considered an information system, generically called IT-System, with the responsibility of access one or more MSU networks.

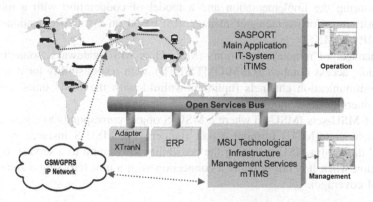

Fig. 2. General system architecture of the proposed approach.

A MSU network is established by a group of solidary MSUs with a particular process or set of transport processes. In the context of the current approach, the aim is focused on the validation of an interface or interfaces proposed as an open framework.

This validation focuses on the MSU network management key component, itself an IT-System installed in containers or other mobile (nomadic) resources. This component, called MSU Technological Infrastructure Management Services (mTIMS) has the responsibility to provide access services to each of the distributed units (remote) MSU transparent to communication failures or periods when the units are turned off (for maintenance or other reason). The iTIMS is responsible for the management of groups of transponders associated to specific transport processes. It uses services implemented by the mTIMS it-system.

Thus, the architecture of the IT-System, mTIMS (Fig. 3), includes the following main modules:

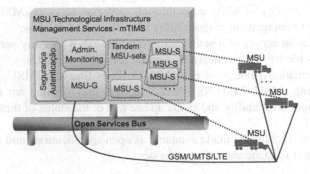

Fig. 3. TIMS component architecture and its connection to MSU network.

i. Security and authentication mechanisms to access, either by users, or by other IT-Systems;

ii. Monitoring the implementation and a model of cooperation with a monitoring infrastructure for maintenance management based on open specifications such as SNMP or JMX;

iii. A manager of remote connections (MSU-G or MSU-gateway), sometimes with multiple access numbers (GSM/UMTS/LTE), with responsibility for management of communication channels (uplink/downlink) with the MSU units installed in containers or other mobile resources;

iv. Set of MSU-sets (MSU-S) where a MSU-S object corresponds to a surrogate of a physical unit (MSU) forming a pair (tandem). A MSU-S instance extends the capabilities of a MSU including the possibility to respond to a service to obtain a location when it is not possible a connection with a unit (crossing a zone without GSM coverage).

The pairing type (tandem) between a physical unit with a unique identifier (UID-MSU) with its MSU-S-UID, which is associated with the same unique identifier, makes available an MSU with extended capabilities and this runs in a computing platform with potential unlimited resources (e.g., using cloud computing). The management of the life cycle of a MSU unit should ensure that the state of the surrogate unit is consistent with the physical unit, in particular, always an action occurs by a manual process. If the unit is shut down permanently (by a permanent fault) the respective MSU-S should also be eliminated, staying for the purposes of historical information the registration of the "slaughter" together with other information related to their working state.

For an enhanced management of MSU devices in different application contexts (different IT-Systems from different stakeholders) is introduced the concept of MSU groups. An IT-System can access more than a set of MSU devices.

3.1   The MSU-Surrogate (MSU-S) as Abstraction Module of the Device MSU

For each device (MSU) installed on some mobile resources (container, truck, wagon, etc.) there is an instance of a model that represents it (surrogate), Fig. 4. Essentially an MSU-S maintains updated information regarding an MSU, its equal (surrogate). Such an information update depends on the policy adopted for communication with an MSU, which is constraint by the energy consumption. Although the proposed approach has been designed having as key mission the autonomy of a unit through harvesting techniques, the energy should be managed as part of a policy of reducing consumption by which the number of communications between an MSU and the mTIMS system should be maintained in minimum.

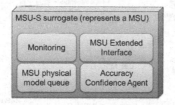

Fig. 4. MSU-S unit (surrogate) architecture.

Either because long periods without communication or because the unit is in a location without access to the communications network or yet because the unit is turned off (e.g. for maintenance), it is intended that an IT-System (client) can access the information of an MSU device. That is, it is the responsibility of the mTIMS system to maintain a MSU-S set equal to a MSU set, so that through a MSU-S a client could "see" the corresponding MSU in its approximate state by inference of attribute of values that may have been modified by a state change of the respective MSU. This approximate state may refer to the geo-position of the MSU device. That is, until there is a new communication of the respective MSU, the corresponding MSU-S can respond with an inferred position, by calculation or application of some heuristics as to give the position with a certain degree of confidence associated. An example could be an MSU device associated with a container moving between point A and B.

Knowing the last position, the azimuth (direction), the direction of movement, speed and geographic information/roads, a computational agent infers at each instant the position value with an associate degree of confidence. The architecture of a MSU-S module that virtualizes a MSU device, consists of the following key components:

i. A sequence of states of a virtualized MSU device (MAX_STATES_QUEUE, maximum number of ills states, one for each access to an MSU device);
    An extended interface related to the interface of a device (MSU), i.e., an interface of a virtual device MSU-S, such that the computing capacity that is executed allows a set of functionalities difficult to implement in the corresponding device;

ii. An evaluation module on the degree of trust of attributes of a MSU provided by its virtual view, when the values are not updated for more than a MSU_DeltaUpdate time, defined by configuration.

3.2 Open Interfaces of the Proposed Approach

In SoaML model, Fig. 5 depicts the main open interfaces to various levels of cooperation. The proposed approach considers a set of interfaces to be implemented for access by IT-Systems, either by the demo application of the current approach or other approaches. The open interfaces are as follows:

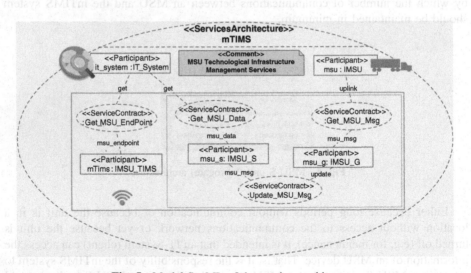

Fig. 5. Model SoaML of the services architecture.

- mTIMS Interface
  - Communication interfaces with mTIMS system to obtain the reference of a particular MSU-S, and later access through the operations provided by a MSU-G:
    - IMSU_S - access interface to a virtual representation of a MSU device;
    - IMSU_G - interface that allows obtain, upon client application authentication, an end point for a MSU_S that allows access to information of the respective MSU.

- Uplink/Downlink (MSU) Interface
  - Access interface to a MSU, through its MSU-G (gateway) in the uplink operation;
  - Updating attributes interface of a MSU, through the respective MSU-G (gateway) in the downlink operation.

The interfaces considered a minimum set of functionalities. The objective of the proposed approach is the definition of a generic interface even without considering specific requirements arising from the evaluation of one or more application domains.

The messages exchanged between services (producers and consumers) have been described through messages models directly convertible to eXtensible Markup Language (XML) and based on the Scheme Definition (XSD) grammar.

The proposed models represent a first approach to an initial version of an open specification for the distributed computing responsibilities (the connected intelligent things). It is expected that more complete and robust models are proposed as validations identifies features that were not considered but important to the required completeness of critical operating solutions.

3.3 Characteristics of MSU Device

The developed autonomous locator is self-sufficient, with a rechargeable built-in "battery", being the corresponding blocks diagram depicted in Fig. 6(a). It integrates GPS and GSM/GPRS technologies and other sensors such as accelerometer, temperature and real time clock. The locator, whose prototype is shown in Fig. 6(b) is intended for market of goods transport and further to harvest energy from the vibrations and the sun, which is one of the innovative aspects that presents itself to the sector. The locator will integrate the DSRC-MDR technology (radio technology used in the Via Verde toll identifiers) thus enabling the unit to detects tolls in all countries that use the radio frequency identification technology (5.8 GHz) TC270 DSRC-MDR. This information will be relevant for logistics operators or logistics parks because they allow accurately track cargo passage sites, without using GPS or GSM network. This potential collaboration involving highway concessionaires (as another collaborative stakeholder) has motivated the promotion of synergies with the ECoNet platform [10]. Nevertheless, the focus of the project is to develop the power generation system ("Energy Harvesting") which will load the "battery" extending the unit life. This will prevent battery exchange after few months of use (when battery exchange is not possible, often results in the loss of devices).

To complement the system, it will be developed a "central system" with georeferenced maps for display the devices and all data sent by the remote units. The map chosen was the OpenStreetMap since it has a worldwide coverage and have not running costs. As far as other options are concerned, e.g. as the possible use of GoogleMaps, the choice of OpenStreetMap, beyond being made available in an open source model (Open Source), allows operation in offline mode. The current "central/back-office system" is presented in Fig. 7, where start/end and trip events, as well as, the electronic

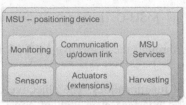

(a) The MSU Architecture

(b) The Unit developed by the
SASPORT Project

Fig. 6. The MSU unit.

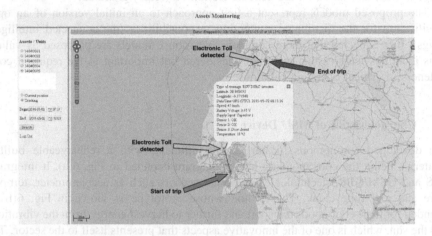

Fig. 7. A view of the monitoring web interface.

tolls detected with DSRC-MDR technology are shown. The unit under development
has as main requirements the low cost and low energy consumption. Thus the computing platform chosen was a microcontroller with enough computing power to perform the various unit control functions but without the capability to support an
operating system.

To implement the GSM/GPRS communications was chosen the BG2-W module
from Gemalto (former Siemens and former Cinterion) since it is a module with
worldwide coverage (Quad-Band), small size, low cost and low power consumption.

Being available the GSM and GPRS technologies means that could be used the
following communication approaches: SMS - communication limited to 160 characters
to a mobile device; Data - communication via GPRS over the Internet. Of both types of
communications should be privileged data communication due to low cost and ease of
integration with the central computing platforms that integrate geo-referenced maps.
However the SMS communication has the advantages of having a lower consumption
due to reduced communication time. The GPRS communication has as main characteristic the fact of being billed by volume of data rather than the communication time.
On the other hand, reducing the transmitted data minimizes the communication time
and thus increases the device autonomy.

4 Conclusions

The architecture of the proposed approach bases its open framework on the possibility of allow multiple suppliers for an MSU device. For this to happen is necessary that the uplink/downlink messages between a MSU device and an IT-System gateway (MSU-G) be standardized, especially in the accuracy of the fields semantics that constitute the message. This would promote the participation in group or groups of standardization related to the field of transports or logistics so that the product that emerges from this project can gain international visibility and credibility.

The standardization of interfaces at the "back office" system level, the mTIMS system, assumes a dimension of industry promotion in terms of IT-Systems. In fact, the separation between the system (infrastructural IT-System) and the proposed system considered here concerned with the management application of a network of MSU devices, aims at a contribution to a system framework of open IT-Systems. We define a system of open systems (SoS), where one IT-System for which each subsystem has a market competitor. This is a complex challenge being that the mapping between requirements and capabilities of an IT-system is not of simple formulation, nor the establishment of a closed framework for standardization (full). In any case, the proposed approach aims to be an initial contribute in a validation of a modular framework contributing to an open SoS in a framework of development and operation management of transport, logistics, and other related processes.

The IMSU-TIMS interface in which we can consider as a more relevant interface the IMSU-S access interface to a virtual MSU device, would establish a standard framework for a manager of a network of MSU devices (potentially from different vendors). The architecture and interfaces proposed leave a set of open questions to be developed in specialized projects, concerned with a device perspective in their physical and functional characteristics, or in the perspective of the development of integrated systems for the management of transport processes. Such SoS, while being a complex distributed system have open challenges/questions unanswered as follows:

- Definition of a reference model for component "Accuracy Confidence Agent" responsible for presenting a virtual interface of a MSU device, having the responsibility to reply with attribute values with a degree of confidence associated when the image of the physical MSU device is delayed by a given time;
- The suggestion of the concept of MSU sets (groups) for a more efficient management of a MSU devices network (eventually involving multiple transport companies) requires a modeling work to be reflected in the proposed interfaces;
- The transport processes may involve more than one company which configures the need to formalize a collaborative network where companies (organizations) with different cultures of organization/processes and technology have to coordinate their collaborative processes. These involve the infrastructure component (MSU) and the IT-Systems component responsible for coordinating the collaborative processes (exchange/sharing messages) and internal activities of the organization;
- Model of integrated maintenance management through standardized monitoring interfaces that are able to be integrated with specialized IT-Systems of operation/maintenance management;

- Integration of MSU devices with other embedded devices (on-board), e.g. integration of the tachograph system with a MSU in a container transported by the respective vehicle (tractor), requires the development of an open framework that enables interoperability between devices from different manufacturers where the interception of a set of functionalities is not null (potential redundancy, e.g., multiple GPS modules), or implement additional functionalities.

Acknowledgments. This work was partially supported by the national founded QREN I&DT individual n°. 24715 (SASPORT) project. By the Administration of the Port of Lisbon (APL) through the EU MIELE founding, and by Brisa Innovation and Technology, through a yearly research grant. It was also partially supported by FCT, through IDMEC, under LAETA UID/EMS/50022/2013. The models definition and design received a valuable contribution from Paula Graça.

References

1. Gubbi, J., Buyya, R., Marusic, S., Palaniswami, M.: Internet of things (iot): a vision, architectural elements, and future directions. Future Gener. Comput. Syst. **29**(7), 1645–1660 (2013)
2. Mattern, F., Floerkemeier, C.: From active data management to event-based systems and more. In: Mattern, F., Floerkemeier, C. (eds.) From the Internet of Computers to the Internet of Things, pp. 242–259. Springer, Berlin (2010)
3. Athreya, A.P., DeBruhl, B., Tague, P.: Designing for self-configuration and self-adaptation in the internet of things. In: 9th International Conference on Collaborative Computing: Networking, Applications and Worksharing (Collaboratecom), pp. 585–592 (2013)
4. Dias, J.C.Q., Calado, J.M.F., Osório, A.L., Morgado, L.F.: Intelligent transport system based on RFID and multi-agent approaches. In: Camarinha-Matos, L.M., Picard, W. (eds.) Virtual Enterprises and Collaborative Networks, pp. 533–540. Springer, Boston (2008)
5. Dias, J.C.Q., Calado, J.M.F., Osório, A.L., Morgado, L.F.: RFID together with multi-agent systems to control global value chains. Ann. Rev. Control **33**(2), 185–195 (2009)
6. Meier, A., Lorie, R.A.: A surrogate concept for engineering databases. In: 9th International Conference on Very Large Data Bases, pp. 30–32, San Francisco, CA, USA (1983)
7. Waldo, J.: Virtual organizations, pervasive computing, and an infrastructure for networking at the edge. Inf. Syst. Front. **4**, 9–18 (2002)
8. Afsarmanesh, H., Camarinha-Matos, L.M., Ermilova, E.: VBE reference framework. In: Camarinha-Matos, L.M., Afsarmanesh, H., Ollus, M. (eds.) Methods and Tools for Collaborative Networked Organizations, pp. 35–68. Springer, US (2008)
9. Camarinha-Matos, L.M., Afsarmanesh, H.: A framework for virtual organization creation in a breeding environment. Ann. Rev. Control **31**(1), 119–135 (2007)
10. Osório, A., Camarinha-Matos, L.M., Afsarmanesh, H.: Enterprise collaboration network for transport and logistics services. In: Camarinha-Matos, L.M., Scherer, R.J. (eds.) PRO-VE 2013. IFIP AICT, vol. 408, pp. 267–278. Springer, Heidelberg (2013)
11. Kosch, T., Kulp, I., Bechler, M., Strassberger, M., Weyl, B., Lasowski, R.: Communication architecture for cooperative systems in europe. IEEE Commun. Mag. **47**(5), 116–125 (2009)
12. Lewis, G., Morris, E., Simanta, S., Smith, D.: Service orientation and systems of systems. IEEE Softw. **28**(1), 58–63 (2011)

Collaborative Networks and Active Knowledge Architectures - A Road Building Case

Sobah Abbas Petersen[1](✉), Frank Lillehagen[2], Minh Vu Bui[3], and John Krogstie[3]

[1] SINTEF Technology and Society, Trondheim, Norway
Sobah.Petersen@sintef.no
[2] Commitment AS, Lysaker, Norway
[3] Department of Computer and Information Systems,
Norwegian University of Science and Technology, Trondheim, Norway

Abstract. The planning, designing and building of roads is an extensive process that takes several years and involve several actors from industry and the public sector. This paper reports the collaboration with the Norwegian Road Authority on using the Active Knowledge Architecture approach and Visual Modelling methods to support road planning, design and building. The experience is based on the work conducted on real parts of the E6 Motorway, being built north of Trondheim, Norway. The purpose of the knowledge architectures presented in this paper is to improve collaboration and to share knowledge among all the stakeholders in the process. Road planning projects will benefit from agile collaborative networks and active knowledge bases built by knowledge models and architectures. Important lessons learned include the need for holistic design methods, instant data-driven collaboration, and agile approaches and work environments for continuous planning, design and building.

Keywords: Collaborative networks · Active knowledge architecture · Road planning and building · Holistic design · Model-based architecture-driven solutions and visual models

1 Introduction

The planning, designing and building of roads is an extensive process that takes several years and involves several actors from industry and the public sector. The current practices take the approach of different phases in the process where different actors are involved. The procedures and other relevant knowledge are documented in a set of handbooks. While the desire to make the process more effective, a change may take time, and perhaps involve new ways of working and leveraging the knowledge of the actors. The interactions and alliances among the actors could benefit from ideas addressed by researchers in collaborative networks [1] and knowledge visualisation approaches such as Enterprise Modelling, e.g. [2] and Active Knowledge Architectures [3]. This paper reports the collaboration with the Norwegian Road Authority on using Active Knowledge Architectures and visual modelling to support road planning, design and building.

© IFIP International Federation for Information Processing 2015
L.M. Camarinha-Matos et al. (Eds.): PRO-VE 2015, IFIP AICT 463, pp. 297–308, 2015.
DOI: 10.1007/978-3-319-24141-8_27

During the last 25 years, novel enterprise concepts, agile approaches, IT methods and digital technologies have been developed and applied for new application areas and purposes. Improving the business processes of public organizations, capturing, enhancing, and visualizing data and information flows are common challenges.

Industry sectors, in particular the aerospace and automotive sectors, have been very active participants in networked enterprise R&D projects; for example in several European projects such as ATHENA [4]. However, the public sector has only recently become engaged in such collaborative research projects. The reasons why most public sector agencies are slow in adopting novel approaches, methods and technologies, and innovation platforms are probably due to the size of the organizations and the fact that strategic and business objectives and values to be delivered are decided in political programs. This knowledge is not directly accessible or visible to the project planners, designers and developers of technologies or the various stakeholders such as the citizens.

The experiences presented in this paper are from the public sector of road planning and building. The main objectives of the research work performed were to explore Active Knowledge Architecture (AKA) driven work environments for road planning, design and building. The focus of this paper is on the many key roles of the Norwegian Road Authorities, and their need to improve knowledge sharing and competence management among road entrepreneurs and suppliers and the various stakeholders of the process. An ongoing road building project was selected for testing the approach and gathering of experiences and work practices. The work reported in the paper are based on a Masters thesis [5].

2   Planning and Building of Roads – Current Practices

The experiences presented in this paper describe a real case on building roads, based on information contributed by The Norwegian Road Authorities (SVV, Statens Vegvesen in Norwegian). The road planning and building process is shown in Fig. 1. As most public sector projects, it is a layered approach, where each layer is managed and executed by horizontal slicing of activities. The tasks are shown in the top row, whereas the main actors involved per task are shown in the bottom row.

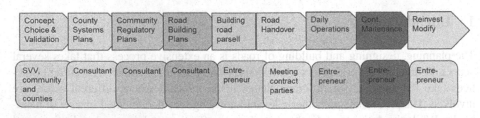

Fig. 1.   Traditional horizontally sliced road planning and building process

Projects start with Concept Choice Validation (CCV), a methodical government evaluation in the early phases of major road projects and major transport systems in rural areas and cities. In a CCV, all transportation and citizens' needs and societal influences are considered as are the possible solutions and their main concepts. The evaluation and the following quality assurance measures form the knowledge base for decision making and the scope for road planning based on county plans or community regulation plans covering the entire transportation sector.

The main knowledge is in the minds of people assigned to the major roles as road owner, consultants and entrepreneur as indicated in Fig. 1. Supporting the people is a series of elaborate documents maintained and produced by SVV. Currently, there are 153 documents and the road owner, consultants and entrepreneurs must be familiar with the contents of these documents. They are divided into three categories:

- 11 building norms documents describe the principles for building roads for annual average traffic, type of transportation, and operational rules;
- 37 legislative and prescriptive documents for planning and building roads;
- 105 documents with SVV approved guidelines and data collected from experiences in building and maintaining roads.

These handbooks provide the necessary information and data for planning, project execution and building of roads, including support for decision making in the planning stage. Most of these handbooks have close to 200 pages.

SVV, as owner, is responsible for all strategic planning of roads, building and management, and for communication with the stakeholders and users, from community and county service providers to the common citizen. Arriving at an agreed plan and concepts that are accepted by all parties can take many years and costs hundreds of millions of Norwegian kroner. Planning, data collection, design and knowledge sharing are major challenges and most of the time, the actual costs of planning and constructing the road is much higher than the respective budgets.

A specific section of the E6 Motorway, north of Trondheim Airport at Stjørdal, was selected as the case for modelling the first knowledge architecture for road planning and building. The SVV officials from the Trondheim project office, as responsible road builders, were the main sources of planning and building competence and provided the domain knowledge for our modelling efforts. However they were not involved in the modelling itself.

The questions they wanted answers to were:

- Can SVV implement faster, more effective planning and improved understanding and communication among stakeholders involved?
- Does the AKM technology give significant time savings in planning and building, improved knowledge sharing, and a more holistic understanding of the road planning and building tasks?
- Will AKM capabilities improve collaboration in design and building, enable knowledge sharing and reuse, and support competence transfer for rapid team building?

3   Modelling Road Knowledge Architectures

Some illustrative examples of the models produced and an overall structure of the relevant knowledge architectures are described. The main objectives of the modelling, the resulting architectures, and architecture-driven solutions are to investigate the possibility to represent the main knowledge as active models, and get initial feedback from the core stakeholders on the potential of the approach including:

- How active knowledge architectures might improve the planning and building of roads, and enhance the present knowledge base,
- Show support for holistic thinking, design principles, and novel road design methodologies supporting collaborative planning, design and execution,
- Show how existing handbooks, processes and community and county plans can become valuable knowledge models,
- Show support for traceability, decision/support, predictability and reuse, and autonomous data and knowledge management,
- Enable faster and easier access to knowledge and data, and work-centric views providing improved collaboration and execution,
- Show that planning, design, construction and operation architectures can be built, used and maintained by users applying simple graphic modelling

3.1 Active Knowledge Modelling

Active Knowledge Modelling (AKM) is based on the nature of Enterprise Knowledge Spaces, and practical Work and Collaboration Spaces [3, 6]. Most of the AKM ideas and design methodologies have evolved through experiences in practical modelling projects with leading international enterprises such as Volvo Cars, Boeing Aircraft, and US Air Force (see [3] for descriptions). AKM can be used to create AKAs of enterprises. Of particular importance to AKA are the properties of practical workspaces, such as reflective views of enterprise knowledge, repetitive task-patterns, replicable templates, and reusable knowledge models. AKM emphasises visual models that bring together different concepts and their dependencies that are easily visualised by different roles in role-specific workspaces. Such models facilitate adaptation of methods and contents to produce role-specific views.

3.2 Modelling for Road Planning

Modelling is ideally performed by a team of people that include several roles, e.g. [7]. The roles that were involved in this work were:

- The Owner: the ones responsible for the road building architecture and for contracting consultants and entrepreneurs.
- Modelling Expert: someone who could provide expert knowledge in modelling process, methods and tools.
- Facilitator: someone who is experienced in using the selected modelling process and tool and facilitating the modelling process.
- Modeller: develop the enterprise models in the selected tool during the modelling of architecture.
- Domain Experts: someone who could provide knowledge about the domain under consideration, such as bridges and tunnels, which is basis for modelling.

In this case, however, it was not possible to have all these members as active members of the modelling team simultaneously. The owners, SVV, were also the domain experts. Due to time constraints on their part, they guided the modeller, mostly the Masters student and modelling experts who were the advisors, to the relevant handbooks on road design and building, which served as the main source of domain knowledge. Several meetings were held between the modelling team and the owners to verify if the model was relevant for them and contained relevant and correct domain knowledge. The owners included four people with competencies from working with road planning and building, who had over 25 years of experience.

METIS[1] was selected as the modelling tool as it is based on the ideas of AKM and is also the preferred tool by the modelling experts based on their experiences.

4   The Initial Model

The model was designed to represent the knowledge required to execute the processes identified in the CVV shown in Fig. 1, and to support the different roles involved in the processes. An overview of the model is shown in Fig. 2. The left hand side of the model contains generic information that applies to all roads and this information was obtained mostly from the relevant handbooks and discussions with the owners and domain experts. The contents of this part of the model were structured to represent the governing rules and regulations for the specific road. Planning processes and references to similar projects, the goals and expectations from the project owner's perspective and from roles that should be involved were modelled. The right hand side of the model contains the actual road case, i.e. contents specific to the particular part of the road between Havnekryss and Kvithammer. This part contains the specific governing information for that project, the work processes and tasks and the corresponding roles and the road building plan. One of the rationales of this structure for the model is to enable reuse of information and experiences so that similar road projects can use parts of this model as a start for their specific models.

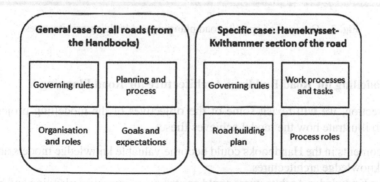

Fig. 2. Overview of the model

An overview of the actual model that was created is shown in Fig. 3. The lines between different objects indicate relationships among the objects and how they relate

---

[1] The METIS tool is now Troux Architect. For tool information see www.troux.com.

to or depend on each other. On the right hand side of the model which shows the specific model for the road section Havnekrysset – Kvithammer (the label translated as "Architecture for building plan Havnekrysset – Kvithammer"), there are numerous lines across the different contents in the model; e.g. the work processes and tasks are assigned to roles, the plan indicates which work processes are responsible for which parts and the plan is governed by rules and regulations. The viewing and filtering mechanisms of METIS make it possible to handle large models such as these with many relationships. The left hand part of the model (the label translated as "Architecture for planning and building roads") shows the generic information from several handbooks that are relevant for building the road section of interest which is modelled on the right hand side.

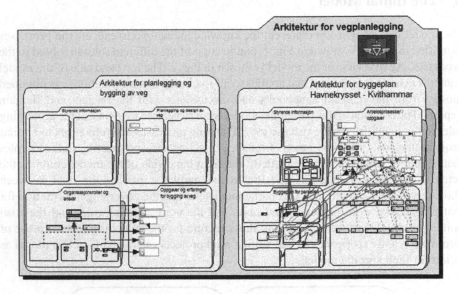

Fig. 3. Generic and specific road planning and building architectures

4.1   Modelling for Road Building: Architecture for Road Planning

In this section, we will revisit some of the objectives of the modelling project from Sect. 3 to illustrate how the model achieves these:

- The contents in the Handbooks could become valuable knowledge models and reusable knowledge architectures.
- Active Knowledge Architectures could contribute to improved planning and building of roads through enhancing the visualization and sharing of knowledge among the people.

The governing information that is required for most roads and transport related projects are documented as Handbooks, which are currently available and textual documents, in paper and online. Accessing the right information from these Handbooks requires experience and knowledge about the domain and can take time.

As mentioned earlier, the left hand side of the model shown in Fig. 3 contains generic information about road building. Parts of this model are shown in Figs. 4 and 5 where the left part of the both figures show governing information from these Handbooks. These specific parts refer to the relevant documents (live links are available from the model). How this governing information is used in the planning and designing of roads is shown in Fig. 4 while Fig. 5 how the project owner's tasks are governed to ensure that the project's goals and expectations are met.

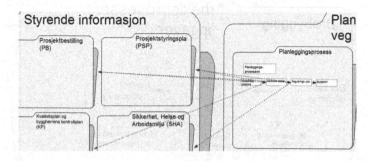

Fig. 4. Contents of handbooks used in planning

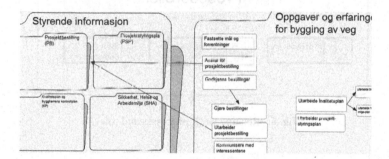

Fig. 5. Contents of handbooks used in meeting the goals of the project

During the discussions with the team from SVV, they highlighted the various public and private institutions that may be involved with project, which ranged from the police to private entrepreneurs. Similarly, the competence and expertise varied from technical to legal and design experiences. And most importantly, since these are often fairly large projects that span a long time period, (for example, there are cases that have spanned in the range of 30 years from the concept to the actual road in operation), the original planners, contractors of technical experts may not be around for the complete lifetime of the project. Thus, the need for making the knowledge visible and accessible to all became more and more evident throughout the project.

The information that is required to plan, design and build the specific road section is modelled in the right hand side of Fig. 3. As can be seen from the model, there are several relationships across the model which relate the different concepts. A simple example of such relationships is shown in Fig. 6. For example, the specific road section include a bridge and the process project description (the task "prosjektering") involves the roles of bridge building manager, the bridge expert and SVV's bridge planner. Similarly, externalisation of the knowledge from documents, handbooks or contracts, adapted and shared among several institutions and roles, enhances the existing knowledge among the people responsible. This facilitates the increase of competences among the individuals and teams, and sharing of knowledge. This in turn enhances the planning and execution of the project.

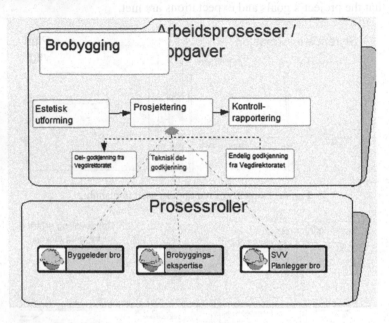

Fig. 6. Relating work processes and roles

4.2 Collaborative Networks

The example process shown in Fig. 7, that for "skilting" or road signs, shows that the process involve actors from different organisations. The automatically generated relationship matrix shows how two sets of concepts relate to each other; e.g. the relationships between the different processes and roles, where the arrows in the cells show a relationship between two objects. The vertical axis shows the activities for creating a road sign such as the approval of the sign by SVV and the police and the announcement from the Municipality. The horizontal axis shows the actors that are involved, such as the Police, the Municipality and the producers of the road sign itself.

Almost all the processes in road planning, designing and building involves several actors from different organisations and this can be considered as a set of Virtual Enterprises [8] or Collaborative Networks [9]. Some of the most important features of Virtual Enterprises and Collaborative Networks include the communication and sharing of information among the collaborating partners. The characteristics of such organisations become relevant for road building also. Moreover, due to the long time span, the chances

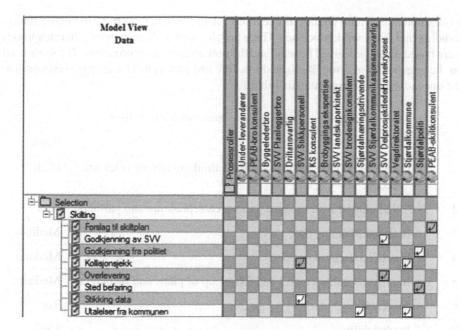

Fig. 7. Relationship matrix of processes and roles from the model

that the individual actors may change. Also, since different actors are involved in the different phases, there is a need to support the active participation of new actors and ensuring the transfer of the relevant knowledge across the actors. The AKM approach, through visualisation of knowledge, could provide the necessary knowledge base for the actors that are involved by providing them an overview of the project activities, their task descriptions and other relevant information for their work. This should contribute to a more effective working practice and better collaboration among the actors.

Matrices such as these can be used to make various stakeholders aware of their roles and responsibilities and possibly to provide notifications as necessary. As can be seen from the figure, each activity involves several institutions and roles and the challenges in ensuring that all actors are aware of their roles in a timely manner can be challenging.

Whereas the initial model presented is not used in work execution, it has earlier been reported e.g. in [3] how models can be provided for users in model-driven work environments to be directly accessible and further evolved capturing new knowledge from the different stakeholders of the project.

4.3   Feedback on the Initial Model from SVV

The validation of the model was done through regular meetings and getting feedback from the domain experts. Due to the lack of time and modelling experience of the expert from SVV, there was no opportunity for them to use the model. In total, six people from SVV participated in three meetings during the project period and the model was presented to them every time. During the final meeting, they were asked to respond to a questionnaire, which contained questions related to collaboration, increased understanding and faster work processes. Three people from SVV responded; their responses were based on the perceived benefits and the potential of the approaches. The scale used on the questionnaire is top, high, medium, low and minimal. The average responses to the questionnaire are presented in Table 1.

Table 1. Summary of the questionnaire responses

	Questions	Score
1	Enhanced collaboration and holistic thinking among roles and people	High
2	Collaboration with external parties, entrepreneurs and partners	High
3	Reduced planning time	Medium
4	Improved decision-support	Medium
5	Improved quality control and follow up of plans and resources	Medium
6	Traceability	Top
7	Predictability	High
8	Better understanding of approaches, methods and alternatives	Medium
9	Competence transfer	High
10	Support for training of new employees and partners	High
11	Improved data, knowledge management and viewing	Top
12	Reuse of architectures, models and knowledge assets	High

The responses to questions 1 and 2 indicate that modelling is a means to support collaboration across stakeholders and collaborative networks such as those that would exist between SVV and the entrepreneur that is contracted. Questions 3–7 relate to reducing the time taken for the project and if improved decision support and quality control. The responses to these questions were Medium while they all agreed (responded Top) that the model helped to improve traceability. They also gave a high score to support for competence transfer and support for training new employees. Similarly, improved data and knowledge management received a top score. Given that we have only feedback from very few people that has seen the initial model, and not been yet able to work within a model-generated workspace, this is only tentative input of course. However, it would be beneficial to have the model and the approach evaluated by a larger and more varied group of people.

Considering the fact that the validation was performed based on a 3 month modelling effort by a student, we regard these validations as good indications that model-based, architecture driven approaches and solutions have the potential to answer the questions they had asked.

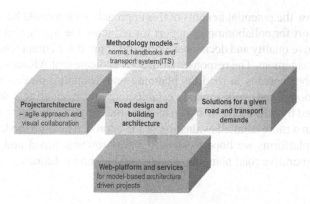

Fig. 8. Future road building reference architectures

5 Experiences and Lessons Learned

Many experiences and practices learned are already included in Sect. 3. For the SVV people participating in modelling the planning and building architectures, developing and using enterprise knowledge models was a new experience.

AKAs must be modelled from different perspectives: an agile approach capturing the workspaces, actions and decisions, of the roles designing the solution architecture and developing and adapting the methods to be applied. Emergent solutions and open extendable modeling and execution platforms are the other two fundamental knowledge dimensions, but there are more dimensions that will determine the design and construction rules of roads, other products and services.

Connecting the people that possesses the leading knowledge and experience from practical project work is always a major challenge as these people are always busy with ongoing projects. Organizational structures should include role-oriented structures, complementing the hierarchies and networks. Roles should be designed in order to create the best workspace tasks, views and data [10, 11].

The four dimensions described in Fig. 8 are composed of reflective views and repeatable task-patterns [12]. Views from each of the above dimensions are mutually meta- and operational views for each other. The work plan is the meta-view for the work performer, and the performance is the meta-view for the planner.

The project architecture, the road design and building architecture are independent architectures, but share many common knowledge models, like the overarching community transport strategy, design methods and role-oriented workspaces. Road planning, design and construction should be further researched to test out new collaborative design methods, applying holistic design principles and methods.

6 Summary

Knowledge models were created by a modelling team for the Norwegian Road Authorities, with focus on a specific road section. The responses to a questionnaire indicate that the customer saw the potential benefits of this approach, which could be summarised as enhanced support for collaboration, support for reducing the time taken by SVV to do the work, improve quality and decision making and support for competence transfer and knowledge management. The responses from SVV indicate that AKAs and AKM could provide a number benefits in road the planning and designing processes. We plan to enhance this model and work towards establishing and evaluating role-based workspaces supported by AKAs. We also plan to show the enhanced model to more potential users and obtain a more detailed evaluation of the approach and the model. With access to more open platforms we hope to show the way towards novel and agile ways of designing collaborative road planning, design and building solutions.

References

1. Camarinha-Matos, L., Afsarmanesh, H.: Classes of collaborative networks. In: Putnik, G.D., Cunha, M.M. (eds.) Encyclopedia of Networked and Virtual Organizations, pp. 193–198. IGI Global, Hershey (2008)
2. Vernadat, F.B.: Enterprise Modelling and Integration Principles and Applications. Chapman and Hall, London (1996)
3. Lillehagen, F., Krogstie, J.: Active Knowledge Modelling of Enterprises. Springer, Heidelberg (2008)
4. ATHENA: Advanced technologies for interoperability of heterogeneous enterprise networks and their applications. ftp://ftp.cordis.europa.eu/pub/ist/docs/directorate_d/ebusiness/athena.pdf. Accessed 14 June 2015
5. Bui, V.M.: Aktive kunnskapsmodellering for planlegging og bygging av veg. Department of Computer and Information Science, Norwegian University of Science and Technology, Trondheim (2013)
6. Lillehagen, F.: The foundations of AKM technology. In: 10th International Conference on Concurrent Engineering (CE), Madeira, Portugal (2003)
7. Persson, A., Stirna, J.: Towards defining a competence profile for the enterprise modeling practitioner. In: van Bommel, P., Hoppenbrouwers, S., Overbeek, S., Proper, E., Barjis, J. (eds.) PoEM 2010. LNBIP, vol. 68, pp. 232–245. Springer, Heidelberg (2010)
8. Petersen, S.A.: Virtual enterprise formation and partner selection: an analysis using case studies. Int. J. Networking Virtual Organ. 4(2), 201–215 (2007)
9. Camarinha-Matos, L., Afsarmanesh, H.: Collaborative networks: a new scientific discipline. J. Intell. Manuf. 16, 439–452 (2005)
10. Jørgensen, H.D., Krogstie, J.: Active models for dynamic networked organisations. In: Dittrich, K.R., Geppert, A., Norrie, M. (eds.) CAiSE 2001. LNCS, vol. 2068. Springer, Heidelberg (2001)
11. Krogstie, J., Jørgensen, H.D.: Interactive models for supporting networked organisations. In: Persson, A., Stirna, J. (eds.) CAiSE 2004. LNCS, vol. 3084, pp. 550–563. Springer, Heidelberg (2004)
12. Sandkuhl, K., Stirna, J.: Evaluation of task pattern use in web-based collaborative engineering. In: Proceedings of the 34th EUROMICRO. IEEE (2008)

Innovation Networks

Collaboration for Innovation Networks: Towards a Reference Model

Christopher Durugbo[✉] and Andrew Lyons

Management School, University of Liverpool, Liverpool L69 7ZH, UK
{christopher.durugbo,a.c.lyons}@liverpool.ac.uk

Abstract. Practitioners and scholars have argued that external collaboration has become fundamental to how organisations function. There is also an emerging rhetoric on the imperatives of innovation for competitiveness. This amplifies the relevance of innovation networks that allow partners to pool resources and share expertise. Consequently, an understanding of collaboration within these networks is crucial to better managing the complexities and uncertainties that underlie how organisations and individuals can collaborate to innovate. Along these lines, this paper has analysed the nature of collaboration in 12 real-world innovation networks with the aim of a developing a reference model. The analysis showed that in order to maintain resilience, the network design and orchestration in these networks are technology-oriented. In addition, the collaborative competencies and capabilities were found to be service-oriented to provide the mentoring, business support, technological, and scientific needs that underlie the formation of these innovation networks.

Keywords: Collaborative networks · Innovation · Resilience · Virtual organisation · Services

1 Introduction

Sustaining competitive advantage of operations is a major challenge for modern firms. This is due to a variety of existing and emerging uncertainties that make it difficult to extrapolate from the past and to make forecasts for the future. *Behaviourally*, several strategies have been adopted by organisations to maintain competitiveness. Significantly, there is evidence to suggest that from the 1990s onward, organisations have increasing shifted their main focus from efficiency and quality to innovation [1]. *Structurally*, companies are also changing their focus from knowledge gathering within a single organisation to knowledge rich distributed processes and arrangements that co-opt multiple stakeholders. The effect has been a gradual rise in corporate partnering and increasing reliance on different forms of collaboration with external entities [2]. Here, the imperatives for maintaining competitive advantage has forced companies to pool resources within intra- and inter-organisational networks in endeavours that create a critical mass of participants for survival. There are also arguments that this behavioural and structural shift has also been at play in manufacturing where firms have transitioned from global production networks targeted at new markets and lower cost production sites, to global innovation networks motivated by knowledge potentials [3].

© IFIP International Federation for Information Processing 2015
L.M. Camarinha-Matos et al. (Eds.): PRO-VE 2015, IFIP AICT 463, pp. 311–322, 2015.
DOI: 10.1007/978-3-319-24141-8_28

These arrangements are set to share risks, gain access to new markets and technologies, speed up product introduction to markets, learn from partners, and pool complementary skill [2].

Although there has been increased research and practice in innovation networks, there are still major gaps in knowledge on the intricacies and permutations of these forms of networks. For instance, related studies have highlighted paucity in research on government sponsored innovation clusters [4]. Others have conceptualised and examined organisational [5] and individual [6] challenges of designing and managing innovation aggregations. In an attempt to enhance research in this area, this study is motivated by the characteristics of collaboration that triggers and sustains the structure/behaviour of innovation networks.

The aim of this paper is to develop a reference model of collaboration for innovation networks. Reference model is used in this context, as a purpose-relevant representation for use in construction of other management models [7]. Such models have been widely used in the conceptualisation and representation of collaboration-related phenomena such as collaborative networks [8], supply chains and networks [9], collaborative value webs [10], and coalition interoperability [11]. In these models, researchers explore the nature of phenomena for use in detailing aspects such as strategy, process, information technology, and so on. With this in mind, this research is guided by the following research question: What is the nature of collaboration for innovation networks?

The rest of this paper unfolds as follows. §2 will outline the background for the research. §3 and 4 will present the research method and findings respectively, and 5 will conclude by highlighting the study limitations, contributions, implications and some unanswered questions that may offer useful paths for further research.

2 Research Background

In an attempt to answer the research question, the theoretical development began with the review and analysis of the background for the research. For this, literature was used to analyse collaboration and innovation networks. Particular attention was paid to current understanding and factors of the key factors that underlie these concepts and this insight served as the foundation for developing the conceptual framework for this research.

2.1 Collaboration

Collaboration is a key feature of a process when it involves more than one participant in durable and pervasive relationships [12]. It is frequently used to mean working together in group(s) to achieve a common task or goal. This task or goal is often beyond the capabilities of the collaborating participants and collaboration is typically achieved through activities for coordination, decision-making and teamwork [12–14]. Accordingly, research has shown that arrangements for collaboration are shaped by competencies and capacities [15].

Collaborative competencies are the resources (knowledge, skills and support) that serve as the basis for working together to achieve a goal. Attitudes towards group work are also important in collaboration competencies that can be oriented towards: dictatorships in which interactions are directed or dominated by a few individuals, mutuality in which interactions are managed by a set of individuals for solving uni-, inter- or multi-disciplinary problems, and exclusivity in which individuals negotiate and work with others (similar or dissimilar specialties) to achieve goals.

Collaborative capacities, on the other hand, are the practices that enable work across intra- and inter-organisational levels and boundaries irrespective of temporal and spatial separations. These practices encourage durable and pervasive relationships and processes that are necessary for gaining the full commitment of individuals to a shared mission [16]. Effective collaborations, based on these relationships and processes are assessed in terms of collaborative capital i.e. 'who we know and how well we work together' [15].

Focusing on innovation through collaborative competencies and capacities, firms have been able to: (i) move from traditional linear attitudes for executing process to more contemporary concurrent approaches, and (ii) tackle the problematic 'over-the-wall' phenomena i.e. intrinsic organisational barriers that were created due to process demarcations for functions such as manufacturing and marketing. Accordingly, the benefits of such focus has been increased competitiveness through: (i) greater awareness of potential cumulative knowledge from key stakeholders such as customers and staff, (ii) increasing informal interactions among company personnel and (iii) challenges for understanding and resolving differences between team members and groups [13].

2.2 Innovation Networks

Citing Van de Ven [17] and Swan et al. [1, p. 263] defined innovation that takes place in networks as "the development and implementation of new ideas by people who over time engage in transactions with others in an institutional context." In other words these networks have innovation imperatives or outputs that lie at the heart of transactions or networking. Thus, a key challenge for organisations is to cope with the increasingly complex nature of innovation processes in tandem with increasing number and diversity of innovation network actors [4]. There is also an implied 'voluntary' nature of such networks that allow for resources to be mobilised and strategic alliances to be dynamically created [5].

It is for this reason that scholars have suggested that the locus of innovation in modern day organisations is situated in networks for internal and external collaboration [2]. These networks enable companies not only to retain competitive advantage but also to progressively add and accumulate value for stakeholders. There are also suggestions that these networks are characterised by innovation that is achieved through collaborative creativity, an ethos of collaboration that is underscored by a strict ethical code, and communication established by direct-contact networks [18]. However, network benefits can only outweigh advances with the closed innovations in large corporations when resources are distributed efficiently by partners [6].

Theoretically, scholars have suggested that for innovation network arrangements to generate outputs, two determined need to be considered: network design and network orchestration [5, 6]. For both determinants, networking takes centre-stage as a social process that enables knowledge sharing among partners [1].

According to Dhanaraj and Parkhe [6], an important determinant of innovation networks is the network design. This design is reflected in (i) network membership as determined by the size and diversity of participants and ties, (ii) network structure in relation to density of topology and autonomy of participants, and (iii) network position with respect to centrality of topology and status of participants. Structurally, the diffusion of knowledge in innovation networks is shaped by cohesion and centralisation factors [19]. Cohesion refers to how participants in the innovation network are related to each other and centralisation concerns how hubs (highly connected participants) emerge in innovation networks. The former influences network connectively while the latter affects network influence – impact on the overall network performance. Inevitably, there is a case to be made for these networks to be "flatter, less bureaucratized and more decentralised, even virtual, organizational arrangements with key areas of expertise (e.g. IT) often being provided externally" [1, p. 263]. Consequently, it has been suggested that innovation networks are typically characterised by low-density and high-centrality [6].

The orchestrating of innovation networks is also another issue that requires management for knowledge mobility, innovation appropriability and network stability [6]. The output of this orchestration is often in the form of value for participants and economic growth in a wider context [4]. Network orchestration or governance [5] depends on contractual arrangements between partners [3]. With these arrangements in place, collaborations can then be monitored according to administrative mechanisms and adjusted with regards to project developments. For instance, studies have explored contractual arrangements and used insights from findings to advocate for the importance of innovation champions (i.e. individuals who informally advance the goals of innovation) in the orchestration of innovation networks [5].

3   Research Method

The study applies a theory-building methodology [20] in a multi-case study [21] that was undertaken in two main stages: conceptualisation and case study.

During the conceptualisation stage, a review of literature was conducted to analyse the concepts of collaboration and innovative networks. Insights from this review were then used in the formulation of conceptual framework, as presented in §2, for use in the subsequent stage of the study. Drawing on the extant literature, Fig. 1 presents the conceptual framing of collaboration in innovative networks. The model argues that innovation imperatives are the major factors that these networks are built on. These factors in turn necessitate competencies and capabilities for collaboration as well as design and orchestration for networks.

Next, using the conceptual framework from Fig. 1, an exploratory study of collaboration for innovative networks was conducted with twelve real-world innovative networks (I-nets). These case I-nets (ShoreTel Innovation Network (ShoreTel I-net),

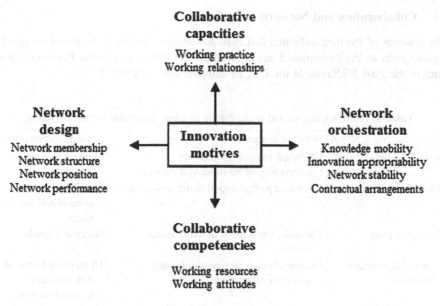

Fig. 1. Research model

Water Innovation Network (Water I-net), Genomics Innovation Network (Genomics I-net), Regional Accelerator and Innovation Network (Regional Accelerator and I-net), iNnovation Network Liverpool (i-net Liverpool), Food and Drink Innovation Network (Food and Drink I-net), Co-operative Councils Innovation Network (Co-operative Councils I-net), Menu Innovation Network (Menu I-net), Quality Insights is the Quality Innovation Network (Quality I-net), i-net: innovation networks Switzerland (I-net Switzerland), Roanoke-Blacksburg Innovation Network (Roanoke-Blacksburg I-net), and European Business and Innovation Network (European Business and I-net)) are set at industry or regional levels for various goals as summarized by Table 1. These, case I-nets were purposefully sampled, as is often the case for qualitative studies [22], by focusing on innovation motives of organisation and institutions. Data was gathered through secondary sources [23] (specifically webpages, annual reports, press releases and literature) and examined using content analysis [24] to present network and innovation orientations due to collaboration in these cases. The study is therefore based on an exploratory approach that generalises at a level of theory as opposed to statistical representativeness or significance.

4   Findings

The next subsections present the main findings from the analysis. First, the findings of network and innovation orientations due to collaboration are presented. Next, insights from the analysis are used in the development of a reference model.

4.1   Collaboration and Network Orientation

The analysis of the data indicated that network designs tended to be based on specific regions such as the Genomics I-net in Northern Switzerland and the Food and Drink I-net in the East Midlands of the UK, as summarised by Table 1.

Table 1. Network design and orchestration in case innovation networks (i-nets)

Case	Network design	Network orchestration
ShoreTel I-net	US-based technology industry community of 93 industrial partners	Shoretel as focal partner
Water I-net	UK-based partnership of water innovators	Peterborough city council and anglian water
Genomics I-net	Canadian consortium of 10 research centres	Genome Canada'
Regional accelerator and I-net	Oregon alliance of 8 academic and economic institutions	10 member board of directors and regional mayors
I-net Liverpool	UK-based community made up of hundreds of individuals and organisations from Liverpool	Liverpool city council
Food and drink I-net	UK-based food consortium of academic organisations in the East Midlands	The food and drink forum
Co-operative councils I-net	UK-based collaboration between 23 local authorities	6 member executive oversight committee
Menu I-net	UK-based knowledge exchange for the food industry	Inside foodservice
Quality I-net	US community of health-care providers in New Jersey, Delaware, Pennsylvania, West Virginia and Louisiana	6 member board of directors
I-net Switzerland	Switzerland-based public private partnership	Management board supported by an advisory board
Roanoke-Blacksburg I-net	Virginia community consisting of hundreds of individuals and organisations	10 member board of directors
European business and I-net	Europe-wide community of professionals	21 member board of directors

For network orchestration, the focus in case I-nets was on boards of directors for governance or focal organisations (Shoretel (ShoreTel I-net), Peterborough City Council and Anglian Water (Water I-net), Liverpool city council (I-net Liverpool), and The Food and Drink Forum (Food and Drink I-net)) that are governed themselves by boards of directors. The boards act in dictatorships style arrangements in which committees are set up to help discharges duties. For instance an Executive Committee, Audit and Investment Committee, Programs Committee, and a Governance, Election and Compensation Committee were all set up by the Genomics I-net board. Advisory Committees at I-net Switzerland and Genomics I-net were also important for getting strategic and visionary advice and expertise for research and development.

The data showed that network designs were characterised by varying levels of membership according to subscription or level of expertise. For instance in the ShoreTel I-net had two levels of membership: a foundation-level membership for information and tool provision, and an alliance-level membership for validating, documenting and marketing interoperability. Similarly, at the European Business and I-net, membership was according to: quality-certified business and innovation centres, incubators, accelerators and other support organisations, and associate members that support the development and growth of innovative entrepreneurs, start-ups and SMEs. Generally, distinctions were made between founding (or core) partners and associates that participate in mutual or exclusive arrangements.

4.2   Collaboration and Innovation Orientation

Overall, the analysis found two main focal points of collaborative goals for innovation. The first was *regional-focus* and the attitudes tended to be on causes that impacted the position of unions (European Business and I-net), countries (Genomics I-net) or states (Regional Accelerator and I-net, Quality I-net, and Roanoke-Blacksburg I-net) on a global scale, or enhanced the quality of life of communities (Co-operative Councils I-net, Water I-net, and I-net Liverpool). The second was *industry-focus* and this often originated from specific regions but was targeted as novel approaches to delivering and marketing specific goods, services and technologies (ShoreTel I-net and Menu I-net). Both orientations were found in I-net: Switzerland and the Food and Drink I-net where the focus was on innovative IT from Northern Switzerland and food/drink from the East Midlands respectively.

The analysed data showed that collaborations in the case I-nets were technology-oriented irrespective of the goals and motivation for collaboration. The technologies as suggested by Herstad et al. [3] are embodied in the resources and exchanges between partners. Additionally, the study found that these technologies play important roles in the innovation network competencies. In all case I-nets, orientations were not only according to pooled capabilities and competences but were also on 'networks of networks' i.e. establishing and communicating the international collaborative linkages that would be available to potential network partners. Support for capabilities was provided through avenues such as training and mentoring while capacities were maintained through web portals, conferences and other knowledge exchange events, as summarised by Table 2.

Imperatives for collaboration were also for ground-breaking work with potential impacts for humanity and in such cases the network design centred on creating a cluster of specialised organisations. For instance, the Genomics I-net focused on ten research centres, termed 'nodes', within the British Colombia, Alberta, Ontario and Quebec

Table 2. Collaborative competencies and capacities in case innovation networks (i-nets)

Case	Collaborative competencies	Collaborative capacities
ShoreTel I-net	Partnering of technology companies	Web portal Partner conferences
Water I-net	Water utility company with the supply chain	Web portal Signposting to investment/funding opportunities
Genomics I-net	Assembling of highly-qualified personnel and leading-edge technologies used in genomics and metabolomics	Web portal Commissioned groups
Regional accelerator and I-net	Start-up ecosystem of connected entrepreneurs, investors and resources	Web portal Working groups formed by the local board partners
I-net Liverpool	Commissioners, service providers, user-led organisations, creatives, and technologists	Web portal iNnovationXchange uNconference Round tables Hatching and matching event
Food and drink I-net	Community of food experts	Web portal Booster workshops for SMEs
Co-operative Councils I-net	Local authority subject matter experts	Web portal Workshops and conferences
Menu I-net	Group menu development managers and group executive chefs	Web portal awards Forums Social programmes
Quality I-net	Network of medical institutes and healthcare strategists	Web portal knowledge exchange events and webinars
I-net Switzerland	Technology field experts of ICT, life sciences, Medtech, Cleantech and nanotechnology	Web portal Partner and technology events
Roanoke-Blacksburg I-net	Start-up ecosystem of connected entrepreneurs, investors and resources	Web portal Outreach and awareness events
European business and I-net	Team of experts and business and innovation centres	Web portal Online and offline networking events and technologies

regions. In others, the focus was on community building endeavours with opportunities for networking and access to talent, capital and infrastructure.

4.3   Towards a Reference Model

Figure 2 presents a proposal for a reference model of collaboration for innovation networks. The model mainly captures sets of management models for structural design and behavioural support. It consists of sub-models that capture relationship development, support services, technology embodiments, network board, working committees, and subscribed partners. There are also rationales according to innovation, task and network imperatives.

Task imperatives are the motives that necessitate service support and relationship development in pursuant of collaboration goals. These services included technical services for technologies (e.g. network design validation) or scientific research (e.g. proteomics), organisational services that provide business (e.g. idea generation and

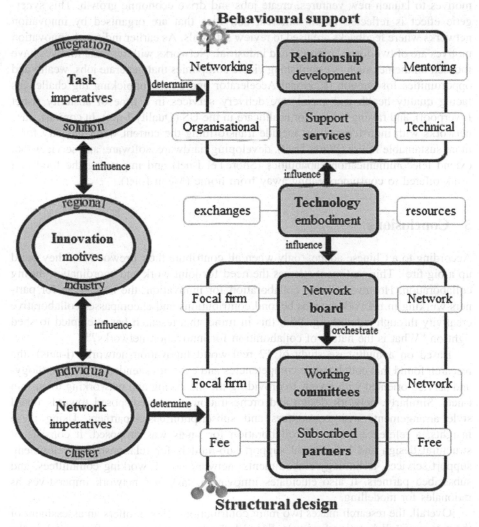

Fig. 2. Reference model of collaboration for innovation networks

networking) and process support. Tasks imperatives concern how businesses bring together ideas and expertise together with a view to delivering solutions. This involves interacting, exchanging information and creating synergies with peers as well as translating co-operative policy and principles into practice.

Network imperatives are the motives that shape the design and orchestration of networks. This concerns how network designs reflect involvement of individuals for equal partnership to shape and strengthen communities. It also considers clusters or hubs of organisations, institutions and regions for generating collective power for the advancement of cause and ground-breaking work. This focus has been captured by studies that examine the innovations that emerge when industry and academe collaborate in networks for economic growth in specific geographical areas [4].

Task and network imperatives ultimately impact and are impacted by innovation motives to launch new ventures, create jobs and drive economic growth. This synergetic effect is reflected in the different activities that are organised by innovation networks where feedbacks are used to review set goals. As earlier indicated, innovation motives are of two forms: regional and industrial. Networks with regional motives have focused on themes such as establishing viable companies that generate jobs, wealth and opportunities for Oregon (Regional Accelerator and I-net), unpicking big challenges facing quality health and social care delivery services in a time of austerity (I-net Liverpool), and raising the bar for healthcare in the US (Quality I-net). In contrast, case networks with industry motives include transforming the current water industry for a more sustainable future (Water I-net), developing hardware, software, and services that extend telecommunication capabilities (ShoreTel I-net) and improving the food and drink offered to consumers eating away from home (Menu I-net).

5   Conclusions

According to a Chinese adage, 'only when all contribute their firewood can they build up a big fire'. This sentiment stresses the need for joint work and coordination during collaboration. However, during collaboration for innovation, the imperative for partners working in network extends beyond contributions and encompasses collaborative creativity through networking. With this in mind, this research has attempted to shed light on "What is the nature of collaboration for innovation networks?"

Based on a multi-case study of 12 real-world innovation networks (i-nets), the research found that collaborative competencies and capacities tended to be technology- and service-oriented with a view to providing the mentoring and networking to sustain i-nets. Similarly, network design and orchestration were predisposed towards board style arrangements with committees and subscription-bases partners. Using these insights, a reference model of collaboration for i-nets was proposed. It consists of structural design and behavioural support sub-models for relationship development, support services, technology embodiments, network board, working committees, and subscribed partners. It also elucidates innovation, task and network imperatives as rationales for modelling.

Overall, the research makes two main contributions. First it offers an assessment of the nature of collaboration for i-nets. Second, the research proposes a framework in the form of a reference model for use the in construction of other management models such as those that focus on collaborative resilience, risk and performance. Along these lines, the research contributes to the rhetoric on competitive advantage realised through collaboration but offers a prescriptive model to aid collaborative network managers in developing a grounded foundation for coping with uncertainties.

Fundamentally, this research has focused on secondary sources as avenue for the exploratory analysis of these i-nets. Further empirical work is therefore needed to qualitatively and quantitatively study the underlying themes uncovered in this study. In spite of this limitation, the analysis and insights from this study has offered a reference model for designing and managing collaborations in i-nets. As firms strive to work innovatively, using innovation network resources and delivering innovative results, the behavioural support and structural designs agreed with collaborating partners will need to ensure task imperatives for integration and network imperatives for cluster-oriented work are technology-embodied.

References

1. Swan, J., Newell, S., Scarbrough, H., Hislop, D.: Knowledge management and innovation: networks and networking. J. Knowl. Manage. 3(4), 262–275 (1999)
2. Powell, W.W., Koput, K.W., Smith-Doerr, L.: Interorganizational collaboration and the locus of innovation: networks of learning in biotechnology. Adm. Sci. Q. 41(1), 116–145 (1996)
3. Herstad, S.J., Aslesen, H.W., Ebersberger, B.: On industrial knowledge bases, commercial opportunities and global innovation network linkages. Res. Policy 43(3), 495–504 (2014)
4. Levén, P., Holmström, J., Mathiassen, L.: Managing research and innovation networks: evidence from a government sponsored cross-industry program. Res. Policy 43(1), 156–168 (2014)
5. Klerkx, L., Aarts, N.: The interaction of multiple champions in orchestrating innovation networks: conflicts and complementarities. Technovation 33(6), 193–210 (2013)
6. Dhanaraj, C., Parkhe, A.: Orchestrating innovation networks. Acad. Manage. Rev. 31(3), 659–669 (2006)
7. Becker, J., Delfmann, P.: Reference Modeling: Efficient Information Systems Design Through Reuse of Information Models. Springer, Heidelberg (2007)
8. Camarinha-Matos, L.M., Afsarmanesh, H.: Collaborative Networks: Reference Modeling: Reference Modeling. Springer, Heidelberg (2008)
9. Huan, S.H., Sheoran, S.K., Wang, G.: A review and analysis of supply chain operations reference (SCOR) model. Supply Chain Manage. Int. J. 9(1), 23–29 (2004)
10. Yang, T.A., Kim, D.J., Dhalwani, V., Vu, T.K.: The 8C framework as a reference model for collaborative value webs in the context of web 2.0. In: Proceedings of the 41st Annual Hawaii International Conference on System Sciences, pp. 319–319. IEEE, January 2008
11. Tolk, A.: Beyond Technical Interoperability-Introducing a Reference Model for Measures of Merit for Coalition Interoperability. Old Dominion University, Norfolk (2003)
12. Durugbo, C., Hutabarat, W., Tiwari, A., Alcock, J.R.: Modelling collaboration using complex networks. Inf. Sci. 181(15), 3143–3161 (2011)
13. Durugbo, C.: Work domain analysis for enhancing collaborations: a study of the management of microsystems design. Ergonomics 55(6), 603–620 (2012)

14. Michaelides, R., Morton, S.C., Michaelides, Z., Lyons, A.C., Liu, W.: Collaboration networks and collaboration tools: a match for SMEs? Int. J. Prod. Res. **51**(7), 2034–2048 (2013)
15. Beyerlein, M.M.: Beyond Teams: Building the Collaborative Organization. Jossey-Bass/Pfeiffer, San Francisco (2003)
16. Kvan, T.: Collaborative design: what is it? Autom. Constr. **9**(4), 409–415 (2000)
17. Van de Ven, A.H.: Central problems in the management of innovation. Manage. Sci. **32**, 590–607 (1986)
18. Gloor, P.A.: Swarm Creativity: Competitive Advantage Through Collaborative Innovation Networks. Oxford University Press, Oxford (2005)
19. Van der Valk, T., Chappin, M.M., Gijsbers, G.W.: Evaluating innovation networks in emerging technologies. Technol. Forecast. Soc. Change **78**(1), 25–39 (2011)
20. Dubin, R.: Theory Building. Free Press, New York (1978)
21. Yin, R.K.: Case Study Research: Design and Methods, 4th edn. SAGE Publications, California (2009)
22. Miles, M.B., Huberman, A.M.: Qualitative Data Analysis: Grounded Theory Procedures and Techniques. Sage Publications, London (1994)
23. Stewart, D.W., Kamins, M.A.: Secondary Research: Information Sources and Methods, vol. 4. Sage, California (1993)
24. Krippendorff, K.: Content Analysis: An Introduction to its Methodology. Sage, California (2012)

Innovation Ecosystems:
A Collaborative Networks Perspective

Ricardo J. Rabelo[1(✉)], Peter Bernus[2], and David Romero[2,3]

[1] Federal University of Santa Catarina, Florianópolis, Brazil
ricardo.rabelo@ufsc.br
[2] Griffith University, Brisbane, Australia
p.bernus@griffith.edu.au, david.romero.diaz@gmail.com
[3] Tecnológico de Monterrey, Monterrey, Mexico

Abstract. Innovation ecosystems (IE) have increasingly gaining importance due to their potential to leverage regional development. In a previous research, authors have translated into processes how current IEs have been built or emerged. This process-based model can be used for building new or support the analysis of existing IEs. In order to evaluate the completeness of this model, this paper presents its mapping against the ARCON reference model considering that an IE can be seen as special type of Collaborative Network. Given the particularities of IEs, this paper also provides some elements of reflection that may be taken into account in future ARCON evolutions.

Keywords: Innovation ecosystems · Collaborative networks · Reference model

1 Introduction

Innovation ecosystems (IE) have been nowadays considered as the most prominent driver to be built up and nourished to reap the benefits of innovation. This reflects a paradigm shift, whereupon innovation is becoming a centrepiece of a socio-economic development model for cities and regions [1]. An IE can be defined as an environment and economic development and diffusion model formed by an ecology of actors whose goal is to create, store and transfer knowledge, skills and artefacts which define new technologies, enable technology development and innovation, made up of inter-connected institutional entities (e.g. industry, academia and government) participating in the IE, bound together by social interactions and culture [2, 3].

Building an IE is a more complex task compared to other environments that are typically less open and more controlled, like incubators, technology and science parks, innovation habitats and centres, or virtual organisation breeding environments (VBE) [5, 6]. When seen as a whole, this *organic* task comprises different and independent but interrelated activities that must be performed carefully considering different tangible and intangible matters. Such activities (being implicit or deliberate, emergent or planned, static or evolving, loosely or tightly managed) span the IE's life through all stages of its evolution [7].

L.M. Camarinha-Matos et al. (Eds.): PRO-VE 2015, IFIP AICT 463, pp. 323–336, 2015.
DOI: 10.1007/978-3-319-24141-8_29

An analysis of literature reveals no consensus about the required lifecycle phases, involved processes, their recommended sequence or stages of evolution; nor is literature definitive about the actors and enabling elements most likely to play the major roles in building an IE [8]. Most of the consulted works focus on some specific phases; e.g., how to qualify different actors; how to analyse a region to better identify its business vocation; how to conduct innovation processes inside the IE; etc. This lack is also evident in research projects that deal with enabling innovation[1].

This paper extends and complements previous work by the authors [7], which identified and represented processes that were involved in building and sustaining existing IEs. However, in order to both serve as a guide for future IE building, and for refinements of current IEs, it is important to check how complete the devised model is. Therefore, this paper is not about innovation models themselves. Adopting as the initial hypothesis that IEs can be seen as a Collaborative Network (CN) [10], authors organised and mapped the identified processes against ARCON (*A Reference model and Modelling framework for Collaborative Networks*) [11], which is seen as the most relevant model for CNs. One of the advantages of analysing IEs from the CN perspective is the possibility to apply the huge bunch of knowledge on collaboration-based networks when investigating the several issues of IEs.

The remaining part of the paper is organized as follows. Section 2 summarizes the adopted research methodology. Section 3 identifies the differences and commonalities between IEs and CNs. Section 4 gives an overview about the IE model. Section 5 maps this model against ARCON. Section 6 discusses this mapping, highlighting at which extent ARCON can be used to model IEs. Section 7 presents the conclusions.

2 Basic Research Methodology and Underlying Concepts

This qualitative research work was carried out based on *conceptual analytical* method according to Järvinen's taxonomy of research methods [12]. The work includes three research actions to achieve its goals: (A) the study of IEs as a type of CN; (B) the mapping of the devised process model against ARCON and the identification of possible gaps in the former; and (C) the identification of IE specific details that could be incorporated into ARCON in order to help its users when specifically applying it for the creation of future IEs.

For (A) a systematic literature review was performed, looking at definitions of IEs and conceptual foundations of CN-like networks. For (B) ARCON was studied and compared against the IE lifecycle process model. Authors highlight the diversity of terminologies used when describing/characterising what an IE is. For (C) the commonalities and particularities of IEs against ARCON were identified.

In terms of the present treatment, a combination of terminology established in the systems engineering community ISO 15288 [13] and enterprise engineering community

---

[1] e.g. The European projects *BIVEE, ComVantage, IMAGINE, CoVES, Laboranova, PLENT, GloNet* and *SmartNets* [9] have tackled innovation with different models, platforms and scopes, basically supporting the collaborative development of products and related services mainly for the manufacturing sector. They essentially focus on the "ecosystem" *operation* stage and not on how to build it.

ISO 15704 [14] was used. Thus, by a *process* (*P*), we mean a collection of inter-related *activities* (*a$_i$*) that transform physical goods and/or information (the input) into output by performing a value adding *function* (*F*). Activities in a process are performed by *resources* (*r$_j$*), which in turn are *entities* considered to be systems capable of performing a set of (more elementary) functions (*f$_{j,k}$*).

3 Innovation Ecosystems and Collaborative Networks

In order to better understand the nature of these 'ecosystems' and if they can be considered as a type-of CN, we looked at literature for definitions of an IE (see below) to compare these against the definition of CNs:

- "An environment with economic agents and economic relations as well as the non-economic parts, such as technology, institutions, sociological interactions and the culture" [3]
- "Networks that provide mechanisms for goal-focused creation of new goods and services tailored to rapidly evolving market needs, with multiple, autonomous and independent institutions and dispersed individuals for parallel innovation" [15]
- "Independent factors working together to enable entrepreneurs and allow innovation to occur in a sustained way in a particular location" [16]
- "An environment and economic model formed by actors whose goal is to enable technology development and innovation", made up of institutional entities participating in the ecosystem, bound together by social interactions and culture [2, 3] (paraphrased)
- "An environment that aligns independent actors, regulations and supporting elements to leverage actors playing their roles in an organised and collaborative way towards developing innovations" [17]
- "An open, dynamic, sustainable and evolving networked business environment, which catalyses and drives the transformation of ideas into valuable outcomes under varied business models, supported by capital and by heterogeneous actors' knowledge and infrastructures, constrained by policies, regulations, governance and culture" [7]
- "The inter-organisational, political, economic, environmental, and technological systems of innovation through which a milieu conducive to business growth is catalysed, sustained and supported" [...] "It is characterised by a continual re-alignment of synergistic relationships that promote harmonious growth of the system in agile responsiveness to changing internal and external forces" [18].

Elements of an IE include [2, 4, 8, 15, 19]: *Actors* (government, universities, industry, supporting institutions and specialised people, entrepreneurs, financial system, customers and civil society, and their [social and economic] relationship, playing various roles throughout the IE's life); *Capital* (financial assets provided by some actors); *Infrastructure* (physical, technical conditions and general resources to support the IE and the innovation developments 'inside' of it); *Regulations* (laws and rules that frame the IE functioning and innovation environment); *Knowledge* (existing supporting theoretical foundations, tacit and explicit, formal, informal and specialised knowledge that are used, generated (and eventually organised and managed), made available, and learned along the innovation value chain); *Ideas* (intentional thoughts that trigger innovation actions and around which the whole IE works).

Three additional elements impact the way the IE operates [7]: *Interface* represents the channel to support the interaction between the IE's participants with external actors, considering their usually significant heterogeneity; *Culture* refers to the mind-set of people and organisations combined to support and easy innovation initiatives and to solve related problems [4]; *Architectural Principles* refers to the way the IEs' elements are combined, orchestrated and the culture element is also reflected in them.

The IE's dynamics makes actors assume multiple, but not fixed or pre-defined roles, in the different stages and involved phases of IE life.

A Collaborative Network (CN) is defined as [10] "a network constituted by a variety of entities (e.g. organisations and people) that are largely autonomous, geographically distributed, and heterogeneous in terms of their: operating environment, culture, social capital, and goals" [...] "CN focus on the structure, behaviour, and evolving dynamics of networks of autonomous entities that collaborate to better achieve common or compatible goals" [...] "interactions are supported by computer networks" [...] "CN collaboration derives from the shared belief that together the network members can achieve goals that would not be possible or would have a higher cost if attempted by them individually".

Based on these definitions and related literature [4, 15, 18, 20], we argue that an *Innovation Ecosystem is a CN* as it has all essential CN characteristics, namely: formed by autonomous, independent, distributed and heterogeneous actors [...] that behave, interact and collaborate with each other with different roles [...] in a socio-technical network [...] within a fertile, spatial and evolving environment [...] to overcome individual capability limitations, maximise resource usage, and share risks and costs, [...] so as to better achieve common/compatible goals [...] regarding the different involved cultures [...] and intrinsic network dynamics. Although not explicitly mentioned in the above CN definition, *trust* is also a crucial issue in IEs.

As a matter of fact, it is not the name or borders of the network that turn it into a CN, but rather what and how things happen inside of it.

There are many other dimensions to characterise a CN, like if it is mono or multi-sectorial, long-term or grasp-driven, regionally or globally focused/placed, etc. However, when looking at more specific features of typical IEs, some major differences can be pointed out. The ARCON reference model identifies fourteen basic types of CN [11]. Two of these are the most similar to IEs: Business Ecosystem and Virtual organisation Breeding Environments (VBE) long-term alliances. An IE is a broader concept and is a more open and dynamically emerging environment than a Business Ecosystem (in the ARCON reference model characterised similarly to an industrial cluster). Original VBE concepts [21], its so-called 'second generation' [22] and inter-played CNs [23] still represent 'closed-world' type of alliances, although allowing multi-sectorial companies and inter-VBE collaboration to better support the creation of *virtual* enterprises/organisations.

It is important to highlight that it is not our goal here to verify if an IE is 'better' or not than e.g. a VBE. Instead, the point is that IEs seem to be a *particular* type of CN suitable to achieve certain strategic goals and objectives. The main similarities and differences between IEs and other CNs include:

- CN original definition stands for having computers networks as the means to support interactions among members. Although ICT can be very much variable in type and usage intensity, and regarding its current proliferation in the society and organisations, it is rather difficult to imagine IE's members interacting and doing their work without using ICT reasonably intensively, in the same way as other types of CNs.
- An IE is not always created as a methodologically planned and induced initiative of some actors. There are several cases (e.g. Silicon Valley) which have simply emerged as a result of a set of regional factors. In cases of more planned initiatives, its building is far from being linear or sequential. Its building phases are very much decoupled from one to another, and processes' phases and actors evolve at different pace and independently from the other ones.
- An IE typically embraces many kinds of actors, existing infrastructures and even other CNs. Because there is no physical or organisational border, IEs embrace universities, private R&D labs, funding agencies and banks, etc., besides previously established industrial clusters, innovation habitats and VBEs. Therefore, IEs can be considered as a 'logical' environment on top of existing CN and other non-CNs alliances. IEs can also interplay with other ones.
- Actors can perform several different roles throughout the IE's life, having plenty of members' capabilities overlapping.
- Actors may be different in nature, internal processes, stages of evolution/maturity level, and value systems. Therefore, an IE can be seen as a heterogeneous system of systems. Although being independent entities, actors may perform actions related to sustaining the entire IE and not only to the operational actions related to various innovation initiatives, e.g., some actors help other actors to be created and evolve.
- The so-called 'minimum level of preparedness' that each actor should have to collaborate is much less formalised, controlled and homogenous than in other types of CNs. Although 'preparedness' can be used as one important criterion for partners selection or suggestion, practice in IEs shows that this is mostly resolved 'on the fly'.
- Joining and exiting of actors can be dynamic and even unnoticed. IE boundaries are intrinsically 'elastic'. This means having only general and less formal governance and performance management models: the IE manages *itself* in an organic manner rather than being managed by some central authority. Due to cultural factors and implicit social rules it is unlikely for a formal governance to strongly coerce members and system behaviour.
- IEs involve another level and nature of outcomes. Besides generating physical outcomes, less tangible or more abstract impacts are just as important. This requires the identification of adequate performance indicators aligned to the IEs' goals, but observable by all as a feedback mechanism.
- An IE is devoted to conduct, leverage and sustain *innovation* and to boost business and (*real* rather than *virtual*) enterprises creation;
- The creation of Virtual Enterprises/Organisations (VE/VO) can be seen as a possible consequence – and not as an ultimate purpose – of a given innovation initiative. There are four differences compared to 'classical' VE/VO: First, innovation can happen anytime in the IEs' phases and processes performed by actors involved in, creating multiple and simultaneous value chains. Second, an innovation initiative includes

partners not having 'common' goals in the strict sense. Actors have their own intrinsic interests aligned to the type of 'system' they belong to. Therefore, when a CN is defined to *'achieve common or compatible goals'*, in the context of IEs perhaps a more appropriate formulation might be as *'support the achievement of mutually beneficial but independent/aligned goals'*. Third, innovation outcomes not necessarily refer to final physical goods to be delivered or ready commercialisable ideas. Sometimes the goal is to test a concept or technology; intermediate results may be exploited in different ways and by another VOs; etc. Fourth, the VE/VO composition can vary depending on the innovation needs, the required path and the innovation model in use. A significant part of a VE/VO is created 'on the fly', rather than follows the classic, usually linear and coupled steps of *opportunity identification :: VO/VE characterisation and planning :: partner search and selection :: negotiation :: contracting :: launching VE/VO*. Many other 'sub' VE/VOs can emerge as the result of such dynamics.

- The classical role of the so-called 'VO Coordinator' does not necessarily exist. Coordination is achieved through organic negotiations between stakeholders as defined by the needs of the business and exploitation plan. This kind of network may use multiple network brokers and orchestrators who are in charge of finding the most suitable partnerships as the innovation project goes on.

All these particularities make IEs extremely difficult to build and integrate (including at the ICT level); they are perhaps the most complex type of CN when considering those fourteen types identified in ARCON.

4   The Innovation Ecosystem Model

This section presents the lifecycle phases and processes involved in the building of an IE (Fig. 1), and were inspired by the description [21] of VBE evolution. The IE's stages of life are named according to ARCON [11]. In Fig. 1 processes are presented in a condensed way as the details are not essential to achieve this paper's objective. A very detailed description of each process, and how they were identified and derived from the current body of knowledge on IEs, can be found in [7].

When discussing the processes involved in creating, operating, changing, etc. of a system (such as an IE or in general a collaborative network) it is customary to categorise these processes according to the level of abstraction at which they consider that system. This is done by defining (from abstract to concrete) lifecycle 'processes' that define the identity, develop the concept, specify the requirements, and design, build, operate, and decommission the system. These types of processes are called lifecycle *phases*, due to the fact that their instances are repeatedly executed, often in parallel, and there is considerable amount of feedback (constraining relationships) involved. In the context of IEs, lifecycle processes cannot be seen only from the classical engineering perspective, where processes are always deliberately performed. In the present organic context, processes are often related to social phenomena, which in turn are largely unpredictable, dynamic, unstructured, emergent, and are only up to some extent observable and manageable.

A *system* can evolve throughout its *life* in *stages*, and each stage can involve the execution of the same type of lifecycle processes many times over.

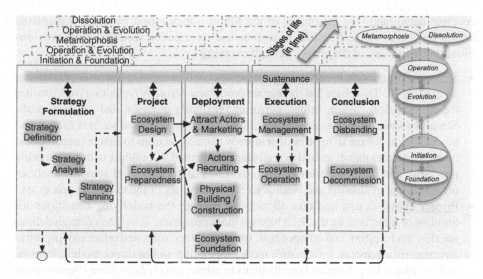

Fig. 1. Innovation ecosystem: a) lifecycle phases and b) stages of life

The *evolution* of a system may involve various kinds of change, like the joining of new members, replacement of parts of the system, creating new connections and relationships, learning, restructuring, developing new assets that enable previously impossible functions, etc., so a system evolves throughout its life, at the same time as it is operating. Part of this evolution includes the improvement of the system lifecycle processes themselves. Improvements include changes in maturity, emergent or induced growth, learning and gaining experience, making autonomous decisions within the IE. Improvement may also be due to external events, or feedback from internal processes, or the external environment that cause or enable processes to change.

Both the system as a whole and supporting subsystems have *stages of life* that together cover their respective lifespans, and each have a respective *lifecycle*, that consist of their specific (lifecycle) processes (types).

Each phase has processes (e.g. *Project* consists of *ecosystem design* and *ecosystem preparation* processes) and activities (the set of actions performed within each process). Process scopes are not always perfectly determined and the control and information flow can vary due to the intrinsic non-linearity of enacting an IE (represented as dashed lines in Fig. 1).

These processes are continuously performed/instantiated throughout the stages of the IE life. The IEs is initially devised, prepared, set-up and launched (*initiation and foundation*), it reaches operation and gradually evolves as it goes (*operation and evolution*), and may need deep changes in its identity (*metamorphosis*), or can even reach closure (*dissolution*). Note that we define 'metamorphosis' as substantial change in some of the identity attributes of the IE, but still the result of such deep transformation is rooted in the IE's earlier existence. If this were not so, then we would talk about 'dissolution'.

What follows is a description of the lifecycle phases. Note that the name 'phase' of 'lifecycle phase' suggests that these 'phases' consider the IE on different levels of abstraction. If we go from left to right in Fig. 1, these processes reveal more and more concrete detail, and – as the phases of the Moon – they repeat by being instantiated during the stages of the IE's life, as well as use information feedback from previous instantiations of any of the phases through evolving cycles.

- Strategy Formulation Phase: take strategic decision of creating a new or reinforcing an existing IE. This phase has three main processes: *Strategy Definition* (re)identifies the IE's mission, vision, values, performs feasibility analysis, and strategic goals. *Strategy Planning* defines actions plans and milestones, critical success factors and key indicators for the IE to be built or already running, actions to ensure preparedness of actors, defines mandates and overall plans, dedicated IE-building or transformation programs, and projects. *Strategy Analysis* refers to the variety of strategic analyses informing the evaluation and feedback of the outcomes of the two other processes.
- Project Phase: design and take all steps to prepare the underlying conditions for building or transforming the IE. It has two main processes: *Ecosystem Design* defines the IE's 'architecture', its components, types of actors, roles and relationships, infrastructure requirements, governance model, operating and business models, bylaws, code of ethics, incentives and mechanisms to attract actors. *Ecosystem Preparedness* defines a plan of actions related to preparing involved actors, infrastructures, laws and regulations to cope with the IE's requirements, mid- and low level specifications, along the future stages of evolution.
- Deployment Phase: formally establish the designed IE, transform specifications into infrastructures and populate with real actors. This has four main processes: *Actors' Attraction and Marketing* designs and executes actions to publicise the IE to attract qualified actors. *Actors' recruiting* aims to attracting participants according to preparedness directives and rules. *Physical building* makes available suitable facilities to support the diverse types of actions required throughout an innovation's lifecycle, following the requirements and guidelines indicated in the design sub-process. *Ecosystem foundation* refers to the official organisational foundation of the IE, when pertinent. Depending on the deployment model and taxation laws as well as legal incentive mechanisms, this can involve a legal or more formal establishment of the IE, or in the other extreme case this may simply take the form of an 'announcement'.
- Execution Phase: is the set of processes involved in the operation of the entire IE. It has two main processes: *Ecosystem operation* consists of the activities involved in creating and bringing to successful conclusion various innovation initiatives, as carried out 'inside' the IE. *Ecosystem Management* includes management activities of the IE, and can cover two levels: the strategic management of the IE itself (identifying opportunities, threats, issues, etc., and initiating other relevant lifecycle processes as above); the tactical and operational management of the IE. This process involves dealing with human resources, financial, organisational, technological, governance issues, and is likely to be a distributed collaborative set of activities, rather than being concentrated into a management role performed by any one particular organisational or individual actor.
- Conclusion Phase: this phase is basically responsible for handling issues that deeply impact the continuation of the IE's life. This phase has two main processes: *Ecosystem Decommission* refers to handling the coming and going of actors within the IE along its life cycle. *Ecosystem Disbanding* refers to a gradual exiting of actors

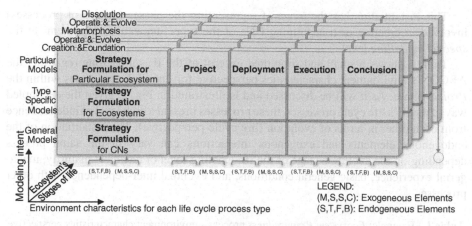

Fig. 2. The innovation ecosystem lifecycle phases framed by the ARCON model

from the IE business environment due to e.g. strategic changes and general disagreements.

- Sustenance Phase: this phase is responsible for handling the future evolution and viability of the IE, managing the IE's life cycle. This phase has one main process, but which crosses, impacts and receives feedbacks from all the other sub-processes. *Ecosystem sustainability* corresponds to *tactical and strategic* management levels that *all* phases have when performing their actions.

5   Mapping ARCON and Innovation Ecosystems

ARCON is a reference model and modelling framework directed to collaborative networks. It intends to be used as a basis for derivation of other specific models for particular cases in various types of CNs, helping to understand the involved entities and significant relationships among them [11].

For the purpose of modelling all features of CN components, ARCON considers three perspectives [11]. The first one (ARCON *lifecycle*) addresses the timing of CN's life stages: *creation, operation, evolution, metamorphosis* and *dissolution*. The second perspective (*'environment characteristics'*) focuses on capturing the CN's general features. This perspective in turn includes two so-called subspaces: The *endogenous elements* sub-space embraces the internal CN elements' characteristics and are classified into four dimensions: *structural (S), componential (C), functional (F)* and *behavioural (B)*. The *exogenous interactions* sub-space handles the logical surrounding of CNs and are also classified into four dimensions: *market (M), support (S), societal (S)* and *constituency (C)*. The third perceptive (*'modelling intent'*) refers to the different goals one may have when modelling a CN, addressing the three possible intents: *general representation, specific modelling,* and detailed specification/*implementation modelling*. Figure 2 presents a very general 'instantiation' of ARCON.

This instantiation has the *intent* of representing the phases (groups of processes) involved in creating or transforming CNs of the type 'innovation ecosystem' at the *specific modelling* level.

Table 1 shows a small and simplified excerpt of the IE's modelling regarding the ARCON's environment characteristics perspective for one of the processes within the *Project* phase. As it will be discussed and is illustrated in Fig. 2, given the decoupled way of the IE's life cycle processes, these processes present a high level of independence from each other in terms of evolution (life cycle perspective). The instantiation of the endogenous elements and exogenous interactions can vary in the same process depending on the evolution stage of the IE, existing level of technical maturity, managerial experience, basic general conditions, and eventual inter-dependence with other processes.

Table 1. Example: *Ecosystem Preparedness* process - environment characteristics perspective

Innovation ecosystem *endogenous* elements sub-space

Structural	Componential	Functional	Behavioural
Active entities **Actors:** universities, … **Roles:** member, service provider, coacher, … *Concepts* **Relationships:** funding, … …	***Passive entities*** **Human resources:** recruiter, orchestrator, … **Knowledge resources:** members profile and competency info, … …	***Actions*** **Processes:** eco membership mgmt., strategic mgmt., … *Concepts* **Methodologies:** training method, coaching method, …	***Concepts*** **Behaviour:** business culture, governance principles, … **Contracts and Agreements:** … **incentives and sanctions:** …

Innovation ecosystem *exogenous* interactions sub-space

Market	Support	Societal	Constituency
Mission statement: Eco mission, vision, goals, … **Marketing strategies:** … **Market interactions:** strategic customers, new members, …	**Network social Nature:** profit-oriented eco, … *Interaction parties* **Support entities:** Certification entities, … …	**Network legal identity:** Legal Name: "Eco Great" Values and principles: free commerce, free competition, … …	***Network identity*** **Attracting factors:** Attracting and recruiting strategies, **Rules of adhesion:** … …

6   Discussion

Having in mind the differences between IEs and other CNs (see Sect. 3), it could be observed that the usual way of using ARCON as a process-based methodology seems not applicable at all here, because lifecycle processes are normally performed in parallel in a decoupled way, and not sequentially, refining the outcome in an evolutionary manner throughout the stages of the IE's life.

Although decoupled, activities of these processes may be circularly dependent on one another. This can be easily understood by differentiating between activity as in *process (type) definition* (meaning 'activity type') and activity as in *process instance* (meaning 'activity instance'). This feedback in turn can be affected by the different pace and implementation success of each process' activities and policies. This means that an IE does not evolve linearly and harmoniously.

Therefore, modelling innovation systems should perhaps be done looking at each individual process level and not at once as if it was a "monolithic" block. This suggests a very high level of complexity – perhaps not being truly and tightly manageable – as each "step" of every single evolving stage is different among the phases/process as the processes evolve in a non-synchronised and non-linear way. A possible approach for this is to see the IE's processes from the *fractal* point of view, where each process might be independently (although not in an isolated manner), modelled as the image of the whole.

Processes' activities need specific and proper instantiations for the given IE instance, with consideration of the maturity levels of technical and management capabilities, local conditions, culture, planned goals, and the required and available investments. Actors' involvement in each process in terms of intensity of participation and roles can also vary due to emergent leaderships. In the case of the *operation* processes (the phase where innovation projects are usually performed), the derivation of particular models is probably only feasible if done by the people involved, using a library of elementary process definitions, such as described in Malone's Process Handbook [24]. This is because every single innovation project is carried out differently, in terms of partners, innovation model, (eventual) supporting ICT tools, governance model (if any), planned outcomes, IPR and transfer mechanisms, etc. In other words, there might be innumerable possible instantiations. Therefore, given the intrinsic "elasticity" and dynamics of IEs, it is an open point how feasible it is to derive a complete instance of a particular model, even via ARCON.

Other issues have to be tackled from wider views, as business models for example. Considering its role in terms of regional development, business models for IEs can be as many and should be handled at regional level, at the IE (as an entity) level, at the processes level, and at the individual innovation's level. Less tangible issues, like culture, are extremely critical in IEs. They are difficult to be understood and hence modelled. In this aspect, ARCON leaves to the "derivers" the option of using whatever tools and approaches when intending to derive particular instances of CNs; e.g. via soft modelling methods [11].

Another aspect refers to the terminology and underlying semantics of the evolution stages. The building or the emergence of an IE does not start from scratch and via an explicit trigger. Instead, it is established after a usually long process of seeding and cultivation of a multitude of disparate actors and supporting elements and conditions, without having a moment where such environment can be considered as ready to start from that point on. In this sense, and inspired by the terminology used in [4], a more proper term might be *'induce, seed and cultivate'* instead of *'initiation and foundation'*. As mentioned, innovation-related actions can happen 'everywhere' throughout the IE's phases, and not only during the so-called 'operation' phase. The IE as a whole and its components constantly evolve. All this should be handled in such way the created catalysing environment remains sustainable. More proper terms for that might be as *'nourish & sustain'* instead of *'operation & evolution'*. Deeper changes in an IE can indeed happen, both due to endogenous or exogenous factors. This may impact an IE to significantly modify its general identity, profile and focus, policies, structures, etc., to adapt to the new scenario. As such, the term: *'metamorphosis'* seems adequate for this stage. On the other hand, this kind of 'reset' in the IE does not happen suddenly. Instead, it is a gradual process that can take years, so processes involved in metamorphosis may start during operation, before change manifests as a stage.

'Dissolution' also happens differently in an IE. Considering the type of actors and existing infrastructures, IEs are likely to never 'disappear'. At a more daily level, individual members can come and go freely as the IE operates, some businesses and start-ups may go bankrupt, etc. At a more strategic level, an IE can lose its vitality as actors – the key ones in more particular – start disbanding the system for many possible reasons. This 'vanishing' event can be gradual and may take years, and even after that, some actors would remain in the region and could go back to be active again in any moment. Therefore, more proper terms for this stage might be as *'decommissioning & disbanding'*. Summing up, where creation, operation, evolution and metamorphosis share the same semantics in IEs as in CNs, the same thing is not true at all in the dissolution stage.

7   Conclusions

This research work has presented an analysis of how innovation ecosystems (IE) fit the CN foundations. In a previous research a bottom-up approach was applied with the aim of describing the set of processes that have been carried out when building IEs. In order to evaluate how complete the devised process-model is regarding future derivations and considering some intrinsic characteristics of IEs, ARCON was used as the reference model to be checked against in a top-down approach.

Based on literature review and on CN foundations, we could deduce that IEs share CN's essentials and so they can be considered as another CN type.

After mapping our process model for building IEs against the ARCON reference model, we could verify that all ARCON aspects were present in the devised model regarding the *general representation* and *specific modelling intent* levels. Therefore, we conclude that our model is complete in terms of phases, stages of evolution as well as of endogenous and exogenous elements. This is important as the so-developed model does not intend to be a 'recipe' to build IEs. On the other hand, given a particular case, the model can be used by stakeholders as one basis to analyse, enhance or better sustain existing IEs, and be considered when conceiving future IEs. Thanks to the holistic and complete view of the whole IE building process and its life cycle, the devised model can help stakeholders to better plan and manage the time, resources allocation, and the degree of complexity of actions in different stages of IE building. This all can be helpful for predicting points of higher risks, and to prevent the whole system from achieving undesirable states.

In this research we could observe that the *specific* IEs model has a set of particularities not detailed by ARCON, as discussed in Sect. 6. IEs have a number of particularities when compared to the other fourteen types of CNs used as the basis for the ARCON conception. They are built in a decoupled and non-linear way throughout independent although inter-related phases. Processes evolve at a different and autonomous pace rather than in common cycles of global evolution. We believe that these aspects, with careful conceptual definitions (phases, processes, process and activity types and instances), would benefit the users of ARCON as a reference model.

This paper is the result of an ongoing research. Next short-term steps include the development of a more formal model of the IE and its processes, comprising the mix of deliberate and emerging decoupled processes regarding the IE evolution, and the formalisation of business models at all the involved levels.

Acknowledgements. This work has been partially supported by CNPq - The Brazilian Council for Research and Scientific Development funding agency.

References

1. OECD: Innovation to strengthen growth and address global and social challenges (2012). http://www.oecd.org/sti/45326349.pdf
2. Jackson, D.: What is an Innovation Ecosystem?, pp. 1–12. National Science Foundation, Arlington (2011)
3. Mercan, B., Gökta, D.: Components of innovation ecosystems: a cross-country study. Int. Res. J. Finan. Econ. **76**, 102–112 (2011)
4. Hwang, V.W., Horowitt, G.: The Rainforest - The Secret to Building the Next Silicon Valley. Regenwald Publishers, USA (2012)
5. Romero, D., Molina, A.: Virtual organisation breeding environments toolkit: reference model, management framework and instantiation methodology. J. Prod. Plan. Control **21**(2), 181–217 (2010)
6. Molina, A., Romero, A.: (University) Technology parks toolkit: knowledge transfer and innovation - the Tecnológico de Monterrey experience. In: 19th International ICE-Conference on Engineering, Technology and Innovation, pp. 1–10 (2013)
7. Rabelo, R.J.; Bernus, P.: A holistic model of building innovation ecosystems. In: 15th IFAC Symposium on Information Control in Manufacturing, Ottawa, Canada (2015)
8. Mercier-Laurent, E.: Innovation Ecosystems. Wiley, New York (2011)
9. CORDIS: http://cordis.europa.eu/projects/home_en.html
10. Camarinha-Matos, L.M., Afsarmanesh, H.: Collaborative networks: a new scientific discipline. J. Intell. Manuf. **16**, 439–452 (2005)

11. Camarinha-Matos, L.M., Afsarmanesh, H.: A comprehensive modeling framework for collaborative networked organizations. JIM **18**(5), 529–542 (2007)
12. Järvinen, P.: On Research Methods. Opinpajan kirja, Tampere (2004)
13. ISO 15288: Systems and Software Engineering – System Lifecycle Processes (2008)
14. ISO 15704: Industrial Automation Systems – Requirements for Enterprise Reference Architectures and Methodologies (2000; Amd 1. 2005)
15. Durst, S., Poutanen, P.: Success factors of innovation ecosystems: initial insights from a literature review. In: CO-CREATE 2013, pp. 27–38. Aalto University (2013)
16. Lawlor, A.; Woodley, M.: Innovation ecosystems. The economist insights (2014). www.economistinsights.com/sites/default/files/barclays_1.pdf
17. Spolidoro, R.: Innovation habitats and regional development driven by the triple helix. In: IX Triple Helix International Conference, Silicon Valley, pp. 1–23 (2011)
18. Rubens, N., Still, K., Russell, M.: A network analysis of investment firms as resource routers in Chinese innovation ecosystem. J. Softw. **6**(9), 1737–1745 (2011)
19. Carayannis, G., Barth, D., Campbell, D.: The quintuple helix innovation model: global warming as a challenge and driver for innovation. J. Innov. Entrepreneurship **1**(2), 1–12 (2012)
20. Lundvall, B., Johnson, B., Andersen, E.S., Dalum, B.: National systems of production, innovation and competence building. Res. Policy **31**, 213–231 (2002)
21. Afsarmanesh, H., Camarinha-Matos, L.M.: On the classification and management of virtual organization breeding environments. Int. J. Inf. Technol. Manage. **8**(3), 234–259 (2009)
22. Afsarmanesh, H., Camarinha-Matos, L.M., Msanjila, S.S.: Models, methodologies, and tools supporting establishment and management of second-generation VBEs. IEEE Trans. Syst. Man Cybern. **41**(5), 692–710 (2011)
23. Camarinha-Matos, L.M., Ferrada, F., Oliveira, A.: Interplay of collaborative networks in product servicing. 14th IFIP Working Conference on Virtual Enterprises, pp. 52–62 (2013)
24. Malone, T.W., Crowston, K.G., Herman, G. (eds.): Organizing Business Knowledge: The MIT Process Handbook. MIT Press, Cambridge (2003)

Innovation from Academia-Industry Symbiosis

Paula Urze[1,2(✉)] and António Abreu[3,4]

[1] FCT/UNL, Faculdade de Ciências e Tecnologia da, Universidade Nova de Lsboa,
Lisbon, Portugal
pcu@fct.unl.pt

[2] CIUHTC – Centro Interuniversitário de História das Ciências e da Tecnologia, Lisbon, Portugal

[3] ISEL/IPL – Instituto Superior de Engenharia de Lisboa do Instituto Politécnico de Lisboa,
Lisbon, Portugal
ajfa@dem.isel.ipl.pt

[4] CTS – Uninova - Instituto de Desenvolvimento de Novas Tecnologias, Almada, Portugal

Abstract. Anchored on a systemic perspective of innovation and particularly on the triple helix model, which highlights the state, university and companies as central players, this paper aims to discuss the factors that enable or constrain the processes of innovation, using the system thinking approach to understand the academia-industry symbiosis. The paper's empirical section is based on a case study on Portugal's major highway management concessionaire. In order to ensure a "healthy" co-innovation environment, the archetype studied emphasizes the need to implement coordination mechanisms such as communication routines and metrics to monitor collaborative behavior in addition to the need to develop global goals that align the efforts of the partners.

Keywords: System thinking · Triple helix · Collaborative networks · Innovation and case study

1 Introduction

Today, companies in global markets need to achieve high performance levels and competitiveness just to stay "alive". Recent studies point out that a growing number of innovations introduced in the market come from networks that are created based on the core competences of each member.

In a collaborative environment, the existence of cooperation agreements, norms, reciprocal relationships, mutual trust and common infrastructures allows members to operate more effectively in pursuit of their goals. Partners "split the innovation value chain" into various tasks where the assignment of these tasks to each partner is based on the identification of resources that hold lower costs, and better skills and/or access to specific knowledge, in order to make the outcome more competitive [1].

Furthermore, the synergies created by "confrontation" of different perspectives and sharing experiences in a "healthy" collaborative environment, lead to the reinforcement of innovation flows [2]. The aim in such an innovation environment is to establish mutually beneficial relationships through which new products and services are created, often in close interaction with the customers.

© IFIP International Federation for Information Processing 2015
L.M. Camarinha-Matos et al. (Eds.): PRO-VE 2015, IFIP AICT 463, pp. 337–344, 2015.
DOI: 10.1007/978-3-319-24141-8_30

It is frequently mentioned by many industrial managers that a poor understanding of the drivers that underpin the innovation processes in a collaborative environment is an obstacle for a wider acceptance of this paradigm.

Based on an academia-industry perspective, this paper helps identify and discusses the relevant drivers and barriers that support "healthy" innovation in a collaborative context.

2   Drivers and Barriers in Industry-Academia Collaboration

Although collaborative networks have this great potential to both create value and boost innovation, several empirical studies show that many of today's joint ventures fail. According to Lee [3] several types of co-innovation networks can be identified taking into account the diversity of entities that make up the collaborative network such as large companies, SMEs, Universities and research centers, where the roles of each player and the strength of the links differ. Looking at the academia-companies link, there are many types of links that depend on the respective goals and the institutional arrangements. Collaboration to support co-innovation activities can be more or less intense, and also may be formal or informal.

In terms of time one can find short-term and long-term collaboration agreements. Short-term collaborations generally consist of on-demand problem solving with predefined outcomes. Long-term collaborations are associated with joint projects, often allowing companies to contract a core set of services and to periodically re-contract for specific deliverables in a flexible way. Long-term collaborations are more strategic, providing a multifaceted platform where companies can develop a stronger innovative capacity in the long run [4].

The purpose of this section is to address the key factors identified in the literature that are involved in Academia-Industry collaboration. Table 1, shows these factors.

Despite the potential gains obtained from the collaboration between academia-industry several barriers have been identified in the literature which helps to discuss ways of overcoming these constraints to the innovation processes (see Table 2).

3   Models to Understand the Innovation Processes

The National Innovation System theory has attained a dominant position, but over recent decades there have been several new perspectives, which give emphasis to the systemic conception of innovation. Carlsson [12] developed the concept of the technological system in the early 90s.

Leaving aside the national approach, Carlsson and Stankiewicz [13] defined a technological system as a network of agents interacting in a specific industrial or economic area, within a set of infrastructures involved in the generation, dissemination and use of technologies. The literature on regional systems of innovation has grown rapidly since the mid 90s and this time also witnessed the development of the concept of the sectorial system of innovation [14]. Some of the crucial ideas inherent in the innovation system concept (vertical interaction and innovation as an interactive process) emerge in Porter's industrial clusters, as well as in Etzkowitz and Leydesdorff's [15] Triple Helix (TH) theory.

Table 1. Innovations Drivers.

		Drivers of co-innovation	References
Motivation for companies to collaborate with Universities/Research Centers		Saving costs – access to equipment and physical facilities	[5, 6, 7]
		Risk Reduction - Access to highly qualified personnel	
		Reduction of innovation time – access to new technologies and processes.	
		Ability to recruit qualified researchers	
		Develop an innovation culture	
		Increase the qualification level of employees	
		Improve public image in society	
		Access to funding from R&D funding programs	
		Source of information for new ideas	
		Increase product quality	
		New business opportunities	
Motivation for Universities/Research Centers to collaborate with companies		Access to industry funding	[6, 7, 8]
		Access to industrial data	
		Access to technical knowledge with special impact on research and teaching activities	
		Enhancing an entrepreneurial culture	
		Facilitate graduates' integration into the job market	
		Postgraduate training in an industrial context	
		Access to updated technical knowledge	
		Join networks of knowledge creation and utilization	
		Reward systems based on amount of technology transfer	
		Support the creation of spin-offs	
		Feeling of accomplishment when working with industry/ Good publicity for the university	

The TH theory highlights the state, university and companies as influential players in the NIS. The TH improves on this (national) innovation model, because it no longer requires the assumption ex ante of national or regional systems for its integration [16]. The TH Model was developed as a result of the convergence and crossing over of the three worlds: research, business and government, which used to be very much separated.

The most recent step in the TH debate has been the concept of the TH system of innovation. This step was introduced and has been integrated into the system as an analytical framework that synthesizes the key features of TH interactions, defined according to the systems theory as a set of components, relationships and functions [17]. In this new design, among the components of the TH System, a novel distinction has been made between: (1) R&D and non-R&D innovators; (2) "single-sphere" and "multi-sphere" (hybrid) institutions; (3) individual and institutional innovators. The new strategic relationships between components have been synthesized into five main types of operations: (1) technology transfer, (2) collaboration and conflict moderation, (3) collaborative leadership, (4) substitution, and (5) networking. This perspective provides an explicit framework for the systemic interaction between TH actors, which was lacking up to now, and a more fine-grained view of the circulation of knowledge flows and resources within and among the spaces, helping to identify blockages or gaps. Thus, the TH system will generate new combinations of knowledge, resources and relationships which will in turn improve innovation theory and practice. The role of universities in this conceptualization

Table 2. Innovations Barriers.

		Barriers to co-innovation	References
Barriers for companies to collaborate with Universities/Research Centers		Absence of established procedures to collaborate with industry	[9, 10, 11]
		Lack of information about what universities do	
		University researchers don't fit in with business culture	
		Joint projects could imply more risk	
		Lack of understanding about university expectations	
		Long-term orientation of university research	
		Universities seeking to immediate disseminate findings	
		Knowledge production cycles are shorter and well defined in terms of technical results	
		Different perception of the R&D product (more applied research)	
		Companies need products and services that can be sold in the market	
		Companies believe that R&D needs to remain secret to be competitive	
Barriers for Universities/Research Centers to collaborate with companies		Different perception of the R&D product (more theoretical research)	[9, 10, 11]
		The nature of the research is not linked to industry's interests and needs	
		University needs to produce scientific results	
		University needs to publish results	
		Knowledge production cycles are longer and less defined in terms of technical results	
		Potential conflicts with industry in terms of IPRs	
		Industry developed knowledge is geared to the market	
		Industry imposes delays in dissemination of research outcomes and publications	
		University is extremely oriented to pure science	
		Difficulty in finding companies with adequate profile	
		Short-term orientation of companies' research	

is often mentioned as its "third mission". In fact, the concept of the entrepreneurial university is central to the TH model. As universities forge links, they can combine separate parts of knowledge and bring them together to innovate. Collaborative links with the other innovation actors have improved universities 'production of scientific research over time. Moreover, entrepreneurial universities are now educating organizations as well as individuals and also have an enhanced capacity to generate technology that has shifted their position from a traditional source of human resources and knowledge to a new source of technology generation and transfer. Rather than only serving as a source of new ideas for existing firms, universities are now combining their research and teaching capabilities into new formats and triggering the establishment of new companies, especially in advanced areas of science and technology.

4   System Thinking to Support the Dynamics of Co-innovation

According to Hakansson and Snehota [18], to ensure the success of the TH model it is crucial to understand and develop mechanisms to coordinate the complex interactions among university, industry and government, which is impossible to achieve when using linear approaches.

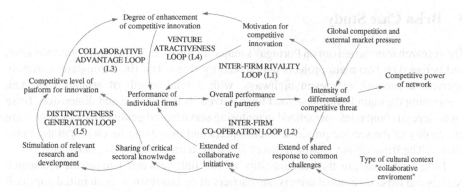

Fig. 1. Cluster dynamic model.

The tendency to apply models where analysis of the reality is mainly based on a linear approach, where the system behavior and its dynamic is explained through a series of one-way relationship events, together with the predisposition to ignore feedback and delays, might all be obstacles to grasp a better understanding of the dynamics of innovation processes.

Brown and Smith [19] developed a model based on a systems thinking approach to understand the dynamics within networks, as shown in Fig. 1. Based on this model the behavior of the network is determined by its causal structure rather than by specific events. This model tries to describe how a successful network might develop and the changes in network behavior and company interaction that might be perceived at each stage. The model consists of several loops that are used to build different stages of the network's development and impact on the performance of both individual firms and all the firms in the network.

An important aspect of the system thinking approach is that certain patterns repeat themselves, allowing an "archetypes" portfolio to be built.

The systems archetypes provide a basic form to describe generic stories and scenarios that can be applied to distinct contexts and environments. Each archetype is built based on a causal loop diagram and offers a common language to understand the behavior and dynamics of a particular system over time. The archetypes can be used to support the decision-making process in two distinct contexts: as a diagnostic tool, it can help managers understand the dynamics of a specific set of behaviors or events that have emerged over time. As a prospective tool, it can help managers identify undesirable behaviors in advance.

The most common systems archetypes are the following: Success to the Successful, Limits to Growth (also known as Limits to Success), Accidental adversaries, Tragedy of the Commons, Growth and Under Investment Attractiveness Principle, Fixes that Fail (also known as Fixes that backfire), Escalation, and Shifting the Burden (also known as Addiction). Considering that at any given time a company is in a state of dynamic equilibrium, the drivers underpinning the innovation processes and the barriers opposing it can be represented using causal loop diagrams.

5   Brisa Case Study

The research was carried out on Portugal's major highway[1] management concessionaire, and is based on two main projects undertaken by Brisa. The Brisa company currently operates a network of eleven highways, with a total length of around 1096 km, comprising the main Portuguese road links. Given its importance and dimension, Brisa owns several companies specialized in motoring services and geared towards improving the quality of the service provided to customers and increasing its own operating efficiency. The Brisa co-innovation network is a long-term collaborative network.

In order to analyze the sustainability of the link between Universities/Research centers and Brisa in terms of drivers and barriers of co-innovation, as an initial approach an effort was made to find some similarity to the most common systems archetypes mentioned in literature. Taking into account the data collected and the archetypes causal loop diagram, the choice fell on the Accidental adversaries Archetype, whose Causal Loop Diagram is illustrated in Fig. 2.

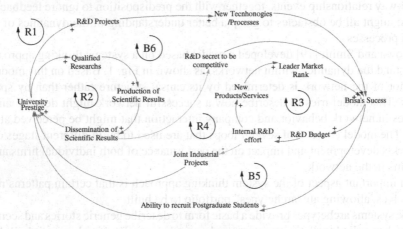

Fig. 2. Influence diagram showing the drivers and barriers of innovation.

The application of the Accidental adversaries Archetype to this analysis backs up the following explanation: initially, Research Centers/Universities and Brisa begin a relationship with the best of intentions on both sides, with the purpose of maximizing their respective strengths and minimizing their weaknesses. From the perspective of the University/Research Centers, the main goal was to increase their level of prestige. Brisa's goal was to increase the success of its business.

In the first stage, University/Research Centers establish an alliance with Brisa that benefits both parties. This is a virtuous reinforcing dynamic (R1) – in order to increase their prestige, University/Research Centers carry out R&D projects and the outcome of the R&D projects (new technologies and processes) increases Brisa's

[1] These results are based on research carried out in the project – DiInov - Dinâmicas de trans-
ferência de conhecimento em rede de inovação, FCT/UNL, BRISA, ISEL/IPL, 2015.

success. Furthermore, the growth of Brisa's success increases the possibility of recruiting postgraduate students, which creates more prestige for the University/ Research Centers. The two reinforcing loops R2 and R3 illustrate the actions taken by University/Research Centers and Brisa to improve their growth, the University's prestige and Brisa's success.

However, the problem might arise when one or both parties take some action that looks perfectly reasonable from their perspective. By seeking improvement through R2 and R3, University/Research Centers and Brisa suppress the effects of R1 and establish the negative-effect reinforcing loop R3, which in turn completely takes over B5 and B6. For instance, the dissemination of scientific results based on industrial data may compromise Brisa's competitiveness. The impact of these harmful actions may merely create a sense of frustration and antipathy between the parties, who remain partners, or it may get to the point of turning them into hostile adversaries.

The balancing loop B5 is formed by: Brisa's success, ability to recruit postgraduate students, University prestige, qualified researchers, production of scientific results, R&D secrecy to be competitive, and Brisa's success.

6 Conclusions

This paper discussed the systems thinking approach and the general systems archetypes applied to co-innovation in a collaborative context. The development of models to gain a deep understanding of the dynamics of the co-innovation processes in collaborative environments will not only help to better understand the area, but also contributes to a broader adoption of the collaborative networks' paradigm as a way to develop capabilities that will enable companies to respond quickly to market needs.

In order to ensure a "healthy" co-innovation environment, the archetype studied emphasizes the need to implement coordination mechanisms such as communication routines and metrics to monitor collaborative behavior in addition to the need to develop global goals that align the efforts of all parties involved.

Some preliminary steps in this direction, inspired by system thinking concepts, were presented. Initial results illustrate the applicability of the suggested approach.

References

1. Abreu, A., Macedo, P., Camarinha-Matos, L.M.: Towards a methodology to measure the alignment of value systems in collaborative networks. Innovation in Manufacturing Networks, pp. 37–46. Springer, US (2008)
2. Urze, P., Abreu, A.: System thinking to understand networked innovation. In: Camarinha-Matos, L.M., Afsarmanesh, H. (eds.) Collaborative Systems for Smart Networked Environments. IFIP AICT, vol. 434, pp. 327–335. Springer, Heidelberg (2014)
3. Lee, S., Park, G., Yoon, B., Park, J.: Open innovation in SMEs—an intermediated network model. Res. Policy **39**(2), 290–300 (2010)
4. Koschatzky, K., Stahlecker, T.: New forms of strategic research collaboration between firms and universities in the German research system. Int. J. Technol. Transf. Commercialisation **9**(1), 94–110 (2010)

5. Dooley, L., Kirk, D.: University-industry collaboration: grafting the entrepreneurial paradigm onto academic structures. Eur. J. Innov. Manag. **10**(3), 316–332 (2007)
6. Lee, Y.S.: The sustainability of university-industry research collaboration: an empirical assessment. J. Technol. Transf. **25**(2), 111–133 (2000)
7. Decter, M., Bennett, D., Leseure, M.: University to business technology transfer—UK and USA comparisons. Technovation **27**(3), 145–155 (2007)
8. Hall, B.H. University–industry partnerships in the United States. In: Contzen, J.-P., Gibson, D., Heitor, M.V. (eds.), Rethinking Science Systems and Innovation Policies. Proceedings of the 6th International Conference on Technology Policy and Innovation. Purdue University Press, Ashland, OH (2004)
9. Rohrbeck, R., Arnold, H.: Making university-industry collaboration work - a case study on the Deutsche Telekom Laboratories contrasted with findings in literature. In: ISPIM, Conference, - Networks for Innovation, Greece (2006)
10. Ramil, M., Senin, A.: Success factors to reduce orientation and resources related barriers in university industry R&D Collaboration particularly during development research stages. In: Global Conference on Business and Social Sciences, Procedia Social and Behavioral Sciences, vol. 172, pp. 375–382 (2014)
11. Bekkers, R., Freitas I.: Catalysts and barriers: factors that affect that affect the performance of university-industry collaborations, Conference on Innovation, Organisation and Sustainability and crises, Aalborg (2010)
12. Carlsson, B.: Technological Systems and Economic Performance: the Diffusion of Factory Automation in Sweden. Springer Science, Business, Media, New York (1995)
13. Carlsson, B., Stankiewicz, R.: On the nature, function and composition of technological systems. J. Evol. Econ. **1**(2), 93–118 (1991)
14. Lundvall, B.-Å., Borras, S.: Science, technology, innovation and knowledge policy. In: Fagerberg, J., Mowery, D., Nelson, R.R. (eds.) The Oxford Handbook of Innovation. Oxford University Press, Norfolk (2005)
15. Leydesdorff, L., Etzkowitz, H.: The triple helix as a model for innovation studies. Sci. Public Policy **25**(3), 195–203 (1998)
16. Leydesdorff, L.: The triple helix model and the study of knowledge-based innovation systems. Int. J. Contemp. Sociol. **42**(1), 12–27 (2005)
17. Ranga, M., Etzkowitz, H.: The triple helix systems: an analytical framework for innovation policy and practice in the knowledge society. Ind. High. Educ. **27**(4), 237–262 (2013)
18. Snehota, I., Hakansson, H. (eds.): Developing Relationships in Business Networks. Routledge, London (1995)
19. Smith, M., Brown, R.: Exploratory techniques for examining cluster dynamics: a systems thinking approach. Local Econ. **24**(4), 283–298 (2009)

A Conceptual Framework for Mobile Service Value

Garyfallos Fragidis[1,2(✉)] and Dimitri Konstantas[2]

[1] Faculty of Business and Economics, Technological Education Institution of Central Macedonia,
Terma Magnisias, 62124 Serres, Greece
garyf@teicm.gr
[2] Faculty of Social Sciences, University of Geneva, UniMail en Battelle, Geneva, Switzerland
Dimitri.Konstantas@unige.ch

Abstract. Mobile services have unique characteristics and can provide opportunities for added value, new types of value and new ways of value configuration.
Mobile cloud computing can boost the development of mobile services. In this
paper we provide a user-driven and usage-oriented perspective on mobile services, especially when they are provided via the cloud. We examine the different
perspectives on mobile services and outline models of mobile service provision.
Mobile services are regarded as embedded in the daily activities of the mobile
user in order to attain personal objectives. We provide an integrated view on
mobile services that combines technological and usage aspects and emphasizes
on value creation. This work helps understand better the provision, usage and
value creation in mobile services and can provide new research and practical
opportunities for developing new service models in mobile environments.

Keywords: Mobile service · Mobile cloud computing · Service value · Value co-
creation

1 Introduction

The substantial progress in mobile technologies and the wide availability of wireless
Internet has driven to an increasing popularity of mobile computing. Mobile devices,
especially smartphones and tablets, serve today as a multipurpose tool in everyday life
practices of the people. They are used more and more to provide a variety of services
('mobile services') that go beyond communication and support a wide spectrum of
human activities, including social interaction, entertainment, economic transactions,
business operations, personal time management, data management, learning, healthcare
and a variety of location-aware and context-aware services, such as navigation, tracking
services, emergency services, etc.

A serious obstacle for the further development and use of mobile services stems from
the technological limitations of mobile devices, especially with concern to resources
(battery life, storage space, etc.) and capacity (processing, bandwidth, etc.). Mobile
cloud computing has been developed as a solution to these problems, by marrying
together mobile technologies and cloud computing to extend the benefits of cloud
computing to mobile services and applications. Mobile cloud computing can supposedly

© IFIP International Federation for Information Processing 2015
L.M. Camarinha-Matos et al. (Eds.): PRO-VE 2015, IFIP AICT 463, pp. 345–356, 2015.
DOI: 10.1007/978-3-319-24141-8_31

boost the development of mobile services, as well as enable the development of entirely new types of services [1] and become the dominant model for mobile applications in the future [2]. Huang et al. [3], for instance, give a perspective of the 'service of the future' as a combination of people needs, the physical environment surrounding people and the virtual environments with which people interact. Research in the areas of ubiquitous and pervasive computing (e.g. [4]) recognizes the central role of the user in the interaction with cyber-physical systems, as a part of their everyday life practices.

In this paper we provide a user-driven and usage-oriented perspective for mobile service, especially when it is provided via the mobile cloud. We acknowledge that mobile services are embedded in people's everyday life practices. For this, we introduce concepts from service management to explore the meaning of service value, analyze the role of the user and examine the interaction, collaboration and co-creation of value between the user, the service provider and the mobile cloud actors that facilitate the provision of mobile service.

The emphasis on the mobile cloud is founded on its significance as a new technological approach that can empower the mobile user in his everyday activities and can support the emergence of novel distributed and collaborative models of service provision and consumption [2]. Notice that the business and usage or user aspects of the mobile cloud computing remain marginal in the literature (e.g. [4, 5]).

The purpose of this paper is to provide a framework that integrates concepts from mobile cloud computing on the one hand and service management on the other hand in order to understand better the usage and value creation in mobile services. Without good knowledge of the usage aspects of the mobile service, companies are prone to fail to support their customers and they may be missing opportunities for the development of new services and new business models.

The paper contributes in the literature in the following ways: first, it analyzes concepts and models of mobile service provision and explains the roles and activities of the different actors. Second, it integrates in the analytical framework the human aspects of mobile service regarding the usage and value creation with the computing operations for the provision of mobile service. Third, it introduces concepts of mobile service provision as a cyber-physical phenomenon that includes computing operations and value creation activities from the part of the user. Fourth, it provides a bridge between the technological, business and use aspects of mobile services and supports the better understanding of the relevant concepts.

The rest of the paper is organized in six sections. In the next section we present an overview of mobile services and mobile cloud computing, by emphasizing on the use aspects of services and the service models. In section three we analyze the different perspectives on the concept of mobile service and we describe the related mobile service models. In section four we provide an integrated view on mobile service provision that combines technological and usage aspects, regards mobile service provision as a cyber-physical phenomenon and emphasizes on real world effects and value creation. In section five we develop a conceptual framework for the provision, usage and value creation and co-creation in mobile services. The paper concludes with the main points of this work and the research implications.

2   Mobile Services and Mobile Cloud Computing

Mobile services are services that can be accessed and used with the use of mobile technologies and mobile devices, such as smart phones, tablets and other wireless devices. The great advantage of mobile services comes from their ability to support the mobility of the user. They are characterized by ubiquity, localization, improved personalization and increased convenience [7, 8] and, thus, they are different from other e-services and physical-world services [9]. Under certain circumstances [10], mobile services can provide new types of value (e.g. location-aware services), new ways for value configuration (e.g. real-time interaction with friends and other users who share the same context), rich experiences (e.g. context-aware services that adapt to the situation of the user) and opportunities for more added value (e.g. receiving service any time and especially at the moment it is needed). Satyanarayanan [11] describes the vision of mobile computing as "information at your fingertips anywhere, anytime".

Mobile cloud computing has been developed as the integration of mobile computing and cloud computing with the purpose to bring the benefits of cloud computing into the mobile environment [12, 13]. Cloud computing is a new computing paradigm [14, 15] that is based on the use of Internet infrastructure for the provision or sharing of computing resources, hardware and software, 'as a service', that is on demand and on temporary basis. Cloud computing has been recognized as the 'next generation computing infrastructure' [13] and a 'new economic and business computing paradigm' [16].

With the explosion of mobile applications in the first place and the supplementary support of cloud computing in the provision of mobile service, the significance of the mobile cloud computing was amplified. Mobile cloud computing can bring new types of services and it offers ample business opportunities [11].

The literature of mobile services and mobile cloud computing suffers from ambiguity. Yang et al. [12] distinguish three major approaches in the literature for mobile cloud applications: (a) extending the access of cloud services to mobile devices; (b) enabling mobile devices to work collaboratively as cloud resource providers; (c) augmenting the execution of mobile applications on portable devices using cloud resources. In the first approach, users access with their mobile devices software/applications "as services" offered on the cloud, with all the computation and data handling being performed in the cloud. The second approach makes use of the resource at individual mobile devices to provide a virtual, ad hoc and local mobile cloud environment. The third approach uses the cloud resources for the execution of the operations on mobile devices. We can gather that, from a usage point of view, mobile cloud applications can support the access of services offered in the cloud, while from a computing point of view, they can enable mobile devices to work collaboratively as cloud resource providers or augment their operations by using cloud resources.

Regarding the typical service models of cloud computing [15], the mobile cloud is most often considered as a SaaS model, when it is used to access software offered on the cloud, and it is considered as IaaS or PaaS model, when it is used to augment the capability of mobile devices through partial or full offloading of the computational operations and data storage from the mobile devices [12]. Qi and Gani [16] describe three basic mobile cloud computing service models that are based on the role of the mobile device. In 'mobile as a service consumer' (MaaSC), which is the most common model, the mobile device receives computing functions as single direction service from other actors that operate on the cloud. In 'mobile as a service provider' (MaaSP) the mobile device becomes the service provider of information or computing capacity through the cloud. 'Mobile as a service broker' (MaaSB) is a special case of MaaSP, because the mobile device provides services to other mobile devices or sensing nodes in its proximity.

In the literature we can find several examples of mobile cloud applications and services. Here we are interested in those that include user's involvement and provide direct benefits to the user. Common examples refer to mobile crowdsourcing [2, 11], collective sensing [3], location-aware and context-aware services [3, 17, 18], pooling mobile resources and sharing applications between mobile devices [19, 20].

3 A Service Terminology and Service Models in Mobile Environments

The discussion about the mobile service provision is prone to serious misunderstandings as concerns the meaning of the term 'service' when one adopts a user-driven and usage-oriented approach. The source of misunderstandings is the multiple dimensions of the concept of service and in particular the different uses of the term in computer science and in business science [21, 22]. Besides, there are different approaches in running mobile cloud applications [12] and commercial hype in mobile cloud computing [23]. In this section we attempt to clarify the concept of service in the mobile cloud. In particular, we distinguish between mobile service for the user and computing service for the operation of the mobile device in the mobile cloud. We name the former 'mobile service' and the later 'mobile cloud service'.

A 'mobile service' is an electronic service that can be provided, accessed and used with the use of mobile technologies and mobile devices. Mobile services are used by users in commercial transactions, business operations, learning, healthcare, entertainment/multimedia, gaming, social networking and collaboration, augmented reality, searching/querying, etc [5, 13, 23, 24].

A mobile service can be the mobile version of an e-service (as the term is described in [21]), or it can be provided only in a mobile form, such as some kinds of location-aware and context-aware services. Likewise, a mobile service can be the mobile counterpart of a physical world service, or it can be only in mobile form.

A mobile service is an electronic in nature service that is produced and consumed by real world entities: business entities, as service providers, produce and provide mobile services as a part of their business functions; end-users as individuals consume mobile services in their everyday life practices. Thus, mobile services produce a real world effect.

Service providers can offer mobile service directly to the end user with the use of mobile computing technologies and Internet and wireless technologies. In addition, they can provide mobile service via the cloud, with the use of cloud resources and cloud

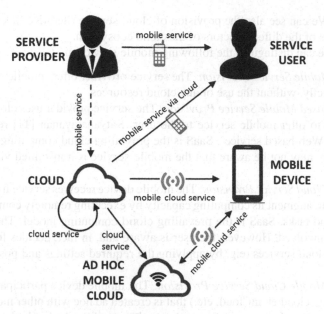

Fig. 1. Provision of mobile service and mobile cloud service

computing technologies. In most cases, the user does not know (and perhaps does not care) about the way mobile services are transmitted and received by his mobile device. These relationships can be seen in Fig. 1.

A 'mobile cloud service' is a computing service that is provided with the use of mobile computing technologies and cloud technologies and consumed by the mobile device of the user to run more efficiently and effectively mobile applications and provide mobile service to the user. For instance, in order to provide navigation service (mobile service) to the user, the mobile device uses cloud resources for processing location-aware data (mobile cloud service). Examples of mobile cloud services are related to the access, transmission and storage of data in the cloud, the outsourced execution of computing operations of the mobile device, the use of security services, etc. Mobile cloud services exist only in the virtual world of the cloud and serve the augmented operations of the mobile devices.

In Fig. 1 we see two approaches for mobile cloud service. In the first case the mobile device receives computing service from the cloud for the augmented execution of computing tasks. In this case we have basically a two-level architecture for the provision of cloud-based service that is consumed by mobile devices. In the second case the mobile device participates in a local and ad hoc cloud environment that exploits distributed operations and opportunism and enables mobile devices to work collaboratively by pooling resources and sharing operations.

In Fig. 1 we can see the distinction between the cloud and the ad hoc mobile cloud. In the literature the term mobile cloud is used frequently as a general term to refer broadly to cloud services for mobile applications. However, in most cases it is simply cloud service that is offered to mobile devices, adjusted to the requirements of mobile computing. We can see also the provision of cloud service (iterative link) as a part of the operations of the different actors of the cloud ecosystem.

Is sum, we can distinguish the following mobile service models:

(a) *Direct Mobile Service Provision*. The service provider offers mobile service to the user directly, without the use of any cloud resources.
(b) *Cloud-Based Mobile Service Provision*. The service provider uses cloud resources in order to offer mobile service to the user. Satyanarayanan [11] refers to it as 'mobile Web-based service'. SaaS is the prevailing cloud computing model here. The users may not be aware that the mobile service is transmitted via the mobile cloud.
(c) *Mobile Cloud Service Provision*. The mobile device receives service from the cloud in order to augment its computing capacity by executing remotely computing operations and tasks. SaaS is the prevailing cloud computing model. The user is not directly involved. However, the user is aware and, in fact, decides for the use of mobile cloud services (e.g. by applying the required settings and possibly paying a fee).
(d) *Ad-hoc Mobile Cloud Service Provision*. The mobile device participates in a local cloud (e.g. cloudlet, mCloud, etc.) that is created ad hoc with other mobile devices and cloud-based resources in proximity. The mobile device both receives and provides computing services in the ad hoc cloud; for instance, it offers computing capacity because it holds bigger battery resources and uses the bandwidth of another smartphone in the ad hoc cloud, because it provides cheaper or faster Internet access. All cloud computing models can be applied here (SaaS, IasS and possibly PaaS). As in the previous case, the user is not directly involved, but is aware of the participation in the ad-hoc mobile cloud.

4   An Integrated View on Mobile Service

Mobile devices function in an autonomous way in mobile cloud computing, when they interact with other devices or mobile cloud resources to receive or provide service. In addition, they have their own objectives, such as reduce energy consumption or improve the quality of connection to the Internet. However, their objectives and their operations are closely related to the provision of mobile service to the user and they must serve the needs of the user. Mobile services and mobile cloud services are supplementary. It is difficult to see the mobile device in separation of the user, his activities and intentions. The mobile device is simply the smart and multi-functional tool that enables people receive service in a flexible way in their daily life practices, anytime and anywhere.

The combination of service concepts from the real world and the computing world introduces the idea of mobile service provision as a cyber-physical phenomenon. This idea is not new in the literature of mobile cloud computing. Huang et al. [3] suggest a user can be represented by a virtualized entity in the cloud, through his mobile device, an approach that can introduce a "next-generation mobile cloud computing service model" in that both physical systems and virtual systems are seamlessly integrated through virtualization technologies to provide service. The connection between a cyber-physical system (CPS) and cloud computing is envisaged also by Simmon et al. [26], who cast the term 'Cyber-Physical Cloud Computing' (CPCC). Moreover, research in the areas of ubiquitous computing, pervasive computing and the Internet of Things include also the user (as a human being) in the conceptualization of the cyber-physical framework. The National Institute of Standards and Technology (NIST) uses the term 'Smart Networked Systems and Societies' (SNSS) to describe the network of connected computing resources, things and humans [26]. Humans participate as an integral part of SNSS, especially through social networks, and social networking services allow people to access, store and share their real-life experiences. Conti et al. [4] place humans at the center of the 'Converged Cyber-Physical World', as humans use several computing devices in their everyday life practices. Likewise, Zhuge [27] suggests people live and develop in a 'Cyber-Physical Society', which is a multi-dimensional complex of the cyberspace, the physical space and the social space. Huang et al. [3] suggest mobile devices have a dual character and operate in the physical world as cyber-physical system (CPS) and in a virtualized mobile cloud as cyber-virtual system (CPV).

The development of an integrated view on mobile service that combines techno-logical and usage aspects and emphasizes on real world effects and on value creation requires inevitably to include explicitly the user and his context in the analytical framework. The mobile service should be seen as an embedded part in the life of the user that supports human activities and attains personal objectives. Hence, the mobile device facilitates the provision of mobile service and intermediates and connects the physical world of the user with the virtual world of the electronic systems. In sum, the mobile device can be seen as a cyber-physical system and the mobile service provi-sion as a cyber-physical phenomenon.

This approach can have important implications for value creation in mobile service environments and can provide new research and practical opportunities. For instance, the interconnection of the cyber and the physical worlds enables the observation and measurement of human behavior, which can allow the analysis, modeling and experi-mentation with human behaviors, reveal behavioral patterns and support a dynamic adaptation of service provision [4]. Understanding better the individual and how it uses mobile service in the daily life practices is a key requirement for understanding service value, improving service provision and developing new services and new service models.

Input from the service management literature can help understand better the concept of mobile service. Recent research in service management focuses on the role of the service consumer/user and on the creation and co-creation of value. Service value is created by users in their everyday practices [28], or co-created with the providers [29]. Service providers do not create value, but they only offer service, as a 'value proposition' and as input in the value creating process of the users. Service providers can also support and facilitate the users in their value creating processes.

The mobile technologies have some value potential, but value is created by the user only when the mobile service is used. If it is not used for some reason (e.g. technological restrictions, computing failures, security issues, wrong settings in the mobile devise, ignorance of user for the existence or the usage method of the service, etc.), then it creates no value at all. In addition, the same service will bring different value to different users.

For instance, the value of the mobile cloud services varies for different mobile devices, with different technical features, or for the execution of different tasks that have different computing needs.

Value is created in the context of the user. The notion of the context includes anything that characterizes the situation of the user [30]; key dimensions of the context refer to the time and location. The context is a key characteristic of mobile service and offers plenty opportunities for the development of personalized services and further service innovations [31]. Mobile devices are in most cases strictly individual and, therefore, mobile services can be personalized to each user. Hence, besides contextual, value of mobile service is highly personalized and experiential.

5   A Conceptual Framework for the Provision, Usage and Value Creation in Mobile Services

In this section we present a conceptual framework for the provision and usage of mobile service and the creation and co-creation of value in mobile service. The framework considers mobile service provision as a cyber-physical phenomenon that is enabled by mobile devices and facilitated by mobile cloud technologies and resources. The proposed framework is depicted in Fig. 2.

The *Service Provider* is the business entity that provides Mobile Service. The key activity here is the provision of Mobile Service. Mobile Service can be provided directly by the Service Provider or with the support of Cloud Service, provided by a Cloud Actor. The Service Provider makes a Value Proposition to the User through the offer of the Mobile Service. The Value Proposition describes the potential uses and value of the Mobile Service.

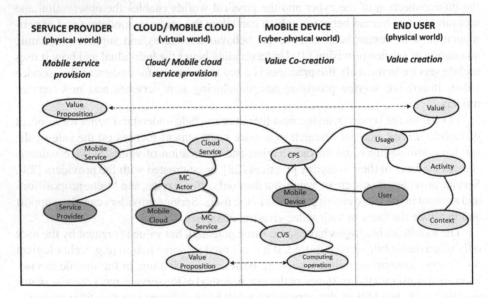

Fig. 2. A conceptual framework for value creation and co-creation in the mobile cloud

The *User* is the human entity that consumes Mobile Service through the use of a Mobile Device. The basic activity of the User is the creation of value. Value is created by the User as an outcome of the meaningful Usage of Mobile Service, which takes place as a part of the daily Activities of the User in the Context of his life.

The *Cloud/Mobile Cloud* refers to the general cloud computing idea and infrastructure. It is a middle layer between the User and the Service Provider and facilitates the provision of Mobile Service to the User. The key activity here is the provision of computing service as Cloud Service and Mobile Cloud Service. Cloud Service supports the provision of Mobile Service by the Service Provider. Mobile Cloud Service supports the virtualization of the operations of the Mobile Device in the Mobile Cloud. The MC Actor is a resource (i.e. network, infrastructure, platform or software) and service provider of Cloud Service or Mobile Cloud (MC) Service. Value Proposition of MC Service refers to the potential use and value of MC Service and it is a key selection criterion for MC Service.

The *Mobile Device* serves as an interface of the User in order to receive Mobile Service and participate in the Mobile Cloud. It is a middle layer that refers to: (a) the interaction of the User with the Service Provider, directly or through the Mobile Cloud, in order to receive Mobile Service (as Cyber-Physical System), and (b) the computing operations of the Mobile Device (as Cyber-Virtual System) in order to interact with other MC Actors and receive or offer MC Service. The key activity is the co-creation of value, as a result of the interaction of the User with the Service Provider and possibly other Users. Value co-creation exists also when Mobile Devices interact with other Devices and MC Actors and they work collaboratively in the mobile cloud.

Mobile Cloud Service is based on the dynamic pooling, sharing and composition of resources and it can be even more interactive and collaborative than Cloud Service. For instance, while in cloud computing the client regularly receives services only, in the mobile cloud the client usually both receives and provides services. In certain cases, such as in mobile crowdsourcing, value is always co-created as a result of the active participation and contribution of a large number of users.

6   Conclusions

Mobile devices, especially smartphones and tablets, are used today more and more to provide a variety of mobile services. In this paper we analyzed the concept of service in mobile environments and distinguished between 'mobile service' on the one hand as an electronic service that is provided through mobile devices and with the use of mobile technologies and possibly cloud computing technologies, and 'mobile cloud service' on the other hand as a computing service for the improved performance of the mobile device through the virtualization of its operations in the mobile cloud. Based on this distinction and on the complementary relationship between mobile service and mobile cloud service, we analyzed mobile service provision as a cyber-physical phenomenon. At the end we developed a conceptual framework for mobile service provision and for the creation and co-creation of value in the mobile cloud.

This paper integrates concepts from mobile cloud computing and service management and provides a user-driven and usage-oriented perspective for mobile service that explains mobile service provision, value creation and value co-creation. The paper integrates the human-related aspects for the use of service and the creation of value with the computing operations for the provision of the mobile service. Certain concepts of the service management literature, especially for the creation and co-creation of value, are relevant in mobile cloud computing.

The conceptual framework provides some key concepts for the analysis and the better understanding of the usage of mobile service by the user. Understanding better the service user and how he creates value in his context and in his daily life practices, in which mobile service is naturally embedded, is a key requirement for the creation of service value, for service improvement and for the development of new services and new service models.

Future research can develop further and refine the proposed conceptual framework, as well as explore its practical implications. For instance, it can be used for the analysis of use and the identification of use patterns of mobile services (e.g. who uses them, when, where, with what application and technologies, with what resources, with whom else, for what reason, etc.). Such use patterns can be useful for the service improvement and the development of new service. In addition, use patterns can be used for the assessment of the mobile service models in terms of the technological restrictions and limitations in the use of mobile cloud services, the functional requirements and the motivation of the users to receive mobile cloud services and share their resources in the mobile cloud.

References

1. Smura, T., Kivi, A., Töyli, J.: A framework for analyzing the usage of mobile services. Info **11**(4), 53–67 (2009)
2. Fernando, N., Loke, S.W., Rahayu, W.: Mobile cloud computing: a survey. Future Gener. Comput. Syst. **29**(1), 84–106 (2013)
3. Huang, D., Xing, T., Wu, H.: Mobile cloud computing service models: a user-centric approach. IEEE Netw **27**(5), 6–11 (2013)
4. Conti, M., Das, S.K., Bisdikian, C., Kumar, M., Ni, L.M., Passarella, A., Zambonelli, F.: Looking ahead in pervasive computing: challenges and opportunities in the era of cyber–physical convergence. Pervasive Mob. Comput. **8**(1), 2–21 (2012)
5. Rahimi, M.R., Ren, J., Liu, C.H., Vasilakos, A.V., Venkatasubramanian, N.: Mobile cloud computing: a survey, state of art and future directions. Mob. Netw. Appl. **19**(2), 133–143 (2014)
6. Leimeister, S., Riedl, C., Böhm, M., Krcmar, H.: The business perspective of cloud computing: actors, roles, and value networks. In: 18th European Conference on Information Systems (ECIS), Pretoria, South Africa (2010)
7. Heinonen, K., Pura, M.: Classifying mobile services. In: Proceedings of Helsinki Mobility Roundtable. Sprouts: Working Papers on Information Systems, vol. 6, no. 42 (2006). http://sprouts.aisnet.org/6-42
8. Rowley, J.: An analysis of the e-service literature: towards a research agenda. Internet Res. **16**(3), 339–359 (2006)
9. Baldauf, M., Dustdar, S., Rosenberg, F.: A survey on context-aware systems. Int. J. Ad Hoc Ubiquit. Comput. **2**(4), 263–277 (2007)
10. Verkasalo, H.: Contextual patterns in mobile service usage. Pervasive Ubiquit. Comput. **13**(5), 331–342 (2009)

11. Satyanarayanan, M.: Mobile computing: the next decade. ACM SIGMOBILE/Mob. Comput. Commun. Rev. **15**(2), 2–10 (2011)
12. Yang, L., Cao, J., Yuan, Y., Li, T., Han, A., Chan, A.: A framework for partitioning and execution of data stream applications in mobile cloud computing. ACM SIGMETRICS/ Perform. Eval. Rev. **40**(4), 23–32 (2013)
13. Dinh, H.T., Lee, C., Niyato, D., Wang, P.: A survey of mobile cloud computing: architecture, applications, and approaches. Wirel. Commun. Mob. Comput. **13**(18), 1587–1611 (2013)
14. Youseff, L., Butrico, M., da Silva, D.: Toward a unified ontology of cloud computing. In: Proceedings of the Grid Computing Environments Workshop, Austin, Texas, USA, November, pp. 1–10 (2008)
15. Mell, P., Grance, T.: The NIST definition of cloud computing (2011)
16. Qi, H., Gani, A.: Research on mobile cloud computing: review, trend and perspectives. In: Second International Conference on Digital Information and Communication Technology and it's Applications, pp. 195–202 (2012)
17. O'Sullivan, M.J., Grigoras, D.: User experience of mobile cloud applications-current state and future directions. In: IEEE 12th International Symposium on Parallel and Distributed Computing (ISPDC), pp. 85–92 (2013)
18. Lin, C.Y., Hung, M.T.: A location-based personal task reminder for mobile users. Pers. Ubiquit. Comput. **18**(2), 303–314 (2014)
19. Dihal, S., Bouwman, H., de Reuver, M., Warnier, M., Carlsson, C.: Mobile cloud computing: state of the art and outlook. Info **15**(1), 4–16 (2013)
20. Huerta-Canepa, G., Lee, D.: A virtual cloud computing provider for mobile devices. In: Proceedings of the 1st ACM Workshop on Mobile Cloud Computing and Services: Social Networks and Beyond (2010)
21. Baida, Z., Gordijn, J., Omelayenko, B.: A shared service terminology for online service provisioning. In: Proceedings of the 6th International Conference on Electronic commerce, pp. 1–10 (2004)
22. Cardoso, J., Voigt, K., Winkler, M.: Service engineering for the internet of services. In: Filipe, J., Cordeiro, J. (eds.) Enterprise Information Systems. LNBIP, vol. 19, pp. 15–27. Springer, Heidelberg (2009)
23. Liu, F., Shu, P., Jin, H., Ding, L., Yu, J., Niu, D., Li, B.: Gearing resource-poor mobile devices with powerful clouds: architectures, challenges, and applications. IEEE Wirel. Commun. **20**(3), 14–22 (2013)
24. Wang, Y., Chen, R., Wang, D.C.: A survey of mobile cloud computing applications: perspectives and challenges. Wirel. Pers. Commun. 1–17 (2014)
25. Wan, J., Liu, Z., Zhou, K., Lu, R.: Mobile cloud computing: application scenarios and service models. In: 9th IEEE International Wireless Communications and Mobile Computing Conference, pp. 644–648 (2013)
26. Simmon, E., Kim, K.S,, Subrahmanian, E., Lee, R., de Vaulx, F., Murakami, Y., Zettsu, K., Sriram, R.D.: A vision of cyber-physical cloud computing for smart networked systems. NIST (2013)
27. Zhuge, H.: Cyber-physical society—the science and engineering for future society. Future Gener. Comput. Syst. **32**, 180–186 (2014)
28. Grönroos, C., Voima, P.: Critical service logic: making sense of value creation and co-creation. J. Acad. Mark. Sci. **41**(2), 133–150 (2013)
29. Vargo, S.L., Lusch, R.F.: Service-dominant logic: continuing the evolution. J. Acad. Mark. Sci. **36**(1), 1–10 (2008)

30. Abowd, G.D., Dey, A.K.: Towards a better understanding of context and context-awareness. In: Gellersen, H.-W. (ed.) HUC 1999. LNCS, vol. 1707, pp. 304–307. Springer, Heidelberg (1999)

31. De Reuver, M., Haaker, T.: Designing viable business models for context-aware mobile services. Telematics Inform. 26(3), 240–248 (2009)

Supporting Collaborative Innovation Networks for New Concept Development Through Web Mashups

Luís C.S. Barradas[1(✉)], Eduarda Mendes Rodrigues[2], and João J. Pinto-Ferreira[3]

[1] DIMQ, Escola Superior de Gestão e Tecnologia, Instituto Politécnico de Santarém,
Complexo Andaluz, Apartado 295, 2001-904 Santarém, Portugal
claudio.barradas@esg.ipsantarem.pt

[2] DEI, Faculdade de Engenharia, Universidade do Porto, Rua Roberto Frias, s/n,
4200-465 Porto, Portugal
eduardamr@acm.org

[3] DEIG, Faculdade de Engenharia, Universidade do Porto, Rua Roberto Frias, s/n,
4200-465 Porto, Portugal
jjpf@fe.up.pt

Abstract. The new concept development is a critical stage of the innovation process that can be seen as a new knowledge creation process. This paper presents a new approach and a software tool for a collaborative new concept development. Our approach considers Collaborative Innovation Networks as ecosystems for new knowledge creation and integration, and Web Mashups as supporting platforms for the development of virtual co-learning and knowledge co-creation environments. The achieved results confirm the utility and efficacy of the software tool and allow foreseeing its suitability for use in educational contexts.

Keywords: Collaborative innovation networks · Learning · Web mashups

1 Introduction

Innovation plays a central role within businesses because it is seen as a way of sustainable competitive advantage creation. Initially rooted in R&D and based only on organizations' internal knowledge, the innovation models have evolved to the current open and networked models. Today, the locus of innovation is no longer the individual or the organization, but, increasingly, the network where the firm is embedded [1]. External socio-economic agents such as clients and users of products and services are significant sources of knowledge, especially in the Front End of Innovation (FEI). User communities are an important locus of innovation and can increase the productivity in the development, test, and diffusion of innovations. Information Technologies (IT) and the Web 2.0 have come promote and facilitate the creation of innovation communities. *User Innovation Networks*, *Peer Production*, *Community-Driven Innovation* or *Crowdsourcing*, are terms often used to describe the innovation by virtual user communities. Table 1 presents a summary of IT tools that operationalize the mechanisms [2] typically used to acquire user's knowledge for innovation. On the one hand, current approaches are not entirely effective because

© IFIP International Federation for Information Processing 2015
L.M. Camarinha-Matos et al. (Eds.): PRO-VE 2015, IFIP AICT 463, pp. 357–365, 2015.
DOI: 10.1007/978-3-319-24141-8_32

they limit user participation to idea generation and design of simple products. On the other hand, the supporting IT tools may not also be totally efficient in knowledge structuration and systematization, two key requirements for easy knowledge transfer [3, 4]. Moreover, these tools are not entirely effective in the exploration of the tacit knowledge latent in people's mind. The linear text format typically used to express ideas makes difficult the establishment of connections between ideas.

Table 1. User innovations promotion mechanisms in the front end of innovation

Mechanisms	Operationalization	Studies
Idea contests (Ideagoras, Ideariums, Ideatubes)	Knowledge brokers applications	[5]
	Social media platforms; SNS platforms	[6, 7]
Product related discussion forums	Discussion forums	[2]
Communities of creation	Social media platforms; SNS platforms	[2, 4]

In the contemporary context, the integration of external and internal knowledge to organizations through collaborative approaches is a critical factor for successful innovation. Thus, a collaborative model that integrates clients, innovative users and partners in the development of new concepts can increase the chances of creating products or services commercially attractive. Notwithstanding, the integration, absorption and application of this external knowledge require mastering a set of dynamic capabilities where the absorptive capacity (learn, integrate and apply the acquired knowledge) plays a central role. Firms with a higher absorptive capacity show a strong capacity of learning with their partners.

This paper is structured as follows. Section 2 presents some background concepts. Section 3 presents our approach and a software tool for a collaborative new concept development. Section 4 presents tests and results. Finally, Sect. 5 presents the conclusions.

2   Collaborative Innovation Networks, Knowledge Dynamics, and Web Mashups: Background Concepts

2.1   Collaborative Innovation Networks

A Collaborative Innovation Network (COIN) [8] is a social construct that is used to describe innovative teams or groups. COINs are powered by *swarm creativity* - their structural mechanism - and are defined as auto-organized cyber teams of auto-motivated people that share a common vision and use the Web to collaborate, sharing ideas, information and work, aiming to create something new. The underlying concept builds on the premise that, the creative production that results from the open share of ideas and work within a group, is exponential greater than the sum of individual creative production of each element of the group [8, 9]. In fact, the underlying premise is tightly related to the foundations of the Collective Intelligence (CI) concept. COINs are the core of a knowledge ecosystem that encompasses some other virtual collaborative communities (learning and information), through which the generated knowledge flows until reaches the virtual world. They can emerge spontaneously outside or within firms. Internal COINs can cross firm's boundaries and include external members and even other firm's members. Thus, a COIN can be considered, in a natural way, a productive innovation ecosystem powered by CI that leverages and integrates external and internal knowledge to firms. Under this view, COINs can work as enablers or facilitators of the absorptive capability in organizations.

2.2 Knowledge Dynamics and Learning

In knowledge management (KM) related literature [10, 11], knowledge is commonly classified along two dimensions [12]: *tacit knowledge* (TK) and *explicit knowledge* (EK). TK is personal, context-specific, composed by intuitions, mental models unarticulated or technical competencies. EK is articulated, codified and can be transmitted in natural or symbolic language and computationally processed [11].

Knowledge creation is a complex social process that involves the acquisition, replacement and reconfiguration of existing knowledge structures in entities (individuals, groups or organizations). The SECI model [11] explicitly addresses the social nature of knowledge creation dynamics and comprises two dimensions: (1) *epistemological*, which describes TK to EK conversion and vice versa; (2) *ontological*, which describes knowledge transformation and flow between individuals groups and organizations. Thus, knowledge creation is a spiral process that builds on four stages of knowledge conversion (TK → EK; EK → TK): Socialization; Externalization; Combination and Internalization. Socialization is a social process and consists of sharing TK through communication. Externalization is an individual process and refers to the expression and translation of TK into tangible media such as text, concepts or models (EK). Combination is a social process and consists in the conversion of EK into more complex sets of EK by means of sorting, combining, adding and categorizing. At last, Internalization is an individual process that involves the conversion of newly created knowledge (EK) into TK through reasoning and reflection, *i.e.*, learning. This process is iterative and takes place in a shared place known as *ba* that defines the context in which knowledge is created.

Individual learning occurs in the Internalization stage. Group learning occurs in the Socialization stage. Once internalized, the explicit knowledge becomes part of the individual's knowledge base and becomes an asset for the organization.

2.3 Web Mashups as Learning and Knowledge Management Supporting Tools

The openness and participatory nature of Web 2.0 changed the way that people use the Web allowing peer production, sharing and collaboration harnessing CI. Users, prior content consumers become content producers. Rapidly, the web became a huge repository of information and knowledge (opinions, know-how, etc.) in the form of knowledge artifacts. An intrinsic feature of Web 2.0 applications is the openness of their APIs, which

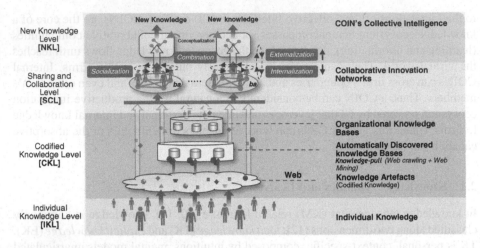

Fig. 1. A conceptual framework for harnessing the collective intelligence in COINS

allows the development new applications based on those exposed interfaces. These are known as Web Mashups – composite Web applications that allow extend original functionalities or the combination of data from different sources into a new presentation, giving rise to new sets of data, information and knowledge representations. Web Mashups have been exploited in support of Web-based learning and KM. As supporting platforms for learning contexts, Web Mashups are capable to integrate and enable the learning functions that the learning process depends on [13]. In the scope of education, several studies [14] showed the benefits of Web Mashups for the construction of Personal Learning Environments. In the scope of KM, the literature shows practices of analysis [15] and attempts of use of Web mashups in the development of KM tools [16]. These platforms provide a solid support for personal KM and informal learning [15, 16].

3   Supporting Collaborative Innovation Networks for New Concept Development Trough Web Mashups

Supported by the concepts presented in the previous section, we derived a conceptual framework (Fig. 1) for the development of new concepts in FEI, harnessing CI of COINs. The framework assumes the new concept development process as a new knowledge creation process [17] and the Web as a vast repository of individual knowledge representations in the form of knowledge artifacts.

Around a seminal idea about a new concept of a product or service, a group need or a market need, a COIN can emerge. Its members can join in a virtual shared space (*ba*) and start to collaborate by sharing ideas, know-how, experiences and opinions (Socialization) around a shared vision that is mapped into a plan (NKL) and codified as a shared conceptual structure (Externalization). The externalized knowledge can be combined or supported by/with knowledge embedded in knowledge artefacts distributed and available on the Web (videos, images, Web pages, RSS feeds, etc.) or located in organizational knowledge bases (design schematics, models, product's data, etc.). Web knowledge artefacts can be manually or automatically selected and aggregated and then manually combined and recombined (mashup) giving origin to new and more complex knowledge artifacts (Combination). The analysis and reflection on the conceptual structure collaboratively created, promote knowledge endogenization (Internalization), *i.e.*, learning. The process is iterative and stops when a common understanding about the new concept is reached, which can be translated as new knowledge that results from the CI of COIN members. This new knowledge can, in fact, promote the organizational learning once it may help improving organization's technology, processes and structure and consequently, acquire market competitive advantage.

3.1 A Web-Based Software Tool for New Concept Development

The conceptual framework provided a base for the development of a collaborative Web-based software tool aiming to support COIN's activities in the new concept development in the FEI. The tool builds on a set of ontology-based knowledge management services [18] that provide an effective management of COINs' activities and resources. The system relies on a multi-layer modular architecture (Fig. 2) in which three major modules stand out: (1) *Collaboration Module*; (2) *User Mashup Builder Module*; (3) *Mashup Middleware*. The Collaboration Module operationalizes a virtual collaboration space (*ba*) providing users with communication tools, real-time collaboration and a shared whiteboard used for the co-construction of the shared conceptualization which is shaped by an extended concept map, where the shared concepts can be supported by Web Mashups. The User Mashup Builder Module provides functionalities for setting up searches and combination of results into a single and new representation – a mashup. Finally, the Mashup Middleware provides an interface layer for fetching and pre-processing data.

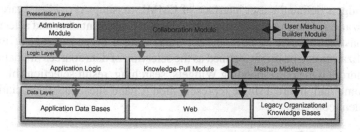

Fig. 2. Simplified high-level architecture of the software tool

3.2 The Mashups Development Process

The mashup development process is performed in two levels (Fig. 3). The first level (low level) is supported and operationalized by the Mashup Middleware which

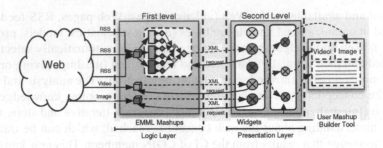

Fig. 3. Mashup development process

establishes an interface between data sources and data presentation by providing data access and data pre-processing. Data pre-processing can be simple consisting of data cleaning and filtering followed by data structuring in a normalized format; or it can be far complex involving data acquisition from different sources, data cleaning, data filtering, data integration/combination through *union*, *join* or *sort* operations and subsequent data structuring in a normalized format. This subsystem is supported by an open mashup platform known as *Enterprise Mashup Platform* that allows describing low-level mashups in EMML (Enterprise Mashup Markup Language), an XML dialect. The module provides multiple data access methods (REST, WS, JDBC, and POJO), supports multiple data formats (XML, JSON e Java Objects) and several data processing methods (EMML flow control structures, XPath, and JavaScript). EMML mashups are hard-coded and developed by software developers.

The second level (high level) is operationalized by the User Mashup Builder Module. This module builds on three components (Fig. 4): (1) *Resources Library* [a], which provides access and represents the EMML mashups available on the Mashup Middleware; (2) *Mashup Dashboard* [b], which hosts the mashup widgets selected in the Resource Library; (3) Composer [c], which allow the composition and combination of widgets selected resources into a single representation.

The Widgets define the user interface of EMML mashups providing search queries parameterization (filtering and sorting criteria), results presentation and selection.

The construction of user mashups for supporting a given concept of the shared conceptualization can be briefly defined as the selection of data sources [a], data source's modeling through the corresponding Widgets, searching, result selection [b], composition and combination into a single representation [c] and subsequent association to the correspondent concept.

4   Testing and Results

Two tests were conducted aiming to verify the utility, quality and efficacy of the software tool. The first test was performed in the form a real-time collaborative session, involving persons geographically dispersed (Portugal and Brazil). The main objective was to verify the system stability in the collaborative construction of a shared conceptualization. The second test was performed within a real business environment and had as a goal the

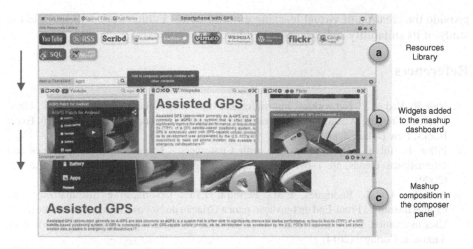

Fig. 4. The user interface of the *User Mashup Builder Module*.

collaborative development of a solution to an existent identified problem. Data was collected by semi-structured interviews with the members of the involved teams. Data analysis was done by qualitative methods using the dimensions and measures for information systems evaluation proposed in [19].

The tool revealed to be efficient in supporting the problems in both contexts. Especially on the second test, the software tool was able to bridge an existing gap related with the process of idea enrichment/maturing. Beyond this, the involved participants identified several positive aspects that can be classified into two levels: *individual* and *organizational*. In the individual level, the promotion of the individual learning and networking were pointed out as two value-added features. The richness, comprehensibility, format and accuracy of information were the factors identified as enablers for an easy learning and knowledge transfer. In the organizational level, the results achieved (in the second test) produced a positive impact on the environment which can be translated as an improvement in business process and subsequent cost reduction.

5   Conclusions

This paper presented a new approach that relies on Web Mashups as supporting tools for the process of new concept development in the FEI. The results obtained in both performed tests showed a positive impact on learning and new knowledge creation processes. COINs are very productive knowledge creation ecosystems and may integrate internal and external persons to organizations. By fostering and nurturing these networks through a collaborative platform of this nature, one can promote new knowledge creation by integrating external and internal knowledge to organizations, facilitating thus the absorptive capacity and consequently, the innovation.

The contributions of this work are tightly related to learning and knowledge creation through reflection. The developed software tool revealed the ability to

364   L.C.S. Barradas et al.

provide the creation of virtual learning environments. Future work will include the study of its suitability and extension to educational contexts.

References

1. Nair, R., Vedak, V.: Networking, Innovation and Innovative Culture. In: Muncherji, N., Dhar, U. (eds.) Creating Wealth Through Strategic HR and Entrepreneurship, pp. 405–416. Excel Books, New Delhi (2009)
2. Piller, F., Ihl, C.: Open Innovation with Customers - Foundations, Competences and International Trends, pp. 1–69. Technology and Innovation Management Group, Aachen (2009)
3. Barradas, L.C.S., Rodrigues, E.M., Ferreira, J.J.P.: Co-criação e Sistematização de Conhecimento no Front-End de Inovação para a Criação de Novos Conceitos, no contexto da User Innovation. In: 14ª Conferência da Associação Portuguesa de Sistemas de Informação, Santarém, Portugal (2014)
4. Standing, C., Kiniti, S.: How can organizations use wikis for innovation? Technovation **31**, 287–295 (2011)
5. Sousa, M.C.: Open Innovation Models and the Role of Knowledge Brokers. Inside Knowledge. Wilmington Publishing & Information, London (2008)
6. Friedrich, P.: Web-based co-design - social media tools to enhance user-centred design and innovation processes, p. 306. Ph.D. School of Science, Aalto University School of Science, Espoo (2013)
7. Duin, H., Jaskov, J., Hesmer, A., Thoben, K.-D.: Towards a framework for collaborative innovation. In: Cascini, G. (ed.) CAI. IFIP, vol. 277, pp. 193–204. Springer, Heidelberg (2008)
8. Gloor, P.A.: Swarm Creativity: Competitive Advantage Through Collaborative Innovation Networks. Oxford University Press, New York (2006)
9. Gloor, P.A., Cooper, S.M.: The Coming World of Swarm Creativity. In: Gloor, P.A., Cooper, S.M. (eds.) Coolhunting: Chasing Down the Next Big Thing. AMACOM, New York (2007)
10. von Krogh, G., Ichijo, K., Nonaka, K.: Enabling Knowledge Creation: How to Unlock the Mystery of Tacit Knowledge and Release the Power of Innovation. Oxford University Press, New York (2000)
11. Nonaka, I., Konno, N.: The concept of 'Ba': building a foundation for knowledge creation. Calif. Manage. Rev. **40**, 40–54 (1998)
12. Polanyi, M.: The Tacit Dimension. Anchor Books, Garden City (1967)
13. Boss, S., Krauss, J.: Power of the mashup - combining essential learning with new technology tools. Learn. Lead. Technol. **35**, 12–17 (2007)
14. Drachsler, H., Pecceu, D., Arts, T., Hutten, E., Rutledge, L., van Rosmalen, P., Hummel, H., Koper, R.: ReMashed – recommendations for mash-up personal learning environments. In: Cress, U., Dimitrova, V., Specht, M. (eds.) EC-TEL 2009. LNCS, vol. 5794, pp. 788–793. Springer, Heidelberg (2009)
15. Weber, S., Thomas, L., Ras, E.: Investigating the suitability of mashups for informal learning and personal knowledge management. In: Workshop on Mashup Personal Learning Environments (MUPPLE 2008), Maastricht, Netherlands (2008)
16. Bitzer, S., Ramroth, S., Schumann, M.: Mashups as an architecture for knowledge management systems. In: 42nd IEEE Hawaii International Conference on System Sciences, Hawaii (2009)

17. Barradas, L.C.S., Ferreira, J.J.P.: Mashup enabled dynamic capabilities in the fuzzy front-end of innovation. In: Quintela Varajão, J.E., Cruz-Cunha, M.M., Putnik, G.D., Trigo, A. (eds.) CENTERIS 2010. CCIS, vol. 110, pp. 228–237. Springer, Heidelberg (2010)
18. Barradas, L.C.S., Rodrigues, E.M., Ferreira, J.J.P.: Deriving an ontology for knowledge management in collaborative innovation networks. Int. J. Innov. Learn. (in press)
19. Steinhuser, M., Smolnik, S., Hoppe, U.: Towards a measurement model of corporate social software success-evidences from an exploratory multiple case study. In: 44th International Conference on System Sciences (HICSS 2011), pp. 1–10. IEEE, Hawaii (2011)

A Flexible Collaborative Innovation Model for SOA Services Providers

João F. Santanna-Filho, Ricardo J. Rabelo[(⊠)],
and Alexandra A. Pereira-Klen

Department of Automation and Systems Engineering,
Federal University of Santa Catarina, Florianópolis, SC, Brazil
joao.santanna@posgrad.ufsc.br,
ricardo.rabelo@ufsc.br, xandaklen@gmail.com

Abstract. Software sector plays a very relevant role in current world economy. One of its characteristics is that they are mostly composed of SMEs. SMEs have been pushed to invest in innovation to keep competitive. Service Oriented Architecture (SOA) is a recent and powerful ICT paradigm for more sustainable business models. A SOA product has many differences when compared to manufacturing sector. Besides that, SOA projects are however very complex, costly and risky. This can be mitigated if SMEs can innovate together. This paper presents an innovation model to assist groups of disparate SMEs to work together towards providing a SOA-based software product. The model is flexible and adaptive to every innovation project. Final considerations about the work are presented at the end.

Keywords: Collaborative innovation · Software services · SOA

1 Introduction

Software sector plays a very relevant role in current world economy as a means to face several of societal challenges [1]. However, being typically constituted by SMEs (Small and Medium sized Enterprises), most of them use to have many problems to be sustainable in the increasing competitive, globalized and innovation-driven market [2].

In the software sector, SOA has introduced a new outlook on system design, implementation and integration, and has been increasingly adopted (as services-based applications) by software developers and customers in general [3]. In SOA, all system's features are regarded as independent and self-contained software modules – called software services or just services – that jointly form a virtual single logical unit to create products and processes [4].

However, SOA projects are complex, risky and costly, and its adoption impacts both customers and providers at many techno and non-techno dimensions [3].

Software innovation is a key factor to increase SMEs competitiveness nowadays [5]. This paper exploits the premise that SOA providers SMEs can mitigate the mentioned barriers if they innovate together, collaboratively, towards developing a SOA-based solution/"product", although mostly in the form of prototypes. This has the potential to endow them to develop novel software solutions or gathering existing

© IFIP International Federation for Information Processing 2015
L.M. Camarinha-Matos et al. (Eds.): PRO-VE 2015, IFIP AICT 463, pp. 366–376, 2015.
DOI: 10.1007/978-3-319-24141-8_33

services and solutions from other companies to more effectively and flexibly attend to new and larger demands and wider markets. Such SMEs are here seen as software services providers (SSP), i.e. independent organization that owns and provides software services' implementations and descriptions as well as the respective technical and business support throughout a given SOA solution's life cycle [4, 6].

In a previous work, authors have proposed an innovation model for SOA providers [7]. However, after further evaluations by some IT companies, it was realized that it could not support at all the required flexibility in the development path as each SOA product, as an innovation project, is unique and there is not a single model to follow.

A sort of innovation models has been presented in the literature. However, it was not found out anyone devoted to SOA/software sector and that consider software services' providers as autonomous SMEs that can participate in all phases of the innovation process, flexibly, collaboratively, as a network. This is also important as a SOA/software "product" is different than manufacturing, in terms of e.g. development stages and methodologies, supporting constructs, physical deployment, SLA treatment, software/services quality, and product contracting, access and usage [6]. This paper presents a newer model so as to cope with these requirements.

This work has been conducted as an essentially action-research, qualitative, deductive and applied research, strongly grounded on literature revision.

The paper is organized as follows. Section 1 has introduced the problem and research goals. Section 2 presents a brief review of the main basic foundations used in the proposed model. Section 3 presents an analysis of related works. Section 4 presents the proposed innovation model. Section 5 presents some results of a preliminary assessment of the model. Finally, Sect. 6 presents final consideration about the research done so far and next steps.

2 Basic Concepts

Innovation Models. Literature presents several definitions of innovation. In this work we have considered it as "the implementation of a new or significantly improved product (good or service), or process, a new marketing method, or a new organizational method in business practices, workplace organization or external relations" [8].

An innovation model can be defined as the general conceptual construct that helps organizations to set up the innovation framework, to develop the innovation itself and to manage its progress and results (adapted from [9]). In general, it basically describes the main phases and processes necessary to carry out an innovation throughout (and typically via) a so-called funnel. These processes often comprise: generation and ideas selection; concept development; concept evaluation/selection; concept design and specification; implementation; and exploitation (adapted from [10]).

Innovation models have evolved from linear to open and network models, and can go back and forth through each stage. Evaluation actions (through gates) are normally added between each stage in way to restrict process' continuation. Processes can be executed sequentially or in parallel. Different types of actors can be involved along the innovation process with variable roles, being intra-organizational members or external partners, like ad-hoc business partners, supporting institutions and customers [11].

Regarding this paper's goal, two innovation models are relevant. *Open innovation* model is based on a more ample collaborative environment where ideas both from the company and third parties are taken into account in some parts of the innovation process to add value to what has been conceived [12]. The *Network* model considers an environment that is composed of a set of complementary and independent organizations that work on a given innovative idea regarding their core expertize [13].

Collaborative Networks (CN). CN has arisen as a prominent paradigm to underpin strategic alliances that are focused on a more intense and fluid collaboration among autonomous organizations. Its vision relies on allowing organizations to keep focused on their skills and aggregating competencies and sharing resources with other organizations in order to meet businesses in a better way [14]. In order to support a higher agility in the formation of an innovation network, the concepts of two types of CN are used. A Virtual Organization (VO) can be characterized as a temporary alliance formed by autonomous and heterogeneous organizations that join their complementary core-competences and resources to better attend to a given demand, dismantling itself after all its legal obligations have been accomplished. VOs are originated from long-term alliances, the Virtual organization Breeding Environment (VBE). A VBE can be defined as a long-term association of organizations (companies, etc.) which have the willingness, enough preparedness and trust, and that share common principles to collaborate. It is assumed in this work that SSPs are members of a VBE-like alliance.

A collaborative innovation network is defined as "*a long-term or temporary cluster of disparate and autonomous organizations with the willingness to collaborate towards exploiting together an individual or collective business vision by sharing ideas, knowledge, work, computing and services assets, as well as costs, risks and benefits, supported by ICT, and grounded on trust, preparedness, governance and IPR*" [15].

Service Oriented Architecture (SOA). A SOA "product" typically comprises services of several natures, like business services, infrastructure, security, interoperability, orchestration, wrapped legacy systems' functionalities, etc., deployed and provided under different models [4]. Web services are one of the most currently implementing technologies in SOA [4].

Likewise traditional software engineering methodologies, SOA also has a lifecycle, covering a number of developing phases [4], spanning from the analysis to delivery and management. However, these phases have to be dealt with in a different way as: (i) the final result of a development process within an innovation initiative is usually a prototype, proof of concepts, etc., and where some existing software/services from SSPs can also be reused for the given purpose; i.e. it is a not a bundled product; (ii) likewise typical SOA development processes, collaborative innovation involves disparate SSPs, having different practices, working cultures and sometimes non-common objectives in terms of exploitation plans, (iii) SOA is not a mere technological paradigm. Instead, it is an approach to help companies to better achieve its strategic goals. The model should provide means to bring the business perspective into the software innovation process; (iv) besides supporting the provision of the services themselves, a SOA solution should look after its life cycle as a product as well as the general non-software services required to support its life cycle (e.g. local integration, ESB configuration, training, maintenance, etc.), i.e. the set of respective business models. In other words, SOA deeply involves management too, at several levels [16].

3 State of the Art Review

A literature review was carried out mainly via the SLR methodology, looking for articles that essentially tackled SOA, innovation, SMEs and networks. The search also comprised the *CORDIS* EU's research projects database. None works were found out that covered that at all. However, five papers and seven projects presented some similarities and have provided some useful insights for the proposed innovation model.

In terms of papers, in a resumed way: in [10] an innovation model for manufacturing products and related services have been devised, identifying the most important innovation processes, but without considering *software* services and a high dynamics in the network formation. In [18] a supporting language to express the value delivery and services chain for the general area of services was proposed. In [19] authors stressed the obstacles for SMEs to collaborate towards jointly handling e-business transactions. In [20] authors proposed a framework and typology to understand the services innovation (but not of software) as a wider and multidimensional evolutionary process. In [21] a model-driven collaborative development platform for SOA-based e-business systems was proposed, but without considering innovation processes and networks of companies.

In terms of EU funded projects [22], *BIVEE, ComVantage, IMAGINE, CoVES, Laboranova, PLENT and GloNet* have tackled innovation at different perspectives and levels, but devoted to the manufacturing and general services sectors. Some of them consider open innovation, some don't. *GloNet* is the only one that has specifically applied the network innovation model using the virtual organization concept. None of these projects are devoted to software innovation or SOA areas though.

4 Proposed Innovation Model

The innovation process can be triggered on customer request or prospectively (by one or more partners) with the aim to attend foreseen new businesses or to improve a previous SOA products. Innovation outcomes can evolve and be exploited according to what was set up in the governance model. Cycles of developments, prototyping, etc. can be necessary until a result can be considered as ready for representing the initially envisaged SOA product. During the development partners can reuse their existing software services assets and also share them with other members [23].

A set of premises are adopted to frame the envisaged innovation scenario: selected members may participate along the entire innovation process and associated software development cycle; this participation, stage of that, and decision power should respect the respective VO governance model; companies can/should enter to, operate in, and exit from the collaborative innovation network in different moments and number of times, both in the normal operation of the network and when problems, changes or severe conflicts take place; the innovation process involves creativity and some unpredictability [24]. These premises were adapted to the envisaged collaborative innovation, flexible, and SME- and SOA-oriented scenario.

In order to cope with the desired flexibility, we brought inspiration from the *Design Thinking* method [25] and of its three innovation "spaces" (*immersion, idealization and prototyping*) and innovation stages. This was complemented and adapted (including processes' terminology) with the six classical processes suggested in [11] regarding the specificities of the envisaged scenario. Besides considering the SOA development requirements along the whole innovation processes and spaces, one of the processes is devoted to software development itself. For that, we have adopted and adapted the processes proposed in [4, 16]. Governance issues were regarded mainly considering the works of [17, 26, 27]. Regarding the intrinsic nature of software development process, there is no simple progression, being often necessary to go back to earlier stages in order to overcome problems and need for revisions, in non-linear cycles. In other words, each innovation is treated as a unique initiative with no predefined paths.

The collaboration within a VO is carried out along four phases/life cycle: Creation (starting phase, when it is created, partners are selected and the network is configured for the business); Operation (when the VO effectively runs, executing and managing the required activities and partners towards reaching its goals); Evolution (performed when problems take place during the Operation phase and that can hazard the VO success); and Dissolution (ending phase, where the VO finishes its activities) [14].

4.1 The Innovation Model

The proposed innovation model is to support the development of the SOA product, from the initial ideas exchange to its final delivery/deployment (Fig. 1). There are three spaces through which all the actions are carried out.

The execution path within each space is flexible, i.e. each innovation initiative has particular requirements that determine its flow. Because of that, each process is seen as a kind of decoupled building block, which is linked with others to define the given innovation's path and the set of activities that have to be executed. This also means that a given space (and so some of its processes) can be revisited in cycles, or that some of the processes may not be performed. The whole team of companies, also considering the governance model associated to the given innovation initiative, is the responsible to set up the path on-the-fly and to make the necessary changes when needed. That is why there are no arrows in the model as the flow, cycles and sequence can vary from project to project. Briefly, the spaces and processes are as follows, and they have *not* to be understood as sequential steps.

First space: *Ideas development space*

- *Idea Analysis*: one or more companies from the VBE-like alliance can propose a joint innovation to the alliance's committee (or a kind of board *if* any), which will firstly evaluate the idea's potential. At this moment the idea is just generally presented.

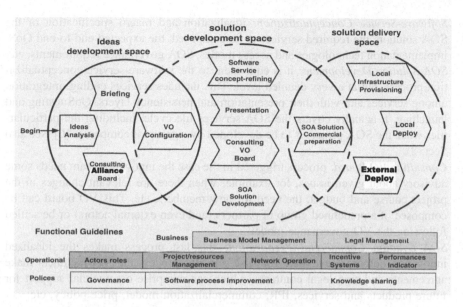

Fig. 1. The proposed innovation model. Source: authors.

- *Briefing:* the idea is detailed presented, describing the necessary technologies, potential partnerships, estimated ROI, foreseen market, etc.
- *Consulting Alliance Board:* process triggered in the case the innovation team needs some advisory about given issues. Although it can depend on how the governance model had been set up when the alliance was founded, the board usually does not have the power to cancel an initiative. It is usually formed by some selected members and can also involve external actors. The main goal here is to try to anticipate problems or to identify major issues and possible solutions before keeping going on.
- *VO Configuration:* formation of the VO that will develop the innovation. It usually includes subprocesses, like partners' search and selection, negotiations of several matters, the VO governance model setting up, the agreement on revenue mode, and IPR contracts signature. VO members may have different decision powers and internal top level committees can be created. This can also comprise the definition of performance indicators and metrics upon partners and the innovation process itself.

Second space: *Solution development space*

- *Presentation:* a more complete project plan and ICT technological analysis are conceived and the initially devised business model (if any) is refined. This is done by the involved companies' managers and can also be helped by some external expert actors, depending on the VO governance model specification. This process also includes discussions on issues like IPR and ownership, technology transfer, accounting, and knowledge gaps in the VO and in the alliance.

- *Software-Service Conceptualization:* idealization and macro specification of the SOA solution, the required services to be composed, the expected end-to-end QoS, implementation technologies and access modes, SOA governance requirements, etc.
- *SOA Solution Development:* it is equivalent to the software-service conceptualization process, but at a very detailed level. This includes services coding, integration among services and with their presentation and persistency layers, QoS testing and launching. It actually covers the SOA/services life cycle, including the particularities when the SOA project is to be developed by a group of companies [6] (see also Sect. 2).
- *Consulting VO Board:* process triggered in the case the innovation team needs some advisory about given issues, for example, when there are relevant changes in the project course and budget, the need for new members, etc. This VO board can be composed of a predefined group of partners (and even external actors) or be settled following the VO governance model.
- *SOA Solution Commercial Preparation:* this last process makes the idealized innovation outcomes available for "use". In this process the VO members make agreements and sign legal contracts, which can comprise commercial support for future products and services, IPR, commercialization model, price policy, etc.

> Third space: *Solution delivery space*

- *Local Infrastructure Provisioning:* preparation and hiring of the required infrastructure for the SOA solution at the customer, third part, some specific member, or at the alliance's site regarding the agreed business model, contracts and QoS requirements.
- *Local Deployment:* making the physical deployment of the SOA solution at the customer's site once the infrastructure is ready.
- *External Deployment:* making the deployment (e.g. in a cloud) of the SOA solution. The third space may be not executed depending on the development results and even on the initiative's goals. For example, partners might only be interested in developing a mockup to better evaluate some concepts even though some potential customers might be invited to assess it. On the other hand, this space can be partially visited when e.g. such prototypes require some deployment in external clouds to evaluate end-to-end QoS.

In general terms, a more human-driven approach tends to prevail in the first space, and a process-driven approach in the second and third ones as software development and delivery processes are usually much more structured. As such, in each space, there are different notions of: budget, time and human resources allocations; the need for research and even the involvement of research institutions; and the involvement of customers, experts and other supporting institutions (like IPR offices).

The nature of discussions, type of involved and required knowledge, information flow, type of responsibilities, etc., are different in each process and space. Regarding that, the innovation initiative behaves more like as the *network* type inside the first space and more like as the *open* innovation type in the second and third spaces. In terms of governance model, while the *all-ring no-core* and *buyer-driven* models [26] are likely to prevail in the first space, this tends to be more *core-ring with coordination firm* and *information-driven* [27] in the second and third spaces. Likewise in the traditional *funnel*-based models, where *gates* are used to decide about the continuation of the innovation project, the proposed model also has this equivalent concept. Actually, the innovation initiative can be interrupted, radically changed or just stored (for further usages) anytime in any of the spaces/processes. Performance indicators can be used to support this decision [28], following the governance model. All processes can be audited and authorized knowledge can be stored, also following the governance model.

4.2 Functional Guidelines

Functional guidelines (FG) are supporting and reference constructs of the model. Members of the innovation initiative require methods, techniques and tools to help them executing processes' activities along the collaborative innovation regarding that SMEs' managers are often not much aware of which issues are more likely to be taken into account in each process. The model does not offer the concrete methods themselves. Instead, they should be chosen by each alliance or VO regarding existing practices, available financial resources, prepared people, etc. For example, if VO members realize that they indeed need some support in terms of (the FG) *Project Management* in a given process (or space), they can select the *PMBOK* methodology and the *MS Project* as the specific software tool after an analysis by the members.

FGs are actually associated – as an abstract reference – to each model's processes. For example, thanks to the FGs, partners can become aware that (FGs) *actors' roles* and *network operation* governance issues are important to have in mind in the *VO configuration* process.

There are ten main FGs. They were identified and categorized via an inductive method over a number of papers on innovation, [2, 29] in more particular:

Business level: FGs more related to the business and strategic aspects:

- *Business Model Management:* foundations to help partners checking if innovation results are aligned with the defined business model and innovation goals.
- *Legal Management:* help partners checking if the innovation follows the required legal frameworks, contracts, IPRs and services ownerships.

Operational level: support to the daily operation of innovation developments:

- *Actors' roles:* help partners checking if partners' rights, duties and roles settled in the alliances and VO's governance models are been followed.
- *Network Operation:* it is also related to the governance model, helping the observation of the power and structural elements of decision-making along the innovation process.
- *Project/Resources Management:* supports the issues related to manage the innovation process as a project, including associated e.g. financial, material and human resources.
- *Incentive Systems:* checking if the collaboration incentives are being correct applied to partners, also regarding general performance and adherence to the project's goals.

- *Performance Indicators:* selection and application of adequate indicators to measure and manage the performance of the innovation projects and partners.

Policies level: FGs related to general relations among the VO, the VO with other actors (internal or external to the alliance), and with customers:

- *Governance:* rules to set up how the innovation will be managed, including partners' roles, responsibilities, boundaries of actions and actors autonomy.
- *Software Process Improvement:* models, standards, specifications and methodologies to guarantee the use of more proper practices of software and services development.
- *Knowledge Sharing:* to guarantee that the necessary information and knowledge to support the innovation are properly organized and shared, that lessons are learned, etc.

These FGs and their placement along the innovation process should however be seen as a reference. Regarding the particularities of the given innovation initiative in terms of e.g. existing culture, type of customers, current business models, and regional/national/international accounting and legal frameworks' requirements, FGs can support processes at different levels and can have different degrees of importance. Besides that, other FGs can be added to the model if needed by the particular case.

5 Preliminary Evaluation

This model was preliminary evaluated by a group of experts on SOA from a cluster of ICT/SOA providers placed in the South of Brazil. Actually, such users have been participating since the early stages of the model development, helping in the identification of requirements. A survey was prepared using the *GQM* method [30] and the method was presented and a set of typical business cases were exemplified. In this first stage the questions of the survey focused on the processes and basic assumptions of the innovation model. The questions were made using the *Likert* scale and free-response questions. For all the experts, all processes were considered as necessary. For most of them the most critical processes are the *Ideas Analysis* and the *VO Configuration*, and the general *SOA delivery space* due to commercialization aspects as they are particular to customers and there can be several providers involved in. The experts called the attention to the governance issue and the complexity it can have, at the alliance, VO and SOA levels.

About if software services providers in the near future tend to provide joint solutions in order to reduce costs and risks and increase the chances of better addressing the market, around 75 % agreed on that. About if more and more ICT companies can become part of larger IT ecosystems in the near future to take advantage of complementarities and additional scale, around 85 % agreed on that.

6 Final Considerations

This paper has presented current results of a research which aims at conceiving an innovation model devoted to support collaborative innovation among SMEs of software/services providers related to SOA products. Collaborative innovation has the potential to leverage new degrees of sustainability for software and SOA SMEs. The proposed model has been developed in the light of Collaborative Networks foundations, enabling SMEs to work as a network, sharing assets, resources, costs, risks and benefits. A Virtual Organization (VO) represents the group of SMEs that jointly develop an innovation. This work has also identified the most important supporting constructs to consider throughout the innovation process and VO life cycle. Such constructs, called as functional guidelines, help companies to allocate resources and to be aware of the different levels of complexities along the collaborative innovation life cycle. It could be noticed that dealing with the envisaged scenario which combines collaborative innovation between disparate and independent SMEs, SOA and software sector particularities, flexibility in the processes, etc., is complex. Regarding it was not found in the literature an innovation model for this scenario, the proposed model should be taken as an initial contribution, even because it was not truly validated yet. As the model was conceived based on more generic and reference innovation models, we believed it may be also used in the traditional software sector. However, some activities inside of some processes should be adapted, in more particular the SOA solution development process and the software delivery.

Next short-terms steps of this research include new rounds of assessment and practical evaluation of the model towards its validation.

Acknowledgements. This work has been partially supported by CNPq - The Brazilian Council for Research.

References

1. Kramer, W.J., Jenkins, B., Katz, R.S.: The Role of the Information and Communications Technology Sector in Expanding Economic Opportunity. Economic Opportunity Series, pp. 1–52. Harvard College, Cambridge (2007)
2. Munkongsujarit, S., Srivannaboon, S.: Key success factors for open innovation intermediaries for SMEs: a case study of iTAP in Thailand. In: Proceedings in Technology Management in the Energy Smart World (PICMET), pp. 1–8 (2011)
3. Zhiqiang, N.: Credibility evaluation of SaaS tenants. In: Advanced Computer Theory and Engineering, pp. 488–491 (2010)
4. Papazoglou, M.P.: Web Services and SOA, Principles and Technology. Pearson, London (2012)
5. Rosenbusch, N., Brinckmann, J.: Is innovation always beneficial? A meta-analysis of the relationship between innovation and performance in SMEs. J. Bus. Ventur. **26**, 441–457 (2011)
6. Cancian, M.H., Rabelo, R.J., Wangenheim, C.G.V.: Collaborative business processes for enhancing partnerships among software services providers. Enterp. Inf. Syst. **9**, 1–26 (2015)
7. Santanna-Filho, J., Rabelo, R.J., Pereira-Klen, A.A.: An innovation model for collaborative networks of SOA-based software providers. In: Camarinha-Matos, L.M., Afsarmanesh, H. (eds.) Collaborative Systems for Smart Networked Environments. IFIP AICT, vol. 434, pp. 169–181. Springer, Heidelberg (2014)
8. OCDE: Oslo Manual: Guidelines for Collecting and Interpreting Tech Innovation Data. OCDE, Paris (2005)
9. Tidd, J., Bessant, J., Pavitt, K.: Innovation Management. Willey, New York (2001)

10. Du Preez, N.D., Louw, L.: A framework for managing the innovation process. In: Proceedings of International Conference on Management of Engineering and Technology, Portland, USA, pp. 546–558 (2008)
11. Rothwell, R.: Successful industrial innovation: critical factors for the 1990s. R&D Manage. **22**, 221–240 (1992)
12. Chesbrough, H.: Open Innovation: The New Imperative for Creating and Profiting from Technology. Harvard Business Press, Boston (2003)
13. Rycroft, R., Kash, D.: Self-organizing innovation networks: implications for globalization. Technovation **24**(3), 187–197 (2004)
14. Camarinha-Matos, L.M., Afsarmanesh, H.: Methods and Tools for Collaborative Networked Organizations. Springer, New York (2008)
15. Santanna-Filho, J.F., Rabelo, R.J, Pereira-Klen, A., Bernus, P., Romero, D.: Leveraging collaborative innovation in SOA-based software providers networks. In: Proceedings 21st ICE/IEEE International Technology Management Conference, pp. 1–9 (2015)
16. Lewis, G.A., Smith, D.B., Kontogiannis, K.: A research agenda for service-oriented architecture (SOA): maintenance and evolution of service-oriented systems. CMU/SEI-2010-TN-003 (2010)
17. Rabelo, R.J., Costa, S.N., Romero, D.: A governance reference model for virtual enterprises. In: Camarinha-Matos, L.M., Afsarmanesh, H. (eds.) Collaborative Systems for Smart Networked Environments. IFIP AICT, vol. 434, pp. 60–70. Springer, Heidelberg (2014)
18. Berre, A., Lew, Y., Elvesaeter, B.: Service innovation and service realisation with VDML and ServiceML. In: Proceedings of 7th IEEE International Enterprise Distributed Object Computing Conference Workshops, pp. 104–113 (2013)
19. Hoyer, V., Christ, Oliver: Collaborative e-business process modelling: a holistic analysis framework focused on small and medium-sized enterprises. In: Abramowicz, W. (ed.) BIS 2007. LNCS, vol. 4439, pp. 41–53. Springer, Heidelberg (2007)
20. Belussi, F., Arcangeli, F.: A typology of networks: flexible and evolutionary firms. Res. Policy **27**, 415–428 (1998)
21. Li, Y., Shen, J., Shi, J., Shen, W., Huang, Y., Xu, Y.: Multi-model driven collaborative development platform for service-oriented e-Business systems. Adv. Eng. Inform. **22**, 328–339 (2008)
22. CORDIS. http://cordis.europa.eu/projects/home_en.html
23. Perin-Souza, A., Rabelo, R.J.: Services discovery as a mean to enhance software resources sharing in collaborative networks. In: Camarinha-Matos, L.M., Pereira-Klen, A., Afsarmanesh, Hamideh (eds.) PRO-VE 2011. IFIP AICT, vol. 362, pp. 388–399. Springer, Heidelberg (2011)
24. Hwang, V., Horowitt, G.: The Rainforest: The Secret to Building the Next Silicon Valley. Regenwald Publishers, California (2012)
25. Mootee, I.: Design Thinking for Strategic Innovation: What They Can't Teach You at Business or Design School. Wiley, New York (2013)
26. Storper, M., Harrison, B.: Flexibility, hierarchy and regional development: the changing structure of industrial production systems. Res. Policy **20**, 407–422 (1991)
27. Gereffi, G., Humphrey, J., Sturgeon, T.: The governance of global value chains. Rev. Int. Polit. Econ. **12**, 78–104 (2005)
28. Rogers, M.: The definition and measurement of innovation. Melbourne Institute of Applied Economic and Social Research, Working paper no. 10/98 (1998)
29. Van Zyl, J.: Process innovation imperative. In: Proceedings of IEMC 2001 - Change Management and the New Industrial Revolution, pp. 454–459 (2001)
30. Basili, V.R., Caldiera, G., Rombach, H.D.: The goal question metric approach. In: Encyclopedia of Software Engineering. Wiley, New York (1994)

Governance in Collaborative Networks

Towards a Collaborative Networks Governance Framework

Sébastien Truptil[✉], Anne-Marie Barthe-Delanoë, Tiexin Wang,
and Frédérick Bénaben

Université de Toulouse- Mines, Albi, France
{truptil,barthe,tiexin.wang,benaben}@mines-albi.fr

Abstract. Nowadays Collaborative Networks (CN) have to evolve in an unstable world and therefore appear, change and disappear quickly. Although IT solutions like SOA can support these evolutions, there is a lack of governance at the business layer. This lack relies on the poor (i) aggregation of data to information, (ii) comparison of CN vision of the world and real world, (iii) sharing of partner's objectives. Moreover, organizations have to manage exponential growth in the amounts of data with the development of Internet of Events. Therefore, organization should not manage information with an empirical approach. This paper aims to define a Collaborative Networks Governance Framework (CNGF) in order to support CN. CNGF manages (i) snapshots, which are timestamp pictures of the world, (ii) indicator function, which transforms sets of data into information, (iii) agility function, which describes partners' objectives and (iv) analysis function in order to evaluate the performance of CN.

Keywords: Governance · Collaborative network · Big data · Internet of Events

1 Introduction

Since the 70's, Collaborative Networks of Organizations (CNO) have evolved from single workshops collaborative situations to inter-organizational collaborations [1]. This evolution could be easily explained by the development of new technology. Indeed, a set of heterogeneous organizations, geographically distributed, could instantaneously exchange information in order to achieve common or compatible goals thanks to computer networks. Nevertheless, organizations are still heterogeneous by nature (mission, equipment, culture, vocabulary, etc.). To be efficient, they have to collaborate, or at least coordinate their actions, in order to build a coherent way to reach the shared goal of the CNO.

Although the new technologies have pushed the boundaries of CNO, in terms of variety of forms, geographical distribution, variety of data to manage, the CNO life cycle is always composed of five main stages [2]:

1. **Creation:** can be divided into two parts, namely (i) initiation and recruiting, dealing with the strategic planning and (ii) foundation, dealing with the constitution and start up

L.M. Camarinha-Matos et al. (Eds.): PRO-VE 2015, IFIP AICT 463, pp. 379–387, 2015.
DOI: 10.1007/978-3-319-24141-8_34

2. **Operation:** the "normal" stage of the CNO existence.
3. **Evolution:** when small changes in membership, roles, or daily operating principles happen.
4. **Dissolution:** when the CNO ceases to exist.
5. **Metamorphosis:** when major change in objectives, principles, and membership take place, leading to a new form of organization.

The need for information management all along the CNO lifecycle is obvious as underlined in [3]. Even if it is exposed with a manufacturing point of view in [3], the Challenge 3 could be defined in any domain: *"Challenge 3: "Instantaneously" transform information gathered from a vast array of diverse sources into useful knowledge for making effective decisions"*.

This challenge is crucial to ensure the success of CNO especially due to the fast development of new technology that produces amounts of data. Indeed, amounts and variety of data arose from the development of domain ontologies and the development of Internet of Event (IoE). According to [4, 5], IoE could be divided in four sources:

1. *Internet of Things:* all physical objects connected to the network. This includes all things that have a unique id and a presence in an Internet-like structure. Things may have an Internet connection or tagged using Radio-Frequency Identification (RFID), Near Field Communication (NFC), etc.
2. *Internet of Location* refers to all data that have a spatial dimension. With the uptake of mobile devices (*e.g.* smartphones) more and more events have geospatial attributes.
3. *Internet of People:* all data related to social interaction. This includes e-mails, Facebook, Twitter, forums, LinkedIn, etc.
4. *Internet of Content:* all information created by humans to increase knowledge on particular subjects. This includes traditional web pages, articles, encyclopedia like Wikipedia, YouTube, etc.

According to [6], the information management all along the CNO lifecycle could refer to a big data challenges. Indeed, "Big data is a set of techniques and technologies that require new forms of integration to uncover large hidden values from large datasets that are diverse, complex, and of a massive scale"[6] and Big Data is characterized by 4V: volume, variety, velocity and value. Value refers to the process of discovering huge hidden values from large datasets with various types and rapid generation of more valuable information that is similar to the challenge 3.

Talia [7] pointed out that obtaining useful information from large amounts of data requires scalable analysis algorithms to produce timely results. As researchers continue to probe the issues of big data in cloud computing, new problems in big data processing arise from the transitional data analysis techniques. The speed of stream data arriving from different data sources must be processed and compared with historical information within a certain period of time. Such data sources may contain different formats, which makes the integration of multiple sources for analysis a complex task [8].

Moreover, due to the heterogeneity of organizations and the CNO lifecycle, the information management has to be defined without requesting a change for the organization. Therefore a middleware is needed [9] and, as explain in [10], target architecture for this middleware is Service Oriented Architecture (SOA). SOA is composed of several components and the SOA governance is in charge to manage the lifecycle of the middleware.

Even if there is lots of work on the SOA governance [11–13], the alignment between organization (business aspect) and SOA (technical aspect) starts from processes and there is a lack concerning the information management, especially how to generate valuable information from incoming data, and process adequacy with the objectives of cross-organization.

A framework is proposed in this paper in order to fill the previous lack. This framework is a novel approach to reach the goal to manage data and information in order to help CNO to make effective decisions all along their lifecycle. This approach aims to define a business governance as an extension of the SOA governance in a Service Oriented Architecture.

The remainder of this paper is divided into two sections. Section 2 identifies the objectives of the framework in order to list the required functionalities and before concluding, Sect. 3 presents the architecture of the framework.

2   Objectives of the Framework

In order to reach the Challenge 3 and thus to help CNO to make effective decisions, the aim of the framework is to build snapshots of the reality. The idea of snapshots is to have pictures of the world state that is composed of all information related to a specific CNO context. There are at least three kind of snapshots:

- *Situational snapshot* is a picture of the world state and it is independent from CNO activities.
- *Expected snapshot* is a picture of what the CNO expect to obtain after executing activities.
- *Forecast snapshot:* what the situational snapshot or expected snapshot looks like in future.

By comparing information embedded into each snapshot, the CNO could make effective decision. Figure 1 represents an overview of the comparison principles over the time.

To illustrate the benefits of the comparison, it is possible to take a common example as in criminal stories. A murderer exists; his picture is the *situational snapshot*. Policemen don't know exactly how the murderer looks like but based on gathered information, they build a facial composite, which is the *expected snapshot*. If the facial composite is closed to the picture, the policemen have a chance to capture the murderer. Another example is when you are looking for someone for a long time; it is possible to generate a new picture, the *forecast snapshot*, thanks to accelerated ageing models based on a picture or a facial composite.

Another example in CNO context could be the following: several organizations want to produce together a product and so they define a production process. Based on this process, the supplier has to finish a part of the product two weeks after the beginning of

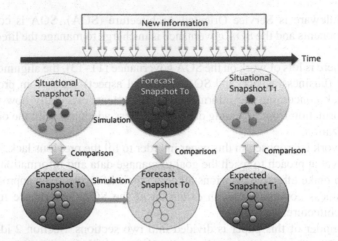

Fig. 1. Overview of the use of snapshots in order to help CNO to make effective decisions.

the process but it has a technical malfunction. Therefore thanks to a comparison of forecast snapshots, it is possible to find the impact at the end of the process and thanks to comparison between situational and expected snapshots, it is possible to detect the problem as soon as possible.

Nevertheless, each snapshot depends on time. Therefore, snapshots have to be either changed directly by user or indirectly by the use of IoE, results of CNO activities.

Therefore, the framework has to propose the following functionalities:

– Compare snapshots.
– Propose forecast snapshot (based on simulation).
– Transform data into information (in order to update snapshot).

These functionalities have to be built in compliance with the problematic of heterogeneity of data and the evolving aspects of CNO. Therefore it is necessary to generate and manage snapshots by transforming and combining amounts of data without manual effort.

3 CNO Governance Principles

3.1 Snapshot and Models

This section describes the architecture of the proposed framework in order to fit with the functionalities identified in the previous section. The main purpose of the framework is to manage snapshots in order to update and compare them. Therefore, each snapshot needs to be understandable to the same (or at least similar) structure. For this reason, a model will represent each snapshot because a model "represents reality for the given purpose; the model is an abstraction of reality in the sense that it cannot represent all aspects of reality. This allows us to deal with the world in a simplified manner, avoiding the complexity, danger and irreversibility of reality" according Rothenberg [14]. However to be comparable, a model has to be written according to a specific language, shared by several users, called metamodel [15].

Accordingly, each snapshot is a model and each model is conform to a metamodel. Nevertheless it is obvious that defining one metamodel able to cover all CNO contexts is a pipe dream. But for one given CNO context, it is possible to have one metamodel describing all information. For this purpose, the framework is based on the core-meta-model presented in [16], which is an extendable metamodel from generic concepts of collaboration to a definition of specific context (such as road management in winter period).

Finally, the objectives of the CNO governance are (i) to update models based on information provided by users, IoE or CNO activities, (ii) to compare models, (iii) to simulate in order to build forecast models and (iv) to design collaborative behaviour in order to merge, when it is needed, the expected and situational models.

The last point is in conformity with the lifecycle of CNO, especially the creation, evolution and metamorphosis stages. The chosen model to represent the collaborative behaviour is the process model in BMPN. Indeed, process model aims to capture the different ways in which a case can be handled. Process model is composed of ordering activities and could be described with temporal properties, creation and use of data and resources [17]. Hence, the simulation could be based on process model in order to build forecast models. Moreover, on-going research works [18] and [19] propose a methodology to build collaborative processes based on collaborative aims.

3.2   Framework of CNO Governance

Figure 2 represents the proposed framework. It is divided into three main layers in order to support all the previous identified functionalities and thus reach the aim of *"Instantaneously" transform information gathered from a vast array of diverse sources into useful knowledge for making effective decisions".*

Agility layer:

Numerous authors largely discussed the notion of agility. The Collins dictionary defines agility as the power of moving quickly and easily. For Badot [20], agility is a reconfiguration of the system to satisfy a need of adaptation. For other authors, such as Kidd [21], Lindberg [22] and Sharifi [23] agility is a need of flexibility, responsiveness or adaptability. In logistics, flexibility is seen as "the ability to meet short-term changes" [24] and is differentiated to the over time adaptation in response to a change [25]. Therefore, the agility layer of the framework is in charge to ensure (i) the assessment of the need for CNO to evolve or to metamorphose, (ii) the help to adapt the CNO.

Hence the agility layer is divided into three components:

- *Model comparison:* this component evaluates at any time the divergence between the expected model and the situational model. If the value of the divergence is higher than a threshold value, an alert is sent to the detection component.
- *Detection:* this component is in charge of analysing the divergence and thus defining the new objectives of the CNO. This analysis is possible because the situational model and the expected model are defined based on the same metamodel. The result of this analysis is sent to the collaborative process design component.

– *Collaborative process design* is the component in charge of adapting or defining new collaborative process. This deduction is based on the result of the detection component. The result of this component is composed of two models, which are (i) the collaborative process and (ii) a mapping between CNO activities and objectives. This second model will be reuse in the Updating layer (see below) in order to update the expected model.

This layer was defined in previous research works. The mechanisms of the model comparison and detection components were described in [26], and [18, 19] present a solution for the collaborative process design component.

Simulation layer:

This layer aims to produce a forecast model of the situational model and of the expected model, in order to apply the agility layer to the two forecast models. Hence it is possible to anticipate, instead of react, an evolution.

The two forecast models are obtained thanks to manipulation of existing information, e.g. existing model, or by the result of a simulation. The idea of this layer is inspired from the results of the European funded CRISMA project [27].

Updating layer:

This layer has a simple but difficult objective to achieve: build both situational and expected model from data. The difficulties arise in the variety and the amount of data

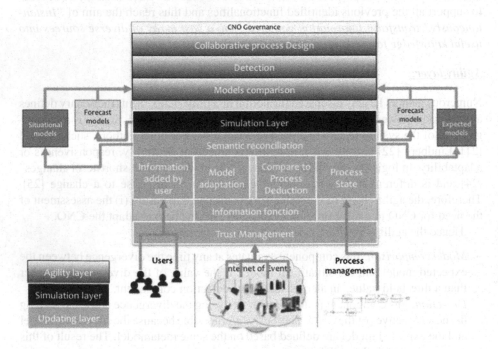

Fig. 2. Overview of the CNO governance framework.

sources. Three main kinds of data sources could be identified (i) IoE, (ii) data from users or their ontologies and (iii) the achievement of CNO activities, e.g. the progress of the collaborative behaviour. This variety of data sources implies issues concerning (i) Trust management, especially regarding IoE (especially Internet of person), (ii) comparison of data due to the heterogeneity of semantics and levels of description, e.g. granularity issue.

In order to achieve this simple objective, the Updating layer is divided into seven components:

- *Trust Management:* this component aims to filter no-trustable data. For instance, if a sensor always sends the same expected value during one second, thus we have a Dirac delta function. This value may be wrong and the governance does not have to take it into account. Trust management is more complex than just this example as explains in [28].
- *Information function:* this component is the key point of the governance. It aims at transforming data to information. This component is compliant with Big Data challenges [6] to automatically define the transformation from data to knowledge. However, it is possible to manually define information function that transforms data into information. For example, if sensors could send the heart rate and another could send the body temperature of a human being, it is possible to deduce if the human being is ill or not. Indeed, if his/her body temperature is above 39 °C (fever) and his/her heart rate is above 120, so he/she is ill.
- *Model Adaptation:* this component is used to update the situational model. Based on information generated by Information function component, the situational model is updated thanks to principles defined in [26].
- *Compare to process deduction:* this component is used to update the expected model. As described in [26], this update is possible thanks to information generated by Information function component and the model defining mapping between CNO activities and objectives.
- *Process state:* this component is used to also update the expected model based on the progress of collaborative process. This is allowed thanks to the model defining mapping between CNO activities and objectives.
- *Information added by user:* this component allows user to directly add, remove or modify information from the situational or expected models.
- *Semantics reconciliation* is needed because we cannot assume that each user and/or each information function will generate information based on a coherent glossary or taxonomy. A semantics reconciliation component is used with the aim to unify semantic as well as the level of description, e.g. the granularity level, of information. This component is based on work described in [29].

4 Conclusion and Next Challenges

This paper presents a framework for CNO governance that aims to support CNO all along their lifecycle. Especially, the objective of the governance is to "Instantaneously" transform information gathered from a vast array of diverse sources into useful knowledge for making effective decisions. In order to achieve this objective, the idea is based on snapshots of the reality that allow CNO to make a comparison between the situational state and the expected state from the CNO point of view. This comparison is possible if data provided by various heterogeneity sources could be filtered (using trust principles), aggregated, and transformed into information.

In order to achieve the objectives of the governance, a three-layers architecture is proposed. The agility layer aims at detecting divergence between CNO behaviour and reality and then deducing a new version of the CNO behaviour. The simulation layer aims to make forecast in order to anticipate evolution. The updating layer is the key point of the governance. It aims to manage a huge number of data from various sources in order to produce information usable by other layers.

This framework is based on the result of three PhD works, two on the agility layer and one on the updating layer. Each PhD provides theoretical solution and a demonstrator. Our future work consists in merging the demonstrator and developing the simulation layer.

References

1. Camarinha-Matos, L.M., Afsarmanesh, H.: Classes of collaborative networks. In: Putnik, G.D., Cunha, M.M. (eds.) Encyclopedia of Networked and Virtual Organization, pp. 193–198. Hershey, New York (2008)
2. Camarinha-Matos, L.M., Afsarmanesh, H.: Collaborative networked organizations – concepts and practice. Comput. Ind. Eng. **57**, 46–60 (2009)
3. Camarinha-Matos, L.M., Afsarmanesh, H., Galeano, N., Molina, A.: Collaborative networked organizations–concepts and practice in manufacturing enterprises. Comput. Ind. Eng. **57**(1), 46–60 (2009)
4. van der Aalst, W.M.P.: How people really (like to) work. In: Sauer, S., Bogdan, C., Forbrig, P., Bernhaupt, R., Winckler, M. (eds.) HCSE 2014. LNCS, vol. 8742, pp. 317–321. Springer, Heidelberg (2014)
5. van der Aalst, W.M.P.: Data Scientist: The Engineer of the Future. In: Proceedings of the I-ESA Conference, volume 7 of Enterprise Interoperability, pp. 13–28. Springer (2014)
6. Hashem, I.A.T., Yaqoob, I., Anuar, N.B., Mokhtar, S., Gani, A., Khan, S.U.: The rise of "big data" on cloud computing: review and open research issues. Inf. Syst. **47**, 98–115 (2015)
7. Talia, D.: Clouds for scalable big data analytics. Computer **46**, 98–101 (2013)
8. Assuncao, M.D., Calheiros, R.N., Bianchi, S., Netto, M.A., Buyya, R.: Big Data Computing and Clouds: Challenges, Solutions, and Future Directions. arXiv preprint arXiv:1312.4722 (2013)
9. Wiederhold, G.: Mediators in the architecture of future information systems. Computer **25**(3), 38–49 (1992)
10. Papazoglou, M.P.: Service-oriented computing: concepts, characteristics and directions. In: 4th International Conference on Web Information Systems Engineering (WISE 2003), Rome, Italy, pp. 3–12 (2003)
11. Niemann, M., Eckert, J., Repp, N., Steinmetz, R.: Towards a generic governance model for service oriented architectures. In: AMCIS 2008 Proceedings, p. 361 (2008)
12. Marks, E.A.: Service-Oriented Architecture (SOA) Governance for the Services Driven Enterprise. Wiley, New York (2008)

13. Adam, S., Doerr, J.: How to better align BPM & SOA–ideas on improving the transition between process design and deployment. In: 9th Workshop on Business Process Modeling, Development and Support (2008)
14. Rothenberg, J.: The nature of modeling. In: William, L.E., Loparo, K.A., Nelson, N.R. (eds.) Artificial Intelligence, Simulation, and Modeling, pp. 75–92. Wiley, New York (1989)
15. Object Management Group, Meta Object Facility (MOF) Specification, Version 1.4 (2002)
16. Lauras, M., Benaben, F., Truptil, S., Lamothe, J., Mace-Ramete, G., Montarnal, A.: A meta-ontology for knowledge acquisition and exploitation of collaborative social systems. In: International Conference on Behavior, Economic and Social Computing (BESC) pp. 1–7 (2014)
17. van der Aalst, W.M.: Business process management: a comprehensive survey. ISRN Software Engineering (2013)
18. Mu, W., Boissel-Dallier, N., Bénaben, F., Pingaud, H., Lorré, J.P.: Collaborative mediation information system design based on model-driven business process management approach. Enterprise Interoperability VI, pp. 139–150. Springer International Publishing, Berlin (2014)
19. Montarnal, A., Barthe-Delanoë, A.-M., Bénaben, F., Lauras, M., Lamothe, J.: A PaaS to support collaborations through service composition. In: IEEE International Conference on Services Computing (SCC), pp. 677–684 (2014)
20. Badot, O.: Théorie de l'entreprise agile. L'Harmattan, Paris (1998)
21. Kidd, P.T.: Agile manufacturing: forging new frontiers. Int. J. Hum. Factors Manuf. 5, p343 (1994)
22. Lindberg, P.: Strategic manufacturing management: a proactive approach. Int. J. Oper. Prod. Manag. 10, 94–106 (1990)
23. Sharifi, H., Zhang, Z.: A methodology for achieving agility in manufacturing organisations: an introduction. Int. J. Prod. Econ. 62(1–2), 7–22 (1999)
24. Sheffi, Y.: Demand Variability and Supply Chain Flexibility, Entwicklungspfade und Meilensteine moderner Logistik, Glaber, pp. 87–113 (2004)
25. Mc Cullen, P., Saw, R., Christopher, M., Towill, D.: The F1 supply chain: adapting the car to the circuit-the supply chain to the market. Supply Chain Forum 7, 14–23 (2006)
26. Barthe-Delanoë, A.M., Truptil, S., Bénaben, F., Pingaud, H.: Event-driven agility of interoperability during the Run-time of collaborative processes. Decis. Support Syst. 59, 171–179 (2014)
27. Dihé P., Scholl M., Schlobinski S., Hell T., Frysinger S., Kutschera P., Warum M., Havlik D., DeGroof A., Vandeloise Y., Deri O., Rannat K., Yliaho J., Kosonen A., Sommer M., Engelbach W.: CRISMA ICMS Architecture Document V2 (2014). http://www.crismaproject.eu/deliverables/CRISMA_D322_public.pdf
28. Afsarmanesh, H., Camarinha-Matos, L.M., Msanjila, S.S.: On management of 2nd generation virtual organizations breeding environments. Ann. Rev. Control 33(2), 209–219 (2009)
29. Wang, T., Truptil, S., Benaben, F.: Semantic approach to automatically defined model transformation. In: Enterprise Interoperability VI, pp. 127–138 (2014)

Evaluating Collaboration and Governance in SME Clusters

Teresa Taurino[✉]

DIGEP – Departmento of Management and Industrial Engineering, Politecnico di Torino,
Corso Duca degli Abruzzi 24, 10129 Turin, Italy
teresa.taurino@polito.it

Abstract. The need of collaboration among SMEs and improving governance has been perceived by the European Commission and by individual countries that promote since some years new organizational transformations of industrial-service systems into sustainable networks. The proposed paper is intended to address: How a manager of an individual SME, aiming to join an existing cluster, can evaluate a cluster that could be a "collaborative environment" for his small business; which main characteristics of the cluster governance have to be analyzed; which network structures appear to be preferable with a mutual profit? To help the manager to answers to these questions, the proposed work establishes a Cluster Reference Framework (CRF) structured in three dimensions: (i) the types of SME clusters; (ii) the types of governance (management) committee; (iii) the different ways of creating a network of small businesses, depending on whether or not there is a promoter or an independent will.

Keywords: SME clusters · Graph representation · Collaboration · Management committee

1 Introduction

The need for strengthening cooperation among SMEs and improving networking has been perceived of interest by the European Commission [1] and by individual countries [2] that promote, since some years, new organizational transformations of industrial-service systems into sustainable networks.

The industrial network systems, in Europe, rise from different needs and with different characteristics [3, 4]. The Italian industrial districts and the UK clusters of SMEs have in common the characteristic to be agglomerations of SMEs from the same geographic area. The development of the network [5] can be determined by the possibility to easily supply raw materials, the presence of a big local market and the availability of a high level of expertise in a specific manufactured sector. In France, it is common to find "Pole of Competitiveness" as well as the "Scientific Parks" in Greece. This kind of networks rise thanks to national or regional governments incentives to develop a common project. In other countries, like Germany, the SME networks rise around a leading firms that have the characteristics to pull all the SMEs in the market.

© IFIP International Federation for Information Processing 2015
L.M. Camarinha-Matos et al. (Eds.): PRO-VE 2015, IFIP AICT 463, pp. 388–397, 2015.
DOI: 10.1007/978-3-319-24141-8_35

The promotion of the clustering or networking of companies can be reached according different routes:

- stimulated by local training centers that helps the enterprises to create an organic product service system in order to meet better the demand of the labor market;
- driven by the need to share the resources and to collaborate in order to face the adverse market environments;
- the local public administration, or agencies/associations for industrial and commercial development SME asks SMEs to strengthen cooperation, often during times of crisis.

"A product service-system" is composed by products, services, resources, buildings and personnel that continuously work to be more competitive, to satisfy the needs of the market by paying attention to the environmental impact with less effort with than a traditional business models [6].

Despite the pressure towards cooperation, many SME managers have maintained their individualistic position: this has reflected in many dramatic crises and closures of small businesses, especially in recent years [7, 8].

Consequently the problem discussed in the proposed paper is intended to address the following questions: How does a manager of an SME assess whether an existing cluster could be a "friendly environment" for his small business? What organizational characteristics of the cluster have to be analyzed? Which network structures appear to be preferable such as the SME would fit into the existing network with mutual profit? In order for the manager to look for answers to these questions, the proposed work establishes a Cluster Reference Framework (CRF) structured in three dimensions:

- the types of SME clusters, modeled in terms of standard networked graphs, such to allow an easy view of the networked links connecting SMEs;
- the types of management committee, that should assure cooperation among the SMEs together;
- the different ways of creating a network of small businesses, depending on whether or not there is a promoter or an independent will.

Even considering only these three dimensions, they offer criteria for analysis and evaluation of a SME cluster ("marginal analysis"). However, considering them in pairs, other points of view for the analysis are obtained:

(a) taking into account the pair <network type; type of committee> one can get information about organizational transformation applicable to the network;
(b) from the analysis of the pair <network type; procedures for setting up the network> design tips arise;
(c) in addition, an analysis of the pair <type of committee; how to build> can give information on sustainability of the network.

The paper will motivate in detail the CRF, and show its practical utilization by a SME manager. To this aim, the paper is organized as follows. The introduction of a model of a SME cluster, by making evidence to the two components above mentioned, namely types of networks connecting the partner SMEs together, and types of cluster management is in Sect. 2. Depending on these two components, a classification of the different SME clusters can be standardized. Section 3 will illustrate a three-dimensional framework, namely the mentioned Cluster Reference Framework – CRF, where the types of networks, the types of management organizations and the different ways to create a network of small enterprises will be respectively referred to each dimension. The potential practical utilization of the proposed framework will be discussed by showing how the presented framework can support a specific analysis of a SME manager. Section 3 will also illustrated a preliminary application of the CRF, by analyzing the three types of dimensions for a number of SME clusters, based on data collected during the European project CODESNET [17] and stored in the CODESNET archive. The European project CODESNET (COllaborative DEmand and Supply NETwork) aimed to create a virtual environment to promote the development of SME network. During the project, a huge number of data and information concerning more than 100 SME networks have been collected. CODESNET has relied on the contribution from both enterprises and academia partners since this synergy is considered a strong point in order to guarantee stability in a network organization.

2 Modeling a SME Cluster

Three important aspects must be taken into account in the modeling of SME networks [9, 10]:

- the management of the network in terms of functionalities that can assure efficiency, effectiveness and economy in all the SMEs belonging to the network;
- the structure of the connections among the SMEs, that means the type of their relationships;
- the reasons at the origin of the aggregation of multiple companies in a common network.

2.1 Main Functions and Management Organization of a SME Cluster

The management organization of a SME cluster can be represented by a "functional scheme" that represents the main functionalities and that shows how the committee of the cluster can receive contributions from the partners of the cluster, can generate products and financial strategies and can translate strategies into action plans able to satisfy customers orders by using the cluster structure to produce. In the next Fig. 1, the functional scheme is presented: "A" denotes the operations control loop; "B", the performance evaluation loop; "C", the finance management loop; "D", the partners' interactions management loop.

In practice, the real application of all these management functions depends on the type of cluster committee. Consequently, it can be stated that the presence of a particular type of committee characterizes a SME network defining the robustness and the possibility of a real future development. With reference to the cluster analysed in the project CODESNET, you can recognize the following types of the Management Committee:

- Industrial management committee, i.e. a committee composed by the top managers of the most important enterprises included in the cluster: among the managers, a coordinator is usually nominated. This is the case of small and mid-size enterprises operating in the manufacturing sector, as automotive, aerospace, electronic ones; in this organization, all the management functions of Fig. 1 are applied.
- Administration management committee, i.e. a committee composed by administrative directors or, more generally, by administrative staff, of some companies in the cluster, with the task of monitoring costs and revenues on behalf of individual companies, and of reporting to external funders (function C in Fig. 1). This can be the case of clusters having a leading enterprise, whose aim is to monitor financial flows without completely removing autonomy to other SME of the cluster.
- Marketing-oriented committee, i.e. a committee made up of directors of marketing for some companies, with the task of managing specific marketing initiatives, such as exhibitions, promotional campaigns or advertising (function A in Fig. 1). This is the case of SME clusters of the jewelry sector.
- Political committee, i.e. a committee composed by representatives of the municipalities where the SMEs belonging to the cluster are located; this is the case of some clusters operating in the agro-food sector, as in production of wine. A political committee is a

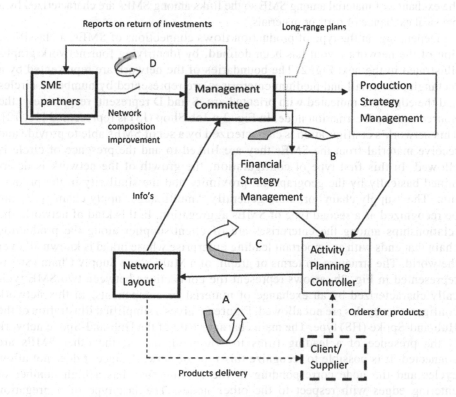

Fig. 1. Schematic model of an industrial SME network.

committee that can implement at most promotional functions, but does not have operational duties.

- No committee, i.e. a form of weak interaction, partly marketing – oriented and partly characterized by a political and social nature, with the sole purpose to create a market to the SMEs.

2.2 Models of the Network of SMEs

A network of SME can be easily modelled by a graph G = (V,E), where V is the set of vertices and E is the set of edges or arcs. Each vertex corresponds to a SME of the cluster and the edges correspond to the links among the SMEs.

The SME-to-SME connections can have different characteristics:

1. can represent the connection between a client and a supplier and in this case the links is mainly characterized by the flow of parts from a SME to another;
2. can be the exchange of information and from one SME to another into a cluster information system;
3. can be the transfer of orders either between SMEs or between a SME and a common centre, as part of a cluster management organization.

In this analysis of manufacturing SME networks, we will refer to a graph representing the exchange of material among SME so the links among SMEs are characterized by a physical exchange of parts or materials.

Depending on the type of production flows connections of SMEs, a classification of the network layout has been defined, by identifying four network graphs illustrated in the next Fig. 2. The boundaries of the network are represented by a rectangle; the small and medium enterprises are represented by numbered circles and the edges are indicated with oriented arc. S and D represent, respectively, the Source and the Destination node. In Fig. 2 a Job Shop (JS) is represented [11, 12]. This network's configuration is characterized by a set of SMEs able to provide and receive material from the SMEs they are linked to and the presence of circle is allowed. In this first type of configuration, the growth of the network is determined basically by the geographical proximity and the similarity in the production. The "supply chain" or, more generally, "multi-stage supply chain" [13] can be recognized as a second type of SMEs aggregation. In this kind of network, the relationships among the enterprises are of client/supplier along the production chain that ends with an important leading enterprise whose brand is known all over the world. The structure, in terms of graph, of a Multi-stage Supply Chain (SC) is represented in Fig. 2b: arrows represent the connections between two SME typically characterized by an exchange of material or components. In this network configuration cycles are not allowed. Figure 2c gives a simplified illustration of the Hub-and-Spoke (HS) type. The main characteristic of the Hub-and-Spoke network is the presence of a leading firms to whom almost all the other SMEs are connected. It is possible to recognize this type of network since it does not allow cycles and the node corresponding to the leading firm has a high number of entering edges with respect to the other nodes. The last type of aggregation

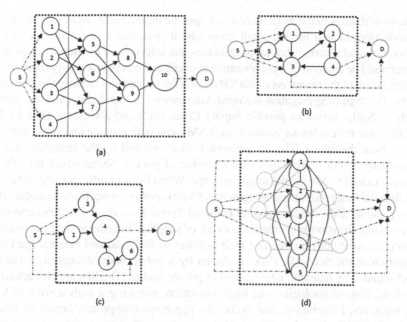

Fig. 2. Graph representation of the four network types.

proposed has less ruled interactions that permit to recognize the aggregation. This type of networks is mainly exploited by high-tech production and/or service supply where the nature of such aggregation is mainly oriented to R&D. This configuration is named Scientific Park (SP) [14, 15] and, in terms of graph representation, the nodes can be considered as inserted in a pre-existing with very flexible and more informal connections. To differentiate these potential connections from the classical ones, we represent them as switches on the graph edges. An example of the Scientific Park network is shown in Fig. 2d.

The typical feature of a Scientific Park is that each node is connected directly with the source and the destination nodes due to the pre-existing network. Furthermore, all possible edges between nodes can be activated or interrupted at any time. The exchanges between such companies do not concern materials or components but rather exchanges of information (knowledge, data, models, ideas) and services, thanks to the underlying network of partners specialized in ICT (Information and Communication Technology) and support to the innovative activities.

2.3   Models of a SME Cluster Dimension Dynamics

The differences in the creation and in the structure of the enterprise clusters give rise to different types of SME networks, as it has been presented in [15, 16] where an overview of clusters in some European countries has been illustrated. In some countries, like Italy, Germany and UK, the enterprises networks have raised in an autonomous way, pushed either by the companies themselves, or by industry organizations. In countries like France and Greece, the national or local governments have promoted investment programs to push the aggregation of SME into networks. The free aggregation of SMEs can occur either in a territory with no boundaries (if there are no specific requirements from logistics needs of the production) or in a limited small geographical area, due to the necessity of a strict collaboration and a strong sharing of resources and information or the exchange of parts or materials. The creation of a collaborative network can be autonomously induced by the strategic vision of the managers of the SMEs in order to plan and manage their production activity. This type of aggregation is named Autonomous or Marshallian and two particular models of SMEs networks prevail: Supply Chain (SC) and Job-Shops (JS). In the JS network, since the circles are allowed, each SME can both provide and receive products/ services from the others. The SC network is characterized by the presence of a chain composed by two or more stages with a number of parallel SMEs which provide products/services to the SMEs in the following stage. When firms of different size and different strength in the final product market agree to activate together connections depending on one (or few) leading SME we can speak of Hub-and-Spoke networks. In the HS networks one or two leading firms push to create a network of suppliers in order to drag the production and increase their performance and their position on the local and external market. The aggregation of the Scientific Parks is driven by a public body through a collaborative project founded by national, international or private bodies. The SPs are characterized by high skills, high technologies, and high innovation, requiring a high sharing of knowledge, resources, information, and skills. The aggregation approach cannot be based on autonomy of SMEs: large investments are required as well as an accurate selection of both SMEs and the personnel of high qualification to be employed.

3 The Cluster Reference Framework - CRF

The three main aspects of a SME cluster model, namely SME network type, management organization, and cluster creation, define three dimensions of a frame as in Fig. 3. This frame can be seen as a three-dimensional matrix, each internal box is associated to a triplet: <network type; type of Management body; network's agreement>. Said triplet specifies a SME cluster type. In each box, the names of some SME clusters (among the ones stored in the CODESNET archive) can be located: then, each box offers to a SME manager a set of preliminary information for evaluating if joining the considered network type could be of some interest for his/her SME. The real utilization of the schematic model of Fig. 3 can be realized by considering some Italian industrial districts. In the next Table 1 a set of data of Industrial networks belonging to the CODESNET archive are given.

3.1 Example of Application

An example of specific analysis has been done by referring to the manufacturing sector, with attention to districts producing shoes. The manager of a SME of this same sector, aiming to join a district, has at disposal the "archive" illustrated in Fig. 3. He will use the archive boxes tagged with the word "product = shoes", thus obtaining the following Table 1.

The selected boxes, however, are referred to different triplets, and then the manager receives the following information:

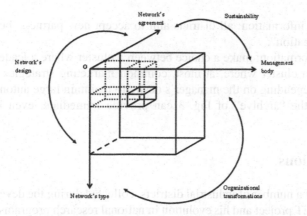

Fig. 3. Schematic model of CRF.

(a) Fermo's District:
- Network type = Hub and Spoke;
- Management body = none (existence of leading firms);
- Network creation = free aggregation.

(b) Vigevano's District and Lucca's District:
- Network type = Supply Chain;
- Management body = none (no leading firms in the chain stages);
- Network creation = free aggregation.

(c) Verona's District and San Mauro Pascoli's District:
- Network type = Supply Chain;
- Management body = Marketing-oriented committee;
- Network creation = free aggregation.

In summary, manager asking for joining suggestions can get:

Table 1. Selected industrial district from the CODESNET "archive".

District name	Network type	Management body	Network creation
Fermo	HS	None – existence of leading firms	Free aggregation
Vigevano	SC	None – No leading firms	Free aggregation
Lucca	SC	None – No leading firms	Free aggregation
Verona	SC	Marketing-oriented committee	Free aggregation
San Mauro Pascoli	SC	Marketing-oriented committee	Free aggregation

- A common information: all districts aim to accept new partners, being born from "free aggregation".
- Specific information: make a choice between a cluster where a leader will plan the future and a cluster where, at most, common marketing strategies could be plan together. Depending on the manager's desire to maintain large autonomy and to be supported, the "archive" of Fig. 3 can provide immediate, even if preliminary, suggestions.

4   Conclusions

The analysis of a number of industrial districts, collected during the development of the EU CODESNET project and his evolution in national research programs, gave rise to a complete model of an industrial SME cluster, with three main complementary aspects (and model components): SME network cluster, management committee, and cluster creation dynamics. A graphical three dimensional representation of the cluster model has been presented. This same representation has to be interpreted as an "archive" of cluster data/information. This archive is useful tool for a manager who aims to join a cluster, but wants to take its decision based on a sufficient view of the cluster main characteristics.

In summary, manager asking for joining a district can get the following suggestions:

- As general information: all districts aim to accept new partners, if they have been born from "free aggregation";
- As specific information: make a choice between a cluster where a leader will plan the future and a cluster where, at most, common marketing strategies could be planned together.

The two above suggestions (that could be improved by taking into account of the district management body as well as of the district dimensions, as number of components and number of connections among them) can help the manager to take a decision, even if preliminary but sufficient to give him main lines to contact the district representative and negotiate for a potential joining agreement.

References

1. Villa, A., Bruno, G.: Promoting SME cooperative aggregations: main criteria and contractual models. Int. J. Prod. Res. **51**(23–24), 7439–7447 (2013)
2. Bruno, G., Villa, A.: An ontology-based model for SME network contracts. In: Herrero, P., Panetto, H., Meersman, R., Dillon, T. (eds.) OTM-WS 2012. LNCS, vol. 7567, pp. 85–92. Springer, Heidelberg (2012)
3. Villa, A., Antonelli, D.: Strengthening SME network governance. In: Villa, A., Antonelli, D. (eds.) A Road Map to the Development of European SME Networks, pp. 61–69. Springer, London (2009)
4. Antonelli, D., Taurino, T.: Identifying and exploiting the collaboration factors inside SMEs networks. Int. J. Networking Virtual Organ. **9**, 382–402 (2011). ISSN: 1470-9503

5. Taurino, T., Antonelli, D.: Analysis of potential collaborations in SME networks. In: INCOM 2009 - 13th IFAC Symposium on Information Control Problems in Manufacturing, Moscow, Russia (3–5 June 2009)
6. Goedkoop, M., van Haler, C., Te Riele, H., Rommers, P.: Product service-systems, ecological and economic basics. Report for Dutch Ministries of Environment (VROM) and Economic Affairs (EZ) (1999)
7. Tomlinson, P.R., Fai, F.M.: The nature of SME co-operation and innovation: a multi-scalar and multi-dimensional analysis. Int. J. Prod. Econ. **141**, 316–326 (2013)
8. Antonelli, D., Caroleo, B., Taurino, T.: Pattern recognition from data collection on industry networks. Syst. Sci. **33**, 81–90 (2007). ISSN: 0137-1223
9. Taurino, T., Antonelli D.: An insight into innovation patterns of industrial districts. In: 6th CIRP International Conference on Intelligent Computation in Manufacturing Innovative and Cognitive Production Technology and Systems, 2008, Naples, Italy (23–25 July 2008)
10. Markusen, A.: Sticky places in slippery space: a typology of industrial districts. Econ. Geogr. **72**(3), 293–313 (1996)
11. Coe, N.M.: A hybrid agglomeration? The development of a satellite-Marshallian industrial district in Vancouver's film industry. Urban Stud. **38**(10), 1753–1775 (2008)
12. Bogataj, M., Grubbstrom, R.W., Bogataj, L.: Efficient location of industrial activity cells in a global supply chain. Int. J. Prod. Econ. **133**(1), 243–250 (2011)
13. Villa, A., Taurino, T., Ukovich, W.: Supporting collaboration in European industrial districts – the CODESNET approach. J. Intell. Manuf., 1–10 (25 February 2011). doi:10.1007/s10845-011-0516-6
14. Boja, C.: Clusters models, factors and characteristics. Int. J. Econ. Pract. Theor. **1**(1), 34–43 (2011)
15. Villa, A., Taurino, T.: Cooperative agreements for SME network organization. In: Villa, A. (ed.) Managing Cooperation in Supply Newtwork Structures and Small or Medium-Sized Enterprises, pp. 19–34. Springer, London (2011)
16. Villa, A., Taurino, T.: SME networks and clusters: an approach to their performance evaluation. In: Villa, A. (ed.) Managing Cooperation in Supply Network Structures and Small or Medium-Sized Enterprises, pp. 65–88. Springer, London (2011)
17. CODESNET: COllaborative DEmand and Supply NETwork, European Coordination Action, EU-funded project EU FP7

A New Insight in the SMEs Internationalization Process

Eric Costa[1,2(✉)], António Lucas Soares[1,2],
and Jorge Pinho de Sousa[1,2]

[1] INESC TEC – INESC Technology and Science,
Campus da FEUP, Rua Dr. Roberto Frias 378, 4200-465 Porto, Portugal
eric.m.costa@inesctec.pt,
als@fe.up.pt, jsousa@inescporto.pt
[2] FEUP – Faculty of Engineering, University of Porto,
Rua Dr. Roberto Frias S/N, 4200-465 Porto, Portugal

Abstract. There is growing evidence that internationalization of small and medium enterprises (SMEs) has become a priority to gain competitive advantage. However, SMEs still face major challenges and obstacles during these processes. This paper proposes a model of collaborative networks for internationalization processes of SMEs, mediated by industrial enterprise associations (IEAs), in order to improve decision-making processes. First, a systematic literature review (SLR) was performed to study the impact that networks and collaboration have in the decision-making process of internationalization. Then, the model was developed using adequate information and knowledge management tools. Finally, to understand the relevance of the proposed model, data were gathered through interviews to key persons in companies of the IT/electronics and textile industries. Results showed that collaborative networks can represent an important facilitator in the internationalization of SMEs and that IEAs can have a fundamental role for promoting collaboration in this domain, between associated SMEs.

Keywords: Internationalization · Collaborative networks · Decision-making · Systematic literature review · Interviews

1 Introduction

Small and medium enterprises (SMEs) are the backbone of the economy in most of the countries around the world, and they can significantly contribute to restoring growth by entering into new market opportunities provided by developed and emerging economies. There is growing evidence that internationalization of SMEs has become a key requirement to gain competitive advantage [1, 2]. Some of the major motivations for going international are profit and growth goals, competitive pressures, foreign market opportunities, expansion opportunities, and domestic saturation [3–5]. However, SMEs still depend largely on their domestic markets and face challenges and obstacles during their internationalization processes. Among all difficulties in managing internationalization processes, SMEs face significant barriers related to the lack of capital, lack of adequate information and knowledge, and lack of adequate state support [6, 7].

© IFIP International Federation for Information Processing 2015
L.M. Camarinha-Matos et al. (Eds.): PRO-VE 2015, IFIP AICT 463, pp. 398–410, 2015.
DOI: 10.1007/978-3-319-24141-8_36

Information and knowledge are seen as key resources for facilitating SMEs international expansion, reducing risk and uncertainty, and increasing creativity in decision-making [8]. From another perspective, it has been found that collaborative networks can represent an important facilitator in the internationalization of SMEs, particularly by nurturing knowledge sharing [9]. However, there is clearly a lack of comprehensive and systematic studies investigating how SMEs can access, organize and use the information generated in a collaborative network context, and how they can collaboratively convert this information into knowledge to support decision-making in internationalization processes.

This paper proposes a model of collaborative networks for internationalization processes of SMEs, designed to improve decisions in those processes and to increase their export propensity. A systematic literature review (SLR) was first performed to study the impact that networks and collaboration have in decision-making processes of SMEs internationalization. Then, from the results obtained with the SLR and following some suggestions for future research in the literature, the model of collaborative networks for internationalization was constructed. The main distinguishing factors of this approach are that the model considers Portuguese industrial enterprise associations (IEAs) as the context for collaboration and is based on state-of-the-art information and knowledge management models, to significantly improve collaborative decision making in internationalization processes. To have a first feeling on the relevance of the model, three interviews were performed with companies with experience in these processes.

This study contributes to the body of knowledge in internationalization by providing a new model for SMEs to undertake internationalization processes in collaborative networks. Based on the feedback from experienced companies, the authors believe that the model can bring significant benefits for SMEs to internationalize, benefiting from the valuable resources that networks can bring for the process, and somehow overcoming the barriers of lack of adequate information and knowledge in decision-making. Moreover this work will hopefully represent an additional opportunity for further research and discussion in international scientific meetings.

2   Research Methodology

The research methodology applied for this study was composed by three parts: (i) systematic literature review (SLR); (ii) model proposal; (iii) interviews.

2.1   Systematic Literature Review

A SLR was used to study the impact that networks and collaboration have in internationalization decision-making processes. The intention of using a SLR was to move away from traditional narrative or descriptive reviews of the literature, creating a basic framework for a more in-depth analysis of the literature by adopting a replicable, scientific and transparent process [10]. The underlying literature review methodology followed a five-step approach, as proposed by [11, 12]:

Step 1:   **Questions formulation.** The research questions to be answered by this work were defined using the CIMO model [11] (Context, Intervention,

Mechanisms, and Outcomes) and are the following: how do networks and collaboration influence the internationalization process of SMEs? How do networks and collaboration affect the decision-making process?

Step 2: **Locating studies.** Two databases were used: Web of Science and Scopus. These databases cover a significant proportion of the published material on internationalization, including the most relevant peer-reviewed journals on the area. The search criteria used was: *(decision* OR "decision making" OR "decision-making") AND (internationali*) AND (collaborat* OR "collaborative networks" OR network*)*

Step 3: **Study selection and evaluation.** Inclusion and exclusion criteria were defined to select the studies to be included in the review. Only English and published peer-reviewed articles were included in the review. A 5-year time horizon was established (2010–2014) and some specific areas were considered, such as International Relations, Engineering, Operations Research, Business Management and Economics. After checking duplicates, titles and abstracts of the selected articles were analyzed for relevance. Articles eligible for review had to fulfil three main criteria: (i) articles had to be focused on SMEs and on the area of management studies; (ii) articles had to be empirical (qualitative and quantitative studies) rather than theoretical or conceptual; (iii) articles had to be focused on the influence of networks and collaboration in internationalization processes of SMEs, with specific emphasis on decision-making processes. The application of these criteria reduced the number of articles for analysis and synthesis to 16 (Table 1)

Step 4: **Analysis and synthesis.** The 16 papers obtained in this way were analyzed more in detail to extract and store information and cross tabulating the studies, in order to identify a set of key issues. For this purpose, a data extraction form in Excel was created

Step 5: **Reporting and using the results.** Section 3 of this paper formally presents the SLR results

2.2 Model Proposal

With the results of the SLR, and based on the future directions for research proposed in the literature and on the authors' knowledge and experience, a model is proposed in

Table 1. Summary of the study selection and evaluation (date of search: March 2014)

Criteria	Web of Science	Scopus	Total
Database analysis	180	195	375
Date range	91	99	190
Document type	72	75	147
Subject area	60	35	95
Language	58	34	92
After checking duplicates	-	-	81
Title and abstract analysis	-	-	16

this paper (Sect. 4). This model is expected to support the internationalization processes of SMEs in collaborative networks contexts. The model is focused in IEAs addressed as collaborative networks for internationalization. SMEs operating in industrial sectors with more uncertain environments might have larger information requirements than other SMEs operating with less amounts of uncertainty [2]. Thus, two types of industrial sectors will be considered as the target for implementation of the model: (i) the IT and electronics industry that operates in a quite uncertain context; (ii) the textile industry where more certain and foreseen environments are expected.

2.3   Interviews

To understand the relevance of the proposed model and to validate the idea before starting to apply it in a real world context, some interviews were performed, this providing a first feedback from potentially interested companies.

Semi-structured interviews were carried out with three Portuguese companies (one from the IT/electronics industry and two from the textile industry) in order to discuss previous internationalization experiences and to evaluate the role of IEAs in those processes. Personnel with experience in internationalization processes were interviewed, with an average duration of each interview of approximately one hour. A semi-structured interview guide was used and all conversations were recorded and transcribed. The open-ended style of interview allowed the respondents to describe their experiences and ideas freely, without being limited to standardized categories [4]. Section 5 describes the main findings of the performed interviews

3   SLR Findings

All the 16 analyzed papers had their focus on the influence of networks and collaboration in internationalization processes of SMEs. In fact, to limit the number of papers for analysis, emphasis was made on studies specifically approaching decision-making processes in internationalization.

The research methods most frequently adopted in the papers were interviews, questionnaires and surveys, with 13 of the 16 papers using those methods to obtain data for their studies. This kind of empirical research is very common in studies of internationalization: authors prepare different types of questions, and mainly approach companies' entrepreneurs, managers and key informants with experience in internationalization processes.

From the results of the SLR it can be concluded that, undoubtedly, SMEs need to form alliances, collaborate with different entities and use resources from their social and business networks, to be successful in internationalization processes. This conclusion can be generalized for almost all kind of companies from different types of industries or sectors: born global firms[1] [3, 13], manufacturing firms [14–16], service

---

[1] "Born global firms" is a term used in the internationalization literature, applied to firms aiming for international markets right from their birth or very shortly thereafter [3, 13, 20].

firms [17–19], and start-ups [20, 21]. According to this literature, an SME can establish collaborative networks for internationalization purposes with quite different types of intermediaries (Table 2).

Table 2. Types of intermediaries for collaborative networks in internationalization

Intermediaries	References
Local partners (distributors, subcontractors and customers)	[3, 6, 8, 13, 15, 17, 19, 20, 22]
Competitors	[13, 17, 19, 23]
Managers' contacts from previous jobs or experiences	[3, 13, 19, 24]
External parties	[14, 16]
Foreign firms	[13, 18, 19, 21]
Institutional agencies	[8, 25]
Consultants	[8]
Personal network, family and friends	[8, 13, 19, 21, 24, 25]
Government bodies	[8, 13]
Strategic allies and affiliated companies	[16, 22]

The knowledge, experience, information and learning from business partners, network relationships and collaborations, are resources that can be very useful for making decisions in internationalization, and which have influence on first entries into markets and on selection of host countries. Table 3 presents the reasons for establishing collaborative networks in internationalization processes.

From the SLR results, it has been found that networks can represent an important facilitator in the internationalization of SMEs, in quite different ways such as:

Table 3. Reasons for establishing collaborative networks in internationalization

Reasons	References
Achieve rapid international expansion and growth	[3, 8, 13, 17, 19–22]
Obtain information about foreign markets	[8, 14, 16, 19, 20, 25]
Explore how quickly an international opportunity can be exploited	[8, 19, 20]
Create strategic alliances or cooperation agreements	[13, 20]
Provide access to new knowledge	[3, 8, 13–17]
Create a source of learning	[16, 17, 22, 25]
Foster the decision to enter the export market	[8, 13, 16–19, 22]
Build up a distribution and commercialization network abroad	[18]
Increase export propensity	[13, 18, 21, 22]
Reduce information asymmetry	[8]
Reach target niches across international markets	[19]
Assist in mitigating the costs and risks of cross-border activities	[6, 19, 23]
Reduce uncertainty	[6, 13, 25]
Compensate the lack of financial resources	[13]
Assist in the selection of foreign entry modes	[3, 6, 8, 13, 19, 22]

(i) providing important channels of information and knowledge to decision-makers; (ii) influencing the approach adopted by SMEs' leaders; (iii) influencing decisions on foreign market selection and entry mode; (iv) allowing to increase international commitment; (v) overcoming resource constraints. In despite of this, there is a lack of comprehensive and systematic studies investigating how SMEs can access, organize and use the information generated in a collaborative network context, and how they can collaboratively convert this information into knowledge to support decision-making in internationalization processes. This is in line with some findings and future directions for research, as proposed in the literature:

- there is a lack of comprehensive and systematic studies investigating how SMEs can acquire and use information generated in a network context, to achieve higher levels of internationalization [2, 8];
- only limited studies show results on how SMEs can convert information into knowledge, for decision-making towards internationalization [26, 27];
- there has been a limited development of methods and techniques to improve the decision-making process of internationalization of SMEs [1];
- most of the literature on internationalization of SMEs is centered on companies acting in isolation, with only few studies considering collaborative internationalization processes [28].

4   A Model of Collaborative Networks for Internationalization

A model of collaborative networks for internationalization processes of SMEs is proposed in this paper, as a way to address some of the issues and future directions for research identified in the literature. The objective of creating this model was to contribute to the internationalization of SMEs, mainly in what concerns the associated decision-making processes. The general hypothesis is that information models and technologies, by providing information collected from heterogeneous sources and mediated by favorable collaborative contexts, positively influence the decision-making capabilities in the internationalization processes of SMEs. This paper is the first formal presentation of the model, providing a brief description of the approach and methods, as well as some of the expected impacts.

Introduction and Baseline Research. Managing effectively the information in internationalization decision processes is, for many companies, a critical success factor that has been addressed in the literature, in different ways and perspectives. It has in fact been shown that information is crucial for more rational decision-making [8], to manage international complexity and ambiguity [29], to reduce risks and uncertainty [26], and to stimulate awareness of foreign market opportunities [30]. There are also studies on the importance of the role of information in the creation of internationalization knowledge [17, 31], as well as on demonstrating that cooperation and networks are facilitators of internationalization [19, 32]. In spite of this, surprisingly there is a clear lack of exploratory studies on how state-of-the-art information management models and technologies can be used to improve collaborative decision-making in the internationalization of SMEs. Moreover, there is no sound reporting on the benefits of systematic networking and collaboration in internationalization.

Approach and Methods. The model was designed to be general, but it was instantiated and assessed by involving two Portuguese IEAs that contribute to the internationalization process of SMEs. IEAs can play a facilitating role to promote collaboration between SMEs, providing services and information to support the internationalization of their associates. The model will allow IEAs to assist SMEs in accessing and interpreting information, decide on the best internationalization strategy, and join competencies with other SMEs, to maximize the success of their internationalization processes. Actively involving IEAs in SMEs internationalization processes is, to the best of the authors' knowledge, an innovative contribution of the proposed model.

The model will encompass novel information management tools, in order to support collaborative internationalization decisions and processes. These information management models and technologies will allow SMEs to search, collect, integrate, organize and visualize information from different internet accessible, heterogeneous public and private sources, to be used and adapted in the different contexts where they are embedded. The concept of "information internalization" will be considered in the development of the solution. As information and knowledge are complementary and transformable, SMEs should find ways to transform information into knowledge in order to enhance the internationalization process. Information internalization is the process of absorbing both tacit and explicit information into the organization and translating it into knowledge, to be then applied with some specific purpose [33]. Therefore, in this model, a model will be developed in the context of firms acting in collaboration, exploring the following modes of information internalization: socialization, combination, externalization, and internalization [34].

Additionally, to improve the effectiveness of decision-making in the internationalization of SMEs, a collaborative decision support system (DSS) will be designed, based on multi-criteria decision-making approaches and on business intelligence. This DSS will support activities related to market selection, choice of partners and resources, assessment of risks and negotiation. The "business intelligence" concept will also be used for gathering, analyzing and distributing information, and also to support the strategic decision-making process [35]. Figure 1 presents the rationale of the model.

According to some future research directions identified by [2, 8, 27], there is a need to explore how different contexts would result in different information and knowledge requirements for SMEs to internationalize. Dutot et al. [2] stated that SMEs in industries operating in more uncertain environments might have greater information requirements than SMEs in more "deterministic" environments. Therefore, to test and validate the model, the developed solutions will be applied to case studies addressing SMEs of two different types of industrial sectors: (i) the IT and electronics industry, which operates in a quite uncertain context; and (ii) the textile industry, where more certain and foreseen environments are expected.

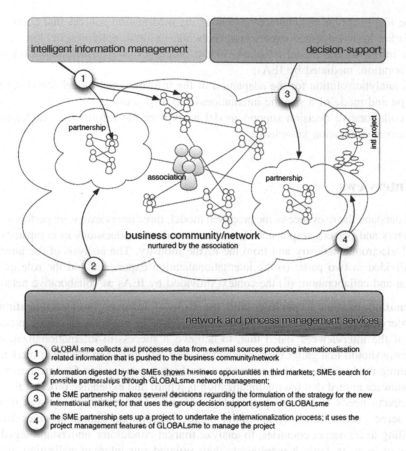

Fig. 1. Rationale of the proposed model

The strength of the model depicted in Fig. 1 lies in the combination of three valuable components for supporting enterprise networks: information, decision-making and collaboration. The rationale of the model use is a set of SMEs joining efforts through networks creation and collaborative process management services, to access high value added information and knowledge about internationalization conditions and to perform collaborative decision-making on the development of internationalization strategies. All these processes are facilitated by IEAs.

Expected Impacts. The main expected results and impacts of the model are:

- a description and explanation of the factors influencing the management of information that is relevant for internationalization purposes;
- a comprehensive characterization of the decision processes involved in the internationalization of SMEs and on how the IEA influences those processes;
- a description and explanation of the factors influencing the implementation of collaborative processes for internationalization;

- the identification and characterization of the information sources that contribute to market knowledge and experiential (network, cultural, entrepreneur) knowledge;
- an informational model adaptable to the processes of internationalization in collaboration, mediated by IEAs;
- an analytic solution for the adaptation of the informational model according to the type and mode of a specific internationalization process;
- a collaborative decision support model to explore the information model and the internationalization knowledge.

5   Interviews

To understand the relevance of the proposed model, three interviews were performed with managers and persons responsible for internationalization decisions in companies from the IT/electronics industry and from the textile industry. The analysis of the interviews was divided in two parts: (i) the internationalization experience and the role of information and collaboration; (ii) the context provided by IEAs as collaborative networks.

Internationalization Experience and the Role of Information/Collaboration. All the interviewed companies have a lot of experience in internationalization processes. One of the interviewees stated that, to achieve a successful internationalization, the company should first gain experience and be well established in the home market, thus becoming ready for launching innovation products or services in foreign markets. All interviewees agreed that internationalization is a hard and expensive process, for which a company needs to be well prepared in advance. Financial capacity was therefore considered crucial since, at an initial stage, internationalization involves frequent travelling to the target countries, to analyze market conditions, understand legislation, and participate in fairs. Nevertheless, they pointed out internationalization as being essential for the growth of their companies.

Regarding the issue of sharing information with other companies or entities, the interviewees stated this is an interesting, viable and useful activity. They considered that companies might be willing to share information and knowledge about previous internationalization experiences, with companies wanting to start to internationalize in particular to markets where some experience has already been accumulated. This will provide a clear idea about the internationalization process, the problems and barriers to face, and all the particular aspects of some specific target countries.

In what concerns the involvement with other companies in collaborative networks, some believe that the collaboration of experienced companies with less experienced companies in internationalization projects, will increase their competitiveness, visibility and presence in the market. Moreover, as SMEs face more difficulties in internationalization processes, they could create joint ventures with each other to increase their chances of success. Yet, the interviewees of one of the companies suggested that, to collaborate, companies should be of equal size and have common interests, since companies with a different economic power will probably have different requirements and objectives, with different approaches, values and resources. They have also stated that in a process of internationalization, when approaching a new market, there should be a budget, a strategy and an outflow of resources to be adequately matched for companies to collaborate.

The Context of IEAs as Collaborative Networks. The three studied companies are associates of IEAs in their industrial sectors. All the companies agreed that IEAs should be more active in supporting their associates, as they can surely have an important role for the development of better internationalization processes. One interviewee considered that IEAs can act as disseminators of information and competences of their associates, thus promoting the creation of collaborations and of good synergies between companies. This would be particularly useful in launching internationalization processes together, as well as in exploring and creating new international opportunities.

One of the main problems faced by these companies is the lack of information and knowledge about certain markets. The interviewees consider that, in a first stage, IEAs may play an interesting role as "information aggregators", analyzing different markets and pointing paths to follow, and showing the reality of each market. At a later stage, IEAs may promote discussion and meetings between their associates, seeking the alignment of strategic objectives and the set-up of joint initiatives and investments in a given market, thus sharing costs and risks.

6 Conclusion

This study aims at contributing to the internationalization processes of SMEs, by presenting a new perspective on these processes and a new model of collaborative networks for internationalization. The next paragraphs present the main conclusions of the work, as well as some suggestions for further research possibly to be developed in future scientific meetings and conferences in this area.

From the results of the performed SLR, it has been found that collaborative networks can represent an important facilitator in the internationalization of SMEs, particularly by nurturing knowledge sharing, obtaining information about foreign markets and achieving rapid international expansion and growth.

From the responses obtained with the interviews, it is clear that IEAs might have a more active role in the internationalization processes of their associates. IEAs can have a fundamental role in fostering collaboration between associates, promoting both dissemination of opportunities and establishment of relationships.

The model proposed in this paper contributes to the scientific knowledge on SME internationalization by addressing how SMEs can establish collaborative networks for internationalization processes. It also contributes to the field of information and knowledge management, with the development of approaches and techniques to support these management activities for internationalization decision-making in collaborative networks. In this study the context used for collaboration is formed by Portuguese IEAs, which, to the best of the authors' knowledge, has never been addressed in previous research.

This paper shows that the management of internationalization is a research area that can be further explored with concepts and approaches based on topics of collaborative networks, and information and knowledge management. Researchers of these areas can bring new insights and contributions for the internationalization of SMEs, as well as for the internationalization of multinational enterprises (MNEs), with the creation of new business models and concepts [36–39] that, among other contributions, can provide an important support to internationalization.

Acknowledgments. This research was financed by the North Portugal Regional Operational Programme (ON.2 - O Novo Norte), under the National Strategic Reference Framework (NSRF), through the European Regional Development Fund (ERDF), and by national funds, through the Portuguese funding agency, Fundação para a Ciência e a Tecnologia (FCT), within project NORTE-07-0124-FEDER-000057.

References

1. Schweizer, R.: The internationalization process of SMEs: a muddling-through process. J. Bus. Res. **65**, 745–751 (2012)
2. Dutot, V., Bergeron, F., Raymond, L.: Information management for the internationalization of SMEs: an exploratory study based on a strategic alignment perspective. Int. J. Inf. Manag. **34**, 672–681 (2014)
3. Andersson, S.: International entrepreneurship, born globals and the theory of effectuation. J. Small Bus. Enterp. Dev. **18**, 627–643 (2011)
4. Hutchinson, K., Alexander, N., Quinn, B., Doherty, A.M.: Internationalization motives and facilitating factors. Qual. Evid. **15**, 96–122 (2007)
5. Kiss, A.N., Williams, D.W., Houghton, S.M.: Risk bias and the link between motivation and new venture post-entry international growth. Int. Bus. Rev. **22**, 1068–1078 (2013)
6. London, K.: Multi-market industrial organizational economic models for the internationalization process by small and medium enterprise construction design service firms. Archit. Eng. Des. Manag. **6**, 132–152 (2010)
7. Djordjevic, M., Sapic, S., Marinkovic, V.: How companies enter international markets: presentation and analysis of the empirical research. Actual Prob. Econ. **7**, 331–342 (2012)
8. Child, J., Hsieh, L.H.Y.: Decision mode, information and network attachment in the internationalization of SMEs: a configurational and contingency analysis. J. World Bus. **49**, 598–610 (2014)
9. Musteen, M., Francis, J., Datta, D.K.: The influence of international networks on internationalization speed and performance: a study of Czech SMEs. J. World Bus. **45**, 197–205 (2010)
10. Tranfield, D., Denyer, D., Smart, P.: Towards a methodology for developing evidence-informed management knowledge by means of systematic review. Br. J. Manag. **14**, 207–222 (2003)
11. Denyer, D., Tranfield, D.: Producing a systematic review. Organizational Research Methods, Sage, Beverly Hills (2009)
12. Wong, C., Skipworth, H., Godsell, J., Achimugu, N.: Towards a theory of supply chain alignment enablers: a systematic literature review. Supply Chain Manag. Int. J. **17**, 419–437 (2012)
13. Kaur, S., Sandhu, M.S.: Internationalisation of born global firms: evidence from Malaysia. J. Asia Pacific Econ. **19**, 101–136 (2013)

14. Aspelund, A., Butsko, V.: Small and middle-sized enterprises' offshoring production: A study of firm decisions and consequences. Tijdschr. Voor Econ. En Soc. Geogr. **101**, 262–275 (2010)
15. Hultman, J., Johnsen, T., Johnsen, R., Hertz, S.: An interaction approach to global sourcing: a case study of IKEA. J. Purch. Supply Manag. **18**, 9–21 (2012)
16. Peng, Y.-S.Y.S., Yang, K.P.K.-P., Liang, C.C.C.-C.: The learning effect on business groups' subsequent foreign entry decisions into transitional economies. Asia Pacific Manag. Rev. **16**, 1–21 (2011)
17. Casillas, J.C.J.C., Acedo, F.J., Barbero, J.L.J.L.: Learning, unlearning and internationalisation: evidence from the pre-export phase. Int. J. Inf. Manag. **30**, 162–173 (2010)
18. Castellacci, F.: Service firms heterogeneity, international collaborations and export participation. J. Ind. Competition Trade. **14**, 259–285 (2014)
19. Ibeh, K., Kasem, L.: The network perspective and the internationalization of small and medium sized software firms from Syria. Ind. Mark. Manag. **40**, 358–367 (2011)
20. Cannone, G., Ughetto, E.: Born globals: a cross-country survey on high-tech start-ups. Int. Bus. Rev. **23**, 272–283 (2014)
21. Kollmann, T., Christofor, J.: International entrepreneurship in the network economy: Internationalization propensity and the role of entrepreneurial orientation. J. Int. Entrep. **12**, 43–66 (2014)
22. Torkkeli, L., Puumalainen, K., Saarenketo, S., Kuivalainen, O.: The Effect of Network Competence and Environmental Hostility on the Propensity of SMEs to Internationalise. Emerald Group Publishing Limited, School of Business, Lappeenranta University of Technology, Lappeenranta (2011)
23. Malik, T.: First mover, strategic alliances and performance: context of turmoil in China. Chin. Manag. Stud. **6**, 647–667 (2012)
24. Zucchella, A., Servais, P.: The internationalisation process of small- and medium-sized firms and the liability of complexity. Int. J. Entrep. Small Bus. **15**, 191 (2012)
25. Santos-Alvarez, V., Garcia-Merino, T.: The role of the entrepreneur in identifying international expansion as a strategic opportunity. Int. J. Inf. Manag. **30**, 512–520 (2010)
26. Nguyen, T.D., Barrett, N.J., Fletcher, R.: Information internalisation and internationalisation —evidence from Vietnamese firms. Int. Bus. Rev. **15**, 682–701 (2006)
27. Fletcher, M., Harris, S.: Knowledge acquisition for the internationalization of the smaller firm: content and sources. Int. Bus. Rev. **21**, 631–647 (2012)
28. Hong, P., Roh, J.: Internationalization, product development and performance outcomes: a comparative study of 10 countries. Res. Int. Bus. Financ. **23**, 169–180 (2009)
29. Hsu, W.-T., Chen, H.-L., Cheng, C.-Y.: Internationalization and firm performance of SMEs: the moderating effects of CEO attributes. J. World Bus. **48**, 1–12 (2013)
30. Zhou, L., Wu, W., Luo, X.: Internationalization and the performance of born-global SMEs: the mediating role of social networks. J. Int. Bus. Stud. **38**, 673–690 (2007)
31. Saarenketo, S., Puumalainen, K., Kyläheiko, K., Kuivalainen, O.: Linking knowledge and internationalization in small and medium-sized enterprises in the ICT sector. Technovation **28**, 591–601 (2008)
32. Ciravegna, L., Lopez, L., Kundu, S.: Country of origin and network effects on internationalization: a comparative study of SMEs from an emerging and developed economy. J. Bus. Res. **67**, 916–923 (2014)
33. Knight, G.A., Liesch, P.W.: Information internalisation in internationalising the firm. J. Bus. Res. **55**, 981–995 (2002)
34. Nonaka, I., Takeuchi, H.: The Knowledge-Creating Company: How Japanese Companies Create the Dynamics of Innovation. Oxford University Press, New York (1995)

35. Rouhani, S., Ghazanfari, M., Jafari, M.: Evaluation model of business intelligence for enterprise systems using fuzzy TOPSIS. Expert Syst. Appl. **39**, 3764–3771 (2012)
36. Aguilera, C., Castañeda, A., Guerrero, F.: Past, present and future of the Andalusan aeronautical cluster. Network-Centric Collaboration and Supporting Frameworks. IFIP, vol. 224, pp. 583–590. Springer, US (2006)
37. Imtiaz, A., Hauge, J.B.: Enriching collaboration among Eastern European SMEs through dedicated virtual platform. Pervasive Collaborative Networks. IFIP, vol. 283, pp. 567–576. Springer, US (2008)
38. Jansson, K.: An innovation and engineering maturity model for marine industry networks. In: Camarinha-Matos, L.M., Pereira-Klen, A., Afsarmanesh, H. (eds.) PRO-VE 2011. IFIP AICT, vol. 362, pp. 253–260. Springer, Heidelberg (2011)
39. Jansson, K., Karvonen, I., Uoti, M.: Towards collaborative alignment of engineering networks. In: Camarinha-Matos, L.M., Xu, L., Afsarmanesh, H. (eds.) Collaborative Networks in the Internet of Services. IFIP AICT, vol. 380, pp. 467–474. Springer, Heidelberg (2012)

Collaborative Communities

Territories as Collaborative Networks: Concepts and Elements of Commitment

João Alberto Rubim Sarate[1] and Janaina Macke[1,2(✉)]

[1] Faculty Meridional, IMED,
R. Senador Pinheiro, 304, Passo Fundo 99070-220, Brazil
{joao.sarate,janaina.macke}@imed.edu.br
[2] University of Caxias do Sul (UCS),
R. Francisco Getúlio Vargas, 1130, Caxias do Sul 95020-972, Brazil
jmacke@ucs.br

Abstract. The present study aims at analyzing a territory according to collaborative network concepts. It highlights the degree of members' commitment with a collaborative project. The research was conducted in a collaborative network in southern Brazil. The quantitative survey highlighted the three dimensions of commitment: continuance, affective and normative. Affective commitment was the most significant for the continuation of the collaborative network project. The research provides practical and academic contributions and demonstrates how collaborative processes can depend on a territory's specific resources.

Keywords: Collaborative networks · Territory · Commitment

1 Introduction

One of the major challenges of current studies on local development is related to the processes of endogenization and construction of new development strategies. If, in one hand, we see the decline of traditional industrial regions, on the other, we have seen the emergence of a new paradigm, such as the service innovation. This dialectical movement has been contributing to significant changes in the theories and practices of territorial development.

This work has focused on emerging forms of cooperation; such forms are called collaborative networks that consist in entities (people and organizations) autonomous, geographically distributed and heterogeneous with respect to its environment of operation, their culture, their goals and their capital [1]. It is precisely because of the capacity to promote collaboration in order to work collectively, that the collaborative networks concept can role a key position in the development of a territory.

The associative capacity depends on the degree that communities, groups and businesses share norms and values and are prepared to subordinate individual interests to those of larger groups. From these shared values trust emerges [2].

Collaborative networks organizations are structured primarily to make a favorable position against the competition. Therefore, internal resources presented in the group should be valued because they can become the source of competitive advantages [3–6].

© IFIP International Federation for Information Processing 2015
L.M. Camarinha-Matos et al. (Eds.): PRO-VE 2015, IFIP AICT 463, pp. 413–420, 2015.
DOI: 10.1007/978-3-319-24141-8_37

From the perspective of territorial development, the process of building a competitive territory can be considered dependent on specific features in the territory. Resources should be understood as material assets and relational assets. An activity is territorialized when "its economic viability is rooted in assets (including practices and relations) that are not available elsewhere and that cannot be easily or quickly created or imitated in places that do not have them" [7].

However, working together can be challenging and risky. Often organizations can have a good performance when working alone and show poor performance when they work together. This means that before deciding to join a network, organizations must be prepared to collaborate in order to be ready to react quickly and take advantage of business opportunities [8, 9].

In the case of territories analyzed as collaborative networks, this is especially relevant. It is common to face some difficulties in collaboration processes, in terms of resources, individual's contributions evaluation and lacks of commitment. In fact, a system of common values development is a significant element for the sustainability of collaboration, for it allows the key elements identification that create value in the network, avoiding misunderstandings and promoting the formalization of a shared understanding [10].

The study objective is to analyze the degree of commitment of a territory with its development project through collaborative networks, so as to identify strategies that can strengthen and sustain the collaborative process.

After a literature review and the presentation of the research context, the method section explains the sample as well as methods for data collection and data analysis. The subsequent findings section provides a descriptive overview on the thematic areas. The final section discusses the findings and concludes on the insights gained from this study.

2   Theoretical Background

The analysis of the territories centred on the concepts of territorial economy. Its fundamental elements concern the collective construction of the territory, based on its population daily lives, their work-related activities and family life. The territories and networks surveyed were considered as socioeconomic and political projects [11–13].

Networks have their own way to structure the relationship between the territory's cooperative and antagonistic forces. They are instruments that enable to control power and disputes and are likely to function as integration and exclusion tools in differentiation processes [14].

Collaborative networks are organizational forms based on the collaboration between its members, according to a specific shared goal. A collaborative network organization (CNO) is a form of emerging organizational setting that involves mutual engagement of participants to solve a problem together, which implies mutual trust, and therefore takes time, effort and dedication. A CNO can be created from a regional grouping of companies that already have a longstanding relationship and a cultural history [15].

In this sense, organizational commitment refers to identification with the organization, through the belief and acceptance of company's values and goals and through the desire to remain a member of the company making efforts for the benefit of the organization [16]. In addition, commitment has three main features: strong belief in the goals and values of the organization, willingness to make an extra effort on behalf of the company and a great desire to join and belong to the company [17].

The most accepted view on organizational commitment refers to the psychological state that characterizes the relationship among employees and the company that implies the decision to continue being part of the company. In this study, we consider three components of organizational commitment: (i) affective commitment: related to peoples' emotional involvement and their identification with the organization, (ii) continuance commitment: related to perceived costs of leaving the organization; (iii) normative commitment: related to the feeling of obligation to remain in the organization [18, 19].

Once the concept of organizational commitment is extended and applied to the inter-organizational context of collaborative networks, identities are constructed from the interaction between networks and the territory. Given the networks' reciprocal character, the territory has even more relevance. The interaction between them requires intercultural exchange and new communication skills [14]. The key for thinking about the creation of collaborative networks is negotiation and intercultural communication skills, supported by inter-organizational commitment.

3 Method

This study was conducted at an agricultural business network, located in Southern Brazil. The survey was applied to 210 employees from companies that are members of this network. We aimed to correlate the amount of interorganizational commitment with the collaborative network project.

The territory is part of the Serra Gaúcha region, located in the state of Rio Grande do Sul (Southern Brazil). It is a region formed mainly by descendants of Italian immigrants who arrived in Brazil between the years 1875 and 1930. The region is characterized by the presence of small family farms, in part, due to the fact it is the largest wine region of Brazil with about 40,000 hectares of vineyards.

The sample was non-probabilistic, which was chosen for convenience. This work is an exploratory study that used quantitative approach. Exploratory research has the main purpose to develop, modify and clarify concepts and ideas [20]. This study is based on the survey method, using the questionnaire as a technique for data collection.

In order to measure interorganizational commitment we used the 7-item scale developed by Meyer and Allen [18], which was translated and applied in Brazil by Rego et al. [19]. Before formal survey, we ran a pre-test with fifteen members of the network. We used the software PASW statistic 18, to analyze data. The statistics chosen were the descriptive, the factorial and the correlation analysis.

The choice of this referential work was because of the similarity of some features of the context previously discussed by the authors with the reality of companies to be surveyed. The geographical proximity between industries and their integration and relevance in local communities reinforce this choice.

4 Discussion

The data were submitted to factor analysis using PCA (Principal Component Analysis), with varimax rotation and pairwise treatment (considered all valid observations of each variable) for the missing data. The index of Kaiser-Meyer-Olkin (KMO) adequacy of the sample was 0.903 and the Bartlett's Test of Sphericity - (significant to 0.001) indicated the factorability of data.

Results of factor analysis suggested that interorganizational commitment is explained by three factors, with 63.623 % of total variance explained. The Cronbach's Alpha for this scale was 0.922 that represents a satisfactory range for an exploratory study [21]. It is possible to conclude that the items in each dimension of the construct are suitable for measuring the interorganizational commitment into territories (Fig. 1).

Continuance Commitment 0.906[*]	Affective Commitment 0.862[*]	Normative Commitment 0.730[*]
Cost of leaving the network	Emotional attachment to the network	Feeling of obligation to the network
Cost of change	Strong beliefs in the networks' goals and values	Moral and ethical obligations
Previous investment in the network	Readiness to support other members	Cultural values
Result of a cognitive evaluation process	Need to maintain their membership	Degree of professional socialization
	Integration into the network	

* Cronbach's Alpha.

Fig. 1. Elements of interorganizational commitment dimensions and Cronbach's Alphas.

The factorial analysis resulted in three elements. Those adapted from Meyer and Allen [18] and Rego et al. [19] remained within the same concepts, which contributed for the construction of the concept of inter-engagement. The percentage of explained variance was 63.63 %, which means that the variables chosen and the resulting factors can explain 63.63 % of the inter-organizational commitment.

Cronbanch's alpha values were calculated in order to test the consistency of the variables in each factor. The ideal alpha value in social sciences exploratory researches should be higher than 0.6 [22].

The first factor identified was instrumental commitment, with an alpha value (0.906) considered excellent [23]. Its variables obtained the lowest average (from 1.74 to 2.31), which means that in the context studied the degree of instrumental commitment was notably low. The cost of leaving the network was relatively low in the analysis of the degree of commitment.

Instrumental connection is linked to proximity to or the availability of resources and territorial assets that interest or benefit the individuals [13]. These resources and assets are employed in the context of collaborative network. When the relationship is predominantly instrumental, the cost of moving can be high because it would imply in the loss of some advantage that the territory can provide to the individual [18]. In this particular case, the costs of an eventual departure from the collaborative network were low.

Affective commitment derives from identity bonds built over time. Its variables obtained the highest average (2.64 to 4.25), suggesting that links with the territory are essentially affective, the result of experience and acquired knowledge. The relationship between individuals and the area of the collaborative network includes objective and subjective aspects, which tend to increase over time [11, 24]. In the case studied, the strong emotional bonds indicate that members tend to remain in the collaborative territory even in dire situations.

The third factor, normative commitment, concerns the links established by reciprocal ties, the normative sense of duty of living in the territory in order to repay what might have been gained from it [11]. Its variables presented averages between 2.40 and 3.60, indicating that the development achieved through the collaborative network generated a moral sense of obligation to remain in it [18].

One aspect that was appeared relevant was the difference between the levels of network commitment of people who work with the family and other employees who have no family ties to the owners of the companies associated with the network.

As we can see in Fig. 2, the commitment levels are higher for those working in the family business. The analysis of variance (ANOVA test) was significant for the three factors ($p = 0.000$ for continuance; $p = 0.002$ for affective; $p = 0.000$ for normative), which indicates that the family ties are significant important for the network commitment.

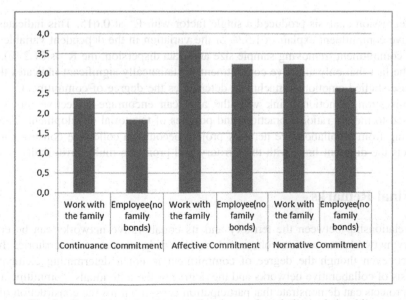

Fig. 2. Commitment levels according types of workplace relationships.

This explains the high level of affective commitment, because it mixes family with labor relationships, while sharing common life projects. On the other hand, this result points to a challenge: as the collaborative project matures, the need for more professional relationships increases and consequently, the need to achieve the commitment of new members without family ties.

In the region, dominates a workaholic behavior, cultural heritage of immigrants who believed that with work, everything is achieved. The obstinacy combined with an entrepreneurial vein, has become an unmistakable mark of the immigrant. This cultural aspect is predominant in the region and overlaps with other cultural differences.

Linear regression was applied in order to analyze how each group of variables was related to the general perception of commitment: the variable number 41 of the data collection tool - "Overall, I feel committed to the territory".

Variables were considered significant when $p < 0.05$ (probability of error of 5 %). Beta is the relative significance of each variable and determines their order of importance in the same factor [22]. Value R^2 indicates the degree of explanation of the set of variables in relation to the general perception of the degree of territorial commitment. In order to perform linear regression, the stepwise regression was used. Such method considers as entry criterion of the variables in the model, their significance level [21] (Table 1).

Table 1. Linear regression model

Model	R	R^2	R^2 adjusted	Error	Durbin-Watson
1	0.784	0.615	0.612	0.838	2.198

Regression analysis produced a single factor with R^2 at 0.615. This indicates that affective commitment explains 61.5 % of the variation in the dependent variable territorial commitment (removing sample size and data dispersion, the R^2 is 61.2 %).

The fact that only affective commitment is statistically significant indicates that in the case studied emotional attachment determines the degree of commitment.

This strong emotional link with the area can encourage collective movements opposed to merely rational practices and policies of territorial development. The area resulting from a collaborative network project becomes a collective construction that respects the different links with the territory and promotes multi-territoriality [24].

5   Final Remarks

The relationship between the territory and its collaborative networks can be contradictory: networks can act as a cohesion element or they can transgress territories. In this respect, even though the degree of commitment is not a determining element, the analysis of collaborative networks and the degree of the individuals' commitment with their projects can demonstrate that participation is essential for the construction of new territorial scales.

This study maintains that engaging practices happen on an instrumental, normative and affective level, and configure an "ideal way of living" in an area. Residents depend on local resources and believe in remaining in the territory. The way of living is, in this case, the attitude of the individuals in relation with the space they inhabit.

Through which mechanisms the process of building a collaborative network can be understood? Being the territory something "alive", how the sharing of resources should be considered? Such questions can lead to the identification of elements and methods able to encourage the establishment of new collaborative networks. Firstly, it is necessary to recognize that networks are not homogeneous; they function as connectivity spaces, a reticular formation that can preside over some kind of sociability that minds specially the level of affective commitment.

National policies for territorial development prioritize rational aspects much to the detriment of emotional and affective elements. Collective movements opposed to purely rational policies of territorial development are possible. The present study argues that divergent perceptions on territorial development projects should be considered, given that the concept of territory encompasses collective construction and respect for the different relationships within it.

Acknowledgments. This work is being supported by the Faculty Meridional (Faculdade IMED), University of Caxias do Sul (Universidade de Caxias do Sul - UCS), the Coordination for the Improvement of Higher Education Personnel (Coordenação de Aperfeiçoamento de Pessoal de Nível Supeior - CAPES), and the National Counsel for Scientific and Technological Development (Conselho Nacional de Desenvolvimento Científico e Tecnológico - CNPq).

References

1. Camarinha-Matos, L.M., Afsarmanesh, H.: Collaborative networks: a new scientific discipline. J. Intell. Manuf. **16**, 439–452 (2005)
2. Fukuyama, F.: Trust: the Social Creation Virtues and the Creation of Prosperity. Free Press, New York (1995)
3. Wernerfelt, B.: A resource-based view of the firm. Strateg. Manag. J. **5**, 171–180 (1984)
4. Prahalad, C.K., Hamel, G.: The core competence of the corporation. Harward Bus. Rev. **68**, 79–91 (1990)
5. Barney, J.: Firm resources and sustained competitive advantage. J. Manag., Greenwich. **17** (1), 99–120 (1991)
6. Penrose, E.T.: The Theory of the Growth of the Firm. Oxford University Press, New York (1995)
7. Cassiolato, J.E., Szapiro, M.: Arranjos e Sistemas Produtivos e Inovativos Locais no Brasil. In: Lastres, et. al. (eds.). Promoção de sistemas produtivos locais de micro, pequenas e médias empresas. UFRRJ/IE/REDESIST, Rio de Janeiro (2002)
8. Camarinha-Matos, L.M., et al.: Collaborative networked organizations: concepts and practice in manufacturing enterprises. Comput. Ind. Eng. **57**(1), 46–60 (2009)
9. Rosas, J., Camarinha-Matos, L.M.: An approach to assess collaboration readiness. Int. J. Prod. Res. **47**(17), 471–4735 (2009)
10. Camarinha-Matos, L.M., Macedo, P.: A conceptual model of value systems in collaborative networks. J. Intell. Manuf. **21**(3), 287–299 (2010)

11. Pecqueur, B.: A guinada territorial da economia global. Política & Sociedade: Revista de Sociologia Política. **8**(4), 79–105 (2009)
12. Mollard, A., Pecqueur, B., Hirczak, M., Rambonilaza, M., Vollet, D.: Le modèle du panier de biens: grille d'analyse et observations de terrain. Économie Rurale **308**, 55–70 (2008)
13. Bolba-Olga, O., Grossetti, M.: Socio-économie de proximité. Cinquièmes Journées de la Proximité. Bordeaux, juin (2006)
14. Silva, R.H.A.: Sociedade em Rede: cultura, globalização e formas colaborativas (2004). http://www.bocc.ubi.pt/pag/silva-regina-sociedade-em-rede.pdf
15. Camarinha-Matos, L.M., Afsarmanesh, H.: The Virtual Enterprise Concept. Infrastructures for Virtual Enterprises: Networking Industrial Enterprises. Kluwer Academic Publishers, Boston (1999)
16. Mowday, R.T., Porter, L.W., Steers, R.M.: Employee-Organizational Linkages: the Psychology of Commitment, Absenteeism, and Turnover. Academic Press, New York (1986)
17. Fiorito, J., Bozeman, D.P., Young, A., Meurs, J.A.: Organizational commitment, human resource practices, and organizational characteristics. J. Manag. Issues. **19**(2), 186–207 (2007)
18. Meyer, J.P., Allen, N.J.: A three-component conceptualization of organizational commitment. Hum. Resour. Manag. Rev. **1**(1), 61–89 (1991)
19. Rego, A., Cunha, M.P., Souto, S.: Espiritualidade nas organizações e comprometimento organizacional. RAE eletrônica **6**(2), 1–27 (2007)
20. Yin, R.K.: Case Study Research: Design and Methods. Sage Publications, Thousand Oaks (1994)
21. Hair, J.F., Babin, B., Money, A.H., Samoul, P.: Essentials of Business Research Methods. Leyh Publishing, LLC (2003)
22. Malhotra, N.: Pesquisa de marketing: uma orientação aplicada, 4th edn. Bookman, Porto Alegre (2007)
23. Pestana, M.H., Gageiro, J.N.: Análise de Dados para Ciências Sociais: A Complementaridade do SPSS, 4ª edn. Sílabo, Lisboa (2005)
24. Haesbaert, R.: O mito da desterritorialização: do "fim dos territórios" à multiterritorialidade. Bertrand Brasil, Rio de Janeiro (2009)

Towards an Enterprise Social Network to Support Inter-organizational Collaborations

Sarah Zribi[1](✉), Aurélie Montarnal[2], Frédérick Bénabén[2], Matthieu Lauras[2],
Jacques Lamothe[2], Michael Bailly[3], and Jean-Pierre Lorré[1]

[1] Linagora, 75, Route de Revel, 31400 Toulouse, France
{szribi,jplorre}@linagora.com
[2] Mines Albi – University of Toulouse, Campus Jarlard, Route de Teillet, 81000 Albi, France
{aurelie.montarnal,frederick.benaben,matthieu.lauras,
jacques.lamothe}@mines-albi.fr
[3] Linagora, 80, Rue Roque de Fillol, 92800 Puteaux, France
mbailly@linagora.com

Abstract. Since the 2000s, social networks have grown spectacularly until they are now regarded as indispensable and introduced as a daily practice of millions of users. Enterprises have become aware of the need and the importance of these collaborative tools, and the concept of Enterprise Social Network (ESN) has now emerged. As such, OpenPaaS is an innovative ESN that aims at facilitating inter-organizational collaborations. In this sense, this paper describes the new OpenPaaS platform to address current issues of ESNs: (i) the management and exchange of large amount of data during inter organizational collaborations; (ii) the ability of the system to provide synchronous communications between collaborative partners; and finally, (iii) the establishment of transverse collaborations. This last point is a key feature of OpenPaaS, which goal is to automatically generate new inter-organizational coalitions by deducing collaborative processes in response to an opportunity of collaborations brought by any enterprise of the ESN.

Keywords: Enterprise social network · Collaborative platform · Support for inter-organizational collaborations · Inter-enterprises process deduction

1 Introduction

Social Networking has emerged with the development of a new technology, "Web 2.0", when it became possible for web users to participate actively in the production and disseminating content. They are shifting the Web to turn it into a participatory platform, in which people not only consume content but also contribute and produce new content [5]. Over the past few years, Social Networks (SN) have attracted much attention from the web users and they have grown spectacularly until begin now regarded as indispensable and having deeply penetrated our lives.

Companies have become aware of the need and the importance of SN collaborative tools and the concept of Enterprise Social Networks (ESN) has nowadays emerged. However, social working inside organizations is still a wild place that is looking for the

© IFIP International Federation for Information Processing 2015
L.M. Camarinha-Matos et al. (Eds.): PRO-VE 2015, IFIP AICT 463, pp. 421–428, 2015.
DOI: 10.1007/978-3-319-24141-8_38

right implementation models. In this context, this paper aims at proposing a new Enterprise Social Network OpenPaaS that is open-source and supports both inter- and intra-organizational collaborations.

The remainder of this paper is organized as follows. Section 2 presents a brief state of the art on the topic of Enterprise Social Networks and existing collaborative platforms. In Sect. 3, we sketch an overview of the proposed architecture. Sections 4 and 5 describe the main characteristics of OpenPaaS. Thereafter, Sect. 6 illustrates an implementation of practical use case study. Finally, the last section concludes and gives insights of future works.

2 Enterprise Social Networks

Enterprise Social Networks allow creating or developing friendly or/and professional ties between people. They don't have a unique or fixed form: they are customized to the needs of the organization. In [7], Altimeter defines ESN as a set of technologies that creates business value by connecting the members of an organization through profiles, updates, and notifications.

Various ESN solutions are available (more than 80 according to the last census of Bébin in [8], but only 29 are interested in social collaboration). According to authors in [1–4], *IBM Connections, Jive SocialBS, NewsGator, Telligent, Confluence, Microsoft SharePoint 2010, Yammer, SocialText, Webex Social* and *Open Text* are among the most important existing solutions.

However, all the aforementioned solutions are proprietary and our principal focus is open-source. Among the existing open-source ones, we find *Buddypress, Elgg, Lovdbyless, Ning, Statusnet* and *People Aggregator*. Although those solutions consider the main collaborative concepts resulting from Social Networks, the establishment of a transverse collaborative communication was not treated.

3 Overall Architecture

We illustrate the overall architecture of OpenPaaS in Fig. 1. Our approach consists on a PaaS (Platform as a Service) technology dedicated to enterprise collaborative applications deployed on hybrid cloud. It provides an innovative Enterprise Social Networks that innovates both at collaborative level by its capacity to leverage heterogeneous cloud technologies at the IaaS (Infrastructure as a Service).

Within OpenPaaS Platform, a set of collaborative services is made available in an IaaS infrastructure. The ESN is itself a service available in SaaS (Software as a Service) and serves as a point of access to applications deployed in the PaaS. Video Conferencing, messaging, calendar management and file sharing services are included in OpenPaaS platform and are presented in the next section. Moreover, our proposed platform provides Profile and Collaboration Editors tools in order to facilitate the definition of collaborative workflows adapted to the enterprise's needs. Furthermore, OpenPaaS platform includes a Roboconf module that allows both applications deployment and auto-adaption of the infrastructure.

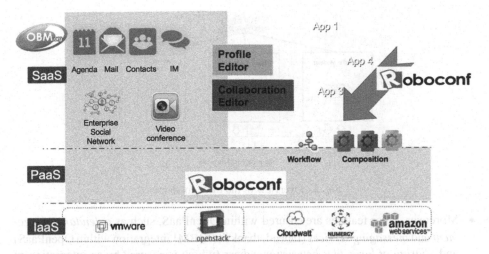

Fig. 1. OpenPaaS platform.

4 OpenPaaS Collaborative Framework

4.1 Social Interaction Services

OpenPaaS is a reliable social platform in the cloud. Its main contexts of collaboration are:

- *Community*, which is comprised of members, has a name, can have an avatar and a description. Its main space is an activity stream (compatible on mobile phones) where members can exchange several kinds of messages. Moreover, it has an intrinsic rule regarding the visibility of information that is shared inside. Four types are considered (open, restricted, private and confidential): an open community allows every one to read and to add content, whether or not users are part of the community; a restricted one allows everyone to see the content but only members can contribute; non-members of a private community can only see its name, avatar and description; finally a confidential community is invisible for all users that are not members. Membership to a community depends on its type. For open ones, the user can freely join it. For the other types, a membership request shall be sent by the user and, then, be validated or denied by the community manager (CM), or an invitation is sent by a CM to a user to become a member who decides whether to accept or not.
- Project. While communities result from an organic self-organization of the users, a *project* is more tied to the activity of the company. As such, a project has a start and end dates. Besides, project's members can be users or/and communities.
- *Conference* consists on a short-lived collaboration. It includes instant messages and WebRTC (Web Real-Time Communication) videoconference.
- *Synchronization with external contacts lists,* which allows to import contacts from an existing database in order to invite them to join. Currently, OpenPaaS can be connected to Google Contacts API.

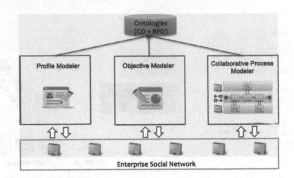

Fig. 2. Overview of the three modelers.

- Moreover, other features are ensured within OpenPaaS, such as *calendar management* and *messaging services* (Indeed, thanks to OBM[1] integration within OpenPaaS) and *Sharing of large files between members* (which is ensured by an integration of LinShare[2] within OpenPaaS in order to allow user to add and share files with other users).

4.2 Automated Creation of New Collaborations

In addition, a collaborative module has been implemented and aims at facilitating new inter-organizational collaborations: it gathers knowledge on collaborative contexts and needs (profiles and objectives of collaboration) through two modelers and exploits it to create new collaborations: (i) the Profile Modeler lets the enterprises describe their business capabilities (e.g. produce cars) and (ii) the Objective Modeler offers a way to propose new collaborative objectives (e.g. buy cars) and answers to them by setting up the corresponding optimal (e.g. on cost, delivery time, quality criteria, etc.) collaboration (i.e. selecting the best partners to answer the objectives, and order their corresponding capabilities into a business process). A last Collaborative Business Process Modeler allows the users to adapt the latter process and to orchestrate it on the later run-time phase. Figure 2 illustrates these three parts of this knowledge-based system.

In [9], authors explain the interaction of these three modelers with two ontologies as structured knowledge bases: the Collaborative Ontology (CO) provides a decomposition of collaborative objectives into sub-objectives, and for each objective the corresponding capabilities to execute in order to fulfill it; the Business Field Ontology (BFO) has been implemented since the latter objectives of the CO remained very generic (e.g. "Buy" which doesn't make the difference between "Buy cars" or "Buy candies"). The CO has been populated y adapting the MIT Process Handbook OWL version [10], and the BFO results from the decomposition of the international business activities in the ISIC Classification (International Standard Industrial Classification of all Economic Activities) [11].

---

[1] OBM: http://obm.org/.
[2] Linshare: http://en.linagora.com/produits/linshare.

As a first step, the capabilities, described via the Profile Modeler, are represented by their "intrinsic" name, and their inputs and outputs. The capability itself is linked to a capability of the CO, and the input and the output are linked with business fields of the BFO. Then, the objectives described via the Objective Modeler are represented with a link to an objective of the CO and are linked with a specific domain of the BFO. The third step is executed in back office: it is based on an Ant Colony Optimization algorithm (ACO) that exploits the knowledge included in the ontologies and also gathered by the Profile and Objective Modelers. The overall mechanism of this algorithm can be found in [9]. This ACO allows selecting the optimal set of partners to answer the objectives of the collaboration, and their capabilities. The sequencing of these capabilities into a process is achieved according to a right-to-left process: if one of the outputs of the selected capabilities matches the business field of the objective of the collaboration, it is considered as the final capability of the process. Then, capabilities are linked one to each other by making a correspondence between the input of a capability and the output of the previous capability. The deduced process can be downloaded as a file, which can now be opened, analyzed and potentially adapted by the users in the Collaborative Process Modeler.

For a better understanding of these steps, a use-case is given and detailed in the next section.

5   Use Case Validation

In order to constitute the fulfillment of the OpenPaaS platform, to illustrate the work, we present hereafter a practical use-case that meets the needs of the company Super-Cookie that produces cakes with fruits, and which is actually looking for a new collaboration to supply the fruits.

First of all, we start by creating a collaboration context: a use case participant creates a community inside the ESN and chooses its visibility. Second, he/she invites other people to join. Those who respond by accepting are considered as members and can start sharing messages inside the community's activity stream. They use the most simple type of message, that is basically a text, attachments and, if the permission is granted, geolocalisation. Each message appears on the community activity stream. Any member of the community can answer the root message, thus creating a discussion thread. In the use case, members conclude that they need help to choose some enterprises to work with, and they decide to use a collaboration opportunity modeler.

5.1   Profile Modeler

In Fig. 3, SuperCookie declares to be able to "place order" and link it to the corresponding capability of the CO. From a business field point of view, the input of this capability refers to the "Combined office administrative services" and the output to "Wholesale of food and tobacco" and "Processing and preserving of fruits and vegetables". Basically, this means that SuperCookie is able to send order for buying high amounts of fruits. For the rest of the illustrative case, it is assumed that many enterprises have already described their capabilities in their own profiles.

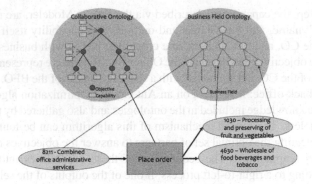

Fig. 3. Example of capability description.

5.2 Objective Modeler

The Objective Modeler lets the companies of OpenPaaS to propose new opportunities, for which they need to set up a collaboration (select partners, and deduce the corresponding optimal process). The Fig. 4 describes such an objective: here, SuperCookie would like to "buy". As this objective is very generic, the users indicate that the purchase refers to the "wholesale of tobacco" since they would like to buy high amounts of food products, and precise it with "processing and preserving of fruits and vegetables".

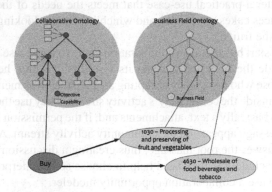

Fig. 4. Example of a collaborative objective.

5.3 Collaborative Process Modeler

Finally, the ACO performs the selection of the optimal set of partners and their activities to execute, and order them into a process. This process can be seen in Fig. 5. Two companies will take part of the process (SuperCookie and FruitCompany), during the following supply process. A Mediation Information System Pool is directly dedicated to the IT system so that the process can be orchestrated after that the users have adapted this process if needed.

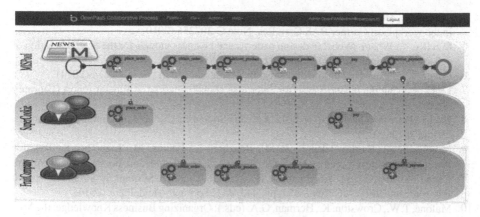

Fig. 5. Example of a deduced collaborative process.

6   Conclusion

This paper presents an innovative Enterprise Social Network which originality relies on its ability to support and facilitate intra- and inter-organizational collaboration by many ways. First, it provides a complete package of social services that helps coordinating the daily working life of the collaborators by providing easy way to share various types of information. This contribution to the current offers of social and professional networking platforms fits a deep need of the companies today, by providing easy-to-use tools. More than facilitating coordination among collaborators, it also provides a service to create new collaborations to fit current business opportunities of the OpenPaaS' users. The optimal selection of partners (and consequently of their capabilities) can, for example, help the enterprises in their bidding process: it can indeed be performed on a very large scope of candidate partners and thus provides quickly an efficient set of partners. Then, the sequencing of these capabilities into a business process that can be opened in a modeler lets the companies to easily adapt it (according to their specific preferences), and then orchestrate it. Besides, works industrialization should be taken in order to stabilize and improve its usability for a wide number of users. Furthermore, to enrich OpenPaaS's features collaborative real-time services (e.g. editing text documents, spreadsheets, business process modeler) need to be studied.

References

1. Portela, A.: Implantation et usages d'un réseau social d'entreprise: l'expérience d'Astral (2012)
2. Koplowitz, R., Brown, M., Dang, J.: The Forrester Wave™: Enterprise Social Platforms, Q3 2011 (2011)
3. Lecko: Réseaux sociaux d'entreprise (tome 4): urbanisation du SI Social: entre gouvernance, technologie et usage (2012). http://www.lecko.fr/etude-reseaux-sociaux-d-entreprise-tome-4.html

4. Drakos, N., Mann, J., Rozwell, C., Austin, T., Sarner, A.: Magic quadrant for social software in the workplace. Gartner RAS Core Res. Note G **207256** (2010)
5. O'reilly, T.: What is Web 2.0: design patterns and business models for the next generation of software. Commun. Strat. (1), 17 (2007)
6. Cavazza, F.: Panaroma des médias sociaux. Mediassociaux.fr. 19 mai 2014 (2014)
7. Li, C.: Making the business case for enterprise social networks. Altimeter report (February 2012)
8. Bébin, H.: Le marché du RSE en 2012. Réseaux Sociaux et Collaboratifs Internes ou Étendus. 26 juin 2012 (2012)
9. Montarnal, A., Barthe-Delanoë, A.-M., Bénaben, F., Lauras, M., Lamothe, J.: Towards automated business process deduction through a social and collaborative platform. In: Camarinha-Matos, L.M., Afsarmanesh, H. (eds.) Collaborative Systems for Smart Networked Environments. IFIP AICT, vol. 434, pp. 443–451. Springer, Heidelberg (2014)
10. Malone, T.W., Crowston, K., Herman, G.A. (eds.): Organizing Business Knowledge: the MIT Process Handbook. MIT press, Cambridge (2003)
11. United Nations and Statistical Division: International Standard industrial classification of all economic activities (ISIC). United Nations, New York (2008)

Collaborative Networks Dynamics and Social Capital: A Brazilian Case

Janaina Macke[1,2(✉)] and João Alberto Rubim Sarate[1]

[1] Faculty Meridional (IMED),
Researcher at Master Program in Business Administration,
R. Senador Pinheiro, 304, 99070-220 Passo Fundo, Brazil
{janaina.macke,joao.sarate}@imed.edu.br
[2] Researcher at Master Program in Administration,
University of Caxias do Sul (UCS),
R. Francisco Getúlio Vargas, 1130, 95020-972 Caxias do Sul, Brazil
jmacke@ucs.br

Abstract. The ability to mobilize resources through collaborative action is understood as the social capital present in a territory. The presence of social capital can indicate how a collaborative network can be managed. Using a quantitative method, this article aims to analyze the social capital present in collaborative networks, by accessing the case of three collaborative networks in southern Brazil. The results show that social capital can be analyzed according to four factors: proximity, territorial anchorage, reciprocity and collective memory. The elements found can indicate barriers or motivators for the operation of collaborative networks.

Keywords: Collaborative networks · Social capital · Survey · Brazil

1 Introduction

Potential partners in a collaborative network (CN) are expected to collaborate with each other in problem solving processes, in the compliance with operational standards, in the establishment of forms of cooperation, in the acceptance of agreements, building trust among its members. This collaboration process requires effort, time, dedication, and disagreements might occur. Transparent governance benefits from an incentive system that encourages proactive participation and recognition of individual contributions [1].

New researches demonstrate that elements, such as values, trust and norms can influence collaboration processes, shape networks and members' behaviors in a significant way and, consequently, indicate the chances of success (or failure) of collaborative networks. On the other hand, competence or technologic affinities can be important during the preliminary stage of the development of a network [2].

One element of social theory that highlights the potential of a collaborative network is the social capital [3], because it represents the "sum of the actual and potential resources embedded within, available through and derived from the network of relationship possessed by an individual or social unit" [4]. In this sense, social capital is a strongly competitive resource, enhancing the individual and collective capacities through collaborative practices.

© IFIP International Federation for Information Processing 2015
L.M. Camarinha-Matos et al. (Eds.): PRO-VE 2015, IFIP AICT 463, pp. 429–436, 2015.
DOI: 10.1007/978-3-319-24141-8_39

Social capital favors collective actions due to the dynamics and density of inter-actions, changes and learning processes. These learning processes, on its turn, define the ability to intervene and manage change processes, allowing people to act as active agents rather than as merely passive recipients of outside demands [5, 6].

The present paper aims at identifying and analyzing elements of social capital present in collaborative networks, focusing on local aspects and on the links among collaborative networks and the territories in which they are located. By analyzing these elements, we expect to contribute to the debate on inter-organizational issues, such as the elimination of obstacles generated by the environment and/or other organizations which might hamper collaboration processes.

2 Theoretical Background

Social capital is a set of informal norms and values common to the members of a specific group which allow cooperation among them.

Since its creation, the concept of social capital is being used to explain specific social phenomena. Most researches have focused on its role in the human capital development [7, 8], in economic performance [9], in regional [10] and national development [11].

In a study that relates social capital and intellectual capital, Nahapiet and Ghoshal [4] propose three social capital macro-dimensions: structural, relational and cognitive. However, such analytical division does not exclude the existence of a close association between their main features.

The structural dimension of social capital is related to the presence or absence of interactions between the members and the configuration or morphology of the network by describing the standards of connections through variables, such as density, con-nectivity, network configuration, stability, and ties. The relational dimension describes the kind of personal relationship developed through a history of interactions. This concept focuses on aspects that influence behaviors, such as trust and distrust, norms, obligations, expectations and identity. Finally, the cognitive dimension refers to resources that originate shared visions, interpretations and systems of meaning, mainly codes, shared narratives, values, and other cultural elements. Some authors believe that the cognitive dimension is not sufficiently explored in the literature [4].

The promotion and strengthening of solid networks of relationships based on trust, reciprocity and values is more easily done in a micro rather than in macro society where relationships tend to be more formalized and impersonal. In this sense, it is necessary to analyze the three main characteristics of the collaborative processes that contribute to the creation of a territory [12]:

(a) the society and the community are in balance. The main characteristic is an economy that is autonomous in relation to politics and the functioning of society itself, which brings out the concept of territorial anchorage;
(b) historicity (collective memory), i.e. the social construction of collective cognitive reserves and the learning ability of the agents involved;
(c) reciprocity which determines the relationship between the agents recognized by their life beyond purely commercial transactions.

Pecqueur's elements [12, 13] can be associated with Putnam's [14] and Coleman's ideas [7]. The characteristics of the regionalized production model lead to the establishment of a new local/global relationship around which territorial anchorage and non-spatial production are complexly articulated. In other words, the territory becomes central to the coordination of collaborative actions among players interested in solving unprecedented problems [12]. This can be achieved by the mobilization of the existing social capital and the promotion of collaborative networks.

Local agents able to activate and evaluate the area's social capital, as well as, to change generic into specific resources are increasingly important. Specific resources are unique and differentiated and, consequently, difficult to transpose or translate, being one of the keys to territorial competitiveness and development.

3 Method and Context

Data was collected through survey in order to identify and analyze the social capital elements present in collaborative networks and its relation with the territory.

The authors conducted an extensive literature review in order to identify the most significant studies on social capital [4, 15, 16], collaborative networks [1] and territories [12, 17]. The variables to be used in the survey were decided upon after meta-analysis.

All items were measured using a five-point Likert scale (1 = strongly disagree; 2 = somewhat disagree; 3 = neither agree, nor disagree; 4 = somewhat agree; 5 = strongly agree). Before formal survey, we conducted semi-structured interviews with three experts in collaborative networks and social capital theory to validate our scale items (these experts are researchers and professors of graduate programs and members of the Social Theory Research Group). We also ran a pre-test with ten respondents.

The survey was conducted in three Brazilian collaborative networks (Caminhos de Pedra, APROBELO and APROVALE) immersed in the same regional culture. These collaborative networks are located in three areas of the Serra Gaúcha region, state of Rio Grande do Sul (Southern Brazil). The APROVALE (Association of Producers of Fine Wines of the Valley of Vinhedos) consists of 31 wineries, and 43 members to support tourism, including hotels, hostels, restaurants, handcraft and antique shops. The APROBELO (Association of Producers of Fine Wines of Monte Belo) comprises 11 wineries; the Caminhos de Pedra Association has 23 members, including restaurants, hostels and small family businesses.

The networks have a diversified economy, and are located in the largest wine-producing region of Brazil (with approximately 40,000 ha of vineyards). The region is also characterized by family farms and lower mechanization level, because of the mountainous terrain. Nowadays, rural wine tourism is also an economic resource being explored.

The survey was conducted with employees and company owners. The sample of 206 respondents was chosen by convenience [18]. We used the software PASW statistic 18, to analyze data descriptive and factorial analysis.

4 Results and Discussion

The responses were submitted to PCA (Principal Component Analysis) factor analysis with varimax rotation and pairwise treatment (considering all valid observations of each variable) for missing data. The Kaiser-Meyer-Olkin index (KMO) of sampling adequacy was 0.837 and Bartlett's test of sphericity (significant 0.001) indicated the factorability of the data. The answers submitted to descriptive analysis revealed averages ranging between 2,158 and 4,356, with standard deviations from 0.906 to 1.836.

The Cronbach's alpha measured for the instrument with the 23 social capital variables resulted in 0.829, demonstrating excellent internal consistency of analyzed variables [19]. Moreover, few cases of missing values were observed.

The final factor analysis resulted in four elements; the percentage of explained variance was 54.52 %, which means that the variables chosen and the resulting factors can explain 54 % of the area's social capital of the collaborative networks studied. Applied social researches consider that a good result: the classic study of social capital in Australian communities conducted by Onyx and Bullen [15], whose factor analysis explained 49.3 % of the variance, is a reference in social capital measurement.

In order to check the consistency of the variables in each factor, values for Cronbanch's alpha were calculated. The ideal value in social sciences exploratory studies should be higher than 0.6 [20]. Considering the whole instrument, Cronbach's alpha was 0.833.

The fourth factor presented an Alpha value considered low (0.567). Its removal was not recommended given the significant reduction it would cause in the explained variance and even in the KMO index.

The first factor identified was *proximity* with alpha of 0.813, which is considered a very good result [19]. The variables in this factor concern the participation in associations and organizations, volunteering, participation in the community's festivals and celebrations. These variables are related with situations that promote the coming together of people and groups, either by shared goals (associations/organizations) through volunteer work or at parties and celebrations (Table 1).

The literature describes an oscillatory movement because the coming together is not a "state" but a "tension". It does not abolish the distance and it is defined by oppositions [21].

The question of proximity can also be understood through the analysis of the three mechanics of social capital (bonding, bridging and linking). A significant difference between bridging and bonding, for example, indicates the distance between heterogeneous groups in the same way that low linking levels indicate the presence of asymmetric power relations [15]. "Taking part in a network" allows discussion of common problems, exchange of information and practical experience, facilitated by territorial proximity. This aspect is decisive for the development of innovations and the building of a sense of inhabiting.

The second factor, *territorial anchorage*, displays a set of variables in which the collaborative network illustrates the sense of experiencing the territory. The social approval of the territory and its resources and the collective investment and believe in its development characterize territorial anchorage.

Table 1. Social capital elements in collaborative networks

Variables	1	2	3	4
11 – I participate in the network	0.797			
12 – I do volunteer work	0.794			
17 – I participate in parties and celebrations	0.790			
13 – I believe that people treat well those arriving from outside to work in the network		0.708		
16 – The rich and poor live well together		0.627		
15 – I feel proud to work to the network		0.599		
19 – The local government supports local development		0.584		
20 – I consider locals trustworthy		0.505		
22 – I believe in the future of the territory		0.480		
2 – I can count on other members to take important decisions			0.773	
8 – I would not have made it without the help of others			0.677	
7 – People help each other in the territory			0.561	
1 – Co-workers are friends				0.712
14 – I can share a family meal at least once a day				0.706
4 – The children and grandchildren are encouraged to follow traditions				0.499
6 – I know local history				0.452

Source: present study

The variable "people treat well those coming from outside" shows willingness to accept the "different" and indicates a certain degree of openness (51 % of the respondents worked for the network and also reside in the territory). The coexistence between rich and poor suggests that, despite economic differences, there is a movement towards the horizontalization of the social relationships.

The variable "feel proud to work to the network" obtained the best performance. Even those who do not live in the area, feels connected through the work. To consider people trustworthy is a key indicator of the presence of social capital; trust allows the establishment of informal standards systems, which facilitates the coordination of existing regional resources, strengthening territorial anchorage. Finally, to "believe that the territory has a future" summarizes the belief that it is worth investing in collaborative network, i.e. there is adherence of individuals and groups to future projects.

The third factor, *reciprocity*, relates to the feeling of obligation one feels to return a favour and to the social embarrassment of anyone who does not cooperate or violates agreed norms [14]. To count on neighbours to take important decisions, to recognize other people's help (and be socially compelled to repay it) and to consider that the organization is a place of exchange (mutual assistance) are reciprocity indicators. In the literature, norms of reciprocity and participation systems are the main evidence of the presence of social capital.

The fourth factor is designated as *collective memory*, due to variables that show the families' efforts so their children and grandchildren follow customs and are aware of the region's history. The other two variables - consider co-workers friends and share a family meal at least once a day – seem, at first, unrelated to the others. However, when we analyzed the difference between the responses of resident and non-resident workers we realized that the residents perform better, i.e. "work" seems to be the link between the variables. Working and living in the same territory offer more opportunities to share family meals and to work with the family, which encourage the teaching of values and customs and contribute to the preservation of the territory's collective memory.

Among the factors found, three had already been reported in the literature [12] as essential to the process of collective construction. The authors identified these elements through the analysis of groups and of specific literature. Pecquer's typology [12] failed to include an element (factor 1 in this study), which the authors linked to the concept of proximity.

5 Final Remarks

This study allowed the identification of the members' perception about their interactions and purposes, in other words, the social dynamic. The interaction between members and organizations appears to broaden options to reach common interests and projects, and to break through bureaucratic barriers. The idea is to preserve the group's heterogeneity and seek flexibility, focusing on cooperation without eliminating constructive conflict and competition [22].

Social capital is not disconnected from historical or geographical influences. Therefore, the results were strongly influenced by the context in which they were inserted. Analyzing the main evidences according to that theoretical framework, the authors could collect evidences about the dynamics of collaborative networks and their links to social capital.

The present study identified and analyzed the elements of social capital in territories with collaborative networks based on four main factors: proximity, territorial anchoring, reciprocity and collective memory. In an initial stage, usually technical skills were essential to the network's functioning. Nevertheless, research on the role of social players in territorial building can contribute to broaden the debate on the role of collaborative networks in local development.

The theoretical contribution of the paper is the identification of a new element necessary for the maintenance of collaborative networks in communities: the concept of proximity. Moreover, from the practical perspective, the study provides a social capital assessment tool to access social capital levels in collaborative networks.

Many questions remain to be answered, such as: how to develop new ways of network management capable of dealing with the territorial multiplicity in which we are inserted? How to reinstate a territorialization concept that means not only "controlling" the space, but also its production and experience taking into consideration the collaborative networks?

In conclusion, social capital is not an instrument to be used in isolation, nor it claims to be the single tool to understand the role of collaborative networks embedded in a territory. The authors expect that this study can contribute to the reflection on the obstacles to the establishment of collaborative networks.

Acknowledgments. This work is being supported by the Faculty Meridional (Faculdade IMED), University of Caxias do Sul (Universidade de Caxias do Sul - UCS), the Coordination for the Improvement of Higher Education Personnel (Coordenação de Aperfeiçoamento de Pessoal de Nível Supeior - CAPES), and the National Counsel for Scientific and Technological Development (Conselho Nacional de Desenvolvimento Científico e Tecnológico - CNPq).

References

1. Camarinha-Matos, L.M., et al.: Collaborative networked organizations: concepts and practice in manufacturing enterprises. Comput. Ind. Eng. **57**(1), 46–60 (2009)
2. Rosas, J., Camarinha-Matos, L.M.: An approach to assess collaboration readiness. Int. J. Prod. Res. **47**(17), 471–4735 (2009)
3. Macke, J., Vallejos, R.V., Faccin, K., Genari, D.: Social capital in collaborative networks competitiveness: the case of the Brazilian Wine Industry Cluster. Int. J. Comput. Integr. Manufact. **25**(1), 1–8 (2012)
4. Nahapiet, J., Ghoshal, S.: Social capital, intellectual capital and the organizational advantage. Acad. Manage. Rev. **23**(2), 242–266 (1998)
5. Barquero, A.V.: Desenvolvimento endógeno em tempos de globalização. Editora UFRGS, Porto Alegre (2002)
6. Albagli, S., Maciel, M.L.: Capital social e desenvolvimento local. In: Lastres, II.M.M., Casssiolato, J.E., Maciel, M.L. (eds.) Pequena empresa: cooperação e desenvolvimento local, pp. 423–440. Relume Dumará, Rio de Janeiro (2003)
7. Coleman, J.S.: Capital in the creation of human capital. Am. J. Sociol. **94**, 95–120 (1988)
8. Loury, G.: Why would we care about group inequality? Soc. Philos. Policy **5**, 249–271 (1987)
9. Baker, W.: Market networks and corporate behavior. Am. J. Sociol. **96**, 589–625 (1990)
10. Putnam, R.D., Leonardi, R., Nanetti, R.Y.: Making Democracy Work: Civic Traditions in Modern Italy. Princeton University Press, Princeton (1993)
11. Fukuyama, F.: Trust: The Social Creation Virtues and the Creation of Prosperity. Free Press, New York (1995)
12. Pecqueur, B.: A guinada territorial da economia global. Política Soc. Rev. Sociol. Política **8** (4), 79–105 (2009)
13. Pecqueur, B.: O desenvolvimento territorial: uma nova abordagem dos processos de desenvolvimento para as economias do Sul. Raízes **24**(1), 10–22 (2005)
14. Putnam, R.D.: Bowling Alone: the Collapse and Revival of American Community. Simon & Schuster Paperbacks, New York (2000)
15. Onyx, J., Bullen, P.: Measuring social capital in five communities. J. Appl. Behav. Sci. **36** (1), 23–42 (2000)
16. Woolcock, M.: Social capital for social policy: lessons from international research and policy. In: Policy Research Conferation, Otawa (2005)
17. Wu, W.: Dimensions of social capital and firm competitiveness improvement: the mediating role of information sharing. J. Manage. Stud. **45**(1), 122–146 (2008)
18. Hair, J.F., Babin, B., Money, A.H., Samoul, P.: Essentials of Business Research Methods. Leyh Publishing, LLC (2003)
19. Pestana, M.H., Gageiro, J.N.: Análise de Dados para Ciências Sociais: A Complementaridade do SPSS, 4ª edn. Sílabo, Lisboa (2005)
20. Malhotra, N.: Pesquisa de marketing: uma orientação aplicada, 4th edn. Bookman, Porto Alegre (2007)

21. Lefebvre, R.: La 'proximité': nouveau capital social au chevet de la démocratie? In: GRIS (Groupe de Recherche Innovations et Sociétés). (ed.). Le Capital social: actes du colloque organisé par le GRIS, pp. 167–180. Université de Rouen, Rouen (2004)
22. Loyola, E., Moura, S.: Análise de Redes: uma Contribuição aos Estudos Organizacionais. In: Fischer, T. (ed.) Gestão contemporânea, cidades estratégicas e organizações locais, pp. 53–68. FGV, Rio de Janeiro (1996)

Information and Assets Sharing

Green Virtual Enterprise Breeding Environments Bag of Assets Management: A Contribution to the Sharing Economy

David Romero[1,2(✉)], Ovidiu Noran[2], and Hamideh Afsarmanesh[3]

[1] Tecnológico de Monterrey, Monterrey, Mexico
david.romero.diaz@gmail.com
[2] Griffith University, Gold Coast, Australia
ovidiu.noran@griffith.edu.au
[3] University of Amsterdam, Amsterdam, The Netherlands
h.afsarmanesh@uva.nl

Abstract. Green Virtual Enterprise Breeding Environments (GVBEs) are long-term strategic alliances of green enterprises and their related support institutions aimed at offering the necessary conditions to efficiently promote and establish common working and sharing principles with the intention of creating sustainable (shared) value in a collaborative way. The Sharing Economy (SE) is founded on the principle of maximising the utility of assets and other shareable resources by means of renting, lending, swapping, bartering and giving them away in order to avoid their idle existence, and is currently being facilitated by emerging collaborative business ICT infrastructures in the marketplace and society. The SE provides the ability to GVBE members to unlock the untapped social, economic and environmental value of their underutilised assets and other shareable resources towards higher resource efficiency. This paper explores the enabling role of the GVBE bag of assets as a virtual and physical warehouse, including collaborative procurement and shareable assets management strategies, in order to facilitate the sharing of tangible and intangible resources between GVBE members. The GVBE bag of assets is put forward as a novel internal sustainable business model, based on a conceptual framework, taking advantage of idle assets and other shareable resources within the breeding environment in order to save costs and generate new revenue streams (economic), make efficient use of resources (environment) and create deeper social connections – trust – among member enterprises (social).

Keywords: Collaborative networks · Green virtual enterprises · Bag of assets · Sharing economy · Industrial ecology · Sustainability · Shared value

1 Introduction

The *Sharing Economy* is founded on the principle of maximising the utility of assets and other shareable resources by means of renting, lending, swapping, bartering and giving them away in order to avoid their idle existence [1] and is currently being facilitated by emerging collaborative business ICT infrastructures in the marketplace [2] and

© IFIP International Federation for Information Processing 2015
L.M. Camarinha-Matos et al. (Eds.): PRO-VE 2015, IFIP AICT 463, pp. 439–447, 2015.
DOI: 10.1007/978-3-319-24141-8_40

society [3]. The *Sharing Economy* provides the ability to organisations and individuals to unlock the untapped social, economic and environmental value of their under-utilised assets and other shareable resources towards higher resources efficiency. Such resource efficiency strategies (e.g. virtuous business value cycles) are known as the *Circular Economy* [4] and *Collaborative Consumption* [1] by the economists, and as *Industrial Ecology* [5] by the engineers. Complementarily, these concepts focus on enabling links/exchanges/sharing of information, materials, water, energy, technology, services and/or infrastructure, and any other possible tangible or intangible asset, including by-products, based on collaboration and sharing strategies supported by shared/communal use of assets, logistics, expertise and knowledge transfer within a collaborative network [6, 7].

This paper explores the enabling role of the *GVBE bag of assets* [6, 7] as a virtual and physical warehouse, including collaborative procurement and shareable assets[1] management strategies in order to facilitate the sharing of tangible and intangible resources between *GVBE members*. The GVBE bag of assets is put forward as a novel internal sustainable business model, based on a conceptual framework, taking advantage of idle assets and other shareable resources within the breeding environment in order to save costs and generate new revenue streams (economic), make efficient use of resources (environment), and create deeper social connections – trust – among member enterprises (social).

2   Green Virtual Enterprises and Their Breeding Environments

A *Green Virtual Enterprise Breeding Environment (GVBE)* is a long-term strategic alliance of green enterprises[2] and their related support institutions aimed at offering the necessary conditions (human, financial, social, infrastructural and organisational) to efficiently promote and establish common working and sharing principles with the intention of creating sustainable (shared) value[3] in a collaborative way [6–8].

From a *functional* point of view, *GVBEs* focus on sharing information, resources, responsibilities, risks and rewards to jointly plan, implement and evaluate sustainable initiatives and collaborative endeavours [10]. From a *behavioural* point of view, *GVBEs* focus on adopting common governance rules and bylaws [11] and a common ontology [12] in order to reduce the barriers towards successful collaborations. From a *structural* and *componential* point of view, *GVBEs* focus on developing common interoperable infrastructures [2] and creating a resource pool (bag of assets) with different tangible and intangible shareable resources in order to eliminate redundant assets within the

---

[1] A shareable (tangible) asset is characterised by its high acquisition price, low availability and low frequency of use.

[2] A *Green Enterprise* is an enterprise that strives to meet the triple bottom line by ensuring that all products, processes, manufacturing and logistics activities in its business operation address the sustainability principles [6, 7].

[3] *Sustainable Value* is the long-term shareholder value created as a scalable source of competitive advantage by embracing opportunities and managing the risks/benefits associated with their economic, environmental and social developments [9].

GVBE and manage their ownership costs in an efficient way [6, 7]. As a result, a *GVBE* can be considered as an intelligent network for competences and *resources (assets) management* contributed by various green enterprises aiming to combine their green capabilities in order to develop triple top-line[4] strategies for creating sustainable (shared) value – though *GVEs creation* [6, 7], as addressed below.

"*Green*" *VBEs* in particular are aimed at facilitating the sharing and recycling of assets and other resources with the intention of creating *industrial symbiosis* [5] links/exchanges and shared/communal use of assets between their members [6, 7].

A *Green Virtual Enterprise (GVE)* is a short-term and dynamic coalition of green enterprises that may be tailored within a *GVBE* to respond to a single sustainable value creation opportunity to deliver new green products to the market by means of dynamic forward supply networks creation (see F-GVEs [14]), or to capture the value that may exist in a product or by-product, by recovering it temporarily during its mid-life for service provisioning or at the end of its life for reuse, repair, remanufacturing, recycling or safe disposal by means of dynamic reverse supply networks (see R-GVEs [15]).

3   GVBE Bag of Assets and the Sharing Economy

The *GVBE bag of assets* provides collaborative procurement and shareable assets management services to the *GVBE members* in order to develop economies of scale and scope, and enable an 'inter-organisational' sharing economy (see Fig. 1).

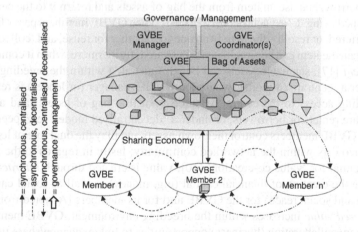

Fig. 1. GVBE bag of assets: a sharing economy scenario

Collaborative procurement services [16] aim to ensure GVBE members improved security of supply through aggregated buying power; exploit economies of scope within

---

[4] A *Triple Top-line Strategy* establishes three simultaneous requirements for sustainable activities: financial benefits for the enterprise, natural world betterment, and social advantages for employees. Though this is sometimes called the triple bottom-line, triple top-line stresses the importance of initial value rather than after the fact effects [13].

the breeding environment through bundling where there are significant costs common to different products or services in a supply chain; strengthen the negotiating position in contracting with suppliers; reduce prices through economies of scale; share procurement costs for buyers and reduced bidding costs for suppliers through a single tendering process; share the costs associated with gathering price and market information; facilitate improved management of suppliers and contracts at a strategic level for contracts agreed by the GVBE management and GVE coordinator(s); deliver service and process improvements through the adoption of best practice; reduce fragmentation, number of contracts and unnecessary complexity for the breeding environment; ensure all collaborative procurements adopt the highest standards in terms of safety and environmental protection; better decision making through cross-GVBE members and external price benchmarking; and more consistent application of best practice, innovation and enhanced opportunities for learning [adapted from 16].

Meanwhile, *shareable assets management services* aim to create a resource pool that in the sharing case of tangible assets may include transportation vehicles (e.g. collaborative logistics), physical spaces (e.g. shared warehouses, excess space), infrequent-use items (e.g. event equipment), durable goods (e.g. productive assets), etc., and in the sharing case of intangible assets, individuals' knowledge, skills and services (both business and software services), data, time and experiences, with the intention of maximising the return on capital investments and maintaining a shareable knowledge and skills base.

Shareable assets can have different dimensions according to [17], based on their nature and *lifecycles,* assets can be 'synchronously shared' when the GVBE members can rent, borrow, and use an item from the bag of assets and return it to the central pool when finished using it, 'asynchronously shared' when GVBE members pass off – gifted, traded, bartered, or resold – the item from one to the other for reuse, and 'collaboratively shared' when the item can be simultaneously shared; furthermore, when it comes to their *management* [17], shareable assets can be administrated within the breeding environment under a 'centralised model' where the GVBE manager (or lender) is responsible for providing access to the central resource pool (the bag of assets) and all GVBE members are renters or borrowers, or under a 'decentralised model' (e.g. peer-to-peer) where the GVBE members control their own assets and play the dual role of lenders and renters/borrowers within the networked community; lastly in regards to the shareable assets potential for 'value co-creation' [10], value is created through *interactions* [17] that enable the creation of financial capital (e.g. money) as well as social capital (e.g. reputation and social reach) for the GVBE and for its members [Adapted from 17].

As *shared value* increases within the breeding environment, GVBE members will discover new collaboration (business) opportunities to link/exchange/share their assets and value-added activities to gain competitive advantage and sustainable organisational performance [18].

3.1   Towards a GVBE Bag of Assets Framework and Lifecycle

A *GVBE bag of assets* represents a new long-term collaboration (business) opportunity, namely: the *Sharing Economy* [1], aimed at making 'business sense' of the efficient use of common and shareable assets within the untapped internal B2B breeding environment sharing marketplace. Therefore, the *GVBE bag of assets creation* will be triggered as an internal collaboration (business) opportunity to create a resource pool that will be gradually built-up with the GVBE members' shareable assets and joint purchases and investments in common assets.

Similar to the GVE creation framework [6, 19] and according to GERAM - ISO/IS 15704 guidelines [20], the *GVBE bag of assets creation framework* (see Figs. 2 and 3), on its 'shareable assets' pillar, starts with the identification of a set of shareable assets between the GVBE members within an open or predefined conceptualised scope that will trigger and justify the resource pool and its related services creation. Next, the collaboration (business) opportunities identified will be characterised (requirements design) in terms of their 'economic drivers' (e.g. monetise excess and idle inventory, increasing financial flexibility, access over ownership, etc.), 'ecological drivers' (e.g. reduction of ecological and carbon footprints, etc.) and social drivers' (e.g. asset-light business paradigm, collaborative consumption, etc.). Following, a first rough architectural design of the GVBE bag of assets taxonomy will be defined (e.g. based on business and accounting principles – current assets, long-term investments, fixed assets, intangible assets, other assets) together with its sharing governance model (e.g. own-to-mesh vs. full mesh, community diversity vs. company control, adoption vs. appropriability of benefits, informal contracting vs. formal contracting, trust by reputation vs. trust by commitment, non-market mediated vs. market mediated, social capital vs. individual benefits, identification avoidance vs. perceived ownership [21]) and business models (e.g. sharing plan, sharing method(s), sharing investment, cost and profit model(s)). Subsequently, GVBE members willing and suitable to participate (as sharing users, sharing suppliers and/or broker(s)) in the long-term *Sharing Economy* collaboration (business) opportunity should be searched and selected according to the degree that their shareable assets profile (e.g. shareable assets inventory, trust level [22], etc.) matches the GVBE bag of assets scope. Then the rough taxonomy and sharing governance and business models should be detailed and agreed by the GVBE members through a negotiation process that aims to embed social (shared) value creation into contracts and agreements. Finally, the GVBE bag of assets operation should be launched.

For the particular situation of the GVBE bag of assets dissolution, shareable assets already count with an specific ownership by the GVBE members (sharing suppliers), so decommissioning efforts will be centred in common assets jointly purchased.

On its 'collaborative procurement' pillar, the *GVBE bag of assets creation framework* starts with the identification and conceptualisation of the potential participant pool to get involved in the collaborative purchasing opportunities. The GVBE members interested will begin communication and information exchange concerning their (individual) planned purchases in order to identify similar commodities in the same market – a broker may support this coordination action. Next, the collaborative purchase will be characterised (requirements design) in terms of number of participants involved, their size, their geographic location, their purchasing volume, etc. in order to use the appropriate mechanisms to obtain additional discounts or rebates beyond the initial volume-driven lower per-unit pricing. Following, a first rough architectural design of the total purchase size and individual bundles will be calculated as well as expected benefits for the participant GVBE members. Subsequently, GVBE members will confirm their

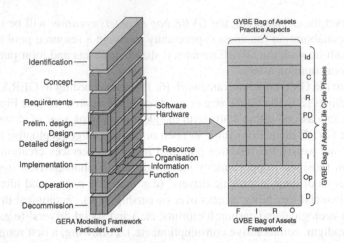

Fig. 2. Modelling concept [6, 19, 20] for the GVBE bag of assets framework

Fig. 3. GVBE bag of assets creation framework pillars

participation in the collaborative purchasing opportunity. Then the rough collaborative purchase order will be <u>detailed</u> and transform into a request for quotation that will trigger concurrent negotiation processes with the suppliers, responding to a call for tenders issued by the GVBE manager or GVE coordinator, until an agreement is reached and a contract is signed. Finally, the winning supplier will issue an invoice and the GVBE members will expect the purchase within the time frame agreed in the collaborative procurement <u>operation</u>.

3.2 GVBE Bag of Assets Management Practice Aspects

The *GVBE bag of assets management practices* may include function-wise, the following bundle of services, related to the *shareable assets management:* setup and update of the shareable assets taxonomy, shareable assets inventory management, reservation and scheduling of shareable and common assets, assignment/re-assignment of shareable and common assets, logistics and distribution of shareable assets, and monitoring of shareable and common assets utilisation (e.g. tracking assets condition, lifecycle cost, performance measurements, etc.). Resources-wise (and related to *GVBE members' participation management),* the services bundle may include: shareable assets contributions and utilisation accounting, shareable and common assets financials (e.g. purchase, payment and invoice systems) and rewarding mechanisms to stimulate the internal B2B breeding environment sharing marketplace. Organisational-wise (and related to the *GVBE bag of assets governance*), the service bundle may include support for 'centralised' and 'decentralised' control and management models. Finally, information-wise the *GVBE bag of assets services bundle* should be supported by an information management system as detailed below.

3.3   GVBE Bag of Assets Information Management System

First generation *GVBE bag of assets management systems* [23] were mainly focused on storing and sharing intangible assets (e.g. documents, software tools, and other knowledge items); they were implemented as 'content management systems' providing services (functionalities) for the GVBE members, such as: subscribing/unsubscribing, publishing information (metadata), viewing information (browsing and sorting) and support for GVBE member(s) reward. In this first generation, the GVBE bag of assets management was mainly a task for the GVBE manager and GVE coordinator(s), responsible for collecting 'reference information' that could support future better decision-making and efficient business processes execution.

Second generation *GVBE bag of assets management systems,* empowered by the Internet of Things [24] paradigm, aim to enable a repository supporting the collection and dissemination of common and shareable assets-related information, capable of offering advanced functionalities or services for assets availability, assets conditions, assets tracking and assets usage, cost tracking, cash flow forecasting and financial reporting. In this second generation, in a centralised management model, *brokers* play a new supporting role for the GVBE manager and GVE coordinator(s) as 'matchmakers' of the supply and demand for common and shareable assets within the breeding environment, closing deals, and scheduling and tracking their utilisation. On the other hand, in a decentralised GVBE bag of assets management model, assets' sharing becomes every breeding environment member's business.

As a result, a *GVBE bag of assets management system* can be seen nowadays as a B2B e-marketplace within the breeding environment, based on a collaborative business ICT infrastructure (online platform), capable of creating reciprocal economic value by increasing assets utilisation through online accessibility and community sharing, as well as environmental and social value by reduced ownership overhead and stronger collaboration.

4   Conclusions and Further Research

The *Sharing Economy* attempts to define a wide range of collaborative (business) practices whose central characteristics are the ability to save or make money, reduce ecological footprints and strengthen social ties. This paper has put forward the concept of *GVBE bag of assets* as a novel internal sustainable business model based on sharing idle assets and other under-utilised resources and collaborative procurement strategies within a breeding environment in order to save costs, co-create shared value, efficiently utilise resources and deepen the trust among GVBE members. Moreover, the ongoing research work has introduced a proposal for a GVBE bag of assets conceptual framework to be further developed.

The transition to an 'assets sharing economy' as a corporate practice is not an easy task; nevertheless, GVBEs collaborative culture and common infrastructure present promising social, economic and technological drivers and enablers [25] such as the desire for cooperation, sustainability, shared value co-creation, social networking, and collaboration platforms.

References

1. Botsman, R., Rogers, R.: What's Mine is Yours: How Collaborative Consumption is Changing the Way We Live, HarperBusiness (2010)
2. Rabelo, R.: Advanced collaborative business ICT infrastructures. In: Camarinha-Matos, L.M., Afsarmanesh, H., Ollus, M. (eds) Methods and Tools for Collaborative Networked Organizations, pp. 337–369. Springer, New York (2008)
3. Andersson, M., Hjalmarsson, A., Avital, M.: Peer-to-peer service sharing platforms: driving share & share alike on a mass-scale. In: International Conference of Information Systems (2013)
4. Ellen MacArthur Foundation. Towards the Circular Economy: An Economic and Business Rationale for an Accelerated Transition. McKinsey & Co. Commissioned Report (2012)
5. Huber, J.: Towards industrial ecology: sustainable development as a concept of ecological modernization. J. Environ. Plann. Policy Manage. 2(4), 269–285 (2000)
6. Romero, D., Molina, A.: Green virtual enterprises breeding environment reference framework. IFIP AICT 362, 545–555 (2011)
7. Romero, D., Molina, A.: Green Virtual enterprise breeding environments: a sustainable industrial development model for a circular economy. IFIP AICT 380, 427–436 (2012)
8. Afsarmanesh, H., Camarinha-Matos, L.M., Msanjila, S.S.: Models, methodologies, and tools supporting establishment and management of 2nd Gen. VBEs. IEEE Trans. Syst. Man Cybern. Part C Appl. Rev. 41(5), 692–710 (2011)
9. Short, S.W., Rana, P., Bocken, N.M.P., Evans, S.: Embedding sustainability in business modelling through multi-stakeholder value. IFIP AICT, Part I 397, 175–183 (2013)
10. Camarinha-Matos, L.M., Afsarmanesh, H.: Collaborative networks: value creation in a knowledge society. IFIP 207, 26–40 (2006)
11. Romero, D., Giraldo, J., Galeano, N., Molina, A.: Towards governance rules and bylaws for virtual breeding environments. IFIP 243, 93–102 (2007)
12. Afsarmanesh, H., Ermilova, E.: Ontology engineering for VO breeding environments. In: 9th International Conference on the Modern Information Technology in the Innovation Processes of the Industrial Enterprises, pp. 124–137 (2007)
13. Tueth, M.: Fundamentals of Sustainable Business: A Guide to the Next 100 years. World Scientific Publishing Co., Hackensack (2010)
14. Romero, D., Molina, A.: Forward - green virtual enterprises and their breeding environments: sustainable manufacturing, logistics and consumption. IFIP AICT 434, 336–346 (2014)
15. Romero, D., Molina, A.: Reverse – green virtual enterprises and their breeding environments: closed-loop networks. In: Camarinha-Matos, L.M., Scherer, R.J. (eds.) PRO-VE 2013. IFIP AICT, vol. 408, pp. 589–598. Springer, Heidelberg (2013)

16. Sellafield Ltd.: Objectives of Collaborative Procurement. http://suppliers.sellafieldsites.com/procurement-opportunities/nda-shared-service-alliance/
17. Latitude and Shareable: The New Sharing Economy: A Study by Latitude in Collaboration with Shareable Magazine. http://latdsurvey.net/pdf/Sharing.pdf (2010)
18. Haanes, K., Arthur, D., Balagopal, B., et al.: Sustainability: The 'Embracers' Seize Advantage, MIT Sloan Management Review and The Boston Consulting Group (2011)
19. Camarinha-Matos, L.M., Oliveira, A.I., Ratti, R., Demšar, D., Baldo, F., Jarimo, T.: A computer-assisted VO creation framework. IFIP **243**, 165–178 (2007)
20. ISO/IEC.: Annex A: GERAM - ISO/IS 15704:2000/Amd1:2005: Industrial Automation Systems - Requirements for Enterprise-Reference Architectures and Methodologies (2005)
21. Smolka, C., Hienerth, C.: The best of both worlds: conceptualizing trade-offs between openness and closedness for sharing economy models. In: 12th International Open and User Innovation Conference (2014)
22. Msanjila, S.S., Afsarmanesh, H.: Towards establishing trust relationships among organizations in VBEs. IFIP **243**, 3–14 (2007)
23. Afsarmanesh, H., Camarinha-Matos, L.M., Msanjila, S.S.: Virtual Organizations Breeding Environments: Key Results from ECOLEAD. IFAC-CEA (2007)
24. Rosemann, M.: The internet of things: new digital capital in the hands of customers. Bus. Transform. J. **9**, 6–15 (2013)
25. Bockmann, M.: The shared economy: it is time to start caring about sharing: value creating factors in the shared economy. In: 1st IBA BT Conference (2013)

Modelling Interactions Between Health Institutions in the Context of Patient Care Pathway

Sabri Hamana$^{(\boxtimes)}$, Vincent Augusto, and Xiaolan Xie

UMR CNRS 6158 LIMOS, Centre for Biomedical and Healthcare Engineering,
MINES Saint-Etienne, 158 cours Fauriel, 42023 Saint-Etienne cedex 2, France
{sabri.hamana,augusto,xie}@mines-stetienne.fr

Abstract. Health systems around the world have been continuously subject to many questions about their performance. In order to improve the functioning of such systems, Health Information Systems (HIS) and Technologies (HIT) are deployed to support patient care pathways and ensure information exchange between health structures, actors of patient care. The aim of this paper is to propose a generic modelling framework for describing the exchange of information between health institutions in the context of patient's care, concerning a given chronic pathology. The purpose is to facilitate building of flow models starting from the proposed modelling framework, those models will be used to support quantitative evaluation through discrete event simulation, useful to evaluate the impact of communication between health institutions on patient care pathway. This work is a part of a research project entitled e-SIS ("Assessment in Health Information Systems"), project funded by the French health ministry (DGOS) as part of its research program called PREPS ("Research Program on Performance of Healthcare Systems").

Keywords: Patient care pathway · Hospital · City health facilities · Information systems · Interactions · Generic modelling framework

1 Introduction

Health systems around the world are in crisis because of the increase of care expenditures whereas resources become limited [1]. The French health system is constrained in the same way and faces since many years an increase mainly related to care spending which can be explained, in part, by the increase in care demand due to the population aging and also the increase of the number of people with chronic diseases. On the other hand, the increase in health spending is explained by the many frontiers that separate the French health system and generate costs: the barriers, now considered as non-quality, could explain up to 15 % unjustified costs [1], the main partitioning being between hospitals and private practitioners.

To tackle this problem, it is important to reorganize the health system around the patient's care pathway [2]. Given that the hospital represents itself a care pathway, organized and coordinated by the hospital information system, it seems judicious to export that model outside the hospital walls, by implementing e-health platforms and

© IFIP International Federation for Information Processing 2015
L.M. Camarinha-Matos et al. (Eds.): PRO-VE 2015, IFIP AICT 463, pp. 448–455, 2015.
DOI: 10.1007/978-3-319-24141-8_41

the interfaces between such platforms and all the information systems of health institutions within a territory. The goal consists in having a health information system which is computerized and integrated, enabling the continuity of care and the traceability in patients' pathways. Such approach is motivated by the fact that organizational problems related to patient care (delays between health-care stays, ruptures in patient pathway...) are primarily related to a lack of communication between health institutions, which lead to a lack of coordination between the different health actors involved in the patient's care [3].

This work is a part of a research project entitled e-SIS (French acronym for "Assessment in Health Information Systems"), project funded by the French health ministry (DGOS) as part of its research program called PREPS (French acronym for "Research program on performance of health-care systems"). The project aims to assess the impact of information systems on creating value in health facilities.

As regards the quantitative evaluation of HIS, there is no study that takes into account, at the same time, human, organizational and technological aspects of an IS and their impacts on values' creation within health institutions [4]. Whereas for the modelling of HIS, some authors have proposed flow models which were described using graphical formalisms such as UML [5] and 3LGM^2 [6], except that these models describe only the flow of electronic information among computer systems within an IS, neglecting thus the human and organizational aspects. Other authors, for their part, have proposed models to exclusively describe patients' flows through their care pathway, using formalisms such as BPMN, SADT or also Petri Nets [7, 8]. Therefore, there has not been, to our knowledge, a modelling framework that jointly describe the flows of patients and information within a one and only model representing a health institution or territory.

Thus, before achieving such evaluation, a modelling work of cancer care system should be performed upstream. For that reason, we decided to implement a modelling framework based on the process approach. Then starting from the proposed modelling framework we belt a flow model which will support the quantitative analysis (through discrete event simulation), the ultimate objective being to evaluate the impact of information exchanges between a hospital and a city health facilities on patient cancer pathway.

This paper is organized as follows: position of the problem is presented in Sect. 2. A generic modelling framework for describing the management system of information exchanged between health institutions within the context of patient pathway is described in Sect. 3. Finally, conclusions and perspectives are given in Sect. 4.

2   Position of the Problem

Anyone who is suffering from a chronic disease, such as cancer, follows a double care pathway: (i) In-hospital, within a hospital centre or a specialized centre for cancer care, and (ii) out-hospital, within city health facilities (General Practitioners (GP) offices, biological analysis laboratories, rehabilitation care facilities, hospital at home structures...). The role of hospitals is to provide a highly specialized diagnosis and treatment, which will be supported by an out- hospital care, provided by city health facilities.

On the other hand, patient's care at a health facility (hospital or city facility) requires external medical information provided by other health facilities; patient's care at that facility will also create, by the same occasion, medical information that will be required as a result of patient care in other health facilities. It is noteworthy that the exchange of information between institutions is done through one or more communication interfaces (e.g. postal mail, secure electronic messaging, shared patient record, etc.), each interface being characterized by a cost, related to resources used to transmit information, as well as an information delivery delay.

Given that the actual literature does not provide models or tools that allow assessing quantitatively the impact of information systems on patient pathway, the aim of this work is to propose a generic modelling framework for describing both patient pathway and the exchange of information between health institutions in the context of patient's care, concerning a given chronic pathology. Such framework should be compact and simple enough to be used by any stakeholder to build the specific model of a patient pathway including all HIS available in the environment. The resulting model can be used to support risk analysis and discrete event simulation, in order to assess the impact of health institutions' communication on the patient care pathway.

3 A Generic Modelling Framework for Describing the Management System of Information Exchanged Between Health Institutions Within the Context of Patient Pathway

In the perspective of assessing the impact of interactions between the hospital and the city health facilities on patient's cancer pathway, we have decided to implement a generic modelling framework for describing the management system of medical information which are exchanged between health institutions within the context of healthcare for patients suffering from a chronic disease. This modelling framework uses the process approach as a modelling method, as well as the BPMN (Business Process Model and Notation) as a graphical formalism with, however, some modifications made on that formalism. Furthermore, any model built starting from the proposed modelling framework will be represented according to two views: (i) a « Patient pathway » view and (ii) a « Shared health information system » view. The aim of such modelling structure is to increase the readability of the model and therefore the intelligibility of the described system.

(i) **The « Patient pathway » view**: described on one hierarchical level, it makes explicit all healthcare processes that can compose a patient pathway regarding a given disease (e.g. medical consultation, biological analysis examination, surgery, etc.) as well as the articulating of these processes, i.e. the various possibilities of process sequences. In order to illustrate our point, we will give the example of the patient's cancer pathway (see Fig. 1). The figure below describes the cancer patient's pathway through the processes that compose it: the red area constitutes the in- hospital care, while the green area will constitute the out-hospital care (within city health facilities).

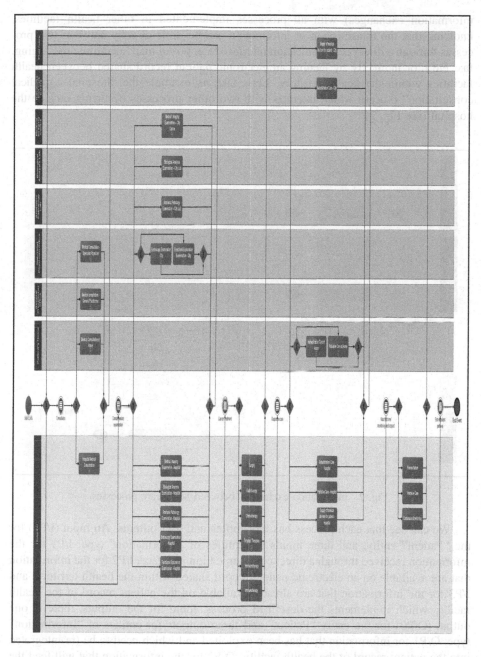

Fig. 1. The cancer patient's pathway (Color figure online)

(ii) The « Shared health information system » view: described for its part on three hierarchical levels:

Level 3: representing the highest level of abstraction, it allows describing for each process, implemented within a given health facility, its potential interactions (or information exchanges) with all processes implemented in other health facilities, knowing that the transmission of information can be done directly between two processes through a direct communication interface (e.g. postal mail, electronic messaging, fax, etc.), or indirectly by feeding an electronic patient record shared between health facilities within the health territory. Let's take as example the "hospital's medical consultation" process which interacts with two other processes occurring outside the hospital (see Fig. 2).

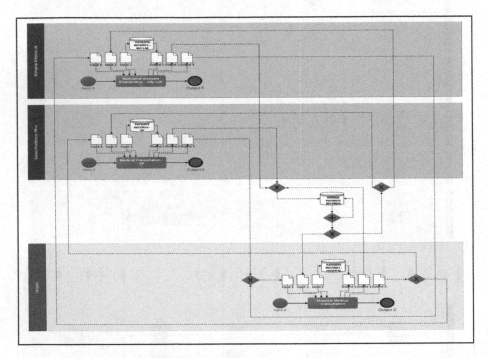

Fig. 2. Information exchanges between healthcare processes

We can see that each process has four inputs and four outputs. An input (I/P0) for the "Patient" entity, and three inputs for entities of "Information" type: I/P1 for the information received through a direct communication interface, I/P2 for the information that are available on an electronic patient record shared within the health territory, and I/P3 for the information that are already available on the patient record of the health facility which implements the described process. Idem for the outputs, there is one output (O/P0) for the entity "Patient" and three outputs for entities of "Information" type: O/P1 for information that has been exploited and which need to be (re)integrated into the patient record of the health facility, O/P2 for the information that will feed the electronic patient record shared within the health territory, and finally O/P3 for the information transmitted to another process via a direct communication interface (postal mail, fax…).

Level 2: describes each process from the view of the shared health information system, i.e. from the view of the management of medical information received or sent by the described process. The management of these information is performed through the concatenation of a number of dedicated activities which are (at most) in number of seven: (1) Receive an information, (2) Integrate an external information into the patient record, (3) Retrieve the patient record, (4) archive the patient record, (5) Consult an external information, (6) Produce an information and (7) Communicate an information (see Fig. 4). We can distinguish in that figure the four inputs and the four outputs of the process. We can also distinguish two types of transitions: the ones with an arrow in solid line correspond to patient flows, while dotted arrows represent information flows. Furthermore, we can see that the execution of some activities may require synchronization between the "patient" entity and an "information" entity such as for the activity "Consult an information".

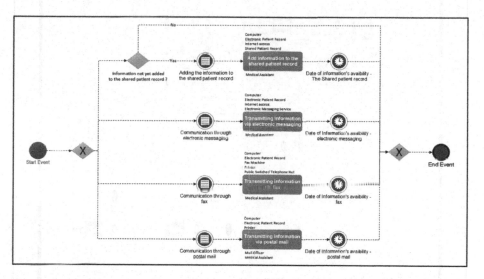

Fig. 3. The implementing procedures of the activity "Communicate an information" within the context of a medical consultation at a hospital

Moreover, it is important to emphasise the generic nature of that level which allows describing any healthcare process from the point of view of the shared health information system, regardless the degree of development of the facility's information system (a paper or an electronic patient record, a non-integrated or a highly integrated computer system, etc.).

Level 1: finally, this level allows describing the implementing procedures of each activity composing a given process: each activity has at least one implementing procedure, each procedure is characterized by a delay and a cost related to the mobilization of human, hardware, software and network resources which are necessary for its achievement. Example: The implementing procedures of the activity "Communicate an information" for the process "Medical consultation" within a hospital having an electronic patient record (see Fig. 3).

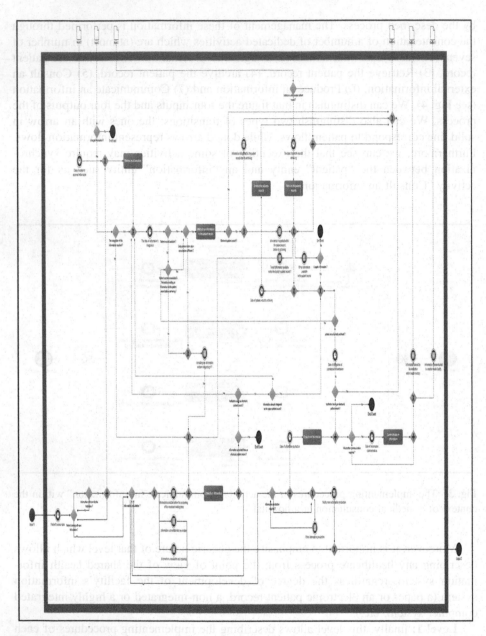

Fig. 4. The generic description of a healthcare process from the view of the shared health information system

4   Conclusion

In this paper we proposed a new framework based on the process approach for patient pathway and information modelling. We first defined the context of the study in the e-SIS project. Then we presented the basics of the modelling framework which allows describing the management system of information exchanged between health institutions within the context of patient pathway. The resulting models will be used to support simulation for performance evaluation.

In future work we are currently working on the development of a rigorous methodology to propose a performance evaluation of the health information system on the regional level. Such quantitative evaluation will be performed taking into account (i) patient quality of care, (ii) working conditions of health-care professionals, and (iii) economic evaluation of health structures.

Acknowledgments. The authors would like to thanks practitioners from the Centre Léon Bérard: L. Perrier, P. Biron, T. Durand; CH Sens: S. Aloui; Centre Jean Perrin: A. Doly.

References

1. Bourret, C.: Partager l'information pour dépasser les frontières institutionnelles et professionnelles ou le défi des réseaux de santé dans le système de santé français. In: 35th Annual Conference Information Sharing in a Fragmented Word (2007)
2. ARS Centre (The Regional Agency for Health - Centre region, France). Stratégie nationale de santé et enjeux régionaux d'une médecine de parcours; Comment améliorer le service rendu au patient. Première journée des rencontres de la santé (2013)
3. Caillavet-Bachellez, V.: «Le parcours de soins du patient: un dispositif fédérateur pour les Communautés Hospitalières de Territoire (CHT)», Ecole des Hautes Etudes en Santé Publique (EHESP) (2010)
4. Yusof, M.M., Papazafeiropoulou, A., Paul, R.J., Stergioulas, L.K.: Investigating evaluation frameworks for health information systems. Int. J. Med. Inform. **77**(6), 377–385 (2008)
5. Spyrou, S., Bamidis, P., Pappas, K., Maglaveras, N.: Extending UML activity diagrams for workflow modelling with clinical documents in regional health information systems. In: Connecting Medical Informatics and Bioinformatics: Proceedings of the 19th Medical Informatics Europe Conference (MIE 2005), pp. 1160–1165. Geneva, Switzerland (2005)
6. Winter, A., Brigl, B., Wendt, T.: Modeling hospital information systems (part 1): the revised three-layer graph-based meta model 3LGM2. Methods Inf. Med.-Methodik Inf. Med. **42**(5), 544–551 (2003)
7. Augusto, V., Xie, X.: Modélisation et analyse de flux par la simulation en milieu hospitalier: état de l'art. In: Conférence Gestion et Ingénierie des SystEmes Hospitaliers (GISEH), Luxembourg (2006)
8. Ozcan, Y.A., Tànfani, E., Testi, A.: A simulation-based modeling framework to deal with clinical pathways. In: Proceedings of the Winter Simulation Conference, pp. 1190–1201. Winter Simulation Conference (2011)

Secured and Efficient Information Exchanges in Collaborative Networks: The Singular Information System

Cédrik Béler[✉] and Bernard Grabot

Université Fédérale de Toulouse Midi-Pyrénées, LGP-ENIT-INPT, 47 Avenue d'Azereix,
BP 1629 65016 Tarbes Cedex, France
{cedrik.beler,bernard.grabot}@enit.fr

Abstract. Information exchange is the object of intensive research from quite separated communities, dealing for instance with connected objects, interoperability of industrial information systems, personal information systems or data security. A unified framework, defining the conditions of interrelations of elementary information systems, could allow to address these problems with a holistic view. In that purpose, we suggest the concept of Singular Information System (SIS) and give the basic principles allowing the connection of two SIS. We show then how exchanges of information between objects, persons and organizations may benefit from such a unified paradigm.

Keywords: Information system · Personal information system · Collaboration · Interoperability

1 Context: Information Sharing in Collaborative Networks

Collaborative Networks (CN), i.e. networks of autonomous organizations that collaborate to better achieve common or compatible goals [1], are now considered as the best solution for coping with the uncertainty of the markets and with an increased competition. For a company, the interest to belong to such networks is to extend its competences and share risks, allowing to benefit from opportunities that the company could not address alone. Information sharing is quite commonly considered as an essential condition for maintaining collaborative relationship between partners [2]. What information should be shared and how is an important problem for long-term relationships, but becomes critical when organizations want to create a short term relationship. In this context, the mass of digital information created today by individuals, organizations and connected objects may result in an uncontrolled flow of information. Breaches in confidentiality and inefficient communication, resulting in an increased risk, are possible consequences in collaborative networks. A reason of this situation is that even if the interoperability of organization's information systems, personal information systems and connected objects are "hot" topics now, no framework has yet been proposed that would provide a unified, secured, centralized and controlled way for exchanging information between "carriers of information" of different levels. To the difference with many works focusing on the interoperability of the information systems of organizations, we

© IFIP International Federation for Information Processing 2015
L.M. Camarinha-Matos et al. (Eds.): PRO-VE 2015, IFIP AICT 463, pp. 456–463, 2015.
DOI: 10.1007/978-3-319-24141-8_42

suggest choosing as central component the dedicated and private information system of an entity (object, individual or organization), that we call the *Singular Information System (SIS)*. The qualifying term "singular" was chosen to strongly underline the uniqueness of such IS. SIS are owned by only one entity and contains only information the entity wants to store in a secure and private manner. Therefore, each SIS is singular by its content and by its nature. Collaboration between SIS is achieved through their interconnection resulting in (singular) information transactions.

The aim of this communication is to present this prospective work by explaining the basic principles allowing SIS to communicate, focusing here on applications linked to collaborative networks.

2 Related Works: From Collaborative Organizations to Singular Information Systems

The interest of process modeling for describing the internal behavior of an organization is now universally recognized. Comprehensive modeling tools like ARIS [3] allow to link process activities to the organizational elements performing these activities (services, departments), then to persons belonging to these elements of organization. It is not anymore enough: many papers have shown the interest of building communities for taking benefit from external experience, within or outside the company. The success of professional social networks is an illustration of this new propensity [4]. In that case, the distinction between the individual and professional social networks may become unclear. Therefore, there is in our opinion a need for clearly defining a personal information system, and investigating how it feeds personal or professional "consumers of information" in a controlled way, respecting the basic principle that personal data may be used by external entities only under permission. The page of an individual or organization in a social network can be considered as an embryonic SIS regarding the functionalities but most of the time, control and privacy are not guaranteed. Clarifying the relationships between a person and an organization is not the single utilization of SIS: "connected" or "intelligent" objects [5] will be more and more present in companies. Their embedded simplified information system may also be considered as a SIS, and their relationship with the SIS of persons and organizations may be managed according to the same principles. So, the SIS can be considered as the private information system of an entity (object, individual or organization), allowing the entity to keep control over all information transactions in which it is involved. In this paper, only the personal and organizational level is tackled.

The idea of personal information system is not new. Vannevar Bush's 1945 Memex vision (namely memory extender) was the description of an analogical computer where people could store and link information together [6]. Recently, an implementation of Memex was realized with MyLifeBits [7], a lifetime store of everything a person could encounter in his life. These systems are limited to person and do not enable collaboration. Recent considerations of the problems related to information dissemination have raised a new literature related to personal information systems. Ann Cavoukian [8] proposes for instance a new paradigm called Privacy By Design (PbD) that aim at considering privacy as the raw building block of an information system. Close to this point of view are alternative social network tools distributed as open-source solutions, built with privacy as first principle (e.g. Diaspora [9], Heartbeat [10] or Safebook [11]). Interesting works on the development of personal information systems, called Personal Data Store/Server (PDS), Personal Data Vaults/locker (PDV) or Personal Cloud, can also be found [8]. Some recent initiatives (Mydex [12], Meeco [13], sdX [14], etc.) share the same goals of data storage and exchange security and privacy with different design choices. Even if these tools are said to facilitate information exchange, they essentially focus on data storage and data aggregation, and stay essentially at a personal level (even if some of them, like Meeco or Mydex, include the relationship of the customer with organizations).

Several works focus on the collaborative aspects of information exchange in organizations and are by the way good inspirations even if they do not consider persons as a first principle which is essential to us. Besides all works on Collaborative Information Systems ensuring interoperability between several exogenous IS, let us note one initiative. Federated Information System [15] is the evolution of federated database system which is a multi-database system in which every node in the federation maintains its autonomy on the data. A set of export schemas (derived from local schemas) through which the data is made available to other specific nodes are the underlying working principle. The way information is exchanged is interesting but the SIS approach is more global and not limited to a given context. Instead of exporting internal IS database models, SIS rely on messaging between SIS according to a given protocol ideally without considering IS internals. Moreover, the unicity of a person, an organization is again not considered.

Another recent tendency is BYOD (Bring Your Own Device) in cloud environments allowing people to bring and use their own devices in work contexts. Indeed, personal devices (smartphones, tablets, …) associated to Cloud environment and smart assistant (like Apple or Google ecosystems) tend to be potential SIS but they have inherent limitations (business model based on data disclosure or proprietary model without guarantee in the long term). More over, BYOD is a rather practical approach that raises several security issues [16] and promotes the multiplication of entry points which is clearly in opposition to what SIS envisions.

Finally, some other recent researches fostered around the idea of privacy exchange of information seem to be good foundations for the development of SIS. The Minimum Exposure Project [17] aims at controlling information sharing and capitalization for an entity both in input (filtering data input) or output (data exposure frequency and duration). This underlying limited data collection principle seems essential to limit the dissemination of information (a well known privacy principle) but also to have a fine control on incoming information. Also, Trusted Cells as component of smart objects (trusted devices) are an interesting approach to ensure privacy relevant application [18]. Finally, asymmetric architectures like MetaP have been suggested for connecting secured and unsecured networks [19] and could be of high interested to interconnect SIS through Internet.

In the next sections are defined SIS principles and abstract models so as to show how interconnected SIS can improve agility of CN and therefore their resilience regarding communication inefficiencies.

3 SIS Architecture and Principles

A SIS is a private and dedicated information system that would be the unique place where is recorded the whole "digital life" of an entity (object, individual, organization, network of organizations, government…). It has the ambition to provide a scalable framework able to link individuals, smart objects and organizations. As a consequence, the required global functionalities of a SIS should be:

- global querying and data/information/knowledge mining,
- anonymous data publishing,
- distributed secure sharing (users must get a certified proof of legitimacy for the credentials exposed by the participants of a data exchange eventually using a third-party),
- secure usage and accountability (users must not loose control over their data through data sharing),
- service offering or acceptation (local push opportunities, ads, love market,…),
- collaboration facilities (automatic update of information about other SIS, distributed planning of collaborative processes between SIS partners…).

The core of the system is the private information stream (life data stream) capturing each piece of information (data, pictures, videos…) that the singular entity wants to store. All recorded information is private by default, leveraging todays legal limitations of classical IS to store personal information, according to the PbD principles. A "view" on the SIS can be created for a certified partner, according to the respective roles of the entity and its partner. Several SIS, when interconnected, define a network of SIS called INTERSIS (Interconnection of Singular Systems).

SIS dedicated to persons, organizations or objects share the same architecture. Conceptually, a SIS is composed of a private core and of information views extracted from the private core to structure information of interest, used internally or shared with other SIS. Private core singular information must only be accessible by his owner and contains only singular information.

Singular information structuration is important to be able to do generic lookup on past information, but also to perform information and knowledge inference at the owning entity level (assistant dimension of SIS). Singular information (SInfo) can be considered as a personal digital trace and is essentially a wrapper on usual kind of data (structured or unstructured data, files, applications logs…). Meta information is added in a generic manner (geospatial and temporal information on the information input, with an extensive use of tags that express the context of the information). Useful information can be added in an information container without being conformant to a data model. SInfo have several properties: they can be composed forming a tree where leafs are raw types (composition), evolution and history must be accessible (versioning), several variations may represent the same information according to different detail level (variation) and one SInfo could be the synthesis of several others (synthesis). Raw types may be text, picture, video, sound, website snapshot… An information view is a particular kind of SInfo that may be dynamic (for example, the age of a person could be a view extracted from his singular information "date of birth"). Singular information views and singular information structuration will be deeper studied in future works so as to validate its universality and scalability.

Collaborative dimensions are managed through SIS interconnections. For such purposes, SIS basic structure includes collections of persons, organizations and objects/resources with which the owner has authorized exchanges of information in given situations. Information exchange is materialized by singular information transactions and consists in: (1) extracting a view from singular information, (2) defining the term and conditions of the exchange (limited data collection principle) and (3) establishing the transaction according to a secured communication protocol.

Several types of interactions are possible. The first kind is the exploitation of the SIS itself by the owning entity (information mining, digital assistance...). Other kinds of interaction may be defined depending on the entities that are engaged in any singular information transaction. There are transactions between similar entities: (a) person to person (PtP), (b) organization to organization (BtB), (c) object to object (OtO) and transactions between different kinds of entity: (d) person to organization (PtB), (e) person to object (PtO) and (f) object to organization (OtB). Each of these interaction classes is a potential CN use case, but the most important are BtB and PtB, the former underlying each potential collaborative role in the supply chain for instance, while the latter implements each potential role a person can have regarding an organization.

Of course, it is not reasonable to imagine that every organization and person on earth would adopt at short term the SIS paradigm and this is why one major requirement of SIS is the interoperability with legacy IS (for people, organizations and smart objects). Moreover, although the basic idea is to interconnect SIS, it is not viable to imagine an always-connected system, hence SIS has to "work offline". Eventually, SIS could be most of the time disconnected, only initiating a communication when necessary, without being connected to an unsecured network like Internet (e.g. if a person wants to exchange information with an organization like a hospital, the connection can be done physically). SIS "proxies" can be introduced as a mean to deal with non universality and sporadic connections. A proxy is a classic pattern in computer science, whose intent is to provide a surrogate for another object to control access on it. They can be considered as "smart and authorized views" on external information systems associated to objects, persons, and organizations. Actually, a SIS owner can "see" what another entity "sees" of itself by exploring its associated proxy (however he has no clue on what was filtered). When disconnected, a SIS proxy acts as a non-synchronized system. It can represent entities that are not SIS (legacy system for which bridges can be developed) but also non-connected SIS. SIS proxies, when interconnected, have of course much more potential. This connection is necessary to establish/resume information transactions, which is the core functionality of INTERSIS. Also, to deal with the sporadic functionalities, information transactions have to be asynchronous, i.e. there can be pending transaction, initiated when disconnected, and resumed once connected. Information update is done only when all SIS engaged in a transaction are connected.

Defining a proper communication protocol so as to meet the requirements of singular information transactions will be a very important challenge in future works.

4 Collaboration Through SIS

In this section, more details are given on the organizational SIS, and a collaborative use case is introduced through a planning assistance tool.

Imagining SIS for persons and objects is more straightforward than for organizations because of the complex nature of an organization (composed of services, departments and ending with persons). An organization has a main global SIS but also includes a composition of other SIS: several organizational SIS reflecting its organization (companies, subsidiaries, services, working group...), several personal SIS according to the role of persons (governance, employees, stockholder, final customers...) and several SIS for objects of interest (resources that are shared and smart objects). One important aspect to consider is that personal SIS is the main entry point for organizational SIS (for instance, a CEO access his organizational SIS through his personal SIS). The organizational SIS can be more volatile than the organization structure, i.e. it can be created on the fly according to a specific task that needs a specific organization (project group for instance). When the task is over, the SIS is dismantled and absorbed by the parent SIS. By default, it is possible to include all SInfo of the former SIS, but clever inclusions can be done depending on what lesson learned are interesting to store (is it the result of the project or eventually the process followed that we are interested in?). Temporary creations of organizational SIS are also possible for working groups that are a federation of people and/or organizations (i.e. outside an organization perimeter).

To illustrate the collaboration facilities that SIS provide, one major tool is the planning assistant, which is a basic but very important application of all SIS. Its functioning is illustrated on Fig. 1 and rests on the SIS Timeline Paradigm that serves as support to plug applications to one SIS. The SIS internal architecture makes a clear distinction between three temporal dimensions: past, present and future. SIS is primarily a unified communication framework but its first purpose is to help organization, so this temporal distinction is very useful in that respect. The past dimension is about storing the singular information stream to reuse it later (global querying, information view creation/extraction...). Storing SInfo is an important requirement and so as to ensure privacy and control, it is possible to choose between different providers (todays encrypted cloud services for instance).

"Present" corresponds to the basic usage of a SIS and consists in the conversion of future planned activities to digital traces stored as singular information belonging to the "past" dimension. Coupling between future activities and current activity could be of great assistance to infer and classify automatically new SInfo. Let us remark that singular information is not always converted from a planned activity. Indeed, an activity can start without being planned. Figure 1 also symbolized activity treatments that result always in new SInfo (one that can be a summary of the activity done, or one logging the fact that the activity was postponed or cancelled).

One important aspect of the present dimension is the "offline gap", meaning some activities or tasks may be started when the SIS is not used. So when resuming a SIS, each application has to provide facilities to roll out the timeline until the last usage so as to give the possibility to enter SInfo asynchronously as if it was done inline.

"Future" is mainly about planning tasks. In todays world, it is a real challenge to reconcile our career and private life. Applying SIS to planning through singular

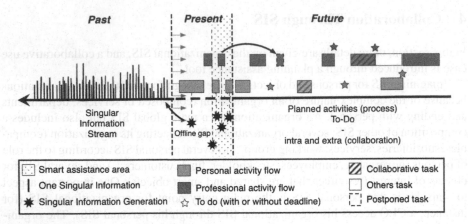

Fig. 1. SIS timeline paradigm applied to planning

information transactions seems promising as it enables an up-to-date and efficient view on every planning of interest (personal, organizational…). Of course, this is possible if you have an authorized (full or restricted) view on another SIS planning. On Fig. 1 is depicted a personal and a professional activity flows. Note that there are potentially as many activity flows as you have personal/object SIS. The limited data collection principle applies here too. One can decide to share only some activities with some persons or some organizations or to share free time intervals on specific durations. One can set up an activity that engage someone else and, once accepted, he will be notified in near real time on all possible (authorized) evolutions. For instance, somebody can assign a task to you and it will appear in your planning. Once started, the responsible could know if it is started (if you have authorized this transaction) and once finished, the responsible could receive specific information like the time spent on the activity, eventual encountered problems, etc. Again the power of SIS is that you send only what is needed or what you think is relevant. Nothing prevent yourself from recording lots of information and keeping most of them private at the end.

5   Conclusion and Perspectives

The uncontrolled access of information created by the daily life of individuals and organizations clearly set confidentiality and efficiency problems. The first elements of Singular Information System have been described in this communication, with the aim to give to each entity a permanent control on its digital information, while increasing the interoperability between entities, which seems to be now a non negotiable requirement of our modern life. We strongly believe such systems would greatly enhance the agility of collaborative networks by improving reactivity.

Having one logical entry point per entity aggregating all life information exchanges regardless their context (personal(s), professional(s), …) is according to us an important foundation to cope with today explosion of data exchanges: it considerably leverages interoperability and complexity issues while preserving privacy. Of course, this require a strong paradigm shift which could be considered infeasible as one may think that everybody, every organization, every smarts objects should embrace this paradigm to succeed. Of course, this is not the purpose of SIS and this why we envision SIS proxies as a way to manage under the same interfaces legacy IS and SIS.

As a prospective work, SIS approach needs several additional developments and refinements. Next step will be the development of personal SIS applied in the context of SME so as to share productivity information (processes, activities, ...) between a project manager and employees. In the same time, theoretical developments will be conduced regarding singular information structuration and information transaction definition (as the underlying communication protocol).

References

1. Camarinha-Matos, L.M., Afsarmanesh, H.: Collaborative networks: a new scientific discipline. J. Intell. Manufact. **16**(4–5), 439–452 (2005)
2. Nyaga, G.N., Whipple, J.M., Lynch, D.F.: Examining supply chain relationship: do buyer and supplier perspectives on collaborative relationships differ. J. Oper. Manage. **28**, 101–114 (2010)
3. Scheer, A.W.: ARIS: Business Process Modeling. Springer, Berlin (2000)
4. Grabot, B., Mayère, A., Lauroua, F., Houé, R.: ERP 2.0, what for and how? Comput. Ind. **65**(6), 976–1000 (2014)
5. Meyer, G.G., Främling, K., Holmström, J.: Intelligent products: a survey. Comput. Ind. **60**(3), 137–148 (2009)
6. Bush, V.: As We May Think. The Atlantic. Reprinted in Life magazine (1945)
7. Gemmell, J., Bell, G., Lueder, R., Drucker, S., Wong, C.: MyLifeBits: Fulfilling the Memex Vision. In: ACM Multimedia, pp. 235–238. Juan-les-Pins, France (2002)
8. Cavoukian, A.: A privacy by design approach to an individual pursuit of radical control. In: Digital Enlightenment Yearbook: the Value of Personal Data, pp. 89–101. IOS Press, Amsterdam(2013)
9. Diaspora*. https://diasporafoundation.org
10. Heartbeat. https://ind.ie
11. Cutillo, L., Molva, R., Strufe, T.: Safebook: a privacy-preserving online social network leveraging on real-life trust. IEEE Commun. Mag. **47**(12), 94–101 (2009)
12. Mydex. https://mydex.org
13. Meeco - sovereignty for all. https://meeco.me
14. sdX: the building blocks of small data apps. http://smalldata.io/#sdx
15. Afsarmanesh, H., Camarinha-Matos, L.M.: Federated information management for cooperative information. In: 8th International Conference on Database and Expert Systems Applications (1997)
16. Morrow, B.: BYOD security challenges: control and protect your most sensitive data. Netw. Secur. **2012**(12), 5–8 (2012)
17. Anciaux, N., Nguyen, B., Vazirgiannis, M.: The minimum exposure project: limiting data collection in online forms. ERCIM News **90**, 41–42 (2012)
18. Anciaux, N., Bonnet, P., Bouganim, L., Nguyen, B., Popa, I., Pucheral, P.: Trusted cells: a sea change for personal data services. In: 6th Biennial Conference on Innovative Database Research (CIDR) (2013)
19. Allard, T., Nguyen, B., Pucheral, P.: METAP: revisiting privacy-preserving data publishing using secure devices. In: Distributed and Parallel Databases (DAPD) (2013)

Business Processes

Supporting Business Processes for Collaborative Alliances of Software Service Providers

Maiara Heil Cancian[✉], Cleber Pinelli Teixeira,
and Ricardo J. Rabelo

Department of Automation and Systems Engineering,
Federal University of Santa Catarina, Florianópolis, Brazil
{maiara.cancian, cleber.pinelli}@posgrad.ufsc.br,
ricardo.rabelo@ufsc.br

Abstract. Software sector has become a very important and increasing competitive sector, being mostly composed by SMEs. Enhancing partnerships at a more valuable business level can help companies to attend to wider markets in a more sustainable and agile way taking advantage of assets that they would not have if working alone. One strategy to reach this is via collaborative networks. However, companies should be prepared for that. One of the first issues is to understand more deeply what working collaboratively actually means in businesses and how to support it. This article presents the set of business processes that need to be handled in a collaboration among software service providers throughout its lifecycle. Final results are discussed at the end.

Keywords: Collaboration · Business process · Software services

1 Introduction

The software industry has nowadays become a very important and increasing competitive sector. In Europe, for instance, there are more than fifty thousand SMEs within the ICT (Information and Communications Technology) sector [1], being mostly composed of small and medium-sized enterprises (SMEs). SMEs, however, usually have much difficulties to engage general conditions to be competitive, lacking more advanced and sustainable models [2].

In the software sector, SOA (Service Oriented Architecture) [3] has arisen as a prominent paradigm for wider and more sustainable business models. It has introduced a new outlook on system design, implementation, integration and agile partnerships, and has been increasingly adopted (as services-based applications) by software developers and customers in general [4]. SOA and services-oriented market is already very representative and can reach up to US$22 billion in the next years [5].

In SOA, all system's features are regarded as independent and self-contained software modules – called *software services* or just *services* – that jointly form a virtual single logical unit to create software products and processes [3]. SOA is an architectural style that supports loosely coupled software services to enable business agility and

L.M. Camarinha-Matos et al. (Eds.): PRO-VE 2015, IFIP AICT 463, pp. 467–478, 2015.
DOI: 10.1007/978-3-319-24141-8_43

flexibility. These services are made available by *software services providers* (SSP), which are independent organizations that own and provide software services' implementations and descriptions as well as the respective technical and business support throughout a given SOA solution's life cycle [3]. *Web services* are one of the most currently implementing technologies for SOA [3].

Regarding their intrinsic nature and goals, SOA projects are very complex, risky and costly. A big operational or strategic mistake in a given SOA project may even hazard the SME survival.

An alternative to decrease these obstacles but keeping companies' sustainability is to work collaboratively with other SSPs, as a network [6]. Collaborative Networks (CN) [7] leverages many competitive advantages. They allow its members to overcome individual limitations and to maximise the utilization and sharing of resources and assets (of many types) while risks and costs are shared, so as to better achieve common/compatible goals regarding the different members' culture [6, 7].

In order to support the envisaged collaborative scenario among disparate SSPs, two types of CN are of particular importance in this work: VO (*Virtual Organization*) and VBE (*Virtual organization Breeding Environments*). A VO is characterized as a temporary alliance formed by autonomous and heterogeneous organizations that join their complementary core-competences and resources to better attend to a given demand. VOs are originated from long-term alliances, the VBE. A VBE can be defined as a long-term association of organizations (companies, etc.) which have the willingness and enough pre-conditions to collaborate towards creating VOs with the most adequate partners in a more agile and trustful way [7].

In the CN scenario, working collaboratively means a practice to be introduced by companies in their daily routines. Focusing on the *business process* perspective, this work identifies and synthetizes which business processes are required to support the collaboration among SSPs that are members of VBEs. In general terms, it is assumed that a VO will be formed to represent every collaboration initiative among SSPs no matter its purpose (e.g. joint innovation, joint training, joint marketing, joint development of services-based software solutions, etc.).

Related works have proposed reference models and processes for creating and managing VBEs and VOs. However, they are (on purpose) generic and not devoted to any particular sector (although most of them have been based on manufacturing setor). Besides that, the scenario envisaged in this paper deal with "extended" VBEs, a "federation alliance", which logically embraces different VBEs (although can be applied to single VBEs), other alliances, individual companies and even independent professionals which develop and share their software services in a governed and collaborative cloud-like shared services repository [6, 8].

Regarding the massive SME nature of SSPs, the relevance of knowing more precisely these processes are: (i) processes are many and SMEs managers are usually not aware of them; (ii) managers can more properly evaluate how prepared they are to indeed start collaborating more effectively and so which measures should be put in place for that; (iii) processes have interdependencies and different levels of implementation complexity and practices; this process list helps SSPs' managers to plan their gradual introduction in this larger scale collaborate scenario regarding current maturity level and priorities.

This article is organized as follows: Sect. 1 has introduced the problem and intended contribution. Section 2 explains the adopted methodology. Section 3 presents the state-of-the-art review. Section 4 presents the set of collaborative processes. Section 5 discusses about the current main findings of this research.

2 General Methodology

In order to gather a coherent and comprehensive set of business processes to support collaboration among SSPs this research was conducted as action-research, qualitative and applied work, strongly grounded on literature revision.

The literature review was mainly conducted applying the SLR (*Systematic Literature Review*) methodology [9] over the *IEEExplore, ACM Digital Library, Compendex/Engineering Village* and *ScienceDirect* scientific databases, collecting papers published in journals and conference proceedings in the period of 2002:2013 on long-term and more formal enterprising strategic alliances. 308 works were initially retrieved and a subset of that was considered as relevant for the purpose of this research was selected. A special attention was given on trying to identify the works which dealt with SMEs and software and services sectors.

Five steps were carried out to achieve this research's results. First, gaps and existing knowledge in the state-of-the-art about supporting processes for VBE-like alliances were identified (see next section). Second, applying an inductive approach, 28 papers were selected as the basis to generate an initial generalized list of business processes. Considering that there are too few VBE alliances already deployed over the world, more "classical" and very studied long-term alliances (namely clusters) were analyzed in terms of how (processes and actors) they have been created, managed and sustained. Due to space restrictions, these 28 papers are not shown in the references. Third, regarding that classic clusters do not handle some VBE process, a second study (upon other 14 selected papers) was executed to complement and adapt that list for the VBE context in a first step, and for the software services in a second step. Fourth, this list was compiled and refined by a working group, composed of some experts in the involved areas. Fifth, the list was finally evaluated by those experts and evaluated by some users, applying a questionnaire over the Internet (*expert panel* technique).

3 State-of-the-Art Review

The goal of this review is twofold: to identify gaps, and to gather and take advantage of existing models and processes to generalize and adapt to the envisaged scenario.

After evaluating related works it was observed that none of them have dealt with processes to the software services sector. On the other hand, several works have provided important related outcomes. For example, Afsarmanesh et al. [10] proposed a VBE reference model identifying a comprehensive list of required elements, but without identifying which business processes should be considered to support them. Romero et al. [11] identified a list of processes along the collaboration life cycle, but at a too generic level. Rabelo et al. [12], Krogstie [13], Franco et al. [14] and

Camarinha-Matos et al. [15, 16] adopted the VBE concept as a wider and logical federation of providers to cope with that wider services-based digital business ecosystems, but also without identifying the required business processes. Cancian et al. [17] have elicited the processes and practices for SSPs that want to develop a joint SOA solution, but just assuming that companies would come from a federation. Other works have proposed processes for dealing with collaboration but focused on single issues. For example, Danesh and Raahemi [18] focused on services management; Haines and Rothenberger [19] on how to glue different services in cohesive SOA solution; Svirska et al. [20] on the supporting services infrastructure; Santanna-Filho et al. [21] on innovation among SSPs; BS 11000 British Standard only handles collaborative bidding processes [47]. In terms of EU funded projects, for instance, ECOLEAD [6] DBE [22], COIN [23] and GLONET [24] have developed platforms and visions to support collaboration among (also) software providers, but without identifying which more concrete processes are necessary to support when creating and maintaining the alliance.

4   The Collaborative Processes

After the analysis and generalization (as described in Sect. 2), a list of 22 business processes has been identified, reflecting the processes that are involved in a collaboration among SSPs throughout the VO life cycle. Therefore, it is not related to the processes involved in the creation, management and dissolution of VOs, but rather how collaboration activities span along this.

Objective
Management of inter-organizational trust (in terms of e.g. reputation, financial health, performance, competences, etc.) so that the Federation's members, customers and supporting institutions can be confident about the existing transparency, honesty and interpersonal relationship values.
Extended Description
Considering that a federation is a long term alliance and independent of its aiming sector and size, one of the aspects to be discussed is the trust management. In order to provide the trust between partners in a Federation some elements should be managed. Those are transparency, honesty and interpersonal relationship values [...].   The trust is defined as an expectation that others will behavior in a not opportunistic way [...], or in a committed way not only with their tasks, but with the group [...]. The trust management deals with the management of trust between organizations, including either a basic evaluation level of individual trust or between members of different organizations [...]. Partners need to trust to each other enough in order to allow and/or to facilitate the collaboration. A low level of trust increases the "transactions costs", requiring an additional set of protection actions against unknown partners. In order to measure the level of trust a careful evaluation analysis criteria is necessary. (...)
References
[...] Msanjila, S.S., Afsarmanesh, H. *Towards Establishing Trust Relationships among Organizations in VBEs.* In *Establishing the Foundation of Collaborative Networks*, 2007. Springer, pp 3-14.

Fig. 1. Partial example of a process' complete description

Table 1. List of processes

Process	Objective
Trust management [10, 25]	Inter-organizational trust management of (in terms of e.g. reputation, financial health, performance, competences, etc.) so that the alliance's members, customers and supporting institutions can be confident about the existing transparency, honesty and interpersonal alliance's values
Governance management [14, 26, 27]	Definition of rules, decision making criteria, responsibilities and autonomy levels that should be set up upon the alliance's members, customers and other supporting institutions regarding current contracts and businesses. This process affects all the other ones directly, although with different degrees of intensity
Quality management [28]	Management of quality aspects upon the alliance's members of their software services and supporting non-software services. This involves organizational-related aspects (e.g. members' reputation, services trustworthiness and QoS), software maturity models and certifications as means to selecting providers and SLA (Service Level Agreement) specifications, and general quality of supporting institutions
Legal issues management [29]	Management of all legal aspects related to the alliance establishment. It also provides legal support to all issues, conflicts, transactions and collaborative processes that are carried out among the alliance's members, customers, supporting entities and eventual external actors
Performance management [11, 30]	Management of the general performance of every alliance's member and supporting institutions by means of qualitative and quantitative indicators, following the specifications indicated in the governance process. It is a basis for some other processes, like membership, competence and knowledge management
Membership management [11, 31]	Management of all issues related to the integration, accreditation, disintegration, rewarding, and categorization of members and supporting entities within the alliance
Collaborative project management [32]	Management of collaborative projects that can be done by and among the alliance's members or in connection with supporting entities and customers. Examples of collaborative projects include the creation of virtual organizations, collaborative innovation, collective purchasing, joint training, and shared inventory management. This also involves financial, human resources, project planning, risk management, among many other aspects typical in project management
IPR management [33]	Management of the rights, duties, rewarding, royalties, etc., related to intellectual property rights (IPR) associated to innovations (of any type), licenses, patents, etc., developed inside the alliance environment

(*Continued*)

Table 1. (*Continued*)

Process	Objective
Competence management [30, 31, 34]	Management and permanent updating of information about technical and human capabilities and capacities of each member and supporting entities. It can also have an active role, feeding the strategic management process with such information for strategic plan feasibility analysis
Financial management [26, 35]	Management of the activities to rise, allocate and use monetary resources over the alliance, regarding risk analysis and strategic plan. It also includes cash flow, accounting, tributary planning, general payments, invoicing and other financial related actions
Contract management [36]	Management of all contractual documents and legal issues to support the formal entrance and exiting of members, customers and supporting entities to/from the alliance. It also involves the establishing, reviewing and cancellation of all current SLAs (Service Level Agreement) associated to all members' software services as well as related negotiations among its members, customers and supporting entities
Information management [37]	Management of all information (and their life cycle) that is generated, stored and made available inside the alliance as a support to all other processes. This information can be used by the members, customers and other supporting institutions according to the governance process
Knowledge management [38]	Management of all knowledge (and their life cycle) that is generated, stored, organized, combined, and made available inside the alliance as a support to all other processes. This knowledge can be used by the members, customers and other supporting institutions according to the governance process
Inheritance management [10, 39]	Management of activities related to gathering, storing, refining, integrating and re-using information and knowledge from/about/along all actions and transactions among members, customers and supporting institutions for future usage and continuous improvement
Strategic management [40, 41]	Management of the alliance's value system, bylaws, sustainability and competitiveness via e.g. SWOT analysis and BSC. It also comprises activities related to KPI and general performance indicators (seeing the alliance as a business); evaluation of members' alignment; strategic liaisons with supporting entities, new customers and markets; alliance's life cycle management, its metamorphosis and even its closure
Innovation management [21, 42, 43]	Management of activities, resources and results throughout the innovation life cycle developed in the scope of the alliance by its members and partnerships in terms products/services, processes, marketing and business

(*Continued*)

Table 1. (*Continued*)

Process	Objective
Marketing and commercial management [11]	Management of the activities related to all commercial practices derived from the strategic and marketing plans considering the alliance as a business organization. Marketing acts as a process over the commercial activities to help the alliance to achieve its business goals
Bag of assets management [11]	Management of the activities responsible to handle the access and maintenance of all existing alliance's assets (e.g. information, knowledge, practices, partners' profiles, customers' information, software services and general tools, etc.). The access to it from certain members, supporting institutions, customers and other external actors depends on the governance process and bylaws
Interoperability management [23, 30]	Management of all levels of interoperability (data, applications, processes and models) required to support a proper communication among the members, customers and other supporting institutions so as to better conduct businesses, covering the many involved perspectives (organizational, legal, accounting, technological, etc.)
Infrastructure management [12, 44]	Management of the activities related to the ICT infrastructure, human staff, physical facilities and other general infrastructures to administrate the alliance
Services management [34, 45]	Management of all kind of software services (at application, communication, infrastructure, integration, orchestration, security, etc., levels) provided by or under responsibility of the alliance, its members and supporting institutions. It includes services' life cycle and SOA governance management, and the management of the non-software-based services provided by supporting institutions
Security management [46]	Management of all access, communication and security policies involved in the general transactions among members, customers and supporting entities

By business processes it is generally meant as the set of inter-related activities and resources involved in the accomplishment of organization's goals. Each process is expressed in a table form (Fig. 1) identified by its core objective and by an extended description, which was conceived after a refinement of similar definitions and semantic interpretations. Only the most relevant sources of supporting references are presented in the end of each process. Figure 1 shows an excerpt of the *Trust Management* process.

Table 1 presents the 22 elicited business processes. Due to space restriction, only their short description (objective) is presented. Their complete and detailed descriptions can be accessed in https://sites.google.com/site/federationmanagement/.

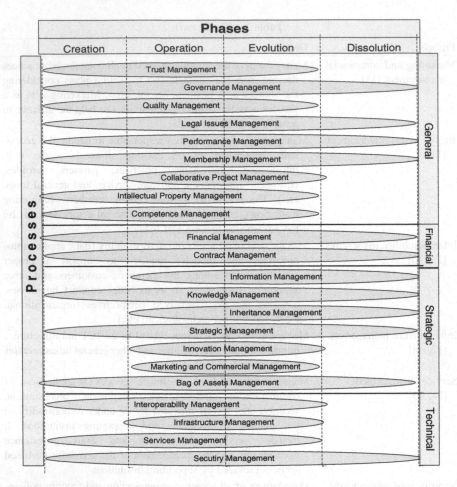

Fig. 2. Processes positioning along the alliance's life cycle

Processes were positioned along the alliance's life cycle (Fig. 2) so as to help managers in the planning of activities, resources allocation and priority processes, as well as to reason about impacts and implementation time. This placement considered the authors' experience as well as what the set of related papers and other general references on CN talked about. They were empirically categorized into four groups regarding their most intrinsic nature.

5 Conclusions

This paper has presented a list of business processes required to handle when more ample digital ecosystems of SSPs have the willingness to work collaboratively in a more intense, formal and systematic way so as to benefit from the sort of competitive advantages provided by Collaborative Networks.

Each business process was evaluated by a group of experts and some analyses can be made upon such processes. For example, none of the processes were considered as unnecessary by them. For most of the experts the processes related to trust, governance, legal aspects, project management and interoperability/integration are the first ones to be implemented or tackled from a more technical point of view. In terms of implementation complexity by companies, this was quite variable as it depends on local expertizes, "legacy" practices and culture, existing ICTs, and life cycle phase. About if SSPs tend to provide joint solutions in the near future in order to reduce costs and risks as well as to increase the chances of better addressing the market, around 75 % agreed on that. About if more and more ICT companies can become part of larger IT eco-systems in the near future to take advantage of complementarities and additional scale, around 85 % agreed on that. Another conclusion is that some processes are in fact similar to the ones found in other alliances, and there are other processes that are more related to software services and the federation scenario.

Although comprehensive and can be used by SSPs' managers as a useful guideline, the listed processes and life cycle positioning should however be taken as a *reference* and not as a definitive or mandatory view instead. Their deployment can vary depending on local factors, existing culture, already deployed processes, current business priorities, customers' needs, financial conditions, etc., as processes are different in terms of complexity, implementation costs and required human resources. One consequence of this is that processes could not be described at activities level as this can vary from one alliance to another. On the other hand, most of the identified processes deal with very known issues to which best practices can be used to more detailed define the usual activities to be supported within each process. For example, when dealing with strategic planning, BSC method can be used as a reference.

A business process-based perspective is only one among some others that should be dealt with by SSPs when working within networks. Therefore, perspectives like the socio-economic, the general business context, organizations' preparedness, among others, should complement the analysis that was done.

The proposed list of business processes was not yet validated in real or near-real alliances, although it has considered published material also about real cases. Anyway, SOA, software-services-based alliances and digital ecosystems are relatively new areas for SMEs, still having many open points and implementation challenges. Actually, there are too few real deployments of VBE-like long-term examples upon which more historical and consistent analysis could be taken as a reference.

Next short-term main steps of this research include a deeper validation activity by world-wide experts and in some real alliances, trying to also getting a more accurate notion of implementation complexity, importance and inter-relation among processes.

Acknowledgements. This work was partially supported by CNPq and Capes Brazilian research agencies.

References

1. Office, U.M.: UK IT Association. http://www.ukita.co.uk/about-ukita/about-ukita.html (2013)
2. Kramer, W.J. Jenkins, J., Katz, R.S.: The role of the information and communications technology sector in expanding economic opportunity. In: Economic Opportunity Series. Harvard University, Cambridge (2007)
3. Papazoglou, M.P.: Web Services & SOA. Principles and Technology, Pearson (2012)
4. Choi, J., Nazareth, D.L., Jain, H.K.: Implementing service-oriented architecture in organizations. J. Manage. Inf. Syst. 26(4), 253–286 (2010)
5. INFOWORLD 2012: Cloud Computing Deep Dive. http://www.infoworld.com/d/cloud-computing/cloud-computing-in-2012-infoworld-special-report-187077
6. Perin-Souza, A., Rabelo, R.J.: Services discovery as a means to enhance software resources sharing in collaborative networks. In: Proceedings of 12th IFIP Working Conference on Virtual Enterprises, pp. 388–399, Springer, Berlin (2011)
7. Camarinha-Matos, L.M., Afsarmanesh, H.: Collaborative networks: a new scientific discipline. J. Intell. Manufact. 16, 439–452 (2005)
8. Rabelo, R.: Advanced Collaborative Business ICT Infrastructures. In: Camarinha-Matos, LM, Afsarmanesh H, Ollus M (eds) Methods and Tools for Collaborative Networked Organizations, pp. 337–370. Springer, New York (2008)
9. Kitchenham, B., Pretorius, R., Budgen, D., Pearl Brereton, O., Turner, M.: Systematic literature reviews in software engineering - a tertiary study. Inf. Softw. Technol. 52(8), 792–805 (2010)
10. Afsarmanesh, H., Msanjila, S.S., Ermilova, E., Wiesner, S.: VBE management system. In: Camarinha-Matos, L.M., Afsarmanesh, H., Ollus, M. (eds.) Methods and Tools for Collaborative Networked Organizations, pp. 119–154. Springer, New York (2008)
11. Romero, D., Molina, A.: VO breeding environments & virtual organizations integral business process management framework. Inf. Syst. 11(5), 569–597 (2009)
12. Rabelo, R., Gusmeroli, S., Arana, C., Nagellen, T.: The ECOLEAD ICT infrastructure for collaborative networked organizations. In: Proceedings of 7th IFIP Working Conference on Virtual Enterprises, pp. 451–460. Springer, New York (2006)
13. Krogstie, J.: Modeling of Digital ecosystems - challenges and opportunities. In: Camarinha-Matos, L.M., Xu, L., Afsarmanesh, H. (eds.) Collaborative Networks in the Internet of Services, pp. 137–145. Springer, Berlin (2013)
14. Franco, R.D., Ortiz Bas, A., Gomez-Gasquet, P., Rodriguez Rodriguez, R.: Open ecosystems, collaborative networks and service entities integrated modeling approach. In: Camarinha-Matos, L.M., Xu, L., Afsarmanesh, H. (eds.) Collaborative Networks in the Internet of Services, pp. 74–83. Springer, Berlin (2013)
15. Camarinha-Matos, L.M., Afsarmanesh, H., Cardoso, T.: Service federation in virtual organizations. In: Proceedings of 11th International Conference on Digital Enterprise, pp. 305–324, Kluwer (2001)
16. Camarinha-Matos, L.M., Ferrada, F., Oliveira, A.I.: Interplay of collaborative networks in product servicing. In: Camarinha-Matos, L.M., Scherer, R.J. (eds.) PRO-VE 2013. IFIP AICT, vol. 408, pp. 51–60. Springer, Heidelberg (2013)
17. Cancian, M.H., Rabelo, R.J., Wangenheim, C.G.: Supporting processes for collaborative SaaS. In: Proceedings of 14th IFIP Working Conference on Virtual Enterprises, pp. 183–190. Springer, Berlin (2013)

18. Danesh, H.M., Raahemi, B: A framework for process management in service oriented virtual organizations. In: Proceedings of 7th IEEE International Conference on Next Generation Web Services Practices, pp. 12–17 (2011)
19. Haines, M.N., Rothenberger, M.A.: How a service-oriented architecture may change the software development process. Commun. ACM **53**(8), 135–140 (2010)
20. Svirska, A., Ignatiadi, I., Briggs, J. Agent-based service-oriented collaborative architecture for value chains of SMEs. In: Proceedings of 2nd IEEE International Conference on Digital Ecosystems and Technologies, pp. 161–167 (2008)
21. Santanna-Filho, J.F., Rabelo, R.J., Pereira-Klen, A.A.: An innovation model for collaborative networks of SOA-based software providers. In: Proceedings of 15th IFIP Working Conference on Virtual Enterprises, pp. 169–181. Springer, Berlin (2014)
22. DBE Ecossystem. http://www.digital-ecosystems.org/cluster/dbe/ref_dbe.html. Accessed February 2015
23. COIN. http://www.coin-ip.eu. Accessed April 2015
24. GLONET. http://www.glonet-fines.eu/2-glonet. Accessed January 2015
25. Msanjila, S., Afsarrnanesh, H.: Assessment and creation of trust in VBEs. In: Msanjila, S., Afsarrnanesh, H. (eds.) Network-Centric Collaboration and Supporting Frameworks, pp. 161–172. Springer, New York (2006)
26. Romero, D., Galeano, N., Giraldo, J., Molina, A.: Towards the definition of business models and governance rules for virtual breeding environments. In: Romero, D., Galeano, N., Giraldo, J., Molina, A. (eds.) Network-Centric Collaboration and Supporting Frameworks, pp. 103–110. Springer, New York (2006)
27. Romero, D., Galeano, N., Molina, A.: Towards governance rules and bylaws for virtual breeding environments. In: Camarinha-Matos, L.M., Afsarmancsh, H., Novais, P., Analide, C. (eds.) Establishing the Foundation of Collaborative Networks, pp. 93–102. Springer, New York (2007)
28. Alonso, J., de Soria, I.M., Orue-Echevarria, L., Vergara, M.: Enterprise collaboration maturity model (ECMM) - preliminary definition and future challenges. In: Popplewell, K., Harding, J., Poler, R., Chalmeta, R. (eds.) Enterprise Interoperability IV, pp. 429–438. Springer, London (2010)
29. Romero, D., Rabelo, R.J., Molina, A., Baldo, F.: Value co-creation & co-innovation strategies in collaborative networks: emergence in different industrial domains. pt.slideshare.net/davidromerodiaz (2001)
30. Ermilova, E., Afsarmanesh, H.: Competency modeling targeted on promotion of organizations towards VO involvement. In: Camarinha-Matos, L.M., Picard, W. (eds.) Pervasive Collaborative Networks, pp. 3–14. Springer, New York (2008)
31. Ermilova, E., Afsarmanesh, H.: Competency and profiling management in virtual organization breeding environments. In: Ermilova, E., Afsarmanesh, H. (eds.) Network-Centric Collaboration and Supporting Frameworks, pp. 131–142. Springer, New York (2006)
32. Jansson, K., Karvonen, I., Ollus, M.: Governance and Management of Virtual Organizations. In: Camarinha-Matos, L.M., Afsarmanesh, H., Ollus, M. (eds.) Methods and Tools for Collaborative Networked Organizations, pp. 221–238. Springer, New York (2008)
33. Sebrae/NA. What is Intellectual Property? [in Portuguese]. http://www.sebrae.com.br/customizado/inovacao/acoes-sebrae/consultoria/propriedade-intelectual/17-propriedade-intelectual-1/BIA_17 (2013)
34. Kai, T., Jian, Z., Bo J.: Framework for SaaS Management Platform. In: Proceedings of 7th IEEE International Conference on E-Business, pp. 345–350 (2010)

35. Romero, D., Galeano, N., Molina, A.: Virtual organisation breeding environments value system and its elements. J. Intell. Manufact. **21**(3), 267–286 (2007)
36. Camarinha-Matos, L., Afsarmanesh, H., Ollus, M., Oliveira, A.: Agreement Negotiation Wizard. In: Camarinha-Matos, L.M., Afsarmanesh, H., Ollus, M. (eds.) Methods and Tools for Collaborative Networked, pp. 191–218. Springer, New York (2008)
37. Gartner. New Realities of IT. Stanford, USA. http://www.gartner.com/technology/home.jsp (2010)
38. Jain, P.: Knowledge management for 21st century information professionals. J. Knowl. Manage. Pract. **10**(2), 31–49 (2009)
39. Romero, D., Rabelo, R.J., Molina, A.: On the management of virtual enterprise's inheritance between virtual manufacturing & service enterprises: supporting dynamic product-service business ecosystems. In: Proceedings of 18th International Conference on Concurrent Engineering, pp. 1–11 (2012)
40. Sturm, F., Kemp, J., Joode, R.: Towards strategic management in collaborative network structures. In: In: Camarinha-Matos, L.M., Afsarmanesh, H. (eds.) Collaborative Networked Organizations, pp. 131–138. Springer, New York (2004)
41. Serrano, V., Fischer, T.: Collaborative innovation in ubiquitous systems. J. Intell. Manufact. **18**(5), 599–615 (2007)
42. Tidd, J., Bessant, J., Pavitt, K.: Innovation Management. Wiley, Hoboken (2001)
43. Senano, V., Fischer, T.: Contribution of pervasine intelligence to collaborative innovation processes. In: Senano, V., Fischer, T. (eds) Network-Centric Collaboration and Supporting Framework, pp. 93–100. Springer, New York (2006)
44. Camarinha-Matos, L.M., Afsarmanesh, H.: Elements of a base VE infrastructure. Comput. Ind. **51**(2), 139–163 (2003)
45. Wu, B., Shuiguang, D., Ying, L.: Reference models for Saas oriented business workflow management systems. In: Proceedings of IEEE International Conference on Services Computing, pp. 242–249 (2011)
46. Stihler, M., Santin, A.O., Marcon, A.L., Fraga, J.S.: Integral federated identity management for cloud computing. In: Proceedings 5th International Conference on New Technologies, Mobility and Security, pp. 33–40 (2012)
47. The British Standards Institution: BS 11000 Collaborative Business Relationships – Product Guide. UK, 12 p. (2015)

Machine Learning Agents in the Cloud to Support Smart Business Process Management

Samia Gamoura[1(✉)], Laurent Buzon[2], and Ridha Derrouiche[3]

[1] Agenor-I, 1, Place Colonel Fabien, 69700 Givors, France
samia.gamoura@gmail.com
[2] ESCE – International Business School,
6 Cours Albert Thomas, BP 8242, 69355 Lyon Cedex 08, France
laurent.buzon@esce.fr
[3] EVS-UMR5600, 158 Cours Fauriel, 42023 St-Etienne Cedex 2, France
ridha_derrouiche@esc-saint-etienne.fr

Abstract. In Virtual Enterprise, Business Processes Management is regarded as one of the most concerns of managers and academic researchers. Managing flows complexity and actors requirements in terms of high quality in less time, make this management more and more complex and push specialists to explore new promising ways. Like these researchers, we present in this paper, a modelling and simulating software toolkit called BP-EMC^2 based on a generic framework baptized H-BPM. We propose a solution using machine learning agents operating in an AGR (Agent-Group-Role) organization within the Cloud. Furthermore, this paper includes a real case study of Adecco® business process deployed into its Cloud solution.

Keywords: Business process · Multi agent system · Virtual enterprise · Modelling · Simulation · Cloud computing · Machine learning

1 Introduction

Since the beginning of the 90's, inter-enterprises collaboration stills growing and generates new organizations patterns. Today, competition is no more limited in the internal organization but is extended in the whole enterprises network. These new kind of relationships created is called Virtual Enterprises (VE) focused on sharing Business Processes (BP). Here we situate our purpose to address an important issue in Business Processes Management (BPM): 'Collaboration'. The main topic considered in this paper is according to the collaboration strategies and how these strategies could be deployed overall BPM within Virtual Enterprise Network (VEN).

One from the huge number of methods and techniques used as a support for collaboration in VEN is Multi Agents Systems (MAS). As in many other business areas, such as medical, image processing, astronomy, etc. this paradigm of Distributed Artificial Intelligence (DAI) provided an efficient way to propose solutions and simulation of complex issues. Furthermore, we explain a new advanced kind of agents called Machine Learning Agents (MLA), able to use Machine Learning

© IFIP International Federation for Information Processing 2015
L.M. Camarinha-Matos et al. (Eds.): PRO-VE 2015, IFIP AICT 463, pp. 479–488, 2015.
DOI: 10.1007/978-3-319-24141-8_44

(ML) algorithms efficiently within the Cloud environment in order to extract and predict the best way of providing collaboration to companies.

2 Business Processes in Virtual Enterprises

VEs can achieve their business objectives only through effective collaboration between the autonomous enterprises that comprise them. A key requirement for theses VEs is called 'Collaborative BP' that explicitly captures and manages the functional and contractual relationships between VE's partners.

2.1 Virtual Enterprises Networks

As a formal definition, VEN is a temporary alliance of enterprises that aim to share resources and skills in order to respond better and faster to emerging opportunities in the market, based on a technical infrastructure and information technologies [1].

In Fig. 1. we illustrate the VEN concept with a network of companies created to design and manufacture a new type of stool [2].

The next section deals with the essential elements of BPM to identify concepts and approaches that aim to design an efficient tool to help VEN partners to manage and improve their cooperation.

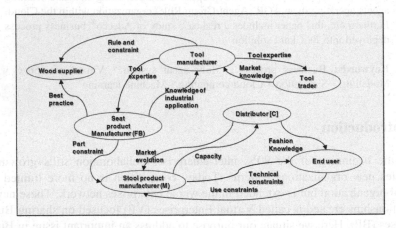

Fig. 1. An example of VEN of a stool supply chain

2.2 Business Processes Management Methodologies

As mentioned by the Object Management Group (OMG) in [3], the primary goal of BPM modelling is to provide a notation that is readily understandable by all business users, from the draft of the initial business analyst, to the technical developers responsible for implementing the technology that will perform those processes, and finally, to the business people who will manage and monitor those processes. The state-of-the-art shows three main modelling methodologies: One-Thing Approach (OTA) [4], View-Based Approach (VBA) [5] and Holistic Process Methodology (HPM).

The main idea behind the HPM approach is that domain specific process models are required both to capture the contents of a process based application and to present a process model in a user-friendly way. The assumption is that this application is composed of single activities that have to be executed in a certain order [6].

According to our framework, we choose to use this last methodology for several reasons: agility, wide usage and user-friendly feature to insure business people requirements.

3 Multi Agent Systems and Machine Learning

Systems based on a set of software agents commonly named MAS have been used widely following an exponential trend during recent ten years, and this is mainly due to their potential in understanding various group behaviors such as swarms and flocking. In industry and business applications, in domains as several as manufacturing [7], war gaming [8], satellite clusters [9] and so on. Furthermore, a number of development environments and frameworks are actually available, i.e. SWARM® [10], JADE® [11], JACK® [12], etc. appeared. Computer science architects and program designers believe that this paradigm called Agent Oriented Programming (AOP) is the next step forward from Object Oriented Programming (OOP) [13].

In the following section, we begin by positioning MAS in terms of its business uptake. We know that there is a lot of research works, ideas, and projects, but the uptake of the technology is not as rapid or as pervasive as its advocates anticipated [13]. In the configuration MAS-BP, one of the bright works is that one of Fleischermann et al. in [14]. According to authors, the emerging paradigm of the subject oriented BPM by MAS is to augment MAS models with a process-centric layer that preserves autonomy and concurrent interactions. Another remarkable work was published by Bonfante et al. in [15] inspired by the same principle of the MAS layer above the process layer. The proposed architecture is composed of a layer between BP and Web canals.

3.1 Agents and Predictive Machine Learning Algorithms

Research works, publications, books, projects, applications in the area of Machine Learning Agents (MLA) are numerous, especially in recent works concerned by Big Data phenomenon: [16, 17], etc. ML techniques can be classified according on several criteria to several classes. These techniques are to be coupled to learning classes according to the data nature where the learning type could be supervised or unsupervised.

The most widely used technique is the last one; Q-Learning; also called Reinforcement Learning (RL), easy to implement and convergence is guaranteed. This is one of the reasons that push us choosing it to predict our agents' actions.

4 Cloud Computing in Business Process Management Context

Nowadays, Cloud computing is the fundamental change happening in the field of IT. The special report published by the National Institute of Standards and Technology (NIST) in US [18] provides a clear understanding of Cloud computing. It provides a simple and unambiguous taxonomy of three service models available to Cloud consumers: Cloud Softwares As A Service (SaaS), Cloud Platform As A Service (PaaS) and Cloud Infrastructure As A Service (IaaS).

This paper presents an organized snapshot of the challenges faced by scientists and professionals in designing and deploying BPM within VE in the Cloud. Our background study encompasses both classes of systems: for supporting update dynamic BPM and for ad-hoc analytics and decision support using intelligent tools within SaaS Cloud platforms.

Since 2010, big numeric companies propose industrial software products for BPM in the Cloud, such Oracle Fusion Middleware 11 g by Oracle® [19]. A 'Cloudified' BPM allows what is called 'Unified Collaboration' or 'Social BPM' which becomes increasingly more and more important, especially with the IT virtualization phenomenon. Distributed nature of Cloud reinforces the need for process visibility and collaboration, especially as systems and people are distributed. Also, BPM should leverage optimized structure and management of 'Cloudification'.

All these reasons have guided our decision to locate our platform on the Cloud, with services offered in SaaS with appropriate rights management. This particular part of rights management and security will be presented in further publications topics.

5 Framework Proposal BP-EMC²

In this work, we look at the issue of BPM in VE of nowadays, with new challenge of 'Cloudification'. As we already introduced, we have chosen to automate the dynamic monitoring of changes in processes by AGR machine learning agents (Fig. 2).

For experimental needs and validation, we worked on an industrial case study of Adecco® recruitment process shared with its partners; HP® and Renault® in a VE context (we call this VE Adecco® & Co.). In the following sections, we will describe step by step how we design and build our solution by using this case study, without exposing deep details.

5.1 Building Smart BPM Model in the Cloud

We regard a process as a collection of activities that consume some inputs in order to produce some outputs based on HPM (as discussed previously in Sect. 2.2) .in the process life management as detailed in the following steps:

Step 1. Managing Process Life Cycle (PMLC) by Holistic Approach (H-BPM): The BPM life cycle is constituted by a set of activities and the model has to define a

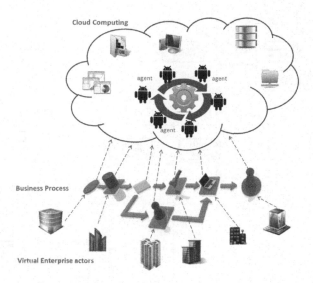

Fig. 2. Machine learning agents in the cloud for BP-EMC^2

clear guideline how a process must be performed. To design our model named H-BPM, our concern was to notice all key concepts in the life cycle model offered in HPM methodology. Thus, we consider some of them:

- **Item:** three types of items; Actor (a reactive or proactive entity which can act and initiate an activity of launch events, such as human task, automatized task, application module, etc.), Object (a passive entity which is handled by actors, such messages, documents, products, etc.) and Event (all events defined in BMPN such as 'timer', 'start and 'end' events).
- **Configuration:** a set of items with related parameters define a configuration. It is the set of all the elements contained in the BMPN relative to a time reference.
- **Time guide-based:** The life cycle is marked by a time stamp. During this cycle, multiple configurations may exist following time.
- **Version:** each item in the configuration is mentioned by a version, and the configuration itself is versioned (Fig. 3).

Step 2. Introducing Machine Learning algorithm in H-BPM agents' behavior: As discussed previously, we introduce a Machine Learning algorithm to give ability to our agents to be adaptive and predictive to augur better actions to help human and system. We implement ML based on Q-Learning algorithm where each agent has a history as a sequence of state-action-rewards.

Step 3. Modelling H-BPM components: Our built model is based on autonomous agents, with whom we aim to understand and study the behavior actors within BPM. In our proposed platform, agents are necessary to initiate and drive the execution of processes. Based on key concepts described previously, we design our system components based on three main entities: Actors, Events and Objects.

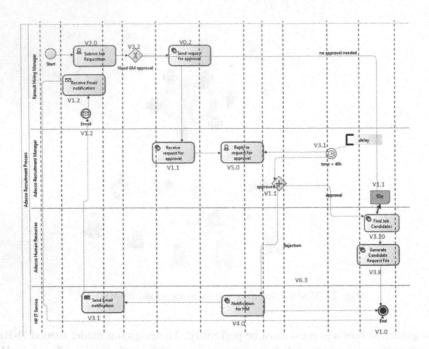

Fig. 3. Recruitment BPM in Adecco® & Co. modeled by H-BPM (by IBM-Bonitasoft® 6.5.1)

Pools in H-BPM should be designed as 'Roles' entities. And agents indicates 'Actors', Objects are designed by 'Objects' and finally events are defined as 'Events' for agents' input/output flows. Actions performed by actors in H-BPM are implemented in 'Roles' (Fig. 4).

Based on this presented model H-BPM, we baptize a software toolkit BP-EMC² as 'Business Process – Evolutive Management by Collaborative agents in the Cloud'. The remaining part in the next section is devoted to the description of this toolkit.

6   Experimental Validation of BP-EMC²

The software platform was designed and conducted in JAVA®. Following the study of both platforms SWARM® and JADE®, this last was chosen because of the following advantages: it is a platform FIPA compliant (meaning feature ensures interoperability with protocols and standards); it manages the task achieving parallelism; it allows reusability and all imported libraries are free software.

6.1   BP-EMC² Features: Case Study Adecco® & Co. Recruitment BPM

Our toolkit named BP-EMC² is a generic model of BPM with agents as we conceive it. The framework embeds two modules: 'Modelling module' where we can configure the system and the 'Simulation module' which is a Graphical User Interface (GUI) that

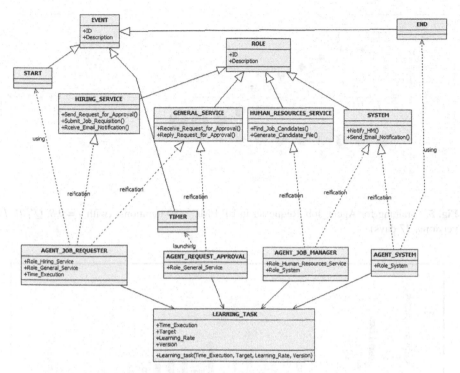

Fig. 4. Learning with AGR in H-BPM (by StartUML 5.0.3®)

uses the parameters defined in the model described in the previous section for illustration, analysis and numerical and graphical monitoring of experimental scenarios.

During our simulations campaigns, our main objective was to provide proofs that agents in BP-EMC^2 have the ability to improve overall BPM in terms of time execution and targets. Using predictive agents in the Cloud should provide a high target level with short time execution. Thus, we considered described metrics: *Time Execution* (TE) and *TarGet* (TG) according to time-line represented by *Versions* (V).

In order to compare our proposition with a solution without agents, we refer to SAS® (the Business Intelligence (BI) software) extracted Key Performance Indicators (KPI) data in figures below. Used KPI are: *'AD KPI'* as 'Action Duration KPI' (cf. Figure 6) and *'AQ KPI'* as 'Action Quality KPI' (cf. Figure 7).

6.2 Discussion

As we see on the both trend curves in figure Fig. 5, both indicators *TE* and *TG* tend to stabilize and to optimize values. When, after several iterations we get close values, we speak of stability. At the *11th* iteration, the average execution time of the action *Agent_Job_Requester* is *2.9* h with a *TG/action* indicator of *0.08/10* ~ *80* %, and this is satisfactory and maintained for next versions. Then, if we compare this (Fig. 5) with extractions in figures Figs. 6 and 7, we can notice that the average time per action *moy*

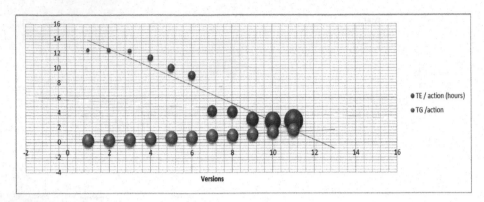

Fig. 5. Training for Agent_Job_Requester in BP-EMC^2 (*50* iterations) (with $\gamma = 0.8$, $Q^0[0]$, *11* versions, *17* days)

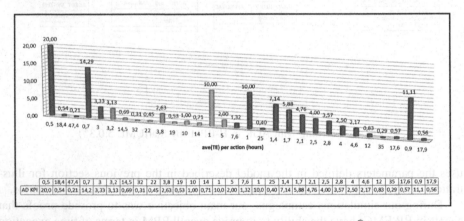

Fig. 6. Extraction of *AD KPI* for a month (*30* days) (by SAS$^®$ Software)

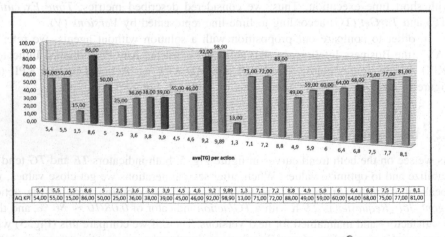

Fig. 7. Extraction of *AQ KPI* for a month (*30* days) (by SAS$^®$ Software)

(TE)/action may be slightly more interesting *(0.5 to 1 episode)* but with a mediocre quality indicator *TG* of *5.5 /10* ∼ *55 %* in longer global time execution *(30 days vs 17 days)*. Also, we have not insurance that this will be maintained as there is no system for experience storage and management (no memory). As we see, these values vary and may worsen from an episode to another.

These results are admittedly preliminary but very promising: Learning agents helped refine the convergence to a more optimal BPM model. This convergence is reached after a number of versions obtaining a short execution time with a high quality indicator. These results may be similar to a conventional BPM (without the use of Machine learning agents Results), but can take more time longer and without any insurance of stability.

7 Conclusion

This paper attempts to address the issue of collaboration in the area of Virtual Enterprises which concerns Business Process Management under Cloud Computing requirements. As technology evolves, flexibility of BPM adapts to new requirements. Processes can be managed at anytime from anywhere and optimization allows to adjust processes to Cloud SaaS context. Our toolkit called BP-EMC² (Business Process – Evolutive Management by Collaborative agents in the Cloud), tries to provide a complete platform for BPM partners to face new IT challenges. We believe that, our work may be an efficient tool to reduce complexity and provides the flexibility required for any BPM in Virtual Enterprise.

References

1. Roşu, S.M., Drăgoi, G.:Virtual enterprise network general architecture. In: 8th IEEE International Conference on Communications (COMM), pp. 313–316. IEEE Press, New York (2010)
2. Buzon, L., Bouras, A., Ouzrout, Y.: Knowledge exchange in a supply chain context. In: IFIP 18th World Computer Congress, TC5/WG5.5: PRO-VE'04, 5th Conference on Virtual Enterprises, pp. 145–152. Kluwers Academics Publishers, Dordrecht (2004)
3. Business Process Model and Notation (BPMN), Version 2.0. http://www.bpmn.org/ (2011)
4. Vogel, O., Arnold, I., Chughtai, A., Kehrer, T.: Software Architecture: a Comprehensive Framework and Guide for Practitioners. Springer, Heidelberg (2011)
5. Hentrich, C., Zdun, U.: Patterns for process-oriented integration in service oriented architectures. In: 11th European Conference on Pattern Languages of Programs (2006)
6. Dori, D.: Object-Process Methodology: a Holistic Systems Paradigm. Springer, Heidelberg (2002)
7. Liu, Q., Gao, L., Lou, P.: Resource management based on multi-agent technology for cloud manufacturing. In: IEEE 2011 International Conference on Electronics, Communications and Control, pp. 2821–2824. IEEE Press, New York (2011)
8. Tan, X., Lai, S., Wang, W., Zhang, M.: Framework of wargame CGF system based on multi-agent. In: IEEE International Conference on Systems, Man, and Cybernetics. pp. 3141–3146. IEEE Press, New York (2012)

9. Schettera, T., Campbella, M., Surkab, D.: Multiple agent-based autonomy for satellite constellations. J. Artif. Intell. **145**, 147–180 (2003)
10. SWARM® Project under GNU Lisence. http://www.swarm.org
11. JADE® Framework under LGPL Lisence. http://jade.tilab.com
12. JACK® Software under AOS Group Lisence. http://aosgrp.com/products/jack
13. Jarvis, D., Jarvis, J., Rönnquist, R., Lakhmi, C.: Multiagent Systems and Applications. Springer, Heidelberg (2013)
14. Fleischmann, A., Metasonic, A.G., Pfaffenhofen, G., Kannengiesser, U., Schmidt, W., Stary, C.: Subject-oriented modelling and execution of multi-agent business processes. In: IEEE International Joint Conferences on Web Intelligence (WI) and Intelligent Agent Technologies (IAT), vol. 2, pp. 138–145. IEEE Press, New York (2013)
15. Bonfante, M.C., Paz, J.P., Castillo, A.: Multi-agent system for integration process business and ontologies for the government online strategy. Int. J. Appl. Sci. Technol. **7**(4), 19–25 (2014)
16. Rand, W.: Machine learning meets agent-based modelling: when not to go to a bar. In: Conference on Social Agents: Results and Prospects (2006)
17. Kotsiantis, S.B.: Supervised machine learning : a review of classification techniques. J. Emerg. Artif. Intell. Appl. Comput. Eng. (2007) (IOS Press, Amsterdam)
18. Liu, F., Tong, J., Mao, J., Bohn, R., Messina, J., Badger, L., Leaf, D.: NIST Cloud Computing Reference Architecture. NIST Special Publication (2011)
19. Connaughton, M.: Business Process Management and Cloud Computing. Oracle Middleware 11 g Forum (2011)

Separation of Decision Modeling from Business Process Modeling Using New "Decision Model and Notation" (DMN) for Automating Operational Decision-Making

Thierry Biard[1(✉)], Alexandre Le Mauff[2], Michel Bigand[2], and Jean-Pierre Bourey[2]

[1] Université Paris-Saclay – Laboratoire Génie Industriel – CentraleSupélec, Grande Voie des Vignes, 92290 Châtenay Malabry, France
thierry.biard@centralesupelec.fr

[2] Université Lille Nord de France – Ecole Centrale de Lille, Cité Scientifique, CS 20048, 59651 Villeneuve d'Ascq Cedex, France
alexandre.lemauff@centraliens-lille.org,
{michel.bigand,jean-pierre.bourey}@ec-lille.fr

Abstract. This paper presents Decision-making in Collaborative Networks and enlarges the differences between strategic-tactical and operational decisions. The common way of representing decisions into classical BPMN diagrams is shown, with its drawbacks. The new OMG's standard DMN (Decision Model and Notation) is introduced, with its context and its main elements. Then, the association between BPMN and DMN is detailed and the advantage of their separation is illustrated into examples. At last, the related experiments (already done and future works) are demonstrated: a graphical editor for modeling and an automatic code generator from a Model-To-Text transformation.

Keywords: DMN · Decision model notation · BPMN · Business process management · Model to text transformation

1 Decision-Making in Collaborative Networks

Decision-making is an important concern for Collaborative Networks (CN). Several papers already published address strategic-tactical decision-making, as Join/Leave/Remain a CN [1]. A few papers address operational decision-making as Demand and Capacity Sharing [2]. This paper is about a contribution to operational decision-making, directly linked to business processes.

The environment, the scope and the impact of decision-making are different depending on whether the decisions are strategic-tactical or operational. The predefined environment of operational decision usually leads to integrate them into business processes. Once it is done, due to their high frequency, there is an interesting opportunity to automate the operational decision-making. The main differences between strategic-tactical and operation decisions are listed into Table 1.

© IFIP International Federation for Information Processing 2015
L.M. Camarinha-Matos et al. (Eds.): PRO-VE 2015, IFIP AICT 463, pp. 489–496, 2015.
DOI: 10.1007/978-3-319-24141-8_45

Table 1. Strategic-tactical versus operational decisions (from the authors)

Type of decision	Strategic-tactical	Operational
Environment	Uncertain	Predefined
Scope	Global (to Local)	Local (to Global)
Term impact	Long	Short
Process oriented	Low	High
Decision-making	Human with decision support system	(To be) Automated
Frequency	Low	High
Period	Years-months	Real time
Decision example	Join/Leave/Remain	Capacity sharing
Object example	CN entity	Sales order

2   Decision Modeling Inside Business Process Diagrams

In recent years, BPMN (Business Process Model and Notation [3]; version 1.0 was published in 2003) has become the adequate notation for modeling business processes. BPMN Orchestration Diagram has even supplanted UML (Unified Modeling Language [4]) Activity Diagram for describing business processes, because BPMN provides modeling elements that are missing in UML and that are useful at business level, such as inclusive gateways and compensations. BPMN Orchestration Diagram is supposed to be simple and understandable by many people, among them the business stakeholders.

In fact, especially with all the features proposed by the version 2.0.2, BPMN Orchestration Diagram can become complex. The possibilities offered by its gateways for drawing multi-criteria decisions can lead to represent a business process model as a labyrinth. Indeed the result is that decisions are often drowned into these complex BPMN orchestration diagrams. One main consequence is the coupling increase between the decision elements with the process model: a slight modification on decision rules may have a strong impact on the whole process model. Here is a simple example of such Orchestration Diagram (Fig. 1).

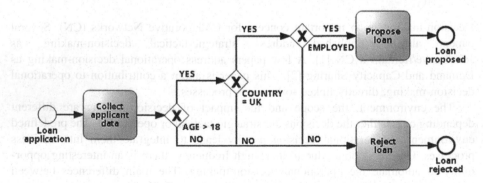

Fig. 1. Classical BPMN orchestration diagram with cascading gateways

3   "Decision Model and Notation" (DMN)

3.1   New Standard Proposed by OMG

It exists now a solution for simplifying these complicated BPMN Orchestration Diagrams with multi-criteria decision. This solution is demonstrated in this paper.

This innovation was proposed last year by the OMG (Object Management Group): its "Decision Model and Notation" (DMN) specification [5] proposes a new way for modeling decisions, which can be now extracted for business process BPMN models.

This new standard DMN is not isolated. On the contrary, it can rely on the vocabulary defined in SBVR (Semantics of Business Vocabulary and Business Rules [6]) and the objectives defined in BMM (Business Motivation Model [7]), others OMG's standards. However, DMN is above all interfaced with BPMN 2.0.2. Only the strong association between DMN and BPMN is detailed further in this paper.

DMN is supported by software companies, but also by KU Leuven University. Note that, although the final version 1.0 of DMN specification was approved by OMG's board in December 2014, it is the beta version 1.0, published in February 2014, which is still available en OMG's web site.

3.2   DMN Diagram Elements

A DMN model, aka Decision Requirements diagram, can be drawn using four graphical elements: Input Data, Business Knowledge, Decision and Knowledge Source (this last one is optional and is used for quoting external references). The other ones are mandatory (Fig. 2).

Component		Description	Notation
Elements	Decision	A decision denotes the act of determining an output from a number of inputs, using decision logic which may reference one or more business knowledge models.	Decision
	Business Knowledge Model	A business knowledge model denotes a function encapsulating business knowledge, e.g. as business rules, a decision table, or an analytic model.	Business knowledge
	Input Data	An input data element denotes information used as an input by one or more decisions. When enclosed within a knowledge model, it denotes the parameters to the knowledge model.	Input data
	Knowledge Source	A knowledge source denotes an authority for a business knowledge model or decision.	Knowledge source

Fig. 2. Decision requirements diagram elements (from OMG specification)

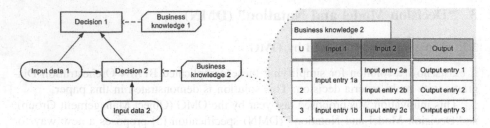

Fig. 3. A simple decision requirements diagram (from OMG specification)

DMN is supposed to be understandable by stakeholders, as business users. The fact is that its graphical representation is quite simpler than BPMN one, because DMN has neither gateways nor events, for instance (Fig. 3).

You will notice that the Decision is the Output Data (aka the chosen option), which is determined from Input Data, potentially other sub-decisions, and pre-defined business logic described into Business Knowledge, using preferably Decision Tables, as shown on the right side of above Fig. 3.

3.3   BPMN + DMN Association Principle

Business Processes and Decisions can now be modelled separately, using BPMN and DMN respectively [8]. The multiple gateways into the BPMN Orchestration Diagram, often nested in cascade, are now replaced by a unique task as "Make a decision" that returns the result. It is a Business Rule Task, with a small Decision Table symbol on its top left corner (Fig. 4).

Fig. 4. Business rule task (BPMN)

3.4   BPMN + DMN = Separation of Concerns

The main advantage of having two different BPMN + DMN models, decoupling Decision-making from Processes, is the Separation of Concerns (SoC). SoC is an old (1974) best practice coming from computer science [9].

These loosely coupled models can evolve independently from each other and can even be supported by different stakeholders, according to their needs and skills (IT people and business analysts for instance). Each model (Business Process or Decision) can consider the other one as a black box, exchanging data against decision.

These models respect the main required property for a good Separation of Concerns: they have their own consistency; to understand one model, it is not necessary to know the other one. Moreover, Decision-making context can be explicitly detailed into the DMN diagram. Sub-decisions can be reused into several decisions too. This capitalization can lead to Knowledge Management (KM).

3.5 BPM + DMN Separation Applied to Collaborative Networks

Here is a couple of examples (willingly simplified), first a classical BPMN Orchestration Diagram without DMN, then a new BPMN Orchestration Diagram with DMN Decision Requirements Diagram, associated together via a Business Rule task (Figs. 5 and 6).

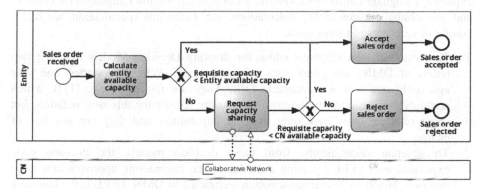

Fig. 5. Classical BPMN orchestration diagram without DMN

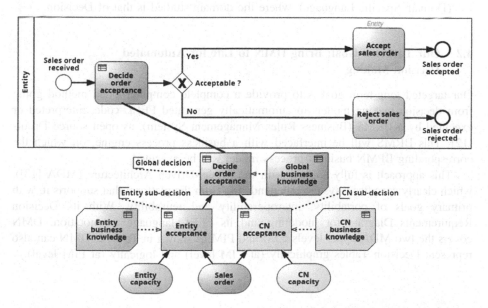

Fig. 6. New BPMN orchestration diagram with DMN decision requirements diagram

Besides reorganizing the diagrams, this implementation of Separation of Concerns seems to be interesting for Collaborative Networks (CN): a main decision could be split into several sub-decisions made by each entity and made by the CN as a whole.

4   DMN Related Experiments

4.1   Our Reached Goals: Graphical Editor and Automatic Code Generation

The OMG specification of DMN provides both a metamodel of DMN and an expression language called FEEL (Friendly Enough Expression Language) for defining and assembling decision tables, calculations, etc. From this specification, we had a couple of reached short-term goals:

1- To create our own graphical editor for drawing Decision Models (the first two letters of DMN), compliant with this metamodel. When we started one year ago, only one tool was available [10]. They are ten now (e.g. [11]), which certainly demonstrates the interest of software editors for this new notation, but some of these tools have only drawing capabilities and they are not free of charge.

2- To generate automatically, from these decision models, the decision code expressed with FEEL by using a model driven engineering approach and more precisely Model-to-Text transformation technique. In DMN, FEEL is the language for Notation (the third letter of DMN). FEEL stands for Friendly Enough Expression Language. Our approach is to consider FEEL as a DSL (Domain-Specific Language), where the domain studied is that of Decision.

4.2   Our Targeted Goal: Bring DMN to Life for Automated Decision-Making

Our targeted long-term goal is to provide a complete computer-aided method going from decision-making models to automatically generated FEEL code, interpreted or executed by a BRMS (Business Rules Management System), as open source Drools [12]. This BRMS will be interfaced with a business process engine, on which the corresponding BPMN business process model will be executed.

This approach is fully aligned with the Model-Driven Architecture (MDA [13]), which clearly specifies a system independently from the platform that supports it, with primary goals of portability, interoperability and reusability. With its Decision Requirements Diagram for modeling and its FEEL language for notation, DMN covers the two MDA upper levels CIM and PIM as shown in Table 2. DMN can also represent Decision Tables graphically (at CIM level) and logically (at PIM level).

Table 2. Model-driven architecture (MDA) applied to decision-making

MDA levels	Decision-making
CIM (computation independent model)	DMN (decision requirements diagram)
PIM (platform independent model)	DMN (FEEL considered as a DSL)
PSM (platform specific model)	e.g. DRL (drools rule language)

4.3 DMN Implementation Based on Eclipse Tools

We chose best-of-breed modules for Eclipse Modeling Tools dedicated to model driven engineering:

- Sirius [14] to create our graphical DMN modeling tool (without programming but with advanced setting),
- Acceleo [15] to generate FEEL code by using a Model-to-Text transformation (with programming and advanced setting too).

Below is a couple of screen captures about what we have done with theses Eclipse modules. DMN graphic elements special shapes are for the moment replaced by colours: it is a temporary solution without Java programming (Fig. 7).

This is an example of FEEL code generation from the above DMN model: on the left, there is M2T (Model-To-Text Transformation Language) code [16]; on the right, the FEEL code automatically generated from the above DMN model (Fig. 8).

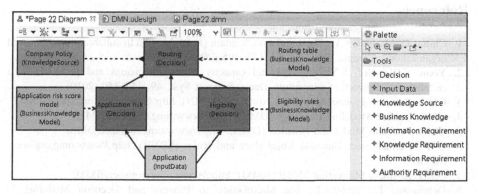

Fig. 7. Graphical DMN modeling tool with Sirius module

```
FEEL (                                                      FEEL (
    [ac.knowledgeRequirement.requiredKnowledge.name/]          Routing table (
    [for ( anInformationRequirement : InformationRequire           Application risk,
    [if (anInformationRequirement.requiredDecision.name.           Eligibility,
        [anInformationRequirement.requiredDecision.name/           Application
    [/if]                                                      )
    [if (anInformationRequirement.requiredInput.name.ocl   )
        [anInformationRequirement.requiredInput.name/][i
    [/if]
    [/for]
    )
)
```

Fig. 8. Model-to-text (FEEL) transformation with Acceleo module

5 Conclusion and Future Work

The separation of Decision Modeling from Business Process Modeling is a good principle, whatever the models, notations and languages are. It will enhance agility when changes are required, in reducing their impact, among them the risk of failure, and in increasing the resilience of the Information System (IS).

Our contribution is to present DMN as a relevant standard for Decision-making. However, DMN cannot deal with uncertainty and is limited to pre-defined decisions made from known criteria. The emphasis is now on operational Decision-making.

DMN makes it possible to represent Decision Models with sub-decisions, business knowledge, input data and knowledge sources distributed over various CN entities. Therefore, DMN can model decentralized and collaborative operational Decisions, based on standard and international specification. The decision models, shared on-line by all entities, can provide the transparency required by Collaborative Networks.

DMN is already usable for modeling these decisions, in separating them from business processes and applying the principle of separation of concerns. In a few months, due to Model-To-Text transformation, its FEEL code will be runnable and it will be possible to automate operational Decision-making, in a fast, reliable and repeatable way from business processes already modelled.

References

1. Chituc, C.-M., Nof, S.Y.: The Join/Leave/Remain (JLR) decision in collaborative networked organizations. Comput. Ind. Eng. **53**, 173–195 (2007)
2. Yoon, S.W., Nof, S.Y.: Demand and capacity sharing decisions and protocols in a collaborative network of enterprises. Decis. Support Syst. **49**, 442–450 (2010)
3. OMG: Business Process Model and Notation (BPMN). http://www.omg.org/spec/BPMN/
4. OMG: Unified Modeling Language (UML). http://www.omg.org/spec/UML/
5. OMG: Decision Model and Notation (DMN). http://www.omg.org/spec/DMN/
6. OMG: Semantics of Business Vocabulary and Rules (SBVR). http://www.omg.org/spec/SBVR/
7. OMG: Business Motivation Model (BMM). http://www.omg.org/spec/BMM/
8. Debevoise, T., Taylor, J.: The MicroGuide to Process and Decision Modeling in BPMN/DMN: [Building More Effective Processes by Integrating Process Modeling with Decision Modeling] (2014)
9. Dijkstra, E.W.: On the role of scientific thought. http://www.cs.utexas.edu/users/EWD/transcriptions/EWD04xx/EWD447.html
10. Decision Management Solutions: DecisionsFirst Modeler. http://decisionsfirst.com/
11. Signavio: Decision Manager. http://www.signavio.com/products/decision-manager/
12. Red Hat: Drools, Business Rules Management System. http://drools.org/
13. OMG: MDA (Model Driven Architecture) Specifications. http://www.omg.org/mda/specs.htm
14. Eclipse: Sirius. http://www.eclipse.org/sirius/
15. Eclipse: Acceleo. http://www.eclipse.org/acceleo/
16. OMG: Model To Text Transformation Language (M2T). http://www.omg.org/spec/MOFM2T/

Application of Process Mining and Semantic Structuring Towards a Lean Healthcare Network

Dario Antonelli and Giulia Bruno[✉]

Department of Management and Production Engineering, Politecnico Di Torino,
Corso Duca Degli Abruzzi 24, 10129 Turin, Italy
{dario.antonelli,giulia.bruno}@polito.it

Abstract. Modern healthcare systems are evolving towards a complex network of interconnected services. The increasing costs and the conversely increased expectations for high service levels leveraged the birth of healthcare monitoring activities and the proposition of numerous performance evaluation indicators. Generally, the adopted performance measures allow to draw a picture of quality, equity, appropriateness and efficiency of the medical care at different levels: caregiver, hospital, local health authority, region. The role of network organization and its impact on the performances is largely underestimated. It is difficult to build a Value Stream Mapping of the healthcare network because of the number and complexity of care and diseases followed. The study tries to overcome this issue. Starting from a database of the accesses to the services in a local health agency, the activity flow diagram is produced by using a process mining software, Disco. A knowledge structured by means of an ontology allows to describe the logic behind the health service provision. The resulting process flow chart is the base for the identification and amendment of redundant and non value added flows among services.

Keywords: Process mining · Healthcare network · Ontology

1 Introduction

Worldwide there is an increasing number of initiatives aimed at introducing a standardized and centralized information management in healthcare organizations (hospitals, medical centers, drugstores) through digitalization of medical data. It is proven that digital tools like the electronic health records provide benefits to both patients and physicians by improving health care efficiency [1]. The availability of the medical history of the patient's accesses to medical centers will allow both the physicians to express meaningful analyses at the patient level (e.g., searching for similar patients based on their medical history or predicting future events in care pathway) and the system manager to operate at the organizational level (e.g., discovering which are the most accessed resources or which are the anomalous managements of patients) [2]. Therefore the analyses are intended to improve the quality of services offered to citizens while to reducing costs and wastes. Since the data volume is very high, and it is expected to grow dramatically in the years ahead, for healthcare organizations it is

© IFIP International Federation for Information Processing 2015
L.M. Camarinha-Matos et al. (Eds.): PRO-VE 2015, IFIP AICT 463, pp. 497–508, 2015.
DOI: 10.1007/978-3-319-24141-8_46

vitally important to acquire the available tools, infrastructure, and techniques to leverage big data effectively. The enormity and complexity of collected medical data present great challenges [3].

The format of medical data and the data base structure is a serious issue preventing their use for operation managements applications. Data describe the healing pathway of the patient and do not give direct evidence of the process flow in terms of process times, queues, unproductive times, etc. To have a better insight of the process flow, data should be elaborated by process mining.

Process mining aims at extracting process knowledge from event logs which may originate from different kinds of systems, e.g., enterprise information systems or hospital information systems [4]. Typically, these event logs contain information about the start/completion of process steps together with related context data (e.g. actors and resources). Previous works addressed the problem of analyzing single entities (e.g., a hospital department) by applying techniques of data/process mining and simulation [4–7]. In these cases, existing processes are compared with the medical knowledge to determine whether the pathway of a patient within the structure is correct. However, the analysis of a single entity is limitative, because it does not consider the previous history of the patient and thus it is not able to evaluate the quality of the healthcare system as a whole.

Before applying the process mining techniques, it is important to merge data of different nature to collect the patient movements inside the network. In order to merge heterogeneous data, we need a controlled vocabulary in term of set of ontologies to give data a meaning despite the different original data structure. After the merge of data, it is possible to apply a process mining tool, to automatically reconstruct the movements of patients inside the network. This analysis is useful both to analyse the changes in patient flows depending on age or gender of patients and to discover the bottleneck and waste of the system, toward a lean restructuring of the healthcare process.

The overall objective of this paper is to contribute in giving medical managers an accurate and deep understanding of the healthcare network functioning. There are several contributions: the first contribution is the definition of an ontology of the healthcare network: general concepts and relationships. Then, starting from the data organized in the model, the process mining analysis is used to extract information for the network evaluation. To make the methodology more concrete, the real data collected by an Italian Healthcare Territorial Agency (HTA) is exploited as a case study. The preliminary results we obtained proved the applicability and the usefulness of the proposed approach.

2 State of the Art

There is an evolving trend in recent years that has modified the healthcare system from a few nodes hospital based organization to a branched network of service centers spread on the territory [8]. Furthermore the approach to disease treatment is now based on integration among the different agents of the care system. Therefore there is a convergent trend towards a network of centers that delivery integrated care [9].

The integration of different aspects of healthcare system has been a subject of study by many authors in the field of operations management [10–12] and several authors highlighted the benefits of integration both in terms of quality of care as in terms of lean organization [13–15]. Drawbacks are equally reported but are mainly due to lack of cooperation and commitment of the healthcare personnel [16, 17].

The analysis of healthcare network by using the operations management models is not effective as in the industrial environment where the process activities and the flow of material are utterly defined. The production is substituted by care pathway, that is far less deterministic. Products are substituted by patients that are free to move along the process flow at their will (or even to abandon care and consequently interrupt the flow of activities). To extract performance variables to be a guidance in the process management, it is necessary to have recourse to other methods, like data mining techniques [18, 19]. If time is not a monitored output, the focus is on pattern extraction in order to detect the most frequent medical treatments undergone by patients [20–22]. These techniques do not give a comprehensive view of the processes in act in the healthcare systems.

On the other hand, process mining can be applied to healthcare data to identify the processes and derive meaningful insights from the complex temporal relationships existing between activities and resources involved in processes [23]. For example, process mining was applied to a hospital emergency service in a public hospital in Portugal to identify regular behavior, process variants, and exceptional medical cases in [24], and to a hospital in Belgium to model the activities related to breast cancer treatment in [25]. It was also applied to perform a comparative analysis across four hospitals in Australia [23]. We follow these previous works, but we applied process mining to extract the movements of patients among the different centers of a Healthcare Territorial Agency (HTA), in order to perform a comparative analysis among different patient segments.

3 Healthcare Network Ontology

The ontology used in our work has two aims: firstly to model the entities and relationships needed to collect data coming from a healthcare network, and secondly to provide the controlled vocabulary in order to merge data coming from heterogeneous sources. For the first aim, we define a model as a UML class diagram, after the carefully analysis of the data available in Italian HTA. For the second aim, we reused the controlled vocabularies previously developed relevant for our purpose, i.e., ICD10 [26] for disease classification, MDC [27] for the major diagnostic categories, DRG [28] for diagnosis related group and ATC [29] for drug classification.

The UML class diagram representing the healthcare data collected by the HTA is reported in Fig. 1. A service is any kind of healthcare service provided to a citizen, form examinations to drugs to hospitalizations, while a user is any person who access the healthcare system. A prescriber is a physician who can do prescription of services to the users, while a provider is a structure that provides one or more services. For each provider, the list of services it provides is known. A prescription represents the information of the specific services that a prescriber prescribes to a user, and a provision stores the information of services provided by providers to the users. This is a very general model that is valid for all the healthcare territorial agency [30].

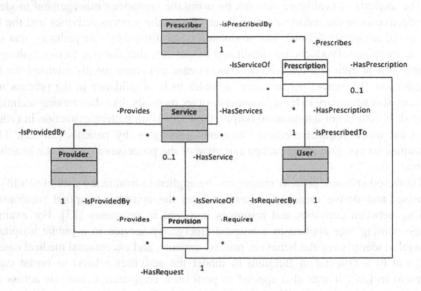

Fig. 1. Main entities of the healthcare network ontology.

This UML class diagram can be represented in the form of an ontology, where each entity is a class, with the corresponding relationships linking the classes. Then, for each entity, it is possible to specify the hierarchical tree of concepts at increasing detail levels which represent the knowledge related to the services, providers, users and prescribers of the HTA [31]. This information constitutes the HTA ontology that will be used to select the data of interest for the following analysis.

In a HTA, three types of providers can be identified: (i) the medical centers without hospitalization capacities, (ii) the hospitals and (iii) the drugstores. The existence of three providers determine the existence of three type of services, i.e., (i) the examinations, (ii) the hospitalizations and (iii) the drugs. For each kind of service, a further hierarchy can be defined. The examinations can be further specified based on the medical branch they belong, the hospitalizations based on the diagnosis-related group (DRG) and the major diagnostic category (MDC), the drugs based on the anatomical therapeutic chemical (ATC) classification. The prescribers can be divided in two categories, i.e., the general physician and the specialist physician. The users can be divided based on their pathology, represented by their exemptions code. These hierarchical structures are shown in Fig. 2.

The information stored in the ontology is used to extract from the database the subset of data relevant for the analysis.

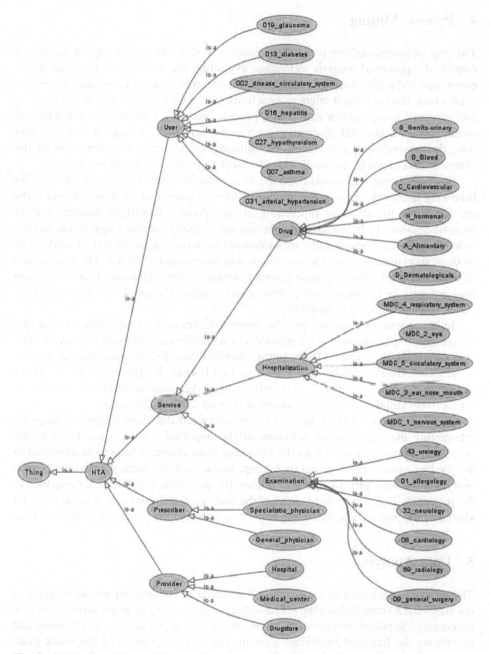

Fig. 2. Hierarchical levels of the healthcare network ontology, built with the Protégé ontology editor (http://protege.stanford.edu).

4 Process Mining

The goal of process mining is to extract process models from event logs. It includes a family of a-posteriori analysis techniques exploiting the information recorded in the event logs. Typically, these approaches assume that it is possible to sequentially record events such that each event refers to an activity (i.e., a well-defined step in the process) and is related to a particular case (i.e., a process instance). Furthermore, some mining techniques use additional information such as the performer or originator of the event (i.e., the person/resource executing or initiating the activity), the timestamp of the event, or data elements recorded with the event (e.g., the size of an order).

Process mining was already applied in healthcare systems, trying to answer the following questions: (i) what are the most followed paths and what exceptional paths are followed? (ii) are there differences in care paths followed by different patient groups? Standard paths are the activities that are typically executed by patients and the order of them. Exceptional paths are anomalous activities due to the way of working of medical specialists or related to specific patient characteristics or not. The comparison of the behavior of different patient groups is another interesting issue. This comparison may not only be interesting for patient groups within a hospital but also for similar patient groups in different hospitals.

In this paper, we applied process mining techniques to reconstruct the actual movements of patients among the providers of a Healthcare Territorial Agency. To this aim, we exploit the software Disco (https://fluxicon.com/disco/), a commercial process mining tool, freely available under an academic license. It exploits the Fuzzy Miner algorithm for process mining [32], which uses significance/correlation metrics to interactively simplify the process model at desired level of abstraction.

The core functionality of this tool is the automated discovery of process maps by interpreting the sequences of activities in the imported log file. According to the process mining paradigm, at least the following three elements have to be identified in the file log: case id, activity, and timestamp. In our analysis, since we are interested in analyzing the movements of patients among the providers, the case id corresponds to the patient id. The activity is an event of the process, thus in our case it is the provider visited by the patient. The timestamp is the date in which the patient visits the provider.

5 Data Analysis

The database considered as a case study contains data collected by an Italian HTA in the 2007–2012 years. Indeed, the HTAs collect data about the supplied services for cost accounting. Supplied service data represent an essential resource in planning and monitoring the Regional Healthcare System. Data for the analysis of diagnostic pathway are selected from the data warehouse: Hospital Discharge Records, Ambulatory Care Records, Emergency Department Records, Ambulatory Care Records. They are composed of personal data and clinical data section, so that it was possible to merge anonymized personal and clinical data, to collect all databases in a single MySQL database by means of a PHP routine that automatically import data.

In order to focus our study on a specific pathology, we extracted from the database the log file of all the patients suffering from asthma for year 2007. The aim is to analyze the mobility of patients across the different medical centers placed on the territory. The data refer to a total of 451 asthma patients who accessed medical centers, divided in 207 males and 244 females. Regarding the age of patients, 155 are younger than 36 years, 333 are between 36 and 65 years old, and 63 are older than 65 years.

Before attempting any process mining it was necessary to preprocess the data in order to simplify them, by skipping unnecessary low level activities and by merging the significant low level activities in singular high level ones. We used the knowledge deriving from the ontology of Sect. 3 to preprocess the data. An example is the log describing the accesses to a laboratory for executing analyses. Whether the analyses are executed on the same patient, the same day, for the sake of operations management, they can be safely converted in a singular access to one activity.

After preprocessing, we performed two alternative segmentations of the dataset, one based on gender and the other one based on age, in order to highlight the effect of both factors on the process flow diagram. Each segment was imported in Disco to perform the process mining. For readability reasons, only the 30 % of activities involved and the 10 % of the path between activities are shown in the results. These percentage grant to cover at least the 90 % of the data, since there are many centers that are accessed only one or two times, and thus are not relevant for the analysis.

From the analysis of the first segmentation, it can be noticed that the some similarities exist between the two obtained graphs (Figs. 3 and 4). The first one is that in both cases there is a "hub center" which is the most accessed by both genders, since the majority of patients perform examinations only in this center. Another similarity is that the processes usually do not involve more than two different centers (the hub center and one of the other centers). Despite these similarities, the graphs also show some differences. First of all, the number of visited centers is different: male patients visit 12 different centers, while female patients visit 21 different centers, thus showing a higher mobility of female patients.

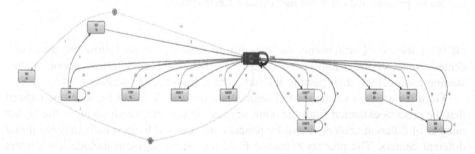

Fig. 3. Process flow extracted by Disco on the male segment, all the ages considered.

Also the frequency of accesses is different. Figure 5 reports the number of accesses to each center for the male segment and the female segment (the hub center is not reported since its accesses are significantly higher than the others: 1348 for male and

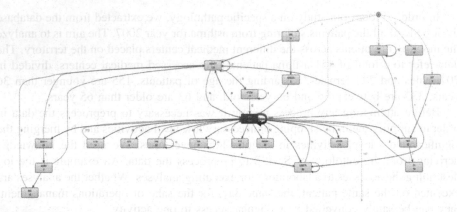

Fig. 4. Process flow extracted by Disco on the female segment, all the ages considered.

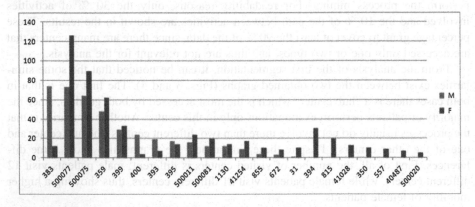

Fig. 5. Different numbers of accesses to medical centers by male patients (blue bar at the left) and female patients (red bar at the right) (Color figure online).

1820 for female). Furthermore, the majority of male processes follow the path "hub center - other center - hub center", while the female process follow various paths, starting for a center, then passing the hub center, followed by another center.

From the analysis of the second segmentation (Figs. 6, 7 and 8), it can be noticed that the process extracted from the adult segment is the one which includes the higher number of different centers visited by patients and also the longest pathways involving different centers. The process extracted from the senior segment include less centers and shortest paths. This can be due to the low mobility of elder patients with respect to the others. The number of accesses to medical centers of each of these three segments is reported in Fig. 9.

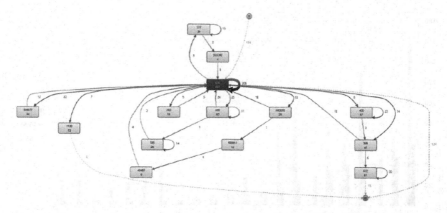

Fig. 6. Process flow extracted by Disco on the young segment for all the genders.

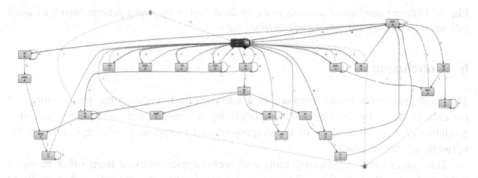

Fig. 7. Process extracted by Disco on the adult segment for all the genders.

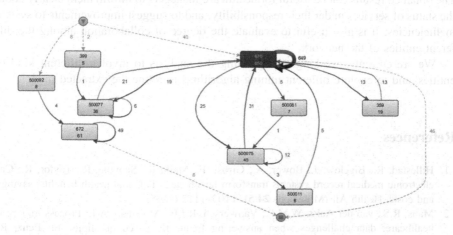

Fig. 8. Process flow extracted by Disco on the senior segment for all the genders.

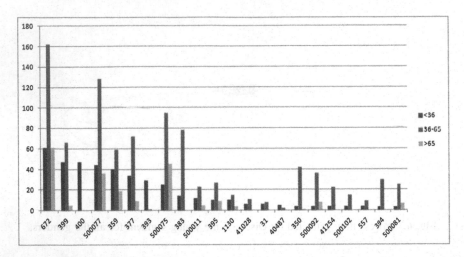

Fig. 9. Different numbers of accesses to the medical centers by young patients (first bar), adult patients (second bar) and senior patients (third bar).

6   Conclusion

The evaluation of a health network is a complex task because the management of patients is done by entities not controlled by a central unit, with the result that guidelines for the evaluation of the diagnostic and therapeutic pathways through the network are not available.

This paper aims at adapting tools and technologies derived from other research fields and using them firstly to obtain a model of a healthcare network, and secondly to perform a meaningful analysis of the mass of data produced by a healthcare network. The obtained results can be useful for healthcare managers to inform them clearly about the status of services under their responsibility, and to suggest improvements to system inefficiencies. It is also useful to evaluate the degree of collaboration among the different entities of the network.

We are currently working on extending the analysis to involve different kind of entities, and to explore different mining algorithms to refine the extracted model.

References

1. Hillestad, R., Bigelow, J., Bower, A., Girosi, F., Meili, R., Scoville, R., Taylor, R.: Can electronic medical record systems transform health care? Potential health benefits, savings, and costs. Health Aff (Millwood) **24**(5), 1103–1117 (2005)
2. Mans, R.S., van der Aalst, W.M.P., Vanwersch, R.J.B., Moleman, A.J.: Process mining in healthcare: data challenges when answering frequently posed questions. In: Lenz, R., Miksch, S., Peleg, M., Reichert, M., Riaño, D., ten Teije, A. (eds.) ProHealth 2012 and KR4HC 2012. LNCS, vol. 7738, pp. 140–153. Springer, Heidelberg (2013)

3. Sun, J., Reddy, C.K.: Big data analytics for healthcare. In: Proceedings of the 19th ACM SIGKDD International Conference on Knowledge Discovery and Data Mining, p. 1525 (2013)
4. Mans, R.S., Schonenberg, N.H., Song, M., van der Aalst, W.M.P., Bakker, P.J.M.: Application of process mining in healthcare – a case study in a dutch hospital. In: Fred, A., Filipe, J., Gamboa, H. (eds.) BIOSTEC 2008. CCIS, vol. 25, pp. 425–438. Springer, Heidelberg (2011)
5. Coelli, F.C., Ferreira, R.B., Almeida, R.M.V.R., Pereira, W.C.A.: Computer simulation and discrete-event models in the analysis of a mammography clinic patient flow. Comput. Methods Programs Biomed. **87**(3), 201–207 (2007)
6. Di Leva, A., Femiano, S.: The BP-M* methodology for process analysis in the health sector. Intell. Inf. Manage. **3**, 56–63 (2011)
7. Cardoso, E.C.S., Guizzardi, R.S.S., Almeida, J.P.A.: Aligning goal analysis and business process modelling: a case study in healthcare. Int. J. Bus. Process Integr. Manage. **5**(2), 144–158 (2011)
8. Wan, T.T.H., Wang, B.B.L.: Integrated healthcare networks performance: a growth curve modeling approach. Health Care Manage. Sci. **6**, 117–124 (2003)
9. Lenz, R., Reichert, M.: IT support for healthcare processes - premises, challenges, perspectives. Data Knowl. Eng. **61**(1), 39–58 (2007)
10. Scott, W.R.: The organization of medical care services: toward an integrated theoretical model. Med. Care Rev. **50**(3), 271–302 (1993)
11. Ahgren, B., Axelsson, R.: Evaluating integrated health care: a model for measurement. Int. J. Integr. Care **5**(e01), (2005)
12. Tjerbo, T., Kjekshus, L.: Coordinating health care: lessons from Norway. Int. J. Integr. Care **5**(e28), (2005)
13. Axelsson, R., Bihari, A.S.: Integration and collaboration in public health: a conceptual framework. Int. J. Health Plann. Manage. **21**(1), 75–88 (2006)
14. Bazzoli, B.J., Chan, B., Shortell, S., D'Aunno, T.: The financial performance of hospitals belonging to health networks and systems. Inquiry **37**(3), 234–252 (2000)
15. Provan, K.G., Milward, H.B.: Do networks really work? A framework for evaluating public-sector organizational networks. Public Adm. Rev. **61**(4), 414–423 (2001)
16. Hurtado, M.P., Swift, E.K., Corrigan, J.M.: Crossing the Quality Chasm: a New Health System for the 21st Century. National Academy Press, Washington (2001)
17. Cesarini, M. Mezzanzanica, M. Cavenago, D.: ICT management issues in healthcare coopetitive scenarios. In: Information Resources Management Association International Conference (2007)
18. Lin, F., Chou, S., Pan, S., Chen, Y.: Mining time dependency patterns in clinical pathways. Int. J. Med. Inform. **62**, 11–25 (2001)
19. Batal, I., Fradkin, D., Harrison, J., Moerchen, F., Hauskrecht, M.: Mining recent temporal patterns for event detection in multivariate time series data. In: ACM SIGKDD Conference on Knowledge Discovery and Data Mining (2012)
20. Baralis, E., Bruno, G., Chiusano, S., Domenici, V.C., Mahoto, N.A., Petrigni, C.: Analysis of medical pathways by means of frequent closed sequences. In: Setchi, R., Jordanov, I., Howlett, R.J., Jain, L.C. (eds.) KES 2010, Part III. LNCS, vol. 6278, pp. 418–425. Springer, Heidelberg (2010)
21. Antonelli, D., Baralis, E., Bruno, G., Chiusano, S., Mahoto, N.A., Petrigni, C.: Analysis of diagnostic pathways for colon cancer. Flex. Serv. Manufact. J. **24**(4), 379–399 (2011)
22. Antonelli, D., Baralis, E., Bruno, G., Cerquitelli, T., Chiusano, S., Mahoto, N.A.: Analysis of diabetic patients through their examination history. Expert Syst. Appl. **40**(11), 4672–4678 (2013)

23. Partington, A., Wynn, M., Suriadi, S., Ouyang, C., Karnon, J.: Process mining for clinical processes: a comparative analysis of four Australian hospitals. ACM Trans. Manage. Inf. Syst. **5**(4), 1–18 (2015)
24. Rebuge, A., Ferreira, D.R.: Business process analysis in healthcare environments: a methodology based on process mining. Inf. Syst. **37**(2), 99–116 (2012)
25. Poelmans, J., Dedene, G., Verheyden, G., Van der Mussele, H., Viaene, S., Peters, E.: Combining business process and data discovery techniques for analyzing and improving integrated care pathways. In: Perner, P. (ed.) ICDM 2010. LNCS, vol. 6171, pp. 505–517. Springer, Heidelberg (2010)
26. ICD10: http://www.who.int/classifications/icd
27. MDC: http://health.utah.gov/opha/IBIShelp/codes/MDC.htm
28. DRG: http://www.cms.gov/Research-Statistics-Data-and-Systems/Statistics-Trends-and-Reports/MedicareFeeforSvcPartsAB/downloads/DRGDesc05.pdf
29. ATC: http://www.whocc.no/atc_ddd_index
30. Antonelli, D., Bruno, G.: Healthcare network modeling and analysis. In: Camarinha-Matos, L.M., Afsarmanesh, H. (eds.) Collaborative Systems for Smart Networked Environments. IFIP AICT, vol. 434, pp. 691–698. Springer, Heidelberg (2014)
31. Antonelli, D., Bellomo, D., Bruno, G., Villa, A.: Evaluating collaboration effectiveness of patient-to-doctor interaction in a healthcare territorial network. In: Camarinha-Matos, L.M., Xu, L., Afsarmanesh, H. (eds.) Collaborative Networks in the Internet of Services. IFIP AICT, vol. 380, pp. 128–136. Springer, Heidelberg (2012)
32. Günther, C.W., van der Aalst, W.M.P.: Fuzzy mining – adaptive process simplification based on multi-perspective metrics. In: Alonso, G., Dadam, P., Rosemann, M. (eds.) BPM 2007. LNCS, vol. 4714, pp. 328–343. Springer, Heidelberg (2007)

Performance and Optimization

A Performance-Based Scenario Methodology to Assess Collaborative Networks Business Model Dynamicity

Raúl Rodríguez-Rodríguez[✉], Juan-José Alfaro-Saiz, and María-José Verdecho

Universitat Politècnica de València, Camino de Vera s/n, 46022 Valencia, Spain
{raurodro,jalfaro,mverdecho}@cigip.upv.es

Abstract. In today's business marketplace many enterprises collaborate forming a collaborative network (CN) in order to achieve competitive and sustainable advantages. In this context, CNs should have not only well-defined business models but also mechanisms and tools that help them out to assess such business models as well as other CN operations at their early stages. Due to shorter life-cycles and to the current fierce competition such an evaluation should be made as quickly as possible and analyzing real data rather than based on opinions and subjective judgments. This paper presents the application of a methodology that allows such an assessment as well as the generation of business scenarios based on the performance of the CN. Then, it first defines the appropriate CN key performance indicators (KPIs), gathering data for a certain time-period; then, it applies multivariate techniques to this data, identifying relationships between the KPIs, and being able to build the timely evolution of the CN based on this data; next, it is able to design a business scenario based on the timely evolution that the CN should have according to its business models and operations results achieved so far. With all this additional information decision-makers could decide whether the CN's business models succeeded or not so far and what actions to take in order to achieve the future desirable scenario.

Keywords: Scenarios · Business models · Collaborative networks

1 Introduction

Design, implementation, re-definition and sustainability of business models are complex tasks. However, these are key tasks when aiming to stay in business in a sustainable manner for a long time. Nowadays, when competition is fiercer than ever and business environments are turbulent ones there is a need to evaluate, under a dynamic approach, whether a business model is and, what it is more important, will be successful. When bringing this thematic to the Collaborative Network (CN) context, it becomes more complex, as CNs requires of more organizational skills and capabilities to do so than in single companies. Therefore, the business model dynamic assessment issue is one of the most serious research gaps to be covered within the current literature. Then, recently some authors [1, 2] affirmed that an orientation towards experimenting with and exploiting new business opportunities was the key to cope with dynamicity. In addition, organizations achieving coherence between leadership, culture, and employee commitment are in the

© IFIP International Federation for Information Processing 2015
L.M. Camarinha-Matos et al. (Eds.): PRO-VE 2015, IFIP AICT 463, pp. 511–517, 2015.
DOI: 10.1007/978-3-319-24141-8_47

first line regarding business models knowledge and, extensively, success. Experimenting is directly liked to innovation, which is of great importance when aimed to develop a sustained business model. However, there is a lack of models/methodologies that clearly propose an approach to link CNs experimentation results and CNs performance. Additionally, the current approaches do not integrate a business scenario methodology within a solid and complete performance measurement system.

Then, this paper applies a methodology that will help to CNs decision-makers to assess, in its early stages, whether a business model is successful or not and whether it will, based on real recent performance, be successful in both the short and the medium-term. This will be made through the development of business scenarios based on applying multivariate statistical techniques to real data as gathered by sound performance indicators. The outcome of this methodology will help to decide whether to pursue the defined CN business model, and other important CN operations, or not. The main results of applying this methodology to a CN are highlighted, as well as final conclusions, future research work and generalization of the findings.

2   Scenario Planning and Performance Measurement

Even though it is widely accepted that the usage of scenario planning is very beneficial for organisations, this has not been totally proved. In fact, there are several works that aim to establish links between scenario planning practices and benefits. Chermack [3] proposed fourteen different hypothesis that aimed to demonstrate the existence of correlation between scenario planning and other factors such as firm performance, improved decision making or learning. Additionally, [4] revised several case studies, empirical studies and theoretical works that evaluated scenario based decision-making processes. Real world evaluations lacked measures of verification, which usually turned out to be subjective ones. On the other hand, theoretical evaluations involved rationales difficult to properly assess. Finally, it is stated that when evaluating a decision-making method, the human component should be carefully taken into account.

Therefore, a system that somehow combined the implementation of scenarios within a performance measurement system (PMS) would be of great utility to decision-makers. In this sense, and even though in the last years several important supply chain PMS have been developed – i.e. [5–7] - none of these works do enable effective mechanisms to incorporate scenarios application. At the individual enterprise context something similar happens, as there are only two works that have dealt in some deep this idea. Fink et al. [8] developed a called "future scorecard" in which some consideration is given to the possibility of developing a scorecard that possesses an additional input with the information and conclusions derived from environmental analysis. On the other hand, Othman [9] establishes that a balanced scorecard could be linked with scenario planning by taking into account a future state or scenarios to be reached when formulating the PMS strategy. Both of these works are theoretical and do not go beyond, as they neither propose a structured method nor provide experiences derived from application.

Hence, the methodology developed by Rodriguez-Rodriguez et al. [10] incorporates business scenario generation within a PMS. In order to do this, it is based on real data coming from the PMS, as collected by the key performance indicators, to design the different business scenarios. Therefore, decision-makers have available scenarios based on real data coming from their own PMS and they can therefore project this data to achieve the future position of the organisations. Moreover, they will know in advance what values should take the different indicators in order to reach this future desirable position and, extensively, will be able to react and propose and apply actions that will make this possible. This methodology applies multivariate techniques such as Principal Component Analysis and Partial Least Squares to find combination of inter-related KPIs and to project them in order to define the future business scenario.

This methodology was applied to organisations but not yet to CN. This paper presents next the main results of applying it to the key performance indicators regarding the business models and operations of a CN.

3   Application

The above mentioned methodology has been implemented in a specific CN in order to be able to design business scenarios that will help to decide not only to what extent a business model is being profitable and effective but also to decide whether to modify it or not. A Spanish furniture manufacturer and a home appliances company form such a CN. These two companies have kept business relationships for the last two decades and know each other very well. They combine different products in order to offer to customers different combinations of their products. Moreover, customers will have available a combination or pack of products whose value proposition exceeds the traditional single-company one. It is important to point out that these two companies are the core ones of the CN, but this involves to many other organisations that come from the raw material suppliers to the own final customers. Additionally, this study was carried out when the CN was already stated and working and therefore metrics collected data from different key business models indicators, as well as from other parts of the CN, rapidly. Therefore, decisions made as a result of the experimentation, calculated performance business scenarios, were expected to have an impact in the short-term.

Then, it was initially needed to define key performance indicators able to measure, control and monitor not only business models activities and changes but also other important parts of the CN regarding both its customers and operations. Therefore, a list of 15 key performance indicators was defined. These are shown in Table 1. The business models key performance indicators were defined following [1].

Some of these KPIs were quite abstract and a great effort was made in order of not only properly collecting the data but also creating a standardize process accepted by the partners. Then, many KPIs were collected via experts' analysis instead of direct feeding from some databases. For instance, KPI number 1 was collected once the experts analysed whether there was any knowledge strategy change compared to the previous situation, as defined in the immediate previous time period. In order to do so, experts had to analysed different points and results from the CN carrying out different activities: developing a questionnaire, monitoring the evolution of the CN regarding financial results, personnel perception or knowledge transfer and comparing the obtained results with the situation in which, according to its strategic formulation and business model, the CN should be.

Table 1. CN key performance indicators

Id.	KPI
1	Number of knowledge strategies changes
2	Improvement of the degree of contextualization of multi-disciplinary knowledge
3	Improvement of the service level
4	Improvement of the customer involvement level
5	Improvement of the customer fidelity degree
6	Improvement of the delivery time
7	Decrement of the life cycle time-to-market
8	Improvement of the customer satisfaction degree
9	Improvement level of the GRI indicators related to sustainable production
10	Number of collaborative product designs
11	Improvement of the number of additional business services offered
12	Improvement of the degree of collaborative innovation
13	Improvement of the degree of perceived quality
14	Improvement in of sales achieved (% turnover)
15	New business opportunities discovered

Then, these KPIs were collecting data over a six-months time period. The operative phase of collecting the data was not an easy task. First of all, it was necessary to homogenize the frequency of the data from the KPIs. In other words, some KPIs were regularly collected (i.e. weekly frequency for the KPI number 3 of increment of service level) whereas others were collected in a more dilated way (i.e. every two months for the KPIs 1, 2 or 9).

Then, some initial data treatment was performed on such data (statistics, frequency homogenization), having available an initial data set. Such a data set formed an initial data matrix to which Principal Component Analysis was applied, obtaining different principal components. The principal components are constituted by KPIs that interrelated. For this study, the two first principal components were retained, as they explained the 82 % of the initial data variability. The indicators forming these two first components were the following.

- PC1. Indicators number: 3, 6, 7, 9, 10, 13 and 14
- PC2. Indicators number: 1, 2, 4, 5 and 8.

Therefore, the PC1 could be representing the operational evolution of the CN whereas the PC2 could be representing the business model control and customer situation of the CN. It is necessary to point out that the KPIs not included within either PC1 or PC2 were forming other PCs that were not retained for this study.

Then, a monthly time evolution of these KPIs was obtained and the observed trend can be seen in Fig. 1.

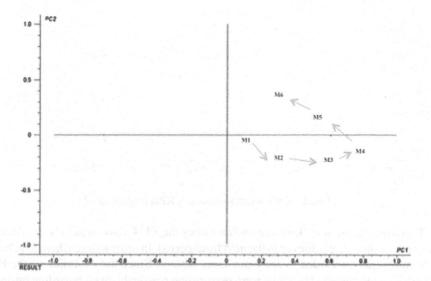

Fig. 1. CN timely evolution

Then, from this time evolution, it can be seen that for the two first periods of time (M1, M2) the evolution of the PC1 is positive (growths) whereas the PC2 decreases. This means that the CN was positively growing regarding its operations (as measured by the KPIs that form the PC1) and decreasing regarding its business model and customer situation, as captured by PC2. Then, it can be observed a change in this trend in the periods M3 and M4, where PC1 still grows but slower than before and the PC2 stabilizes its decrement. Finally, in the periods M5 and M6 PC2 grows positively whereas the PC1 decreases its value. At the end of M6, the situation was by one hand that the CN was obtaining a good response in terms of the PC2 (business model and customer situation) coming from a bad starting; on the other hand, the CN was performing worse than initially regarding its operations.

With this information, the decision makers had to decide what they wanted to achieve in the next period(s) of time. Since the KPIs related to business models were performing well in the last periods, they decided to generate a scenario where the CN operations improved, maintaining the positive growing trend of PC2. Then, the PCA was applied again providing some future values to the KPIs of both PC1 and PC2. This application was performed several times until the future scenario (E), as shown in Fig. 2, was achieved.

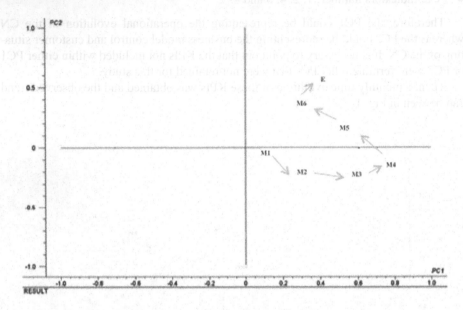

Fig. 2. CN's scenario based on KPIs projection

Therefore, decision-makers knew what values the KPIs associated to both principal components should be achieved in the next time-period. In order to force them to achieve such values, they accorded to carry out some actions. Since the evolution of the PC2 was positive they decided that they were performing reasonably well regarding business model and customer situation and focused therefore on modifying the trend of PC1. In doing so, they decided to apply, among others, the next actions:

- Supervise and re-organise the design team.
- Look for new first-tier suppliers.
- Application of lean manufacturing techniques.
- Improve customer participation in the design and first units production processes.

As pointed out before, these actions were indicated to act and achieve results in the short-term. However, the effect of these actions may take time and it should be monitored and re-adjusted if necessary over-time.

4   Conclusions

This work has presented the main results of applying a methodology for designing scenarios based on performance for CNs. This methodology allows to decision-makers to decide whether the CN's business models and operations have being achieved so far. In the application presented, after applying Principal Component Analysis, two principal components were retained for the study, representing both the operational evolution of the CN and the business model control and customer situation of the CN. These two principal components were represented over a period of time of six months, being able to determine whether the expected objectives were being achieved or not. The principal component 2 of business model control and customer situation had a good positively growth trend whereas the principal component 1 of CN operations was decreasing in value. This lead to decision makers to design a future desirable business scenario, which would bring to the principal component 1 to positively growth in the next time periods. Additionally, adequate actions to make that the KPIs inherent to the principal component 1 would get the position defined for the business scenario were stated.

This application can be generalized for any CN that has got KPIs defined and wants to analyse the timely evolution of its performance, as a result of the timely evolution of some principal components formed by different CN KPIs. Besides, such a CN can also define one or some scenarios and associated actions to be taken within the CN.

Future research work could focus on linking together the KPIs that constitute the different principal components with the CN strategic objectives; this would lead to a representation of the timely evolution of CN at the strategic levels.

Acknowledgments. This work has been developed within the research project called "Design of business scenarios to improve the efficiency and management of industrial supply chain" (reference GV/2013/045).

References

1. Achtenhagen, L., Melin, L., Naldi, L.: Dynamics of business models – strategizing, critical capabilities and activities for sustained value creation. Long Range Plann. **46**, 427–442 (2013)
2. Chesbrough, H.: Business model innovation: opportunities and barriers. Long Range Plann. **43**, 354–363 (2010)
3. Chermack, T.J.: Studying scenario planning: theory, research, suggestions, and hypotheses. Technol. Forecast. Soc. Change **72**, 59–73 (2005)
4. Harries, C.: Correspondence to what? Coherence to what? What is good scenario-based decision making? Technol. Forecast. Soc. Change **70**, 797–817 (2003)
5. Gunasekaran, A., Patel, C., Tirtiroglu, E.: Performance measures and metrics in a supply chain environment. Int. J. Oper. Prod. Manage. **21**, 71–87 (2001)
6. Bullinger, H.J., Kühner, M., Hoof, A.V.: Analysing supply chain performance using a balanced measurement method. Int. J. Prod. Res. **40**, 3533–3543 (2002)
7. Folan, P., Browne, J.: Development of an extended enterprise performance measurement system. Prod. Plann. Control **16**, 531–544 (2005)
8. Fink, A., Marr, B., Siebe, A., Khule, J.-P.: The future scorecard: combining external and internal scenarios to create strategic foresight. Manage. Decis. **43**, 360–381 (2005)
9. Othman, R.: Enhancing the effectiveness of the balanced scorecard with scenario planning. Int. J. Prod. Perform. Manage. **57**, 259–266 (2008)
10. Rodriguez-Rodriguez, R., Saiz, J.J.A., Bas, A.O., Carot, J.M., Jabaloyes, J.M.: Building internal business scenarios based on real data from a performance measurement system. Technol. Forecast. Soc. Change **77**, 50–62 (2010)

Performance Measurement for the Design of Product-Service Systems

Khaled Medini[✉], Sophie Peillon, Xavier Boucher, and Hervé Vaillant

Ecole Mines de Saint-Etienne, Henri Fayol Institute, Saint-Etienne, France
{khaled.medini,peillon,boucher,vaillant}@emse.fr

Abstract. Resources depletion, emerging competition, and increasing individual customer requirements are among the most common trends shaping nowadays manufacturing industry. Product-Service Systems (PSS) are put forth as a potential means for meeting these challenges due to their intrinsic characteristics such as dematerialization, multi-actor perspective, inimitable service know-how, and customer closeness. The scope of this paper falls under a wider topic relating to the development of PSS solutions for the steel sludge treatment sector. More specifically, the paper reports on a combined performance measurement and PSS design approach to support the decision making process on the PSS implementation. The approach takes into account the need for a collaborative effort among the PSS value network actors to successfully implement PSS offers. A case study from the sludge treatment sector is used to illustrate the synergies between performance measurement and decision making, in the PSS context.

Keywords: Product-Service systems · Decision making · Performance · Sludge treatment · Recycling

1 Introduction

The last few decades witnessed a paradigm shift through the development and spread of servitization and Product-Service System (PSS) concepts. Goedkoop et al. [1] define PSS as 'a system of products, services, networks of 'players' and supporting infrastructure that continuously strives to be competitive, satisfy customer needs and have a lower environmental impact than traditional business models'. Since then, most contributors have broadly adopted this definition. As already stressed by many authors such as Goedkoop et al. [1] and Meier et al. [2], PSSs are generally delivered by a network of partners. A PSS is the result of a value co-production process within such a partnership. Therefore, PSS business models call for a continuous collaboration process that involves both the buying and the selling organizations, and other external and complementary partners. The stakeholders, whether they are producers, retailers, customers or end-of-life managers, require connected economic interests and shared vision of desirable outcomes for a system resource optimization [3]. The scope of this paper falls under a wider topic relating to the development of PSS solutions for the steel sludge treatment sector. More specifically, the paper reports on a combined performance measurement and PSS design approach to support the decision making process on the PSS implementation. The approach takes into

© IFIP International Federation for Information Processing 2015
L.M. Camarinha-Matos et al. (Eds.): PRO-VE 2015, IFIP AICT 463, pp. 518–525, 2015.
DOI: 10.1007/978-3-319-24141-8_48

account the need for a collaborative effort among the PSS value network actors to successfully implement PSS offers. A case study from the sludge treatment sector is used to illustrate the synergies between performance measurement and decision making, in the PSS context. The novelty of this paper lies in the use of performance measurement and analysis at the PSS design stage. The remainder of the paper is organized as follows: Sect. 2 sheds more light on performance measurement from a PSS perspective. Section 3 describes the proposed approach combining PSS design and performance measurement. Section 4 illustrates the approach with a case study. Conclusions and research perspectives are detailed in Sect. 5.

2   Performance Measurement from a PSS Perspective

Performance measurement is a well-established concept in the operations management literature. The ultimate goal of the current research is to extend performance measurement to the PSS context; in particular by supporting the decision making process during PSS design.

Performance measurement definition and issues relating to PSS. Performance measurement is an activity aimed at reaching predefined goals that are derived from the company's strategic objectives by using performance indicators (PIs) [4]. A PI is a variable that expresses quantitatively the effectiveness or efficiency or both, of a part of or a whole process or system against a given norm or target [5]. Performance measurement represents the concrete formulation of firm's strategic choices and has been closely related to supply chain and extended enterprise [6]. Lohman et al. [4] highlighted the need to measure the supply chain performance as a whole and to be able to drill down to different measures and different levels of details. Folan and Browne [6] assume that performance measurement has moved towards examination of the organization as a whole and impacting to a greater extent upon strategy. They assume that performance measurement would have an impact outside organization (i.e. external environment).

Among the difficulties shaping the performance measurement in the PSS context, and in extended enterprises at large, is the decentralized nature of the value network leading to uncontrolled growth in indicators. Basically, this stems from the connection of several companies to deliver the PSS [7]. This potentially leads to inconsistencies among the indicators used by the value network actors. The impact on the decision making is thus obvious as the performance is evaluated from single points of view. A multi-actor based indicators system reflecting all points of view of the value network actors is thus required and would be of much support to the PSS network management, which is a crucial task for the PSS [7]. Such indicators systems can act as a common platform from which all members of the value network can draw knowledge [6, 8].

Performance Measurement as a Support for the Decision Making Process. As the performance measurement has evolved from measuring and monitoring to supporting decision making, proper tools and methods should be created as substitute of historical data [4, 6, 8]. Consistently with the above evolution, simulation is among the most used approaches to support the decision making. It allows replicating the actual behaviour of the real system at different granularity levels, ranging from value network actors down to production and service delivery activities. As such, the simulation, be it a discrete-event, an agent-based or a system dynamic based one, is a corner stone of the performance measurement, and thus of the decision making process [9, 10], and the performance indicators are its backbone. Several research works used the simulation to support the decision making process in the context of PSS [10–12]. Among the most common questions addressed in this context is the shift from a mere product oriented offer to a PSS oriented offer. The simulation here supports the performance measurement by evaluating different envisioned shifting scenarios using quantitative measures. Yet, in order for the decision makers to measure and improve the performance of their production systems, firms or even supply chains, there is a need to capture the most impacting performance drivers and align the decision making process with them. Consequently, several methods and tools have been used to deal with this appealing concern of exploiting performance measurement by decision makers. An example of these are multi-criteria decision methods which allow to combine a set of performance measures into a fewer ones, or even a single holistic index [13]. Another relevant means for understanding the most impacting performance drivers are decision trees which are the result of different classification algorithms [14]. These trees allow for a quick and clear graphical representation of the impact of different decision levels. The nodes of the trees represent the performance drivers, classified in order of their relevance; the most relevant drivers are linked to the root of the tree, while drivers with the lowest importance are at the bottom. The branches are labelled with the separating input variables (i.e. drivers).

3   A Combined Design and Performance Measurement Approach for the PSS

This section reports on a combined design and performance measurement approach for PSS. Unlike the traditional and most common performance measurement systems, the current approach uses performance measurement a-priori, as a supporting tool for the decision making process regarding the relevance of PSS solutions and delivery systems. The foundations of the current approach are detailed further in [4, 6, 10, 12]. More specifically, the methodological guidance combines the steps of building and using performance measurement systems [4] with the methodological support for defining PSS scenarios [12]. The performance measurement is enabled by a simulation approach inspired by Medini et al. [10]. The combined approach is structured in four steps which are detailed in the following.

Context Analysis combines the firm's mission, objectives and functional areas relating to these objectives, in keeping with [4]. More broadly, context analysis consists in understanding the company's industrial context and competition factors. This relies on semi-structured interviews with the PSS key actors. This step provides insights into the

PSS development opportunities and the main strategic capabilities of the involved actors with regards to the PSS.

Usage Analysis and Scenario Prioritization are needed in order to define different PSS variants based on the possible different uses of the PSS, and to identify the value-creation potential for the actors involved (provider, customer, and other stakeholders). This step relies primarily on semi-structured interviews, brainstorming, and questionnaires to capture expectations of both customer and other actors of the PSS value network. Afterwards, several scenarios are defined consistently with the expected uses of the PSS. Each of the scenarios is defined by a combination of actors and roles within the value network. Finally these scenarios are filtered in order to narrow the scope of the subsequent quantitative evaluation. The filtering criteria stems from the context analysis and the stakeholders' experience, and are defined during face-to-face meetings.

Select or Develop Performance Measures consistently with the firm's objectives behind the PSS implementation. More specifically, this step aims to define the performance indicators for each actor involved, then identify physical and financial flows that should be modelled in order to enable indicators calculation by use of simulation. Then, questionnaires are built upon these models and are used for data collection. Indicators should comply with the multi-actor perspective, meaning that the final set of performance measures should accommodate the points of view of all the actors of the PSS value network.

Evaluate Scenario Performance: this step is critical in supporting the decision making process as it provides an evaluation of several alternative scenarios, thus helping to put the focus on the most interesting ones according to the performance measures. To this end, a three-stage process is deployed:

- *Building an Experimentation Plan* is concerned with the a priori identification of potential performance drivers according to PSS actors' know-how.
- *Evaluating Scenario Performances* uses simulation to compute the performance measures, based on replication of the real operations within the PSS production and delivery network.
- *Identification of Performance Drivers* is performed out of the simulation results. The tools used at this stage are decision trees, which form an efficient and comprehensive tool to identify the impact of different decision levels on the performance. Thresholds can be defined based on this analysis, in order to specify the circumstances under which the PSS implementation would be potentially successful.

4 Illustrative Case Study

Usually, machining sludge generated by manufacturers is collected and treated by specialized companies. The envisioned PSS solution is built around a briquette-making equipment which allows the compacting and briquetting, and makes the sludge reusable.

The compacting and briquetting result in two reusable products, (i) briquettes, which can be sold to and used by smelters, and (ii) cutting fluid extracted from the sludge, which can be used by the manufacturers themselves. The actors involved in the envisioned PSS value network are: (i) an equipment provider (i.e. briquette-making), (ii) manufacturers producing sludge and representing potential customers of the envisioned PSS solution, and (iii) smelters using electric arc furnaces for melting steel scrap and other metals who are potential customers of the produced briquettes.

Context analysis relies on semi-structured interviews with manufacturers, (who generate different types of sludge), with equipment provider, and with smelters. The interviews resulted in the identification of several alternative organizational scenarios that were filtered to come up finally with 6 relevant ones. The current paper is limited to the two following ones:

- U1a: the briquette-making equipment is sold to a manufacturer who is in charge of the compacting, briquetting and maintenance operations, retrieves cutting fluids and sells briquettes to smelters.
- S1a: the briquette-making equipment remains the provider's property, and the manufacturer pays for its use in his premises according to a "rental" contract. The equipment maintenance can be included as a service in the contract and is then performed by the briquette-making equipment owner; otherwise, it is considered as an internal activity of the manufacturer.

The selection of proper performance indicators was straightforward since the main concerns of the involved actors (i.e. equipment provider, manufacturer, and smelter) relate basically to costs and benefits. In the following, the analysis will be focused on the profit indicator, which is a result of the above ones. A deterministic continuous simulation model is used to evaluate the performance of the scenarios and is implemented under Excel in Visual Basic language. The back bone of the simulation model is a set of mathematical equations depicting the interdependencies between the physical and financial flows [10]. The simulation inputs are data about the value network activities (e.g. cost, input and output flows), contracts (e.g. duration, installation costs, and ascribed services), services (e.g. costs), market (e.g. scrap cost, market demand, sludge characteristics), roles (e.g. actors responsibilities in terms of services and activities). The aim of the evaluation is to identify the main economic performance drivers for the value network actors, so as to provide a support for the decision making process of these actors regarding PSS implementation alternatives. To this end, an experimentation plan was adopted and is represented in Fig. 1, showing the combination of the input variables for each of the two scenarios. The simulation horizon covers a 10 years period.

The simulation results are processed using the R software[1] and the Analysis of Variance (ANOVA) method [15]. The output is structured in three regression trees representing the performance drivers of the profit indicators. Figure 2(a) indicates that organizational scenarios are the main drivers of the equipment provider profit. Generally, the PSS scenario (S1a) allows for more profit which ranges from 80k €

---

[1] http://www.r-project.org/.

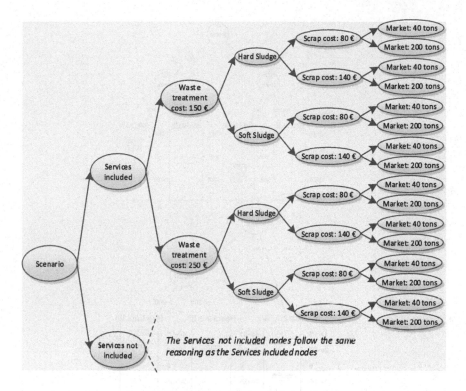

Fig. 1. Experimentation plan

when services are not included in the offer, to 130k € when they are included. The sales scenario (U1a) allows for a lower profit which culminates at about 60k €, when the services are also offered in addition to the sale contract. Manufacturers' and smelters' profits are mainly impacted by the market volume, as shown in Fig. 2(b) and (c); the bigger are the market volumes, the higher is the generated profit. The other drivers of profit for these two actors are the waste treatment cost (wCost) and the scrap cost (sCost), respectively. The manufacturers profit reaches its highest values when waste treatment costs are high.

Indeed, the PSS helps avoiding the costs that are traditionally incurred by the manufacturers when they want to get rid of their produced sludge. Further on, for the smelters, the scrap cost is an important driver, after the market. This is explained by the fact that smelters profit comes from the savings generated out of purchasing the briquettes at a lower price than traditional steel scrap, thus the higher the scrap costs are, the higher is the smelters profit.

The above analysis provides the different value network actors with some useful inputs regarding their decision making process, through the most relevant drivers for profit. The focus can thus be put on these specific drivers to define trade-offs taking into account all the actors points of view and thus easing the implementation of a win-win PSS solution.

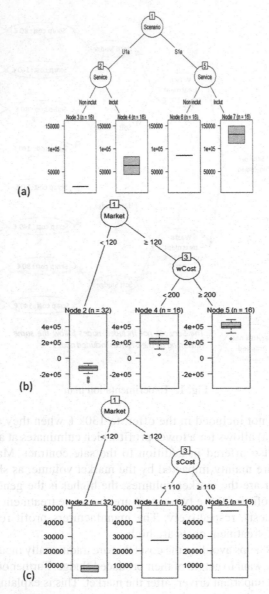

Fig. 2. Regression trees of the (a). equipment provider profit, (b). manufacturers profit, (c). smelters profit

5   Conclusion

The current paper reports on a combined performance measurement and design approach to support the decision making process and thus mitigate the uncertainty at the PSS design stage. The basic prerequisite of this approach is a strong collaboration among the PSS stakeholders from the early design phases of PSS solutions. The case study shows the ability of the approach to determine the key performance drivers for the PSS actors and to identify the most relevant PSS value network configurations prior to the PSS implementation. The current work, however, has limitations and thus, opens further research perspectives. First of all, the performance system implemented (based on the industrial consortium requirements) can be enriched further with other indicators in order to better reflect the service perspective. Additionally, the simulation model opens many opportunities regarding the quantification of uncertainty and its impact on performance measurement. Basically, this would strengthen the decision-aid provided to PSS actors.

References

1. Goedkoop, M., et al.: Product service systems – ecological and economic basics. Report for Dutch Ministries of Environment (VROM) and Economic Affairs (EZ) (1999)
2. Meier, H., Roy, R., Seliger, G.: Industrial product-service systems—IPS2. CIRP Ann. Manuf. Technol. **59**(2), 607–627 (2010)
3. Xing, K., Ness, D., Lin, F.: A service innovation model for synergistic community transformation: integrated application of systems theory and product-service systems. J. Clean. Prod. **43**(3), 93–102 (2013)
4. Lohman, C., Fortuin, L., Wouters, M.: Designing a performance measurement system: a case study. Eur. J. Oper. Res. **156**(2), 267–286 (2004)
5. Fortuin, L.: Performance indicators – why where and how? Eur. J. Oper. Res. **34**(1), 1–9 (1988)
6. Folan, P., Browne, J.: A review of performance measurement; towards performance management. Comput. Ind. **56**(7), 663–680 (2005)
7. Morlock, F., Dorkaa, T., Meier, H.: Performance measurement for robust and agile scheduling and control of industrial product-service systems. Procedia CIRP **19**, 154–159 (2014)
8. Morlock, F., Dorkaa, T., Meier, H.: Concept for a performance measurement method for the organization of the IPS^2 delivery. Procedia CIRP **16**, 56–61 (2014)
9. Mourtzis, D., Doukas, M., Psarommatis, F.: Design and operation of manufacturing networks for mass customisation. CIRP Ann. Manuf. Technol. **62**(1), 467–470 (2013)
10. Medini, K., Boucher, X., Peillon, S., Matos, C.D.: Product service systems value chain configuration - a simulation based approach. In: Proceedings of the CIRP IPSS 2015, Elsevier, Saint-Etienne, France (2015a)
11. Marquès, G., Chalal, M., Boucher, X.: PSS production systems: a simulation approach for change management. In: Emmanouilidis, C., Taisch, M., Kiritsis, D. (eds.) Advances in Production Management Systems, Part II. IFIP AICT, vol. 398, pp. 377–384. Springer, Heidelberg (2013)
12. Medini, K., Moreau, V., Peillon, S., Boucher, X.: Transition to product service systems: a methodology based on scenarios identification, modelling and evaluation. In: Camarinha-Matos, L.M., Afsarmanesh, H. (eds.) Collaborative Systems for Smart Networked Environments. IFIP AICT, vol. 434, pp. 143–150. Springer, Heidelberg (2014)
13. Medini, K., Da Cunha, C., Bernard, A.: Tailoring performance evaluation to specific industrial contexts – application to sustainable mass customization enterprises. Int. J. Prod. Res. **53**(8), 2439–2456 (2015)
14. Theil, H.: Principles of Econometrics, p. 736. Wiley, New York (1971)
15. Speed, T.P.: Introduction to fisher (1926) the arrangement of field experiments. In: Kotz, S., Johnson, N.L. (eds.) Breakthroughs in Statistics, pp. 71–81. Springer, New York (1992)

Including the Evaluation of the Compliance to Delivery Dates into a Performance Analysis Concept

Hendrik Jähn[✉]

Department of Economic Sciences, Chemnitz University of Technology,
Thüringer Weg 7, 09126 Chemnitz, Germany
hendrik.jaehn@wirtschaft.tu-chemnitz.de

Abstract. The delivery date is one of the most important performance parameters of a business contract. In order to guarantee the customers' satisfaction and sustainable success it is essential to keep the fixed delivery date. Therefore a performance measurement system needs to be applied. In the following a specific approach for the performance analysis for Virtual Enterprises is introduced. Hereby both the comprehensive approach for performance analysis and the procedure for the evaluation of the compliance to delivery dates are considered. This concept allows an adaptive applicability which is necessary to support the short-term management of order-specific configured Virtual Enterprises within smart networked environments.

Keywords: Virtual enterprise · Performance analysis · Delivery date · Collaborative network model

1 Motivation

The agreement of an exact delivery date represents an essential part in a contract between supplier and customer. Adherence of the delivery date should have highest priority for the supplier as deviations from the agreed delivery date often entail far-reaching consequences for the buyer. This may also lead to negative consequences for the supplier, e.g. in form of contractual penalties or loss of customers. In connection to Virtual Enterprises/collaborative systems, adherence of the delivery date gets even higher importance by a particularly close and time-referenced cooperation.

Deviations of the delivery date represent a serious problem field as buffer time can hardly be planned. In that context the research question arises how to analyze and evaluate the adherence of the delivery date in networked production structures. As a relevant research methodology it represents one part of a comprehensive approach for the analysis of enterprise-related performances. That approach allows a consideration of different performance parameters, e.g. product quality, response time, price and soft-facts. The analysis is realized related to value-added processes. That means conduction is done separately for each production process or transaction. This form of modeling represents an essential precondition for the value-added-related performance analysis. As major research objectives are to be mentioned a high degree of flexibility and adaptability in combination with clear rules for the evaluation.

© IFIP International Federation for Information Processing 2015
L.M. Camarinha-Matos et al. (Eds.): PRO-VE 2015, IFIP AICT 463, pp. 526–534, 2015.
DOI: 10.1007/978-3-319-24141-8_49

2 Regulatory Framework

2.1 Towards a Performance Analysis Approach

For the realization of the performance analysis in Virtual Enterprises a comprehensive model has been developed [1]. That approach both includes value-added process neutral and value-added process-related process steps. The structure of the model and the interdependencies of the steps are displayed in Fig. 1.

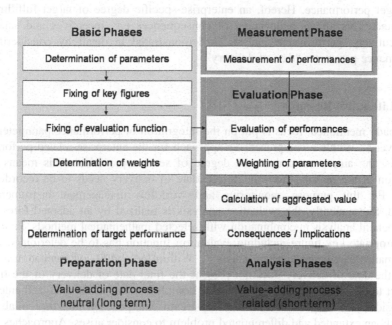

Fig. 1. Performance analysis approach.

The performance analysis approach includes the measurement, evaluation and analysis of relevant services performed by an enterprise operating in a collaborative network based on selected performance parameters. Herein, special attention is paid to aspects relating to one specific value-added process. This operational perspective allows acquiring cognitions about services performed by an enterprise after finishing a value-added process. Hereby, consequences, e.g. concerning the allocation of profit shares can be deduced in case of an unsatisfactory performance of an enterprise [2].

The primary task of the performance analysis approach is to determine the degree of services performed by an enterprise. For this purpose, primarily quantitative methods are applied. The result is considered by the implementation of incentive and sanction mechanisms. Herein, methods for the calculation of profit shares play a specific role. Within this context, it is necessary to analyze the services performed by the enterprises based on selected and relevant performance parameters [3].

The determination of performance parameters is realized by the involvement of an adapted Balanced Scorecard. Performance parameters considered within the performance analysis are the price, date of delivery, response time, product quality, reliance and cooperation climate [1]. The last two parameters form soft factors, whose perceptions primarily have to be quantified through appropriate methods. Each of those performance parameters is characterized by a specific key figure. For the evaluation of the services performed, specific evaluation functions, similar to utility functions, are applied. In order to regard their different relevancies, the evaluations can be weighted individually. By multiplying weighting and level of utility, aggregated utility values are calculated, similar to the value benefit analysis. The sum of the aggregated utilities of all performance parameters represents the actual performance. This can be compared to the target performance. Hereof, an enterprise-specific degree of target fulfillment is calculated. This allows a deviation of consequences e.g. incentives and sanctions. Consecutively, performance analysis is demonstrated in detail by considering the performance parameter "date of delivery".

2.2   Literature Research

As already mentioned, focus is put on the integration of performance parameter "date of delivery". Within a comprehensive approach for the enterprise-related performance analysis, the aim is to analyze the degree of service provision. This means that a deviation of the realized from the agreed date of delivery needs to be recorded correctly. For this purpose, monitoring and workflow management instruments are applied. Subsequently, the evaluation analysis is realized by an adapted form of the value benefit analysis in combination with selected mathematical methods. First of all, an appropriate key figure including evaluation function has to be determined for the performance parameter "date of delivery". Within the context of a collaborative network, the date of delivery does not present the final date of delivery of the finished product to the customer, but the respective completion date at the analyzed enterprise. In consideration of possible effects of upstream enterprises within the collaborative network, an extended and differentiated problem to consider arises. Approaches for the evaluation of performances within networked organization structures are available and have been published in a quite unmanageable number.

In this context, one forerunner is *Neely*, who deals with questions concerning the performance measurement in supply chains and networks [4]. Herein, analyses can be arranged from several perspectives [5]. In general, however, it has been observed that primarily medium- and long-term approaches are suggested. Background for this is the financial focus of those approaches with regard to external effects of the company. During the development of those approaches, it is often reverted to the Balanced Scorecard, followed by an adoption of the same in a modified form considering supply chains or networks [6–8]. A more specific focus on performance indicators for collaborative networks based on collaboration benefits can be found in [9]. Most networks exist long term whereas virtual enterprises represent the cooperation of several enterprises for completing a value-added process. This more relevant perspective is focused by Westphal et al. by investigating methodologies of measuring the collaborative performance in virtual enterprises [10]. However, this publication primarily considers soft-facts and therefore is less relevant here. Another publication in that field is [11] which introduces a case study for delivery performance measurement.

3   The Performance Parameter "Date of Delivery"

3.1   Identification of the Key Figure "Adherence to Delivery Date"

The determination of the key figure "adherence to delivery date" respectively "deviation to delivery date" of an enterprise occurs through an evaluation in consideration of the cause or the initiator of the deviation. In general, it has to be distinguished whether the delivery of an enterprise did occur early, on time or delayed. The deviation of the planned/agreed date of delivery l_i^a from the realized date of delivery l_i^r results from the difference of both values and is described as (local) deviation to delivery date or adherence to delivery date Δl_i^l, which leads to Eq. (1):

$$\Delta l_i^l = l_i^r - l_i^a. \tag{1}$$

Δl_i^l is an enterprise-related figure. Depending on the development of the delivery situation, the consequence is, that in case of $\Delta l_i^l > 0$ the delivery is considered as delayed, for $\Delta l_i^l = 0$, the delivery arrived on time and for $\Delta l_i^l < 0$, the delivery occurred early. That interpretation is based on the method of cumulative quantities. That means a delivery on the 20th day while having an agreed delivery date on the 15th day can be interpreted as a delay of 5 days (20 − 15 = 5). By the application of this method, it is possible to calculate an absolute value for the performance analysis. The delivery dates or appointments have to be offset against each other. The decision about the metric should be made depending on the designated accurateness. According to the chosen metric (week, day, hour, minute), the statements concerning the deviation are rough (week) or comparatively accurate (minute) by trend.

To stress the significance of the performance figure "deviation to delivery date" of an enterprise and to allow an activity-based evaluation likewise in the context of the performance analysis, it is necessary to rectify the locally caused delivery adherence of an enterprise Δl_i^l by possible delays by enterprises, which accomplish a previous process step. These enterprises are denoted as "upstream enterprises" $(i - 1)$ in the collaborative network. It is therefore possible that an enterprise will, only because of one late delivery of one or more upstream enterprises, also deliver delayed. Due to this fact, the "upstream delay" Δl_i^v has to be considered as a further influencing value for the performance analysis of that parameter. In the following, the possibilities for the determination of adherences to delivery dates of upstream enterprises are discussed.

If a value-added chain is considered, in general there is only one upstream company (linear process) existent, so that the relevant deviation to delivery date Δl_i^v complies with the deviation to delivery dates of the upstream company Δl_{i-1}^l. In this case, it is valid:

$$\Delta l_i^l = \Delta l_{i-1}^v. \tag{2}$$

Here value Δl_{i-1}^l describes the schedule variance of the upstream enterprise. In case several upstream companies have to be considered (networked process), the specific local delivery delays Δl_{i-1}^l have to be taken into account for all upstream enterprises

$(i-1)$. The delay Δl_i^y, which finally has to be considered herein, is calculated out of the maximum of delays of all enterprises, which are directly preceded within the value-added process. This highest delivery delay of a direct forerunner $max(\Delta l_{i-1}^l)$ represents the delay, which has to be considered for the currently observed enterprise Δl_i^y. The following equation is valid:

$$\Delta l_i^y = max(\Delta l_{i-1}^l). \tag{3}$$

After determination of the locally relevant delivery date variances of an enterprise Δl_i^l as well as the delivery date variance of direct upstream enterprises Δl_i^y, which has to be included for a value correction, the deviation to delivery dates Δl_i, which is the one important input factor for the performance analysis, can be calculated as follows:

$$\Delta l_i = \Delta_i^l - \Delta l_i^y. \tag{4}$$

The value deviation to delivery dates equals the performance figure for the performance parameter delivery date and forms one input variable for the performance analysis. At this stage, one can ask for possible reasons for a schedule variance Δl_i caused by an enterprise. The starting point for arguing is the assumption that within the context of the tender preparation, each enterprise determines an order-specific processing time within the production control, which can be expressed by a corresponding completion date of production. The processing time, which forms the basis of the delivery date fixed in an offer, is t_i^{PTa}. A schedule variance Δl_i, which was caused by the enterprise itself, is expected in cases where the eventually realized processing time of the tender t_i^{PTr} deviates from the planned processing time t_i^{PTa} during the value added process. By this procedure, Δl_i can be calculated alternatively as follows:

$$\Delta l_i = t_i^{PTr} - t_i^{PTa}. \tag{5}$$

Due to the fact that the calculation of the deviation to delivery date of an enterprise is only possible if all delivery dates within the network are known (both offer dates and realized dates), the collection of all performance figures has to be accomplished after completion of the value-added process.

3.2 Measurement of the Key Figure "Adherence to Delivery Date"

By the application of the calculation formulas for the performance figure "(corrected) deviation to delivery date" Δl_i, the result is an accurate time specification. For further processing, in principle two ways are conceivable. On the one hand, it is possible to work with the accurate values of the company-specific schedule variance, which however causes a considerable calculating effort. A further possibility is a provision for the deviation to delivery dates in form of tendential schedule variances. This approach is introduced in the following.

The evaluation function for adherence to delivery dates $f_i(\Delta l_i)$ used for calculating the evaluation credits x_i^l in this approach only considers the influencing factor of the corrected (actually caused) schedule variance Δl_i, whereas local delay Δl_i^l and upstream delay Δl_i^v are input values.

To allow an evaluation/analysis, all potential combinations of those three influencing factors have to be identified. This is to evaluate the practical relevancy. Figure 2 introduces all combinations of the three values Δl_i^v, Δl_i^l and Δl_i which are possible. Consequently, not the accurate deviation serves as the main distinction criterion herein, but only the kind of deviation by trend, whereas "+" signifies a late delivery, "−" an early delivery and "0" represents a delivery in time.

(Δl_i)	(Δl_i^l)	(Δl_i^v)	Description
0	0	0	all deliveries are on time
0	0	-	not possible
0	0	+	not possible
0	-	0	not possible
0	-	-	early delivery, stable conditions
0	-	+	not possible
0	+	0	not possible
0	+	-	not possible
0	+	+	unchanged delay
-	0	0	not possible
-	0	-	not possible
-	0	+	delay has been eliminated, exact delivery date now
-	-	0	enterprise is the first one to cause an early delivery
-	-	-	incoming early delivery, rate has been increased
-	-	+	delay has been changed into a too early delivery
-	+	0	not possible
-	+	-	not possible
-	+	+	reduced delay but still delay
+	0	0	not possible
+	0	-	an early delivery has been changed into a delivery on time
+	0	+	not possible
+	-	0	not possible
+	-	-	incoming early delivery, still early but with a reduced rate
+	-	+	not possible
+	+	0	enterprise is the first one to cause a delay
+	+	-	despite an early delivery enterprise has caused a delay
+	+	+	delay has been increased

Fig. 2. Possible combinations of the input variables.

Starting from these theoretic possibilities, only practically relevant situations are contemplated in the following analysis. This concerns situations which are highlighted in grey.

3.3 Evaluation of the Key Figure "Adherence to Delivery Date"

As it has already been shown, an adjusted value can be determined for the considered value-added process and the analyzed enterprise for the adherence of the delivery date Δl_i. This value has to be transferred to a score evaluation afterwards. Therefore and formally stated, a relation between the adherence to the delivery date Δl_i and the score evaluation x_i^l can be formulated in the form of a mathematic function. This function is called evaluation function. It has to be seen as a utility function in the context of the value benefit analysis.

The method of Lagrange interpolation is intended to determine exact (utility-) functions out of selected relevant combinations of Δl_i and x_i^l given. This procedure allows the generation of a polynomial, which leads through an arbitrary number of points. First of all, selected distinctive points of the function, which has to be determined, need to be defined. Here it has to be considered that the values of the abscissa (x-values) are distributed all about the same considered interval, whereas the probability is increased that a function is generated, which is consistent with the desired process. Normally, the selection of four credits is adequate, whereas two credits shall reflect the relevant exceptional conditions. In a concrete way, full marks are given for exact date adherence taken as an example, while for an exceeding of the maximum justifiable deviation, 0 credits are assigned. The value of 10 is usually given as full marks. Division within the parameters of 0 to 10 makes a significant evaluation possible. At this point, all relevant combinations have been assigned to adequate groups. This leads to a specific evaluation function (6):

$$f_i(\Delta l_i) = x_i^l. \tag{6}$$

Adherence to the date of delivery can be interpreted as one essential characteristic of making delivery of an enterprise, as missing this target will have effects on all downstream processes, so that an influence on the due-date of the final product can be expected.

One possibility for a simplified consideration is the formation of different groups. According to the present modeling, there is an evaluation function, which may be applied for all kinds of combinations of the input parameters from Fig. 2. Seen from a practical perspective, not all kinds may be treated and evaluated the same way. So, it is important for the evaluation whether delays were caused by an enterprise or if existing delays were reduced. Therefore, it is recommended to introduce grouping, which can be evaluated in a similar way but regarding the specific situation. The division into different groups allows for a more detailed observation with a high flexibility regarding potential adjustments. However, a specific evaluation function has to be modeled then for each existing group. This can easily be achieved by means of the Lagrange interpolation.

3.4   Analysis of the Key Figure "Adherence to Delivery Date"

After determining the score evaluation of the performed service, it can be incorporated into the performance analysis. For this purpose, the score evaluations of the remaining performance parameters have to be known. To be able to consider the different meaning of the single performance parameters regarding the whole evaluation, performance parameter related weightings are included.

An actual value of making delivery is calculated from the weighted sum of the single score evaluations, which is then compared to a target value of making delivery. This comparison then allows for a statement if an enterprise has delivered the desired performance in a certain value-added process. If this is not the case, there is the possibility that negative consequences occur for the company, for instance in form of sanction payments or reduced share in profits. However, this subject matter shall not be enlarged upon at this point, as this concerns tasks relating to the whole performance analysis model.

4 Conclusions

An approach for the evaluation and analysis of the performance parameter "delivery date" and its key figure "adherence to delivery dates" has been introduced. It was developed for enterprises operating in Virtual Enterprises. Major advantages are the consideration of different classifications ("groups") for possible scenarios and the development of specific evaluation functions. They allow modeling a calculation scheme dependent on the degree of meeting the agreed delivery date.

The approach represents a quantitative model. Similar models have also been developed for further performance parameters. Therefore, a universal concept for a performance analysis, which relates to the value-added process, is available. This approach allows a complete and comprehensive analysis of the service performed by an enterprise operating in a collaborative network. The introduced approach has consistently been modeled and therefore, it allows for an application related to practical requirements. One limitation is the static character of the approach.

Efforts regarding a realization of the approach from an information-technical point of view as well as its integration into the comprehensive model of the performance analysis are being made currently and represent the challenge for future works.

References

1. Jähn, H.: Value-added process-related performance analysis of enterprises acting in cooperative production structures. Prod. Plann. Control **20**, 178–190 (2009)
2. Jähn, H.: A comprehensive approach for the management of virtual enterprises including performance analysis, provision of incentives and allocation of income. In: Camarinha-Matos, L.M., Scherer, R.J. (eds.) PRO-VE 2013. IFIP AICT, vol. 408, pp. 147–155. Springer, Heidelberg (2013)
3. Jähn, H.: Fundamentals for the development of a performance analysis approach in collaborative networks. In: Camarinha-Matos, L.M., Afsarmanesh, H. (eds.) Collaborative Systems for Smart Networked Environments. IFIP AICT, vol. 434, pp. 521–533. Springer, Heidelberg (2014)
4. Neely, A. (ed.): Business Performance Measurement, 2nd edn. Cambridge University Press, Cambridge (2007)
5. Chendall, R.H., Langfield-Smitz, K.: Multiple perspectives of performance measures. Eur. Manage. J. **25**, 266–282 (2007)
6. Brewer, P., Speh, T.: Using the balanced scorecard to measure supply chain performance. J. Bus. Logistics **22**, 75–93 (2000)
7. Gunasekaran, A., Patel, C., McGaughey, R.E.: A framework for supply chain performance measurement. Int. J. Prod. Econ. **87**, 333–347 (2004)
8. Bhagwat, R., Sharma, M.H.: An application of the integrated AHP-PGP model for performance measurement of supply chain management. Prod. Plann. Control **20**, 678–690 (2009)

9. Camarinha-Matos, L.M., Abreu, A.: Performance indicators for collaborative networks based on collaboration benefits. Prod. Plann. Control **18**(7), 592–609 (2007)
10. Westphal, I., Thoben, K.-D., Seifert, M.: Measuring collaboration performance in virtual organizations. In: Camarinha-Matos, L.M., et al. (eds.) Establishing the Foundation of Collaborative Networks, pp. 33–42. Springer, Boston (2007)
11. Madhusudhana Rao, C., Prahlada Rao, K., Muniswamy, V.V.: Delivery performance measurement in an integrated supply chain management: case study in batteries manufacturing firm. Serb. J. Manage. **6**(2), 205–220 (2011)

Improving the Management of an Emergency Call Service by Combining Process Mining and Discrete Event Simulation Approaches

Elyes Lamine[1,2(✉)], Franck Fontanili[2], Maria Di Mascolo[3,4], and Hervé Pingaud[1,5]

[1] ISIS, Centre Universitaire Jean-François Champollion,
Toulouse University, 81100 Castres, France
{elyes.lamine,herve.pingaud}@univ-jfc.fr
[2] Industrial Engineering Department, Mines Albi,
Toulouse University, 81000 Albi, France
{elyes.lamine,franck.fontanili}@mines-albi.fr
[3] University Grenoble Alpes, G-SCOP, 38000 Grenoble, France
[4] CNRS, G-SCOP, 38000 Grenoble, France
Maria.Di-Mascolo@g-scop.grenoble-inp.fr
[5] CNRS, LGC UMR 5503, 31432 Toulouse Cedex 4, France

Abstract. Each Emergency Medical Assistance Centre in France (SAMU), includes an emergency call service. It provides an adequate and immediate response to medical problems. The processing of the incoming calls can be seen as a collaborative process involving several stakeholders. The control of such a process is crucial. Indeed, the effectiveness of the response to these incoming calls strongly impacts the quality of service of these centres, which is the main information which the government relies for their funding. The aim of this paper is to analyse such a collaborative process, regarding the performance targets requested by the French government. To this end, we suggest applying a new approach, based on the combination of two well-known engineering techniques, in consecutive manner. We will first use process mining techniques to obtain meaningful knowledge about the studied collaborative processes, relying on real data from a French Emergency Medical Assistance Centre. Secondly, we will use a Discrete Event Simulation approach as an effective tool to assess the efficiency of the current management of this emergency call centre and to ask (and answer) some 'what if?' questions to identify possible ways of improving their effectiveness.

Keywords: Emergency call centre · Collaborative process analysis · Knowledge discovery · Process mining · Discrete-event simulation · Key performance indicators

1 Introduction

Since 1986 in France, each administrative department has its own Emergency Medical Assistance Centre (named SAMU in French) whose 24-h service able to provide assistance for all medical emergencies. SAMU works closely with local public services and emergency teams having skills and facilities suitable to many situations.

© IFIP International Federation for Information Processing 2015
L.M. Camarinha-Matos et al. (Eds.): PRO-VE 2015, IFIP AICT 463, pp. 535–546, 2015.
DOI: 10.1007/978-3-319-24141-8_50

Each SAMU has an emergency medical regulation call centre that can be reached by dialling 15 or 112. The origins of phone calls are varied: ordinary people, call centres of firemen, private general practitioners, public or private medical centres. The aim of this centre is to give a suiting answer to the medical problems submitted to it as soon as possible. The action to take in a medical emergency depends on the degree of urgency, ranging from a simple medical advice to the commitment of the Hospital Mobile Intensive Care Units (H-MICU) which are the most potent means of action at the disposal of SAMU call centres.

The processing of the incoming calls may be schematically described as a col-laborative process involving several stakeholders, as show in Fig. 1. There are three kind of human resources devoted to a SAMU call centre to regulate the calls: (1) the Medical Regulation Assistant Operator (AO), (2) the Hospital "regulator doctor" a regulator doctor (RD), (3) the general practitioners of the health care permanence (GP). This collaborative process can be done through four major functions: (1) to receive and sort the calls 24 h a day, (2) to send and coordinate the most suited first aid means as soon as possible, (3) to check the availability of hospital beds to refer the patients to the most appropriate service depending on his/her pathology, (4) to inform the service which will be in charge of the patient for a better welcome.

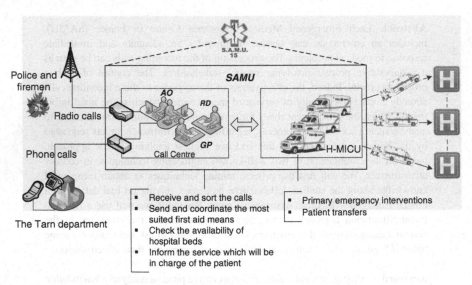

Fig. 1. Operational organisation of the SAMU 81

According to the statistics announced by the National French SAMU [1], a very large number of calls, which currently varies from tens of thousands to several million, is processed each year and continues to increase from one year to the other, despite constant means.

While these figures are impressive, the processing of the incoming calls has been considered, for too long, of minor importance. The search of better response to the patient and better efficiency in the use of resources induces, in France today, to consider this process as crucial for the regulation of emergency medicine. The Speed of response between calling 15 and the actual answering of the call has become one of the top priorities of a SAMU call centres [2, 3]. Indeed, the effectiveness of the response to the incoming calls strongly impacts the quality of service of these centres, on which is the main information which the government relies for their funding [4].

Thus, the improvement of the quality of service in these centres has got an increasing interest in these recent years. It is therefore important to highlight that the quality of service is tightly related to the means made available to the SAMU and the service organization established.

Hence, our present study is focused on the analysis of the performance of the processing incoming calls of such centres with two major aims: 1. To investigate the management of a SAMU call centre and assess the efficiency of the current management of this emergency call centre regarding to the performance targets requested by the French government; 2. To find out some possible ways of improving the speed and quality of service offered by SAMU.

The remainder of this paper is structured as follows: First, in the next section we are going to give an overview of our proposed approach to analyse and ascertain proposals able to improve the current functioning of emergency call services. This approach is based on the sequential combination of two well-known engineering techniques. In the third section, we will focus our endeavour on the presentation of the two first steps of our proposed approach. These steps lie on the use of process mining techniques to obtain meaningful knowledge about the studied collaborative processes, relying on real data from a French Emergency Medical Assistance Centre. In Sect. 4, we will present the main results provided by a Discrete Event Simulation approach as an effective tool to assess the efficiency of the current management of this emergency call centre and discuss some possible ways of improving their effectiveness. Finally in Sect. 5, we will conclude and present some future works.

2 Proposed Approach for Process Reengineering

The deployment of a process reengineering approach is needed to achieve the two objectives mentioned above. Indeed, the aim of process reengineering approach according to [5] *is rethinking and radical redesign of business processes to achieve dramatic improvements in critical, contemporary measures of performance, such as cost, quality, service and speed.*

Roughly speaking, the deployment of process reengineering approach involves three main stages: (1) the discovering stage which aims to reveal how business processes currently operate, (2) the redesigning stage which seeks to find out new ways of organizing tasks, organizing people, able to improve efficiency of these processes; (3) the implementation stage which takes a close interest on how to implement these process changes in an efficient manner.

Traditionally, for the first stage, the discovery of business process models result from a field observation and survey allowing the emergence of knowledge of how the process works which in turn will lead to model the As-Is process in formal process modelling language. However, this traditional approach is time-consuming, as it implies lengthy discussions with workers, extensive document analysis, careful observation of participants, etc. and also it may not provide an accurate picture of business processes, Indeed there often are discrepancies between the actual business processes and the way they are perceived or described by people [6].

As outlined in several works [6–9], Process Mining techniques appear to be an appropriate tool for going beyond the drawback of this traditional process discovery approach. Indeed, process mining is a promising approach to obtain a better understanding about how business process of an organization are currently being performed and this by analysing the historical process data recorded in the information system of the organization. Consequently, we suggest a new process reengineering approach which consists of a synergy of two well-known engineering techniques, in consecutive manner: process discovery technique with discrete Event Simulation method. In particular, after a period of observation and data gathering, we will use a process mining technique to provide an accurate view on the process of the regulation of incoming calls and model how it is really executed by analysing the historical process data recorded in the information system of the call centre.

Based on the output of the process mining technique enactment, we will use a discrete Event Simulation approach as an effective tool to assess the efficiency of the management of the current process and to ask some 'what if?' questions to identify possible ways of improving their effectiveness.

Discrete events simulation is a data-processing tool widely used in industry and by the researchers to reproduce the dynamic behaviour of a manufacturing system studied [10, 11] in order to subject them to predictive experimentation without risk or disturbance of the real life system. More specifically, our proposed approach consists of the following four successive steps, shown in Fig. 2:

1. Data collection and preparation step: it is the starting point of any process mining technique. It consists in looking at historical process data and generating a dataset in the form of so-called event logs that can be used as input for the process mining step.
2. Process mining step: the aim of this step is to discover and construct, from the generate event logs, the process model of the processing of incoming calls of the Medical Assistance Centre. So, the output of this step is the As-is model
3. Model Transformation step: Following an approach grounded in Model-Driven Engineering (MDE), this step aims at generating a computer simulation model from the As-Is knowledge model. The resulting model will be executed on the selected simulation tool.
4. Simulation step: It seeks to ascertain and to assess a couple of scenario for process improvement regarding to the performance targets requested by the French government. The development of the simulation model of our process is carried out with the software Witness[1].

It is worth noting that this proposed approach is not limited to analyse and to enhance an emergency call centre but could be used for any reengineering process

---

[1] http://www.lanner.com/en/witness.cfm.

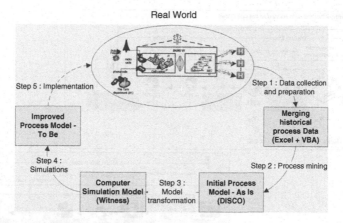

Fig. 2. Proposed system reengineering approach based on the combination of two well-known engineering techniques: process mining and simulation.

needed since a significant time-stamped and valuable data are tracked and closely related to the process execution.

3 The Discovery of the Incoming Call Regulation Process

3.1 Data Collection and Preparation

The generation of a representative activity log is the starting point for process mining techniques. It is the aim of the data collection and preparation step. It includes 1. Searching and extracting useful data about process execution, 2. Structuring and cleaning these data (correcting typos, outliers, and missing values); 3. Converting these data to the format required by the process mining tool.

For our case study, the data gathering was undertaken in the emergency medical call centre of SAMU 81, located in Albi, France. To identify the relevant data needed to be extracted, our method was based on the analysis of the states throughout an incoming call with this call centre. Indeed, many time-stamped data can be found in the information system of this emergency call centre related to call states updates. The main interesting call states for our study are (see Fig. 3):

- An *incoming call* state: it is the initial state which corresponds to a call initiated by an exterior caller to the SAMU ending up at its private automatic branch exchange (PABX). The time of reception of an incoming call is the one of the relevant event tracked by the SAMU IT support system.
- A *rejected call state* consists of an incoming call that has been automatically filtered by SAMU PABX. It could be possibly a number phone among the black list of SAMU or rejected automatically beyond a deadline set.
- A *presented call state* is an incoming call on the verge of being handled by an operator (AO)

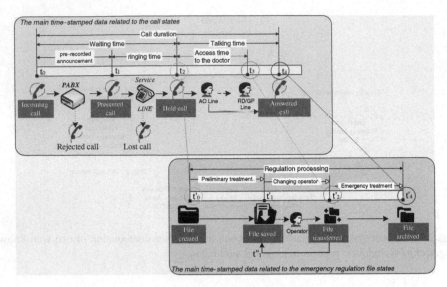

Fig. 3. Generate activity log from call and regulate file states

- A *hold call* state consists of state which a call has been handled by an operator (AO)
- A *lost call* state consists of state which a presented call is neither held
- An *answered call state* it is the final state which corresponds to a call picked up and processed.

Although these states are interesting to discover the incoming call regulation process, it remains a blur to discover milestones between the moment where the call is picked up and the moment where it is hung up. Indeed, a hold call can generate one or several movements corresponding to periods of communication on distinct phone line services.

To overcome this issue, we have enriched our dataset by other useful time-stamped data related to the emergency regulation file states. In fact, when the AO holds the incoming call, he opens a regulation file (RF) and if necessary a medical regulation file (MRF), localizes the request and saves the phone number, evaluates the gravity of the emergency in differentiating a real emergency from a felt one, transmits the call to the regulator doctors. Then, he has to pass the intervention requests on, either after a practitioner's regulation or directly (Reflex Departure) during very few cases according to the service protocols (sudden death, cardiac arrest, death by hanging…). In the IT support system, there also are many data related to the lifecycle of theses emergency regulation file, as depicted in Fig. 3.

Once these data have been collected, we conducted a first cleaning which allowed us to exclude all outgoing calls-related data and to complete some missing information. After we have proceeded to the merger of the two dataset into one log file by linking together information of both dataset that belong to the same process execution. This linking is based on the identification of the phone number and the date of creation of each regulation file and incoming call and several others data as the line service number or the kind of resource (AO, GP, RD) as show in Fig. 3.

3.2 Displaying the Mined Model

The next step was to run the process mining algorithm within Disco tool[2], namely the Christian's Fuzzy miner, to discover the control flow of the incoming call regulation process. The resulting mined model is shown in Fig. 4. It is based on the sequence and timing of the activities in the generate event log dataset.

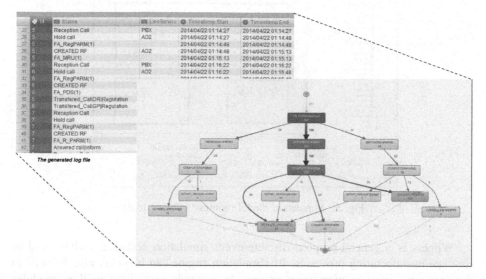

Fig. 4. The resulting mined model of the incoming call regulation process from the generated log file

We can see that there are 267 cases which represent the total incoming calls covered by the chosen timeframe which corresponds on the most critical day (Sunday). We can easy notice that all these cases start with the activity reception call and are served according to the first-come first-served discipline.

The section below presents the statistics deduced from this mined model and in relation to the simulation process model.

4 Simulation Model

4.1 "As-Is" Call Centre Simulation Model

In this section, we present the "As-is" simulation model built with the information discovered from the process mining tool. We decided to focus our simulation study on

---

[2] https://fluxicon.com/disco/.

the (AO) Assistant Operator's activities because the performance of the emergency call centre is mainly dependent on the answer speed of this resource. The call duration of the AO is another KPI we will examine as an outcome of the simulation. The development of the simulation model of our process is carried out with the software package Witness (see a screenshot on Fig. 5).

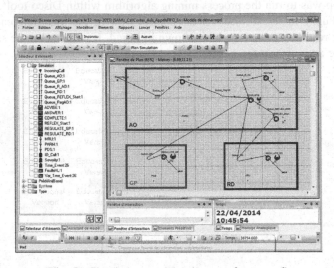

Fig. 5. Simulation model (witness software tool)

Witness is a general-purpose discrete-event simulation software widely used to simulate manufacturing processes. Its simulation engine can however also be used to simulate any service or information process. In our study case, there are three modules (AO, GP and RD) corresponding to the three resources of the call centre (Assistant Operator, General Practitioner and Regulator Doctor). As outlined in the mined model, when somebody calls the emergency number, the incoming call is buffered in a queue "Queue_AO". If the AO is available, he picks up his phone to answer the call. If the AO is busy, then the incoming call is waiting until the end of the process done by the AO. Once a call is held, the AO must open a regulation file and *Complete* information about the patient. After this stage, regarding to the evaluated severity, either the AO (1) keeps the call (severity index = 3, not urgent call) and only gives some advice to the patient or (2) puts the call in the queue "Queue_GP" (severity index = 2, serious call requiring a *Regulation* process by a doctor) or (3) activate a *Reflex* start of an emergency team with a hospital mobile intensive care unit (severity index = 1, life is at risk) if any regulation doctor is not available or transfer the call to the queue "Queue_RD" of the RD.

The speed to answer an incoming call must be as short as possible (less than 30 s is the objective for this kind of service [4]), particularly for severity index = 1.

The simulation study has been carried on the most critical day (Sunday), as it is the day when the number of incoming calls is the highest. Figure 6 illustrates the distribution of 267 incoming calls on 48 slots of 30 min. As far as the incoming call

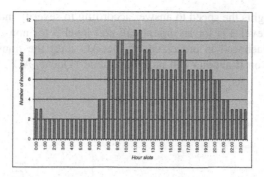

Fig. 6. Incoming calls profile

distribution is concerned, the simulation model is based on statistics from data collected by the SAMU 81.

As presented in Table 1, the processing times of the different activities follow a uniform distribution and have been established thanks to data collected and the outcomes of the process mining step.

Table 1. Processing times

Res.	Activities	Process time (sec.)
AO	ANSWER and SORT OUT	UNIFORM(20,50)
	COMPLETE regulation file	UNIFORM(20,30)
	ADVISE	UNIFORM(100,140)
RD	REGULATE	UNIFORM(300,420)
GP	REGULATE	UNIFORM(300,420)

The simulation runs for 24 h from 00:00 to 24:00. At 00:00, the call centre is empty. The statistics are recorded between the 26th and the 263th call after a warm up period. Figure 7 shows the different values of speed to answer time and processing time (call duration) for all the calls supported by the AO during 24 h.

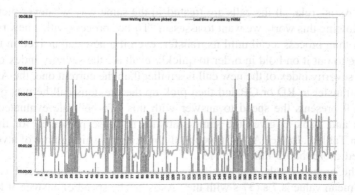

Fig. 7. Speed to answer time (red - thin) and AO's processing time (blue -bold) (Color figure online)

Figure 8 highlights the speed to answer according to severity index (level 1 is for a very serious call, level 2 is for an urgent call and level 3 for non-urgent call). In this "As-is" process, each call is processed by the AO until the transfer or the end of communication, even if another call is in the queue "Queue_AO".

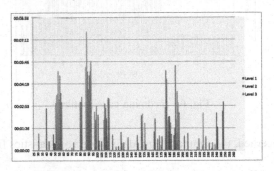

Fig. 8. Speed to answer by AO (As-Is)

Table 2 gives the descriptive statistics for each type of calls according to its severity index. We can see that a very serious call (severity index = 1) can wait more than 5 min whereas the objective is to pick up a call in less than 30 s.

Table 2. Statistics for each severity index of call (As-Is)

| | | Severity Index | | | |
		Level 1 Resuscitation - Emergent	Level 2 Urgent - Less Urgent	Level 3 Non Urgent	All
Number of calls answered by AO		82	90	66	238
Call duration by AO	Mean	00:01:21	00:01:01	00:03:00	00:01:41
	Min	00:00:42	00:00:45	00:02:26	00:00:42
	Max	00:05:56	00:01:18	00:03:35	00:05:56
Speed to answer by AO	Mean	00:00:37	00:00:58	00:00:50	00:00:48
	Min	00:00:00	00:00:00	00:00:00	00:00:00
	Max	00:05:13	00:05:48	00:07:45	00:07:45

4.2   "To-Be" Call Centre Simulation Model

With the "As-is" rule, all the calls are treated in the same way whatever their severity index. Following this work, we want to assess a "To-be" process with a new rule for the AO: rather than process a call until its transfer, even if a new call arrived in the queue, we propose to put it on hold in order to quickly evaluate the severity index of the new call. If the severity index of the new call is smaller than the current one, the AO process it until its transfer to RD or GP and then pick up the previous call he was processing.

Figure 9 presents the speed to answer with this "To-be" rule evaluated with the simulation and Table 3 gives the same statistics as those presented for the "As-is" situation in Table 2. In the "As-is" process, the maximum waiting time of a very urgent call reached more than 5 min (00:5:13).

With the proposed rule, the maximum waiting time does not exceed 1 min 29 s. While the mean value is 7 s (37 s with the "As-is"). The speed of answer of less urgent calls does not highly increase contrary to not urgent calls.

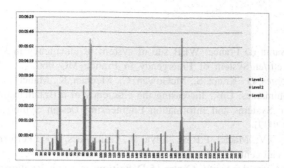

Fig. 9. Speed to answer by AO (To-Be)

Table 3. Statistics for each severity index of call (To-Be)

		Severity Index			
		Level 1 Resuscitation - Emergent	Level 2 Urgent - Less Urgent	Level 3 Non Urgent	All
Number of calls answered by AO		82	90	66	238
Call duration by AO	Mean	00:01:34	00:01:20	00:04:34	00:02:19
	Min	00:00:42	00:00:45	00:02:35	00:00:42
	Max	00:05:56	00:04:37	00:11:38	00:11:38
Speed to answer by AO	Mean	00:00:07	00:00:17	00:00:17	00:00:14
	Min	00:00:00	00:00:00	00:00:00	00:00:00
	Max	00:01:29	00:05:31	00:05:26	00:05:31

To summarize, the simulation study shows that applying this new rule could be the first step to improve the performance of this call centre by taking into account an incoming call in the queue.

5   Conclusion and Future Work

In this article, we describe a new approach for reengineering process, based on the combination of process mining and discrete-event simulation techniques in consecutive manner. We suggest to show the interest of the use of this approach to improve the management of an Emergency Call Service. The applying of the process mining technique allowed us to discover the control flow of the incoming call processing and several others useful figures. The most challenging point was the generation of the log file. In addition, the use of Simulation to analyse the "As-is" dynamic behaviour of the process allows us to identify weaknesses, to identify and implement the best KPI's. Moreover, the main reasons to include simulation in our study is to evaluate "To-be" improvements of the current process as optimizing business rules, effective staff deployment, etc.

The future work can be focused on the use of the simulation to optimize the human resources in relation with the call centre activity. The timetables and work organisation could be considered as control variables. Furthermore, we attend to extend our log files by other useful information to cover all the functions of the SAMU.

References

1. Giroud, M.: Samu de France: WEB site of system of emergency in France. http://www.samu-de-france.fr/en/System_of_Emergency_in_France_MG_0607
2. Bieger, A., Borges, G., Kranz, S., McGowan, C., Meehan, K., Mancuso, L.G., Guerlain, S., de Macedo Guimaraes, L.B.: Increasing the efficiency of a Brazilian emergency response call center. In: Systems and Information Engineering Design Symposium, SIEDS 2009, pp. 125–130 (2009)
3. de Lima, M.A.Q.V., Maciel, P.R.M., Silva, B., Guimarães, A.P.: Performability evaluation of emergency call center. Perform. Eval. **80**, 27–42 (2014)
4. Dreyfus, P.: Activité des Samu -Centre 15 Définitions et standardisation des données. Samu de France (2009). http://www.samu-de-france.fr/documents/actus/155/559/definitions_apl_drm_2009.pdf
5. Hammer, M., Champy, J.: Reengineering the Corporation: A Manifesto for Business Revolution. Harper Business, New York (1993)
6. Rebuge, Á., Ferreira, D.R.: Business process analysis in healthcare environments: a methodology based on process mining. Inf. Syst. **37**, 99–116 (2012)
7. Van der Aalst, W.M.P.: Process Mining. Springer, Heidelberg (2011)
8. Bouarfa, L., Dankelman, J.: Workflow mining and outlier detection from clinical activity logs. J. Biomed. Inform. **45**, 1185–1190 (2012)
9. Caron, F., Vanthienen, J., Baesens, B.: A comprehensive investigation of the applicability of process mining techniques for enterprise risk management. Comput. Ind. **64**, 464–475 (2013)
10. O'Kane, J.F., Spenceley, J.R., Taylor, R.: Simulation as an essential tool for advanced manufacturing technology problems. J. Mater. Process. Technol. **107**, 412–424 (2000)
11. Jacobson, S.H., Hall, S.N., Swisher, J.R.: Discrete-event simulation of health care systems. In: Hall, R.W. (ed.) Patient Flow: Reducing Delay in Health Care Delivery, pp. 211–252. Springer, New York (2006)

Robust Optimization Theory for CO$_2$ Emission Control in Collaborative Supply Chains

Giovanni Felici[1], Toshiya Kaihara[2], Giacomo Liotta[3],
and Giuseppe Stecca[1,2($\boxtimes$)]

[1] Istituto di Analisi dei Sistemi ed Informatica "Antonio Ruberti",
C.N.R., via dei Taurini 19, 00185 Rome, Italy
{giovanni.felici,giuseppe.stecca}@iasi.cnr.it
[2] Graduate School of System Informatics, Kobe University,
l-1, Rokkodai, Nada, Kobe 657- 8501, Japan
kaihara@kobe-u.ac.jp
[3] Center for Industrial Production, Aalborg University, A.C. Meyers Vaenge 15,
2450 Copenhagen SV, Denmark
gl@business.aau.dk

Abstract. Global sourcing in complex assembly production systems entails the management of potentially high variability and multiple risks in costs, quality and lead times. Additionally, current strategies of many companies or environmental regulatory frameworks impose - or will impose - on industries worldwide to take control, among others, of CO$_2$ emissions and related costs generated in supply, production and distribution. Strategic planning should therefore manage multifaceted risks in order to prevent high-costly re-planning. This work addresses the problem of simultaneously controlling CO$_2$ emission, production and transportation costs in supplier-manufacturer echelons. The problem is addressed by using the robust optimization theory applied to network strategic planning. A non-collaborative scenario in which each manufacturer independently selects its suppliers is compared to a scenario in which all the supply-chain actors aim to minimize production, transportation and CO$_2$ emission costs. Computational experiments on realistic instances show positive effects of collaboration on costs, especially in more constrained tests.

Keywords: Supply chain management · Supplier selection · Robust optimization · Sustainability · Collaboration

1 Introduction

Supplier selection is a critical sourcing process with huge impacts on cost, time, and quality performance of manufacturing companies. The implementation of global sourcing programs offers companies to gain significant competitive advantages. However, these programs also expose Original Equipment Manufacturers (OEMs) to multifaceted risks (e.g., late deliveries, financial instability, environmental disasters or negative impacts, security, and safety issues) and hidden costs that make supply chain more vulnerable to supply chain disruptions or poor supplier performance.

© IFIP International Federation for Information Processing 2015
L.M. Camarinha-Matos et al. (Eds.): PRO-VE 2015, IFIP AICT 463, pp. 547–556, 2015.
DOI: 10.1007/978-3-319-24141-8_51

Optimization models for supplier selection (mainly deterministic) have been proposed in the literature but a few of them included operational risks. Operational risks are related to uncertainties in customer demand, supply, and cost, and are opposed to disruption risks which are related to natural or man-made disasters [1]. As pointed out in [2, 3], (operational) risk management approaches can be divided into four categories: risk avoidance aims at eliminating the source of risk; risk mitigation reduces the probability of potential risks; risk sharing, in which cooperation contracts and insurances can be used to share risks with other parties; risk adoption, which is a passive risk taking strategy. Only in the recent years disruptions and uncertainty have been introduced and modeled in formulations including supplier selection (see, e.g., [4]). Beyond the competitiveness, supplier selection hugely impacts on sustainability performance of companies. However, quantitative models for supplier selection still require further research on criteria sets and integration of social and environmental dimensions [5]. In this work we study a robust approach in supply-chain strategic planning dealing with uncertainties in costs which are the uncertain price paid for CO_2 emissions during the production process.

Green supplier selection requires solid environmentally-oriented metrics, collaborative relationships across the supply chain and real-life scenario testing even though the literature seems to demonstrate a raising interest which however is still relatively low [6]. CO_2 emissions can be an effective and clear metric to be embedded in decision making. This is demonstrated by the recent development of models integrating CO_2 in multiple criteria analysis such as Analytic Network Process (ANP) [7], fuzzy multi-objective linear programming and Analytic hierarchy process (AHP) [8]. Multicriteria decision models for supplier selection in collaborative networks (in particular ANP) have been introduced [7, 9] but risks and uncertainty issues have not been addressed. At industry level, the inclusion of CO_2 emissions in supply chain management and in particular in supplier selection is particularly significant for companies relying on energy-intensive processes such as automotive suppliers and manufacturers [10, 11] or transportation and chemical/pharmaceutical industry [5]. Indeed, regulatory frameworks based on carbon taxation or cap-and-trade mechanisms have been already introduced in many countries worldwide [12]. In the future, companies will have to cope with these regulations *de facto*, internalizing the cost of their greenhouse gas emissions. This can also lead to improved environmental performance and cost energy savings involving suppliers [10]. On the other hand, the level of taxation or the trade pricing mechanisms may represent an additional risk factor because of the uncertainty in trends and fluctuations of CO_2 prices (see, for example, [12, 13]).

The objective of this paper is threefold: first, the CO_2 emission cost for companies is integrated into an optimization model to support decision making for supplier selection in addition to production and transportation costs. Second, uncertainty is addressed by using the robust optimization theory, thus exploring several risk scenarios. Third, the impact of collaboration between suppliers and an OEM on the performance of these supply chain echelons is estimated. As exemplary case study, computational tests are carried out on the basis of an instance envisioned for an automotive supply chain [14]. Our approach, which entails robust optimization modeling in operational risks, according to [3], is a risk mitigation strategy which anticipates risks and develops contingency plans. The proposed approach has been selected because optimization allows decision-makers to simultaneously minimize multiple cost components that can be parameterized in scenarios with different constraints. Robust optimization then includes uncertainty in model parameters, thus embedding risk management issues. In our model, multiple supply chain variables and parameters are included and uncertain CO_2 emission cost levels (i.e., trade prices or taxation) are considered as a risk factor. To our best knowledge this is the first optimization model for supplier selection using robust optimization theory and internalization of CO_2 emission costs by comparing collaborative and non-collaborative settings.

The paper is structured as follows. Section 2 presents the suppliers-OEM manufacturing network of the two supply chain echelons. The robust optimization model and the collaboration aspects are introduced in Sect. 3. Computational results are presented and discussed in Sect. 4. Conclusions follow.

2 Manufacturing Network

The manufacturing network consists of a two echelon production-distribution network serving a customer demand clustered in country demand areas. The general (physical) network configuration is presented in Fig. 1.

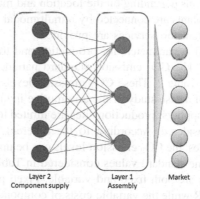

Layer 2   Layer 1   Market
Component supply   Assembly

Fig. 1. Multiechelon production – distribution network.

The central echelon (layer 1) of the modeled supply chain considers the final assembly stage of the production. This layer represents all the final assembly plants controlled by a focal company (OEM). The upstream layer (layer 2) is represented by the suppliers of the main components that have to be assembled into the final products. Figure 1 shows that potentially all the suppliers can provide all the assembly plants with the components and that all assembly plants can produce all the final products and serve the market. However, constraints regarding supply and assembly options have to be met as hereinafter explained.

Usually OEMs (the layer 1) establish supply contracts with a subset of suppliers in order to provide the required production levels and serve the final customers with an agreed service level. More sophisticated strategies could involve partnerships and collaboration between suppliers and/or a single OEM's assembly plant or sets of OEM's plants.

In the modeled network, three assembly plants can produce and deliver at least one of three final products to the market. Each product consists of three major components. The OEM's assembly plants can be supplied by a set of six (competing) suppliers. Suppliers produce specific components. Suppliers, components and product assembly options are specified in Table 1.

Table 1. Component supply and product assembly options.

Supplier (S_i)	Component (C_i)	Product assembly options (P_i)
S_1	C_1	$P_1 = C_1 + C_2 + C_3$
S_2	C_1	
S_3	C_2	$P_2 = C_1 + C_2 + C_4$
S_4	C_2	
S_5	C_3 and C_4	$P_3 = C_1 + C_3 + C_4$
S_6	C_3 and C_4	

Each supplier operates in a specific country. Each country is characterized by specific CO_2 emission levels depending on the location and manufactured components. Suppliers and assembly plants are connected by a multimodal transport network across which road, rail or sea transport services are provided.

The main CO_2 emission parameters for production and transportation are summarized in Tables 2 and 3. The CO_2 emission standard parameters for component production are presented in Table 2. These CO_2 emission levels have been estimated by elaborating on the data of a case study of the automotive industry[1]. In our elaboration, CO_2 emission levels at suppliers' production sites are limited to the lowest (ideal) levels across the countries considered. According to the different locations of sites in the network, in the worst cases, the CO_2 emission levels can be up to approximately 200 % and 270 % higher than the standard values considered in Table 2 for the components.

The production costs are both fixed and variable. Fixed production costs range in the interval 1.80-4 mEUR while the variable costs of components respectively range in

Table 2. CO_2 emissions and cost parameters of production of components.

Components	CO_2 Emission (tCO2/unit)[a]
C_1	0.102
C_2	0.022
C_3	0.05
C_4	0.1

[a]Estimate of standard CO_2 emissions in the countries with the lowest emissions per unit manufactured in the network

[1] http://publications.lib.chalmers.se/records/fulltext/136639.pdf.

the interval 26.5-300 EUR. Transportation costs are specified in Table 3. The carbon price considered is 10 EUR/tCO_2 (see, for example, the 2020 ETS price projections presented in [13]). The considered network costs concern the supply costs and transportation costs between the selected suppliers' sites and assembly plants.

Table 3. CO_2 emissions and cost parameters of transport.

Transport mode	CO_2 Emission (gCO2/tkm)[a]	Transport cost (EUR/tkm)[b]
Road[c]	93.1	0.14
Rail	17.4	0.11
Sea[d]	101	0.009

[a]http://www.developpement-durable.gouv.fr/IMG/pdf/Information_CO2_ENG_Web-2.pdf
[b]http://ec.europa.eu/ten/transport/studies/doc/compete/compete_report_en.pdf
[c]Road, semi-trailer truck with a GCW of 40 tonnes, large volumes, road diesel
[d]Short-sea shipping, Ro-Ro

3 Robust Optimization Approach

Robust optimization is used in mathematical programming to deal with uncertain parameters. With respect to stochastic programming, where some parameters are known through their distribution probability, in robust optimization the parameters are known only through their bounds of variability.

In integer programming, the robust optimization [15] can be defined over cost parameters, constraint parameters (e.g., product weights, arc traveling times, etc.), and known terms (e.g. customer demand values, plant capacities, etc.). The robust optimization aims to find a solution which is feasible and "good" over all the variation scenarios of unknown terms. In particular, some approaches are aimed to find the best solution in the worst case. Our approach is inspired by the work of [15], where robustness is considered inside the mathematical model and a parameter called "robustness budget" will let decide the degree of coverage amongst unexpected events. In the studied case, the unknown parameters are the CO_2 emission costs.

The studied problem can be formulated over a graph $G(N,A)$ where multiple commodities k should be delivered from suppliers to OEM's assembly plants using arcs (i,j). The goal is to minimize the overall production transportation and CO_2 emission costs over a time horizon T. The single time period is denoted with t. The parameters are as follows:

d_{ikt} Demand
fp_{ikt} Activation cost
cp_{ikt} Unit production cost
h_{ikt} Unit holding cost in inventories at node i
IC_{ikt} Inventory capacity
PC_{ikt} Production capacity

ep_{it} Emission factor at node level: the grade of emission of node i with respect to the reference country

ep_k Unit emission cost for product k (reference country at time 0)

et_k Emission cost/km (rail at time 0 =1)

c_{ijkt} Unit travel cost for production k

ft_{ijkt} Arc activation cost for production k

et_{ijt} Emission factor at arc level: the grade of emission of arc (i,j) with respect to the reference arc.

The variables are as follows:

v_{ikt} quantity of product k manufactured in node i in period t

z_{ikt} 1 if k is manufactured in i at time t, 0 otherwise

x_{ijkt} quantity of product k flowing in arc (i,j) in period t

u_{ijkt} 1 if k is flowing in arc (i,j) in period t, zero otherwise

s_{ikt} inventory level of product k in node i in period t, $t \in [0, T]$.

We first describe the non-robust deterministic model. The objective function to be minimized is:

$$z = \sum_{i \in N} \sum_{k \in K} \sum_{t \in T} [z_{ikt} fp_{ikt} + v_{ikt}(cp_{ikt} + ep_k ep_{it}) + s_{ikt} h_{ikt}]$$
$$+ \sum_{(i,j) \in A} \sum_{k \in K} \sum_{t \in T} [u_{ijkt} ft_{ikt} + x_{ijkt}(c_{ijkt} + et_k et_{ijt})] \quad (1)$$

The constraints on flow balancing are:

$$\sum_{j \in \Delta^-(i)} x_{jikt} + v_{ikt} - \sum_{j \in \Delta^+(i)} x_{ijkt} + s_{ik(t-1)} - s_{ikt} =$$
$$d_{ikt} + \beta_{kk'} \sum_{(k,k') \in BoM} (v_{ik't} - s_{ik'(t-1)} + s_{ik't}) \forall i, k, t \quad (2)$$

The constraints on capacity are:

$$s_{ikt} \leq IC_{ikt} \quad \forall i, k, t \quad (3)$$

$$v_{ikt} \leq PC_{ikt} z_{ikt} \quad \forall i \in O^k, k, t \quad (4)$$

$$x_{ijkt} \leq AC_{ijkt} u_{ijkt} \quad \forall i, j, k, t \quad (5)$$

Other constraints are:

$$s_{ik0}, s_{ik(-1)} = 0 \quad \forall i, k \quad (6)$$

$$v_{ikt}, x_{ikt}, s_{ikt} \text{ positive integer}; z_{ikt}, u_{ijkt} \text{ binary} \quad (7)$$

Robust optimization protects against all the possible occurrences of the uncertain values inside given bounds. Here robustness is introduced against the variation of costs of CO_2 emissions for production nodes. The emission factor ep_{it} over time is not fixed and may vary inside the interval $[ep_{it}, ep_{it} + \Delta ep_{it}]$ for $i \in N' \subseteq N$, $t \in [1,..,T]$.

Subset N' and A' contain the nodes for which the unknown variability is considered. Let $\Gamma \le |N'|\, T$ be the "budget of robustness" for emission variability intervals of production. Γ can be explained as the maximum number of variable intervals that are allowed to vary at their maximum and for which robust solution is guaranteed to be feasible. The model considering Γ robustness is named "robust counterpart". The new objective function z' of the robust counterpart model is:

$$z' = z + \max_{\{S_0 : S_0 \subseteq \Gamma, |S_0| \le \Gamma\}} \left\{ \sum_{i \in N, t \in T} \Delta ep_{it} \sum_{k \in K} v_{ikt} ep_k \right\}$$

By using duality theory, the formulation can be rewritten as a standard mixed-integer linear programming (MILP) model adding variables and constraints to hold robust terms and removing the min − max form [15]:

$$z' = z + \Gamma z_0 + \sum_{i \in N', t \in T} p_{it}$$

The complete model would then be:
min z'
s.t (2), (3), (4), (5), (6), (7) and

$$z_0 + p_{it}^0 \ge \Delta ep_{it} \sum_{k \in K} ep_k v_{ikt} \quad \forall i \in N', t \in [1, ..T] \tag{8}$$

$$z_0, p_{it} \ge 0 \tag{9}$$

4   Computational Results and Discussion

The computational experiments have been conducted on two different scenarios: first, a non-collaborative scenario in which each OEM's assembly plant (layer 1 of Fig. 1) runs the optimization separately and sequentially in order to identify the suppliers leading to locally optimal solutions. In the second scenario, a collaborative decision is made between all the OEM's assembly plants of the layer 2 simultaneously in order to jointly select the suppliers minimizing the global system costs. The multi-period model runs over 10 years. The robustness is applied to the CO_2 emission cost of the suppliers' production nodes in order to investigate variability and risks of CO_2 cost impact for production in different countries by focusing on the supplier selection problem. A nominal level of demand and capacity is used in a first experiment (Experiment 1). In the Experiment 2, the demand is supposed to increase by 5 % yearly. However, in the non-collaborative scenario, it is also assumed that the suppliers and carriers allocate no more than 75 % to each assembly plant. In the Experiment 3, the demand is the

Table 4. Comparisons between the non-collaborative and collaborative scenarios.

Experiment 1: Nominal demand and capacity	Non-collaborative scenario (KEUR)	Collaborative scenario (KEUR)	Var. %
Production cost	2,695,705	2,545,705	−5.56
CO$_2$ Emission cost from production	13,974.10	13,974.10	0.00
Transportation	2,418,167	2,418,167	0.00
CO$_2$ Emission cost from transport	3,027.10	3,027.10	0.00
Total costs without robustness	5,130,873	4,980,873	−2.92
Total costs with robustness	5,256,640	5,106,640	−2.85
Robustness contribution ($\Gamma = 1$)	125,767	125,767	0.00
Experiment 2: Increased demand; reduced supplier capacity allocation in non-collaborative scenario			
Production costs	4,117,944	3,268,599	−20.63
CO$_2$ Emission costs from production	21,519.58	18,901.30	−12.17
Inventory costs	583,500	956,250	+63.88
Transportation costs	3,893,614	3,159,373	−18.86
CO$_2$ Emission cost from transport	4,728.39	3,986.67	−15.69
Total costs without robustness	8,621,306	7,407,111	−14.08
Total costs with robustness	8,814,982	7,577,223	−14.04
Robustness contribution ($\Gamma = 1$)	193,676	170,112	−12.17
Experiment 3: Nominal demand; reduced supplier capacity allocation in non-collaborative scenario			
Production costs	2,837,585	2,545,705	−10.29
CO$_2$ Emission costs from production	15,155.07	13,974.1	−7.79
Transportation costs	2,526,145	2,418,167	−4.27
CO$_2$ Emission cost from transport	3,206.29	3,027.1	−5.59
Total costs without robustness	5,382,092	4,980,873	−7.46
Total costs with robustness	5,518,488	5,106,640	−7.45
Robustness contribution ($\Gamma = 1$)	136,396	125,767	−7.79

nominal one (Experiment 1) but the supplier's production capacity allocated to an OEM's plant is up to 33 % in order to be able to potentially cover with 100% of capacity the demand of all the three OEM's assembly plants. The computational results are presented in Table 4.

In the Experiment 1, the total cost savings resulting from the collaboration at OEM level (approximately 3 % in robust and non-robust solutions) moderately support the need for integrated sourcing solutions between assembly sites. In this experiment, the most relevant contribution to cost savings derives from reduced production costs whereas the impact of the variability of CO$_2$ emission costs is negligible. The effects of collaboration on cost reduction are amplified when the demand increases and capacity allocation decisions are more constrained (Experiments 2 and 3). In particular, production, transportation and CO$_2$ emission costs significantly decrease. Especially in the Experiment 2, the cost savings are quite significant and higher than the Experiment 3, which however exhibits positive results.

The collaborative supplier selection based on global cost optimization not only entails important cost savings but produces also a positive effect on risk management related to emission costs. In fact, in the last two experiments, the contribution of the robustness budget emerges in terms of reduction in the budget allocated to the variability of CO_2 cost on the basis of the same demand for suppliers (approximately -12 % and -8 %). Although the total cost of the robust optimization is higher that the non-robust one, the effects of the occurrence of the worst cases may definitely be more harmful in non-robust solutions.

5 Conclusions

This work contributes to the research on collaborative supply chains under risk conditions with consideration of CO_2 emissions by embedding a robustness budget for CO_2 cost uncertainty in the optimization approach for supplier selection, in both collaborative and non-collaborative settings.

The work is inspired by realistic instances and can be useful for: (i) industrial managers, in order to innovate procurement decision-making processes by considering supply-chain partnerships and budgets for uncertainty of variable CO_2 prices or taxes that has, or will have, to be considered according to current or future regulatory frameworks; (ii) policy makers, in order to adjust and test the impacts of variable CO_2 emission trading prices, different pricing mechanisms, carbon taxation schemes or collaboration incentives for supply chain actors.

Test runs are executed over a test instance envisioned in a previous work [14]. We find that the simultaneous, joint decision of OEMs on the selection of the suppliers leads to a cost reduction which varies depending on the experimental setting. When capacity constraints are less tight and the demand does not vary, a reduction in production cost is observed whereas transportation and CO_2 emission costs are substantially unvaried. However, the effects of collaboration on cost reduction are amplified when the demand increases and capacity allocation decisions are more constrained. Collaboration benefits the environmental performance of the sourcing process. In the non-collaborative approach, suppliers sequentially reserve production capacity to OEMs requesting the components. This entails a not optimal allocation strategy. Nominal demand levels in the constrained scenario of capacity allocation produce positive but less significant effects. Robust optimization leads to reduced total costs in all the tests with respect to non-collaborative settings. This entails the possibility to allocate a budget for risks related to CO_2 emissions cost uncertainty from variable trade prices or taxation that can be fully absorbed by the cost benefits from collaboration.

This work has the following limitations: collaboration is not considered horizontally among suppliers and carriers, respectively. Furthermore, transaction costs, which are not considered in the model yet, may lower the potential gain of the collaborative scenario. Future research tasks will aim to identify further instances and additional complexities of the real-life decision-making processes such as, e.g., scarce resources and their impact on collaboration settings. Moreover, the model will be extended to an entire supply chain and possibly integrated with simulation in order to embed dynamicity.

References

1. Tang, C.S.: Perspectives in supply chain risk management. Int. J. Prod. Econ. **103**, 451–488 (2006)
2. Mullai, A.: Risk management system: a conceptual model. In: Zsidisin, G.A., Ritchie, B. (eds.) Supply Chain Risk, pp. 83–101. Springer, NewYork (2008)
3. Hahn, G.J., Kuhn, H.: Value-based performance and risk management in supply chains: a robust optimization approach. Int. J. Prod. Econ. **139**, 135–144 (2012)
4. Sawik, T.: Joint supplier selection and scheduling of customer orders under disruption risks: single vs dual sourcing. Omega-Int. J. Manag. S. **43**, 83–95 (2014)
5. Brandenburg, M., Govindan, K., Sarkis, J., Seuring, S.: Quantitative models for sustainable supply chain management: developments and directions. Eur. J. Oper. Res. **233**, 299–312 (2014)
6. Genovese, A., Koh, S.C.L., Bruno, G., Esposito, E.: Greener supplier selection: state of the art and some empirical evidence. Int. J. Prod. Res. **51**, 2868–2886 (2013)
7. Theißen, S., Spinler, S.: Strategic analysis of manufacturer-supplier partnerships: an ANP model for collaborative CO2 reduction management. Eur. J. Oper. Res. **233**, 383–397 (2014)
8. Shaw, K., Shankar, R., Yadav, S.S., Thakur, L.S.: Supplier selection using fuzzy AHP and fuzzy multi-objective linear programming for developing low carbon supply chain. Expert Syst. Appl. **39**, 8182–8192 (2012)
9. Verdecho, M.J., Alfaro-Saiz, J.J., Rodríguez-Rodríguez, R.: An approach to select suppliers for sustainable collaborative networks. In: Camarinha-Matos, L.M., Boucher, X., Afsarmanesh, H. (eds.) PRO-VE 2010. IFIP AICT, vol. 336, pp. 304–311. Springer, Heidelberg (2010)
10. Lee, K.-H.: Integrating carbon footprint into supply chain management: the case of hyundai motor company (HMC) in the automobile industry. J. Clean. Prod. **19**, 1216–1223 (2011)
11. Lee, K.-H.: Carbon accounting for supply chain management in the automobile industry. J. Clean Prod. **36**, 83–93 (2012)
12. World Bank: State and Trends of Carbon Pricing 2014. World Bank, Washington, DC (2014)
13. Capros, et al.: EU Energy, Transport and GHG Emissions, Trends to 2050, Reference Scenario 2013. Publications Office of the European Union, Luxembourg (2014)
14. Liotta, G., Stecca, G., Kaihara, T.: Optimisation of freight flows and sourcing in sustainable production and transportation networks. Int. J. Prod. Econ. **164**, 351–365 (2015)
15. Bertsimas, L., Sim, M.: Robust discrete optimization and network flows. Math. Program. Ser. B **98**, 49–71 (2003)

A Collaborative Planning Model to Coordinate Mining and Smelting Furnace

Fenemedre Qaeze[✉], Romain Guillaume,
and Caroline Thierry

Université de Toulouse/IRIT,
5 Allée Antonio Machado, 31000 Toulouse, France
{Fenemedre.Qaeze,Romain.Guillaume,
Caroline.Thierry}@irit.fr

Abstract. In this paper, we are interested in the tactical planning problem of mines and smelting furnace. The problem concerns a set of mines with one smelting furnace. We are faced to a multi-actor's context for which a global optimization is not possible due to the independence of the services. This problem is solved using a set of local optimization model of mines bloc extraction and a model of smelting furnace. This paper begin with the state of the art related to the principal problems in mining process. It justifies the novelty of our work. Indeed, this paper aims to discuss on the impact of sharing information between downstream processes and upstream processes. Consequently, after the state of the art, the classical planning process using local optimization and the information sharing process are presented. In the following part, profits generated and related to different contexts. value-creation and approach are compared. At the end of the paper, conclusion and future extensions are presented.

Keywords: Mining complex planning · Information sharing · Coordinated planning

1 Introduction

Mining industry focuses on extraction and transformation of minerals principally in order to produce metals (nickel, iron, gold and copper). These metals are the result of complex processes implying different internal decision-making centers (DCs), themselves linked to other decision-making centers of the supply chain. In this paper, we are interested in the information sharing toward the DCs. Moreover, we focus on a particular key-information which is the value-creation of blocs.

In the literature, the problem of long term planning horizon of mining complex is well studied [1–4]. Nevertheless, to our knowledge, the middle/short term planning horizon is not well investigated [5] whereas it can help to face with uncertainty. The most studied problems are the extraction problems. In the literature [6], it is noted that, due to the nature of the extracted material, a differentiation is made between the problems. Indeed, these different kinds of material have different characteristics depending upon different extraction processes. On the one hand there are the metallic

© IFIP International Federation for Information Processing 2015
L.M. Camarinha-Matos et al. (Eds.): PRO-VE 2015, IFIP AICT 463, pp. 557–565, 2015.
DOI: 10.1007/978-3-319-24141-8_52

ores (iron, copper), the nonmetallic minerals (sand, gravel) and the fossil fuels (coal) and on the other hand the petroleum and natural gas. In this paper we are interested on the metallic ore. The principal problems of the extraction models which aim to determine the ultimate open pit limit [8–10] and the determination of the sequence of extracted bloc [11–13], (see [6] for a revue) are well studied. References [14, 15] propose a global optimization model (extraction and process).

The principal problems studied are the extraction models: determination of the ultimate open pit limit and the determination of the sequence of extracted bloc (see [6] for a recent revue). References [14, 15] propose a global optimization model (extraction and process). The objective of extraction models is to maximize the net present value (value-creation minus the cost of extraction and processing of blocs). Hence, the optimal solution depends on the value-creation of blocs which is difficult to estimate due to the uncertainty on grade elements, selling products price and cost of process which depends on the factory (process cost). References [2, 4, 14] propose models and/or algorithms to take into account the uncertainty on grade and [2] takes into account the uncertainty of prices. To optimize the cost of process, a global optimization approach is proposed by [14]. Nevertheless, a global optimization is not always possible since the mining and the furnace are independent DCs. In this paper we are interested in the coordination of the sequencing decision of bloc and the choice of the process in distributed context at the middle term planning horizon which, to our knowledge, has not been studied yet.

Firstly, the context and the problem are presented. Secondly, we detail the local optimization process. Then, the sharing information process and the possible information sharing (optimistic/pessimistic/average value-creation) is proposed. Then we present the simulation process and the analysis of the results. Finally, conclusion and perspectives are presented.

2 Context and Problem

In this paper we are interested in the coordination of the mining complex. The mining complex is composed of a set of mines which extract blocs and then deliver the extracted blocs to the smelting furnace (see Fig. 1).

Blocs are extracted from each mines, stored and then transported to the production and processing plant. At this first step of the internal supply chain, the extraction process is subject to important decisions of the downstream process. This process consists in determining:

- which bloc will be extracted or not
- the extraction plan (at which period the blocs will be extracted)

The objective of the plant is to satisfy a demand for the end of the planning horizon. The factory reserves the blocs from each mines and blends into one ore mixture. At this step dopants can be added to the ore mixture to satisfy the grade constraints of the smelting furnace. Then the mixture is treated and smelted. From the melted metal different products can be produced using different processes. The choice of proportion

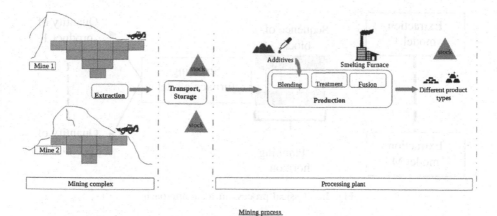

Fig. 1. Global mining complex

of the melted metal sent to a given process is called a production policy (which is defined for the planning horizon).

Noted that, the addition of dopants depends on the grade of the mixed ore mixture which depends on the mining extraction. Moreover the benefit of the factory is impacted by the pair ore mixture production policy since the grade of the element impacts the cost of process to obtain the final product. Nevertheless, the production policy can be chosen only if the sequence of bloc of each mine is known, which needs itself the information on value-creation of blocs. So, our problem is how to coordinate the decisions on the production and the extraction policies.

3   Classical Planning Process Using Local Optimization

In this section we present the classical planning process, [8–13], using local optimization for middle horizon planning (see Fig. 2). The objective of this planning process is to determine the sequence of extracted bloc from each mine and the production policy to apply over whole the horizon. More precisely only one production policy can be applied through the horizon and we must ensure the adequacy between the bloc sequence and the production policy.

The extraction model consists in maximizing the benefit for a horizon $t = 1$ to T under precedence constraints (a bloc cannot be extracted if another bloc has not been extracted before). The benefit is computed using the Eq. 1 where V_b is the value-creation of a bloc b, C_b is the extracting cost of bloc b and $x_{b,t}$ a binary variable which is equal to 1 if the bloc b is extracted at period t zero else. From those optimization, we obtain a sequence of blocs which will be the parameter of the smelting furnace planning model (see Fig. 3).

$$\sum_{b=1}^{B} \sum_{t=1}^{T} (V_b - C_b) x_{b,t}. \tag{1}$$

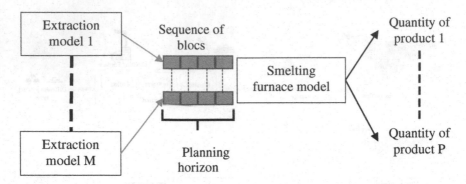

Fig. 2. Classical process in local approach

The smelting furnace model determines the quantity of dopant to be added to the ore mixture in order to meet the element grade target imposed by the smelting furnace and the choice of the production policy. The production policy is a vector of % of the melted metal transformed into a product (% for Product 1, ..., % for Product p). Nevertheless, the quantity of product obtained depends on the production policy and the grade of elements of the melted metal (Fig. 3).

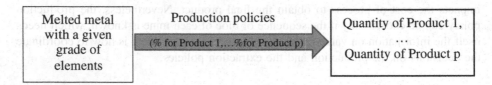

Fig. 3. Production policy

For instance, the mines of nickel can produce ferronickel and matte. To obtain the matte an iron removal is realized on the melted metal while for the ferronickel a desulphurization is realized. Indeed, the quantity of matte obtained depends on the percentage of nickel in the melt metal. The objective is to satisfy the demand of product while maximizing the profit (Eq. 2) where Bt_p is the selling price of product p minus production cost of product p, CI_p is the inventory cost of product p, CB_p is the backordering cost of product p, Cd_e is the dopant cost of element e, $X_{p,t}$ is the quantity of product p produced with the ore mixture extracted at period t, B_p, I_p are respectively the backordering and the inventory of product p at the end of horizon and $Q_{e,t}$ the quantity of dopant of element e used for the ore mixture which is extracted at period t.

$$\sum_{t=1}^{T} \left(\sum_{p=1}^{P} \left(Bt_p \times X_{p,t} - \left(CB_p \times B_p + CI_p \times I_p \right) \right) - \sum_{e=1}^{E} Cd_e \times Q_{e,t} \right). \quad (2)$$

Hence, the optimization at this stage consists in determining: (1) the amount of dopant to be added to the ore mixture at each period and (2) the production policy knowing the sequence of blocs extracted from each mines.

4 Information Sharing Process

The key information of the extracted model which does not depend on the mines is the value-creation of a bloc b since it depends on the decision of smelting furnace (production policy) and of the quality of the blocs from the other mines since the ore mixture has to respect some smelting furnace constraints. To help the mines to estimate the value-creation of a bloc, we propose that the mines share information with the smelting furnace planning to refine the estimation of value-creation of blocs. The questions to be answered are:

1. Which information to be shared (Sect. 4.1)?
2. How to estimate the value-creation (Sect. 4.2)?

4.1 Framework of Information Sharing

The extraction decision-maker (DM) communicates the quality of the extracted blocs (grade of elements) to the smelting furnace DM. From this information the smelting furnace DM computes the value-creation of a bloc taking into account the possible production policy and the respect of smelting furnace constraints (see Fig. 4). This value-creation is communicated to the extraction DM.

In the following Sect. 4.2, we describe how to valuate an extracted bloc taking into account the production decision.

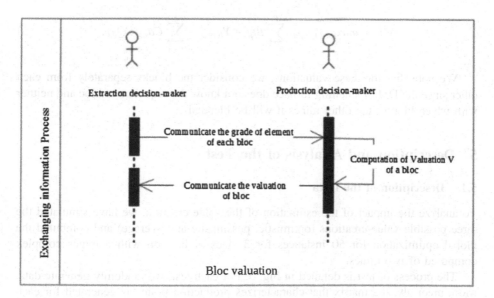

Fig. 4. Sharing information process

4.2   Estimation of Value-Creation Taking into Account Production Decision

The objective of this study is to evaluate the impact of estimation value-creation of a bloc b under uncertainty on the production policies. In this section, we propose three different ways for computing the value-creation of a bloc b. The objective of this study is to evaluate the impact of estimation value-creation of a bloc b under uncertainty on the production policies. The first one is a classical way to aggregate the uncertainty using the average aggregator (noted V_b^{av} for a bloc b) (implicitly it is considered that each production policy has the same probability to be chosen). The second one is the pessimistic evaluation (noted V_b^{pess} for a bloc b). In other words, we suppose that we will use the less profitable policy for this bloc. And, the last one is the optimistic evaluation (noted V_b^{op} for a bloc b). In this case, we suppose that we will use the most profitable policy for this bloc. Equations (3)–(5) are used to compute respectively V_b^{av}, V_b^{pess} and V_b^{op} with pl the index of production policy, $Y_{b,pl,p}$ the quantity of product p for production policy pl produced from the bloc b and $Q_{e,b}$ the quantity of dopant of element e required to satisfy the smelting furnace constraints.

$$V_b^{av} = \frac{\sum_{pl=1}^{Pl} \left(\sum_{p=1}^{P} Bt_p \times Y_{p,pl,b} - \sum_{e=1}^{E} Cd_e \times q_{e,b} \right)}{Pl}. \tag{3}$$

$$V_b^{pess} = min_{pl \in \{1,...,Pl\}} \sum_{p=1}^{P} Bt_p \times Y_{b,pl,p} - \sum_{e=1}^{E} Cd_e \times Q_{e,b}. \tag{4}$$

$$V_b^{op} = max_{pl \in \{1,...,Pl\}} \sum_{p=1}^{P} Bt_p \times Y_{b,pl,p} - \sum_{e=1}^{E} Cd_e \times Q_{e,b}. \tag{5}$$

We note that for these valuations, we consider the blocks separately from each other since the DM of smelting furnace does not know the sequence of bloc and neither with which bloc of the other mines it will be blended.

5   Description and Analysis of the Test

5.1   Description of the Data

To analyze the impact of the estimation of the value-creation, we have simulated the three possible value-creations (optimistic, pessimistic and average) and computed the global optimization for 50 instances for 3 sizes of horizon with a mines complex composed of two mines.

The process of test is detailed in Fig. 5. For each test, we randomly generate data. More precisely, the matrix that characterizes production policy is generated for each test. This matrix gives the quantity of each product p produced for a production policy pl of melded metal satisfying the characteristics on grade of elements. Another matrix that characterizes the grade of elements in an extracted bloc is also generated. This

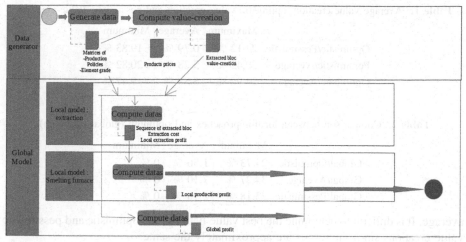

Description of the test Process

Fig. 5. Test process

matrix assigns a percentage of each element e at each bloc b. From these matrices, we compute the three proposed value-creations (a verifier) of blocs using Eqs. 3–5.

A matrix with the value-creation of the blocs is an input of the local model of extraction. The local model of extraction computes the extraction cost and the sequence of the extracted blocs. The sequence of the extracted blocs is an input for the local model of smelting furnace. This local model computes the profit of the production and selling activity. To compute the global profit, we subtract the cost of the extracting blocs to the profit of the production and selling activity (Eq. 6).

$$\sum_{t=1}^{T}\left(\sum_{p=1}^{P}\left(Bt_p \times X_{p,t} - (CB_p \times B_p + CI_p \times I_p)\right)\right) - \sum_{e=1}^{E} Cd_e \times Q_{e,t} - \sum_{b=1}^{B} C_b \times x_{b,t}$$

(6)

To evaluate if it is possible to increase the performances, we compute the optimal solution using a global optimization model which determines simultaneously the extraction sequence, the addition of dopant and the production policy in order to maximize the objective function defined by the Eq. 6.

5.2 Presentation and Analysis of the Result

The Table 1 shows the percentage of gain to use the optimistic evaluation rather than pessimistic, pessimistic rather than average and optimistic rather than average. We can see that optimistic and a pessimistic value-creations are both better than an average value-creation. Which is in contradiction with naive way to aggregate the uncertainty.

More precisely, for the different value-creations and for 50 tests (whatever the problem size), we only have 2 tests in which an average value-creation generates the best profit, so optimistic and pessimistic value-creations are both better at 96 % to the

Table 1. Average value-creation, optimistic value-creation and pessimistic value-creation.

	Maximum	Average	Minimum
Optimistic/Pessimistic	23.12 %	0.79 %	−19.83 %
Pessimistic/Average	30.42 %	5.28 %	−20.82 %
Optimistic/Average	24.96 %	5.88 %	−9.47 %

Table 2. Comparison between local approaches and optimum (global approach).

	Maximum	Average	Minimum
Global/Optimistic	24.73 %	1.56 %	0 %
Global/Average	34.27 %	7.10 %	0 %
Global/Pessimistic	23.18 %	2.16 %	0 %

average. It is difficult to determine the best value between the optimistic and pessimistic value-creations since the results are approximately the same.

In a second step, we compare the three local approaches with the optimum in which the profit is generated by the global approach. Table 2 shows the percentage of gain by using the global optimization rather than one of the local evaluation with different value-creations. It can be noted that, for some tests, the difference between profits generated with an optimistic value-creation (respectively pessimistic value-creation) and global approach is significant (see the maximum of percentage of difference in Table 2: 24,73 % and 23,18 %). In order to reduce the maximum of percentage of difference between local approaches and global approach, an improvement should be made on the optimistic and pessimistic value-creations. This improvement is presented in future works.

It can be observed that optimistic and pessimistic value-creations of extracted blocs generate the highest profits. These generated profits can be considered as near-optimum solutions. As a global approach is not allowed in our context of independent DC that is why to avoid this challenge, local approaches can be preferred.

5.3   Discussion of a General Applicability of the Result

To catch a general applicability of the results, the three principal questions to ask is: how to optimize local approach in order to generate profits that can be considered as near-optimum solutions? Consequently, what information to be shared? And how to compute this information? It will be interesting to find a way of collaboration for the different decision makers, for example using the mining complex network. In order to calculate, the value creation or the bloc to be extracted, the downstream process communicates its needs to the upstream process.

6   Conclusion and Perspectives

To summarize, we have presented previously the problem and the importance of sharing information to optimize the local approach. The description and the analysis of the test presented previously, showed that a good value-creation of the extracted blocs increases profit. Moreover, we stressed that an optimistic and a pessimistic evaluation aggregation of uncertainty is better than the naïve way. /the naive way to aggregate the uncertainty on the production policy can be far from the optimistic and pessimistic evaluation/. In this paper we have investigated the collaboration between each mines with the smelting furnace. As a perspective of a future paper, we are studying uncertainty resulting from the impact of the coordination of the different mines. We call this uncertainty, vertical uncertainty. This coordination between the different mines leads to meet an ore mixture degree which leads to the production of best profit product. Furthermore, the coordination of the blocks extraction from the set of mines could be done in order to minimize the production cost. Thereby, smelting furnace DC would guide all the mines DM by recommending the type of blocs (in terms of grade of element) to be extracted from each mine during the horizon.

References

1. Shishvan, M.S., Sattarvand, J.: Long term production planning of open pit mines by ant colony optimization (2014)
2. Koushavand, B., Askari-Nasab, H., Deutsch, C.V.: A linear programming model for long-term mine planning in the presence of grade uncertainty and a stockpile (2014)
3. Zhang, J., Dimitrakopoulos, R.: Optimising a mineral supply chain under uncertainty with long-term sales contracts. In: Orebody Modelling and Strategic Mine Planning Symposium 2014, Perth, WA, 24–26 November (2014)
4. Asad, M.W.A., Dimitrakopoulos, R.: Implementing a parametric maximum flow algorithm for optimal open pit mine design under uncertain supply and demand (2012)
5. Li, S.-X., Knights, P.: Integration of real options into short-term mine planning and production scheduling (2009)
6. Newman, A.: A review of operations research in mine planning. INFORMS, 222–245 (2010)
7. Gholamnejad, J., Osanloo, M.: Using chance constrained binary integer programming in optimising long term production scheduling for open pit mine design **116**, 58–66 (2007)
8. Dagdelen, K.: Open pit optimization – strategies of improving economics of mining projects through mine planning (2001)
9. Leite, A., Dimitrakopoulos, R.: Stochastic optimization model for open pit mine planning: application and risk analysis at copper deposit (2007)
10. Amaya, J., Espinoza, D., Goycoolea, M., Moreno, E., Prevost, T., Rubio, E.: A scalable approach to optimal block scheduling (2009)
11. Alvarez, F., Amaya, J., Grienwank, A., Strogies, N.: A continuous framework for open mine planning (2010)
12. Askari-Nasab, H., Awuah-Offei, K.: Opem pit optimisation using discounted economic block values (2009)
13. Dimtrakopoulos, R., Goodfellow, E.: Stochastic optimization of mineral value chains - developments and applications for the global optimisation of mining complexes with uncertainty. In: Orebody Modelling and Strategic Mine Planning Symposium 2014, Perth, WA, 24–26 November (2014)
14. Kumral, M.: Multi-period mine planning with multi-process routes (2013)

Integration of Supply Chain Planning with Time and Resource Constrained Project Scheduling Problems for Building's Thermal Renovation Projects

Shadan Gholizadeh-Tayyar[✉], Jacques Lamothe, and Lionel Dupont

Industrial Engineering Department, Toulouse University,
Ecole des mines d'Albi-Carmaux, 81000 Albi Cedex 09, France
{shadan.gholizadeh_tayyar,jacques.lamothe,
lionel.dupont}@mines-albi.fr

Abstract. CRIBA is a project that aims at industrializing thermal renovation processes of buildings. It consists in designing and configuring make-to-order insulated panels that will be installed on the external facade of the buildings to meet the thermal renovation objectives. Our study provides an optimization model that comprehensively plans supply chain network, which delivers insulated panels to the building's worksites, and schedules renovation activity that should be executed at the worksites under the limited quantity of the resources' availability. In this context, integration of supply chain planning problem with resource constrained multi project scheduling problem and time constrained project scheduling is of interest in realizing the decision making tool.

Keywords: Supply chain planning · Resource constrained multi project scheduling problem · Time constrained multi project scheduling problem · Mixed integer programming

1 Introduction

Generally, resource constrained multi project scheduling problem (RCMPSP) is defined as extension of resource constrained project scheduling problem (RCPSP). In RCMPSP the decision makers deal with simultaneous planning of multiple projects that use a common pool of resources for scheduling of their activities whereas in RCPSP one single project is aimed at scheduling while it uses its own dedicated resources. According to [1], nearby 90 % of on-going projects in worldwide are executed in a multi-projects environment. In both RCPSP and RCMPSPs two major types of the constraints are distinguishable: (a) precedency constraints and (b) resource satisfaction constraints [2]. In this context, the activities are forced to use the resources up to the amount that is available on the periods. A modified approach of this hypothesis is considered in Time Constrained Project Scheduling problem, TCPSP, that it supposes additional quantity of the resources has temporarily to be allocated in certain periods, [3].

Furthermore, regarding types of the resources used in projects, two main sorts could be stood out: Renewable and non-renewable ones [4].

© IFIP International Federation for Information Processing 2015
L.M. Camarinha-Matos et al. (Eds.): PRO-VE 2015, IFIP AICT 463, pp. 566–577, 2015.
DOI: 10.1007/978-3-319-24141-8_53

From the viewpoint of renewable resources, we use the approach of TCPSPs. Herein; the availability of the renewable resources such as labor-works, cranes and trucks can increase by renting additional limited quantities on the periods that the demand for these resource types may exceed the available amount by the activities.

From the viewpoint of non-renewable resources, like the basic RCMPSP, consumption of the nonrenewable resources of the model cannot exceed the available quantity. In our case, this quantity is limited by the capacity of supply chain that produces and supplies the resource to the projects' worksites. In this context, our attention is drawn to consider chain of the organizations, which coordinate together, to feed the final required product (the insulated panels in our case) at the projects' worksites and to plan optimally the quantity of materials that should be flowed between the organizations to satisfy projects' worksites on time. Noticeably, such a challenge relates a typical Supply Chain Planning, SCP, problem to the multiple projects scheduling problems.

To the best of our knowledge, integration of supply chain planning problem with resource constrained multi project scheduling problem and time constrained project scheduling is not considered up to now in the literature.

In the rest of this paper, we review the literature. Then, we define use case of the study. The decision making tool and the results are presented in following. Conclusion and future researches will be discussed at the final section.

2 Literature Review

The literature in resource constrained multi projects scheduling dates back to the 1960s. However, RCMPSP has not studied as expensively as single project scheduling [5]. Dealing with multi project scheduling problems distinguishes two main approaches: 1- *Single project approach*, wherein all the projects are joined together to make a single super-project. Herein, a single critical path is regarded in the scheduling of the projects. 2- *Multi projects approach*, in which the parallel separated projects are treated simultaneously while they use the same restricted resources of the management company. Different separated critical paths can be recognized in planning of the projects in multi projects approach.

Considering the multi projects problems with *single project approach* leads the researchers to the literature of RCPSPs. Different extensions of single project scheduling are defined in the literature. As a variant of RCPSPs, TCPSP would remarkably be applicable on practical project scheduling. Therein, a pre-defined due-date is given for completion of the project but it may be too tight to achieve with the resources that are available initially. TCPSP considers an approach that a given project can get complete on time by adding certain additional amounts of the resources [3, 6, 7]. In our study, this idea is utilized as well in order to make closer the completion time of the projects' activities to the expected dates that are regarded. In [6], the authors develop a decomposition method to deal with a TCPSP problem with adjacent resources. Reference [7] provides a two stage heuristic that solves several instances of TCPSPs to optimality.

In order to discover more the other extensions of the single project planning problems, we refer the readers to the reviews [8, 9] and textbook [3].

Besides the variants and extensions, from viewpoint of objective functions, resource constrained project scheduling problems are grouped according to different objectives: (i) Time- based objectives minimizes targets like completion time, earliness, tardiness and lateness [10]; (ii) Quality-based objectives in which maximization of the projects' quality is regarded [11]; (iii) Cost-based objectives where the objective function minimizes the total cost of projects like execution costs, material costs, inventory holding costs, costs related to tardiness or earliness of the project, [12, 13], and the costs of adding supplementary resources in TCPSPs, [3]; (iv) Net present value objectives that they are dealt with when certain pre-defined cash flows happen in the time periods. In fact, net present value maximization of the projects reflexes the time value of money in project scheduling problems, [14]; and, (v) multi objective models that investigate two or more of the above-mentioned objectives simultaneously in one model. In [15] criteria such as time, cost, quality and whole robustness are considered to build the multi objective model for scheduling multiple projects. Based on the importance of different objectives, the proposed model is expected to generate scheduling alternatives. For that purpose, a cloud genetic algorithm is proposed.

Multi projects approach little drew the attention of the researchers, [16]. In [16], the authors justify this choice because (1) it is more realistic, (2) it presents great opportunity for improvement and (3) critically. Within their work, they consider a RCMPSP with two lateness objectives, projects' lateness and portfolio lateness. Set of the priority rules for planning the resources of the model are used by the authors. They distinct several situation, in which priority rules perform poorly. In [17] different resource availability levels are introduced for the multiple projects. In [18], the preemption of the resources is considered for the multiprojects. Reference [19] uses queuing theory for multi project planning.

Dealing with the multi projects planning in both *single project approach*, and *multi projects approach*, engages the researchers with NP-hard problems. In term of computation time of the models, treating with small size of these problems is reasonable by the commercial softwares. In the large size of the problems, more than 50 activities for scheduling [20], application of the heuristics and meta-heuristics reduce considerably the computational time.

From the viewpoint of mathematical modeling, generally two types of the formulation are regarded: discrete time formulation and continuous time formulation. In discrete models the start time of the activities takes integer values whereas in continuous it can take a non-integer value as well. Reference [21] presents two different types of models for each of the mentioned formulations. The authors compare the proposed models with six literature models in 3240 benchmark instances. They define three criteria of good, optimal and feasible to study and rank the proposed models in each of the types. Our model is built based on the discrete time formulation. For the other formulation and developments, we refer the readers to [22].

The last part of the literature relates to the supply chain planning topic, which is considered in our study to plan the procurement of the nonrenewable resources of the problem. The decisions in supply chain planning are made in three levels of operational, tactical and strategic. In operational planning, decision makers try to provide a decisional framework that corresponds to very short periods of time, [23]. Control and procurement planning of necessary materials and short-term transport policy decisions correspond to this level of decision making. The tactical level in supply chain aims to consider the decision that associate with medium terms of planning. They can be considered in the decision making for planning the procurement of required materials, controlling the inventories, planning for production and distribution of the products, [24]. Major and fundamental decisions of network such as locating new facilities among the existing ones, selection of new technologies and selection between potential suppliers are taken into account in strategic level of decision making, [25].

3   Problem Definition and Formulation

3.1   Use Case

This work is a part of a research project, called CRIBA, (Construction et Rénovation Industrialisé Bois Acier). The project is defined in building sector in France to industrialize thermal renovation activities of the buildings. The business is determined to accomplish by designing and configuring make-to-order panels that will be installed on external facades of the buildings to insulate them and to reduce their energy consumption. The main composing elements of the panels are wooden frames, insulation material types, external coating product types and high-insulated carpentries. The carpentries are mainly made from aluminium, PVC and wood. Each composing element of the panels are procured by corresponding suppliers/manufacturers The ready-to-use panels are shipped from the panels' manufacturing unit to different buildings' worksites. Several renewable resources such as labor-works, trucks and cranes should be present at the worksites to make progress on installing the panels. After installation, the former carpentries should be removed from the buildings. In order to respect the sustainability rules regarded in the environmental engagements, the wastes of the worksites are shipped to a recycling center. It is worthwhile to mention that the stocking the panels is not allowed at the thermal renovation worksites, Fig. 1.

3.2   Problem Definition

Our study attempts to present a mid-term comprehensive decision making tool for CRIBA project that is provided by considering the decisions engaged in planning and scheduling of the projects' activities (*project planning*) as well as the decisions faced on procuring the projects' required non renewable resources (*supply chain planning*). Following points represent our attributers for each of the approaches:

From the Viewpoint of Project Planning: the model encompasses a set of w projects which run at different buildings' worksites. Every project has its own specified activities, I_w. For each activity i, a processing time Du_i, earliest start time e_i, latest start time l_i, latest finish time Lf_i and due-date DD_i are attributed which are estimated by project managers. If the due date is not met, a penalty cost $Penc_i$ will be imposed to the system. The predecessor relationship between two activities i and j is denoted by Pre_j.

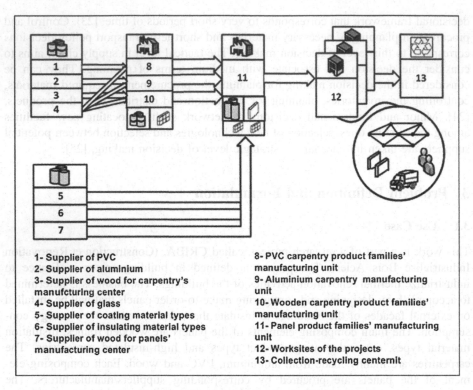

1- Supplier of PVC
2- Supplier of aluminium
3- Supplier of wood for carpentry's manufcturing center
4- Supplier of glass
5- Supplier of coating material types
6- Supplier of insulating material types
7- Supplier of wood for panels' manufacturing center

8- PVC carpentry product families' manufacturing unit
9- Aluminium carpentry manufacturing unit
10- Wooden carpentry product families' manufacturing unit
11- Panel product families' manufacturing unit
12- Worksites of the projects
13- Collection-recycling centernit

Fig. 1. Thermal renovation projects' framework.

In addition, each activity uses certain amount of renewable resources, Dr_{ir}, and non-renewable resources, Dp_{ip}. The nonrenewable resources are supplied to the worksites with a limited capacity of its manufacturer over the different time periods. Meanwhile, Ar_r units of renewable resource r are available to share at the worksites. An additional quantity of renewable resource type r can be rent with cost Rc_r. Relation set φ_{1w} is defined to model a per period cost Pc_w between the beginning and ending activity of the worksite w.

From the Viewpoint of Supply Chain Planning: A network of organizations cooperate together to ultimately satisfy the demand of the worksites for the panels. One single organization is responsible to procure each type of the materials at the supply chain network. The set of the organizations N includes the carpentries' raw material suppliers s_c, the panels' raw material suppliers s_p, the manufacturing units of different carpentry n_c, the panels manufacturing unit n_p, worksites w and wastes recycling center re, ($N = \{s_c, s_p, n_c, n_p, w, re\}$). In the model, $o'(n)$ indicates the articles that are consumed at the organization n, i.e. set of raw materials of the panels rp and set of raw materials of the carpentries rc. Besides, $o(n)$ denotes the articles that are produced at the corresponding organization n. It can be panels p or carpentries c. $N(o)$ is the destination units where a produced article o can be used. In the supply chain network, in order to smooth the flow of products, each carpentry's and panel's manufacturing unit assigns a limited capacity to stock the required raw materials and the finished products, $Caps_{nt}$. Beside of stocking the raw materials and ready-to-use panels, the panels' manufacturing unit stocks some limited quantity of the carpentries as well. $IS_{o'(n),0}$ and $IS_{o(n),0}$ regard the initial stocks. Furthermore; $Cappro_{nt}$ and $Capsup_{o'(n),t}$ are defined to consider production capacity of the manufacturing centers and supply capacity of the organizations. Notation $Pt_{o(n)}$ presents the workload of the production for producing the panels and carpentries at the corresponding manufacturing centers. In order to deal with the delays of the supply chain network, transportation lead-time $Tl_{o(n),n}/Tl_{o'(n),n}$ and production lead-time $Pt_{o(n)}$ are defined. Notation $B_{o,o'}$ is generally used to define the bill of material of the product o'.

Three different type of the costs including transportation costs $QC_{o'(n),n}/QC_{o(n),n}$ production cost $PC_{o(n)}$ and stock costs $SC_{o'(n)}/SC_{o(n)}$ are attended to calculate the total cost of the network.

3.3 Mathematical Formulation

Objective Function: the objective of the model is to minimize total cost of the system execution. It includes different types of the costs:

– *Project Planning Costs* which includes total periodic cost of running the projects till their completion time, (ii) total penalty cost for lateness in completion of the jobs and (iii) total cost of renting the additional renewable resources.
– *Supply Chain Planning Cost* including (v) the total transportation cost for shipping the raw materials and products at the network, (vi) production cost of the panels and carpentry types and (vi) the stock costs, which includes the stocking cost the raw materials and finished products at the carpentries' and panels' manufacturing units.

$$
MinZ = \left[\sum_{w} \sum_{(i,j)\in\varphi_{1w}} (S_j + Du_j - S_i)Pc + \sum_{i} Ltns_i Penc_i + \sum_{r} \sum_{t} R_{rt} Rc_r \right]
$$
$$
+ \left[\sum_{o'(n)} \sum_{n} \sum_{t} Q_{o'(n),n,t} QC_{o'(n),n} + \sum_{o(n)} \sum_{n} \sum_{t} Q_{o(n),N(o(n)),t} QC_{o(n),n} \right]
$$
$$
+ \left[\sum_{n\in\{n_c,n_p\}} \sum_{o(n)} \sum_{t} PQ_{o(n),n,t} PC_{o(n)} \right]
$$
$$
+ \left[\sum_{n\in\{n_c,n_p\}} \sum_{o'(n)} \sum_{t} S_{o'(n),n,t} SC_{o'(n)} + \sum_{n\in\{n_c,n_p\}} \sum_{o(n)} \sum_{t} S_{o(n),n,t} SC_{o(n)} \right] \quad (1)
$$

Constraints:

Supply Chain Design Constraints. Constraints (2)–(4) concern the capacity constraints. Constraints (2)–(4) respectively deal with the production capacity, supply capacity and stock capacity of the organizations.

$$\sum_{o(n)} Pt_{o(n),n} PQ_{o(n),n,t} \leq Cappro_{n,t} \quad \forall\, n \in \{n_c, n_p\},\, t \in T \tag{2}$$

$$Q_{o',n,t} \leq Capsup_{o',t} \quad \forall\, n \in \{n_c, n_p\},\, o' \in O'(n),\, t \in T \tag{3}$$

$$\sum_{o'(n)} S_{O'}(n), n, t + \sum_{o(n)} S_{o(n),n,t} \leq Caps_{n,t} \forall\, n \in \{n_c, n_p\},\, o' \in O'(n) \cup C,\, t \in T \tag{4}$$

Constraints (5)–(8) represent the balance of the flows. Equations (5) and (6) respectively consider the balance for stocked quantity of the finished products and the raw materials at their manufacturing centers considering their consumption, production and transportation. Equations (7) and (8) deal with the initial stocks.

$$S_{o,n,t-1} + PQ_{o,n,t-Pl_o} = \sum_{N(o)} Q_{o,N(o),t} + S_{o,n,t} \quad \forall\, n \in n_c \cup n_p,\, o \in O(n),\, t \in T \tag{5}$$

$$S_{o',n,t-1} + Q_{o',n,t-Tl_{o',n}} = \sum_{o} PQ_{o,n,t} B_{o',o} + S_{o',n,t} \quad \forall o' \in O'(n) \cup C,\, n \in n_c \cup n_p,\, t \in T \tag{6}$$

$$S_{o',n,t} = IS_{o',n,0} \quad \forall n \in n_c \cup n_p,\, o' \in O'(n),\, t = 0 \tag{7}$$

$$S_{o(n),t} = IS_{o(n),0} \quad \forall n \in n_c \cup n_p,\, o \in O(n),\, t = 0 \tag{8}$$

Equation (9) presents the reverse logistic constraints. It guarantees that all the waste produced at the worksites will be shipped to the recycling center.

$$Q_{o'(re),t} = ProQ_{o'(w),w,t-Tl_{o(re)}} \quad \forall t \in T \tag{9}$$

Project Planning Constraints. In this context, constraints (10)–(15) present the activities' scheduling constraints. Constraint (10) guarantees that all the activities of the projects should be executed in a time interval between their earliest start and latest start time. Equation (11) represents that the sum of the activity's execution periods should be equal with its processing time. Constraints (12) and (13) deal with the start time of the activities. Constraint (12) uses the activities' precedence relations for defining the start times. Equation (13) calculates the start time of the activities. Relying on the start times and activity's processing time, constraint (16) relates two decision variables Z_{it} and U_{it}. Constraint (15) deals with the lateness may occur in executing the activities. It is considered by the difference between the due date, which is forecasted for completion of activity i, and the real completion time of activity i.

$$\sum_{t=e_i}^{l_i} Z_{it} = 1 \quad \forall i \in I \tag{10}$$

$$\sum_{t=e_i}^{LF_i-1} U_{it} = Du_i \quad \forall i \in I \tag{11}$$

$$S_j \geq S_i + Du_i \quad \forall j \in Pre_j \tag{12}$$

$$S_i = \sum_{t=e_i}^{l_i} t Z_{it} \quad \forall i \in I \tag{13}$$

$$\sum_{k=t}^{t-1+Du_i} U_{ik} \geq Du_i Z_{it} \quad \forall i \in I, \, t \in \{e_i, \ldots, l_i\} \tag{14}$$

$$Ltns_i \geq S_i + Du_i - DD_i \quad \forall i \in I \tag{15}$$

Constraints (16) and (17) deal with the resources availability constraints. Constraint (16) deals with the requirement of the activities for renewable resources. It guarantees that the demand for renewable resource types of the activities that are executing at a certain time period will be satisfied by the available quantities of these resources and the quantities that probably will be rented. Since panels cannot be stocked on the projects' worksite, Eq. (18) guarantees that the total quantity of the panels that are transported to the worksites over a time period t will satisfy the demand for the panels of activities that are progressing at time period t.

$$\sum_{i \in I_n} Dr_{ir} U_{it} \leq Ar_r + R_{rt} \quad \forall r \in R, \, n \in \{w\}, \, t \in T \tag{16}$$

$$\sum_{i \in I_n} Z_{it} \leq Dp_{i,o'(n)} = Q_{o'(n),n,t} \quad \forall n \in \{w\}, \, o'(w) \in \{P\}, \, t \in T \tag{17}$$

Constraints (21)–(23) represent the variable types that are used at modeling of the problem.

$$U_{it}, Z_{it} \in \{0;1\} \quad \forall i \in I, \, t \in T \tag{18}$$

$$R_{rt}, Ltns_i, Q_{o(n),n,t}, PQ_{o(n),t}, S_{o(n),t}, S_i \in Z^+ \quad \forall o(n) \in O(n), r \in R, i \in I, n \in N, t \in T \tag{19}$$

$$Q_{o'(n),n,t}, S_{o'(n),t} \geq 0 \quad \forall o'(n), \in O'(n), n \in N, t \in T \tag{20}$$

3.3.1   Numerical Results

Parameter setting presented in Table 1 is applied on the model. The problem is solved by using CPLEX algorithm on a notebook with Core i7 CPU, 2.7 GHz processor, 64-bit and 4 GB of memory.

Table 1. Dimension of the indices of the model.

Indices	
i: activities: 1,...,10	*rp*: raw materials of the panels, including:
P: panel types: 1,2,3	insulating materials: 1,2,3
W: worksites: 1, 2	Coating-materials: 1, 2, 3
R: renewable resource types: 1, 2, 3	Wood materials: 1, 2, 3
t: time periods: 1,...,10	*rc*: raw materials of the carpentries, 1,...,4,
C: Product families of the carpentries,	including: PVC, Aluminum, wood and
including:	glass
PVC: 1, 2, 3	
Wooden: 1, 2, 3	
Aluminum: 1, 2, 3	

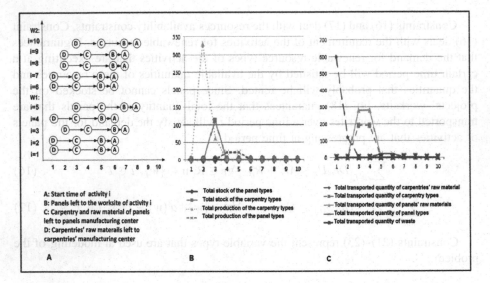

Fig. 2. A: Start time of activities, B: total stock/production quantities and C: total transported quantities of products and raw materials.

Figure 2A depicts the planning events that are engaged with each of the activities, (i.e. events related to start of the activities and also related to the procurement of the demanded consumable resources). Figure 2B presents the total stock and production quantity of all the panel and carpentry types. Figure 2C shows the graphs, which stand out the total quantity of the transported raw materials and products to the destination of use over the different time periods.

For the presented model, a failure in progressing of the thermal renovation activities over the time interval that are forecasted (execution of the activities between e_i and l_i) originates from two kinds of reasons: one can be taken place by the failure of the supply chain network in supplying the resources and the other can be originated from the worksites during the execution of the activities. In this study to deal with the effects of the failure in starting of the activities on the total cost of the system, we carry out sensitivity analysis. For this purpose, we suppose that the earliest start time of the activities be postponed for one unit of time. The results of the sensitivity analysis are presented in Table 2.

Table 2. Results of the sensitivity analysis.

Cost (%) activity	Total running cost in completion time, (i)	Total penalty cost, (ii)	Total resource-add cost, (iii)
1 (in worksite1)	0 %	3 %	0.23 %
2 (in worksite1)	50 %	1 %	0.23 %
3 (in worksite1)	50 %	1 %	0.23 %
4 (in worksite1)	0 %	−1 %	0.23 %
5 (in worksite1)	50 %	1 %	0.23 %
6 (in worksite2)	0 %	3 %	0.23 %
7 (in worksite2)	50 %	1 %	0.23 %
8 (in worksite2)	50 %	1 %	0.23 %
9 (in worksite2)	0 %	−1 %	0.23 %
10 (in worksite2)	50 %	1 %	0.23 %

4 Conclusion and Future Work

In this study a multi project scheduling problem is regarded. Two types of the resources including renewable and nonrenewable resources are demanded by activities to do progress. A common pool of renewable resources with limited availability quantity is shared among the projects. In our model, we consider the possibility of renting additional quantity of the renewable resources, which lets the model to make closer the completion time of the activities, as much as possible, to the expected due dates (Integration of the time constrained project scheduling problems with multiple project scheduling problems). The non-renewable resources of the project are supplied at the worksites by their corresponding manufacturers. Procurement planning of these resources relates the model to the supply chain planning problem. The proposed optimization tool is built based on a case study that is defined by ADEME in context of CRIBA project. The results of solving the model for a small dimension of the problem are obtained by using CPLEX algorithm. A sensitivity analysis is carried out to study the effect of the failure in starting of the activities on different costs of the system.

For the future studies of this research, the authors aim at developing the model by applying the uncertainty modeling approaches such as robust optimization. Using the meta-heuristics to deal with large scale of the problem is also of interest.

Acknowledgement. The authors gratefully acknowledge the Agence d'Envirronnement et Maîtrise de l'Enegrie (ADEME) and SYRTHEA enterprise for founding of this research study.

References

1. Payne, J.H.: Management of multiple simultaneous projects: a state-of-the-art review. Int. J. Proj. Manage. **13**, 163–168 (1995)
2. Badiru, A.B., Pulat, P.S.: Comprehensive Project Management: Integrating Optimization Models, Management Principles, and Computers. Prentice-Hall Inc, Upper Saddle River (1995)
3. Klein, R.: Scheduling of Resource Constrained Projects. Springer, New York (1999)
4. Shirzadeh Chaleshtarti, A., Shadrokh, S., Fathi, Y.: Branch and bound algorithms for resource constrained project scheduling problem subject to nonrenewable resources with prescheduled procurement. Math. Probl. Eng. **2014**, e634649 (2014)
5. Krüger, D., Scholl, A.: A heuristic solution framework for the resource constrained (multi-) project scheduling problem with sequence-dependent transfer times. Eur. J. Oper. Res. **197**, 492–508 (2009)
6. Guldemond, T.A., Hurink, J.L., Paulus, J.J., Schutten, J.M.J.: Time-constrained project scheduling. J. Sched. **11**, 137–148 (2008)
7. Hurink, J.L., Kok, A.L., Paulus, J.J., Schutten, J.M.J.: Time-constrained project scheduling with adjacent resources. Comput. Oper. Res. **38**, 310–319 (2011)
8. Hartmann, S., Briskorn, D.: A survey of variants and extensions of the resource-constrained project scheduling problem. Eur. J. Oper. Res. **207**, 1–14 (2010)
9. Węglarz, J., Józefowska, J., Mika, M., Waligóra, G.: Project scheduling with finite or infinite number of activity processing modes – a survey. Eur. J. Oper. Res. **208**, 177–205 (2011)
10. Baker, K.R.: Minimizing earliness and tardiness costs in stochastic scheduling. Eur. J. Oper. Res. **236**, 445–452 (2014)
11. Icmeli-Tukel, O., Rom, W.O.: Ensuring quality in resource constrained project scheduling. Eur. J. Oper. Res. **103**, 483–496 (1997)
12. Ranjbar, M., Khalilzadeh, M., Kianfar, F., Etminani, K.: An optimal procedure for minimizing total weighted resource tardiness penalty costs in the resource-constrained project scheduling problem. Comput. Ind. Eng. **62**, 264–270 (2012)
13. Rodrigues, S.B., Yamashita, D.S.: An exact algorithm for minimizing resource availability costs in project scheduling. Eur. J. Oper. Res. **206**, 562–568 (2010)
14. Artigues, C., Demassey, S., Neron, E.: Resource-constrained project scheduling: models, algorithms, extensions and applications (2008). http://eu.wiley.com/WileyCDA/WileyTitle/productCd-1848210345.html
15. Browning, T.R., Yassine, A.A.: Resource-constrained multi-project scheduling: Priority rule performance revisited. Int. J. Prod. Econ. **126**, 212–228 (2010)
16. Browning, T.R., Yassine, A.A.: Resource-constrained multi-project scheduling: Priority rule performance revisited. Int. J. Prod. Econo. **126**, 212–228 (2010)
17. Dumond, E.J., Dumond, J.: An examination of resourcing policies for multi resource problems. Int. J. Oper. Prod. Manage. **13**, 54–78 (1993)
18. Bock, D.B., Patterson, J.H.: A comparison of due date setting, resource assignment, and job preemption heuristics for the multiproject scheduling problem. Decis. Sci. **21**, 387–402 (1990)
19. Navi-Isakow, S., Golany, B.: Managing multiple project environments through constant work-in-process. Int. J. Proj. Manage. **20**, 127–130 (2002)
20. Ghomi, S.M.T.F., Ashjari, B.: A simulation model for multi-project resource allocation. Int. J. Proj. Manage. **20**, 127–130 (2002)

21. Kopanos, G.M., Kyriakidis, T.S., Georgiadis, M.C.: New continuous-time and discrete-time mathematical formulations for resource-constrained project scheduling problems. Comput. Chem. Eng. **68**, 96–106 (2014)
22. Hait, A., Artigues, C.: On electrical load tracking scheduling for a stel plant. Comput. Chem. Eng. **68**, 96–106 (2011)
23. Schütz, P., Tomasgard, A.: The impact of flexibility on operational supply chain planning. Int. J. Prod. Econ. **134**, 300–311 (2011)
24. Chen, V.Y.X.: A 0–1 goal programming model for scheduling multiple maintenance projects at a copper mine. Eur. J. Oper. Res. **76**, 176–191 (1994)
25. Chai, J., Liu, J.N.K., Ngai, E.W.T.: Application of decision-making techniques in supplier selection: a systematic review of literature. Expert Syst. Appl. **40**, 3872–3885 (2013)

Impact of Changes in Quality of Deliveries on the Vulnerability of Supply Chains

Leila Sakli[✉], Jean-Claude Hennet, and Jean-Marc Mercantini

Aix Marseille University, CNRS, ENSAM, Toulon University,
LSIS UMR 7296, Marseille 13397, France
{leila.sakli,jean-claude.hennet,
jean-marc.mercantini}@lsis.org

Abstract. The main objectives of the study are to present the vulnerability of the supply chain related to the change in the quality of the products supplied, and propose solutions to mitigate its disturbance. We use ARMA (Auto Regressive Moving Average) time series to model a supply chain with one supplier and one retailer. We then analyze how changes in the quality of products delivered by the supplier may affect the system variables, taking into account the system constraints and the uncertain demand from customers. A quality predictor can then be introduced in the model to improve the resilience of the chain.

Keywords: Risk · Supply chain · Vulnerability · Resilience · Quality

1 Introduction

New technologies and globalization increase the complexity of supply chains and therefore expose them to risks of different types. Faced with uncertainty, supply chains appear more sensitive in the context of competitive pressure, unpredictable and volatile global market demand. In particular, supply chains are sensitive to local disturbances and uncertainties related to demand [1] supplies [2] or information [3, 4]. Several studies have been conducted to analyze the topic of risk especially in the context of the supply chain [5, 6]. In general, risk is a combination of a probability of occurrence of an adverse event and a measure of the severity of the consequences of this event in terms of damage or injury (ISO/CEI73) [7]. The concept of risk is significant only in the presence of targets vulnerable to the effects of hazards induced by accidents [8].

Vulnerability is an intrinsic property of a system. It measures its sensitivity to adverse events. We distinguish endogenous vulnerabilities, which are properties of the companies that make up the supply chain, and vulnerabilities external to the company, at the level of interconnections between companies or flows [9].

In the field of the supply chain, Ou Tang and Nurmaya Musa [10] argue the lack of a difference between uncertainty and risk in the literature. However, as [6] we distinguish between these two concepts. Indeed according to ISO/2009, the risk is defined as the effect of uncertainty on objectives [11]. This definition highlights both the difference and the relationship between the concepts of risk and of uncertainty. Under the effect of uncertainty, a deviation can be positive or negative. In practice, one is

© IFIP International Federation for Information Processing 2015
L.M. Camarinha-Matos et al. (Eds.): PRO-VE 2015, IFIP AICT 463, pp. 578–587, 2015.
DOI: 10.1007/978-3-319-24141-8_54

interested in the negative effect [6]. In this context Wagner and Bode [9] define risk as "the negative deviation from the expected value of a certain performance measure, resulting in negative consequences for the focal firm" [9].

Due to the complex structures of today supply chains, a risk in a company may have consequences for other companies upstream or downstream. It thus threatens the entire chain. The resilient supply chain has the ability to adapt whatever the events to which the chain is subjected. Resilience is "the system's ability to return to a new stable situation after an accidental event" [13]. Taking into account that it is a multidimensional concept, Ponomarov and Holcomb [14] define resilience as "the adaptive capability of the supply chain to prepare for unexpected events, respond to disruptions, and recover from them by maintaining continuity of operations at the desired level of connectedness and control over structure and function" [14]. To preserve the resilience of supply chains, the areas of risk analysis and risk management are currently acquiring great interest, both from the theoretical and applicative standpoints. It is necessary to have indicators of vulnerabilities in the chain to determine the sensitivity of the chain to adverse events and to characterize the system's lack of resilience.

To form a resilient supply chain, the company must select the most reliable suppliers. Product quality is among the key factors in determining the reliability of a supplier, and the quality of a product may critically depend on risks in production, delivery or storage. In this research, we focus on uncertainties about the quality of supplied components and the demand, and try to analyze the vulnerability of the supply chain due to the variation in the quality of the product supplied. In a previous work [5], we have proposed a model based on ARMA time series to study supply chain vulnerabilities under demand uncertainty. The choice of ARMA time series can be argued by the fact that such model takes into account both the random nature of the system and its history.

As shown in the next section, starting from the works of Box and Jenkins [16] for ARMA series and Gilbert [16] for their applications to modeling supply chain dynamics, we have introduced in the model constraints on inventory and supplier capacity. From this non-linear model, we can infer indicators of system vulnerability. After that, we add to this model a quality index. First, the product quality model is supposed ARMA and can be estimated based on the history of deliveries from the same supplier. Next, the product quality model is supposed determinist with random time. In Sect. 3, and to simplify the study, we consider a basic two-stage supply chain consisting of a company and its supplier receiving random demands from customers. The dynamics of the system are studied by simulation, to measure the influence of quality uncertainty and compare the cases when quality variations are anticipated and when they are not, and also to compare between the different models of quality index.

2 Model Development

In this section we start by modeling the supply chain with ARMA. In many cases, supply chains "can be viewed as virtual systems subject to dynamic reconfigurations, through arrival or departure of partner enterprises." [8]. The formulation of the model is as follows. To represent the model of the supply chain, we use the following notation:

D_t: Random demand at period t
$a_{t-1}, e_t, \varepsilon_t$:   White noises
μ: mean demand
I_t: Inventory level at the end of period t
O_t: Order placed at the end of period t
$\hat{D}_t$:   Estimated value of demand at period t
$\bar{I}$:   Maximal storage capacity
II_t: Inventory index at period t
$\bar{O}$:   Maximal quantity ordered from the supplier in one period
OI_t: Order index at period t
z_t: Quality index at period t
$\hat{z}_t$:   Estimated quality index at period t
S: Safety stock level

2.1   Model of the Supply Chain

The modeling of the chain is given by the representation of the demand, the level of stock of each company and the quantity of products or components to be ordered.

When a prime contractor places orders to his supplier, it also transmits information about customer demand. This demand is often of random nature. A mathematical formulation of the demand D_t can be constructed by the method of Box and Jenkins [15] as an ARIMA (p, d, q) (Auto Regressive Integrated Moving Average). The main purpose of this model is to predict the future values of the random demand, taking into account its previous values observed.

$$D_t = \mu + \sum_{k}^{p} \varphi_k(D_{t-k} - \mu) + a_t + \sum_{l=1}^{q} \theta_l a_{t-l}. \tag{1}$$

Based on this representation, Gilbert [16] proposed a linear model of the supply chain by introducing the stock level I_t, and the order quantity O_t at the end of period t according to the forecast demand $\hat{D}_{t+k}$. $\hat{D}_{t+k}$ is calculated by using a forgetting factor α. Starting from a series of stationary demand, Gilbert demonstrated that the stock and order are also ARMA [16]. The ARMA model is a special case of the ARIMA model mentioned above. It treats the stationary series. If the series is not stationary, its variable is integrated until stationarity, hence the letter I in the model name. In the model below, we assume that the order policy is the classical "Order up to policy".

$$I_t = I_{t-1} + O_{t-L} - D_t. \tag{2}$$

and

$$O_t = S - I_t + \hat{D}_t(1) + \cdots + \hat{D}_t(L) - O_{t-1} - \cdots - O_{t-L+1}. \tag{3}$$

By definition, S is the level of safety stock required to limit stock-outs. A study that generalizes this order policy was also proposed by Gilbert and Chatpattananan [17]. The ARMA model also allows the chain to represent a widely known vulnerability in the field of supply chain, known as the bullwhip effect [1, 5, 16]. It represents the amplification phenomenon of demand variability in the stages upstream in the supply chain. The proposed model allows evaluation of the bullwhip effect on the stock and on the order. Note that another phenomenon is also studied in the literature regarding the reverse bullwhip effect. It aims to evaluate the amplification of disturbances in the prices of raw materials on the downward stages and determine its effect on the product's final cost [18].

2.2 The Constrained Model

The model of the supply chain presented above does not take into account the constraints of the companies. In real cases, the company has a limited storage capacity and cannot order more than a maximal amount of products from the supplier. At the other end of the feasibility intervals, the level of the stock and the quantity delivered cannot have negative values. To take these constraints into account, Sakli et al. [5] present a saturated ARMA model, in which the dynamic Eqs. (2)–(3) are replaced by the following non-linear equations.

Inventory equations. Due to the limits on the storage capacity, the current inventory level is computed by:

$$\begin{cases} I_t = \min(I_{t-1} + O_{t-L} - D_t, \bar{I}) \\ I_t = \max(I_{t-1} + O_{t-L} - D_t, 0) \end{cases} \tag{4}$$

Order equations. Due to the limits on the quantity ordered, the current order is computed by:

$$\begin{cases} O_t = \min \quad (S - I_t + \hat{D}_t(1) + \cdots + \hat{D}_t(L) - O_{t-1} - \cdots - O_{t-L+1}, \bar{O}) \\ O_t = \max \quad (S - I_t + \hat{D}_t(1) + \cdots + \hat{D}_t(L) - O_{t-1} - \cdots - O_{t-L+1}, 0) \end{cases} \tag{5}$$

2.3 Representation of the Quality Problem

When a requested quantity is produced or delivered, this amount may not have the desired quality or be delivered within the scheduled time. The variation of product quality can be caused by the production process, but also by the delivery, because of the handling or transport of the goods or by storage. The amount of products that do not meet the desired quality can either be returned to the supplier, be accepted by the company at a lower price, or considered as waste and therefore discarded. This depends on the nature of the goods and the severity of the defect.

Let z_t be an index of the quality of supply in period t. The quality of goods is supposed variable in time. Two cases are analyzed in this study: either z_t is random with variations around a mean value or O_t takes two values: 0 and 1 with deterministic jumps occurring at random times.

Case of random variations. An example of random variations is when z_t is supposed ARIMA (0, 1, 1). In fact, this model of quality must be truncated as follows, to avoid quality values under 0 or above 1.

$$\begin{cases} e_t & N(0,sigma) \\ \zeta_t = h + e_t \\ z_t = \zeta_t \ if \ 0 \le \zeta_t \le 1 . \\ z_t = 1 \ if \ \zeta_t > 1 \\ z_t = 0 \ if \ 0 < \zeta_t \end{cases} \tag{6}$$

Case of deterministic values with random jumps. A typical example of this case is given by formula (7).

$$\begin{cases} z_t = 1 \ if \ 0 \le t < T1 \quad Or \quad if \ T2 \le t < T3 \quad Or \quad if \ T4 \le t \le T \\ z_t = 0 \ if \ T1 \le t < T2 \quad Or \quad if \ T3 \le t < T4 \end{cases} . \tag{7}$$

T1, T2, T3 and T4 are random dates that may be obtained in simulation from uniform laws in given intervals.

$z_t = 1$ is the case when the quantity ordered respects the desired quality. The opposite case, $z_t = 0$ represents the case when the supplier cannot deliver the requested products with the required quality. Such a case may be due to interruption of production (machines' breakdown, strikes, etc.), or transportation problems.

Whatever the law of evolution of z, the dynamic equation of evolution of the stock is constrained by saturation values in the following form:

$$\begin{cases} I_t = \min(I_{t-1} + O_{t-L} * z_t - D_t, \quad \bar{I}) \\ I_t = \max(I_{t-1} + O_{t-L} * z_t - D_t, \quad 0) \end{cases} . \tag{8}$$

It can be noted that the unconstrained model is bilinear. Moreover, integration of constraints as in Sect. 2.2 introduces other nonlinearities. To compensate for the lack of reliability of the supplier, it is possible to adjust the value of the quantity to order based on the predicted quality of delivery. For this, we propose to build a quality predictor, taking value $\hat{z}_t$ at time t. Under this assumption and after introduction of constraints saturation, the equation for the order is:

$$\begin{cases} O_t = \min \quad (\frac{1}{\hat{z}_t} * (S - I_t + \hat{D}_t(1) + \cdots + \hat{D}_t(L) - O_{t-1} - \cdots - O_{t-L+1}), \quad \bar{O}) \\ O_t = \max \quad (\frac{1}{\hat{z}_t} * (S - I_t + \hat{D}_t(1) + \cdots + \hat{D}_t(L) - O_{t-1} - \cdots - O_{t-L+1}), \quad 0) \end{cases} . \tag{9}$$

For example, a predictor $\hat{z}_t$ can be calculated recursively with a forgetting factor f as follows:

$$\hat{z}_t = (1-f) * \hat{z}_{t-1} + f * z_{t-1}. \tag{10}$$

In the previous expression, z_{t-1} is known, measured at time $t-1$ by inspection of the delivery of order O_{t-L+1}, which has just been received at time $t-1$.

Equations (9) tend to increase the order from the supplier up to its maximal capacity. This increase corresponds to the collaboration mechanism between the supplier and the producer to better satisfy customers.

Detecting the saturation of the system further allows the construction of indices that keep in memory the information on the occurrence of saturation.

$$\text{Saturation index of the inventory:} \begin{cases} II_t = -1 & \text{if} \quad I_t = 0 \\ II_t = 0 & \text{if} \quad 0 < I_t < \bar{I}. \\ II_t = 1 & \text{if} \quad I_t = \bar{I} \end{cases} \tag{11}$$

$$\text{Saturation index of the order:} \begin{cases} OI_t = -1 & \text{if} \quad O_t = 0 \\ OI_t = 0 & \text{if} \quad 0 < O_t < \bar{O}. \\ OI_t = 1 & \text{if} \quad O_t = \bar{O} \end{cases} \tag{12}$$

3   A Case Study

The case study concerns a basic two-stage supply chain with a company (producer) and its supplier. The company receives random orders from customers. The demand is supposed ARMA (0, 1, 1) with a fixed delivery lead time L, and is written as follows. Here ε_t denotes as the white noise, representing an additive system disturbance.

$$D_t = \bar{D} + \varepsilon_t. \tag{13}$$

A demand predictor is constructed by recursive forecast with forgetting factor α:

$$\hat{D}_t = (1-\alpha) * \hat{D}_{t-1} + \alpha * D_{t-1}. \tag{14}$$

In numerical examples, the selected value of the forgetting factor is $\alpha = 0.15$. The curves of demand D_t and predicted demand $\hat{D}_t$ are shown in Fig. 1.

To validate the analytical results, we represent the influence of changes in quality in the two cases previously presented. For both cases, the system is simulated with and without a quality predictor given by (10) with forgetting factor $f = 0.55$, to evaluate the accuracy and effectiveness of this predictor to improve the system resilience.

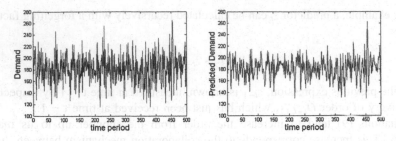

Fig. 1. Curve of demand and predicted demand

3.1 Simulation Under the Multiplicative Quality Disturbance

Firstly, we simulate the system dynamics with a random quality index z_t. The mean value of quality is supposed to be 0.8. Of course, this value is not supposed to be known by the producer, who computes the order value by formula (9).

Simulation Without Quality Disturbance Prediction. The quality index z_t is simulated by formula (6). Figure 3 describes the evolutions of the inventory I_t computed by (8) and the order O_t computed by (9) with $\hat{z}_t = 1$. In this simulation, the quality defects are unknown and there is no prediction of the quality index ($\hat{z}_t = 1$). This figure provides some insights on the system behavior. In particular, it can be noted that the inventory level is often zero and the inventory index (11) takes value -1. It represents the case when demand D_t is greater than the quantity available in stock I_t (Fig. 2).

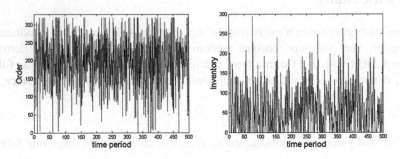

Fig. 2. Order and inventory evolutions with $\hat{z}_t = 1$

Due to the high frequency of stock-outs, it seems necessary to take into account the quality perturbation in the order process.

Simulation with Quality Disturbance Prediction. Under the quality index predicted by formula (10), the system has a less vulnerable behavior. It can be observed on Fig. 3 that the mean value of inventory seems stationary. However, the order values computed by (9) are frequently hitting the maximal delivery level.

3.2   Simulation with Quality Jumps at Random Times

The system is now simulated under random jumps of the quality percentage between 0 and 1 at random times. Again, the system is first simulated without any quality disturbance predictor ($\hat{z}_t = 1$) and with the same predictor as in the previous example ($\hat{z}_t$ given by (10)).

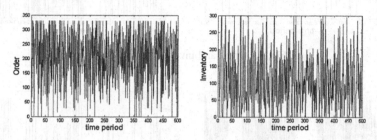

Fig. 3. Order and inventory evolutions

In this numerical example, the dates T1 = 177, T2 = 227, T3 = 395 and T4 = 431 have been chosen at random by uniform laws in given intervals of dates. As shown in Fig. 4, the quality index is 1 between the dates (0: 177), (228: 395) and (432: 500). In these intervals, quality is perfect and there is no defective products discarded. On the contrary, the quality index is zero between dates (178: 227) and (396: 431).

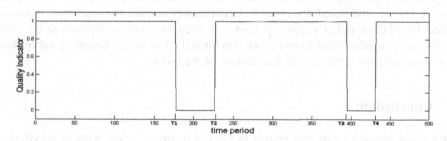

Fig. 4. A curve of quality index evolution with randomly generated commutations

Simulation Without Quality Disturbance Prediction. We have first simulated the system with $\hat{z}_t = 1$ $\forall t \in [0 \quad 500]$. Figure 5 illustrates the order and inventory evolutions without any prediction of the quality index.

Simulation with Quality Disturbance Prediction. To predict the quality index, we use formula (10) again, with forgetting factor f = 0.55. The curve of the estimated index is very close to the quality index of Fig. 4. However, it can be observed on Fig. 6 that the order and inventory evolutions are still strongly disturbed around the dates of the states changes.

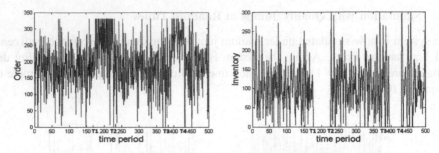

Fig. 5. Order and inventory evolutions

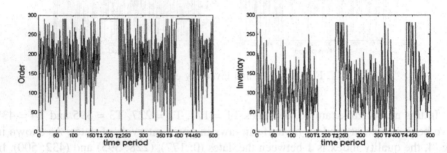

Fig. 6. Order and inventory evolutions

It is clear that the system gets out of stock throughout the supplier interruption period. On the other hand, the order level commonly reaches the maximum threshold value 330 of the supplier's capacity. However, such a systematic increase of the order level during supplier breakdown periods has limited effect on the inventory curve since deliveries are zero regardless of the amount of the order.

4   Conclusion

This paper presented concepts related to risks in a supply chain, namely uncertainty, vulnerability and resilience. We proposed a nonlinear model based on time series ARMA for representing a supply chain, taking into account the constraints of the real system. Then, we simulated the system subject to random disturbances on demand and supply, under positivity and capacity constraints on the quantity ordered and available stock. Two types of quality disturbances from the supplier were simulated. In both cases, it is clear that without taking into account the quality index, the system often is often out of stock and gets into strong disturbance that propagate upward and downward the supply chain. To mitigate that problem, we have proposed to construct a quality predictor, and we have introduced it into the formula for calculating the order quantity. If out of stock, the company orders a larger quantity often equal to the maximum capacity of the supplier. This corrective policy appears to be efficient in the case of random fluctuations of the quality. But its impact is rather limited in the all-or-nothing supply quality case.

References

1. Lee, H.L., Padmanabhan, V., Whang, W.: Information distortion in a supply chain: the bullwhip effect. Manage. Sci. **43**(4), 546–558 (1997)
2. So, K.C., Zheng, X.: Impact of supplier's lead time and forecast demand updating on retailer's order quantity variability in a two-level supply chain. Int. J. Prod. Econ. **86**, 169–179 (2003)
3. Huang, G.Q., Lau, J.S.K., Mak, K.L.: The impacts of sharing production information on supply chain dynamics : a review of the literature. Int. J. Prod. Res. **41**, 1483–1517 (2003)
4. Babai, M.Z., Ali, M.M., Boylan, J.E., Syntetos, A.A.: Forecasting and inventory performance in a two-stage supply chain with ARIMA (0, 1, 1) demand: theory and empirical analysis. Int. J. Prod. Econ. **143**(2), 463–471 (2013)
5. Sakli L., Hennet J.-C., Mercantini, J.-M.: An analysis of risks and vulnerabilities in supply networks. In: Elsevier, Preprints of the 19 th World IFAC Congress, pp. 8933–8938, Cape Town South Africa, IFAC (2014)
6. Manuj, I., Mentzer, J.T.: Global supply chain risk management. J. Bus. Logistics **29**, 133–155 (2008)
7. ISO-IEC guide 73. http://www.iso.org
8. Hennet, J.C., Mercantini, J.M., Demongodin, I.: Toward an integration of risk analysis in supply chain assessment. In: Proceeding of I3 M-EMSS, pp. 255–260 (2008)
9. Wagner, S.M., Bode, C.: An empirical investigation into supply chain vulnerability. J. Purchasing Supply Manage. **12**, 301–312 (2006)
10. Tang, O., Musa, S.N.: Identifying risk issues and research advancements in supply chain risk management. Int. J. Prod. Econ. **33**, 25–34 (2010)
11. ISO 2009. http://www.iso.org
12. Wagner, S.M., Bode, C.: Dominant Risks and Risk management Practices in supply chain. In: Zsidisin, G.A., Ritchie, B. (eds.) Supply Chain Risk: A Handbook of Assessment, Management, and Performance, pp. 271–292. Springer, Berlin (2008)
13. Asbjørnslet, B.E.: Assessing the vulnerability of supply chain. In: Zsidisin, G.A., Ritchie, B. (eds.) Supply Chain Risk: A Handbook of Assessment, Management, and Performance, pp. 271–292. Springer, Berlin (2008)
14. Ponomarov, S.Y., Holcomb, M.C.: Understanding the concept of supply chain resilience. Int. J. of Logistics Manage. **20**, 124–143 (2009)
15. Box, G.E.P., Jenkins, G.M.: Time Series Analysis: Forecasting and Control. Holden-Day, San Francisco (1976)
16. Gilbert, K.C.: An ARIMA supply chain model. Manage. Sci. **51**, 305–310 (2005)
17. Gilbert, K.C., Chatpattananan, V.: An ARIMA supply chain model with a generalized ordering policy. J. Model. Manage. **1**, 33–51 (2006)
18. Rong, Y., Snyder, L.V., Zuo-Jun, M.S.: Bullwhip and reverse bullwhip effects under the rationing game (2008). http://dx.doi.org/10.2139/ssrn.1240173

Network Formation

System of Systems Architecting: A Behavioural and Properties Based Approach for SoS "–ilities" Modelling and Analysis

Vincent Chapurlat[✉] and Nicolas Daclin

LGI2P Ecole Des Mines D'Alès,
69 Rue G. Besse, 30035 Nîmes Cedex 1, France
{Vincent.Chapurlat,Nicolas.Daclin}@mines-ales.fr

Abstract. Architecting a System of Systems (SoS) is a complex task. Capabilities of heterogeneous and interactive sub-systems are composed to fulfil a mission, while preserving, as possible, the autonomy, independence, geographic distribution... of sub-systems and to face up efficiently while remaining as resilient as possible to disturbances and emergent phenomenon. The "–ilities" are relevant non-functional abilities (*e.g.* robustness, resilience, flexibility, adaptability, survivability, interoperability...) for guiding SoS architects and managers to choose and interface sub-systems. The goal is to become able to increase or decrease the value of these "–ilities" thanks to their interest for the SoS mission. The here presented work aims to support resilient SoS design and, in particular, their architecting by proposing a formalised model of property allowing to define and describe an "–ility" and a behavioural modelling approach to evaluate it.

Keywords: System of systems · "–ilities" · Non-functional properties · Resilience · SoS behavioural modelling · Dependencies · Formalisation

1 Introduction

A System of Systems (SoS) is composed of (in most cases, existing) heterogeneous sub systems chosen for their capabilities, assembled and interfaced to interact during a time-frame and to provide capabilities to achieve a mission that each sub system cannot fulfil alone [1]. First, some characteristics of sub systems must be preserved: operational and managerial independence, evolutionary development, geographic distribution, and connectivity. Second, requested interactions induce emergent phenomenon (new properties and behaviours with more or less predictable and unwanted effects) at the SoS level that can favour or affect the achievement of its objectives and mission. Third, it is now recognized, for SoS, the relevance of specific properties called "–ilities". An "–ility"[1] is an *"ability to respond to changes, both foreseeable and unforeseeable"* focusing on *"how the SoS should be and not what it should do"* [2].

---

[1] An "–ility" (plural "–ilities") [5] is *"a developmental, operational, and support requirements a program must address (e.g. availability, maintainability, vulnerability, reliability, supportability"* which are generally non-functional requirements.

© IFIP International Federation for Information Processing 2015
L.M. Camarinha-Matos et al. (Eds.): PRO-VE 2015, IFIP AICT 463, pp. 591–603, 2015.
DOI: 10.1007/978-3-319-24141-8_55

For a SoS, "-ilities" differ from authors, but essentials ones remain: robustness, resilience, flexibility, adaptability, survivability, interoperability, sustainability, reliability, availability, maintainability and safety; each "-ility" can be strongly dependant or influenced by various causes considering SoS context, evolution period of its life cycle and emerging phenomenon. So, architecting a SoS implies to study these "-ilities" and how to increase or decrease their values thanks to their interest for the SoS purpose. Particularly, SoS has to face up, efficiently and accordingly to its mission, to various dynamic contexts in which disturbances can occur due to disruptive actions (from SoS environment or internal sub-systems failures [2]) or to new and enabled technological evolutions i.e., it has to maximise its resilience. The here presented work aims to help and support resilient SoS design, particularly architecting step of the design. Section 2 introduces two approaches for resilient SoS architecting that can be combined with a behavioural modelling approach named OMAG, briefly introduced. In Sect. 3, retained SoS "-ilities" and their interdependence are discussed and formalised. Section 4 illustrates the proposed contributions before concluding.

2 Resilient SoS Architecting

Architecting a resilient SoS means to consider various interdependent "-ilities" and new design approaches. References [3, 4] insists on *"designing for resilience is about creating a system that can bounce back from something no one ever thought would happen"*. Existing approaches are strongly based on system paradigm and follows Systems Engineering principles [24]. In the next we discuss about requested "-ilities" and two approaches.

Various "-ilities" definitions can be found [6–8]. The concept of "-ility" can be used to characterize both SoS and each of its sub-systems. As illustrated in Fig. 1, it is admitted that an "-ility" dynamically vary and is dependant or influenced all along SoS life cycle depending on (1) its characteristics (properties, behaviours and "-ilities"), (2) the characteristics (properties, behaviours, and –ilities) of its sub-systems, and (3) emergent properties and behaviours from sub-systems' interactions.

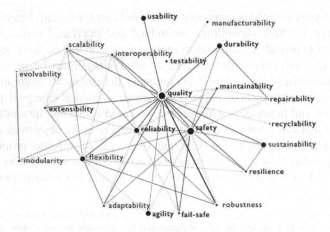

Fig. 1. Overview of "-ilities" dependencies [7]

For instance DoD [6] presents resilience as dependant from robustness, flexibility and protection "–ilities". Following the same dependence principles, robustness depends from reliability, availability, survivability and maintainability. In the same way, the DSTA framework [2] considers two levels of SoS "–ilities": Key SoS "–ilities" (robustness and evolvability) and Key Enabling "–ilities" (flexibility (operational and design) and interoperability) that have been enriched in Fig. 2 by decomposing interoperability definition.

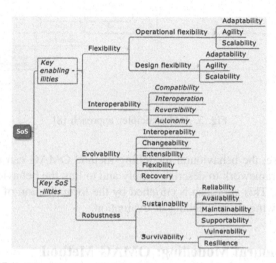

Fig. 2. Key SoS "–ilities" and enabling "–ilities" (inspired from DSTA framework [2])

In both cases, whatever the definition for "-ility" and its interdependence with other abilities of the SoS, an "–ility" remains difficult to conceptualize from a unified manner (that can be even not expected), to handle and to use in confidence in architecting process [9–12].

Concerning SoS architecting approaches, first SAI (SoS Architecting with Ilities) [8] focuses on value sustainment of both functional and non-functional requirements. Figure 3 shows the essential steps of SAI, especially the steps 4 (Generate initial architecture alternatives) and 6 (Evaluate potential alternatives) in which a behavioural model of the SoS architecture is built and executed for evaluating the chosen "-ilities" defined in step 3. Second, DSTA framework [2] is a methodological framework for supporting SoS architecting and a reference framework for choosing the most relevant "–ilities" allowing practitioners and manager to drive and manage efficiently SoS architecting. In both approaches, the SoS architecting phase (i.e., defining strategy, requested operations and scenarios, and specifying architectural alternatives according to a more or less high level of abstraction) is apart from SoS designing phase (for instance, choice and interfacing of sub-systems, validating scenarios). In design phase, several solutions are proposed in [10] to improve various "–ilities" to gain resilience e.g. employing redundancy, reducing complexity or improving reparability. Alternatives solutions must be modelled and compared thanks to an expected value (quantitative or qualitative) level for each "-ility".

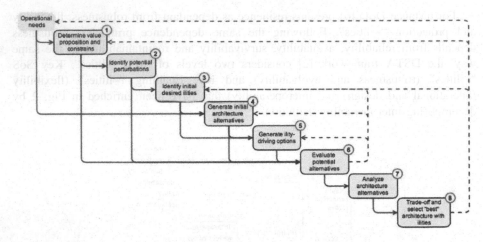

Fig. 3. SAI principles approach [8]

To this purpose, the behavioural modelling method OMAG can support both SAI steps and DSTA framework to describe simply and to link the behaviours of a SoS and of its sub-systems. This approach is enriched by the formalisation of a set of "–ilities" by properties allowing their checking or evaluation.

3   SoS Behavioural Modelling: OMAG Method

OMAG (Operating Modes Analysis Guide) [13] is a behavioural and functional modelling and analysis method allowing:

- System architect to select the **Operating Modes** [14] that characterize a system all along its life cycle.
- To determine gradually the expected **Properties** (functional and non-functional i.e. "–ilities") and **Parameters** of the system when evolving into a mode.
- To determine gradually and to model various **Operational Scenarios**. It is question of a functional model describing the dynamic of a system (what are the expected functions or activities and how they are chained and synchronised?) in a given operating mode. Various modelling languages can be used e.g. BPMN, eFFBD, or use case diagram. In OMAG approach, each operational scenario describes a part of the whole expected functional architecture of the system.

OMAG is based on a graphical grid shown in Appendix, detailed and illustrated in [13]. Briefly, the OMAG principles are summarized in Fig. 4. Considering a system, OMAG requires defining first systems' attributes and to gather them into a *ParametersAndPropertiesSet*. An attribute is modelled as a *Parameter*, a valued and typed data describing time (temporal aspect e.g. maximum delays for reaction), shape (structure e.g. geometric constraints) or space (situation e.g. non-functional expectation) characteristics of any element from the system or its environment.

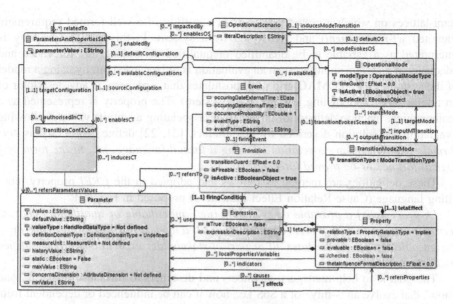

Fig. 4. OMAG main elements meta model (simplified view)

The *ParametersAndPropertiesSet* is set up and grows up gradually all along the architecting process. The set of generic Operating Modes and Transitions is then formalised by the grid and the architect must select those relevant for the system and to be studied. Each transition is characterized by a couple (condition/event) allowing system evolving from an operating to the next. For each mode and transition, architect has to model what are the expected operational scenarios allowed in the studied Mode or induced/expected to fire the transition. Figure 4 shows the main elements of a grid OMAG allowing to describe and link operating modes, operational scenarios associated to each mode, parameters and properties of a system. The result is a behavioural model of the studied system conforms to the underlying mathematical formalism (inspired from Finite State Machine model [15]). Each operating mode is modelled as a state and each mode transition as a state transition. An operational semantic of OMAG grid is given in [13] specifying formally with no ambiguity the interpretation and execution rules of an OMAG grid. This allows then defining and implementing OMAG grid simulation and proof mechanisms not detailed here. These mechanisms allow to model and verify properties (modelling properties as non-functional properties), to approximate "–ilities" values, or to highlight rapidly some disturbing or awkward situations the SoS has to face. This can be helpful for SoS architect who intends to test and compare various SoS architectural alternatives as requested, for instance, in SAI approach.

4   SoS –ilities and –ilities Dependence Modelling: Property Concept

A *'property'* is defined in [18] as "*an entity that can be predicated of a thing or, in other words, attributed to it (also called 'attribute', 'quality', 'feature', 'characteristic' or 'type')*"?. [19] introduced a Property-Based Requirements (PBR) theory based on semi-lattices on which a property formalizes a portion of a well-formed requirement (denoted *wf-requirement*) and be owned by a system. In this case, a property is interpreted as a variable to be quantified or qualified to evaluate the relevance and adequacy of a system solution; such an evaluation is to be carried out by using a model of the system here, an OMAG grid. [20] postulates that a property is any descriptor of an artefact (i.e., a modelling artefact of the system). The property is represented as a mathematical function defined for this artefact, associating a (set of) value(s) allowing evaluating the solution described by this artefact. [21, 22] define a property as *"the formal statement of an expectation by using a formal language, i.e., in the form of a logical formula to be proved later"*.

These definitions are merged as follows and adopted in the *CREI* property modelling language (Cause Relation Effect Indicators) proposed in [16, 17]:

[A property is] a provable or evaluable (i.e., quantifiable or qualifiable) characteristic of an artefact [that is (1) a system S, or (2) a model M of S built for achieving a design objective] that translates all or part of stakeholder expectations to be satisfied by this artefact.

The goal is to help managers, architects and designers to formalise "what is" and "how" can evolve an "–ility" of a SoS i.e., how it can be influenced or dependent from (1) other characteristics of SoS, (2) conditions taking into account external and internal events, but also (3) characteristics related to each sub-systems of SoS or resulting from their interactions.

A *CREI* property is formalized as a composite entity made up of a group of causes (C) correlated with a group of effects (E) via a parameterized and constrained relation (R) between C and E describing the condition and the expected effects under which the property is satisfied. This relationship formally describes how the set of causes C induces a modification in the entire set of effects E. Moreover, a set I of indicators can be associated with R to make property assessable. These indicators are the *observation variable and Design variables*[2] [20]. For the formalization, we define the set Φ as the set of user-defined or predefined properties of the studied system. A *CREI Property CP* is defined as:

$$CP ::= \; < reference_{cp}, \; C, \; R, \; E, \; checkingValue_{cp}, \; [I, \; evaluationValue_{cp}] >$$

With:

- $reference_{cp} \in S$ is a handle (unique) for property proof traceability.
- $C = \{v_i \, / v_i \in ParametersSet \cup \Phi, \, i \in [0; \, card(ParametersSet \cup \Phi)]\}$, *i.e.*, C can be empty $(C = \varnothing)$: the property is then considered to be an *own property*[3], otherwise $(C \diamond \varnothing)$ as a *composite property*[4].
- $E = \{v_j \, / v_j \in F \cup \Phi, \, j \in \,]0; \, card(F \cup \Phi)]\}$ *i.e.*, $E \diamond \varnothing$.
- $R:: = \; < T_p, \; \theta_c, \; \theta_e, \; relationType, \; \theta_i >$, where:

---

[2] An *observation variable* allows modelling an expected performance level or an expected *"i-lity"* level. A *design variable* allows to handle and to set up values corresponding with potential design choices.

[3] An *own property* models expected values of a (set of) Parameter(s).

[4] A *composite property* is to be characterized by the causal relation.

- $T_p = C \cap E$ is the set of variables that may be simultaneously used for describing causes and effects.
- θ_c: T_p^k x C^m x $\mathbb{R}^{+^*n} \rightarrow$ {$True, False$} defines the Boolean function describing the condition under which the causes of C are interpreted. By default, the function θ_c returns $True$ (denoted θ_c = True in the next):
  - $(t_1, ..., t_k, c_1, ..., c_m, r_1, ..., r_n) \rightarrow \theta_c(t_1, ..., t_k, c_1, ..., c_m, r_1, ..., r_n) \in$ {True, False}

- θ_e: T_p^o x E^p x $\mathbb{R}^{+^*q} \rightarrow$ {$True, False$} defines the Boolean function describing the condition under which the effects of E are interpreted. By default, the function θ_e returns $False$ (denoted θ_e = False in the next):
- $(t_1, ..., t_o, e_1, ..., e_p, r_1, ..., r_q) \rightarrow \theta_e(t_1, ..., t_o, e_1, ..., e_p, r_1, ..., r_q) \in$ {True, False}

- At this stage, *relationType* models the relation to be checked: *'C implies E'*, *'C is equivalent to E'*, or *'C influences E'* formalized as follows:
  - *'C implies E'* is defined as the logical function: $\theta_c \implies \theta_e$
  - *'C is equivalent to E'* is defined as the logical function: $\theta_c \iff \theta_e$
  - *'C influences E'* is defined as the function: $\theta_c \dashrightarrow_{\theta_i} \theta_e$. This relation is defined by [23] as "*in knowing with certainty C, we can then deduce E with certainty*", *i.e.*, knowing the values (and their variation) of the causes defined defined in E by defining an *influence factor* $\theta_i \in [-1,1]$ allowing to interpret a beneficial *vs.* harmful influence as follows:
    - $\theta_i \rightarrow 0$: the influence exists between the causes and effects remaining more or less neutral (by default, $\theta_i = 0$);
    - $\theta_i \rightarrow 1$: each variation of the variables used in C induces a variation of the variables used in E, interpreted as beneficial for the system;
    - $\theta_i \rightarrow -1$: each variation of the variables used in C, induces a variation of the variables used in E, interpreted as harmful for the system;
- *checkingValue$_{cp}$* is set to True, else False (*i.e.*, if a checking technique can be applied on the model for proving the property CP and can conclude CP is satisfied, False otherwise, thus providing a counterexample).
- (*optional*) [I, *evaluationValue$_{cp}$*] $I \subseteq ParametersSet$ is a set of indicators that can be evaluated to characterize the truthfulness of the property CP (*e.g.* in case of simulation or for guiding the appraisal): $I = \{i_j / i_j \in ParametersSet, j \in [0, card (ParametersSet)]\}$, where i_j is a *Modeling Variable* extracted from the system model. In case of I is defined, then $CP.evaluationValue_{cp} = \mu(I)$, where μ is the *aggregation function* chosen for the evaluation, *e.g.* μ can be defined by $\mu :: = 1/card(I)^* \sum_I (i.value)$. CP can be considered as satisfied as proposed in [19] *i.e.* $CP.checkingValue_{cp}$ = True if and only if $\forall i \in I$, $i.value \in i.objectif \wedge i.value \in i.valueset$ otherwise not satisfied, *i.e.*, $CP.checkingValue_{cp}$ = False.

As an illustration, we focus on the next on the interoperability of each sub-system making up the SoS, considering the 'key enabling –ility' role of this characteristic [2] and its direct influence on the objectives of resilient SoS architecting project.

For this, we consider (see Fig. 5) there are some dependencies to respect (evaluated by using 5 levels of dependencies from preferred to forbidden) between the operating modes of the SoS and the operating modes of sub-system at each moment, taking into account their dynamical evolution. For instance, when the SoS works and fulfil the mission (SoS is in Operating Mode O3), it seems important (++) that a maximum of sub-systems can be able to provide their own mission, and to operate efficiently (sub-systems have to be preferably in Operating Modes O1 to O5). Some of these sub-systems can also (+) be under deployment (operating Mode D1) for instance if these sub-systems have to replace existing sub-systems at a given moment, assuming then architectural evolution of the SoS. Conversely, it seems inacceptable (–) that a sub-system must be in dismantling operating mode (EL1 or EL2). These interdependencies are, of course, indicative: architect can modify them without any impact on the property formalisation and analysis that follows. Other tables can be built for maintainability, resilience or robustness as expected in [2].

The interoperability characteristic of the SoS is formalized as the property P as follows:

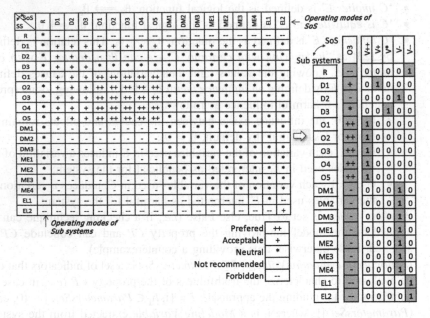

Fig. 5. Operating modes dependencies considering requested interoperability

1. **Cause** : = $\forall OM_{SoS} \in$ OperatingModes(SoS); OMAG grid behaviour is translated into symbolic logico-temporal formulae. Each transition between Operating Modes selected by architect is modelled as an *Elementary Valid Formula* (*EVF*) [26] modified as follows[5]:

   $$EVF :: = (OM_i \wedge event_j \wedge condition_k \supset oOM_l \wedge scenario_m)$$

---

[5] The formula o**A** means that the propositional variable **A** will be true at the next moment in a common logical and unified time scale.

With:

- **OM$_i$** and **OM$_l$** are propositional variables modelling the source and destination operating modes of the transition, and set to True if the studied system is in the corresponding operating mode, false otherwise.
- **event$_j$** and **condition$_k$** are propositional variables set to True if event and condition associated to the transition are True, false otherwise.

The entire list of *EVFs* defines a symbolic and formal description of the behaviour of the OMAG grid. Similarly, a *Unified Valid Formula* (*UVF*) is computed by taking *EVFs* into consideration. Here considered, an *UVF* is the set of conditions i.e. θ_c which specifies how a given Operating Mode *OM* can be activated:

$$\theta_c := UVF(oOM_{SoS}) = \bigvee_{\substack{(p,q,r) \\ OM_{SoS} \wedge event_q \wedge condition_r \supset oOM_{SoS}}} OM_{SoS} \wedge event_q \wedge condition_r$$

2. **Relation** : = (influences); **Indicators** are user-defined and computed including parameters associated to sub-systems *e.g.* the latency time or interoperation time as proposed in [25].
3. **Effect** : = SS$_i$ ∈ SubSystems(SoS); Fig. 5 shows how dependency vectors (denoted V++, V+, V*, V- and V—) are computed regarding each state of the SoS for a top down analysis of the dependence relations. We focus on the preferred states of the sub-system i.e., those characterized by a dependence relation '++'. The state vector V of the SoS (resp. sub-system) is 1×18 vector defined as follows:

$$\exists!k \in [1,18], \left[(V(k) == 1) \underset{SoSisinOMi}{\Rightarrow} \forall j \in [1,18], j \neq k, (V(j) == 0) \right]$$

(there are 18 possible operating modes in the current OMAG grid and the sub-system SS$_i$ must be in one and only one operating mode OM$_k$)
So θ_e is defined as follows:

$$\forall i, \left[(V(OM(SS_i), t) * V^T_{++} == 1) \wedge \neg \prod_{T_k}(condition_i \wedge event_i)] \right.$$
$$\left. \vee [FVU(oOM(SS_i))] \right.$$

Where:

- T$_k$ is the set of output transitions from the preferred operating mode OM of the sub-system SS$_i$ that is preferred when SoS is in operating mode OM$_{SoS}$.
- $(V(OM(SS_i), t) * V^T_{++} == 1) \wedge \neg \prod_{Ti}(condition_i \wedge event_i)] == 1$ iff SS$_i$ is in the state OM and will stay in this state at the next moment or if the state OM will be activated at the next moment.

The same computation process is used for determining θ_e in the case of dependence relation that indicates the operating mode of SS$_i$ is acceptable, neutral, not recommended or forbidden. In the same way, the same computation approach is used in a bottom-up analysis regarding the dependence relations between each operating mode of each SS$_i$ and SoS operating mode.

Simulation (following operational semantics given in [13]), evaluation of parameters and the generation of counter examples provided by checking technique proposed in [26] and developed in [27] are suitable for allowing architect to detect (1) modelling errors or mistakes, (2) unwanted or unexpected behaviour inducing non-functional properties variation. Figure 6 shows a big picture of the overall approach consisting to use OMAG and properties modelling, checking and evaluation in SAI approach.

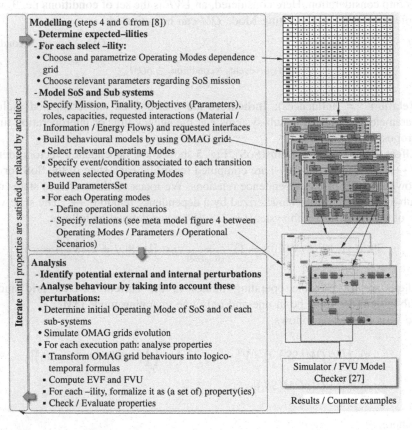

Fig. 6. Overview of the approach (big picture)

5 Conclusion and Perspectives

A demonstrator of the OMAG grid and properties modelling tool is currently being tested. The automated properties building, taking into account various version of dependence tables, properties checking and OMAG grid simulation techniques are under development by using framework developed in [27]. The goal is now to test the overall approach on relevant case studies. The perspective is to enrich the two aforementioned analysis techniques when facing problematic of growing up models' size and complexity (*e.g.* due to number of OMAG to be considered).

Acknowledgement. The authors thank A. Monfouga and R. Blainvillier for their involvement in the development of a demonstrator for modelling OMAG grid.

Appendix: OMAG Grid

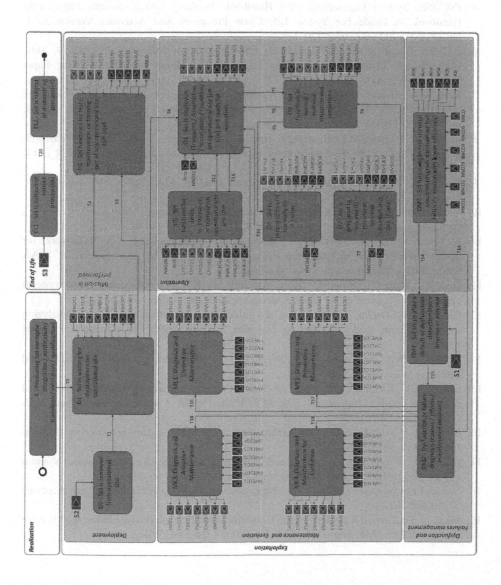

References

1. Maier, M.W.: Architecting principles for systems-of-systems. Syst. Eng. **1**, 267–284 (1998)
2. Shian Chin, K., Eng Yau, P., Kok Wah, S., Chung Khiang, P.: Framework for managing system-of-systems ilities. DSTA Horizons (2013/14)
3. Ferris, T.L.J.: It depends: systems of systems engineering requires new methods if you are talking about new kinds of systems of systems, INCOSE 2006, SoS panel/ (http://www.3milsys.com/sys_of_sys.asp. Accessed 12 July 2011
4. Weck, O., Roos, D., Magee, C.: Engineering Systems: Meeting Human Needs in a Complex Technological World, chapter 4. MIT Press, Cambridge (2012)
5. INCOSE, System Engineering (SE) Handbook Working Group, System Engineering Handbook, A Guide For System Life Cycle Processes And Activities Version 3.2.1, INCOSE TP 2003 002 03.2. (2011)
6. ESD Terms and Definitions (Version 12), ESD Symposium Committee, October 19, 2001, Massachusetts Institute of Technology Engineering Systems Division, Working Paper Series, SD-WP-2002-01
7. Ross, A.M., Rhodes, D.H.: Towards a prescriptive semantic basis for change-type ilities. In: 2015 Conference on Systems Engineering Research, Procedia Computer Science, vol. 44, pp. 443–453 (2015)
8. Ricci, N., Fitzgerald, M.E., Ross, A.M., Rhodes, D.H.: Architecting systems of systems with ilities: an overview of the SAI Method. In: Systems Engineering Research (CSER 2014) (March 21–22 2014)
9. Ross, A.M.: Adaptive and resilient space systems panel. In: AIAA Space 2011, Long Beach, CA (28 September 2011)
10. Vaneman, W.K., Triantis, K.: An analytical approach to assessing emergent behavior is a system of system. In: SEDC 2014, Chantilly, VA (3–5 April 2014)
11. McManus, H.L., Richards, M.G., Ross, A.M., Hastings, D.E.: A framework for incorporating "ilities" in tradespace studies, a collection of technical papers. In: AIAA Space 2007 Conference, vol. 1, pp. 941–954
12. Dou, K., Wang, X., Tang, C., Ross, A., Sullivan, K.: An evolutionary theory-systems approach to a science of the ilities, systems engineering research. In: CSER 2015
13. Chapurlat, V., Daclin, N.: Proposition of a guide for investigating, modeling and analyzing system operating modes: OMAG. In: Complex Systems Design and Management CSDM (2013)
14. Charles, S.W.: System Analysis, Design and Development: Concepts, Principles and Practices. Wiley, New York (2014)
15. Cheng, K.T., Krishnakumar, A.S.: Automatic functional test generation using the extended finite state machine model. In: 30th ACM/IEEE Design Automation Conference, USA (1993)
16. Chapurlat, V.: UPSL-SE: a model verification framework for systems engineering. Comput. Ind. **64**, 581–597 (2013)
17. Chapurlat, V.: Property concept and modelling language for model-based systems engineering (MBSE) context, internal research report (access on demand)
18. Stanford Encyclopedia of Philosophy. http://plato.stanford.edu/entries/properties/. Accessed 31 August 2012
19. Micouin, P.: Toward a property based requirements theory: system requirements structured as a semilattice. Syst. Eng. **11**(3), 235–245 (2008). INCOSE/Wiley

20. Qamar, A., Paredis, C.J.J.: Dependency modeling and model management in mechatronics. In: Proceedings of ASME 2012, International Design Engineering Technical Conference and Computers and Information Engineering Conference, IDET/CIE 2012, USA (August 2012)
21. Dasgupta, P.: A Roadmap for Formal Property Verification. Springer, Berlin (2010). (Bérard et al. 2001). ISBN 978-90-481-7185-9
22. Bérard, B., Bidoit, M., Finkel, A., Laroussinie, F., Petit, A., Petrucci, L., Schnoebelen, P., McKenzie, P.: Systems and Software Verification: Model Checking Techniques and Tools. Springer, Berlin (2001)
23. Pearl, J.: Reasoning with cause and effect. UCLA Cognitive Systems Laboratory, Technical Report (R-265), July 1999. In: AI Magazine, vol. 23(1), pp. 95–111, Spring 2002
24. BKCASE Editorial Board. 2015. The Guide to the Systems Engineering Body of Knowledge (SEBoK), v. 1.3.2 R.D. Adcock (EIC). Hoboken, NJ: The Trustees of the Stevens Institute of Technology. Accessed 23 April 2015
25. Billaud, S., Daclin, N., Chapurlat, V.: Interoperability as a key concept for the control and evolution of the system of systems (SoS). In: van Sinderen, M., Chapurlat, V. (eds.) IWEI 2015. LNBIP, vol. 213, pp. 53–63. Springer, Heidelberg (2015)
26. Chapurlat, V., Larnac, M., Dray G.: Analysis and formal verification of Grafcet (FCCS) using interpreted sequential machine. In: IEEE CESA 1996, Lille, France (July 1996)
27. Nastov, B., Chapurlat, V., Dony, C., Pfister, F.: A verification approach from MDE applied to model based systems engineering: xeFFBD dynamic semantics. In: Complex Systems Design and Management CSDM 2014, Paris, France (December 2014)

Flexibility in the Formation and Operational Planning of Dynamic Manufacturing Networks

Senay Sadic[1,2(✉)], Jorge Pinho de Sousa[1,2], and José António Crispim[2,3]

[1] Faculty of Engineering, University of Porto, Porto, Portugal
{ssadic, jsousa}@inescporto.pt
[2] INESC TEC, Porto, Portugal
crispim@eeg.uminho.pt
[3] School of Economics and Management,
University of Minho, Braga, Portugal

Abstract. The term Dynamic Manufacturing Network (DMN) refers to a new collaborative business model that relies on real-time information sharing, synchronized planning and common business processes. DMNs are operational networks formed among autonomous and globally dispersed partners, and can be seen as the manufacturing industry application of the Virtual Enterprise (VE) concept. Despite their numerous practical benefits such as optimized processes and access to new and global markets, they are particularly vulnerable to disruptions. Any disruption in manufacturing or transportation of products may obviously result in failed orders, thus impacting the whole DMN reliability. Instead of developing stochastic models to deal with uncertainty, as it is usually done, we have rather integrated the concept of flexibility into the tactical and operational planning of such networks. We therefore propose in this work, a multi-objective optimization model that simultaneously maximizes reactive flexibility measures while minimizing total operating costs.

Keywords: Flexibility · Dynamic manufacturing networks · Multi objective optimization

1 Introduction

Global competition, decreased profit margins and market turbulence are forcing supply chains to become dynamic networked structures usually named as Virtual Enterprises (VE), Virtual Organizations (VO), Dynamic Virtual Organizations (DVO), etc. [2]. Within this new paradigm, the concept of Dynamic Manufacturing Network (DMN) has emerged as a manufacturing industry application of VEs that rely on common business processes, real time (or close to real time) information sharing, centralized decision making and optimized operational planning [7, 10].

Despite their numerous benefits such as time savings, cost reduction and visibility, DMNs are hard to plan and vulnerable in their operations [5, 6]. DMN formation requires quick and detailed planning to satisfy demand characteristics (buyer location and expected lead time) through the partner pool (capacities, competencies). Moreover,

© IFIP International Federation for Information Processing 2015
L.M. Camarinha-Matos et al. (Eds.): PRO-VE 2015, IFIP AICT 463, pp. 604–611, 2015.
DOI: 10.1007/978-3-319-24141-8_56

due to the autonomy of partners, a DMN does not completely control their internal operations, this bringing a behavioral risk to its operation. There are also further risk factors that arise from their dispersed structure, such as transportation disruptions and international problems [8]. While facing many disruption risks, reliability is a major performance criterion for DMNs [6]. For these e-commerce based networks, a failed batch not only means a lost order and lost profit, but also possibly significant lost future demand. There is a clear need for mitigating the risks involved in DMN processes.

In this study, reactive flexibility strategies are considered as a factor in DMN planning along with cost. Through integrating two flexibility measures: Slack Time and Slack Capacity into DMN planning, we managed to increase the reactivity of the network to disruptions. For this purpose, a multi-objective mixed integer linear programming (MILP) has been developed. This model aims at finding balanced solutions with minimum total network costs and maximum flexibility.

2   Context

A typical VE goes through a life cycle that is composed of formation, operation, evolution and dissolution stages [11]. In this context, the DMN life cycle is presented in Fig. 1. In the formation stage of DMNs, a business opportunity is received via an e-marketplace, and the DMN formation and planning modules are triggered, to use real time data on partners' capacities and costs. After the network has been formed and the demand has been confirmed, the DMN enters its operation stage. In the operation stage, the DMN monitoring module tracks the execution of the initial plan with the aim of controlling operations.

In case there is a disruption in the execution phase, the necessary actions should be performed to maintain on time delivery [7]. Within the DMN context, we use the term disruption as the deviation from the initial plan, characterized by delays in production or transportation, quality problems, etc. When an operational disruption is tracked and on time delivery is jeopardized, the customer needs to be contacted and recovery actions have to be negotiated. In fact, such a situation will decrease the reliability of the network as perceived by the customer. However, if it is still possible to reconfigure the network, the new real time partner data will be used for re-planning purposes. This may not mean a total reconfiguration of the network, but rather switching partners or transportation modes. Our aim is to do the initial planning by anticipating future disruptions.

For a prompt formation of DMNs, when real time data is available, optimized approaches are required. However, traditional deterministic cost models fail to respond to the flexibility needs of DMNs. A pure cost model may not allow space for reconfiguration if a disruption is detected. Since disruptions are naturally random, and assigning them probabilities is impossible in practice, we chose to increase the reactivity of the network by incurring in a reasonable cost.

3 The Approach

Mixed Integer Linear Programming (MILP) models are commonly used in integrated network formation and operational planning problems, due to their flexibility in encompassing different practical features, and to the reasonable easiness in solving problems to optimality, through commercial solvers. Therefore we have modeled the DMN Planning problem as a deterministic MILP model, with flexibility concerns.

Under the assumption of time independent production and transportation costs, a minimum cost solution is achieved via forward scheduling of the operations. The main reason for adopting forward scheduling is to avoid any stock that would result in extra holding costs for the system. On the other hand, maximum flexibility solution leads to backwards scheduling, selecting all the companies and assigning production as early as possible. However, from a purely economic perspective this is far from ideal. Our aim is to find a trade-off solution, in terms of flexibility measures and cost.

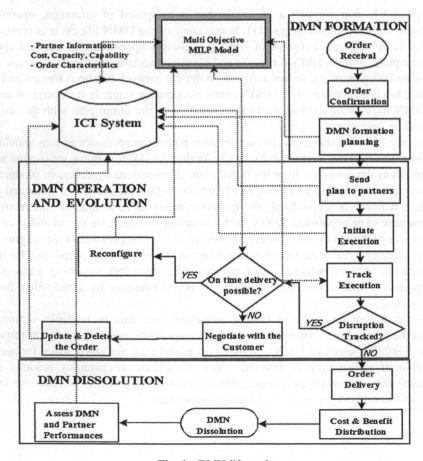

Fig. 1. DMN life cycle

3.1 Flexibility Concerns

Supply chain flexibility can be used as a strategy to deal with potential operational risks and disruptions [3]. Instead of other network formation criteria such as cost, lead time, or quality, flexibility does not represent a fixed performance measure but rather a potential to deal with risks of unknown probability. In the manufacturing context, it can be defined as the capability of a manufacturing system to deal with both internal and external disruptions, while maintaining the competency and profitability levels [4].

In terms of the way to approach risk mitigation, supply chain flexibility strategies can be classified in two main classes: proactive flexibility and reactive (adaptive) flexibility. While proactive strategies are effective in mitigating internal risks, adaptive strategies are utilized to deal with the consequences of disruptions [9]. At this stage reactive flexibility strategies are required to quickly reconfigure the supply chain, in order to compensate disruptions and prevent losses. The reactive (buffering) strategies are safety stock, slack capacity, supplier backups, and slack lead times [1].

In this work we have developed two flexibility measures as total slack lead time and total slack capacity. These two measures will be used as the objectives of the MILP model to maximize total reactive flexibility.

3.2 Model

We present now a generic MILP model to support DMN formation and operational planning. The model is based on the assumption that manufacturing processes of production orders can be broken into several serial production stages.

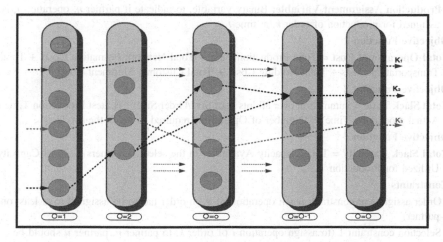

Fig. 2. Network structure

This generic model allows us to change production stages, if different operations are included in the process. We considered a multi-order ($\forall k \in K$), multi-customer ($\forall c \in C$), multi-partner ($\forall n \in N$), multi-echelon ($\forall i \in O$) DMN structure, where each order k goes through manufacturing stages O_k that are a subset of O $(O_k \subset O)$. Moreover, for each operation i $(i \in O)$, there is a subset of partners $(N_i \subset N)$ that are capable of performing operation i. The production allocation and lot sizing decisions will be given within a discrete time horizon, where a unit time period is denoted by t and where the last planning period is denoted as T. The network general characteristics are presented in Fig. 2, and a verbal, synthetic formulation of the model is given in Table 1. To solve the multi-objective problem we have used a weighted sum method.

Table 1. Verbal formulation of the model

Decision variables

• **Production Lot:** Quantity of order k assigned for operation i, at partner n, at time period t

• **Transportation Lot:** Quantity of order k assigned for transportation, from partner n of operation i, to partner m of operation j, at time period t

• **Pre-production Inventory:** Quantity of order k to keep at pre-production inventory of operation i at partner n, at time period t

• **Post-production inventory:** Quantity of order k to keep at post-production inventory of operation i at partner n, at time period t

• **Production Assignment:** Binary variable, to indicate if production of order k is assigned to partner n of operation i, at time period t

• **Transportation Assignment:** Binary variable, to indicate if transportation of order k is assigned, from partner n of operation i, at time period t, to partner m of operation j

• **Manufacturer Selection:** Binary variable, to indicate if partner n is selected for operation i

• **Assignment Variable:** Binary variable, to indicate if partner n, operation i, is assigned for production of order k

• **Production Assignment Variable:** Binary variable, to indicate if partner n, operation i, is assigned for production of order k, at time t

Objective Function 1

Total Operational Cost = Total Production Cost + Total Network Formation Costs + Total Transportation Costs + Total Holding Costs + Total Customer Shipment Cost

Objective Function 2

Total Slack Time = Summation over all lots (Lot Size/Order Size) * (Latest Production Time – Actual production Time) * (Number of Operations required to finish the product)

Objective Function 3

Total Slack Capacity = Total Capacity Available (in the selected partners) – Total Capacity Utilized for Production

Constraints

• Order assignment constraint (each operation of each order has to be assigned to at least one partner)

• Selection constraint 1 (to assign operation i of order k, to partner n, partner n should be selected to be part of the network)

• Selection constraint 2 (if partner n is not included into the network, none of the orders can be assigned to it)

(Continued)

Table 1. (*Continued*)

Decision variables
• Production assignment constraint 1 (to assign operation i of order k at time t to partner n, partner n should be included to production of order k)
• Production assignment constraint 2 (if partner n is not included to production of order k, production cannot be assigned to it at any time period t)
• Production assignment constraint 3 (relating the production lot to binary production decision variables)
• Minimum production lot to initiate production (for each order)
• Capacity constraints for partners
• Minimum total production constraint
• Transportation from a partner is only possible if that partner is included into the network
• Minimum total weight to initiate transportation
• Total transportation capacity constraint
• Flow equation for starting inventories (pre-production)
• Flow equation for finishing inventories (post-production)
• Flow equation for finished orders (inventory or shipment to customers)
• Demand fulfillment
• Transportation capacity constraint from last echelon to customers
• Demand will not be met before due date
• Starting inventories are zero

4 Results

The developed multi-objective MILP model was implemented in and solved with the CPLEX 12.5 optimization software. For assessing the approach, an illustrative network was designed. This network has 3 operations, 6 time periods, and 9 partners, where each echelon has 3 different potential partners to be assessed for assigning production (P1, P2, P3 for operation 1; P4, P5, P6 for operation 2 and P7, P8, P9 for operation 3). Each partner shares their available capacities and detailed costs for the planning horizon. The system also takes into account transportation costs in-between partners. For an easy illustration of the model, we have first considered a single order from a single customer, with a lot size of 200 units to be delivered at time 6. Figure 3 presents three alternative plans we have reached by considering different objective weights. Please note that for this data set, the maximum lead-time is 18, the maximum capacity is 26767, and the minimum cost is 17285 Plan 1, which is the "pure cost" solution, includes one partner per operation (P1, P5, and P12) and forward schedules mainly, with a small slack lead-time of 2.5. Plan 2 is the "pure slack time" solution, where production is totally forward scheduled, with 4 partners (P3, P4, P5, and P10). Plan 3 is a multi-objective solution, with equal weights for each objective, composed of P1, P5 and P12 and has a close to maximum slack lead-time value, with slightly higher cost (5 %). In fact, capacity stays at its minimum (8258) at the balanced solution, since the capacity utilization for this example is low.

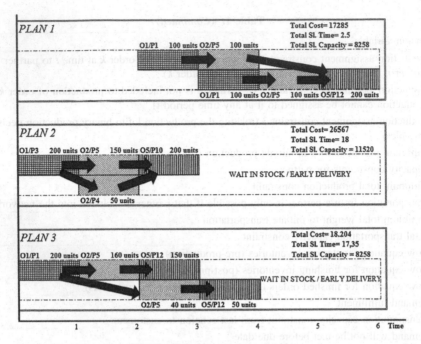

Fig. 3. Solutions to the example

While an increase in *slack time* requires back scheduling and an increasing inventory holding cost, an increase in *slack capacity* requires adding more partners to the network. This is obviously a higher level decision, inducing a higher cost. Further tests also revealed that with multiple orders and high capacity usage, it becomes less costly to include more partners to the network, and split batches among different partners.

5   Conclusions

In this study we have presented a multi-objective model for the formation and operational planning of Dynamic Manufacturing Networks (DMN) that simultaneously minimizes total cost and maximizes reactive flexibility measures. A DMN network is defined as a multi-echelon serial structure, with multiple customers and multiple orders. The total cost function covers production, transportation, holding and network formation costs, from the first echelon to order shipment to the customer. Slack lead time and slack capacity measures were developed, as a way to measure the reactive flexibility of the network. The model allows the decision maker to recognize and understand the trade-offs between cost and flexibility, and to choose the network configuration that best suits to the external conditions, such as how prone the operations are to disruptions and how much the DMN broker is willing to pay for flexibility.

Acknowledgements. This research is partially supported by project "NORTE-07-0124-FEDER-000057" financed by the North Portugal Regional Operational Programme (ON.2 O Novo Norte), under the National Strategic Reference Framework (NSRF), through the European Regional Development Fund (ERDF), and by national funds, through the Portuguese funding agency, Fundação para a Ciência e a Tecnologia (FCT).

References

1. Angkiriwang, R., et al.: Managing uncertainty through supply chain flexibility: reactive vs. proactive approaches. Prod. Manuf. Res. Open Access J. **2**(1), 50–70 (2014)
2. Camarinha-Matos, L.M.: Collaborative networked organizations: Status and trends in manufacturing. Annu. Rev. Control **33**(2), 199–208 (2009)
3. Esmaeilikia, M. et al.: Tactical supply chain planning models with inherent flexibility: definition and review. Ann. Oper. Res. (2014)
4. Gong, Z.: An economic evaluation model of supply chain flexibility. Eur. J. Oper. Res. **184** (2), 745–758 (2008)
5. Li, Y., Liao, X.: Decision support for risk analysis on dynamic alliance. Decis. Support Syst. **42**(4), 2043–2059 (2007)
6. Markaki, O., Kokkinakos, P., Panopoulos, D., Koussouris, S., Askounis, D.: Benefits and risks in dynamic manufacturing networks. In: Emmanouilidis, C., Taisch, M., Kiritsis, D. (eds.) Advances in Production Management Systems, Part II. IFIP AICT, vol. 398, pp. 438–445. Springer, Heidelberg (2013)
7. Papakostas, N., et al.: Organisation and operation of dynamic manufacturing networks, Int. J. Comput. Integr. Manuf. 1–9 (2014)
8. Singh, A.R., et al.: Design of global supply chain network with operational risks. Int. J. Adv. Manuf. Technol. **60**(1–4), 273–290 (2011)
9. Stevenson, M., Spring, M.: Flexibility from a supply chain perspective: definition and review. Int. J. Oper. Prod. Manage. **27**(7), 685–713 (2007)
10. Viswanadham, N., Gaonkar, R.S.: Partner selection and synchronized planning in dynamic manufacturing networks. IIE Trans. Robot. Autom. **19**(1), 117–130 (2003)
11. Wu, N., Su, P.: Selection of partners in virtual enterprise paradigm. Robot. Comput. Integr. Manuf. **21**(2), 119–131 (2005)

Holistic Design of Collaborative Networks of Design Engineering Organizations

Adam Pawlak[1(✉)] and Håvard D. Jørgensen[2]

[1] Silesian University of Technology, Institute of Electronics,
44-100 Gliwice, Poland
adam.pawlak@polsl.pl
[2] Commitment AS, Lysaker, Norway
havard.jorgensen@commitment.no

Abstract. The paper presents a visual knowledge-based approach for designing collaborative networks of engineering design organizations. The novelty of this holistic approach lies in integrated modelling of business, engineering, and learning processes. Distributed design tasks are easier coordinated due to explicit representation of management procedures as visual knowledge models of design flows and workflows. Furthermore, these visual models enable definition of design task patterns that can support design innovation management and learning across distributed teams. Proliferation of this approach in engineering communities is conditioned by availability of appropriate open platforms enabling distributed collaborative design and continuous learning processes in a frame of a collaborative engineering network.

Keywords: Collaborative engineering network · Holistic design · Collaborative network modeling · Active knowledge model · Design house · Design task pattern

1 Introduction

Network-based electronic system design becomes a common engineering paradigm, as a result of ubiquitous access to the broadband Internet and a progress in design engineering technologies [28]. The engineer's workplace gets more and more virtualized [20] with a global access to design resources. This virtualization process transforms both the individual working environment [20], a collaborative work in a distributed team [20], as well as it enables creation of virtual design organizations [6, 7, 30, 31], and additionally networks of collaborating virtual organizations [2], as well as establishment of virtual engineering communities [4, 9]. Network access has a predominant influence on enterprises that deliver design engineering, as a service. These enterprises, called *design houses* achieve a new dimension of flexibility related to the operation on the global market of design resources, partners with complementary competencies, continuous contact with clients, etc. Due to the access to the virtual infrastructures designers' teams from distributed design houses may undertake new innovative complex and heterogonous designs. New design approaches become feasible, like participatory design [13]. Traditional *Computer Aided Design* (CAD) and

L.M. Camarinha-Matos et al. (Eds.): PRO-VE 2015, IFIP AICT 463, pp. 612–621, 2015.
DOI: 10.1007/978-3-319-24141-8_57

Electronic Design Automation (EDA) design disciplines have been especially influenced by the new network-based engineering possibilities [28].

Current systems, like cyber-physical systems [26] are complex and heterogeneous. Their design requires multidisciplinary and usually multi-organizational efforts [20] that integrate diverse design teams from different *design houses* (enterprises) into collaborative networks (CN) that encompass complementary engineering competencies. However, modern design methodologies like, platform-based design focus on system engineering design itself and rather neglect cross-organizational multidisciplinary issues in design flows. Further design challenges include: transformation and integration of models realized by multidisciplinary teams [10], *shared understanding* in distributed teams, engineering knowledge representation [27], as well as use in a design process of *enterprise knowledge* [25]. Due to a *dynamic character* of a design teams' membership, a need for agile learning of team new members becomes evident. Thus a requirement for a holistic and agile design approach that encompasses modeling of a design process of heterogeneous systems realized in networks of collaborating engineering organizations. This approach should comprise enterprise knowledge resources, their structure, business models, as well as feedback from users of designed products.

In the paper we point to the organizational context of complex distributed design processes. They are an essential part of design house knowledge. At the same time, we would like to underline that modeling and management of knowledge of a design house can influence design decisions and can contribute to agile design of more innovative products. In the presented work, visual knowledge models (AKM) have been used to represent multi-organizational, design, product, as well as infrastructural aspects of heterogeneous system design.

2 Design Engineering in Collaborative Networks

Design processes of cyber-physical systems (CPS) are usually conducted in multidisciplinary, often distributed, design teams [26]. Designers realising these design processes necessitate heterogeneous tools from different engineering domains. Mastering interdependencies between digital (cyber) and heterogonous (physical) domains, like: analog, mechanical, or optical design parts that are designed by teams with complementary design competencies constitutes a real challenge. In order to address it companies are motivated to *collaborative engineering,* especially in networks where trust among partners already exists. Inter-organizational collaboration requires an additional care concerning security.

Collaborative networks [2] or *collaborative engineering* networks [21, 27, 31] offer to engineers much broader spectrum of collaboration functionality enabling integration of design teams. The last ones are the most developed form of engineering networks, as they offer advanced engineering collaboration services for designers and tight cross-organizational integration of their tools. Through the evolution of the virtual organization concept [7] from the extended enterprises [3], virtual enterprises, and smart organization [6] concepts until collaborative networks [2], the available support for collaborative engineering was changing [31]. We have distinguished four categories of engineering networks [31]: digital engineering libraries, engineering brokers, engineering networks, and the most advanced collaborative engineering networks. Issues that are central to design engineering in collaborative engineering networks are shortly addressed below.

New techniques for management of distributed tools that support designers in creation of virtual design environments are required. These techniques should enable straightforward integration of engineering design tools and services, like: concept specification graphical tools, compilers, design verification and simulation tools, behavioural, architectural and logic synthesis tools, physical design tools, test generators, product data management systems, and/or databases of predesigned intellectual property components. All these tools and services can be distributed over different Internet sites and platforms. Issues of concern are: portable tool descriptions; management and control of access rights; configuration, registration, search, and invocation of remote tools.

Business aspects of engineering processes, like use of more cost effective technologies compromising some product parameters, like: power consumption, size or weight need to be addressed during the design process. Usually, business process management (BPM) is addressed by economists and managerial staff, who are not involved in design engineering. Integration of their BPM tools with engineering design workflow (WfM) technology is a challenging endeavour [14]. A common modelling paradigm is needed in order to address this challenge. Issues requiring special attention are related to distributed workflows definition, verification, and coupling. Further issues are related to collaboration among dispersed teams' members including synchronous and asynchronous communication, shared understanding, firewalls crossing, and assurance of robust Internet connection. Finally, we point to the need for open platforms that enable engineering in CNs.

3 Modeling of CNs of Design Engineering Organizations

The paper refers to the experiment in modelling of the engineering Collaborative Network (CN) which has been conducted by industrial partners of the MAPPER project (mapper.eu.org). It encompassed two design houses in complementary engineering domains, namely digital and analogue electronics. The industrial design spanned over two countries, Germany and Poland and involved dispersed branches of one company, and an additional academic enabling party responsible for maintenance of the used MAPPER virtual collaborative infrastructure [12]. MAPPER was extensively using the visual knowledge modelling approach based on Active Knowledge Models (AKMS).

The paper reports on the use of this approach to CN modelling that included integration of BPM and engineering WfM. The concept of Active Knowledge Models and its applications in various domains have been covered in the literature [1, 12, 16, 17, 18]. Enterprise architecture modelling, IT governance and BPM are the most common applications.

The additional motivation of this paper is to demonstrate use of the AKM technology in the domain of electronic system design. AKM representation in principle is more general than workflow management. It can thus be applied to representation and modelling of various enterprise processes and products. Engineering processes, including EDA (Electronic Design Automation) ones, can be modelled using AKM. AKM-based design strategy enables capturing in a model, knowledge on: enterprise architecture, design processes, designers' competencies, used tools, IT infrastructure, products, and patterns of good practices. This knowledge is gathered in visual knowledge models, operational models [10], and patterns [23].

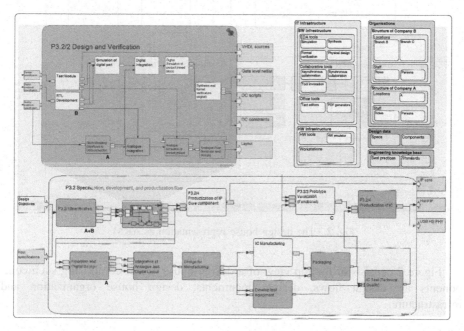

Fig. 1. A visual design of a collaborative network of two design companies

Active knowledge models (AKMs) [18] are visual representations of unfolding and dynamic business knowledge. The models, when supported by an appropriate platform, can be used to *actively* customize the underlying IT infrastructure. AKM models are executed through process enactment and rule engines provided by that infrastructure. In the context of engineering design processes, AKMs can be applied as an active and systematically unfolding knowledge model of the design process and its environment. This knowledge model can integrate: relevant design processes, required human resources with engineering expertise profiles, and appropriate design tools. Such a model, if systematically updated, can simplify transfer of design knowledge concerning a particular design phase to new employees. It supports design knowledge accumulation and transfer through learning patterns around the distributed teams. Furthermore, AKMs can model families of *electronic products* at various levels of abstraction well managing various configurations of product functionality.

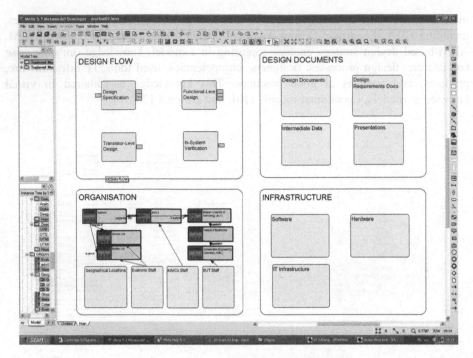

Fig. 2. The design house representation as AKM.

Figure 2 consists of the top view of a design house model comprising such components as: design flows, design documents, design house organization and infrastructure.

4   Towards Holistic Design of CNs of Design Houses

Models of collaborative engineering networks are generally defined as explicit representations of some portions of design houses reality, i.e. their resources in terms of available tools, human experts' profiles, design and verification processes, as well as organizational structures, and collaborative links. Developed knowledge models are actively used during the operation of the system. Models need an appropriate IT infrastructure in order to be developed, managed, stored, and executed. The MAPPER infrastructure [12] has been used in below shortly reported experiments. The infrastructure applies active model configuration in the following ways:

- Model-configured *workplaces* constitute simpler means of interacting with information and knowledge, adapted to the designers' preferences, competences, roles, and responsibilities;
- Portal *navigation* structures reflect model structures;
- Portal and web *services* from other tools can be invoked using general plug-in mechanisms, mapping data from the models to the parameters of the service;

- *Task execution* is used for plugging together solutions for a particular process or task pattern, invoking parameterized infrastructure services for each step;
- *Intellectual property rights* can be protected using a model-configured access control mechanism, as defined in [11].

4.1 Tool Invocation Workflows in TRMS

The Tool Registration and Management Services (TRMS) [15, 24] system comprising three main components: Global Tool Lookup Service (GTLS), Tool Servers (TSs), and Client Applications has been used for tool invocation workflows in the conducted design engineering experiments [23].

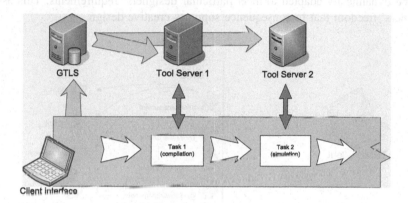

Fig. 3. Tool invocation workflows in TRMS.

Figure 3 illustrates a simplified design scenario based on TRMS. A designer executes a workflow that constitutes a sequence of design tasks. The TRMS Client interface enables a designer to define in a graphical way the workflow of tasks. The simplified workflow consists of two design tasks, namely design compilation and simulation. The first Tool Server is responsible for execution of compilation, whereas the second one executes simulation. Both tool servers have been identified by the GTLS service. A task, being a part of the workflow available at the GUI level, is a representation of a service that is executed at the specified Tool Server.

EDA tools operating in the "batch mode" can also be supported by TRMS which enables their encapsulation and flexible execution. Design data transfer to the tool servers can be facilitated, either through the TRMS Client or through the consecutive use of tools, like CVS.

4.2 Model-Configured Task Execution

The mapping of the high level knowledge models of design flows onto the concrete tasks and workflows that are available through TRMS requires that the atomic tasks of the knowledge models are connected to the TRMS specific workflows or tasks. In consequence, the AKM task execution engine will be able to invoke a particular lower level tool for each process task. The parameterised URL interface of the TRMS applet is used for handling interactive tasks, while automatic workflows may be invoked using the TRMS web service interface. Both these integration mechanisms are supported by the AKM task execution engine.

From the AKM models data and parameters are extracted that are needed as input to TRMS. Definition of mapping between model elements as well as, service input and output parameters, assures that any kind of modelled content may be used by lower level services. Different types of models concerning: documents, organisations and people, design processes and tasks, or product structures can be configured to be used by services. The integration of AKM and TRMS is thus flexibly model-configured, and may be dynamically adapted to meet particular designers' requirements. This assures designers' freedom that in consequence supports creative design.

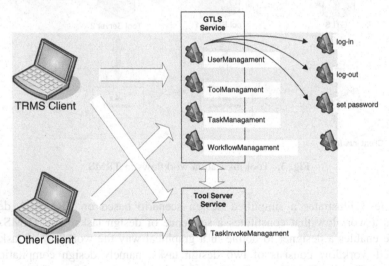

Fig. 4. Model-configured task execution in the MAPPER platform [12].

4.3   Integration of Task Execution and TRMS Workflows

The web services-based architecture of TRMS enables straightforward integration with other web service-based systems. A set of services offered by TRMS includes: search for a predefined task or workflow (group of tasks), as well as task control and execution. Two TRMS Clients independently invoking services from the GTLS server and from the Tool Server are illustrated in Fig. 4. The TRMS Client enables the complete control over the TRMS environment. It supports management of users and tool properties. A designer is supported in building his own visual representation of the environment based on the available web services.

4.4   Design of Virtual Electronic Components in the CN

A distributed collaborative design process aiming at a virtual (Intellectual Property) IP component required for hardware implementation of standard serial communication protocols is shortly described in this section. This design process integrated two electronic design companies from Germany (Recklinghausen) and Poland (Fig. 1) (two branches in Gliwice and Bielsko-Biała). This design process was realised in the collaborative engineering network that was enabled by the MAPPER project infrastructure [12]. The network integrated engineers' workspaces with design tools and remote specialized tools that processed automatically design data upon invocation through the TRMS environment (Figs. 2 and 3).

The IP component design process begins with an informal specification that is agreed upon by both partners. Once a precise specification is defined, both companies precise their design flows and workflows as visual models (AKMs), and agree upon appropriate analogue-digital interfaces. The AKM-based design flows and workflows cover: specification, synthesis, verification, and product preparatory phases for both digital and analogue design flows. Consecutively, designers responsible for particular design phases and tools to be used are defined. The common design workflow defines all design steps at both companies that are needed for designing and production of the designed IP component for standard serial communication. This common design workflow is a result of numerous negotiations between designers and also managers of both companies that are performed using collaboration services of the MAPPER infrastructure (e.g. CURE environment).

The active knowledge model developed for the IP component design integrates a wide spectrum of information and knowledge related to the joint product, namely: the companies' structures, human resources including their competencies, the available IT infrastructure, the project organisation with assigned responsibilities, the detailed structure of the joint product, as well as the project planning with management and design workflows. Figure 2 presents the top-level view of this model for one design organization (design house). The detailed model comprises a very large number of elements, i.e. objects and their relationships that are not easy to comprehend all at once. It is therefore necessary to focus only on the portion of the model at the time. The AKM model browser enables control of visibility of model elements by creating different views with selected model components only.

Further details of the discussed distributed collaborative design process are available in: [22, 23, 25], as well as from *mapper.eu.org* (D15).

5   Conclusions

Modeling of collaborative networks that includes: modeling of partition of design tasks onto different design houses, designers' and resources' allocation enables verification of correctness of design decisions, and in general it supports distributed design processes. The use of active knowledge models has been demonstrated in modeling of organizational, process, product and system aspects of collaborating design houses.

The experiments conducted during the MAPPER project and later the MADONE network [19] have confirmed that Active Knowledge Models constitute an innovative approach to holistic design of CNs due to their support for:

- Multidimensional modeling and management of design house knowledge,
- Integration in a model of organizational, process, product and system aspects,
- Virtual collaboration of designers and their continuous learning processes,
- Creation of meta-models,
- Modeling and generation of configurable model-driven workspaces that support
- collaboration in multidisciplinary design teams,
- Representation of design task patters, and
- Automation of selected design tasks with appropriate infrastructures.

Practical realization of the holistic design methodology depends on the availability of the underlying IT infrastructure for all design houses that are involved in the collaborative network. Community efforts are thus required towards development of open platforms enabling collaborative engineering [19].

Acknowledgments. The authors acknowledge MAPPER project partners and the SUT TRMS team: Paweł Fraś, Tomasz Kostienko, Piotr Penkala, and Marek Szlęzak.

References

1. Active Knowledge Modeling. http://activeknowledgemodeling.com
2. Camarinha-Matos, L.M., Afsarmanesh, H.: The emerging discipline of collaborative networks. In: Camarinha-Matos, L. (ed.) Virtual Enterprises and Collaborative Networks. Kluwer Academic Publishers, New York (2004)
3. CE-NET: A Roadmap towards the Collaborative Enterprise – CE Vision 2010 (2004)
4. Dorn, C., Taylor, R.N., Dustdar, S.: Flexible social workflows - collaborations as human architecture. IEEE Internet Comput. (2012)
5. ECOLEAD Project: A Reference Model for Collaborative Networks, ECOLEAD Project Report D52.3 (2007)
6. Filos, E., Banahan, E.: Towards the smart organization: an emerging organizational paradigm and the contribution of the European RTD programs. J. Intell. Manufact. **12**(2), 101–119 (2001). Kluwer Academic Publishers
7. Filos, E.: Virtuality and the Future of Organisations. European Commission (2004)
8. Global Engineering Networking. xml.coverpages.org/genInitiative.html. Accessed 02, 2014
9. Jeners, J., Prinz, W.: From Groupware to social media - a comparison of conceptual models. PRO-VE **2012**, 416–423 (2012)
10. Jensen, J.C., Chang, D.H., Lee, E.A.: A model-based design methodology for cyber-physical systems. In: 7th International Wireless Communications and Mobile Computing Conference (IWCMC), pp. 1666–1671 (2011)
11. Jørgensen, H.D.: Interactive Process Models. PhD thesis, Norwegian University of Science and Technology, Trondheim, Norway (2004)
12. Jorgensen, H., Johnsen, S.G., Pawlak, A., Sandkuhl, K., Schümmer, T., Tandler, P.: MAPPER collaboration platform for knowledge-intensive engineering processes. In: Abramowicz, W., Tolksdorf, R., Węcel, K. (eds.) BIS 2010. LNBIP, vol. 57, pp. 180–191. Springer, Heidelberg (2010)

13. Kensing, F., Blomberg, J.: Participatory design: issues and concerns. Comput. Suppor. Coop. Work **7**, 167–185 (1998). Kluwer Academic Publishers
14. Kokoszka, A., Siekierska, K., Trung, N.Q., Fraś, P., Pawlak, A.: Are workflow management systems useful for collaborative engineering? In: 2002 ECPPM, eWork and Business in AEC, Balkema Publishers (2002)
15. Kostienko, T., Mueller, W., Pawlak, A., Schattkowsky, T.: Advanced infrastructure for collaborative engineering in electronic design automation. In: Cha, J., et al. (eds.) The Vision for the Future Generation in Research and Applications. Swets & Zeitlinger, Lisse (2003)
16. Lillehagen, F.: The foundations of AKM technology. Enhanced interoperable systems. In: Proceedings of the 10th ISPE International Conference on Concurrent Engineering, Madeira, Portugal (2003)
17. Lillehagen, F., Krogstie, J.: Active knowledge models and enterprise knowledge management. In: Kosanke, K., et al. (eds.) Enterprise Inter- and Intra-Organizational Integration. Springer Science + Business Media, New York (2003)
18. Lillehagen, F., Krogstie, J.: Active Knowledge Modeling of Enterprises. Springer, Berlin (2008)
19. MADONE Network: MADONE: Towards a New Knowledge Base for Collaborative Enterprise Networking. http://madone-network.blogspot.de/
20. Schaffers, H., Brodt, T., Pallot, M., Prinz, W. (eds.): The Future Workspace - Perspectives on Mobile and Collaborative Working. MOSAIC Consortium, The Netherlands (2006)
21. Pawlak, A.: Challenges in collaborative design in engineering networks. In: Cunningham, P., Cunningham, M. (eds.) eChallenges 2010 Conference Proceedings, IIMC International Information Management Corporate (2010)
22. Pawlak, A., Jørgensen, H., Penkala, P., Fraś, P.: Business process and workflow management for design of electronic systems – balancing flexibility and control. In: Lecture Notes in Informatics – Proceedings, vol. P-120. Gesellschaft für Informatik, Bonn (2007)
23. Pawlak, A., Penkala, P., et al.: Distributed collaborative design of a mixed-signal IP component. In: 12th EUROMICRO Conference on Digital System Design Architectures, Methods and Tools, Patras, Greece (2009)
24. Pawlak, A., Fraś, P., Penkala, P.: Web services-based collaborative system for distributed engineering. In: Camarinha-Matos, L., Picard, W. (eds.) Pervasive Collaborative Networks, pp. 463–472. Springer, New York (2008)
25. Pawlak, A., Sakowski, W., Penkala, P., Fraś, P., Grzybek, S.: Distributed collaborative design - a case study for mixed-signal IP core. Przegląd Elektrotechniczny (Electronic Review), Nr 11a/2010, 111–115 (2010)
26. Rajkumar, R., Lee, I., Sha, L., Stankovic, J.: Cyber-physical systems: the next computing revolution. In: Proceedings of Design Automation Conference, Anaheim, USA (2010)
27. Radeke, E.: GEN - global engineering networking. In: Proceedings of Conference on Integration in Manufacturing, Goteborg (1998)
28. Spiller, M., Newton, A.R.: EDA and the network. In: Proceedings of ICCAD'97 (1997)
29. Tellioğlu, H.: Model-based collaborative design in engineering. In: Luo, Y. (ed.) CDVE 2009. LNCS, vol. 5738, pp. 85–92. Springer, Heidelberg (2009)
30. VOSTER Project Report D11.1: VO Concept Source Information (2002)
31. Witczyński, M., Pawlak, A.: Virtual organisations in electronics sector – case study. In: Camarinha-Matos, L., Afsarmanesh, H., Ollus, M. (eds.) Virtual Organisations: Systems and Practices. Springer Science + Business Media Inc., Berlin (2005)

The Development and Adoption of a New Joint Bidding System for Public Contracts in Wales

Andrew Crossley[1,2](✉), Gareth Coles[3], Rhian Edwards[4], Sue Hurrell[5], and Nina Ruddle[5]

[1] ServQ Alliance, Cardiff, Wales, UK
AndrewDCrossley@ServQ.com
[2] University of Bristol, Bristol, UK
[3] Wales Council for Voluntary Action, Cardiff, Wales, UK
[4] Wales Co-operative Centre, Caerphilly, Wales, UK
[5] Value Wales, Welsh Government, Cardiff, Llandudno, Wales, UK

Abstract. The paper describes the adoption of new SME friendly collaborative procurement processes in Wales and reports on some early successes. In 2012 the Welsh Government commissioned a team to research how SMEs could collaborate to access larger public sector contracts. This led to the publication of the new Joint Bidding Guide in 2013. The Guide leads both the selling and buying side through the procurement process ensuring joint bids are assessed in a fair and transparent manner. In 2014 the team was commissioned by the Welsh Government to advise leading procurement professionals in Wales on the adoption of the new Guide and map progress on up to 12 demonstration projects. The demonstration projects total more than €200 million in value.

Keywords: Joint bidding · Procurement · Public sector · Project management

1 Introduction

A major challenge for both micro businesses and Small to Medium sized Enterprises (SMEs) is how to grow efficiently. One possibility is through winning and delivering larger public sector contracts as consortia, often termed Virtual Organizations (VOs), to access higher value contracts than they have historically been awarded individually. There are significant reasons for SMEs and micro-organizations wanting to create VOs [1]. In the context of public sector work, the main advantages are that:

(a) in most of the developed world, public sector contracts offer a wide range of opportunities for SMEs to grow;
(b) there is a high degree of transparency on the tender and selection process;
(c) public sector contracts tend to be financially more secure and less volatile than private sector contracts demanding strong internal and external governance for the VO which can minimize the risk of potential conflict [2];
(d) in many countries public bodies offer strong contract management and align payments to delivery of results either by effort (time) or outcome (success);
(e) well run VO contracts provide good references for future opportunities; and,

L.M. Camarinha-Matos et al. (Eds.): PRO-VE 2015, IFIP AICT 463, pp. 622–630, 2015.
DOI: 10.1007/978-3-319-24141-8_58

(f) public bodies want the best value they can from the supplier base and recognise the high levels of service and innovation that SMEs can deliver.

The paper describes some of the challenges and findings of a three year programme for the design and implementation of a new toolkit for buyers and sellers to the public sector called the Joint Bidding Guide [3]. It demonstrates a practical approach to bidding and awarding larger contracts to VOs working as consortia in Wales.

1.1 The Economy of Wales

Wales is a country within the United Kingdom of Great Britain and Northern Ireland, an EU member state. Its population in 2012 was 3,074,067 and Wales has a total area of 20,782 km^2 [4]. Its population density of 148 people per square kilometre is therefore relatively low compared to the more congested areas of the United Kingdom, most notably the South East around London and the major industrialised cities in the Midlands and North. The majority of the people live in a series of coastal conurbations along the M4 corridor in the South East, together with its hinterlands often known as the Welsh Valleys, and the A55 corridor in the North. Rapid growth of the two corridor communities in the 19th and 20th centuries centred on the abstracting, processing and export of coal, steel and the production of slate mainly for roofing. From the early 1980s some sectors of the Welsh economy have been reinvigorated with advanced technologies in electronics, motor manufacturing, creative and green energy. More recently financial, ICT and support services centred on Cardiff and Swansea have seen rapid growth. The Welsh Government and its agencies have played a major part in encouraging inward investment and created seven Enterprise Zones in Anglesey, Cardiff, Deeside, Ebbw Vale, Haven Waterway, Snowdonia and St. Athan-Cardiff Airport. They are focused on power generation, business services, advanced manufacturing, low carbon development and aerospace.

Employment density is a function of the location and skills availability of the people. The largest companies working in Wales are mainly based along the two economic corridors. Local supply networks tend to be based close to these centres of operation. This means that large areas of Wales remain rural and semi-rural with historic 'market towns' whose economies are traditionally centred on agriculture and tourism. The rural economy makes the most of the countryside and its areas of outstanding natural beauty such as the two national parks: the Brecon Beacons and Snowdonia. Recent advances in high speed broadband and new transport investment will enable more rural and remote economies to participate in the nation's future success.

The Welsh Government plays a major role in the country's economy. Its 2015 budget is €21.4 billion which funds health, education and many public services. Funds are also distributed and spent via local government, the National Health Service and a variety of agencies. The annual spend on external suppliers who contribute to the delivery of public services is €6 billion (28 %). Thus getting more of this delivered by VOs helps grow regional and national employment within SMEs. SMEs share innovation and best practices creating a Welsh Virtual Breeding Environment (VBE) [5] capable of more rapid VO configuration and positioning for future opportunities.

1.2 Small Businesses in Wales

99 % of indigenous businesses in Wales are classed as SMEs (up to 250 employees) of which 95 % are micro businesses (less than 10 employees) [6]. The Welsh Government provides advice and support for small businesses as they are seen as potential catalysts for innovation, growth, new jobs and apprenticeships. A publically funded organization called Business Wales helps train owners and managers of small businesses in a variety of subjects including bidding for public sector contracts. However, the awarding of public contracts is traditionally dependent upon a bidder's revenue, track record and capacity. Hence, working together as extended enterprises, configured as consortia of VEs, can increase the volume and value of opportunities for members to win work from the public sector.

2 Development of Relevant Policy Guidelines

In 2012 the Welsh Government realised that it needed to create a more supportive tendering environment in order for more businesses to be eligible to bid and win larger contracts as collectives of VOs termed consortia. One of the recommendations of the Welsh Government's 2012 Task and Finish Group on micro-businesses was that the Government should encourage micro-businesses to consider consortium approaches to public sector procurement. In 2008 the EU issued a code of practice on improving access for SMEs to procurement contracts [7]. It explicitly refers to the benefits of joint bidding, keeping selection criteria proportionate, and allowing sufficient time for drawing up tenders. These goals are reinforced in the superseding Directive 2014/24 on Public Procurement [8]. The UK Government is an early adopter of the Directive through its Public Contracts Regulations 2015 [9].

Sustainable Development and Sustainable Procurement are vitally important and recognised as the best practice approach by the Welsh Government, ensuring that 'maximum value is achieved for the Welsh pound by delivering the maximum social, economic and environmental benefits'. In its 2012 Procurement Policy [10] the Welsh Government stated that in carrying out procurement activity the public sector will:

(a) Define 'value for money' as ' the optimum combination of whole-life costs in terms of not only generating efficiency savings and good quality outcomes for the organization but also benefit to society and the economy, whilst minimising damage to the environment.' (Principle 3)
(b) Ensure that the 'delivery of added value through Community Benefits policy must be an integral consideration in procurement.' (Principle 4)
(c) Continue to embrace all the principles of Opening Doors - the Charter for Small and Medium sized Enterprises [11]. 'Public bodies should adopt risk based, proportionate approaches to procurement to ensure that contract opportunities are

open to all and smaller, local suppliers are not precluded from winning contracts individually, as consortia, or through roles within the supply chain.' (Principle 5)

Until 2013 there were limited practical guidelines and advice available for small organizations, not-for-profits and charities on how to track opportunities, team up with VO partners then prepare joint bids for higher value public sector tenders. Procurement teams had also experienced challenges in prequalifying and assessing tenders from joint bidding teams. The challenge was how to design, test and validate a new approach to help smaller organizations create effective consortia. They could then access more of the Welsh public sector's €6 billion annual external spend.

3 Joint Bidding Guide Research

Three sponsors from the Welsh Government's team at Value Wales, the Wales Co-operative Centre and the Wales Council for Voluntary Action (WCVA) came together in 2012 to commission research and analysis in order to produce a guide to joint bidding. The 2012 Wales Procurement Policy Statement [10] refers to consortium bidding as a 'means of increasing access to procurement opportunities'. This was a priority issue for the sponsors because:

(a) They had identified that procurement processes can often work against organizations attempting to set up VO consortia to bid for contracts.
(b) In some instances, public money that had previously been awarded as grants was being spent via competitive tendering.

In mid-2012 the Sponsors identified that there was no detailed guidance available that addressed the challenges set out above. Therefore they prepared a joint specification and project budget. This reduced their collective procurement costs and demonstrated practical collaboration between the public and third sectors. A second requirement was to modify the Welsh Public Sector's *SQuID* (*S*upplier *Qu*alification *I*nformation *D*atabase) question set [12] and guidance to make it more suitable for consortia bids.

In September 2012 the Sponsors selected a specialist Cardiff based body with expertise in collaboration, virtual working and alliances to carry out the work. The Sponsors created a Project Board to liaise with the ServQ Alliance. Over five months the programme consisted of: desk research; creating a research database; interviews with successful and unsuccessful consortia; review of best practices, including standards on collaborative business relationships; report drafting; sign off, eventual translation and publication in Welsh and English, in compliance with the Welsh language standards and regulations. The updates to the *SQuID* system were then cross-referenced into the new guide. This created a series of new templates for consortium design and working than both the buying side and the bidding VOs could adopt building a climate of trust and understanding between the respective bodies.

4   Design of the Joint Bidding Guide

The Joint Bidding Guide addresses the technical, organizational, and financial hurdles faced in procurement by both the buying and supplying sides. It is an example of a Wales-based innovation that has potential for widespread application both within Wales and elsewhere, especially within the European Union. It comprises of 18 short chapters with supplementary checklists and assessment tools, a technical glossary, further reading and a set of case studies for reference.

Some examples of the innovations within the Guide are: an evaluation checklist of procurement policy; alignment to BS11000 [13] the most current internationally available standard for collaborative working; a new Procurement Assessment Model (PAM) for Joint Bidding with worked examples; methodologies for measuring 'hybrid' financial reports for consortia; capacity modelling; advice on the relevant timescales needed to encourage more consortia bids; design systems for creating viable consortia; acceptable legal structures for contract, including compliance with competition law; checklists and assessment models to enable potential consortia to score the tender opportunity against 'market position, bidding resources, delivery competence, commercial standing and risk'; configuration and leadership behaviours; trust measurement and due diligence; governance, compliance, intellectual property and asset management; a new approach to integrated risk assessment and planning for consortia with stage gates (see Fig. 1); advice on estimating and pricing for consortia including target pricing and how to share risk and profits; bid planning templates; how to review joint bids, analyse tenders and objectively interview consortia. The entire document was ultimately published on the Welsh Government website on a dedicated Joint Bidding Guide home page [3].

A critical issues raised by both the procurement teams and the VO's potential lead members was how to professionally plan and manage risks. Figure 1 shows the process.

5   Demonstration Projects

The Joint Bidding Guide was formally launched by Jane Hutt AM, Minister for Finance and Government Business for the Welsh Government in October 2013. At the launch the Minister announced that a set of Demonstration Projects would be established to test the Guide's processes. Two such cases are listed below.

Having a high quality guide was the first part of the implementation challenge. It was also critical to promote its use to procurers and consortia bidders. Awareness raising started in 2013 and the Demonstration Programme implemented between mid-2014 and 2015. The key lessons learned from the programme to date are as follows:

(a) *More consistent planning.* Procurers need to configure contracts suitable for VO consortia at the outset. They use the Procurement Assessment Model (PAM) for rapid appraisal of a contract's suitability for consortia working.

(b) *Some modifications to terms of contract are needed.* These are traditionally written based on a lead contractor and its sub-contractors.

(c) *Document review.* Examining tender and specification documentation to ensure it is appropriate for VOs using the updated *SQuID* is critical.

(d) *Allow more time for potential VO consortia to be configured.* Not all potential consortia exist at the time of advertising Prior Information Notices (PINs). Hence signposting the potential of VOs at events is important.

(e) *Provide bid support facilities.* For new VOs bid support is needed to help them through the necessary planning and consortium bid writing processes.

(f) *Best practices, innovation and sustainability.* Additional documentation has been created including a new web site jointly created with the Institute for Collaborative Working [14]. A handbook was written with processes designed using swim lanes following the path of both procurer and VO.

(g) *Promotion outside of Wales.* The Minister highlighted that the best practices were transferable outside of Wales at the Guide's launch. For example, the guide has been referenced at UK national conferences and major events.

5.1 Demonstration Project Case Study 1 in Carmarthenshire

In 2014 Carmarthenshire County Council used the Guide to plan the procurement of a new €3 million framework. Consortia of public and private/third sector organizations needed to work together to design and run an integrated support service called Families First. The contract was awarded in early 2015. Alan Aitken, the Procurement Director was an early advocate of the Joint Bidding Guide. His views are as follows:

"The Welsh Government's Joint Bidding Guide offers practical and straight forward advice to both parties. In Carmarthenshire we have embraced the approach. We were the first Welsh Local Authority to pilot the Guide. From the earliest stages of the project, we could identify clear benefits and a very positive market response to the new Guide. This positive response was confirmed when two consortiums were formed using the Joint Bidding Guide, with the assistance of the Wales Co-operative Centre, in order to specifically bid for the work. It was rewarding to see both consortium bids win business and be awarded contracts as part of the exercise."

5.2 Demonstration Project Case Study 2 in Caerphilly

In 2014 Caerphilly County Borough Council started to procure suppliers for its External Works construction framework agreement. This is a five year agreement with an estimated spend value of €30 million starting in 2015. The works had been tendered in two lots, one lot for works packages below €1 million and one lot for works packages above €1 million. Twelve contractors were accepted on each lot starting in 2015. The Council used the Guide to prepare its tender and a new VO consortium used it to plan its bid. The VO was then awarded a place on the larger value lot. The proposed consortium worked with the Wales Co-operative Centre and Caerphilly County Borough Council's Supplier Development team to ensure a good quality compliant bid was submitted. In line with the latest EU procurement regulations, the successful consortium will be legally constituted as part of the conditions of

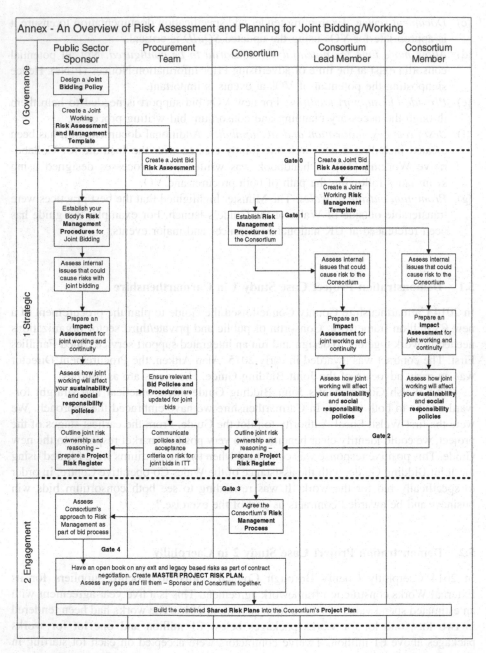

Fig. 1. An overview of risk assessment and planning for joint bidding/working

tender/contract. This is similar to the Italian model [15]. A pathfinder project is being used. Caerphilly's procurement team won a Welsh National Procurement Award in 2015 in part for their innovative work supporting consortia.

6 Conclusions

The paper described the challenges for micro and small to medium sized businesses in accessing larger contracts from the public sector in Wales. From 2012 to 2015 a series of reports, field research and case studies helped shape a new set of processes to help both the buying side (procurers) and the selling side (bidders). In 2012 the Welsh Government and two other sponsoring organizations commissioned a new integrated approach to planning and managing bids from VOs working as consortia. The processes were published as a new document called the Joint Bidding Guide. After its launch a practical follow up project was commissioned to support the public sector and the VOs of micro business/SMEs through a series of demonstration projects. The projects are a mix of national and local procurements with values ranging from €3 million to more than €100 million. They range from large volumes of lower value products such as motor vehicle tyres and hire services, through to large value contracts in construction.

An informed and enthusiastic Steering Group, with expert researchers and practitioners has managed the successful roll out of the Guide. The Guide is strengthened with the 2014 EU and 2015 UK Government procurement regulations. It is tailored for the needs of both the public sector and SMEs to access larger contracts. The Guide is a dynamic document that can change with lessons learnt from the demonstration projects. Updates can be incorporated to maintain it as a practical, well researched toolkit that can help SME's win more business working as VOs in Wales.

Acknowledgements. The Joint Bidding Guide is publically available. Its design and development was part funded by the European Union and the principal Sponsors.

References

1. Camarinha-Matos, L.M., Afsarmanesh, H.: On reference models for collaborative networked organizations. Int. J. Prod. Res. **46**, 2453–2469 (2008)
2. Rabelo, R.J., Costa, S.N., Romero, D.: A governance reference model for virtual enterprises. In: Camarinha-Matos, L.M., Afsarmanesh, H. (eds.) Collaborative Systems for Smart Networked Environments. IFIP AICT, vol. 434, pp. 60–70. Springer, Heidelberg (2014)
3. http://www.Wales.gov.uk/jointbidding. Accessed 12 May 2015
4. http://www.wales.com/en/content/cms/English/About_Wales/Wales_Fact_File/Wales_Fact_File.aspx. Accessed 12 May 2015
5. Paszkiewicz, Z., Picard, W.: Modelling virtual organization architecture with the virtual organization breeding methodology. In: Camarinha-Matos, L.M., Paraskakis, I., Afsarmanesh, H. (eds.) PRO-VE 2009. IFIP AICT, vol. 307, pp. 187–196. Springer, Heidelberg (2009)
6. https://statswales.wales.gov.uk/Catalogue/Business-Economy-and-Labour-Market/Businesses/Business-Structure/Headline-Data/LatestBusinessStructureInWales-by-Sizeband-Measure. Accessed 29 April 2015
7. Facilitating Access by SMEs to Public Procurement Contracts SEC 2193 (2008)

8. Directive 2014/24/EU of The European Parliament and of The Council of 26 February 2014 On Public Procurement and Repealing Directive 2004/18/EC
9. http://www.legislation.gov.uk/uksi/2015/102/pdfs/uksi_20150102_en.pdf. Accessed on 29 April 2015
10. http://gov.wales/about/cabinet/cabinetstatements/2012/welshprocurement/?lang=en. Accessed 29 April 2015
11. https://www.hefcw.ac.uk/documents/about_us/internal_policies/Opening_Doors_Refreshed_English.pdf. Accessed 28 April 2015
12. http://prp.gov.wales/planners/general/phase2/supplierselection/prequalificationquestionnaire/. Accessed 27 April 2015
13. BS 11000-1:2010 Framework specification for collaborative business relationships. British Standards Institute (2010)
14. http://www.jointbidding.org.uk/English/. Accessed 26 April 2015
15. Ricciardi, Antonio, Cardoni, Andrea, Tiacci, Lorenzo: Strategic Context, Organizational Features and Network Performances: A Survey on Collaborative Networked Organizations of Italian SMEs. In: Camarinha-Matos, Luis M., Afsarmanesh, Hamideh (eds.) Collaborative Systems for Smart Networked Environments. IFIP AICT, vol. 434, pp. 534–545. Springer, Heidelberg (2014)

CoDiT: An Integrated Business Partner Discovery Tool Over SNSs

Atia Bano Memon[(⊠)] and Kyrill Meyer

Business Information Systems, Department of Computer Science,
University of Leipzig, Leipzig, Germany
{memon,meyer}@informatik.uni-leipzig.de

Abstract. The success of open innovation alliances depends on the right
selection of business partners. Given the vast representation of business organizations on SNSs and the resulting availability of significant amount of
information about their products and services, the SNSs seem to be a promising
opportunity for the businesses to look for the potential partners. In this regard,
this paper reviews the potential of SNSs for supporting business partner discovery. In order to address the identified inadequacies of SNSs for supporting
business partner search, we present a web based search tool: CoDiT. The CoDiT
system seamlessly integrates the company pages hosted on multiple SNSs by
leveraging the potential of existing social networking APIs. The main premise of
CoDiT system is to support open innovation process – in the 'Find' phase - by
assisting organizations in locating complementary assets through the aggregation and exchange of the information about potential partners available on SNSs.

Keywords: Open innovation · Social media · Social networking sites ·
Business partner discovery · Company pages

1 Motivation

Open innovation, a new paradigm of innovation management, is gaining an increasing
attention in practice and academia. To overcome the dearth of resources and enhance
internal innovation capacity, many firms have started to adapt the open innovation
model whereby they acquire complementary resources and knowledge from outside the
organizational boundaries by establishing co-operations with different types of stakeholders of the value chain. The open innovation efforts of an organization flow through
four phases: Want, Find, Get, and Manage (WFGM) [8, 9]. The WFGM framework
suggests that effective open innovation strategy encompasses four questions; what
external assets are required (Want), what are possible sources of these assets (Find),
which source's assets are superior and how to acquire access to those assets (Get), and
how to coordinate and integrate those assets to meet the objectives (Manage) [9]. The
success of open innovation alliances depends on the right selection of business partners
(sources of complementary assets); which in turn is influenced by the organization's
capacity to identify possible sources of the required assets. Accordingly, the 'Find'
stage of WFGM model needs particular attention from innovation managers in order to
maximize the benefits and chances of the success of open innovation alliances.

© IFIP International Federation for Information Processing 2015
L.M. Camarinha-Matos et al. (Eds.): PRO-VE 2015, IFIP AICT 463, pp. 631–638, 2015.
DOI: 10.1007/978-3-319-24141-8_59

Screening and monitoring the technological environment to search and decide whom to collaborate with is not a trivial task for the organizations. This is particularly true for the companies who are neither equipped with sufficient information sources, nor are they financially capable to run an information system or buy such resources from external providers. Consequently, in order to engage in successful open innovation alliances, it becomes vital for such companies to discover and exploit new channels for collecting information about other businesses.

The current era of digitalized information has brought new ways of information dissemination. One approach to share and acquire information is the paradigm of social networking sites (SNSs). Given the escalating number of business organizations being represented on social networking sites, and the resulting availability of significant amount of information about their products and services, SNSs seem to be a promising opportunity for businesses to look for potential partners. In this context, this paper attempts to evaluate the potential of SNSs for supporting the business partner discovery (Sect. 3). In order to address the identified limitations of SNSs for supporting the business partner discovery, we present the conceptual framework and development of a web-based integrated business partner search tool, CoDiT – Company Discovery Tool (Sect. 4). The CoDiT system is designed to support the open innovation process – in the 'Find' phase - by assisting organizations in locating complementary assets through the aggregation and exchange of the information about potential partners available on SNSs.

2 Methodology

The study is oriented around the design science research methodology proposed by Peffers et al. [7]. Following this methodology, the work discussed in this paper is conducted in two phases. In the first phase of study, we have evaluated the potential of SNSs for supporting business partner discovery. To achieve this task, we have conducted an exploratory study of the structure and searching procedures of company pages facilitated on four distinct social networking sites: Facebook, LinkedIn, Google+ and Xing (a Germany based platform, formerly known as Open Business Club). We have compared these SNSs in terms of four dimensions: (1) the types and pieces of information which can be presented on company pages, (2) the features of the search interface and the underlying search procedures for searching company pages, (3) the search management functionalities offered to the user, and (4) the ways in which a user can interact with the searched company pages. In the second phase of study, with the quest to identify the possible solutions for the identified inadequacies of SNSs, we have assessed the potential of social networking APIs. The existing potential of social networking APIs allows for third party developers to search for and fetch available information from the company pages hosted on social networking platforms. Subsequently, we have exploited this opportunity to develop a prototype of a web based search tool - CoDiT - which seamlessly integrates the company pages hosted on multiple SNSs.

3 Potential of SNSs to Support Business Partner Discovery

Social networking sites have brought a new wave of dissemination of digitalized information, and consequently altered the way businesses communicate within and across the organizational boundaries. Social networking sites have provided many opportunities for the businesses that were either unavailable or very difficult to obtain for most of the organizations on their own [3]. However, effective social media presence of organizations requires specific and appropriate services from the social networking platforms on one hand, and proper strategy and efforts from the organizations on the other hand. To facilitate companies' representation in specific manner, leading social networking sites Facebook, LinkedIn, Google+ and others offer 'company pages' which enable business organizations to display information about them, their products and services, and allow them to interact with their customer community. Nowadays, almost every organization uses one or another social media channel for achieving one or another organizational goal (e.g. promotion of products and/or services, strengthening their relation with customers through easy, timely and direct communication, invading new markets, doing market research etc.). The resulting availability of significant amount of information about the businesses, their products and services on SNSs enables the SNSs to support the dissemination of partnering information. Nevertheless, looking for business partners for B2B alliances is critical and demanding task. Current information models and available services on SNSs pose two main challenges to their potential for supporting business partner discovery:

1. There exists a rich and diverse ecology of social networking sites that vary in terms of their scope and functionality [4]. For instance, where Facebook provides tools more appropriate for networking and communicating with customers, LinkedIn provides more professional services to link with employees [6]. Beside these giant social networking platforms, several other platforms also exist which are more popular in specific parts of world; such as Xing platform which is more popular in Germany and few other countries. All of these platforms work in isolation from each other. As a matter of fact, all companies cannot manage to represent themselves on all platforms or put all information everywhere, useful information remains dispersed and confined to specific platform boundaries. This in turn hampers discovery and information retrieval without actually getting on specific platform. Furthermore, no known service exists for cross platform exchange and/or synchronization of information across multiple platforms.
2. Our exploratory analysis of the structure and searching procedures of the company pages facilitated on four distinct SNSs – Facebook, LinkedIn, Google+ and Xing – yields that every social networking site uses its own platform dependent way for information collection, exploration and presentation. The findings elucidate that each platform collects different pieces and types of company related information, imposes different structure in information collection and presentation, employs varying search procedures, and offers different search management and page interaction functionalities. Table 1 summarizes the features of company pages hosted on four SNSs.

Table 1. Comparison of company page features offered on four SNSs

Facebook	LinkedIn	Google+	Xing
Available information			
Profile, offers, milestones, events, feed, posts, photos, albums, videos	Profile, company updates, employees using LinkedIn platform	Profile, posts, photos, videos, reviews	Profile, updates, reviews, employees using Xing platform and some statistics, jobs
Search interface (search method and depth, query structure and complexity, faceted filtering)			
Direct, Free text (keyword) single valued search over structured data fields without faceted filtering	Faceted, free text, multivalued, full text search with flat, single valued facets on structured data fields with forward highlighting	Direct, Free text (keyword), single valued (with location) search over structured data fields without faceted filtering	Faceted, free text (basic) and structured (advanced), multivalued search over structured data fields with flat (except the location facets), single valued facets on structured data fields with forward highlighting
Search management (Sorting, bookmarking, networking, geographic mapping)			
Individual map	---	Individual and integrated map	Individual map, relevancy and alphabetic sorting
Page interaction			
Like page, post on page, message to page, and like, share and comment any post	Follow page, and like, comment and share any company update	Share or follow page, upload public photo, rate or review page, share any review	Follow, recommend, and rate company, and like, comment and share any update

The dispersion of businesses' information on multiple SNSs, and varying and inadequate search procedures call for their integration together with provision of new or improved services in order to support the discovery of potential business partners for involvement in open innovation alliances.

4   CoDiT System Overview

In this section, we briefly highlight the high-level architecture and implementation of the CoDiT system. Besides enabling simultaneous search over Facebook and LinkedIn platforms, CoDiT is envisioned to provide following functionalities:

F1. Enhanced search interface with business specific features
F2. Consistent and effective view of information with content-oriented metadata
F3. Search management functionalities
F4. Company page interaction

4.1   Approach

Although each SNS confines its collected data within platform boundaries, leading social networking sites have already started exposing their network and related data to other web based services in form of application programming interfaces (APIs). These social networking APIs allow third party developers to access user data [2], and fetch, aggregate and create content according to users' specific interests. The two openly available social networking APIs allowing users to search and manage company pages are the Facebook graph API [1] and LinkedIn companies API [5]. The potential of these APIs makes it possible to develop a web based tool that can seamlessly integrate the company pages hosted on these platform by following three step logic: Fetch, Integrate and Present. The CoDiT is designed to avail this opportunity and thereby aggregates company pages hosted on Facebook and LinkedIn platforms.

4.2   Architecture

As depicted in Fig. 1, the design of CoDiT system is based on a three-tier architecture comprising a user interface (enables the users to execute search query, view results, and manage and interact with the searched company pages), a web server (responsible for executing the search queries, the reading and publishing tasks on the company pages, and the user's bookmarking and networking commands on the local database) and a data layer (consisted of three remote sources - Facebook platform, LinkedIn platform, and Google Maps - and a local database).

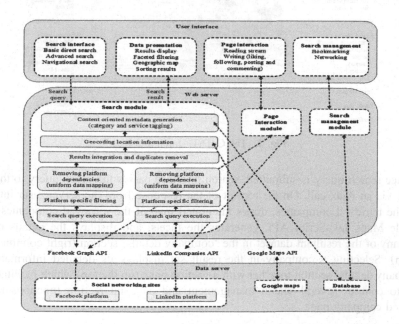

Fig. 1. Conceptual framework of CoDiT

4.3   Implementation

The CoDiT is constructed and configured upon a WAMP (windows + Apache + MyS-QL + PHP) platform. All static content of CoDiT is written in HTML and the local data is stored using MySQL DBMS. For generating dynamic content on user request, it uses JavaScript with Ajax calls. The sorting and filtering of data on client side is achieved using JavaScript Underscore library. The processing of user requests, and database and SNS querying functionalities are achieved with PHP5 scripts. To connect with Facebook and LinkedIn platforms, it uses 'Facebook SDK for PHP' and 'LinkedIn REST API' respectively and retrieves the API outputs in JSON format.

The CoDiT Search Interface: The CoDiT search interface facilitates three types of search: a basic search (direct keyword search which is either full text search – keyword appearing anywhere in company information – or user may restrict the search to one of four fields: name, location, industry, or service of the company), an advanced search (where user can design a search query with combination of different parameters including name, keyword, location, industry, and service), and a navigational search (where user can browse the companies by alphabet, location, industry or service). Figure 2 presents the CoDiT search interface after the execution of a basic keyword search.

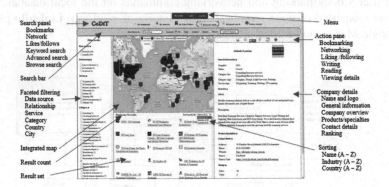

Fig. 2. The CoDiT search interface

Once search query is submitted, search interface passes the given query to the web server via an Ajax call. On the receipt of the response from the server, user interface lists the retrieved companies, draws integrated map of the retrieved companies using Google Maps JavaScript API, generates the facets, and displays the details of first company of the resultant dataset in the 'company details' section (right column of the screen). Selecting a company in the result set displays its detailed information in 'company details' section together with an action pane (on the top) which facilitates the user to commit several search management and page interaction functions for the selected company page.

The CoDiT Search Procedure: The CoDiT system executes the given search query in the following steps (see Fig. 1).

1. Execution of authenticated API calls for searching companies on SN platforms.
2. Filtering of the returned responses from the APIs to discard the pages which do not match with user specified criteria. Facebook response, in addition, is also filtered against the page category to discard the non-business pages.
3. Mapping of the data fields for each company to a uniform data structure to remove the platform dependencies and facilitate a consistent view of information.
4. Integration of the individual data sets together with simultaneous removal of duplicates by matching the name and location of company.
5. Geocoding the locations of companies through the Google Maps geocode service.
6. Generation of the content oriented metadata (category and service tagging) for the retrieved company pages. The metadata is generated on the basis of textual information available in free text fields of the company profile against the predefined category and service lists stored in the local database by using the specific matching algorithms.

4.4 Experiences and Next Steps

We have tested the CoDiT prototype and verified its functionality on a small scale. In its first version, which is discussed here, CoDiT is able to retrieve a data set of around 500 companies for a given search query. Given the partial responses returned by the SNSs, the CoDiT system makes iterative API calls to SNSs in order to maximize the response rate. The iterative API calls increase the response rate, but also raise the response time. To make a trade-off between the response time and response rate, we have set the throttle limits for the API calls per search query. The throttles are set to 1 Facebook graph API call (returning about 300 company pages) and 10 LinkedIn company search API calls (returning 200 company pages). The running time of a search query is approximately 80 s for a simple query and 120 s for a complex query.

Our current experiences with the effectiveness of the CoDiT system indicate that it is capable to achieve the desired goal of assisting companies in their search for sources of complementary assets. It enables the users to determine the suitability of potential partners in an easy and efficient way through the provision of several pieces of content-oriented metadata, faceted filtering, and effective and consistent information visualization. However, the system has not been tested in real innovation settings yet. Another limitation of the current version of the CoDiT system is that the semantical issues with the data aggregation and interoperability of heterogeneous information are only partially addressed. Whilst the system fully supports the 'Find' phase, it provides limited assistance in the next phases of open innovation process.

The CoDiT system is in ongoing process of development and improvement. Currently, it connects two social networking platforms, however, it can be scaled to connect other platforms provided their APIs with required search functionalities are made available by the respective platforms. The future steps include the implementation of the measures (caching of the data and/or batching the API calls) to lower the response time and increase the response rate; inclusion of lexical semantics in service identification of businesses; and a set of experiments in real innovation settings to measure the metrics such as usability, effectiveness and efficiency.

5   Conclusion

In this paper, we have evaluated the potential of social networking sites to support business partner discovery for involvement in open innovation alliances. The major inadequacies of SNSs for supporting business partner discovery include the dispersion of businesses' information on multiple isolated platforms, the cross platform variations in information representation, and lacking of appropriate business specific metadata and searching procedures. In order to address these challenges, we have presented the CoDiT system which allows the simultaneous search for company pages over multiple SNSs in business specific manner. The CoDiT system facilitates enhanced searching procedures and semi-automatic identification of industry and services of companies. The tool is intended to support the open innovation process – in the 'Find' stage - by the aggregation and exchange of partnering information available on SNSs.

The CoDiT system can be applied in two scenarios. One, it can be used as a supportive tool by the innovation managers for searching potential partners for them to involve in open innovation alliances. Two, it can be used by the so-called innovation intermediaries (who function as agents of network formation for business organizations, and assist them in searching and selecting business partners) to look for potential partners for their clients and thereby extend their network. The proposed tool provides two benefits. Firstly, it serves as an efficient and effective method for searching potential business partners. Secondly, it supports the reuse of partnering information already available on SNSs. Therefore, it improves the usability of SNSs and may motivate the representation of business organizations on SNSs.

References

1. Facebook Developers. http://developers.facebook.com/. Accessed 26 February 2015
2. Felt, A. Evans, D.: Privacy protection for social networking apis. In: 2008 Web 2.0 Security and Privacy (W2SP 2008) (2008)
3. Jefferson, C.E., III, Traughber, S. Social Media in Business. How Social Media Can Help Small Businesses and Non-Profit Organizations, pp. 2–3 (2012)
4. Kietzmann, J.H., Hermkens, K., McCarthy, I.P., Silvestre, B.S.: Social media? Get serious! Understanding the functional building blocks of social media. Bus. Horiz. **54**(3), 241–251 (2011)
5. LinkedIn   Developers.   https://developer-programs.linkedin.com/documents/companies. Accessed 2 March 2015
6. Papacharissi, Z.: The virtual geographies of social networks: a comparative analysis of Facebook, LinkedIn and ASmallWorld. New Media Soc. **11**(1–2), 199–220 (2009)
7. Peffers, K., Tuunanen, T., Rothenberger, M.A., Chatterjee, S.: A design science research methodology for information systems research. J. Manage. Inf. Syst. **24**(3), 45–77 (2007)
8. Slowinski, G.: Reinventing Corporate Growth. Alliance Management Group Inc., Gladstone (2005)
9. Witzeman, S., Slowinski, G., Dirkx, R., Gollob, L., Tao, J., Ward, S., Miraglia, S.: Harnessing external technology for innovation. Res. Technol. Manage. **49**(3), 19–27 (2006)

An Ontology Based Collaborative Business Service Selection - Contributing to Automatic Building of Collaborative Business Process

Wenxin Mu[1(✉)], Frédérick Bénaben[2], and Herve Pingaud[3]

[1] Beijing Jiaotong University, Shangyuancun 3, Handian, Beijing, China
wxmu@bjtu.edu.cn
[2] Toulouse University – Mines Albi, Allee de Science, Albi, France
frederick.benaben@mines-albi.fr
[3] Champollion University, Place de Verdun, Albi, France
herve.pingaud@univ-jfc.fr

Abstract. With the world wide inter-enterprise collaboration and interoperability background, automatic collaborative business process deduction might be seen as a crucial researching subject. We design a methodology of deducing collaborative process by only collecting collaborative objectives and partners' business services. The two key problems are: (i) selecting corresponding business services for a set of collaborative objectives; (ii) ordering business services with serializations and parallelization. This paper aims to present solution of business service selection. In order to solve the problem, we defined a collaborative ontology, which contains numerous instances of business services and processes of MIT process handbook. The collaborative ontology contains essential concepts in collaborative situation, and owns process deducing rules and algorithms. We provide a brief illustration of implementation within a SaaS toolkit called Mediator Modeling 2ool.

Keywords: Business process management · Model-driven engineering · Inter-enterprise collaboration · Ontology

1 Introduction

In collaborative situation, all the partners come with collaborative objectives and their own objectives to achieve and business services to share. They expect to combine their own business services with suitable ones from other partners to work towards their common objectives. In addition, collaborative business process is a combination of business functions, which is inter-linked and filled with sequences and orders. With these needs, *objective-oriented business service selection* and *collaborative business process creation* are absolute essentials in collaboration world. Considering self-updating and re-building of collaborative business process, we shall design an automatic way to deal with service selection and process creation in design level. Further more in implementation level, first because the software tool deals with a collaborative situation, all the partners may use the software in the same time or individually. Secondly, in order to interact with other software tools (which is

© IFIP International Federation for Information Processing 2015
L.M. Camarinha-Matos et al. (Eds.): PRO-VE 2015, IFIP AICT 463, pp. 639–651, 2015.
DOI: 10.1007/978-3-319-24141-8_60

developed in our lab), the software should be able to deploy in ESB (Enterprise Service Bus). These lead that the software tool involved in the methodology should be a web service. SaaSs (Software as a Service) seems to be a good solution.

In our lab, Vatcharaphun Rajsiri has created a knowledge-based system for collaborative process specification [1]. This system deduces a BPMN (Business Process Modeling Notation) based collaborative process model automatically with the help of collaborative objective model and MIT process handbook [2]. But this system has weaknesses. First, the system collects only the main goal of whole collaborative network. It leads to lack of partners' objectives and sub-network information. Designing a model, which models all above information, is necessary. Second, the deduced BPMN collaborative process covers only operational level. If in a complex collaborative situation, partners come from different departments and management level. An operational collaborative business process couldn't satisfy partners. According to [3, 4], business process covers strategy, operation and support levels. We arrive at conclusion that target collaborative process should contain strategy, operation and support levels.

A model-driven and ontology based methodology, which take collaborative objectives, partners' objectives and business services as input and deduce collaborative business process as output as automatically as possible, seems to be a good solution in this situation.

For the input, we define objective model and function model to collect basic collaborative knowledge from partners. For the deduction method, collaborative ontology and a set of algorithms and transformation rules is defined. The algorithms manage to link business objectives with business services. The transformations rules help to deduce sequences among business functions. For the output, BPMN based collaborative process cartography is deduced. The collaborative process cartography has three types: strategy, support and operation.

In this paper, we focus on introducing solution of business service selection (dash-line box in Fig. 1). Section 2 first presents definition of objective model and function model. Then it provides a simple example to explain the directions for use of models. Section 3 provides a brief introduction of collaborative ontology. Section 4 gives definitions of business services selection algorithms. Section 5 is a sketch for collaborative process model and collaborative process creation method. Section 6 draws some concluding remarks, discusses the feasibility of our work and outlines our future investigations.

2 Objective Model and Function Model

This section explains the input part of Collaborative Business Process Deduction methodology (CBPD). In Sect. 2.1, we first address the definition of objective modeling elements. Section 2.2 presents the definition of function model. And finally Sect. 2-C illustrates examples of objective model and function model.

2.1   Objective Model

"An objective model is required to facilitate: (i) identification, communication and structuring of business objectives, and (ii) measurement of the level of success in achieving objectives. But individual modeling methodologies focus primarily on selected aspects of objectives representation and measurement." Reference [5] For our individual needs, the objective model here should collect both collaborative main goals and partners' individual objectives. For each collaborative goal, partners are regrouped as sub-collaborative network. Partners also have their own objectives. We come up with a result: a real collaborative situation is like a multi-level pyramid: each level could be decomposed to sub-network until partner, and each level could be abstracted to higher-level collaborative network until the whole collaborative network. With supplementary illustration, because the goal of CBPD is to deduce collaborative process cartography (including strategy, operation and support sub-collaborative processes), we consider that the objectives collected in objective model may set to three types: strategy/operation/support objective.

To summarize, the objective model presented here should be able to (Fig. 1 presents modeling elements and links):

- Model collaborative network, collaborative sub-network and partners' relationships.
- Model collaborative networks' objective, sub network's objectives and partners' objectives.

Classify objective into strategy, operation and support objective.

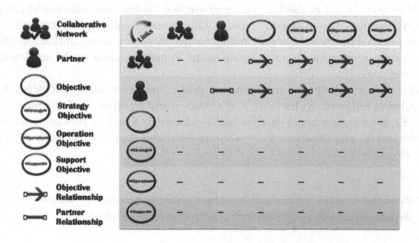

Fig. 1. Objective model elements definition

2.2   Function Model

The requirements for the function model are to get partners' functions, to simplify user's modeling tasks and to decrease user's workload. The function model just collects functions that partners want to share and which can be published to other partners.

We defined an IDEF1 (Integration Definition for Function Modeling) based function model to gather partners' business services.

Standard function model: IDEF0 [6] is reused to present partners' functions. The standard IDEF0 modeling unit is shown in Fig. 2 left part. The modeling unit has input and output message. Controlling message and mechanism controls and support function. The function also could send call message to invoke another function. As shown in the middle of Fig. 2, function main model reuses function unit and controlling message. As shown on the right of Fig. 2, partner columns separate function model. Partner lists its shared functions in correspondence column. Function model reuses function unit, input and output message, controlling message and call message of standard IDEF0 modeling unit.

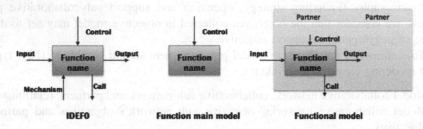

Fig. 2. Function model elements definition [7]

After analysis and evaluation, we found out that the function main model could be partially transferred from objective model. Objectives of collaborative network could be seen as main function. User only fulfills control messages among abstract functions. Transformation equations from objective model to main function model are defined in first-order logic [8].

Due to particularity of transformation rules, first order logic still needs to be expended as followed: (i) Element: X is *Collaborative Network* → *CollaborativeNetwork(X)*; (ii) Relationship: Y is *Objective Relationship* which is between *CollaborativeNetwork* X_1 and *Objective* X_2 → *Objective-Relationship(Y)(CollaborativeNetwork (X_1), Objective(X_2))*.

$$\forall \text{CollaborativeNetwork}(X) \, (\forall \text{ObjectiveRelationship}(\text{CollaborativeNetwork}(X), \text{Objective}(X_1)))$$
$$\rightarrow \exists \text{MainFunctionModel}(X) \land \exists \text{MainFunction}(X_1) \in \text{MainFunctionModel}(X) \tag{1}$$

3   Collaborative Ontology

The collaborative ontology defined in CBPD aims to support business service selection and collaborative process creation. This ontology defines the concepts and relationships involved in collaborative situation. The collaborative ontology must be fulfilled with

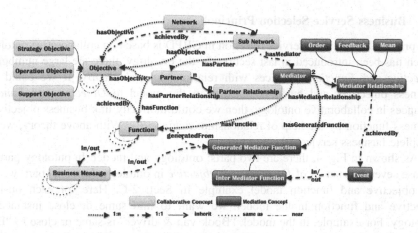

Fig. 3. Collaborative ontology

instances from different business domains (for example, MIT process handbook from manufacture, Score Model from Supply Chain and instances from crisis management) (Fig. 3).

As explained in Sect. 2, the collaborative concepts part of collaborative ontology is seen as two relationships and three main concepts: *Same As/Near By* relationship, *Network*, *Objective* and *Function*. They are detail explained as followed:

- *Same As/Near By* relationship contains two parts: *Same As* and *Near By*. If concept A is Same As with concept B, then concept A equals to concept B. Concept A and Concept B presents the same concept. If concept A is *Near By* concept B, then concept A and concept B are similar. Concept A may present part of concept B. Concept A and concept B may crosse.
- *Network* means all the involved partners and relationships among them. Another close concept is *Sub Network*.
- *Objective* presents business goals of collaboration and partners. *Objective* has relationship: *Same As/Near By* with another *Objective*.
- *Function* equals to business services or function, which are provided by partners. *Function* may own input and output *Message*. Both *Function* and *Message* have self-related relationships: *Same As/Near By*.

In collaborative ontology, collaborative concepts part serves to match collaborative objectives to partners' business capabilities. Mediation concepts part is based on Mediation [9] concept. In this paper, our vision is on business service selection. So process creation part will not be detailed.

4   Business Service Selection Method

In this section, we provide the explanation of business service selection. Section 4.1 presents basic theory of business service selection. The example in Sect. 2-C is re-used. Section 4.2 provides official algorithms of selecting business service.

4.1   Business Service Selection Principal

The principal of business service selection in CBPD is based on collaborative ontology, which has been introduced in last section. In the ontology, there are large numbers of *Objective* and *Function* instances with relationship: *achievedBy*. If we could link business objectives and business function in the model to *Objective* and *Function* instances in collaborative ontology, then we could indirectly link business objective to business function by the help of relationship: *achievedBy*. With above theory, we can complete business service selection task.

As shown in Fig. 4, there are two parts: ontology and model. In ontology part, we choose several instances of *Function* and *Objective* in ontology. In model part, we take the objective and function model example in Sect. 2-C. Here for each business objective and function in the model, we want to find same or close instances in ontology. For example, in the model, "Book van & driver" is same or close to "Book transportation" in the ontology, then we make a link: *Same As/Near By* between them.

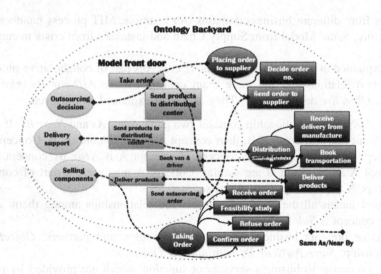

Fig. 4. Making links among models and ontology instances

With all the relationship: *Same As/Near By* in Fig. 4, suitable business functions are selected for business objectives. Figure 5 shows all the results. Business objectives is linked to business functions by relationship: *achievedBy*.

Even though the basic principal of business service selection is defined, there are still some remarks to consider:

- Making relationship: *Same As/Near By* for each business objective and function is quite hard for user. So we provide an Instance Suggestion Mechanism, which could provide suggested ontology instance for user. Section 4.2 Algorithm (1) presents the Instance Suggestion Mechanism algorithm.

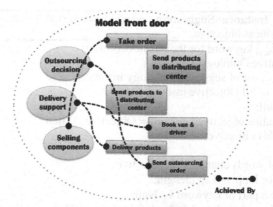

Fig. 5. Deducing links among objectives and functions

- Business objectives and functions defined in the model could also be seen as *Business* and *Function* instances in collaborative ontology for future uses. There should be a self-update mechanism to enlarge the collaborative ontology. Section 4.2 Algorithm (3) explains self-updating mechanism.

4.2   Business Service Selection Algorithms

(1) **Instance Suggestion Algorithm.** Instance suggestion algorithm deals with selecting same or nearest ontology Objective or Function instances for each business objective and function. Algorithm (1) takes keyword of business objective as input, uses collaborative ontology as data and provides a list of suggested ontology instances. This algorithm has three main parts:

- Line 3: finding an *Objective* instance in collaborative ontology which owns the same keyword: objective$_{key}$ as business objective, the instance is added to suggestion list: $L_{suggestion}$;
- Line 6-Line 17: Taking frontal parts of keyword as a new list of keyword: $L_{word}[1]$ to $L_{word}[i]$ (for example, keyword: "send products to distributing center", new keywords: "send products to distributing" and "send products to"), for each new keyword, if finding an *Objective* instance's keyword in collaborative ontology which starts with or contains the new one or contains, then the *Objective* instance is added to suggestion list;

Line 18-Line 23: Taking related two words, which are contained in keyword as a new list of keyword: L_{2words} (for example, keyword: "send outsourcing order", new keywords: "send outsourcing" and "outsourcing order"), for each related two words, if finding an *Objective* instance's keyword, which contains the two words, then the Objective instance is added to suggestion list.

Algorithm (1) Instance Suggestion: provide suggested collaborative ontology instances for business objective.

Input: objective$_{key}$, keyword for the business objective
Data: Collaborative Ontology: CO
Output: L$_{suggestion}$, list of suggested ontology instances
1 A$_{objective}$, array of all Objective instances of CO;
2 L$_{suggestion}$ ← Null;
3 **if** A$_{objective}$ contains objective.keyword = Objective$_{key}$ **then**
4   L$_{suggestion}$ adds objective;
5 **else**
6   L$_{word}$, list of words contained in objective$_{key}$;
7   i, counter for loop ← L$_{word}$.length;
8   word, store a part of keyword ← Null;
9   **for** i from L$_{word}$.length to 3 //Check first three words
10   word = from L$_{word}$[1] to L$_{word}$[i] ;
11   **if** A$_{objective}$ contains objective.keyword starts with word
12   L$_{suggestion}$ adds objective;
13   **end**;
14   **if** A$_{objective}$ contains objective.keyword contains word **then**
15   L$_{suggestion}$ adds objective;
16   **end**;
17   **end**;
18   L$_{2words}$, list of 2 words contained in Objective$_{key}$;
19   **while** L$_{2words}$ has next element: word **do**
20   **if** A$_{objective}$ contains objective.keyword contains word **then**
21   L$_{suggestion}$ adds objective;
22   **end**;
23   **end**;
24 **end**;
25 **return** L$_{suggestion}$;

---

(2) **Objective-Function Mapping.** Objective-Function mapping algorithm is the main part of buiness service selection. The principal has been explained in Sect. 4.1. As shown in Algorithm (2), it takes list of business objectives and list of business functions as input, uses collaborative ontology as data, and outputs list of relationships: achievedBy. The algorithm is explained as followed:

- Line 3-Line 5: starts the mapping from business functions side. If one business function: E$_{function}$ owns relationship: *Same As/Near By* with one ontology *Function* instance: O$_{function}$.
- Line 6-Line 7: if O$_{function}$ owns relationship: *achievedBy* with one ontology *Objective* instance: O$_{objective}$, and if O$_{objective}$ owns relationship: *Same As/Near By* with business objective: E$_{objective}$, then as result: E$_{objective}$ has relationship: *achievedBy* with E$_{function}$.
- Line 8: the relationship is added into the list: L$_{achievedBy}$.
- Line 13 and Line 16: if there is an E$_{function}$, which doesn't find E$_{objective}$, then a relationship: *achievedBy* from Null to E$_{function}$ is created. The relationship is added to L$_{achievedBy}$.

- Line 21: if an $E_{objective}$ is never achieved, then a relationship: *achievedBy* from $E_{objective}$ to Null is created. The relationship is added to $L_{achievedBy}$.

Algorithm (2) Objective-Function mapping: find correspondence business functions for each business objective and create relationship: *achievedBy*.

Input: $L_{objective}$, list of business objectives
       $L_{function}$, list of business functions
Data: Collaborative Ontology: CO
Output: $L_{achievedBy}$, list of relationship
1 $L_{achievedBy} \leftarrow$ Null;
2 $L_{relatedObjectives}$, list of objectives with achievedBy $\leftarrow$ Null;
3 **while** $L_{function}$ has next element: $E_{function}$ **do**
4   **if** $E_{function}$.sameas/nearby!=null **then**
5      $O_{function} = E_{function}$.sameas/nearby;
6      $O_{objective} = O_{function}$.achievedby;
7   **if** $L_{objective}$ contains element $E_{objective}$.sameas/nearby = $O_{objective}$ **then**
8        $L_{achievedBy}$ adds achievedBy($E_{objective}$, $E_{function}$);
9   **if** $L_{relatedObjective}$ doesn't contain $E_{objective}$ **then**
10         $L_{relatedObjective}$ adds $E_{objective}$;
11   **end**;
12   **else**
13        $L_{achievedBy}$ adds achievedBy(null, $E_{function}$);
14   **end**;
15   **else**
16      $L_{achievedBy}$ adds achievedBy(null, $E_{function}$);
17   **end**;
18**end**;
19**while** $L_{objective}$ has next element: $E_{objective}$ **do**
20   **if** $L_{relatedObjective}$ doesn't contain $E_{objective}$ **then**
21      $L_{achievedBy}$ adds achievedBy($E_{objective}$, null);
22   **end**;
23**end**;
24**return** $L_{achievedBy}$;

---

(3) **Ontology Updating.** Ontology updating algorithm deals with inserting business objectives and functions in collaborative ontology as Objective and Function instances with relationship: Same As/Near By. As shown in Algorithm (3):

- Line 2 and Line 3: for each $E_{objecitve}$, if $E_{objective}$ owns relationship: Same As/Near By, then get $O_{objective}$ which is related to $E_{objective}$.
- Line 4 and Line 5: create new ontology instance: O_{new} for $E_{objective}$ and add O_{new} into collaborative ontology.
- Line 6: creates new Relationship: Same As/Near By between O_{new} and $O_{objective}$, and adds the relationship to collaborative ontology also.

Algorithm (3) Ontology Updating: insert business objectives into ontology as instances and created relationship: *Same As/Near By*.

Input: $L_{objective}$, list of business objectives
Data: Collaborative Ontology: CO
1 **while** $L_{objective}$ has next element: $E_{objective}$ **do**
2   **if** $E_{objective}$.sameas/ncarby!=null **then**
3          $O_{objective} = E_{objective}$.sameas/nearby;
4   O_{new} = change $E_{objective}$ to ontology instance;
5   CO adds O_{new};
6   CO adds SameAs/NearBy($O_{objective}$, O_{new});
7   **end**;
8 **end**;

---

5   Implementation

Nowadays, SaaS [10] is very widely used. It allows users to use application in a Web Client as rich application. No complex client site installation is required. According to [11], compared with the traditional way which software is purchased for and installed on personal computers, SaaS has advantages: e.g., investment reduction, performance improvement, time saving, easier collaboration, global accessibility, etc. Considering our own needs, the software tool should be able to deploy on ESB [12], which means the software must be a web service. Because the software deals with a collaborative situation, all the partners may use the software in the same time or individually. This leads to a conclusion. SaaS is a quite good solution for our tool: Mediator Modeling 2ool.

Mediator Modeling 2ool bases on GWT [13] and GeasyTools[1]. Mediator Modeling 2ool supports objective and function modeling. It implements business service selection and collaborative process creation.

Figure 6 is the screen shot of Mediator Modeling 2ool. On the left, there are modeling palette and file explorer. On the right, there are element properties and collaborative ontology instances' tree. In the middle, it is modeling place. We could create objective and function model here. Web browser can directly launch Mediator Modeling 2ool.

In the property window in Fig. 6, if we click on the button beside text field, a window with collaborative ontology instances' tree comes out. User chooses the same as or near by ontology instance for modeling element by dragging the instance form ontology tree to same as or near by lists' windows. After modeling and choosing same as or near by ontology instance, a XML file which contains all the modeling information is saved on the server side. User could save the XML file on local machine too.

For business function, the property also contains semantic annotation. The semantic annotation classifies business function to Service Task, Send Task, Receive Task, User

---

[1] GeasyTools is an open source GWT based API. PetalsLink develops it. The tool helps create graphic elements. It is available on website: http://research.petalslink.org/display/geasytools/GEasyTools +Overview.

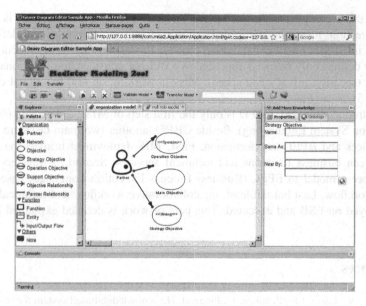

Fig. 6. Mediator modeling 2ool main frame

Task and Business Rule Task. Business functions combined with semantic annotations are reused to semantically select web services, which could implement business functions. This part of work is presented in [14].

6 Conclusion

Collaborative business process deduction methodology (CBPD) aims to provide a collaborative process cartography, which manages process orchestration and business service selection in collaborative situation. The strong points of CBPD are summarized as followed: (i) objective model defines objectives and sub-networks. We could easily verify the small group of partners to complete the task; (ii) objective model could model different levels of partners; (iii) functional table is separated by columns of partner. This allows each partner to fill its own column independently; (iv) collaborative process model is deduced automatically. It saves repeated work and eases heavy workload of user. It also crosses different enterprise modeling standard: from IDEF to BPMN.

However, any system has its weak points. They are summarized as followed: (i) business service selection is half manual and half automatic method. User has to create Same As/Near By relationship from model to ontology instances manually. And then Mediator Modeling 2ool automatically links partners' business functions to collaborative and partners' objectives. (ii) This system bases on collaborative ontology, it means that a collaborative ontology, which holds numerous instances and covers different domains is required.

With the accomplishment of business service selection, the next task is business process creation. It remains the formalization of transformation rules and definition of gateways in BPMN based collaborative process model. Further more, function model of CBPD defines only business function. We did not consider non-functional characterization (security, privacy and speed). Miss is working on non-functional characterization [15].

As introduced in [16], CBPD is only the first step of MISE 2.0 project (Mediation Information System Engineering). Beside CBPD, another two main tasks are semantic web services and BPEL transformation. First, MIS deployment bridges the semantic gap between business functions and technical services. Second, it transfers collaborative process model to BPEL (Business Process Execution Language) based collaborative workflow. Last but not least, the collaborative workflow and technical services are deployed on ESB and executed. This part of work is detailed explained in [14].

References

1. Rajsiri, V., Lorré, J.P., Bénaben, F., Pingaud, H.: Knowledge-based system for collaborative process specification. Comput. Ind. **61**(2), 161–175 (2010)
2. Malone, T.W., Crowston, K., Herman, G.A.: Organizing Business Knowledge: The MIT Process Handbook. The MIT Press, Cambridge (2003)
3. NF EN ISO 9000 Systèmes de management de la qualité - Principes essentiels et vocabulaire, September 2005. http://catdoc.mines-albi.fr:8080/Record.htm?idlist=6&record=19134158124919523309. Accessed 19 January 2012
4. NF EN ISO 9000 X50-130 Systèmes de management de la qualité - Principes essentiels et vocabulaire, October 2005. http://catdoc.mines-albi.fr:8080/Record.htm?idlist=6&record=19143202124919614849. Accessed 19 January 2012
5. Neiger, D., Churilov, L., Flitman, A.: Business objectives modelling. In: Value-Focused Business Process Engineering: A Systems Approach, vol. 19, pp. 1–26. Springer, Boston (2009)
6. Menzel, C., Mayer, R.J.: The IDEF family of languages. In: Handbook on Architectures of Information Systems, pp. 215–249 (2006)
7. Announcing the Standard for Integration Definition for Function Modeling (IDEF0). Draft Federal Information Processing Standards Publication, vol. 183 (1993)
8. Smullyan, R.M.: First-Order Logic. Dover Publications, New York (1995)
9. Benaben, F., Touzi, J., Rajsiri, V., Lorré, J.P.: Mediation information system design in a collaborative SOA context through a MDD approach. In: Proceedings of MDISIS 2008, pp. 1–17 (2008)
10. Sun, W., Zhang, K., Chen, S.-K., Zhang, X., Liang, H.: Software as a service: an integration perspective. In: Krämer, B.J., Lin, K.-J., Narasimhan, P. (eds.) ICSOC 2007. LNCS, vol. 4749, pp. 558–569. Springer, Heidelberg (2007)
11. Wu, B., Deng, S., Li, Y., Wu, J., Yin, J.: Reference models for Saas oriented business workflow management systems. In: 2011 IEEE International Conference on Services Computing (SCC), pp. 242–249 (2011)
12. Endo, A.T., Simao, A.: Model-based testing of service-oriented applications via state models. In: 2011 IEEE International Conference on Services Computing (SCC), pp. 432–439 (2011)

13. Gupta, V.: Accelerated GWT: Building Enterprise Google Web Toolkit Applications. Apress, Berkeley (2008)
14. Bénaben, F., Boissel-Dallier, N., Lorré, J.-P., Pingaud, H.: Semantic reconciliation in interoperability management through model-driven approach. In: Camarinha-Matos, L.M., Boucher, X., Afsarmanesh, H. (eds.) PRO-VE 2010. IFIP AICT, vol. 336, pp. 705–712. Springer, Heidelberg (2010)
15. Zribi, S., Bénaben, F., Ben Hamida, A., Lorré, J.P.: Towards a service and choreography governance framework for future internet. Presented at the I-ESA 2012, Valence, Spain (2012)
16. Mu, W., Bénaben, F., Pingaud, H., Boissel-Dallier, N., Lorré, J.-P.: A model-driven BPM approach for SOA mediation information system design in a collaborative context. In: 2011 IEEE International Conference on Services Computing (SCC), pp. 747–748 (2011)

A Hybrid Syntactic and Semantic Approach to Service Identification in Collaborative Networks

Ehsan Alirezaei[✉] and Saeed Parsa

Software Engineering Group, Iran University of Science and Technology,
School of Computer Engineering, Tehran, Iran
Ehsan.alirezaii@gmail.com, parsa@iust.ac.ir

Abstract. In this paper a semi-automated approach for service identification, considering the requirements of partners in a collaborative network is presented. The requirements meeting the business goals are further applied as a means for building the business process to-be model. Approach begins with process and goal combination and maps action rules to tasks for specific resources for fill the gap between goal model and business model representations. Semantic analysis based on extraction of resource relations and their similarity is second part of main method to service identification. A correlation matrix from extracted weighted task's relations is used as an input of space vector machine. Semantic clustering of pre-processed vector is used for identify partner's services.

Keywords: Service identification · Business process model · Goal model · Collaborative network · Semantic clustering

1 Introduction

Collaborative network defined as "a network consisting of a variety of entities that are largely autonomous, geographically distributed, and heterogeneous in terms of operating environment, culture, social capital and goals" [1]. To achieving collaboration among partners, technical and non-technical approaches should consider. In technical point of view, Service identification is one of the approaches to achieve collaboration among partners. Several researches have suggested service-modeling approaches that can identify and specify service components [2–4]. There are a few automated and semi-automated techniques to identify services based on business tasks [2, 5, 6] that outcomes of most of these techniques are business services that might be quite different from software services. Those techniques are not using combination of syntactic and semantic analysis to identification that this paper suggested to.

We used practical strategy based on existing business processes and goals for service identification. Identification of services by decomposing the business processes into tasks, providing reusable right-grained functionalities, proposed in some methods [7]. A major benefit of this approach is that the identified services satisfy functional needs and objectives [8]. Each task has an action rule to business process that should apply on resources with pre-conditions and post-conditions that we call them goals. Binding

© IFIP International Federation for Information Processing 2015
L.M. Camarinha-Matos et al. (Eds.): PRO-VE 2015, IFIP AICT 463, pp. 652–659, 2015.
DOI: 10.1007/978-3-319-24141-8_61

services to business processes with combining goals could fill the gap of top-down implementation with the bottom-up requirement engineering and implementation. Taking to the account the syntactic approaches of modeling structure it is not enough to fill the gap, so there is also a semantic approach to clustering correlated resources and joining two methods. Based on definition of goal that presented, tasks could be interrelated through the supporting goal for business processes. Therefore, functionality of a target system tracked and traced to business objectives and goals [9]. To identify proper services, combination of business process and goals should analyze [10].

In summary, we can say that to identify appropriate services, cross-organizational business requirements and business change factors should analyze to meet the collaboration objectives and agility [11]. The great benefit of goal driven approaches is that their resulting services have guaranteed fit with the organizations functional needs [12]. To facilitate accessing and manipulation of business resources one or more services could be defined as reusable modules of code. Therefore, business resources are useful to identify services and they classified based on their lifetime, handled by organization units of work [13] and resulting class considered as a candidate service. A resource that shared among business activities has a usage to identifying of activities as a service [14]. In general, a resource indicates a main stable domain abstraction of an enterprise that in certain situations, activities applied to relate a number of those resources commonly. Each service should identify through resource, resource-resource and resource-activity matrixes, those are built to measure the cohesiveness of the service [15]. However, services considered as a reusable set of non-interacting activ ities, which inter-related solely through shared access to one or more resources.

In the method proposed in this paper, three matrices, task-goal, task-resource and task-task applied to detect cohesive and reusable functionalities as candidate services. Services identified as cohesive, independent and reusable components. A service may be composed of set of tasks, which are interrelated through shared access to one or more entities or supporting a same goal. Goal, task and resource may lead to a cluster that shows same class that means an identified service. With considering the efficiency of the final code, some of the candidates selected as services.

The organization of paper is as follows: Service Identification Method described in Sect. 2 in details, with a sample case study. The proposed method presented in some qualification criteria, tasks to services specified, and features has described. A summary to other methods presented in Sect. 3. A summary of the results and future considerations of our research presented at Sect. 4.

2 Service Identification Method

The method proposed in this article identifies services using combined business process and goal models and entities in two syntactic and semantic analysis way. The method consists of some steps that in first main step, the goals and the business process models extracted, and then combined for reaching Business Process (BP) to-be model. Next main step is going to extract the task-task matrix from the combined model. Next main step is using information retrieval based on vector space modeling techniques to building correlation matrix and building groups of tasks as services [16]. Comparing extracted tasks, entities with goals will make possible to identify services. These steps described in detail in the following subsections.

2.1 Creating Combined Business Process and Goal Model

In step one, it assumed BP As-Is models exist, and a job to do is reengineering it from current state to to-be model based on combination of goal models. For achieving this objective and bringing agility to BPs, combination of works [10, 17] used. BPs modeled using BPMN2.0 standard. To create the current BP model of a cross-organization collaboration, that is not part of problem domain in this paper, using experts and process mining techniques could take to account for creating as-is model. Figure 1 shows part of BPMN model as "Purchase part" process with three role and some tasks for each role. It shows how purchase program commits by company experts trough configuring the program, email and comments. Middle-out approach based on existing BPs and main work of it, is bridging the gap between goals and services.

2.1.1 Goal Analysis

In first step, we represent goal model in order to satisfaction of current state relationship. A goal is an action rule, pre-condition and post-condition to an action in BP with roles that should under considerations [16, 18]. Pre-conditions are included "AND" provided statement and Post-conditions are included "OR" provided statement that it helps traceability analysis. From requirement engineering point of view, each request for services is an objective to satisfy that we could classify them in functional and non-functional requirements. These requirements have focus on current and future enterprise goals and define desired features to achieve in the future [19].

For representing goals in informal way that could be traced in hierarchical way and semantic manner, we used KAOS approach to modeling [18] modeling to fill the gap with BPs. In this method, goals hierarchy are refine by "AND" and "OR" operators that each refinement clear the satisfaction of higher goal in hierarchy. Simplicity of KAOS method is the main reason for using its method, and a formal goal definition begins with an assertion of the goal concretion objects. Each goal has informal and formal definitions. Event to complete the process make the traceability of the goal, and satisfaction links are between goal and process. The result of the work is important to us, so we do not enter the details of doing this. As it shows in Fig. 2, the action rules and their hierarchy should satisfy to specific task accomplished like for achieving supporting program's workflow, two providing program and estimating sub-goal should satisfy that each of them represents providing program and sending approved estimation tasks in Fig. 1.

2.1.2 Creating the BP to-Be Model Based on Goals and Tasks

In step 2, gap analysis is performed to extract needed changes in BP model. Tasks, which do not support any goal or sub-goal of organization, should be eliminated. In addition, to support reusability, tasks with a same set of goals can merged in a single task. To identify BP model tasks, which do not cover any system goal and objective,

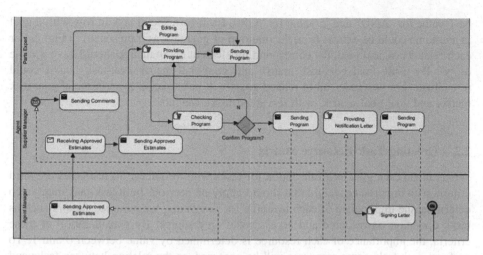

Fig. 1. Part of BP Model (As-Is) for purchase part process [20]

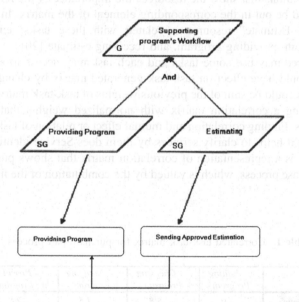

Fig. 2. Goal model map to process task items for creating supplying automation systems

Task Goal matrix should consider with considering goal hierarchy that rows correspond to tasks and columns belongs to goals. Also, each goal analysis should consider clarifying need of task modification or introduction for task alignments. When BP designed in Visual Paradigm tools as it shown in Fig. 1, the tool could help to build task-task matrix and it is one it's outputs. For achieving task-goal correlation matrix, we need goal- goal matrix with weighting of related goals refinement relations it could be 1 value for "AND" and .5 value for "OR". Each correspond task in row with a goal in a column could be extract from the diagram of goal task as it presented in Fig. 2. For each related task and goal, the corresponding element in the matrix should have a value of 'y'. By using final goal-task matrix and goal-goal matrix task-task matrix could re-evaluate. For two tasks, all of related goals will be extracted from the final goal-task matrix and goal-goal matrix, with re-valued tasks weights.

2.2 Creating Task-Resource Matrix

We assumed each goal as a rule action for tasks with resources. So resources are third criteria with importance weight that should apply on pervious built task-task matrix. To determine the importance of each resource for weighting, we assumed factors such as tasks operation on resource and access costs on resource. By consideration of these criteria, the importance of each resource is determined by value between 0 and 1. To perform each task, some resources will be accessed, so the relation between tasks and resources should be considered. In this step, by creating a matrix with rows that show the tasks and columns that show the resources the importance of the relevant entity for each task should be put in the corresponding element of the matrix. In our case study the "Approved Estimate" resource is related with these tasks: editing program, checking program, providing program, and receiving estimate [20].

Each resource may use some tasks and each task may access to some resources. This relation could have effect on task-task generated matrix by changing the values. The final values could be sum of the previous weights of task-task matrixes. In this step we are providing a correlation matrix with normalized weights that could help to identify services. Finding correlation and mutual effect or relation of task in same group and cluster that it helps to clarify services by them does Service identification by this matrix. Table 1 is a representation of correlation matrix that shows purchase program related to purchase process, which is valued by the combination of the first, second, and third matrix.

Table 1. Correlated task-task matrix for purchase part process [20]

	Editing Program	Checking Program	Notifying Program	Provid-ing Program	Sending Comments
Editing Program	0	5.8	1.5	2.8	4
Checking Program	5.8	0	2	3.8	4
Notifying Program	1.5	2	0	1.5	1.5
Providing Program	2.8	3.8	1.5	0	2
Sending Comments	4	4	1.5	2	0

To cluster tasks in vector space machine we used WordNet and aim is finding Pearson correlation coefficient. Similarity function between two tasks "a" and "b" with predefined weight is defined as:

$$Sim(a_m, b_n) = W(R(a_m, b_n))$$

The optimum cluster occurs when cohesion between is minimum tasks as a service is the maximum possible value and coupling is minimum value between tasks in different clusters. For services reusability the optimum way is maximum value of similarity. For vector "V" there is frequency "f" of repeat patterns "p" and in each cluster "c", for "W" the formula is as follows:

$$W(R(a,b)) = \sum_{r_i \in R(a,b)} f(r,a,b) / (\sum_{\alpha \in cj} \sum_{(a,b) \in W} f(a,b,p)) * \sum_{(a,b) \in W} f(a,b,pi)$$

For clarifying the distinction between clusters and their relation, we can use the next formula for cluster "A" and task "t":

$$rel(t,A) = Sim(t,A) - \frac{1}{A} * \sum_{a \in A} Sim(t,a)$$

So there are two results, first for computing similarity between two tasks in vector space, and second for determining relation between a task and cluster. So after distinction between relation and similarities, there will be clusters with some elements that are our tasks, and districted cluster will be known as services. Identified services for the experiment are four clusters:

- *Providing-program with similarity 0.75* service with receiving estimation and preparing program methods
- *Program-notification with similarity 0.62* service with preparing program, email evaluation, email signing, and email evaluation methods
- *Program-evaluation with similarity 0.58* service with program correction, writing comments, sending comments, and comments evaluation methods
- *Email- sending with similarity 0.7* service with email signing, email notification

In the implementing the clustering subject and applying it to the current tasks, we found services with degree of similarity for each one that indicates that each cluster with similar concept and relation to its components.

3 Conclusion

For service identification in a collaborative environment, we presented a syntactic analysis based on hierarchical decomposition task to action rules, task-task matrix and considering the resources that goals act to. For part of semantic analysis we used clustering of identified relations in a task-task matrix by using the appropriate formula. Base of work is on documented existing Businesses processes between partners that help in considering structural relations between tasks and plays the main role in identifying services. In the future work our aim is to find cluster of services base on requests of users and their contexts in a dynamic collaborative environment processes are not documented.

References

1. Camarinha-Matos, L.M., Afsarmanesh, H., Ollus, M.: ECOLEAD and CNO base concepts. In: Methods and tools for collaborative networked organizations, pp. 3–32. Springer, US 2008
2. Rosen, M., Lublinsky, B., Smith, K.T., Balcer, M.J.: Applied SOA: Service-Oriented Architecture and Design Strategies. Wiley, New York (2008)
3. Arsanjani, A., Ghosh, S., Allam, A., Abdollah, T., Ganapathy, S., Holley, K.: SOMA: a method for developing service-oriented solutions. IBM Syst. J. **47**(3), 377–396 (2008)
4. Fensel, D., Bussler, C.: The web service modeling framework WSMF. Electron. Commer. Res. Appl. **1**(2), 113–137 (2002)
5. Jamshidi, P., Sharifi, M., Mansour, S.: To establish enterprise service model from enterprise business model. In: IEEE International Conference on Services Computing, 2008, SCC 2008, vol. 1, pp. 93–100. IEEE (2008)
6. Jain, H., Zhao, H., Chinta, N.R.: A spanning tree based approach to identifying web services. Int. J. Web Serv. Res. (IJWSR) **1**(1), 1–20 (2004)
7. Mani, S., Sinha, V.S., Sukaviriya, N., Ramachandra, T.: Using user interface design to enhance service identification. In: IEEE International Conference on Web Services, 2008, ICWS 2008, pp. 78–87. IEEE (2008)
8. Hubbers, J.-W., Ligthart, A., Terlouw, L.: Ten ways to identify services. SOA Mag. **13**, 1–7 (2007)
9. Levi, K., Arsanjani, A.: A goal-driven approach to enterprise component identification and specification. Commun. ACM **45**(10), 45–52 (2002)
10. Krogstie, J.: Using eeml for combined goal and process oriented modeling: a case study. In: Proceedings of EMMSAD, p. 113 (2008)
11. Iocola, P.: When legacy meets SOA: achieving business agility by integrating new technology with existing software asset. In: 2007 1st Annual IEEE on Systems Conference, pp. 1–8. IEEE (2007)
12. Fareghzadeh, N.: Service identification approach to SOA development. Proc. World Acad. Sci. Eng. Technol. **35**, 258–266 (2008)
13. Rostampour, A., Kazemi, A., Shams, F., Zamiri, A., Jamshidi, P.: A metric for measuring the degree of entity-centric service cohesion. In: 2010 IEEE International Conference on Service-Oriented Computing and Applications (SOCA), pp. 1–5. IEEE (2010)
14. Daghaghzadeh, M., Dastjerdi, A.B., Daghaghzadeh, H.: A metric for measuring degree of service cohesion in service oriented designs. Int. J. Comput. Sci. **8**
15. Yousef, R., Odeh, M.: A new service identification approach based on the riva business process architecture.(Chap 8). In: Frontiers in Information Technology (2012)
16. Kuhn, A., Ducasse, S., Gírba, T.: Semantic clustering: identifying topics in source code. Inf. Softw. Technol. **49**(3), 230–243 (2007)
17. Koliadis, G., Ghose, A.K.: Relating business process models to goal-oriented requirements models in KAOS. In: Hoffmann, A., Kang, B.-H., Richards, D., Tsumoto, S. (eds.) PKAW 2006. LNCS (LNAI), vol. 4303, pp. 25–39. Springer, Heidelberg (2006)

18. Van Lamsweerde, A.: Goal-oriented requirements engineering: a guided tour. In: Fifth IEEE International Symposium on Requirements Engineering, 2001. Proceedings, pp. 249–262. IEEE (2001)
19. Kavakli, E., Loucopoulos, P.: Goal driven requirements engineering: evaluation of current methods. In: Proceedings of the 8th CAiSE/IFIP8, vol. 1, pp. 16–17 (2003)
20. Parsa, S., Amiri, M.J., Lajevardi, A.M.Z.: Semi-automated entity, goals model, and business process model driven service identification. JCSE 11(3), 40–55 (2013)

Author Index

Printed in the United States
By Bookmasters